"HOLLYWOOD'S TOUGHEST SEARCH these days isn't the quest for an unknown to star in the sequel to *Gone With The Wind*. It's the hunt for profits from box-office blockbusters after studio accountants have crunched the numbers."

—Associated Press

"I think of *FATAL SUBTRACTION* as the final chapter in the lawsuit that wouldn't die. It turned into an historic legal battle over the way the motion picture studios keep their books and diddle their talent."

—Art Buchwald
From the Introduction
to *Fatal Subtraction*

"*FATAL SUBTRACTION* IS THE GUIDEBOOK TO HOLLYWOOD DEALMAKING in the nineties. Authors Pierce O'Donnell and Dennis McDougal cut through the tangle of contract doublespeak and studio hot air to explain the real financial issues in movie making. Better yet, they do it with style and wit!"

—Digby Diehl
Playboy

"ONE ABSORBING BOOK . . . PROVOCATIVE . . . SKILLFULLY WRITTEN. A 'FIRST-RATE' and 'candid' depiction of the litigation process."

—*Los Angeles Daily Journal*

FATAL SUBTRACTION

The Inside Story
of Buchwald v. Paramount

– – – – – – – –

Pierce O'Donnell
and Dennis McDougal

DOVE
B O O K S

ISBN 0-7871-0494-9

Printed in the United States of America

Cover design: Rick Penn-Kraus
Cover photography: Yoram Kahana/Shooting Star

DOVE BOOKS
8955 Beverly Boulevard
West Hollywood, CA 90048

Distributed by Penguin USA

First Dove Printing: June 1996

10 9 8 7 6 5 4 3 2 1

To our fellow writers:
First to beget the idea, last to get profits

ABOUT THE AUTHORS

PIERCE O'DONNELL clerked for Supreme Court Justice Byron R. White, and spent three years working with legendary trial lawyer Edward Bennett Williams at Williams and Connolly. In 1981, he formed his own firm, O'Donnell & Gordon, and seven years later, helped found the Los Angeles office of New York's venerable Kaye, Scholer, Fierman, Hays & Handler. He contributed to the *New York Times* Bestselling book *The Private Diary of an O.J. Juror, The Private Diary of Lyle Menendez,* and *Toward a Just & Effective Sentencing System: Agenda for Legislative Reform.*

DENNIS MCDOUGAL is an entertainment industry investigative reporter for the *Los Angeles Times* with over forty journalism awards to his credit. The author of *Angel of Darkness, Mother's Day,* and *In the Best of Families,* for which he received an Edgar Award nomination, McDougal is a former Professional Journalism Fellow at Stanford University.

ACKNOWLEDGMENTS

THERE ARE SO MANY PEOPLE that we want to thank for their contributions to this book and support in the lawsuit that made it possible that we apologize in advance if we fail to acknowledge all of you.

Art Buchwald and Alain Bernheim—two brave men with old-fashioned values and a passion for principle—have given not only their consent but their enthusiastic blessing to this project. We thank them for their courage in letting us report *Buchwald v. Paramount* as it really happened.

The irascible but charming Herman "Mad Dog" Gollob, our dear friend and mentor, is that rare and remarkable editor who can save writers from their own excesses without cutting the heart out of what they mean to say. Thank you, Herman!

We cannot thank enough Pierce's colleagues at Kaye, Scholer, Fierman, Hays & Handler. Besides underwriting the several million dollars of fees and costs that enabled Pierce to represent Buchwald and Bernheim, the firm's partners never faltered in their commitment to the clients and the cause they championed. Special thanks to Peter Fishbein, Fred Yerman, Allan Pepper, Senator Abraham Ribicoff, Gerald Feller, Alan Capilupi, Cliff Hook, Jeff Gordon, Gary Apfel, Barry Lawrence, Hush Sohaili, Aton Arbisser, Ken Freeling, Joseph Hansen, Paul Curran, Milton Handler and Barry Willner.

The Buchwald/Bernheim legal team is an extraordinary band of talented and dedicated women and men who helped us immeasurably: Clara A. "Zazi" Pope, Marsha Durko, Dennis Landry, Suzanne Tragert, Betsy Handler, Bruce Margolius, Michael Malina, Joel Katcoff, Greg Dovel, Jennifer Curran and Mark Hankin.

We are grateful to many others at Kaye, Scholer for their generous assistance: Celine Quarroz, Elinor Martin, Elise Aubé, Colleen Hall, Maryann Spriggs, Asaf Cohen, Billy Lipton, the Word Processing Departments in Los Angeles and New York, and anyone who ever ran the fax machines.

From day one, our agents believed in us and this book. We are forever indebted to Pierce's agents and champions, Joy Harris, Robbie Lantz and Jerry Zeitman, and to Dennis's agent and friend, Alice Martell, whom Dennis insists is actually Annette Funicello.

The spouses and children of writers are invariably the first casualties of any book. It got so bad that our families resorted to putting our faces on milk cartons and cursing our word processors as we ignored them on weekends and family vacations to Ireland and Martha's Vineyard. We apologize for the months we stole from your lives and hope that you understand why we did it. So, thank you Sharon McDougal, Dennis's pal, high priestess, shrink and first-line editor whose aversion to ingesting or sleeping on peas will always make her a princess in her husband's eyes. Thank you Connie O'Donnell, Pierce's best friend and loving critic, who never misses a well-deserved opportunity to bring him gently back to planet Earth. And Meghan and Brendan O'Donnell and Jennifer, Amy and Kate McDougal—you are the proudest legacies that any father could ever want and we love you more than words can ever express.

The rest of our family were stalwart cheerleaders: Carl and Lola McDougal, Mary and Harry O'Donnell, Neal McDougal, Pat McDougal, Colleen McDougal Seligar, Fitz Dearmore, Helen Kay O'Donnell Wahl and Maureen O'Donnell Hibbard.

Pierce's big-hearted sister, Mary Eileen O'Donnell, is a gifted actress who served as our resourceful research assistant. Sandi Duncan was a perceptive proofreader who helped us meet one of our many impossible deadlines.

Dennis is grateful to Shelby Coffey III and those editors at the Los Angeles *Times* who were superb teachers and made the newspaper Dennis's "home" for nearly a decade. The *Times* remains "home" to such fine folk at the top of their profession as Lee Margulies, Barbara Saltzman, Dave Kishiyama, Alan Dirkin, Jim Walters, Stan Williford, Glen Smith, Roger Oglesby, Narda Zacchino, Dave Pecchia, Nina J. Easton, Mark Gladstone, Steve Weinstein, DJ Salem, Bob Sipchen, Larry Armstrong, Terry Pristin, David Fox, Bob Welkos, Elaine Dutka, Katie Sauceda, Connie Koenenn, David Shear, Art Berman and the late John Brownell. And much gratitude to the incredible staff of the *Times*'s Editorial Library—researchers par excellence.

We want to give a big hug to Irv Letofsky—an editor's editor whose caustic humor, fresh ideas, journalistic passion and common sense are sorely missed at the Los Angeles *Times*.

Pierce offers deep thanks to the advisors who guided him through the challenging process of prosecuting the case and writing the book: Danny Arnold, David Rintels, Lynn Roth, Ronald Silverman, Michael Flaherty, Roger Davis, Rudy Petersforf, Paul Maslansky, Max Youngstein, Sid Finger, Ernie Nives, Phil Hacker, Jay Shapiro, David Brown, Howard Suber, Jeff Robin, Nick Winslow, Jesse Kornbluth, Thomas Girardi, Ed Cheramy, Ann Buchwald and the late Ed North. A special thanks is in order to Pierce's pals at the Economic Round Table who encouraged him and provided a forum for testing his ideas.

Dennis acknowledges his debt to the many friends and colleagues who advised, read, commented and/or kept up the applause long after he was dead certain that he could not write another word: Dorothy Korber, Steve West, Patrick Goldstein, Michael Cieply, Larry Lynch, Brian Taggert, Dale Pollock, Jamie Masada, Jack Mathews, Dick Goldberg, Larry Josephson, Leonard Klady, John Horn, Diane Goldner, Brian Zoccola, Bryn Friedman, Alexandra Matisoff, Charles Champlin, Joe Piccherello, Linda Deutsch, Alex Ben Block,

Irv Schwartz, Bill Knoedelseder, Julian Blaustein, Gary Owens, Rhys Thomas, John Wilson, Wayne Rosso, Dave Robb, David Johnston, Peter Bart, Fox Entertainment News and the twin queens of film esoterica, Pat Broeske and Susan King. And posthumous thanks also to the late Jay Sharbutt and Larry Feingold, both of whom abandoned the planet way, way before their time.

Pierce received an outstanding legal education at Georgetown University Law Center and wants to thank all of his professors, particularly Richard Allan Gordon, Sherman Cohn, Joseph Page, William McDaniels and the late Donald Schwartz and Adrian Fisher. A young lawyer was blessed with exceptional mentors whose kindness and encouragement will never be forgotten: the late Edward Bennett Williams, Shirley and Seth Hufstedler, Justice Byron R. White, Dennis Curtis and Paul Wolff.

Writers could not ask for a more supportive publisher than Doubleday. Steve Rubin was the first to perceive the potential for this book, and his enthusiasm, imagination and professionalism were matched by those of his colleagues: Kathy Trager, Ellen Archer, Marly Rusoff, Amy Baron, Lynn Fenwick, Kacy Tebbel, Robert Daniels, Ann Elphick, Harold Grabau and Whitney Cookman.

Susan Werner's fine photography made an invaluable contribution.

Too much of this book was written in hotel rooms and airplanes, and we want to thank the great staffs of MGM Grand Air and the Plaza Athénée Hotel in New York.

We had many sources for this book. In addition to over ten thousand pages of sworn testimony from depositions and court proceedings, over two hundred pleadings, and the notes and memoranda contemporaneously prepared by Pierce and other members of the Buchwald/Bernheim legal team, we had access to over one million pages of documents produced by Paramount, Eddie Murphy and others during the course of pretrial discovery. Our research also included reviewing the hundreds of newspaper and magazine articles and hours of television and radio coverage of the case and reading over one thousand articles and fifty books on the motion picture industry. We also conducted over one hundred interviews, and we are grateful to everyone who spoke to us.

Pierce O'Donnell
Dennis McDougal

Los Angeles
May 11, 1992

The only "ism" Hollywood believes in is plagiarism.
DOROTHY PARKER

FOX   *These* are the films . . . that whaddayacallit . . . that make
           it all worthwhile.
GOULD   . . . I think you're going to find a *lot* of things now, make it
           all worthwhile. I think *conservatively*, you and me, we build in
           to split, minimally, ten percent.
FOX   Of the net.
GOULD   Char, Charlie: permit me to tell you: two things I've
           learned, twenty-five years in the entertainment industry.
FOX   What?
GOULD   The two things which are always true.
FOX   One:
GOULD   The first one is: there is no net.
FOX   Yeah . . . ?
GOULD   And I forget the second one. . . .
DAVID MAMET, *Speed-the-Plow*

Contents

Introduction—May 1992

THE MOST IMPORTANT ASPECT of *Buchwald v. Paramount* to keep in mind is that I did not write *War and Peace*, and Paramount Pictures did not make *Gone With the Wind*.

This lawsuit concerns a two-and-a-half-page screen treatment reduced from the original eight pages. It was something that I wrote as an idea for a motion picture which was eventually optioned by Paramount for Eddie Murphy.

The dispute was never a plagiarism suit but rather a minor breach of contract case which turned into an historic legal battle over the way the motion picture studios keep their books and diddle their talent.

I wish to state that I am not a screenwriter nor do I make my living in the motion picture business. For the past forty years, I have been a newspaper columnist. Occasionally, I have sold something to Hollywood, but it was usually just a story idea and one that did not see the light of day.

For example, I once sold an idea to Richard Zanuck based on a column of mine which suggested that there were not one but five Henry Kissingers, all operating on different world problems. I believe that I received $10,000 for it —which was just about right for a treatment of this kind.

I also want to make it perfectly clear that I have never sued anyone for anything. This was my first experience with the legal system, and I am not sure that I would like to do it as a regular pastime.

The *Coming to America* idea was inspired by a scene I had personally witnessed when the Shah of Iran was being greeted by President Carter on the White House lawn. Surrounding the White House were thousands of Iranian students wearing paper bags on their heads and shouting for the Shah's death. It seemed weird to me since the Shah was paying the students' tuition while they studied in the United States.

In the middle of the ceremony the police tossed tear gas at the demonstrators. But the wind shifted, so that instead of hitting the students, it wafted over to the Shah and President Carter, who both started crying at the same time.

As I saw this drama unfold, the question occurred to me: What would happen if the Shah was overthrown at that moment and wound up in the ghetto? It was a story idea, and it was mine. You don't have to take my word for it. The judge said the same thing.

In Washington I put down eight pages on paper and sent the story to my friend Alain Bernheim in Hollywood. Alain is a Frenchman who had worked in the United States after the Second World War and then moved back to Paris in the forties. He was my closest friend in Paris, my literary agent, and constant companion at Fouquet's restaurant on the Champs Élysées.

Eventually he returned to the United States in the late seventies where he became a producer. We spoke almost every week on every subject. I told Alain about my story.

Alain read it and turned it over to his friend, director Louis Malle, one of the best in the motion picture business. Malle suggested that we cut the treatment from eight pages to two and a half on the theory that, when you're trying to interest a motion picture studio head, "less is more."

I did this. Then someone else suggested that we sell the project to Paramount Pictures for Eddie Murphy. We did this, but Louis couldn't wait for a script so Francis Veber, another excellent director, became interested after another writer's script didn't work. With Bernheim supervising, Paramount hired Veber to write a script.

One of the important things to know about movies is that they have many lives. A film might start out with one writer's idea but is changed and reworked many, many times to accommodate producers, studio heads and, particularly, stars. Those first interested get better offers. Others come into the picture and see the story entirely differently. In many cases, people get involved because they have nothing else to do.

Paramount and Alain's agent, Roger Davis, drew up two contracts—one for him and one for me. My contract was pure boilerplate. No one dreamed the language would change the accounting practices of an entire industry.

I won't go into the details of what happened with the story at Paramount. I only became personally involved much later when I received a call from Bernheim telling me that Paramount had dropped the option on the project. The only explanation we could elicit was that Murphy hated it.

So Alain took it to Warner Bros., where it was optioned for an unknown star.

Everything was going along just fine when the Eddie Murphy people announced that they were doing an original movie about a prince who comes to America and winds up in the ghetto. Bernheim told me that Warner Bros. was going to drop its option. We were out of business.

We sought legal advice and all the lawyers advised us not to do anything about it until the picture was made. Another thing to keep in mind is that it is very difficult to get a good law firm to represent you against a studio in Hollywood. This is because the firms all represent movie studios and find that representing you is either a conflict of interest or a very dangerous idea.

When *Coming to America* was released, it turned out to resemble my story so much that Bernheim and I decided to sue.

The lawyer we found was Pierce O'Donnell.

Pierce came out of Albany, New York, went to Georgetown University Law

Center and worked for the famed Edward Bennett Williams. He is a senior partner with the law firm of Kaye, Scholer, Fierman, Hays & Handler in Los Angeles, and he is a tiger in the courtroom and at the dining-room table.

No one has as much enthusiasm for a case and a client as Pierce. I didn't see him down in three and one half years, and when he called me he never said, "Hello." He always asked, "Are you sitting down?" or "We made legal history today." Pierce is a brilliant lawyer, and when it comes to legal theater, he is a credit to his Irish race. What I liked about him the most was that he always returned my phone calls.

When I met Pierce for the first time, he told me about his breach-of-contract strategy. He also told me that, if he won, the three of us, Bernheim, Pierce and myself, were entitled to 19 percent of the net profits, which would come to billions.

He took the case on a contingency basis and said that all I had to do was pay the expenses. There were two things wrong with the proposition—Paramount claimed that there were no profits, and the expenses came to $400,000 for Bernheim and myself. Whenever we complained to Pierce that a bill was too high, he would say, "Don't pay it."

Once I told Pierce that after we finished suing Paramount for terrible bookkeeping, we were going to sue him for charging us $44 to Xerox one sheet of testimony. He just laughed and said that the trial was costing his firm $2.5 million. I told him, "Don't pay it."

The suing experience is a long, hard one and takes its toll emotionally. Lawyers are hired to win cases no matter how mean and unfair they have to be.

When I got involved, I expected to be in a business dispute that I assumed would be resolved early in the game for a minimal sum of money and, hopefully, an apology.

It didn't turn out that way at all. Paramount decided for reasons of its own to fight. The rumor is that they were afraid to offend Eddie Murphy, whose name was on the picture credits as having written an original story.

I started to lose my sense of humor at the time a newspaper story said that Paramount executives were going to sue me for stealing the idea from Charlie Chaplin's film A King in New York. The lawyer for Paramount, Robert Draper, accused me of being a plagiarist. It was no longer a question of resolving the contract dispute. Paramount wanted to destroy me. Fortunately, the judge threw out the charges, but only after they had gone around the world.

Draper also tried to drag in the race issue. He kept plugging away at the fact that I was white and Arsenio Hall and Eddie Murphy were black, and he got Arsenio to say that all they were trying to do was make a clean, black family picture.

At this point Bernheim leaned over to me in the courtroom and said, "If they wanted to make it a clean family picture, why did they open it with all the virgins washing Eddie's penis?"

The attempt to destroy me left a bitter taste in my mouth. Paramount Pictures' Marty Davis, whom I had known for many years, kept telling my friends he still loved me and bore no malice toward me. He was full of it. Why else would he let his lawyers try to destroy me? One of the discoveries of a suit such as this is that it makes you hurt deeply, and you don't forgive easily.

A few other things I discovered:

It is impossible to recall any facts, including those you have given in deposition.

You want everyone to be interested in your case and to be rooting for you all the time.

When it comes to technical law, a good judge is worth a thousand juries.

Do not count on any money in a lawsuit—this is as true if you win as if you lose.

I bear many grudges in this suit. One is against some of the officers of the board of the Writers Guild of America who promised support but never delivered it. The screenwriters had the most to gain from us winning the suit. They were afraid to get involved. It became so bad that a group of rank-and-file writers, including Larry Gelbart, Neil Simon, David Rintels and others, took out an ad in *Variety* congratulating us and explaining to reporters that they felt they had to do something since the Guild officers were so weak.

Some, though not many, people in Hollywood were angered that we were upsetting the system. They felt that we should shut up and stop being crybabies. This group included lawyers, agents and studio people. At the same time, many studio executives I talked to couldn't believe Paramount's damage control tactics and how they kept sinking into quicksand.

The public was even better. People were rooting for us wherever we went. The only bad experience I had was when my ten-year-old grandson called me. He said that some of the kids in his class were making his life miserable because they had heard that his grandfather was out to get Eddie Murphy.

I said, "Don't let that guy do that to you."

And he replied, "It's not a guy, it's a girl."

When you become involved with something such as this trial, the question arises: Is it worth it?

I think that it is if you believe in what you're doing. There is nothing wrong with getting some money—but it's standing up for what counts that really makes it worthwhile. The system is very difficult to beat, but not impossible.

Pierce, his most able associate, Zazi Pope, and others at Kaye, Scholer, Fierman, Hays & Handler did it, and for that Alain and I are grateful.

Before signing off, I would like to say how much I have admired the courage of Alain Bernheim in this lawsuit. He had far more to lose than I did because he makes his living in Hollywood. He never faltered in his resolve to see it through. I salute him!

So be it. I leave the rest of the book to Pierce and Dennis McDougal. I think of it as the final chapter in the lawsuit that wouldn't die.

I am not responsible for anything they have written although I've been informed by the printers that I am going to be charged $44 a page.

—Art Buchwald

Introduction—May 1996

It seems like yesterday that we first decided to sue Paramount Pictures over *Coming to America*. I recall the very moment the decision was made. I was playing first base for the Chicago Black Sox and had just struck out.

Once I was kicked out of baseball, I tried to talk Charles Lindbergh into putting another seat in the "Spirit of St. Louis." He turned me down. In the meantime the trial dragged on. When Franklin Roosevelt was elected President, the Paramount lawyers started to take depositions. I said I deserved 19 percent of the net, and Adolph Zukor, who was then head of Paramount, said there was no profit.

I thought when America dropped the bomb on Hiroshima that the trial would come to an end. But it continued right through the Korean war.

It dragged on even longer when Paramount asked the Justice Department for relief, claiming our trial was interfering with the shooting of Cecile B. DeMille's *Ten Commandments*.

Finally it concluded in 1992 when we were awarded a handsome sum of money and two tickets to the Knicks game.

Pierce O'Donnell was the architect of our legal battle and spent 45 years proving my contract was unconscionable.

This introduction is what happened as I saw it and how the battle for Net was waged. The rest of the book is Pierce's footnotes.

—Art Buchwald

Prologue

ON A JULY EVENING in 1988, on the Massachusetts island of Martha's Vineyard, Art Buchwald, America's best-known humorist, bought a ticket at the Capawock Theater to see the new Eddie Murphy movie, *Coming to America*. His longtime friend and Hollywood collaborator, Alain Bernheim, had already been given a private pre-release screening at Paramount Studios. When he emerged after two hours in the screening room, Bernheim was fuming.

He had urged Buchwald, who was summering in the seaside town of Vineyard Haven, to see the movie before they decided what to do next. Bernheim was convinced that it was "Art's story" and told him so on the phone, but he wanted the creator to see for himself. Whatever Art decided, Alain would go along.

From the moment the credits began to roll, one name larger than all the others crowded the screen and loomed over the movie title.

EDDIE MURPHY.

In the summer of 1988, the hip, twenty-seven-year-old comic genius was the number one box office star in the world. Murphy had appeared in only six feature films in his short career: *48 HRS.*, *Trading Places*, *Best Defense*, *Golden Child*, *Beverly Hills Cop*, and its sequel, *Beverly Hills Cop II*. But those six films had together grossed over $1 billion. Nobody in Hollywood would dispute that the name that had established Paramount as *the* preeminent studio in the 1980s was . . .

EDDIE MURPHY.

Actor, producer, writer, comedian and, most recently, even a pop music star with a million-selling single called "Party All the Time," Murphy had a management team and staff totaling more than fifty. He was the beneficiary of a five-picture overall deal guaranteeing him $8 million per picture against 15 percent of the studio's *gross* receipts. At the moment, the best star contract in Hollywood was touted in the trade press as belonging to . . .

EDDIE MURPHY, star of *Coming to America*, Paramount's big feature for 1988, aimed at Murphy's army of youthful fans all over the world.

Buchwald, a man of sixty-two, scrunched down into his seat near the back of the tiny theater, feeling uncomfortably old in an audience mainly in their teens or twenties.

Produced by Paramount at a cost of $40 million, with another $30 million allocated for global advertising and distribution of the film's prints, *Coming to America* was the studio's summer blockbuster. Bernheim had sent Buchwald a handful of reviews. Some critics loved it for its raw, simple humor, praising the range of cameo characters that Murphy and sidekick Arsenio Hall played in addition to their chief roles as Prince Akeem (Murphy) and his loyal servant and friend, Semmi (Hall). Murphy portrayed a smarmy nightclub singer, a wisecracking barber and an irritable old man in addition to the prince, while Hall, a hot television talk show host and inexperienced movie actor, was a black preacher, a busty woman and an assistant barber as well as Semmi.

But the reviews were generally negative. "Sticky sweet," said one reviewer. "Not funny," said another. "Predictable," said a third. Even the positive reviews threw in backhanded compliments about Murphy finally portraying a screen character who was not arrogant and angry. *Daily Variety*'s review captured a common criticism:

"Throughout the opulent picture, the prince shows no concern for how much anything costs, tossing money and expensive items in all directions in pursuit of his limited achievements. Much the same can be said for director John Landis' efforts on this project."

The rival trade paper, the *Hollywood Reporter*, was even more trenchant: "dull-witted . . . inept screenplay"; the Blaustein/Sheffield "mushier-than-white-bread script milks only the most obvious laughs from the outlandish situation."

Paramount described the story as a "black fairy tale" about a young, handsome prince from a mythical African kingdom who comes to New York to find a bride, lives in the ghetto where he runs through a series of comic adventures, falls in love with an attractive American woman and marries her back in his royal palace in Africa.

All based on a "story by EDDIE MURPHY."

That's what the credits claimed. But Buchwald began to feel a sense of outrage as he listened to the dialogue. He felt certain that it sprang indirectly from his original idea.

"I want a woman who will arouse my intellect, as well as my loins!" hollered an exasperated Prince Akeem.

"Where will you find such a woman?" asked Semmi.

"In America," said Prince Eddie, brightening with that trademark toothsome grin.

Art Buchwald is not a man easily given to anger. Polite, soft-spoken and gently droll, he is deliberate and temperate in his tastes and manner. He has established an international reputation as a Washington gadfly and much sought-after toastmaster, chiefly because of his wit. Yet he is most familiar to his audiences as perhaps the single best-known newspaper columnist in America.

A short, avuncular man, Buchwald does not seek power or publicity. He prefers the world of ideas to the intrigues of politics, the cutthroat competition of business or the fleeting fame of Hollywood. He would rather poke fun at all of them than play their games.

Art Buchwald's column is read by tens of millions of people twice a week in over 550 newspapers from Miami to Moscow, London to Los Angeles, and Boston to Buenos Aires. His good-natured satire, honed over four decades in papers like the Washington *Post* and the New York *Herald Tribune,* has made him as celebrated in his own way as Eddie Murphy. It just took him a lot longer than it took the wisecracking kid from Roosevelt, Long Island, who laughed and spoke like a prince up on the screen.

"Remember, Semmi: No one here can know that I am royalty," Prince Akeem was confiding to his buddy upon their arrival from Zamunda at JFK International Airport in New York. "We must appear no different than the average man."

Then Prince Akeem walked out in front of a New York cab driver and ordered him to halt.

"You dumb fuck!" screamed the driver, jumping out of his cab and pointing a menacing finger at Eddie.

"Take us to Queens at once!" ordered the prince who, moments before, had ordered Semmi not to appear any different than the average man.

Buchwald felt conspicuously out of place as titters rolled across the theater. "You dumb fuck" was a line he had heard uttered frequently by others in his own lifetime, but it is not his kind of comedy. Buchwald's style can be just as ribald, but without the vulgarity he heard and lived with as far back as his Marine Corps days in the South Pacific during World War II.

He satirized a senator who wore silk stockings and high heels while working on tax reform at home; a Supreme Court justice who took his wife to see *Deep Throat* six times; and a starlet who bathed in Coors with a well-known football player—a football player who appeared in advertisements for Schlitz. Over the years, Buchwald has written columns about Gary Hart's monkey business with Donna Rice, Patty Hearst's closet time with the Symbionese Liberation Army and the pros and cons of Susan Ford engaging in premarital sex.

But his deadpan delivery never contains any four-letter words. Such epithets carry more punch, he learned early on, if they are used sparingly.

His stinging political satire eventually filled thirty-two books and got him elected to the prestigious American Academy and Institute of Arts and Letters. Only two other humorists had ever been named to the academy: New York *Times* columnist Russell Baker and Mark Twain. In 1982, Buchwald was accorded journalism's highest honor when the board of governors of Columbia University awarded him the coveted Pulitzer Prize for commentary.

And now, six years later, he sat in a darkened movie theater surrounded by people who seemed to giggle each time someone uttered the word "fuck," prompting him to wonder again about the absurdity of real life.

Like other journalists before him, Buchwald has done his own share of work in Hollywood. It is a tradition that extends as far back in the annals of the entertainment business as the 1920s and '30s, when popular newspapermen like Ben Hecht, Charles MacArthur, Herman Mankiewicz and Gene Fowler were all lured to Hollywood by the prospect of fame and big money.

In Buchwald's case, however, his flirtations with moviemaking were minimal and unsatisfactory. He wrote a few short treatments outlining concept, principal characters, theme and plot line which were optioned for small change but never produced. While he never adapted any of his work into screenplay form, his 1958 novel, A *Gift from the Boys*, was made into a Columbia Pictures movie. Buchwald invested the money he earned in twenty acres of fallow Orange County property, went back to writing his newspaper column, and paid no further attention to how Columbia developed the screenplay.

When the movie, "based on a novel by Art Buchwald," finally did appear on the big screen in 1960, the name had been changed to *Surprise Package*. It starred Yul Brynner as a big-time gambler who is deported to his native Greece and gets involved with some stolen jewels and a phony king, and it otherwise bore little resemblance to his novel. Buchwald blamed the screenplay.

His opinion about the collaborative art of filmmaking never improved after that. He remained as ambivalent as many other East Coast writers who welcome Hollywood's money at the same time that they fear their work might get translated into drivel by West Coast hacks.

Buchwald knew a lot of people in the film business, including *Roots* producer David Wolper, director Billy Wilder, and MCA/Universal board chairman Lew Wasserman, long considered the single most powerful man in the entertainment industry. And during his stint at the *Herald Tribune* in Paris in the 1950s, he even took a turn at being the in-house film critic.

Once, when he panned the Ingrid Bergman version of *Joan of Arc*, producer Walter Wanger accused Buchwald of sabotaging his movie. Buchwald came back with another column challenging Wanger to a duel.

On assignment for the *Herald Tribune* to interview Katharine Hepburn on location in Venice, he described her disgust over the Italian cigar he was smoking. He tossed it, still smoldering, into a nearby canal and finished interviewing the haughty Miss Hepburn before her next scene for *Summertime*, a comedy being directed by David Lean: She backed accidentally into the water.

In loving, wicked detail Buchwald recalled the flotsam in the water where Hepburn made her big splash: one orange peel, two plums, a pigeon feather, a Popsicle wrapper and . . . Buchwald's half-smoked cigar.

No, Art Buchwald was no stranger to the world of movies. So a few years after his old Parisian pal Alain Bernheim moved to Los Angeles in 1979 and asked Buchwald if he had any movie ideas, Buchwald obliged with an eight-page treatment that he called *It's a Crude, Crude World*.

He got the movie idea from the same place he got most of his column ideas: the daily newspaper headlines. The Shah of Iran had been in Washington during the Carter administration and was caught on the White House lawn, along with President Carter, by tear gas meant for Iranian student protesters assembled on Pennsylvania Avenue. The incident got Buchwald thinking about what would happen if the Shah were deposed while visiting the United States. That, in turn, led him to ponder the humorous possibilities of a king losing his throne while he was out of his country. He also remembered the early days in Paris after the war, when royalty from the former French colonies in Africa seemed to show up in town every week, parading along the boulevards with pomp and ostrich feathers and long convoys of limousines.

What if such a king wound up in the ghetto in Washington, D.C., stranded the same way the Shah had been stranded in Panama?

Bernheim, an ex-literary agent who went to Hollywood to become a producer, loved the idea. Art first wrote an eight-page treatment. On Bernheim's advice, he pared it down to two and a half pages so that, as Louis Malle once advised, it would be simple enough for even a studio executive to understand.

Bernheim optioned the story and eventually sold it in early 1983 to an eager Paramount that wanted Bernheim to develop and produce the movie for Eddie Murphy, using Buchwald's treatment as the starting point.

Buchwald was to get $65,000, 1.5 percent of the net profits, and a screen credit if Paramount made a movie based upon his story. Alain's deal was even more valuable. As producer, he was to earn $200,000 plus 40 percent of the net profits, reducible to 17.5 percent under a studio formula if stars, directors and/or writers were cut in on the profit pie.

The studio promptly changed the title of Buchwald's treatment from *It's a Crude, Crude World* to *King for a Day* and launched full-scale development.

For two years Buchwald—preoccupied with satirizing Ronald and Nancy Reagan and their circle of friends, cabinet members and cronies—had almost nothing to do with the *King for a Day* project aside from the eight-page treatment. Now, as he sat in the Capawock Theater, Buchwald recalled what he considered the essence of his story:

> A handsome young king from a mythical African kingdom comes to Washington, D.C., to trade for arms, ends up in the ghetto of the nation's capital when he is overthrown in absentia, has comic adventures, falls in love with an attractive CIA call girl, regains his throne, and takes his love home to be his queen.

What Buchwald was hearing Murphy and Arsenio Hall say—about traveling to the poorest part of Queens in order to find Eddie a queen—definitely seemed to have been inspired by the story that Bernheim and he had delivered to Paramount five years earlier.

Did Paramount really think that it could fool him? Buchwald wondered. It was so blatant, so cynical, so . . . Hollywood.

Was this the way Paramount treated its friends? Buchwald mused. Before he joined the Marines, when he was still in high school in New York, Buchwald worked in the Paramount mail room. While he was in the South Pacific during the war, Paramount made a great ceremony about sending its drafted alumni, including Buchwald, free cartons of cigarettes. And, more recently, he had spoken at Paramount functions and had become friendly with Martin S. Davis, chairman of the board of Paramount's parent company, Gulf & Western. When Alain first called him about the *King for a Day* deal, Art had felt like he was dealing with family.

Watching the movie, Buchwald was convinced that the concept and main character were his, even if the story line had been altered. The blatant ripoff was galling enough, but Paramount had botched the movie to boot. Saccharine, crude, vulgar, slow-paced . . . and, worst of all, not terribly funny, Buchwald concluded as the end credits rolled.

For several moments after the house lights came up, Art Buchwald sat there, brooding, hurt, angry.

Every summer, the Buchwalds retreat from the pressure cooker life of Washington, D.C., to the Vineyard to write and relax. They live on Main Street in Vineyard Haven across the street from the public library. The unofficial mayor of the town, Buchwald loves to mingle with the residents and tourists, stopping to sign autographs or chew the fat over a back fence.

On his way home that night, he couldn't get one question out of his mind:

Why had Paramount treated Alain and him so shabbily?

Not one to pick a fight, he nevertheless didn't like being cheated, particularly by people he thought he could trust. Should he go to court and fight it out in public with all of the inevitable media attention?

He was torn. To go public carried risks, especially if he lost. To remain silent, on the other hand, would mean compromising his principles as a writer. Friends advised him to "sue the bastards." Ann, his wife, told him to do what he thought was right.

Buchwald had the clout to teach the studios a lesson. And a lawsuit would benefit less famous, younger writers whose ideas, stories and even scripts were too often misappropriated by largely unaccountable studios, production companies and television networks.

The thought of filing a lawsuit, much less playing the part of a hero, disturbed Buchwald. He was the one who wrote about the exploits and foibles of newsmakers, poking holes in pretension. Once he sued, he would be making news.

For a public figure, Buchwald is a private person. No demeaning commercialism for him. No TV commercials, no publicist and no entourage. He is celebrated but not a celebrity; a loner without being alone. Art Buchwald might be a star in some sense of the word, but certainly not in the Hollywood sense. Not yet.

The prospect of spending months in meetings, depositions, and a trial—with all those damn lawyers—was not his idea of fun. In all his years of satirizing big shots from popes to presidents, he had never been sued. Nor had he ever sued anyone for anything. In fact, he had never even testified in a courtroom. But that would all end abruptly if he went public and sued the most powerful motion picture studio in the world, at the same time taking on the biggest movie star of the day.

Buchwald had never met Eddie Murphy, but he admired him. He was a refreshing original on "Saturday Night Live," pricking balloons of convention and stereotyping. In his first two movies, 48 HRS. and *Trading Places*, Murphy was delightful, Buchwald recalled.

Something about the comedian had changed in this latest film, but Art couldn't quite put his finger on just what. There was an air of overconfidence —obvious self-satisfaction—that undermined Murphy's otherwise impeccable timing and gifted mimicry. He was not challenged, and his boredom was evident.

Buchwald was also troubled by the racial implications of a lawsuit accusing Eddie Murphy of plagiarism. Buchwald is a liberal Jewish Democrat who prides himself on a healthy, positive attitude toward civil rights and racial harmony. Stereotyping is anathema to him. But here he would be accusing one of the most famous black entertainers in the world of stealing his idea and implying that he couldn't have come up with it on his own. No matter how cautiously a lawsuit was framed, the media would seize on the fact that Buchwald, a white writer, was suing Murphy, a black star. It was inevitable— and painful to contemplate.

Buchwald wasn't sure that he had the stomach for the fight, for all the publicity and the emotional wear and tear.

He thought about how happy he had been as a writer for the past forty years . . . how complete he felt when he started with a blank computer screen or an empty sheet of paper, and ended a few hours later with another original creation by Art Buchwald.

But he also remembered how he had felt two hours earlier when several hundred people in the Capawock Theater saw a credit that proclaimed that Eddie Murphy authored the story for *Coming to America*.

Reaching home, he headed for the telephone in the kitchen and dialed the number from memory.

"Alain? It's Art. I just saw *Coming to America*. Let's get a lawyer."

Part One

-- -- -- -- -- -- -- --

Fade In

1

Another Celebrity Spat

OUT OF BREATH from my three-mile jog, I bent over to pick up the Los Angeles *Times* lying in the driveway. I cooled off in the kitchen, poured my coffee and turned to "Calendar," the arts and entertainment section. On the second page, under the "Morning Report" column for July 13, 1988, the following caught my eye:

"Eddie Murphy created his movie, 'Coming to America,' solely on his own without any help from columnist Art Buchwald," Murphy's manager Robert Wachs said Monday. "I'm a great admirer of Art, but I don't see how Eddie is responsible. This should just be between [Buchwald] and Paramount's lawyers," Wachs told The Times. But Buchwald, a widely-read humorist whose column appears in The Times, says the star vehicle is awfully similar to a story he wrote three years ago, titled "It's a Crude, Crude World"—and which he subsequently took to Murphy as a movie property. But after spending $500,000 for rewrites on the story, Murphy's production company dropped his story, Buchwald told The Times. "During all this they were telling me that Murphy loved the movie. I'm not saying that they stole my story, but the character is the same. . . . The only difference is that my prince went to Washington [instead of New York]," said Buchwald, who added he first learned of Murphy's movie last October. "And when they were making the movie, Paramount was telling me not to worry, that the movies were different. Well—now I'm worried," Buchwald said. Buchwald said he doesn't want to sue, but will if he has to. Paramount declined to comment Tuesday.

Another celebrity spat in Hollywood. I put it out of my mind. That morning I was far more concerned about a complicated settlement negotiation in a trade secret case I had won in court a year earlier for Zolatone, a paint manufacturer, than I was with some overpaid star bickering over who should get the credit for writing a movie.

Zolatone's complex paint formula had been stolen ten years earlier and used to develop a competitor's strikingly similar paint. Despite a multimillion-dollar judgment, I was having a devilish time getting a final settlement from the stubborn defendant. Unless I could get the defendant to come to some agreement, he would appeal and Zolatone would get stuck with more legal fees, more delays and more expenses.

The case of the purloined paint formula was typical of the kind of law I practiced. Stolen formulas, stolen trade names, stolen concepts, ideas and patents. It happened a lot but rarely made the headlines, the way this Buchwald/Eddie Murphy business had. Since graduating from Georgetown University Law Center in 1972, I had come to learn that sophisticated violation of the Eighth Commandment was, sadly, as American as apple pie.

My practice was national in scope, requiring me to argue cases in courtrooms around the country. I was a trial lawyer and partner-in-charge of the Los Angeles office of Kaye, Scholer, Fierman, Hays & Handler, one of the nation's oldest law firms. Many of my clients included the rich and famous of the business world—Fortune 500 corporations and Forbes 400 individuals whose deals and lawsuits were the bread and butter of my firm's practice. I got my share of the Davids who had been wronged by the system or swindled by one of the Goliaths. And I occasionally defended a so-called white collar criminal too. Accused of fraud or embezzlement, these were the people and corporations whose crimes were committed in the suites instead of the streets.

For the most part, however, my law practice involved complex civil litigation—disputes over money, property and valuable ideas for inventions, television shows and even a movie now and then.

In July 1988, I had been happily married for eighteen years. Connie and I lived with our two preschoolers, Brendan and Meghan, in Altadena, a rustic town of 40,000 at the foot of the San Gabriel Mountains, just a few miles from the route of the Rose Parade in the neighboring city of Pasadena.

I hail from a small town in rural upstate New York near Albany where my three younger sisters and I grew up attending public schools. My father owned the only local liquor store, my mother was the junior high school librarian, and my aunt was the postmaster. Connie and I were college sweethearts, and after college and law and graduate schools, we settled in Los Angeles in 1978. Ten years later, ours was a driven, but comfortable, California lifestyle. We were baby boomers: Connie, the dedicated professional speech therapist in addition to being a mom; me, a lawyer and a dad.

I have been accused of being a workaholic, and it's probably true. By the summer of 1988, I had even hired a full-time driver to cart me to and from my office over an hour away in Century City, near Beverly Hills—not because I fancied a chauffeur as a status symbol, but rather because I found I could squeeze in two extra hours of work on my laptop computer or my car phone while I was stuck in traffic on the eternally clogged Los Angeles freeways.

Connie claims I spend half my life on the phone. She's probably right. I even installed a fax machine in an office next to our bedroom in order to get the very latest information on cases I was preparing. Next to the fax are two computers, one of which is tied into the Kaye, Scholer computers in Los Angeles, New York and Washington.

What made Pierce O'Donnell run? It was a question I rarely asked myself. I was too busy running.

This morning was no exception. I glanced at my watch. Late again. I set aside the show biz gossip of the Los Angeles *Times* and picked up the *Wall Street Journal*, gulping down the rest of my coffee while I picked through the latest litigation news: torts, bankruptcies, contract breaches, and financial disasters that would bore most people to death.

I could have gone on happily settling paint formula cases forever if Art Buchwald hadn't known someone who knew someone who knew me.

One smoggy day two weeks after I had first read about Buchwald's squabble with Paramount, I was working by the pool. I might hold regular office hours in a Century City high rise, but I learned long ago that I do my best preparation in the solitude of my study or sitting by the pool in the shadows of the San Gabriel Mountains.

Connie was gone that morning. So were the kids. The house was quiet and I was zipping through pages of material at a furious clip when the phone interrupted my concentration.

"Yes," I snapped into the portable phone.

"Pierce, old boy. It's Danny."

As we exchanged pleasantries, I wondered why Danny Arnold was calling me at home. Over the decade that I had been his lawyer, I could count on one hand the number of times that he had "bothered" me away from the office. It usually meant the beginning of a roller coaster ride.

"I'm sorry to call you at home when you're hiding out to get some work done. Do you have a few minutes right now?"

For Danny Arnold, I always had time. The man was like a big brother to me. He started writing for the movies when I was still wearing diapers and had made his mark early as one of the genuine pioneers in television. Besides producing two Emmy Award winners in "Barney Miller" and "My World and Welcome to It," Danny had written episodes for more TV programs than half the writers in Hollywood put together. His credits read like two decades' worth of TV *Guide*: "The Real McCoys"; "McHale's Navy"; "The Dinah Shore Show"; "Bewitched"; "That Girl" and on and on. . . .

I had represented him in a half dozen lawsuits involving the entertainment business. Not only had we never lost, I had been so stretched by Danny and gained so many insights about people, negotiating and Hollywood that I often thought I should be paying him.

A self-diagnosed "paranoid with proof," the demanding Bronx native had earned a reputation over forty years in Hollywood as a volatile genius who terrorized insecure television network and motion picture studio executives with his uncompromising insistence on excellence, creative independence and his fair share of the profits. And he practiced what he preached: Danny owned "Barney Miller," and he paid his cocreator, his lead actor Hal Linden and several writer-producers tens of millions of dollars in net profits from the show.

Together, my patron and I battled for five years against Columbia Pictures, his distributor for "Barney Miller." Twice we accused the studio of antitrust violations, dishonest accounting of profits and fraud. Columbia eventually capitulated before trial, paying handsomely in 1986 to get rid of the suit and buy the show from Danny. While Columbia insisted that the terms of the settlement be confidential, the *Wall Street Journal* reported that the sum was about $50 million.

That morning, Danny Arnold had a studio other than Columbia on his mind.

"I have two friends who have a problem and are having trouble finding a lawyer," he said. "I was wondering if you could take just a few minutes and talk with them."

"Sure, Danny. What's the problem?"

"Art Buchwald and Alain Bernheim are old friends of mine, going back to Paris in the late fifties. Alain is a producer who's done a couple of movies. Until about eight or nine years ago, he was a literary agent in Paris. Art has been a client and friend of Alain's for forty years."

I drew a breath, hoping I wouldn't sound too awestruck. Since landing in California, I had met my share of celebrities, cocktail party hotshots and this season's starlets. But Art Buchwald was something else: a genuine American legend.

"I'm a big fan of Buchwald's," I said.

"Have you seen the new Eddie Murphy movie, *Coming to America?*" Danny asked.

"No, I haven't and I doubt I will," I said.

The first reviews were mixed. With two young kids at home, Connie and I did not get to the movies very much anymore.

"Art wrote an original treatment and optioned it to Paramount for an Eddie Murphy movie back in 1983 or so," he said. "Alain was the producer who brought the project to Paramount, and they loved it. Alain was told that Murphy liked it too. Two scripts were written using Art's story. After a couple of years of development, Paramount tells Alain that they're dropping the project because they didn't want to do it."

It started to come back to me.

"Wasn't there something in the *Times* about this a week or two ago?" I interrupted.

"Yeah," Danny replied. "Yeah, it's been all over the newspapers."

"What was the idea? The . . . what do you call it? The story line?" I asked.

"Art's story is about a black African king who comes to Washington to see about getting some missiles, weapons—you know, arms. So while he's attending a White House state dinner he gets overthrown back home. The guy ends up broke in the ghetto, falls in love with a CIA call girl. He gets his throne back, takes her home with him and she marries him."

"That doesn't sound too much like *Coming to America* from what I've read in the reviews," I said flatly.

Danny didn't disagree.

"Look, I don't know if they have a case or not. But they *are* having a goddam awful time finding a decent lawyer to even take a look at it. The studios tie up most of the good law firms in town with conflicts of interest by spreading their business around. You know that."

I sure did know. In fact, I had been the beneficiary of this practice, developing a specialty in suing studios for clients like Danny in the "Barney Miller" case against Columbia. At the time of Danny's call, I was representing NBC in a similar case brought by James Garner and the network against Universal/MCA. In that suit, Garner and NBC successfully battled the giant entertainment conglomerate for a multimillion-dollar share of the net profits on the hugely successful, long-running television series, "The Rockford Files."

In both cases, I wound up with the clients in part because Columbia and Universal had attorneys from almost every reputable entertainment law firm in Los Angeles representing them on other cases. Paramount Pictures, the studio that produced and distributed *Coming to America*, was the same way. The studio might have three or four dozen lawyers on its own in-house staff payroll, but it still farmed out cases all over town. That was one of the subtle but effective ways the tight-knit entertainment industry protected itself from outsiders. I was not too surprised that an out-of-town client, even with the stature of an Art Buchwald, could not find an experienced lawyer who didn't have some obligation to Paramount.

"Do you think that you could call Alain?" Danny asked. "He has the details and, from what he says, some helpful documents."

I was still skeptical, but I wasn't going to admit it to Danny.

"Of course, Danny. I'd be happy to look at it for you. Why don't you have Alain call me and we can set up a meeting?"

"Thanks, old boy," he said. "Both of you will be staying with us at my place in Del Mar next weekend. Maybe you can chat then."

"Sounds fine."

"That's great. He'll be thrilled," said Danny. "See you next weekend."

2

Taking a Hard Line

THE DAY after Danny called, Alain phoned.

He had just spoken with Buchwald the night before, Bernheim told me, and Art had never sounded so angry in the forty years he had known him. They were going to sue. Could I meet with him soon?

The soft-spoken Frenchman reminded me that we had met once before. We had sat together at a dinner honoring Danny Arnold for his charitable work. All I could recall about our first encounter was that Alain was an engaging movie producer with a distinct French accent who was married to an effervescent, chain-smoking delight named Margie.

Alain rattled off more details about the case than the bare-bones description Danny had given me. He told me that Howard King, an attorney he had consulted previously, would send me a couple of hundred pages of correspondence, scripts, treatments and newspaper clippings. Alain was very polite and deferential, but I could tell that he was eager to proceed if I was interested.

A half dozen file boxes brimming with six years of movie development history arrived the next day. The Los Angeles *Times* article and Danny's telephone call didn't begin to tell the story of Bernheim's frustration and Art Buchwald's futile effort to stay out of the fray.

Paramount had signed them up back in 1983 and spent $500,000 over two years to develop two different scripts for an Eddie Murphy feature, based on Art's story. Alain worked first with a promising new writer, Tab Murphy, but his script was ultimately rejected by the studio. Then he turned to Francis Veber, the French director of the hugely successful comedy *La Cage Aux Folles*. For two years, Bernheim shepherded the scripts and rewrites through the preproduction process, all the while getting secondhand reports from top Paramount brass that "Eddie loves Buchwald's idea."

Then something changed.

By 1985 the bloom was off the rose. Paramount's top three executives exited the company: Barry Diller to Twentieth Century Fox and Michael Eisner and Jeffrey Katzenberg to Disney. With no sponsors and an allegedly cool reception from Eddie Murphy after delivery of the second script from Veber, *King for a Day* was now an orphan. The project died on the Paramount lot in March 1985 when, in Hollywood parlance, it went into "turnaround": after one studio abandons a project, the producer has one year to shop it around to other studios in hopes of getting a new contract.

It took over a year, but a determined Bernheim finally interested Paul Maslansky, a producer under contract to Warner Bros., in *King for a Day* after he assured the studio that Paramount had abandoned Buchwald's comedy as a project for Eddie Murphy. Warner Bros. gave Art and Alain contracts that were almost carbon copies of those they had at Paramount. Next, the studio spent $250,000 to develop two of its own scripts. Before Warner Bros. gave the final nod to Bernheim to launch production, however, Paramount announced that Eddie Murphy would soon begin shooting a comedy about an African prince living in a New York City ghetto.

When Bernheim learned of the new project in October 1987, he meekly confronted Paramount's president, Ned Tanen, about the apparent similarity between Buchwald's *King for a Day* and the Murphy movie, then titled *The Quest*. Tanen angrily denied any connection and assured Bernheim that *King for a Day*, then in development at Warner Bros. under the new title *Me and the King*, would not be jeopardized by Murphy's new picture.

Tanen's prediction proved dead wrong. Two weeks after Paramount began filming the Eddie Murphy comedy in New York City, Bernheim received a heavy dose of bad news. In a January 20, 1988 letter, Warner Bros. vice-president Bruce Berman, the creative executive shepherding *King for a Day*, wrote:

> I'm sorry to say that "ME AND THE KING" is not a script that Warner Bros. wants to make. Although it's a premise we always liked, the existence of the Eddie Murphy/ Paramount project in the marketplace makes it difficult for us to proceed with your project. We wish you the best of luck setting up elsewhere.

Everyone has deals fall through. It's a way of life in Hollywood. But not deals that had been as carefully crafted and nurtured and coaxed through good times and bad as had *King for a Day*.

Five years of Bernheim's hard work had gone down the drain. He knew that setting up the project anywhere else was impossible and, undoubtedly, so did

Berman. Once Eddie Murphy did the story, nobody this side of Oz would touch the Buchwald/Bernheim project.

At sixty-seven, Bernheim should have been thinking about retirement. Instead, he was forced to make a tough decision that would have daunted a man half his age. Should he invest more time finding a lawyer and educating him about the history of the case or should he just forget the whole damn thing and get on with his life?

From the very beginning, Buchwald had left everything up to Bernheim. If he wanted to pursue it, fine. If not, that was okay too. After hearing about the Warner Bros. kiss-off, Buchwald told his old friend that Art's was not the big investment. Art had spent only a week or two writing the treatment back in 1982 and his living did not depend on making movies.

Hollywood was Bernheim's turf. The decision to go after Paramount would have to be his.

Bernheim was a mild-mannered, slightly paunchy Frenchman with ruddy cheeks and a ready smile. He was not adversarial by nature. He hated personal confrontation, preferring gentle European persuasion and charm in winning over a reluctant studio executive or a stubborn writer. As a former agent, Bernheim knew the truth of the platitude about catching flies with honey instead of vinegar. After he moved to Los Angeles from Paris in 1979 and produced his first two movies (*Buddy, Buddy* and *Yes, Giorgio*), Bernheim also learned that in Hollywood you got along by going along, not rocking the boat.

People who filed lawsuits or made headline-grabbing trouble for studios were the same people who populated the unemployment lines in Hollywood. There was the paradoxical fate of Cliff Robertson as a memorable object lesson. The actor who won an Oscar for his role in the 1968 film *Charly* blew the whistle on Columbia studio chief David Begelman in the late 1970s. Begelman had forged Robertson's signature on a $10,000 expense check and, it later came to light, on at least two other checks as well. For being a good citizen by revealing the forgery to the police and the studio's board of directors, Robertson was rewarded with ostracism from the mainstream film business and years of being relegated to starring in AT&T television commercials.

Begelman got probation for his crimes and was hired to run MGM/UA.

The loyalty among Hollywood insiders is as fierce and unstinting as that of any Cosa Nostra clan. Hollywood rewards its own and punishes whistle blowers. It was a fundamental truth not lost on Alain Bernheim. At his age, the last thing he needed to hear was "You'll never work in this town again."

Yet Bernheim's smoldering Gallic nature would not allow Paramount and Murphy to get away with what he instinctively felt was literary theft. Still, he thought he could negotiate instead of litigate: strike a quick settlement, get some money for his efforts, and use it to get on with a producing career that started late and inauspiciously. After his pal saw *Coming to America*, he had no trouble persuading Buchwald that they should find a lawyer and quietly explore some out-of-court reparations.

Bernheim turned first to his own lawyer, Marvin Meyer, to investigate a possible claim against Paramount. Meyer, a senior partner in the Beverly Hills firm of Rosenfeld, Meyer & Sussman, did not express much optimism but went ahead and placed a call to Daniel Furie in late January, 1988, about three months after Bernheim's uncomfortable confrontation with Ned Tanen. Furie was one of forty staff lawyers at Paramount and the attorney assigned to handle day-to-day matters for *Coming to America*. Following Bernheim's instructions to go slowly and tactfully with Paramount, Meyer related his client's concerns about the film's similarity to *King for a Day*.

Meyer reported back to Bernheim within twenty-four hours that Paramount was looking into the matter, but it didn't seem too promising at first blush. They would wait and see.

Furie relayed Meyer's message to his boss, Ralph Kamon, the sixty-five-year-old senior lawyer in Paramount's motion picture group. Kamon had been with the studio for more than a quarter century and had seen hundreds of such claims. He knew a routine plagiarism allegation when he saw one. He kicked Meyer's inquiry upstairs without comment to Joshua Wattles, Paramount's hard-charging, newly appointed senior vice-president and head honcho for litigation. From that point forward, Wattles took charge.

Wattles was something of a wunderkind in the corporate inner circle at Paramount. He was not without charm, warmth or civility and came off as a serious, enlightened liberal. He was also ambitious.

Only thirty-seven, the New York City native had joined Paramount in 1981 at the entry-level attorney position in the studio's motion picture group. A music and copyright specialist who quickly impressed his superiors, the aggressive Wattles was also adept at making friends in high places, including Executive Vice-President Richard Zimbert, who became Wattles's mentor and champion. After only a few years of negotiating and drafting contracts, Wattles became a senior attorney. A year or two later, he leapfrogged several lawyers with more seniority, climbing to the post of senior vice-president and deputy general counsel. Reporting directly to Paramount general counsel A. Robert Pisano and Chairman Frank Mancuso, Wattles's influence at the studio was considerable.

Despite his post-hip longish hair and his modified Groucho Marx stride, Wattles could be as abrupt with subordinates as he was deferential to superiors. He was as aggressive and sly on the tennis court as he was in Superior Court. Josh Wattles made no secret of his pride in having attained a position of much influence at such a tender age. Other lawyers, including Universal's Tom Pollock and MGM/UA's Frank Rothman, had risen to the dizzying heights of production president and there was no reason that Wattles himself might not do so someday.

No reason, at least, in early 1988, when he commissioned a comparison of the Eddie Murphy movie to the two Paramount scripts that had been spawned by Buchwald's original story: the one written in 1983 by Tab Murphy, who three years later would be a contributor to the screenplay for *Gorillas in the Mist*, and the second drafted in 1984 by Francis Veber. The shooting script of *The Quest*, the working title of the movie then in production, was written by ex-"Saturday Night Live" writers David Sheffield and Barry Blaustein and was said to be based on a story by Eddie Murphy.

It took two months for Paramount story department analyst Julie Lantz to read the three scripts and write up her conclusions. In mid-March, just as *The Quest* was wrapping up location shooting in Brooklyn, Wattles read Lantz's five-page analysis. She concluded that, while all three scripts used a similar fish-out-of-water premise, "the Sheffield/Blaustein script takes a completely different approach to its protagonist, his adventures in the U.S., and his romance."

Buried in the analysis was "one small point worth noting," she added. There was a plot similarity between Tab Murphy's screenplay and the Blaustein/Sheffield script involving the African prince working in a fast-food hamburger joint. There was also similar dialogue about how hamburgers are put together. Nevertheless, the report confidently concluded, Eddie Murphy's movie "appears to be unique in all aspects of development, and distinctly different from the other two screenplays."

If she had read Buchwald's original treatment for *King for a Day*, however, Lantz made no note of it.

Armed with the analysis, Wattles told Zimbert and Pisano that neither Buchwald nor Bernheim had any legitimate claim. He also passed on the findings to Meyer.

But Alain had already interpreted Meyer's lukewarm interest in the matter as a signal. Neither Meyer nor his firm, which depended for some of its business on the beneficence of the studios, would sue Paramount without an absolutely airtight case. In fact, a firm on the studios' side of the bargaining table wouldn't sue even *with* an airtight case.

In early February, while filming of *The Quest* was still under way and he had yet to hear back from Meyer, Bernheim went to Howard King at the law firm of Gang, Tyre, Ramer & Brown, one of Hollywood's oldest and most prestigious law firms. Bernheim took an instant liking to King, a personable, savvy insider who had fought many a Hollywood legal battle. King interviewed Bernheim and Buchwald and reviewed Buchwald's treatment as well as the Tab Murphy and Veber scripts. He also read through the shooting script for *The Quest*.

King's finding was just the opposite of Julie Lantz's: the characters, setting, plot points and tone were all similar. In fact, he told Art and Alain, he saw similarities in the total concept and feel of all three scripts, as well as Art's story. That Paramount was granting sole story credit to Eddie Murphy for the *The Quest* bordered on laughable. Still, King was unsure whether the similarities were intentional or were merely reflected in the final script as a part of a developing "Eddie Murphy style" that seemed to be inherent in each succeeding movie that the young actor made.

King advised his new clients to seek a quick and quiet settlement. Going to court would be expensive, time consuming, messy. Moreover, what they could get from a jury was limited. Damages would not be more than the reasonable value of Buchwald's idea since that was all that Paramount had agreed to pay when Buchwald submitted his treatment back in 1983. And what was the fair market value of a two-and-a-half-page story, after all?

Plus there was the conflict-of-interest problem. At the outset, King told Buchwald and Bernheim that he would not be able to represent them in court. He was enthusiastic about the case, but his firm had close ties to Paramount and its top executives.

That was okay with Buchwald and Bernheim. They figured that Paramount would promptly settle to avoid bad publicity. So they told King to rattle the saber but, in the end, cut a settlement for a couple of hundred thousand dollars.

King phoned Wattles to tell him that his role would be limited to attempting a settlement so that he could avoid any conflict of interest. Wattles readily consented. After all, Hollywood was a small town where conflicts were inevitable. Today's adversary could be tomorrow's partner, and back scratching was standard operating procedure. Since King and his partners were part of The Club and Paramount might need a favor someday from one of his firm's clients, waiving the conflict was a no-brainer.

Three months passed. King was tied up most of the time in a trial, and *The Quest*, retitled *Coming to America*, went into postproduction. Just as Paramount announced that the comedy was slated for a late June release, settlement talks got under way. Wattles started by offering to share Julie Lantz's analysis of the scripts, but not before he extracted a written agreement from King and his clients that the comparison "will not be used against [Paramount] in any future litigation, if any, [and] will not be disclosed to or discussed with any other persons . . ."

After King put his position on the table, Wattles got tough. He laid out a dozen points in support of Paramount's stance that *Coming to America* didn't resemble any part of Buchwald's treatment. Several of Wattles's statements struck Bernheim and Buchwald as strangely farfetched, if not flat-out lies.

Eddie Murphy claimed he didn't even know a woman named Tamara Rawitt, who had read and commented on Veber's *King for a Day* scripts. In fact, she had promoted several of the star's earlier movies while she was a member of Paramount's publicity department in New York and had later been hired by Murphy's own production company.

Murphy's manager/lawyer, Robert Wachs, had told Bernheim he read half of Francis Veber's script in early 1985. To Wattles, Wachs had denied it.

According to Wattles, Eddie maintained that he developed the concept of a black African prince on his own as far back as Murphy's short-lived TV career on NBC's "Saturday Night Live" in 1982. He had also masqueraded as African royalty in the last reel of Paramount's *Trading Places*. Both portrayals predated Buchwald's *King for a Day*, Wattles noted.

The bottom line, King later told his clients, was that Paramount was taking a hard line. Wattles's strategy was to distance Murphy's story from Buchwald's treatment and from either of the two scripts that were developed from it. To hear Wattles talk, Murphy had never heard of the *King for a Day* project and had no idea who Art Buchwald was. The Paramount party line, King also told his incredulous clients, was that *Coming to America* was the creation of the fertile imagination of Eddie Murphy and no one else.

Up to this point, Buchwald had been more bemused than anything else. As he usually did, he took in the whole scene from the sidelines. But after King reported back from the settlement conference, Bernheim sensed a change in his friend's interest level. Buchwald had a hard time swallowing Paramount's story. During one of their increasingly frequent transcontinental telephone calls, mild-mannered Art Buchwald got bulldog belligerent, insisting that there would be no *Coming to America* without *King for a Day*.

Still, the two partners agreed that a quick settlement remained the best route. Bernheim told King to make a specific offer to Paramount and see if the studio was serious about settling. Three weeks before *Coming to America* opened nationwide in nearly two thousand theaters, King wrote Wattles, graciously thanking the Paramount lawyer for his "detached professionalism" in allowing King to represent Buchwald and Bernheim.

> Alain and Art have what we and they consider to be serious and meritorious claims. Relationships aside, Alain and Art (in particular) are sufficiently upset about what has happened to institute litigation if forced to do so—although that is clearly not their preference.

King then proceeded to lay out a point-by-point refutation of what Wattles had claimed. Some points were made with exquisite, if polite, understatement.

> To Alain and Art, one has to suspend disbelief to accept the notion that Eddie Murphy really doesn't know Tamara Rawitt. Her job title, her proximity to Murphy, and the manner in which she held herself out (at least to Alain) all suggest that she was more than a supernumerary who had very little, if any, contact with Murphy.

The idea that Eddie Murphy himself had never been exposed in any way to the Bernheim/Buchwald project was even more incredible, King said. Even a production behemoth like Paramount didn't throw away a half million dollars on scripts it never even showed to its prospective star.

> The unalterable fact is that Mr. Murphy has done a film in which the lead character and basic story line bear an unmistakable resemblance to the Buchwald submission. Besides, there were just too many people in high places at Paramount who were intimately involved in and actively encouraged the development of this project. Art and Alain cannot now accept the characterization of "King For A Day" as just one of a handful of projects which all had equal standing."

King saved his toughest talk for Julie Lantz's story analysis.

> As for the analysis done by your story department, Alain and Art believe that it is, in many respects, inaccurate and incomplete and more to the point, irrelevant to

the issue at hand. It appears to compare two screenplays which Paramount concededly owns without enough emphasis upon and consideration of the treatment itself. While such an analysis might be more useful in the context of an infringement or plagiarism claim, it begs the issue of whether Paramount honored the terms of its written agreements with Alain and Art arising from the submission of [Buchwald's treatment].

King's bottom-line demand: $600,000 for both clients in exchange for a complete release of all their claims.

Without further comment, Wattles handed over the matter to Paramount's insurance carrier, Fireman's Fund. The studio carried large amounts of liability coverage. When a claim was made and a lawsuit appeared likely, the file went to the insurance company.

So King's demand letter was answered by Kenneth E. Kulzick, who with his partner, Tony Liebig, made his living defending insurance carriers against liability claims. Liebig & Kulzick had successfully handled dozens of similar claims by writers alleging that literary material they had submitted to a studio, network or production company had been used later without permission. But most writers usually could not afford an attorney of Howard King's stature or wound up representing themselves. Most of their claims never made it past first base because they were unable to prove that the studio had access to their treatment or script or that their work was any more than generally similar to a movie the studio had actually released.

Kulzick could be smug and uncomfortably ingratiating at the same time. A garrulous, roly-poly lawyer in his early sixties, he wore a shock of white hair in a pompadour that gave him an aura of Santa without his beard. In his eyes, lawyers were gentlemen first and foremost and needed to comport themselves as such. He would much rather chat informally about his "beautiful young redhead of a wife" than discuss anything so mundane as a client or a lawsuit.

Over the years, Tony Liebig and Ken Kulzick had come to specialize in fending off demands. In his answer to King's demand letter, Kulzick wrote:

> We agree that the correct starting point in considering whether your claims have validity is to compare Mr. Buchwald's treatment with the completed Eddie Murphy film. Having made that comparison, we find the quantum of similarity to be completely insufficient to support legal claims.
>
> We realize that neither Mr. Buchwald nor Mr. Bernheim has had the opportunity to view the completed Eddie Murphy film. We are prepared to arrange a screening for Mr. Buchwald and Mr. Bernheim immediately before the film's public opening and invite you and your associates to attend.
>
> We believe that with all of the facts before all of the people, an early amicable resolution short of court is possible.

In a telephone call to King the same day, Kulzick parroted Wattles's arguments from the month before. But he could not resist adding his own gratuitous observation. Professing to be a longtime admirer of Art Buchwald,

Kulzick suggested that a lawsuit was beneath someone of Buchwald's stature. It was, he said, un-American.

King bit his tongue, but the following day he fired off a blunt response to Kulzick.

> I don't yet understand your comment concerning the propriety of a claim of this nature by a political satirist of Art's standing. Neither Alain nor Art are interested in (as you put it) "stifling freedom of expression." They hoped, even after "Coming To America" was announced, to make their movie elsewhere. Unfortunately, that avenue seems to have been foreclosed. At this point, they merely seek reasonable compromise of a claim which stems from the facts that there was a submission, about which Paramount professed wild enthusiasm, which led to a development deal, which led to development of a project—tailor made for Mr. Murphy—which bears more than passing similarity to the film about to be released.

Three weeks had now passed since King's settlement offer and Paramount had yet to make a counteroffer. Bernheim and King did accept Kulzick's private screening invitation three days before the film's official opening on the Fourth of July weekend. Buchwald, who was at Martha's Vineyard, didn't accept, but awaited word from his lawyer and partner. Their verdict was swift and certain: seeing the movie did nothing to change their minds that Paramount had constructed *Coming to America* on the foundation of *King for a Day*.

Eventually Paramount did make a counteroffer on Buchwald and Bernheim's claim: $50,000 plus a 1 percent interest in "net profits" from the movie which Buchwald and Bernheim could sell back to Paramount in the future for another $50,000. The terms of the settlement, Paramount also insisted, would have to be confidential.

Bernheim, who had spent his entire life either producing films or representing high-octane writers and actors as an agent, felt as though he had been hit in the gut. When King relayed the information to him the same week that the movie opened to huge box office response, Alain was silent for several seconds, shaking his head in a confusion of sadness and anger. Despite Paramount's superficial cordiality and professions of respect, the studio was treating Buchwald and Bernheim like two schleppers with no credentials and less credibility. For Bernheim, the entire matter had moved from the level of money to honor.

By the end of July, when I was interrupted at poolside by Danny Arnold, all negotiations had fizzled. Paramount would not budge off its $100,000 settlement offer, and Howard King's promise to Wattles that he would not be the one to file a lawsuit against the studio ended his role in the case. Because of his own firm's conflict of interest, he reluctantly had to withdraw.

Once again, Buchwald and Bernheim were all alone, looking for a lawyer.

3

Hardball
in Hollywood

FROM WHAT I HAD READ in the files and learned from Alain, I knew one thing for sure: I wasn't going to be their lawyer. Especially when Alain told me that they wanted a contingent fee arrangement: I'd get paid only if I won. The case just didn't strike me as a winner.

But Alain was Danny's friend, and Danny wanted me to give the case a hard look. That much I could do. After all, I told myself, what's a few hours of my time compared to Danny's friendship? Maybe I could recommend it to somebody who *would* take it on contingency. So I went at it, trying to find something encouraging. I first went through the same exercise as Howard King, comparing Art's treatment with the final shooting script for *Coming to America*.

I still refused to plunk down five dollars to see the movie. But what I now read in Art's original story was, at first blush, a completely different—and potentially far better—comedy than what I understood to be the story line of *Coming to America*:

> His Royal Highness, Majestic Ruler, Divine Potentate and direct descendant of Solomon and Sheba, Emperor Josiah Shebach of the African nation of Sheberia makes a State visit to Washington D.C. Because Sheberia happens to be the third largest oil-producing country in the world, the State Department, CIA and White House lay on the super red carpet, which includes military parades, State dinners, and beautiful women employed by the CIA for just such occasions.

Emperor Josiah is a spoiled rotten despot, who treats his subjects rather badly, and foreigners with utter contempt. The three hundred million dollars a day he receives in oil royalties has been spent on palaces, yachts, private airplanes and a tomb for him designed by I. M. Pei. His real purpose for his visit to the United States is to persuade the President to sell him top of the line military equipment from AWACS to nuclear submarines. Without them he feels he has no status as a world leader.

The U.S. is happy to oblige, since the Soviets are flirting with Josiah and CIA reports indicate they are offering the Emperor a bagful of military goodies.

The first part of the movie takes place showing Josiah getting the full treatment from an Oval Office meeting with the President to a ride on an American carrier, with stops at Disneyland, Las Vegas and a topless bar in San Francisco.

Back in Washington after the VIP tour, Josiah is overthrown by his brother-in-law and suddenly from being the most coddled head of state to visit the U.S. in two years, finds himself a non-person, a man without a country. His Minister of Finance takes off immediately—a terrible tragedy since the Minister is the only one who knows the numbers of Josiah's Swiss bank accounts.

The State Department, CIA and White House immediately recognize the new leader of Sheberia and, to make sure the oil will still flow to the West, they refuse to give Josiah asylum and ask him to leave the country as soon as possible.

Alas, Josiah without friends, except one CIA call girl, is booted out of his palatial hotel and left to wander the streets of Washington in his Marshal's uniform. He winds up in the District of Columbia's black ghetto, where he is treated as another crazy black. The second half of the movie deals with the downfall of Josiah as an alien black, who has to deal with life as it really is in the U.S.

After many harrowing experiences, Josiah becomes humbled and a better man. In the meantime the U.S. discovers the new leader of Sheberia is too difficult to live with and the CIA who overthrew Josiah without his knowledge start their plot to return Josiah to the throne. The first step is to find him. He thinks they are looking for him to kick him out of the country and the film ends with a wild chase through Washington. Once captured Josiah is informed of the new plan and decides to accept it, and become a beloved despot and improve the lot of his people with the help of the former CIA call girl whom he will make his Queen.

Several things struck me about Buchwald's treatment. It was simple, direct and wickedly funny. Months later, after I had read it several times, I noticed the phrase "another crazy black" in his reference to the deposed king wandering through the ghetto. When I brought it to Art's attention on the eve of his deposition, he caught it for the first time himself. "It's a typographical error. It should have read 'a crazy black,' " he told me. "I should never type my own stuff."

I reached the same conclusion as Howard King: the dissimilarities far outnumbered the similarities.

Art had a king. Paramount created a prince.

Art's king was despotic. Paramount's prince was sickeningly sweet.

Art's monarch came to America to get military weapons. Prince Akeem, Eddie Murphy's character, came to find a bride.

Art wrote a political satire. Paramount made a romantic comedy.

The plots, settings and supporting characters were different. On the surface, all that the two stories seemed to have in common was a royal black personage from a mythical African kingdom coming to America, having some experiences and going home with an American woman.

Howard King had ruled out plagiarism. I'd done enough copyright cases to see his logic. Federal copyright law protects only the concrete expression of ideas, not the ideas themselves. Nobody can copyright the idea of boy-meets-girl, girl-rejects-boy, boy-and-girl-finally-fall-in-love. But develop the idea into a specific, concrete work, such as *West Side Story*, and presto! The idea is copyrightable.

For centuries, dating back to old English common law, creativity had been encouraged and plagiarism lawsuits discouraged because they jeopardized freedom of artistic expression. Ideas were as free as the air. Stories were not.

Buchwald's treatment fell somewhere in the middle. It was more than a mere idea (African king becomes a fish out of water in American ghetto) but less than a fully developed story with secondary characters, articulated plot points and dialogue.

Assuming he survived Paramount's pretrial efforts to throw his case out of court, Buchwald, I concluded, would probably get blown out of the water in a federal copyright infringement trial. The jury would have to make both a quantitative and a qualitative evaluation of each story element, and his lawyer would have to show substantial similarities between *King for a Day* and *Coming to America*. Furthermore, he'd have to sue under United States copyright statutes. As they used to say back in high school, Buchwald would have to make a federal case out of it. And federal courts didn't pay much attention to plagiarism claims unless there was blatant, out-and-out copying. At that point in time, I didn't see a winning copyright case.

But, as I dug deeper, I did see something else—and I was suspicious. In the stack of letters between Alain and Paramount that began in late 1982 and extended through mid-1985, there were clues suggesting something more than a coincidental connection between Buchwald's story and the Eddie Murphy comedy. Murphy would portray an African monarch who came to America, just as Bernheim and Buchwald first suggested to Paramount in late 1982. All Paramount had to do was get the script right. There were lots of changes to be made in the characters, plot, theme and setting. But, basically, Paramount's ruling hierarchy in early 1983 had flipped over the idea, according to the correspondence.

Now, Paramount was claiming that Eddie independently conceived the idea, even though I had clear proof sitting on my desk that everyone from Paramount Pictures president Jeff Katzenberg to Eddie's own manager, Robert Wachs, knew very well that Alain was developing comedy scripts for Murphy about a black African king in the American ghetto and that it was all based on Art's material.

The trail of development was strewn with strong hints of skulduggery. But that wasn't enough for a lawsuit. I was getting more interested in this case, but I was still a lawyer in search of a legal theory.

Among the missing items in the packet Howard King sent over to me were Paramount's contracts with Art and Alain. I rang up Alain.

"They're standard form contracts," he said, "but if you want to read them, sure. I'll send them over."

I could almost hear him shrugging over the phone:

American lawyers. Why would anyone in his right mind want to pore over the boilerplate bilge in a fifty-page, single-spaced studio contract?

A week later, at Danny Arnold's beach house in Del Mar, I got a chance to tell him.

It was one of those great getaway weekends. Elegant beach house on the Pacific Ocean with its own tennis court and pool. Servants and smart conversation. Horse races at nearby Del Mar. Hobnobbing with the rich and famous —Robert Strauss, Jackie Cooper and diet queen Jenny Craig (whose very presence made me so self-conscious about the forty pounds that I had to lose that I couldn't enjoy dinner).

Connie and I joined Alain and Margie Bernheim as the Arnolds' houseguests. On Saturday evening, Danny hosted a dinner on the beach for Democratic gubernatorial candidate John Van De Kamp, then California attorney general and a longtime friend of mine. I had introduced John to Danny so that John could widen his circle of contacts in the entertainment industry for raising big bucks. After a dinner for thirty guests and the candidate's obligatory "thanks for coming, here's my vision for California" speech, I tugged at Alain's elbow. It was time we talked.

I wanted to get to know Alain better. I also wanted to share some of my latest thoughts. So, as the dinner guests chatted over their desserts, Alain and I walked along the serene, moonlit beach.

I learned during our hour-long stroll that, over the years, Bernheim had been through his own share of pitched battles with the studios. He recalled the actors, writers, producers and directors who stubbornly refused to play the game dictated by the studios and wound up ostracized.

One case in point was Jules Dassin, the brilliant young director of such *film noir* classics as *Brute Force* and *The Naked City* in the late 1940s. Following an appearance before the House Un-American Activities Committee, Dassin found himself blacklisted in 1951. As a matter of conscience, he had refused to tell this panel of elected witch hunters that he wasn't a Red. To the gutless studio chieftains, that was as good a reason as any not to let him make movies. The same people who elected Red-baiting congressmen and senators might not pay to see a movie made by a Red, they reasoned.

Dassin emigrated to Europe and enlisted Bernheim as his agent. Alain got his first front-line lesson in Hollywood blackballing. The oligopoly's tentacles wrapped around the globe. Even in Europe he couldn't get Dassin a job that involved any of the major Hollywood studios.

So, Bernheim remembered, Dassin scraped together his own small nest egg and found a backer willing to put up $60,000 in production money. He went to Greece, hired a local camera crew and filmed his own feature, starring Melina Mercouri, who later became his wife. Because it was a shoestring operation, mostly right out of Dassin's pocket, it took months longer to film than it should have. Dassin, who took no salary, sold off or gave away some of the profits but kept 75 percent for himself—just in case the film hit.

Never on Sunday won the Palme d'Or at Cannes in 1960, the year it was released. Even a McCarthyized Hollywood couldn't ignore Dassin any longer. United Artists bought the distribution rights. Within weeks of the title song winning an Academy Award, Dassin's comedy—about an Athenian prostitute who gave up sex one day a week to attend performances of Greek tragedies on Sundays—became an international box office smash.

Bernheim smiled scornfully at the memory, his dour eyes crinkling at the edges as he remembered his first real lesson in how studios calculate net profits.

Even including Mercouri's up-front $25,000 salary, Dassin's entire price tag for producing *Never on Sunday* was only $105,000, and worldwide box office reports put the take of the film near the $10 million mark. By today's standards, *Never on Sunday* would have qualified as a mini-blockbuster.

Jules Dassin, the blacklisted Hollywood pariah, looked like he was about to clean up in a most capitalistic way. But two years later, when Bernheim went to Arthur Krim, the head of United Artists, to ask for his client's share of the net profits, he was told there were none.

"You're entitled to it, but you must bear in mind," Krim told him, "that we lost money with some other movies. Therefore, we have to compensate for the losers with the winners."

Bernheim had seen or heard of similar cases over the years, but he never stopped being amazed at the bizarre canon of ethics that allowed studios to shaft their most profitable assets—their stars, their storytellers and their directors—while rewarding their most irresponsible and often useless executives.

The David Begelman affair was still the quintessential case in point. David was Alain's friend from the old days and had a hand in the early stages of *King for a Day.* Alain was loyal, but I still was amazed by Begelman's chutzpah and ability to bounce back from scandal. It said more about Hollywood than anything else.

Ten years after his forgery conviction, Begelman was working for Gladden Entertainment, the independent production company that hired Michael Cimino and Mario Puzo to film the box office bomb *The Sicilian.*

The topsy-turvy amorality of Hollywood is a puzzle to outsiders. Everyone is expected to cover for everyone else. That's how it works. Drugs, whoring, gambling, cheating, assault . . . almost any kind of vice is tolerated in the pursuit of power and profit. One of the reasons Bernheim chose to spend most of his career operating out of Europe rather than Los Angeles was because he did not want his two sons growing up in the moral wasteland of Beverly Hills.

From the moment he ended a quarter century of voluntary exile and moved back to Hollywood in 1979, he discovered things had changed considerably since he left Hollywood in 1954 to start his own literary agency in Paris. In those days, the old guard in Hollywood still came to France and Italy and England looking for original ideas and promising stories. Even the worst studio scoundrels in the 1940s and '50s had some honor about them, Bernheim remembered. Louis B. Mayer, Jack Warner, Darryl F. Zanuck . . . they were all cutthroats, but cutthroats with long memories and a code of ethics.

When a Darryl Zanuck signed off on a "deal memo," it was as good as gold, whether written on Fox stationery or a cocktail napkin from a Palm Springs bar. Multi-page contracts usually followed, replete with "wherefores" and "theretos," but the basic deal was as solid as the studio head's signature and handshake. Even with Paramount's legendary tough guy and founder, Adolph Zukor, you knew where you stood if he made a commitment.

In the 1980s, even a producer like Bernheim, who knew the ropes and had been part of the Hollywood scene in one capacity or another for decades, rarely got to talk to studio heads. There seemed to be countless corporate vice-presidents, executive vice-presidents and senior vice-presidents who did the talking for the studio bosses.

Furthermore, it was an article of faith that the easiest and safest word to utter in modern Hollywood was "no." Trying to get a "yes" out of one of the young "development" executives, as the various yuppie vice-presidents were called, was often a double exercise in futility. Even if you got them to green-light a project, a senior vice-president or an executive vice-president up the line could, and usually would, veto it.

There was a time, Bernheim remembered with a sigh, not so very long ago, when all movie projects were somebody's love affair and not "product," "inventory" or just one of a file cabinet full of development deals.

He loved to tell and retell his stories of the Old Hollywood in the late 1940s, when he started out as a junior agent for Famous Artists Agency. His older brother, Michel, had been a stage and film director in France before the war and encouraged Bernheim to go to the United States if he wanted to make his mark in motion pictures. After fighting with the Free French Army during the war, Bernheim tried his hand at stage production in New York with a short-lived American version of Jean-Paul Sartre's grim existentialist play *No Exit.*

From there, Bernheim moved on to Hollywood, and learned the film business at the knee of Famous Artists president Charles Feldman, a Clark Gable look-alike who is still acknowledged as the man who invented "movie packaging." Feldman figured out early that an agency which handled actors, directors and writers could wrest a lot of power away from the studios by simply mixing and matching scripts with stars before they ever got into a producer's hands. That way, a movie project that a Paramount or United Artists or Columbia wanted to make would have to use everyone from the same agency—neatly wrapped in a single package. It meant steady employment for all of Feldman's clients, 10 percent of their earnings for the agency, and lots of clout for Famous Artists when its junior agents, like Alain Bernheim, went knocking at the studio gates.

One rule remained absolutely inviolable in both the Old and New Hollywoods: you had to know somebody to get anything done. People rarely got jobs or made deals in Hollywood, he told me, unless they were part of a network or "family" that played together as often as they worked together.

Movie deals were usually negotiated miles from anyone's office. Bernheim remembered that his first real breakthrough came at the end of one particularly discouraging week of schlepping scripts to the studios in the late 1940s. At a dinner he attended at Feldman's Beverly Hills home the previous week, Darryl Zanuck had asked Alain to come to Palm Springs for the weekend and to play croquet. What he discovered was anything but the tea-and-crumpets game he had learned to play as a child in France.

Director Howard Hawks, restaurateur Mike Romanoff and actor Louis Jourdan were all there. To his surprise, they played *very* serious croquet nearly all night long for big stakes, while Bernheim played the way he had as a kid. To put it mildly, he admitted to me, they cleaned his mallet.

It wasn't losing the money that hurt so much. It was his bruised ego, Bernheim remembered. Their brand of croquet became addictive. The bruised ego was worth it in the long run, though. Bernheim soon found himself facing Darryl Zanuck and his buddies in Zanuck's Palm Springs backyard. What he lost on the croquet course during the weekends he more than made up for when he went calling on studio brass during the week, a hot new book or script under one arm.

In 1954 he made a deal with Otto Preminger that convinced him that his apprenticeship with Feldman was over. After several years of learning how to package movie deals, Bernheim had taken Françoise Sagan's bestseller *Bonjour Tristesse* to Preminger on behalf of French producer Charles Ventura, who had purchased the film rights from the author for $10,000. Preminger paid $150,000 for the rights. In one afternoon, Bernheim had made a 1500 percent profit for Ventura.

It was time to return to the fertile fields of Paris and open his own agency.

For the next twenty-four years, Bernheim conducted most of his successful business in Paris and London, acting as an agent for some filmmakers, such as Jules Dassin, but concentrating most of his efforts on representing writers who wanted their work turned into film. People like Gore Vidal and Françoise Sagan and James Jones . . . and a shrewd, happy-go-lucky American newspaper columnist for the *Herald Tribune* named Art Buchwald.

Their wives were friends first, but it didn't take long after Bernheim's return to Paris for Buchwald and him to become frequent lunch partners. Alain recalled fondly how they loved to sit outside Fouquet's, sipping coffee and admiring the beautiful women. Even after Buchwald returned to America in

1962 to become a Washington-based columnist, they stayed in touch by mail. Once, for Buchwald's birthday, Bernheim surprised him with a leather-bound copy of their written correspondence, titled "A.B. to A.B."

They visited in person whenever Buchwald flew back to Paris, but Bernheim preferred Europe to the United States and tried to avoid making the return trek. Eventually, however, it became apparent that he would have to follow Buchwald's example and come back to America. With each passing year, it got tougher and tougher to sell novels and scripts to moviemakers who operated out of studios located five thousand miles to the west. The nature of the movie business was changing, and Bernheim understood he would have to move back to California if he were going to continue to make a living.

What's more, Bernheim was also growing tired of just being an agent. His mentor Charles Feldman finally sold his agency to become an independent producer of classics like *Bus Stop* and *The Glass Menagerie*. If you could cut the right deal with the studios as an independent producer, you could take in more money on a single movie than you ever could earn in 10 percent commissions as an agent, Feldman had once advised Bernheim. It was time for Bernheim to try his hand at the producing game.

When he closed up shop on the Champs Élysées in 1979 at age fifty-nine and returned to Hollywood as an independent producer, one of the first things Bernheim noticed after a few months in the States was that nobody played croquet anymore.

In the 1980s, they played hardball instead.

The moon was shimmering over the waves as we started back toward Danny's beach house. Alain breathed deeply and smiled. He'd told me his life story and I'd given him a précis of mine. The introductions were out of the way. It was time for a professional opinion on the merits of the Bernheim/ Buchwald case against Paramount.

"Well, counselor, what do you think now that you have had a chance to study the documents?"

"I really haven't had a chance to fully study the case yet," I equivocated, walking toward the beach house a little faster. As our feet sank into the sand, Bernheim showed some of the persistence that had made him the tireless and successful man that he was.

"Oh, I know that you haven't concluded your research and what not," he began. "But what does your gut tell you? Danny tells me that you have good gut instincts."

"My gut tells me that you have a tough copyright case. *Coming to America* is not Buchwald's *King for a Day* in the way that the courts interpret the federal copyright laws."

He stopped and looked at me quizzically. I tried another tack.

"While they are not quite apples and oranges, the fact that they're both fruits is not enough," I said.

"Oh, I see," he said, disappointment flooding his face. "Does that mean that we don't have a case?"

We started moving again, the evening wind picking up behind us and nudging us gently along the strand. Off to the left, ten yards away, the tide was moving in and clouds began to dull the moon.

"Can't we do *anything* about Paramount using Art's idea?" he pleaded. "I know in *my* gut that the studio is protecting Murphy by saying that their big star came up with the idea on his own."

"Look, Alain, I'm sorry. I don't make the law. I agree with you that's probably what happened. But I need evidence, not to mention a plausible legal theory to wrap it in."

I let my words sink in before continuing. The little Frenchman suddenly looked ten years older and I felt very guilty.

"Look: the copyright approach is a dead-bang loser," I said. "You'll get tossed out of federal court so fast that you won't know that you were ever there."

Alain's shoulders started to slump.

"But I may have found something in your contracts," I continued. "It's funny how you can read something several times and not see the obvious."

"What are you saying?" he asked.

"I don't want to get your hopes up too much, so please understand that I just discovered this contract language last night after everyone went to bed: I have not had a chance yet to do any research."

By now we had stopped walking altogether. Alain looked at me with a trusting gaze that I would see many times in the next several years. I slowly, deliberately chose my words.

"Art's contract says, in effect, that if Paramount makes a movie based upon his treatment, it has to pay him a certain amount of money plus 1.5 percent of the net profits. Now, this clause just might be the hook to hang Paramount from. If we can prove that the studio used Art's treatment as the basis for *Coming to America* and that they adapted it during an extended, but unbroken, development process, we might just nail them."

Bernheim nodded as though he understood every word, but I knew he hadn't the foggiest notion of what it was I was driving at.

"So, is this a copyright violation?" he asked.

"No, it would be a simple breach of contract," I said.

He did understand whose contract I was talking about and it was not his.

"What . . . what about my case?" he asked meekly.

I wrapped an arm around his shoulders.

"I've got an idea there too. Your contract says that Paramount is agreeing to hire you as the producer and pay you a lot of money if Paramount makes what your contract calls 'the Picture.' Well, 'the Picture' is defined as Buchwald's *King for a Day*. So, if Paramount made a movie based on Buchwald's treatment, they made *King for a Day* and should have hired you as the producer.

They didn't, so they breached your contract too. In other words, Art and you are contractually a package. At least that's my working theory right now."

"*Fantastique!*" exclaimed this old veteran of the Hollywood wars, clapping his hands.

"Now, Alain, hold on," I cautioned. "I told you that these were only hypotheses. I really have to do some legal research to see what, if anything, the courts have said about the meaning of 'based upon.' I still don't know if this breach-of-contract idea holds water. Please don't assume anything yet."

I had learned the hard way never to arouse a prospective client's expectations. Too many things can go wrong.

"When do you think you might know?" Alain pressed.

"I'm taking the family to New Orleans next week to visit Connie's folks and I've asked one of our associates to research my breach-of-contract notion. I should know something by the time I return. Now let's forget about this for a while. How about some croquet tomorrow morning?"

4

Flying High

AS THE PLANE leveled off at 35,000 feet, I opened my bulging briefcase and faced the grim task of catching up on my reading. Two dozen active cases meant another working family vacation. Connie intermittently read and dozed in the seat next to me while Meghan and Brendan played quietly in the seats behind us. I fished for a file.

I came up with the one fat folder that I was genuinely eager to digest: a file my library staff had prepared containing more than fifty articles and book excerpts about Eddie Murphy, dating back to 1980. During our three-and-a-half-hour flight to New Orleans, I hoped to learn as much as I could from the public record about the man Paramount claimed to be the sole creator of *Coming to America*.

As I dug into my file, the flight attendant stopped at my seat with a stack of magazines. I started to wave her away until I saw Eddie Murphy's face grinning at me from the cover of *People*. I picked it off the top of the stack and put my file folder down on the tray in front of me.

Murphy's face was everywhere in the summer of 1988: on TV, in fan magazines, newspapers, billboards and, of course, theater lobbies . . . a twenty-seven-year-old who bestrode the entertainment world like a colossus. I had a vague idea of who he was and where he came from. Like thirty million other Americans, I had seen him interviewed once on a Barbara Walters special. Of course, Barbara Walters is not exactly Ted Koppel when it comes to grilling her guests. So I had my doubts that I really knew all that much about Eddie Murphy beyond what Paramount Studios and he wanted me and everyone else in America to know.

Leafing through the magazine raised a host of questions: Exactly what was his background and what kind of a person was he? Honest? In touch with reality? Who were his friends and were they really friends or merely opportunistic "yes men" who told him what he wanted to hear? Could he really have conceived the story for *Coming to America* by himself? And had he ever taken credit for something that he did not do?

By the time we arrived in New Orleans, I would have a lot more questions. The real Eddie Murphy was only dimly suggested in a handful of articles and movie reviews. Paramount's publicity department could have written all the rest. In his occasional one-on-one interview, Murphy came off as wary, aloof and frequently angry, but rarely revealing about the biggest question of all:

What makes Eddie tick?

The Eddie Murphy I was to discover in my research was not the Eddie Murphy I saw fielding Barbara Walters' softball questions.

I first knew him as a brilliant, raw talent whose career I had followed as a fan from his very first network performance on "Saturday Night Live." His humor transcended race and class. I found him refreshingly original and funny.

But Alain told me about a very different Eddie Murphy—a spoiled brat on and off camera. He was profane and cocky and, to a Frenchman schooled in the social graces, totally insufferable.

Maybe, I thought. But Bernheim's feelings could also be largely attributable to the generation gap, as well as cultural differences. Alain was entitled to his opinion.

I had to form my own.

And what I learned from my files as I flew to New Orleans was that the official Paramount Pictures biography of Eddie Murphy masked the hardship, loneliness and dedication that molded him into a unique talent.

Edward Regan Murphy was born on April 3, 1961, in the Bushwick section of Brooklyn. His older brother Charles, the firstborn, got the father's first name. But Eddie inherited all the rest, including his dad's middle name. He had Charles Edward Murphy's laugh and lust and driving need to be something more, something better than what his parents were and what their parents were before them.

Charles Murphy was a New York Transit Authority cop by day. But at night and on weekends, he was a stand-up comic, making the rounds of the suburban nightclubs and the roadhouses across the river in New Jersey. Charlie Murphy wanted to be a star.

Charlie did all right for a black from Bushwick with a limited education and three mouths to feed. All that angst was great fodder for his comedy routines: the restraining wife and two howling babies; the free-loading relatives who dropped in and stayed too long; the eked-out living on a meager municipal paycheck.

But it was not all that funny in real life. Charlie began drinking heavily and having affairs with other women. By the time he finally left home, none of it was very funny anymore.

Eddie was only three when his parents' divorce became final.

For the next five crucial years, Eddie's life turned both menacing and wacky.

His mother tried keeping her young family together after Charlie walked out, but she fell gravely ill and had to give the boys up for a time. All his life, Eddie has remembered the ugly months that he had to live in a foster home while his mother recuperated. His foster mother may have simply been the kind of tough disciplinarian that Eddie never had to deal with in his own laissez-faire household, but he remembered her as a "black Nazi." Years later, he credited the woman with turning him into a comedian by making it next to impossible for him to endure in her household without a strong, defensive sense of humor.

The only real relief from his dictatorial foster mother's tyranny was in the TV set. Even when things got better and the family was reunited, Eddie remained a TV junkie, his eyes glued to the set for hours every day and his mind recording the impressions for future playback. Bullwinkle the Moose, Gumby, Bugs Bunny, Laurel and Hardy, Elvis Presley, Jackie Wilson, Martin and Lewis, Bruce Lee, the Beatles, and *West Side Story*, among many others. Of all of them, the King would become his idol.

"I thought Elvis had more presence and charisma than anybody who ever existed," Eddie once remarked.

In the first few years at elementary school, Eddie and his older brother Charlie, Jr., had to learn how to defend themselves against bullies with something other than an uppercut or a right hook. Eddie mimicked his TV heroes in the schoolyard, delivering insults to taunters in a Bugs Bunny drawl or a Speedy Gonzales Hispanic accent. Charlie and he would trade ridicule on the schoolhouse steps or in the hallways—called "doing the dozens"—to demonstrate to would-be tormentors the kind of sarcasm Eddie was capable of delivering if anyone got too close.

When he was eight years old, two things happened that changed Eddie's life forever: his father was killed and his mother remarried.

The death of Charles Edward Murphy was "the worst tragedy ever to happen to me," Eddie would recall in one of his interviews years later.

Charlie Murphy did not die in the line of duty. He died at the hands of a lover. Yvette Wright was only twenty-one when she confessed to the stabbing death of her older boyfriend. It was, according to court records, self-defense: the awful climax of a drunken lovers' quarrel. The court convicted her of manslaughter, but all she served was five years' probation.

Besides Eddie and his older brother, Charles Murphy left twin daughters behind. Wanda and Shondell Murphy were one year old when their mother stabbed their father to death.

Then Lillian Murphy met and married Vernon Lynch. Vernon gave Lillian and her boys stability and a real home. They moved outside of the five boroughs to the predominantly black, working-class suburb of Roosevelt on Long Island, less than an hour from the Big Apple. Vernon also gave her a third son —Eddie's half brother, Vernon, Jr.

Lillian had taken a job as a telephone operator before she met Vernon Lynch. After they married, she stayed on at the phone company, supplementing Vernon's salary as a loading foreman at a Breyer's ice cream plant. For more than a decade after they moved to Long Island, the double-income family that had lived on a shoestring in one of the toughest parts of Brooklyn was now very middle class.

Growing up, when he was not memorizing television shows and movies, Eddie would be in the basement lip-synching the records of his idol Elvis and other singers. He rarely did his homework. It was not a question of his aptitude. He just had his own ideas about what he wanted to do with his life and it had little to do with studies.

Eddie worked hard, mixing impersonations with stand-up gags. At fifteen, he had already started to develop the self-confidence—cockiness, some would say—that became his trademark. Once that year, when lectured by his high school social studies teacher about being unprepared for class, Eddie replied: "One day, I'm going to be as famous as Bob Hope." The funny kid voted most popular boy in his graduating class also prophesied that he would be famous by the time he was nineteen and a millionaire at age twenty-two. He was right on both counts.

Eddie's first club dates were talent shows at the local youth center and high school auditorium where he confronted and conquered stage fright. All those hours of practicing in front of the mirror and in the basement paid off. When he did his first impersonation of Al Green, strutting around the stage like Elvis, the girls started screaming, and Eddie recalled his instant reaction:

"I said, 'Shit, you can't make girls scream doing a lot of other jobs, such as driving an ice cream truck.' . . . I looked *sooo* good to those little girls. They'd squeal at my every move. Looking out at the audience, I knew that I was in show biz for the rest of my life."

Besides talent, Murphy had something else a performer needs: moxie. Eddie hustled club dates the way other teenagers hustle the keys to the family car. At one point, before he acquired an agent, Murphy put his impersonation skills to good use by posing as an agent and calling all over New York and New Jersey to book shows for the hot new comic from Roosevelt, Eddie Murphy.

This was 1976. Adolph Zukor, the founder of Paramount, died that year at age one hundred and three, ending a fabled career. Eddie Murphy was fifteen. He was just getting started.

That year, Eddie found an ad in the Yellow Pages for an agent named Irving "King" Broder. He began hanging around the small-time Catskills talent manager's office and made such a pest of himself that Broder started booking him into clubs. Broder couldn't sign him to a personal management contract until he turned eighteen, but he did find him jobs all over Long Island and taught him about stage presence, rehearsing material and working a crowd. Sometimes Eddie worked for as little as $20 a night at clubs with names like the Blue Dolphin, Mr. Hicks, the White House and My Father's Place.

When Eddie did turn eighteen, Broder got him to sign immediately on the dotted line.

His mother wanted him to go to college and make something of himself. Eddie obliged but dropped out of Nassau Community College after only three weeks of classes in the autumn of 1979. His stepfather wanted him to get a real job instead of bumming around bars and theaters all his life, futilely attempting to break into show business. Even then, he was still boasting about being a millionaire—a *famous* millionaire.

When he was a little more seasoned, Eddie teamed up with two white comedians, Bob Nelson and Rob Bartlett, in a novelty act that Broder booked as The Identical Triplets. When the Triplets act broke up, Eddie struck out on his own, sharpening his impressions and adding Howard Cosell, Bill Cosby and Bruce Lee to his repertoire.

He also listened carefully to the comedy albums of his newest hero, Richard Pryor. After he had made it big, Eddie would acknowledge his debt to Pryor, the man whom he credited as "my only influence. . . . He got status and respect just by being his own outrageous self, on his own terms."

That's exactly how Murphy wanted to make it: on his own terms. When his break came at the Comic Strip, Eddie was ready.

A cover-charge nightclub with fake brick on the interior walls, the Comic Strip was one of several Upper East Side Manhattan joints where the careers of stand-up comics were born.

Bob Nelson, one of the Identical Triplets who often did the Comic Strip amateur-night gig himself, told the owners about Murphy. A former Bronx bar owner named Richie Tienken and a Harvard-educated lawyer named Robert Wachs were the odd couple who operated the Comic Strip. They were not interested in a Long Island teenager who did impressions. In Manhattan, everybody did impressions. The first time Eddie showed up to do his routine, Wachs did not let him perform and threw him out of the club.

But ultimately Eddie swayed both Wachs and Tienken with his tenacity and had the audience howling with his impressions. He was Martin and Lewis, Stevie Wonder and Jackie Wilson, Laurel and Hardy. Mainly, he was shamelessly Richard Pryor, down to the mannerisms and the slightly stooped stage stance.

Tienken and Wachs worked with him, making suggestions: drop that line and stand a little bit differently and show some attitude. Don't blink. Don't linger. Cut to the chase.

Tienken sent him to another Comic Strip club he operated in Fort Lauderdale to hone his material and then brought him back to New York with several fresh new routines.

Within months, Broder heard that "Saturday Night Live" was holding auditions. He sent one of his other comics to the seventeenth floor of Rockefeller Center and asked Eddie if he'd like to try his luck too. Murphy called Tienken and Wachs and asked them to come along.

Eddie tried out with a "Saturday Night Live" talent coordinator, playing three different street-corner blacks. In a replay of a typical Roosevelt High situation, one of Eddie's characters would goad the other two into a fight, then walk away unscathed himself.

Eddie left enough of an impression for a callback and started performing the same routine for anyone who would watch, from talent coordinators to the producer to writers and competing actors. It took five auditions, but he finally landed the "ethnic" slot that had been occupied since "Saturday Night Live"'s inception by veteran comedian and character actor Garrett Morris. Murphy's salary was $750 a week.

From the outset, Eddie Murphy planned *not* to step into Garrett Morris's shoes. He rehearsed his material with his characteristic intensity, vigilantly watching for his main chance. Mr. Moxie did not wait long. He made sure that he got to know the men and women who put the words into his mouth: the writers. Namely, a thirty-one-year-old playwright from Decatur, Alabama, named David Sheffield who was making his own debut as a "Saturday Night Live" writer, and Barry Blaustein, who had begun to team up with the Alabaman in writing sketches. Blaustein, a Long Island native with a degree in broadcast journalism from New York University, told Eddie about a news item he had run across that might make a funny bit for the Weekend Update segment. A Midwestern judge had ruled that a Cleveland high school had to have at least two white players on its basketball team to insure racial balance. What about an outraged black commentator turning the tables on the prevailing wisdom that only tall black athletes can dominate in basketball? It had comic potential, Blaustein told Murphy.

As a result, Eddie's second national TV appearance was in the guise of militant black commentator Raheem Abdul Muhammad. After ranting at the injustice of a system that will not even let blacks control the basketball court, Raheem pulled a huge ghetto blaster from beneath his seat and told the audience:

"I mean, if God had wanted whites to be equal to blacks, everyone would have one of these!"

The audience roared and Eddie Murphy was on his way.

For the rest of the 1980–81 television season, he was on a roll. By the time he turned twenty years old the following April, he was the undisputed star of the new "Saturday Night Live." He was re-signed for the 1981–82 season as a regular cast member at $4,500 an episode—six times what he had been paid his rookie season.

The 1981–82 season became the Year of Eddie Murphy. His two favorite writers were at the helm, and Joe Piscopo, who had become Murphy's closest friend, became his on-camera foil.

One of the twenty million who tuned in each week during that season was veteran screenwriter-director Walter Hill. Four years earlier, Hill had written a script for Paramount Pictures about a jive-talking black convict and a gruff white cop, chasing criminals together through the streets of San Francisco. It was an action comedy that had once been considered for the winning team of Richard Pryor and Gene Wilder, whose *Silver Streak* and *Stir Crazy* hits had made them the black and white Martin and Lewis of the 1970s.

But, as so often happens in Hollywood, interest waned, and the movie had since fallen onto the dusty shelves of the Paramount story department next to hundreds of other optioned scripts that would never be filmed.

Hildy Gottlieb, an agent for International Creative Management, was familiar with Walter Hill and his script. She lived with him, after all.

She was also familiar with Eddie Murphy. Tienken and Wachs had asked ICM to act as Murphy's agency for Hollywood offers. They were his managers, having squeezed King Broder out of the picture after Eddie's initial TV success.

It didn't take long for Gottlieb to convince Hill to think of Murphy as a possibility for the black convict in his script. Hill had seen him run through bits where his comedy appeared to be more acted out than improvised. In more than a decade of moviemaking (*The Long Riders, The Driver, Brewster's Millions*), Hill had learned to spot the difference between a comic actor and a stand-up comic. Based on what he saw the young comic do on "Saturday Night Live," Hill—whose first choice, Richard Pryor, had dropped out—recommended Eddie for the role of the convict Reggie Hammond in *48 HRS.*

Through Hildy Gottlieb, Paramount contacted Richie Tienken and Bob Wachs.

They had just negotiated a $100,000 deal with CBS Records for Murphy to release a comedy record album, replete with the vulgarisms of nightclub humor that he was not allowed to use on "Saturday Night Live." According to Wachs, it was the record deal that cinched the movie role for his client and put him in a position to ask for a fat first-time actor's salary. If Murphy was hot enough to command $100,000 for a first-time album, he was hot enough to earn $200,000 for a first-time movie, Wachs reasoned.

Paramount agreed, but added its own insurance policy with a rider to Murphy's contract that gave the studio an option to make a second film with Murphy for $350,000 if the first one should be successful.

Eddie photocopied the $200,000 check and pinned it to a bulletin board in his dressing room. The photocopy was a tangible focal point for the Eddie Murphy formula: fame + money = success.

Less than eighteen hours after the last "Saturday Night Live" telecast of the 1981–82 season, Murphy was on a plane to San Francisco for location shooting in his first motion picture role. That summer he learned what it meant to be an incipient star—perks ranging from personal aides and drivers to women hangers-on and room service.

Before getting on the plane, Eddie had just been given a raise at "Saturday Night Live": $8,700 an episode for each of the shows in the upcoming 1982–83 season. By the time of his fourth and final season (1983–84), Eddie was pulling in $30,000 per episode. But even $30,000 was chicken feed compared to the salary a movie star earns.

Murphy's eyes turned to Hollywood.

Few actors have made as big a splash in their screen debuts as this twenty-one-year-old did in *48 HRS.* And in the 1980s no one was bigger, more popular or more bankable. His first seven movies for Paramount—*48 HRS., Trading Places, Best Defense, Beverly Hills Cop, Golden Child, Raw,* and *Beverly Hills Cop II*—sold over $1.5 *billion* in tickets, videos, merchandise and cable, pay TV, network and syndicated television licenses. By the time he made *Coming to America* in 1988, Murphy was only twenty-seven, but commanded $8 million in salary per picture, plus a hefty piece of Paramount's *gross* receipts before deducting any expense—a full-partner status reserved for such heavyweights as Sylvester Stallone, Robert Redford and Paul Newman. None of those silly "net profits" for Eddie.

And he wanted to be his own man, to have the total creative control of a filmmaker by writing, directing, producing and starring in his own movies, "like Chaplin used to do. Nobody does that anymore."

Eddie had his share of critics in the black community. While some reviewers praised Murphy for making us laugh at our own racial stereotypes, respected black journalist and film critic Armand White blasted "rich, brash, young Eddie" as the Stepin Fetchit of the 1980s. In a New York *Daily News* column, White castigated Paramount's Golden Child for his racism and sexism, "senseless as well as appalling" jokes about homosexuals, and squandering his talent on stereotypical caricatures to such an extent that he had "become a deeply offensive presence in contemporary movies."

Eddie ignored criticism. Middle-of-the-road comedy was temporizing; he needed to be outrageous to be effective. Otherwise, "I'd just be another face," he insisted. "My comedy is wild and dangerous. I like people to think of me as a comic who takes chances. Richard Pryor is where he is now because of dangerous comedy."

There was no arguing with Eddie that his comedy was dangerous. At various times he managed to offend almost everyone. In his 1987 concert film *Raw*, the most financially successful concert film ever, Eddie antagonized a lot of folks with his mean monologues about grasping "bitches" and sexual infidelity, unrelenting foul language, scatological and sexist humor, and "fag" jokes. The Motion Picture Association of America threatened an X rating until Paramount cleaned it up a little.

Eddie himself later acknowledged, "I look at it now and cringe. It's not so much that I think *Raw* wasn't funny, but I can't believe what I was feeling then."

Eddie's unrelenting stream of profanities in his stand-up routine prompted criticism from Old Hollywood celebrities like Lucille Ball and Red Skelton. Murphy himself told the story about the telephone call from Bill Cosby: "Bill Cosby . . . told me that he didn't like my act. . . . He never saw it."

Eddie's gay bashing was also a staple of his repertoire. While he at first defended his gay jokes ("I poke fun at everybody. . . . It's comedy. It's not real"), he eventually apologized in *Parade* magazine.

His conspicuous womanizing and sexist jokes incurred the wrath of some feminists. Some observers believed that Eddie had a problem dealing with women as equals and not just sexual objects. When *Rolling Stone* wanted to interview Murphy in 1987, the magazine's editor proposed a woman reporter. Manager Wachs rejected her out of hand, explaining: "Eddie wouldn't feel comfortable with a woman, wouldn't be himself. At the house, he runs around in his underwear and the guys are always talking about girls—'Did you fuck her?' Stuff like that."

Eddie's best friends were all men, black men who comprised what he called the Black Pack. The exclusive membership included Paul Mooney (Richard Pryor's head writer for fifteen years), Robert Townsend (comic, actor, film-maker [*Hollywood Shuffle*], and director of *Raw*), Keenen Ivory Wayans (star of "In Living Color" and writer who authored the introduction to *Raw*), and Arsenio Hall (actor, talk show host, comic and closest friend). Eddie occupied the equivalent centrifugal role of Frank Sinatra in his Rat Pack: chairman of the board. And Arsenio's television show became a sort of Black Pack club-house.

Eddie had strong feelings about racism in America.

"A very militant black woman said to me, 'How come no serious black actors get the same kind of deals you get or Richard Pryor gets? How come it's always a comic?' I said because America is still a racist society."

Eddie was tired of getting scripts written by whites. Eddie was tired of seeing only white directors and producers. And Eddie was tired of how blacks were portrayed on television.

"Black people, we didn't have no malt shop like Fonz [in *Happy Days*]," he observed. "Happy days! We got one hero—Martin Luther King. He's the only hero we have. And they killed him. We ain't been having no happy days."

Eddie's moral outrage about the treatment of blacks in the motion picture industry led to two remarkable protests. At the 1988 Academy Awards show, Eddie was the presenter for Best Picture. Sporting tails and a gold medallion, he delivered an unscheduled, rambling diatribe against the Hollywood Estab-lishment. An angry Eddie announced to shocked viewers that he almost did not show because "they haven't recognized black people in motion pictures," only three blacks have won Oscars in over sixty years. At this rate, "we ain't due until 2004."

A year earlier, Eddie had refused to pose for Paramount's seventy-fifth anniversary group photo of the studio's great stars—the likes of Elizabeth Taylor, Robert DeNiro, Tom Cruise and Charlton Heston. The picture, shot with the famous Bronson Avenue gateway entrance into Paramount Studios as a backdrop, was published as part of a *Life* magazine salute to Hollywood in April 1987.

Eddie's reason for refusing to appear in the picture was, again, a racial protest but, as it turned out, a misinformed one.

"It was an historical thing, right? Then I noticed I was going to be the only black face in the picture. So I decided not to do it. I figured 25 years from now, for their 100th anniversary, when they've got a lot more black faces up there, I'll be glad to take part in a picture."

The finished photo was not completely white. Sixty-one of the faces were white, but Oscar winner Lou Gossett, Jr., stood head and shoulders over Penny Marshall and Debra Winger, fourth row back from the camera.

The private Eddie Murphy was a study in stark contrasts.

Despite his notorious womanizing and at least one paternity suit in 1987 by a Los Angeles woman who accused him of fathering her child and offering her $50,000 to have an abortion, the most important woman in his life remained his mother, Lillian. He bought her and his stepfather a beautiful home in Alpine, New Jersey, employed his brother and stepbrother, and took care of his cousins and schoolday friends.

"My family's happiness is the most important thing to me," he admitted to his interviewers. Incongruous as it may seem to those who associate him with the foul-mouthed, brash comic, Murphy has a spiritual side. Raised a Christian, he prays every night, but he is not a religious zealot.

Eddie Murphy is the black Gatsby. He lives in a colonial-style brick mansion in suburban New Jersey. Surrounded by a brick wall and fences, it is a 3.5-acre palatial spread, perched up on a hill and replete with a gym, indoor pool, polished marble floors and each room decorated in a different style. Parked in front of the portico is a blue Rolls-Royce convertible. The place is called Bubble Hill, street jargon for "party" and a fitting nickname considering the steady flow of gorgeous young women imported for Eddie and his friends. His huge bedroom has a makeshift recording studio and an imposing seven-foot-tall oil portrait of Elvis.

At Bubble Hill and everywhere else he went, King Eddie, like Prince Akeem in *Coming to America*, was attended by his court—a collection of managers, relatives, pals and employees. Eddie was their friend and meal ticket. They included his uncle Ray, brother Charlie, cousin Ray, Jr., Ken "Fruitie" Frith and Federoff, the valet.

A Bubble Hill visitor from *Rolling Stone* was struck by the fact that "Murphy does seem to be living out some sort of classic American myth . . . the regal trappings, the zealous security, the sycophantic hangers-on . . . the omnipresent boys, most of whom are on the payroll as bodyguards or assistants. They're always heard saying, 'You're great, Eddie.' "

Known as "Money" around the offices of Eddie Murphy Productions, Inc.,

Murphy was surrounded by yes-men—both at Bubble Hill and on the Paramount lot. Thanks to Eddie, Paramount was the top studio for most of the 1980s. "He is Paramount," a Paramount executive stressed in 1987.

Arsenio Hall, "Little Money," saw the dangers of his best friend becoming an out-of-touch star: "There came a point in his life where if Eddie would say, 'I think I'm gonna shit on the stage,' people would say, 'Yeah, that's funny, Eddie, do shit on the stage.' And these people were on his payroll. He realized a lot of people won't be honest with you anymore when you're Eddie Murphy."

Eddie's entourage had its positive aspects, too. He was a caring boss whose loyalty and generosity to his relatives and friends were admirable. Tim Kazurinsky, Murphy's buddy from "Saturday Night Live," noted: "Eddie's a multinational corporation who many people depend on for their livelihood. That's a burden."

No one depended more on Eddie for his livelihood than Bob Wachs. He was Harvard-educated and a former lawyer at the prestigious firm of Paul, Weiss, Rifkind, Wharton & Garrison who specialized in tax-shelter investments and entertainment law. But Wachs, who never became a partner at Paul, Weiss, had never been a major player in the legal profession. Nevertheless, he had a keen eye for talent and was adroit at negotiating fantastic movie deals for Eddie. By mid-1988 he was making well over $1 million a year as the comanager of Eddie Murphy and the manager of Arsenio Hall, television's hottest new talk show host.

As well as Wachs did for Eddie financially, the nagging question remained whether Wachs was capable of managing the talent side of Eddie's career. Growing disappointment welled up in the mid-eighties with Eddie's choice of scripts and his uninspired performances in *Golden Child*, *Beverly Hills Cop II* and *Coming to America*. Nay-sayers began to equate Wachs with Colonel Tom Parker and Eddie with the ever more reclusive Elvis.

As we touched down in New Orleans, I was just finishing reading a July 2, 1987 *Rolling Stone* article by David Handleman, aptly entitled "Free Eddie Murphy."

Handleman pursued Eddie for months but never got an interview. After describing his unsuccessful efforts, Handleman concluded, "Eddie Murphy lives a strange existence not unlike the one his hero Elvis lived twenty years later in his life—sequestered from reality by his fame, fawned over by courtiers, loved by millions and ultimately alone."

Eddie was all that Alain had said that he was . . . and a whole lot more. He was a talented human being who had been reduced to a commodity. Just like his idol, Elvis Presley, Murphy had been stung and manipulated so often that he trusted no one outside of his immediate circle of friends and family. He was arrogant. No doubt about that. But it looked to me like the arrogance that springs from fear: fear that the bubble will explode, that his jokes might dry up, that he could lose everything on one throw of the dice.

In some ironic way, the biggest box office star in America was desperately afraid that he would not remain on top for long and it was that fear that fueled the quiet desperation beneath his public bravado.

Could that desperation drive him to put his name on another man's story so that he could bask in even more glory than he had enjoyed up to now?

The answer seemed to be a resounding "Yes."

But proving it in a courtroom was another matter.

5

Art in New Orleans

WHEN WE ARRIVED in New Orleans, Connie's mother couldn't wait to tell me that I had a message to call Art Buchwald in Martha's Vineyard.

As it turned out, Art, too, was on his way to bayou country—not for a vacation but to observe the Republican National Convention.

Far from quizzing me like an anxious client, Art chatted over the phone as if we were old friends. In the process, I learned one of his trade secrets: instant rapport with everybody, regardless of who they are or how much power they wield. And we hadn't traded two dozen words before he zinged me.

"You know, Pierce, I'm very depressed," Buchwald sighed in his patented Brooklynese whine.

"Gee, Art, why's that?" I asked with genuine concern.

"Reagan gave me eight great years of material. George Bush is Dullsville. I see a Great Depression descending on the national funnybone if Bush gets elected."

Buchwald told me he had mixed feelings about traveling all the way to New Orleans to mix with a bunch of conservative Republicans. At a minimum, he would get great material for future columns and speeches. But Art was not partisan when it came to satire. He told me that he held out little more hope for the nation's sense of humor should the governor from Massachusetts win the upcoming presidential election.

"Mike Dukakis," he muttered. "There's a real boring guy. I might just have to retire from writing my column and take up a hobby."

"Like what?" I asked, right on cue.

"Like suing Paramount Pictures over *Coming to America.*"

Buchwald paused to let me chuckle, then he said he wanted to meet me in person to discuss his case. But he was characteristically considerate.

"I know you're on vacation. I don't want to mess up your plans."

"No problem," I told him. "How about Sunday afternoon at five? That'll give me a chance to go see the movie."

"You haven't seen it yet?"

"Nope."

It was Art's turn to chuckle.

"You're in for a treat. Five sounds great. I'll be at the Windsor Court. See you in a couple of days."

As I replaced the phone in its cradle, I couldn't help feeling that if this case went to court, Paramount Pictures had a tiger by the tail. I'd seen plaintiffs like Art Buchwald before—even faced them in the courtroom. And they are always the most dangerous kind: a principled plaintiff who's convinced he's been robbed and had his nose rubbed in it.

I already knew from Alain that Art Buchwald didn't care a whit about how much money he could get out of the studio. He just wanted the figure to be high enough to make them squirm. He was a man after the faceless enemy: institutional smugness and the men and women who defended it—right or wrong—against all attacks.

Buchwald didn't want money. He wanted something more precious: vindication.

Two days later, at 5 P.M., I called Art on the house phone in the posh lobby of the Windsor Court Hotel and found him remarkably subdued, compared to the fired-up Buchwald I'd spoken to earlier in the week.

I knew why.

On the drive over to the hotel, the news reports on the car radio had carried details about the death of Edward Bennett Williams. Despite the sunny Southern day, I was gloomy. At forty-one, I was getting too old for heroes, but Williams remained part of my dwindling pantheon. I'd studied under him, admired him, patterned my practice after him in a half dozen different ways.

Ed Williams turned out to be part of our mutual Washington heritage. Buchwald had called him one of his closest and earliest friends along the Potomac. Ed, who had several "best friends," was closest to Buchwald. As I entered the elevator, I wondered if the passing of America's greatest trial lawyer since Clarence Darrow had affected Art the same way it had affected me.

The door swung wide, revealing a five-foot-eight balding bloodhound of a man. His cheeks sagged while his eyes laughed. He had a spreading midriff and thin, graying hair. While I knew Art was a little over sixty, his instant smile seemed to automatically subtract twenty years from his age. He had the rubbery face of a comedian but the manner of a perfect gentleman.

"Come on in. I was just reading the *Times*. Can I get you anything?"

"A Diet Coke, thanks. I had a late night," I sighed.

The previous night we had celebrated Connie's and her best friend's fortieth birthdays and we'd stayed up way past midnight dancing.

"How long you been married?" Buchwald asked.

Eighteen years, I told him.

"Kids?"

In a flash, I had the wallet out, proudly displaying Brendan and Meghan. Art's children were all grown. Ann and he had adopted, he told me. So had Connie and I, I said. A tough job, being a parent, he said, as we talked low key about family for a while.

Art then shifted the conversation to me and my legal background: education, clerkships, friendships. This was a business call after all.

I told him about Georgetown and my Jesuit law school training. When I got to my postgrad days as a law clerk for Supreme Court Justice Byron R. White, he stopped me.

He knew Justice White from his close friendship with Bobby and Ethel Kennedy. They used to have an occasional dinner together, he said.

"I clerked for him back in 1973 and '74," I said.

"Ah. An interesting time to be on the Supreme Court," he said, arching his eyebrows mischievously.

Back in those heady Watergate days, I had seen Justice White operate up close and under extreme pressure. I was there when the justices voted unanimously to force Richard M. Nixon to surrender his incriminating tapes to the Watergate special prosecutor—and his presidency a few weeks later. The big winner was the rule of law in a democracy, and I was privileged to be a witness to the Supreme Court's finest hour.

As Justice White's law clerk, my job was to help him persuade the other eight justices to join his opinions. That's where I really began to learn the art of devil's advocacy, I told Buchwald. I found myself drafting opinions and lobbying other justices' law clerks to get four votes for some positions that I'd never have taken myself. On most issues, I was more liberal than my mentor —from the rights of the accused to the limitations on governmental interference with freedom of expression.

Whether in the courtroom or the highest basketball court in the land—on the top floor of the Supreme Court building—Justice White, a Rhodes scholar, also taught me to be a fierce competitor. He regularly played basketball with his law clerks and I usually drew the dangerous assignment of guarding him. I found myself sprawled on the floor more often than not. White, a former Colorado All-American and All-Pro football player, treated a friendly pickup game of basketball as though it was the NCAA playoffs.

"I got fouled a lot by the justice, but I never got invited to Thanksgiving dinner with the Kennedys," I noted.

Art laughed. He hadn't always been issued such highfalutin invites himself, he said. His voice dropped to a happy whisper as he recalled what it was like being young and single and struggling in Paris back in the days when Byron White was still playing football.

"Life was uncomplicated then. I had a daily column in the *Herald Tribune* and I covered anyone and anything on the Paris scene that happened to catch my eye. I especially got a kick out of interviewing young starlets. Audrey Hepburn. Sophia Loren. Liz Taylor before she got like us."

Art pinched at his expanding waistline and looked at mine.

"You meet Ann in Paris?"

"Yeah. She was a publicist. Great girlfriend for a reporter, uh? We had a crazy courtship. She chased me. I let her catch me."

Art raised his eyebrows a half inch.

I'd spent fifteen minutes with the man and I already felt as though I'd known him for a lifetime. He's good at putting almost anyone at ease, but there's also something special and refreshing about his directness. There's a sophistication to Art Buchwald without the pretense that usually goes with that quality.

And he's funny. He looks funny, he thinks funny, he talks funny.

"You're Catholic, right?" he asked.

"Seven years of Jesuits at Georgetown and I'm still with the Church," I said.

"Ann's Catholic," he said. "In case nobody told you, I'm Jewish."

Theirs was a pre-Vatican II marriage, back in an era when hard-line Roman prelates still blamed the Jews for killing Jesus, Art said.

"It's a miracle our marriage survived through the mid-sixties, when the Church finally absolved the Jews. Now whenever Ann gives me a hard time about not cleaning up after myself or taking out the trash, I dig out my dog-eared set of Vatican II pronouncements and remind her that I've been pardoned."

Art then shifted gears. He tended to get a little quiet when he reminisced about days gone by, particularly the more poignant ones.

"Ann's really very devout," he said softly. "She and Eddie Williams used to go to mass together."

We had avoided the obvious for nearly half an hour. At the mention of his name, Art's smile vanished, his lips pursed and he slowly shook his head.

"I talked with Agnes," Art said quietly, his lower lip quivering ever so slightly between his clipped sentences. "Ed died peacefully last night. He was ready to go. They announced his death during the Redskins game. I guess the arrangements haven't been finalized yet, but he asked me a long time ago to be one of his pallbearers. The funeral's supposed to be Tuesday at St. Matthew's Cathedral. I guess I'll fly back to Washington tomorrow."

Art's best friend had valiantly battled cancer for eleven years. He survived seven operations, painful therapy and numerous predictions about his imminent demise before he finally succumbed. He maintained his grueling, fourteen-hour daily regimen, including morning mass, until a few months before his death.

"I'll be at the funeral too," I said.

I noticed for the first time that the curtains were drawn, preventing the cheerful Southern sun from intruding in the room. Art planted his forehead in his hands, rubbing his temples. He was mourning in his own way.

"How long did you work for Eddie?" he asked softly.

"Three years as an associate and two summers and my last year as a law student," I blurted out proudly before lapsing into a slightly embarrassed silence. I sounded more like a kid talking about his most revered high school teacher than an experienced trial attorney in my own right.

"I remember that I joined the firm right after Ed got John Connolly acquitted on charges of bribery in '75," I said. "I congratulated him on his brilliant defense and he took me aside and whispered: 'Pierce, there's only twelve people in the country who think John Connolly isn't guilty. Thank God that they were all on my jury.' "

Ed never left anything to chance. The facts were never self-evident. They had to be surgically extracted from millions of pages of documents, dozens of interviews of potential witnesses and hundreds of hours with clients.

One of the best illustrations is the John Connolly acquittal. Ed and Michael Tigar, a brilliant associate, spent weeks locked in Ed's conference room with the arrogant, patrician Texan. Ed knew that the former Texas governor and turncoat Democrat, who was shot during the assassination of President Kennedy and served Richard Nixon as Secretary of the Treasury, would be a disaster in front of a Washington jury. His only hope for acquittal was to make Connolly appear to be a humble, ordinary person—a mighty tall order. Ed and Mike practiced with Connolly, screaming and yelling at him and doing everything they could to undo fifty-five years of egomania.

It worked. Connolly's testimony was credible and his demeanor unassuming. Of course, it didn't hurt that Ed destroyed Connolly's chief accuser, Jake Jacobsen, on cross-examination or that he had a star-studded cast of character witnesses attesting to Connolly's fine character, including the Rev. Billy Graham, Congresswoman Barbara Jordan, two of President Johnson's former cabinet officers (Dean Rusk and Robert McNamara), Robert Strauss, and Lady Bird Johnson. When Ed asked Billy Graham what he did for a living, the famed evangelist said:

"I preach the gospel of Jesus Christ across the face of the earth."

When several of the jurors responded "A-a-men!" Ed knew he had a chance.

"Did I ever meet you when you were at Williams & Connolly?" Buchwald asked.

"Not really," I answered. "You used to umpire softball games when our firm played some other firm. Ed pitched. I played third base."

"Yeah? How'd I do?" Buchwald asked.

I thought for a moment, remembering a slightly paunchy, short guy in baggy shorts and knobby knees, chewing on a cigar and leading an ugly bull-dog around on a leash.

"To tell the truth, you were the worst umpire I ever saw. How the hell did you think you could call balls and strikes from behind second base?"

"I couldn't, but it was safer out there," Buchwald fired back.

When I left Williams & Connolly in 1978 and moved to Los Angeles to run for Congress, I never would have suspected that a decade later I would use what Ed Williams taught me to represent one of his best friends in an important battle for the rights of creative talent in the motion picture industry.

Ed was a winner.

Like the two hundred or so other men and women who trained under him, I learned something every time I saw him work his magic on a client, judge, jury or opposing counsel. He understood human nature and seemed to be able to develop a winning argument in the most hopeless of cases.

With his mane of dark hair, big head, imposing physical appearance and booming voice, he was the maestro of the courtroom. He orchestrated a case for the jury the way Leonard Bernstein used to conduct the New York Philharmonic.

For Edward Bennett Williams, the law was not static and unchanging. Winning sometimes meant that you had to push the outside of the envelope —not to distort the law but to help it evolve in a progressive direction that benefited society and, hopefully, your client.

Edward Bennett Williams personified the zealous advocate, fearlessly protecting his client's interests, yet always playing by the rules. He used to say winning unfairly is worse than losing.

"He was my best buddy," Art said finally. "God, did we have a lot of fun together."

I told Art about the day Williams invited me to play tennis with him at the Congressional Country Club near his home in Potomac, Maryland. It was a big honor, and it happened exactly once.

"I was a fairly good player. We played three sets and Ed didn't win a game. He never invited me back again.

"He started hounding me to play squash with him at the Metropolitan Club during our lunch hours. I was lousy. He always trounced me. Always. So, naturally, whenever I brought up tennis, he'd smile and say: 'Let's go play some squash, Pierce.' "

Then, after another pause, Art clapped his hands together and sat up straight in his seat.

"All right," he said. "The case. We've got some business to take care of. Should Alain and I stick our necks out on this or not?"

Two nights earlier, I'd seen *Coming to America* and I now understood what Buchwald had been snickering about over the phone.

"Art, I don't know how to put this gently, so I'll just say it. I can't take your case," I said, mock serious.

Art's face dropped. Then I zinged him.

"Even *I* don't want my name associated with that movie."

Buchwald didn't miss a beat. He hit his forehead with the palm of his hand. "Oh, no, you saw *Coming to America!*" Buchwald exclaimed, his eyes rolling. "It's a real stinker, isn't it?"

"I saw it the other day. Why would *you* want to associate yourself with such a . . ."

"A lot of my friends had the same reaction. But I'm not saying that I wrote what you saw on the screen. I'm not saying that Paramount plagiarized my story. What I *am* saying, I think, is that Paramount took my story and used it to develop *Coming to America*. That's all I'm saying. Now, I'm not a lawyer. You have to tell me whether they can do that and get away with it. If they can, that's it and we drop it. If not, then I want to hear more about what our rights are."

I had been right. This was no laughing matter to Buchwald. He was deadly serious.

"One more thing," Buchwald continued. "I'm not wild about filing a lawsuit. That's not my thing. I know how the press will play it. It'll be Art Buchwald against Eddie Murphy. That isn't it at all, but that's not going to keep me from suing either. So, counselor. Do we have a good case?"

The truth was that Buchwald did have a case. I wasn't about to tell him yes, though, without a whole bunch of "buts" attached to it.

I took off my sports coat, loosened my tie and opened my briefcase. Art leaned back into a corner of the couch, his eyes riveted on me.

"Alain told you that we want a contingent fee arrangment?" Art asked.

"Yes. And if I were you, I'd insist on it too. If you can't find a lawyer who believes in your case enough to put *his* money where his mouth is, you shouldn't waste your time."

It put me in a tough position, however. I had just joined a new firm in January. Kaye, Scholer was one of the oldest and most prestigious in the country, but it rarely took cases on contingency.

"I have to warn you, Art. Our clients usually pay their legal fees the old-fashioned way: by the hour. I'm going to have to get a contingency agreement approved by our billing committee in New York. That means making a compelling case for liability and damages."

"I understand," Buchwald said. "You've got to win the case with your partners before you win it in court."

"That's right. Now, you still want to hear what I think?"

For the next hour, I outlined a simple case of breach of contract for Art. I showed him the "based upon" language in the fine print of his contract and how his contract was linked to Alain's. This wasn't a copyright case, I told him. Forget the word "plagiarism," even though everyone he knew in and out of Washington would be misusing the term if he filed suit.

This was breach of contract: Paramount promised, in writing, to pay him if they made a movie based on his story, and they hadn't paid.

I told Art that Betsy Handler, one of my senior associates at Kaye, Scholer, had managed to dig up two very similar precedents—what we lawyers call cases "on point."

The first involved a series titled "Branded" that ran for two years on NBC during the mid-sixties. Chuck Connors portrayed a former frontier cavalry officer named McCord who was mistakenly blamed for the slaughter of his soldiers in an Indian battle. In the dramatic opening each week, McCord had his saber ritually broken by his commanding officer before he was expelled, in disgrace, from the fort. From that premise, McCord was sent out by the series' creators into the wild West each week, looking to save fair damsels, orphans and other downtrodden people in order to salvage his personal honor.

There was nothing particularly wrong with this show, I told Buchwald, except that a screenwriter named Harry Julian Fink claimed that he had conceived the idea before its producer, Goodson-Todman Enterprises, Ltd. He sued for fraud and breach of contract.

Fink's story, which Goodson-Todman had rejected five years before "Branded," was called "The Coward." It, too, had a so-called "back story" about disgrace during battle. Fink's hero, a man named Dundee, also searched out and helped the oppressed of the world in order to atone for his cowardice. There was one big difference, though: McCord roamed the old West as a kind of vigilante good guy while Dundee roamed the streets of Greenwich Village a century later as a New York cop.

Even so, the Dundee character, as Fink envisioned him, carried the pain of having seen a platoon of his young recruits slaughtered during World War II and, he, too, went through the shame of a court-martial.

"Your courage is worth this much," said a prosecutor in one of the opening scenes of Fink's pilot script. The prosecutor then tossed a nickel at Dundee's feet.

Like McCord, who carried a broken saber with him everywhere he rode, Dundee carried a pocketful of nickels with him everywhere he went in New York, reminding him of the moment in his life when he was declared a coward.

"Fink lost his case in the trial court," I said.

Art's face sagged. I raised my finger in the air.

"But he won on appeal! The court of appeal said Goodson-Todman had to pay if 'Branded' was *based upon* 'The Coward'! Fink had contract language just like yours. And that was way back in 1970." I grinned.

"What about the fraud?"

"No deal on the fraud. Fink made a mistake by not showing that Goodson-Todman's rip-off of his story kept him from selling his pilot to somebody else. Basically, the court said Fink never showed that Goodson-Todman prevented him from taking 'The Coward' to some other outfit to get them to produce it. Hence, no fraud."

Art shot me a look of doubt. He clearly sided with Fink. But he wasn't going to belabor the point at the moment.

"And the other case?"

"*Desny v. Wilder,*" I said.

"Is that Billy Wilder who was the defendant?"

"Yes, the writer-director."

"Billy's an old friend of mine. What did he do?"

It was a landmark decision that protected writers like Buchwald who submit ideas to studios, I said.

"Uh-huh. But what did Billy do?" Art persisted.

"Well, actually, not much. His secretary did most of it for him. A fellow named Victor Desny claimed he dictated an idea for a movie over the phone to Wilder's secretary and that she typed up the notes and gave them to Wilder. That was in November of 1949, when Wilder was working at your favorite studio."

"Paramount?"

"Paramount. Desny's story was about a real incident that happened back in the 1920s in Kentucky, when a guy named Floyd Collins got stuck in a cave. When the newspapers found out about it, they had a field day covering the rescue operations. The biggest splash of all came in the Louisville *Courier-Journal*, and the reporter on the story, who kept getting exclusive interviews from Collins while he was dying down in the cave, won a Pulitzer Prize."

"So he died. This Collins fellow, I mean."

"He died, yes. And all the media hoopla left a bad aftertaste in everyone's mouth. So, jump ahead twenty-five years to 1949 and Desny's trying desperately to sell the story to Billy Wilder. But Wilder doesn't take unsolicited stories from people who ring him up at his office. By 1949 he's already won an Academy Award for *The Lost Weekend* and directed classics like *Double Indemnity*. What's he need stories over the phone for?

"But Desny's persistent and finally gets Billy's secretary to agree to take the story down over the phone. If Paramount uses the story, 'naturally we will pay you for it,' she tells him. He hangs up and waits. For two years he waits. Nothing happens.

"One day in 1951 he goes to the movies to see a new Kirk Douglas picture. It's called *Ace in the Hole* and it's from Paramount, directed by Billy Wilder. And guess what it's about?"

Buchwald touched his fingertips to each other thoughtfully, furrowing his brow as though he were thinking very, very hard.

"Spelunking?"

"Okay, so the trial judge throws Desny out of court, just the way Fink's case was originally tossed out. Fink at least had a written contract. Desny had nothing but Billy Wilder's secretary's word. No contract, said the judge, no legal basis to recover damages."

"Poor Victor." Buchwald frowned.

"Ah, but the California Supreme Court disagreed! Desny was a fighter, apparently, and took the thing all the way to the top. In an historic 1956 decision, the justices held that Desny had an implied contract with Wilder. Desny submitted his idea to him in confidence and Wilder promised to pay the reasonable value of Desny's idea if Wilder used it."

"All this through Billy's secretary?"

"Right. His secretary."

"Jeez. I oughta call Billy up and tell him to get a new secretary. So did Wilder or Paramount really use Desny's idea?"

"We don't know. All that the Supreme Court ruled on was Desny's right to sue. They sent it back to the lower court for trial."

"Right. So what happened?" Buchwald wondered.

"Paramount settled the case and paid off Desny before it ever got into a courtroom. Billy screamed about it, but the studio brass just wanted to get rid of Desny and go on about their business," I replied.

Buchwald smiled broadly, obviously sensing the irony of his situation.

"But they won't settle up on *Coming to America*. I guess Eddie Murphy in the 1980s means more to Paramount than Billy Wilder did in the 1950s," he said. "Let me ask you this, Pierce: does Billy's case mean that I didn't have to have a contract with Paramount in order to sue for using my story?"

"That's right. But you are far better off with a written contract than an implied one for at least three reasons. First, they can't dispute the terms of your contract. They're spelled out in detail. Second, they can't dispute the reasonable value of your idea. Your contract says that if Paramount uses the story as the basis for a movie it has to pay you $65,000 plus 1.5 percent of any net profits."

"Maybe the reasonable value of my story is worth more than that?" Buchwald pressed.

"Maybe. But if you sue to enforce the contract you usually have to live with all of its terms. The third advantage of having a written contract is that Alain is part of the package. Without his $200,000 fee and 17.5 percent to 40 percent of the net, you couldn't economically pursue this case. No matter what the net profits turn out to be, and I haven't done any calculations yet, your contract alone does not justify either you or me filing suit. There's just not enough money in it."

"I'm not in it for the money," Buchwald said. "It would be nice, but I don't need it, and I'm not counting on anything. I care about these bastards ripping me off like all the other writers. But I'm a realist. I know you can't do it unless there's some money in it for your law firm."

While Kaye, Scholer regularly did *pro bono publico* cases, our indigent clients did not include a financially secure Pulitzer Prize winner or a film producer with a lovely home on the edge of Beverly Hills. I might get lucky and get them a no-risk contingent fee deal, but they were still going to have to pay out-of-pocket expenses for court reporter transcripts, photocopying, travel, experts and the like.

"Pierce, if we go ahead with this, you're saying that I don't have to sue Eddie Murphy? Just Paramount. Right?"

"That's right. You signed a contract with Paramount, not Murphy. Paramount produced *Coming to America*. Regardless of whether Murphy was under contract with Paramount as an actor and a writer and used your treatment to create his story, Paramount is ultimately responsible. You might be able to sue Murphy for misappropriating your idea, but why make this case any more complicated than it has to be? In litigation, the motto is the same as the Army's: 'KISS—Keep It Simple, Stupid.' "

"There's another advantage, too," Art quickly interjected. "It might help defuse the race issue. You know: white Buchwald suing black Murphy. I don't need that problem."

"Race has nothing to do with this case," I insisted.

"Pierce, believe me, I know it. You know it. But race will lurk right below the surface if we go ahead. Just watch."

I vowed to myself not to speak ill of Eddie Murphy in public or private if we went ahead. We wouldn't be able to control what the press said, but an upbeat attitude would at least reduce the chances of our being accused of racism.

"One more thing. If we go forward, you need to make me a promise. My friend Erma Bombeck once sued somebody for using her name without permission to endorse some product. Something like that. Anyway, she settled out of court. But she signed one of those confidentiality agreements. To get the money, she had to agree not to talk about how much she got paid. She regretted it, she later told me."

"A 'no comment' clause is pretty standard, especially in Hollywood," I said.

"I know. But I won't sign one. Period. I'm telling you that right now. You need to know that going in. I'm a newspaperman. That type of agreement goes against everything I believe, everything I stand for. The public has a right to know what Paramount ended up paying for violating my contract. So, do I have your word? No confidentiality?"

I thought about trying to argue. I knew it would complicate a settlement down the road. But Art's lower lip was quivering again. This time, it was bulldog determination, not emotion over the memory of a fallen friend. I gave up my objection before ever uttering a word.

"You have my word," I said.

He lifted his Diet Coke off the coffee table and clicked the edge of my glass with his. We toasted to the memory of Ed Williams and to the success of a new lawsuit: *Art Buchwald v. Paramount Pictures Corporation.*

Art smiled, went to the windows and opened the drapes. The afternoon sunlight flooded the room.

6

Dollars
and Due Diligence

— — — — — — — — — — —

SEPTEMBER 1988.

Everyone in the movie business was back from summer vacation in Barbados or Labor Day in Cabo San Lucas. Hollywood was busy again. The new fall TV season was under way, and the editing rooms were buzzing at the major studios with feverish postproduction on Christmas feature releases.

Buchwald v. Paramount was still in preproduction.

My instincts told me that it was a tough case. There was still "due diligence" to perform, entailing a thorough investigation of the facts and legal precedents to see if the case was winnable. I had more to worry about than due diligence, however.

I was new to Kaye, Scholer, and this would be a contingency fee case. To many firms, "contingency" automatically translates into "forget it." Kaye, Scholer was a firm accustomed to being paid by the hour for its time, regardless of the outcome of the litigation. Fortunately, the firm's litigation expertise was in great demand by clients willing to pay our fees, and the firm rarely took cases on contingency. And my own plate was already full with challenging hourly-rate matters.

With clients out there willing to pay $400 per hour, why take on a potentially losing proposition?

The answer was risk and reward. If I could persuade Kaye, Scholer's billing committee, to take the case for 40 percent of whatever Art and Alain won—and they won big—the firm would also win big.

I put this proposition to Peter Fishbein, the chairman of Kaye, Scholer's executive committee and a tough-minded businessman when it came to law firm economics. As a young superstar graduate of Harvard Law School, Peter had clerked for Supreme Court Justice William J. Brennan, Jr., and had later been campaigning with Bobby Kennedy in California just before he was assassinated. A lawyer for theater owners in litigation with the studios, Peter is a tall, athletic litigator who plays tennis with the same ferocity that he represents heavyweights like Herbert J. Siegel in a series of successful battles with Warner Communications, Inc., and Carl Lindner in the Penn Central Corporation takeover. Peter's idea of fun is bicycling three hundred miles across western Europe with his wife Bette.

When I first broached the possibility of taking the case on contingency, still flush from my meeting with Buchwald, Fishbein didn't throw ice water on the idea but he wasn't fired up either. I had only been a partner with the firm for a scant eight months. Though they entrusted their new office to me as the partner-in-charge of a dozen lawyers, I still had a way to go to prove myself by the time the *Buchwald* case came my way. Peter wanted to know how we would be repaid and the estimated amount of net profits. It was clear from Fishbein's wary reception that I was going to have to show this devil's advocate that *Buchwald v. Paramount* was far more of a sure thing before I could take the case.

That meant more sleuthing. And in Hollywood, sleuthing begins on the telephone.

"Hello, Helene? It's Pierce O'Donnell, Art Buchwald and Alain Bernheim's lawyer. Alain suggested that I call you."

"Yes, Pierce. What can I do for you?"

Helene Hahn is the head of legal and business affairs at Walt Disney Studios in Burbank—a wise and businesslike woman in her mid-thirties who represents one of only a handful of women executives who have risen to the upper echelons of the movie business. She is a lawyer and a shrewd studio insider, but most important of all—for my purposes—she was the former vice-president of business affairs at Paramount Pictures during the early eighties.

It was she who negotiated the contracts for both Art and Alain when *King for a Day* was being developed for King Murphy on the Paramount lot.

"Helene, I'm doing some background research to see if Art and Alain should sue Paramount for breaching their contracts. Do you have a few minutes?"

"Sure. But I'd better level with you up front. Even though I'm at Disney now, I still have a pro-studio bias."

"That's okay," I assured her. "I'm interested in the facts, ma'am. Just the facts."

Helene laughed a little and lightened up. We spent the next hour discussing what she recalled about *King for a Day*. She may have a reputation as a tough negotiator but, at least with me, she was cordial, forthright and patient. By the time our conversation was over, she had given me a basic education in how a movie is developed, from first concept to final cut.

"I agree with you that the focal question is whether the movie is 'based upon' Art's sketchy treatment," she said.

"It's not a defined term," I said.

"You're right, Pierce," she said. " 'Based upon' is not defined in the standard contract."

"So what does it mean in the industry?" I asked.

"I'll tell you what it means to Helene Hahn. Development of a movie is pretty linear at a studio. Story, story meetings, revised script, development executive meetings, revised script and so forth. One step builds upon another."

"But it all starts with an idea. Someone saying, 'Let's do a movie about X.' Right?"

"Usually, but not always. You can have a situation where someone comes in with an idea, it goes nowhere and then later someone comes up with a similar idea and the two ideas are merged. Then you have the question of whether the person who is later in time had an independent source for his idea."

"What do you mean by similar idea?" We were getting close to the heart of the matter.

"Well, there's no hard and fast rule. You ask yourself: Is it too close? Was there a link to the past? One of your problems will be proving continuity at Paramount. David Kirkpatrick was the creative executive in charge of *King for a Day*. The project was abandoned and David left a year before Paramount started working on *Coming to America*. So, you have a gap in creative management."

"Thank you. That's very helpful. Let me shift gears for a moment. What do you think it will take to settle the case?"

"You understand"—Helene paused, choosing her words carefully—"that the studio doesn't care if there's a lawsuit. Studios are sued all the time. It's a cost of doing business. Paramount cares about only one thing: protecting its relationship with Eddie. That's the bottom line."

"But Eddie will have to testify, at least at a deposition," I replied.

"And Eddie will be great," Helene fired back. "Remember, he's the actor, not you."

I weighed her sobering words.

"Art's and Alain's contracts guarantee only $265,000 in compensation. Their only upside is the net profits. Any ballpark estimates?"

"What has it done so far?" she asked.

"About $117 million in domestic box office."

"Well, based on Eddie's earlier successes, this movie's strong summer and Eddie's popularity in foreign markets, I'd project Paramount's gross receipts will be $120 million. First, you must take out Paramount's distribution fee of about 35 percent. That's, say, $40 million. Then you'll have a negative cost of $30 million plus 15 percent for overhead. That's another $4.5 million. Then Paramount recoups its distribution expenses. I'll guesstimate that they're about the same as the negative cost so that's another $30 million. What's that total up to?"

I had been writing furiously as she spoke. I did some quick calculating and came up with $104.5 million.

"Okay," she said. "There'll be some interest, so let's use $110 million for Paramount's costs. That leaves a balance of $10 million. But then there's Murphy's and Landis's gross percentages. I'm not sure about their deals, but I know Eddie has a gross deal and Landis probably has some sort of adjusted gross deal."

"What's that mean?"

"It means that their percentages probably eat up all the remaining money, at least if Paramount's gross is only $120 million," she said.

"God! No net profits with worldwide sales of . . . ?"

"Probably over $350 million," she said, finishing my question. "But forget box office and all of that. The only relevant figure is what Paramount gets—the studio's gross receipts."

"But still, Helene," I continued, "that's shocking. No net profits for a movie that's going to do these kinds of numbers? Something's wrong, very wrong, here."

"Look, Pierce: the problem is the gross points," Helene explained patiently. "They gobble up the net. Everyone knows that. It's hardly a secret."

"Maybe not, but it's surely depressing to think that I have no upside going in."

"I understand. You should check out some of my cost estimates and the exact nature of Eddie's and John's participation deals. I could be high."

"I'll do that," I replied. "I have a source who is trying to get me some hard information. Let me ask you this: what would you think would be a good settlement for us?"

Helene thought a moment.

"If I were you, I'd settle for about $300,000," she said.

"Thanks for your time, Helene."

"Good luck, Pierce."

As helpful as she had been, I wasn't sure that she really meant it.

I had money on my mind as I dialed Roger Davis.

One of the three men who ran the William Morris Agency, the world's largest talent agency, Davis was chairman of the executive committee and the man who had negotiated the contracts that Alain and Art signed with Paramount. It was Davis, I surmised, who sat across the table from Helene Hahn back in 1983 and pounded out each clause, each nuance, each crossed *t* and each dotted *i* in the *King for a Day* deal.

Only that's not how it happened at all.

"Alain told me you would be calling," said a pleasant Roger Davis from his office in nearby Beverly Hills. "I want to do anything I can to help. I think what's happened to Art and Alain is disgraceful and I hope you take their case. I think they should sue."

I was feeling better already, until Davis got to the part about the standard development deal. Producers and writers got a specific kind of deal with any or all of the major studios and that was it. No nuances. No special clauses. All *i*'s predotted; all *t*'s precrossed. Given the "take it or leave it" attitude of the studios, Roger's "negotiations" with Hahn had involved the amount of money that Art and Alain would get up front. The rest was boilerplate Paramount contract terms.

At some point after the routine signing of the routine contracts, Davis said, he learned that a script had been submitted to Eddie Murphy, but he couldn't recall where he had heard that.

"From where I sit, the issue of liability is whether a comedy about a black prince in America is protectable," said Davis, a Berkeley-educated lawyer who had practiced entertainment law before joining William Morris.

"I agree."

"If I were you, I'd be concerned about the novelty of the idea," he said.

"If I were contemplating a federal copyright case, I'd share your concern. But I'm not. Even though Art copyrighted his treatment, I have a different theory," I said.

"Implied contract?"

"No, although Art certainly could file a *Desny v. Wilder* claim. I have a different tack: breach of express contract."

"I like it. It's simple and it's exactly what happened. But you're going to have a tough time proving your case. After all, Art's story was how long?"

"Two pages plus a few lines on the next page."

"Well, Paramount's not going to lie down. You're attacking their big star. Paramount will stonewall this case, at least for a while."

That prediction came as no surprise. The studio had already managed to drag out discussions with Howard King for six months.

"Roger, I need some help figuring out whether this case is worth pursuing from a financial standpoint."

"What do they get for up-front money in their contracts?" Roger asked.

"Together they have $265,000," I answered.

"And their combined share of the net?" Roger inquired.

"A maximum of 41.5 percent and a minimum of 19 percent," I told him.

"That's right. I remember now. Well, these are healthy figures," he said.

"Yes, if there are any net profits," I added quickly.

Then Roger said something that heartened me.

"Pierce, there should almost certainly be net profits if the movie continues to do as well as it has already. It's done about $120 million in domestic box office, hasn't it?"

"That's right," I replied, "and it should do as well or better in foreign."

"Eddie always does well overseas." Roger's voice had a reassuring, authoritative tone.

He anticipated that *Coming to America* would earn at least $50 to $100 million more from ancillary sources alone—everything other than domestic and foreign box office. Ironically, by the end of the 1980s, so-called ancillary sources had also become primary sources of profit for a movie. How a movie did on HBO, Cinemax, Showtime, home videocassettes, pay TV, network licensing and syndication to independent or foreign TV stations was at least as important in the late eighties as how it did in theaters.

When it was all over, Roger estimated that there should be at least $10 to $15 million in net profits.

"Good luck," Roger said as we signed off.

I was sure he meant it.

My next call went to Michael Besman.

Where Helene Hahn came off as politely cool and Roger Davis as politely effusive, the thirtyish Besman came off as politely yuppie. He was working with Peter Guber and Jon Peters *(Rainman, Batman)* as one of their development executives on the Warner Bros. lot in Burbank. But, between 1983 and 1986, Besman had been a creative executive at Paramount, reporting to David Kirkpatrick, who at that time had day-to-day responsibility for Eddie Murphy's career.

Besman was "attached," as they say in Hollywood, to Francis Veber while Veber was writing his version of *King for a Day* in 1984 and had attended several story meetings with Bernheim and Veber.

Besman turned out to be as cooperative as Hahn but, unlike Helene, he knew something about the actual development of *King for a Day*. During our half-hour telephone conversation, he told me he thought that Buchwald had a "terrific idea"; that the project had always been earmarked for Eddie Murphy; and that from the very beginning the essence of the story was Eddie playing a black king coming to the United States and ending up a poor man in the D.C. ghetto.

Buchwald's story was the beginning of the creative process, and the story evolved in the customary linear fashion. While Besman never spoke to Murphy or his people about *King for a Day*, he thought that Kirkpatrick had. After he succeeded Jeffrey Katzenberg as head of production in the fall of 1984, Ned Tanen was well aware of the *King for a Day* project, according to Besman. He read the Veber script and ultimately made the decision to scuttle the project.

Spurred on by Besman, I interviewed several others.

Brian Walton, the feisty executive director of the Writers Guild of America West, confirmed that Paramount was obligated, but had failed, to submit Buchwald's treatment when the studio proposed writing credits for the movie earlier that spring. Under the Guild's basic agreement with the studios, Buchwald, if he prevailed in a story-credit arbitration, might be able to force Paramount to recall every one of the more than 2,000 prints of *Coming to America* that were currently in circulation and force the studio to redo the titles of the movie.

Tamara Rawitt was next on the list. A former Paramount publicity department executive in New York from 1981 through 1985, she was now an independent producer. According to Paramount's lawyers, Murphy didn't even know who she was. According to Rawitt, Eddie had personally asked her to move to Los Angeles in 1985 and become vice-president of production and development for Eddie Murphy Productions, Inc.

In a brief telephone interview, an extremely friendly Rawitt told one of my colleagues that she had worked closely with Eddie, Wachs and Tienkin on movie and television development. She arrived in Hollywood shortly before *King for a Day* was dumped, but she did recall seeing on the production chart inside the Eddie Murphy Production offices on the Paramount lot the name *King for a Day* listed among the handful of projects that Murphy was interested in making.

Alain had told me that Rawitt read the script in the spring of 1985 and tried to persuade Murphy to do the movie but could not spark any interest. That was not how Rawitt remembered it, however. She unequivocally denied ever talking to Eddie about *King for a Day* or even reading Veber's screenplay.

Rawitt's recollection was a major disappointment. While I had no doubt that Alain was accurately reporting what she told him in March 1985, I still had no witness who could say that Eddie in fact knew about Buchwald's story. Without that testimony, Paramount could say that Murphy independently created the story with no influence from Buchwald.

I was running out of leads and time. Art and Alain wanted to know if I was going to take the case, and the Kaye, Scholer billing committee back in New York wanted to know if I had a winner worth taking on contingency.

I had to establish that Eddie himself—and not just his manager—knew about Buchwald's story. Neither Hahn nor Besman knew and Rawitt had developed acute amnesia. Obviously, Wachs and Murphy were not going to tell me, and Richie Tienkin had disappeared.

Alain vividly recalled that Jeff Katzenberg had told Alain in 1983 that Murphy liked the Buchwald idea, but that was hearsay. I had to get Katzenberg himself to admit it. And while I could subpoena Katzenberg for a pretrial deposition, the chairman of Walt Disney Studios would hardly grant me an informal interview before I filed suit.

I had one last shot—a long shot, as I thought about it.

David Kirkpatrick had been Eddie Murphy's "keeper" at Paramount. He was the senior vice-president who, along with Bob Wachs, guided Eddie's movie career at Paramount in the early eighties.

In a nasty parting of ways, Kirkpatrick left Paramount in late 1986 to become president of the movie division for a new motion picture company founded by former pop music impresario and film producer Jerry Weintraub

(Nashville, Diner, Karate Kid). Kirkpatrick had remained friendly with Eddie despite his pitched battle with Paramount over his resignation.

While Alain had assured me that Kirkpatrick is a straight shooter, I held out little hope that he would break the conspiracy of silence that protected major stars like Eddie Murphy. Hollywood is an extended insiders' club, where lawyers, agents, managers, and studio and production company executives routinely play musical jobs with each other. I had no reason to believe that David Kirkpatrick, despite his bitter departure from Paramount, was any different.

I called him.

"I understand you were in charge of developing movies for Eddie at Paramount," I began.

"Yes. I was the top executive on the Eddie Murphy account. I reported to Jeff, but I was always involved with all of Eddie's projects."

Kirkpatrick's voice was cheerful and his answers were crisp. He spoke with surgical precision.

"Can you tell me if Eddie was familiar with Buchwald's story?"

"Yes, I can tell you," Kirkpatrick answered without hesitation.

"What can you tell me?" I held my breath.

"I talked to Eddie about the *King for a Day* project. I had conversations with him on four or five occasions. It was always an Eddie Murphy project."

As I wrote down Kirkpatrick's words on my legal pad, I breathed what I hoped was an inaudible sigh of relief. Trying to keep my cool, I pressed Kirkpatrick for details.

"Did Eddie read Buchwald's original treatment?" I asked.

"I don't think so. But Bob Wachs read the Tab Murphy and Francis Veber scripts. And Eddie read some or all of Veber's screenplay. He told me that he did not think the script was strong enough to finish reading it."

I could not believe what I was hearing. Since I was on a roll, I decided to go for broke.

"Tell me, David, did Eddie understand the premise of Art's treatment?"

"Absolutely," Kirkpatrick responded. "He knew the premise and basic story line. We talked about his character and what he could do with it."

The tension inside me that had been building up to this point burst. Relaxing, I put my feet up on the desk and continued my low-key interrogation.

"Was *King for a Day* listed on the project board at Eddie's office on the Paramount lot?"

"Yes," he replied.

"Are you aware of any other direct links between *King for a Day* and *Coming to America?*"

"Well, I don't know if these are links, as you call them. And you realize that I left Paramount in late 1986, quite a few months before *Coming to America* started. But you should know that Jeff Katzenberg and John Landis talked about *King for a Day* at the time Tab Murphy was writing his script, and that Barry Blaustein and David Sheffield, the writers on *Coming to America*, worked for Eddie on 'Saturday Night Live.' Writers on the lot have access to prior material on a project. Of course, I don't know what Blaustein and Sheffield saw or knew."

The more I talked to him, the more impressed I was. He seemed to have no ax to grind. He was just telling the truth as he remembered it: no guile, no posturing, no equivocation. I decided to take a chance and try out my legal theory on him.

"Art's contract has language that says that Paramount must pay him if it produces a movie based upon his treatment. Do you think *Coming to America* is based upon Art's story?"

"That's a matter of opinion," Kirkpatrick said, slowly but thoughtfully. "I have a lot of ambivalence about that issue. Eddie is very gifted. He borrows from his experience. Ideas and thoughts come into his life. He was aware of *King for a Day*. The question in my mind is whether, in his creative experience, Eddie borrowed from *King for a Day* or not. And I can't answer that question for you."

"I guess there's only one person who can," I said.

I now had no doubt that someday I would get to ask Eddie that question myself.

"Anything else?" asked Kirkpatrick.

There was one thing. It was another of Alain's recollections—about an incident in which Katzenberg had remarked to Kirkpatrick about the similarity between *King for a Day* and *Coming to America*.

"Alain's probably referring to the time when Jeff and I went to the movies together in Westwood earlier this year," Kirkpatrick said. "A trailer came up about *Coming to America* and Jeff leaned over to me and said: 'I can't believe this. Who are they kidding? That's *King for a Day*.'"

My heart leaped. The ways that I could exploit that scene in front of a jury . . .

"David, I really appreciate your taking all this time," I said. "Just a couple more questions?"

"Go ahead," he said, his tone still friendly but less matter-of-fact.

"I'm trying to get a fix on the likely range of net profits from *Coming to America*. Based on several other interviews, I've estimated about $15 million, assuming worldwide revenues come in at around $350 million."

"That sounds reasonable," said Kirkpatrick.

"Alain and Art tried to settle, but your former studio offered a ridiculously low amount. Any insights into how I can maneuver this thing for an early settlement?"

"Well, let me tell you how I would be thinking if I were still at Paramount," said Kirkpatrick. "Eddie won't want to be deposed. Neither will Katzenberg. Paramount will worry about embarrassment. If I were you, I'd depose everybody: Murphy, Landis, Katzenberg, Wachs, Hahn, Tanen and Tienkin for starters."

"Do you know where I can find Richie Tienkin?" I asked.

"Not sure. After Eddie fired him in 1987, he's been on the outs with Eddie. He knows a lot. I've heard that he's in the process of settling up with Eddie."

"Have Paramount's lawyers contacted you about this case?" I asked.

"In fact, I have heard from them. In the fall of 1987 before principal photography began on *Coming to America.*"

"Who called?" I asked.

"It was . . . let me think. Yes. It was Josh Wattles and Richard Fowkes. They asked me about the evolution of the project and the location of my files."

Perfect, I thought: right after Alain had lunch with Tanen in the Paramount commissary and Tanen threw his fit about Alain bringing up the similarity between *King for a Day* and *Coming to America.*

"And?" I pressed.

"And I told them what I've told you today," said Kirkpatrick. "No. Wait. I also told them something else."

"What's that?" I asked.

"I told Wattles and Fowkes, 'They're going to sue the shit out of you!' "

My due diligence was over. I was now convinced that the case might be winnable and the damages might be sufficient to justify the risk of a contingent fee. And I really wanted to take the case.

Buchwald v. Paramount promised to be one hell of a fight. In the courtroom, I relished battling for the underdog, and in Hollywood, writers and producers—even of Art's and Alain's stature—were the Davids. And the fact that the studios—the Goliaths—almost invariably won made the case even more alluring.

As a trial lawyer, I had been trained not to get emotionally involved in my client's case. But I knew that I would be violating that rule if I represented Buchwald and Bernheim. I instinctively felt a kinship with Art, Alain and all creative talent in the enduring struggle for power in Hollywood. They had a score to settle, and they needed a champion.

In fact, as I thought more about it, *Buchwald v. Paramount* was not about money. A fundamental principle affecting all men and women who conceived the ideas for movies was at stake. This was a cause, not a case.

But my law partners understandably cared about the money—and so did I. No partner could commit hundreds of thousands of dollars of the firm's resources without prior approval. I therefore prepared in September a sixteen-page memorandum to Kaye, Scholer's billing committee and Peter Fishbein, seeking authorization to represent Art and Alain on a contingent fee basis.

Under my proposal, my law firm would receive 40 percent of any money received from Paramount by way of settlement or trial. Buchwald and Bernheim would pay all expenses, including expert witness fees. We would be partners.

After detailing why I believed that the clients had "an excellent case for breach of contract," I turned my attention to damages. There had to be a significant amount of net profits in addition to the clients' $265,000 in guaranteed payments under their contracts. Otherwise, Kaye, Scholer could not take the case because of the substantial legal fees needed to prosecute the case through trial. We'd have to prepare a complaint, fight motions to dismiss the case, examine Paramount's documents, take depositions, find experts and prepare for trial—all before I made my first appearance before the jury.

All we had was sketchy information with which to estimate net profits. We didn't have hard data on the projected gross receipts, negative (production) costs, distribution expenses, or the magnitude of the back-end payments to Murphy and Landis. Nevertheless, based on my interviews, a usually reliable source who claimed to know Murphy's and Landis's gross participation deals, Bernheim's inquiries, and Fishbein's consultation with some of his theater owner clients, I estimated that our 40 percent share of the minimum 19 percent or maximum 40 percent of the net profits that our clients would get if we prevailed would be more than enough to compensate Kaye, Scholer for its time and risk. I decided to disregard Helene Hahn's prediction that *Coming to America* would never pay any net profits because everyone else with whom we conferred predicted many millions of dollars of net profits. That would mean a big paycheck for Art, Alain, and Kaye, Scholer.

I concluded my memorandum with an assessment of the chances for a quick settlement:

> While we must assume a full-blown case with a trial, the fact of the matter is that a trial is unlikely for several reasons. Several sources indicate that Paramount would like to settle the case before trial because Murphy and several former Paramount executives do not want to go through the hassles of several days of testifying at trial. Without their cooperation, Paramount has a weak defense. . . . Paramount's conduct has been outrageous, and a public trial will be very embarrassing.

I forwarded a copy of my memorandum to Art and Alain. In the cover letter I cautioned them that, "while it would be nice to settle the case in the early going, we should assume a protracted engagement and jury trial."

A week later the firm approved taking the case on a contingency fee basis.

When I called Alain in Paris to tell him the good news, he was exultant. He told me he had just come across an article by Kim Masters in the October issue of *Premiere* magazine entitled "I'll See You in Court!" and suggested that I give it a glance.

One paragraph in particular caught my eye. Months later, I thought seriously about having it engraved in marble and mounted permanently on the wall over my desk:

> Outside of tennis, litigation is probably Hollywood's favorite sport. But before you call your lawyer, think twice. You can win the battle, but lose the war.

7

"Sue Me"

WHILE I WAS PLAYING Philip Marlowe in Hollywood, Art and Alain went about their business.

Alain checked in from Paris, where he was holding forth with the French literati in hopes of snagging an option or two for American film rights to their work. He called my assistant Celine Quarroz with the news that *Coming to America* was as big a hit in France and England as it was in the United States.

And Art had returned to Washington from the Vineyard. Hard at work at his desktop computer, he was banging out columns about the upcoming presidential election as well as a new crisis that loomed on the national horizon: the domino-like collapse of dozens of savings and loan associations across the country. While chronicling the many Quayle-isms that seemed to be creeping into the national lexicon, Art also managed to keep up his speaking engagements at conventions and corporate gatherings.

In early October, a most unlikely CEO asked him to deliver a speech at a charity dinner. His name was Martin Davis, chairman of Gulf & Western, the parent company of Paramount Pictures.

Davis looks like everybody's well-coifed, tastefully dressed grandfather—the kind who is always addressed as "grandfather," however, and never, ever, as "grandpa." Thin, steely-eyed and wearing either a thoughtful frown or an ironic half smirk, Davis has a reputation on both Wall Street and Hollywood Boulevard as a Doberman pinscher in a Brooks Brothers suit. With Marty, you are either his friend or an enemy. If he is your friend, you can ask him to arrange room service for you in the Gobi Desert. If you are his enemy, however, you can expect to make your own funeral arrangements. Art wrote in a note to Howard King, thanking him for his help:

> "I had a wonderful meeting with Pierce O'Donnell in New Orleans. He is dynamite. Even if nothing comes of this, just knowing both of you was worth the experience.
>
> "I hope there is a settlement soon because Martin Davis keeps asking me to do free speeches for him at the Waldorf. He would not think of me unless we were having all these battles."

Howard called me at my office, laughing about the letter and wishing us the best. I was tempted to call Art and ask him what the Davis business was all about, but I was too busy pulling together witnesses, documents and a complaint so that I could get a demand letter off to Paramount and settle the whole thing. I still believed that the studio would come to its senses when its legal department saw what kind of damage we could inflict in court.

But I figured Art must be kidding as usual about Davis. I knew that the chairman of Gulf & Western was a friend, but Davis would hardly be trying to get somebody who was publicly contemplating suing his company to act as a toastmaster. It was obviously another Buchwald fiction.

Letter writing is a dying art form in our electronic age. Much as he loves to kibbitz on the phone, Art Buchwald loves to write letters.

A week after Howard King's call, I got my own note from Art:

> Everything seems to be going very well on the Gulf & Western front. Martin Davis just had a bottle of 1982 Dom Perignon delivered to me, together with a tape (which I am enclosing in case you want it for evidence). He had it made for me. I wrote back to him saying that the fact he had given me such an expensive bottle of champagne clearly indicates he is guilty.
>
> The vice-president for public affairs at Gulf & Western delivered the champagne and the tape on the specific orders of Marty. He seemed a little nervous when I said, "If we win the case, they will probably have to close the Washington office."
>
> Do you get 40% of the bottle? I'd appreciate knowing before I open it.
>
> Ivan Boesky had offered to testify for us, providing we can get 18 months off his sentence. Does this interest you? Please give my regards to your partners.

I held up the enclosed tape cassette labeled "For Art Buchwald's Ears Only." Art wasn't kidding. The toughest thing about working with a world-class leg-puller like Buchwald was knowing when he was serious.

The tape turned out to be a duet taken from the 1951 musical *Guys and Dolls*. In the play, gambler Nathan Detroit and his nightclub dancer/singer girlfriend quarrel incessantly over his frequent forays to the racetrack. The result is a little number called "Sue Me" with the following refrain:

Call a lawyer and sue me, sue me.
What can you do me?
I love you.

From Martin Davis? When I stopped laughing, I called Art in his Washington office.

"What the hell's going on?" I asked.

"Marty wants me to do a speech for him at a Variety Club benefit dinner next January. He's the honoree and they're going to raise a million bucks for poor kids," said Art.

"You're kidding me."

"Pierce. I know we've just started to get to know each other but believe me: I ain't kiddin' on this one. Should I do the dinner?"

"Is it for free?" I asked.

"Yup," Art replied.

I thought for a moment. If he didn't accept, he would be slighting Davis and cutting off a possible channel for settlement. On the other hand, if Art did the dinner, it might appear that he was not serious about his lawsuit. It was a tough call.

"Take the high road," I advised. "Right now, your bitch isn't with Marty personally. It's a good cause. Go ahead. Do it."

"What about the tape? Can we use it as evidence?" Art asked.

It wasn't exactly smoking-gun evidence, but it was pretty inflammatory. In a less litigious frame of mind, I might even have termed it affectionate arrogance. I held the tape cassette up to the lamp and examined it closely.

"Yeah," I finally said into the receiver. "Exhibit A."

"Does that mean you don't want me drinking Exhibit B, counselor?"

"Not yet," I advised. "Let's save it. We'll drink to Marty Davis's health once this thing is over."

◆

The week of the 1988 presidential election, the Associated Press reported that Art and Alain were not the only writer-producer team staking a claim to authorship of *Coming to America*. The others already had filed suit and were now quarreling among themselves as to how much of a share of the booty each should get when they won in court.

> A man who claims to be "Prince Johnny" of Nigeria lost his bid to dismiss a $10 million suit filed by a Canadian who claims Paramount's Eddie Murphy film "Coming To America" was based on his idea.
> Shelby M. Gregory, 38, a Canadian scriptwriter now living in Hollywood, filed the copyright suit against Murphy in July, contending the actor/comedian and two of his employees used his ideas for the film without compensation.
> Lassine Ousseni, an actor-producer who claims to be a Nigerian prince known as "Prince Johnny," sought dismissal yesterday of the suit, claiming that Gregory was his employee and did not have legal standing to file the suit, said his attorney, Francis Pizzulli.

U. S. District Judge A. Wallace Tashima denied the dismissal motion, saying the terms of the employment were unclear, said attorney Kenneth Kulzick, who represents Murphy and Paramount.

The weekend the movie opened, Gregory had filed his suit, claiming that *Coming to America* started out as *Toto, the African Prince*—a treatment he had written and copyrighted back in 1983. According to Gregory, Prince Johnny contacted him, representing himself as an actor-producer, and offered to buy the treatment for $5,000. Gregory claimed he was never paid, even though Prince Johnny took the story to Eddie Murphy Productions and pitched it as a movie. Gregory sued Murphy, Paramount and others for $10 million.

Johnny sued too, but in state, not federal, court. He included his entire name in this lawsuit: Oman Oba Adele Mouftaou Lassine Ousseni-Bellow. In his action Prince Johnny said that he was the true author of the story upon which *Coming to America* was based. It was, at least in part, based on his own royal Nigerian roots, he told newspaper reporters when he called around Los Angeles, trying to drum up media support for his legal action. His pronounced African accent did seem to make him sound like a parody of Murphy's African exchange student in *Trading Places*. When it came time for a hearing on the matter, however, Prince Johnny failed to show up in court and Los Angeles Superior Court Judge Philip Saeta dismissed the suit.

In fact, there were several claims by tangential types, Kulzick told me. They regularly come out of the woodwork after blockbuster hits like *Coming to America* begin to generate publicity, claiming to have written all or a portion of the story, script, dialogue or treatment upon which the film is based. Few of those claims stand up to the legal test of plagiarism and fewer still get beyond the Shelby Gregory or Prince Johnny threshhold stages in the courtroom.

While Paramount disparaged our claim as only one of many frivolous cases, the big difference between those "nuisance" cases and our suit was that Art and Alain had contracts and a paper trail strewn through the filing cabinets and storage vaults of Paramount Pictures Corporation all the way back to the fall of 1982. They also had the resources of Kaye, Scholer behind them. With my pick of the brightest lawyers in the country, I assembled a crack team:

A single parent of an adorable preschool daughter, Marsha Durko is an unflappable litigator under fire. Tall, blond and methodical, she was a pack-a-day smoker in an office of born-again nonsmokers. *Buchwald v. Paramount* didn't help her nicotine habit. I eventually paid an acupuncturist to cure her addiction.

Clara A. "Zazi" Pope, a 1987 honors graduate of Harvard Law School, is the precocious rookie who put her heart and soul into the case and became the kindly drill sergeant for our tiny guerrilla army. A soft-spoken sweetheart with a winning smile, Zazi has the toughness of a foundry worker and the instincts of a hard-nosed city editor.

The team was later bolstered by the addition of Suzanne Tragert, an enthusiastic 1988 Georgetown Law Center alum, and brilliant Michael Malina, my fifty-year-old mensch partner from New York.

Dark-haired and athletic, Suzanne's idea of relaxation is motorcycling the open roads of Southern California with her husband on weekends. On weekdays, she is in the office early and out late: an indefatigable youngster at the bar who conducted her very first depositions as a lawyer with the enthusiasm of a kid in a candy store.

Malina was my brain trust. A burly Harvard Law honors grad with a Park Avenue pedigree, Mike became my chief devil's advocate on every legal issue in the case. A contrarian and a gifted writer who scrutinized every argument for its flaws, he is accustomed to representing oil and pharmaceutical companies and other giants in antitrust actions. So when presented with this unique opportunity to champion a pair of Davids instead of his usual Goliaths, Malina gave my small cadre of young Turks the much-needed perspective of a gray-haired veteran.

The glue of the outfit was an extraordinary paralegal, Dennis Landry, the man who knew how to find anything and keep track of everything. A body builder with an M.A. in comparative literature from UCLA, he spoke German fluently, rode his bicycle to our offices each day and was quite simply the most disciplined person I'd ever met. Under excruciating pressure, he often anticipated our needs for documents, depositions and cases before we even thought of them.

It was now time to engage our adversary. In a letter dated November 10, 1988, to A. Robert Pisano, Paramount's general counsel and former litigation partner with prestigious O'Melveny & Myers in Los Angeles, we fired our opening salvo:

> We represent the above-referenced individuals and corporations (collectively "Buchwald") in connection with various claims against Paramount Pictures Corporation ("Paramount"). Our clients' claims arise out of Paramount's flagrant and continuing breach of its agreements with Art Buchwald and Alain Bernheim, specifically Paramount's shameful and blatant misappropriation of Buchwald's "King for a Day" story treatment. The facts display a shocking and callous disregard for our clients' contractual rights.

This was deliberately tough talk. Paramount had to know that we meant business. In nine pages, I meticulously laid out our case for Paramount's legal department: we would be alleging breach of contract and would be showing a jury how the studio originally signed Art and Alain to make a comedy about Eddie Murphy as an African king living by his wits in an American ghetto and how the studio eventually based *Coming to America* on Buchwald's original story.

I included references to both Billy Wilder's battle over the Floyd Collins story in the making of *Ace in the Hole* and to the "Branded" TV series case that Goodson-Todman Productions lost. Paramount needed to know that, at least twice in the past, appeals courts sided with the little guy over the studio system in contract breach—i.e., story theft—cases. My associates had also come up with at least another dozen precedents, similar to the Wilder and "Branded" cases, all of which gave Buchwald and Bernheim a solid legal foundation.

To add further evidence that I was serious, I heeded David Kirkpatrick's advice and listed eighteen names of Paramount and ex-Paramount personnel I wanted to depose once the suit was filed. The list included Eddie Murphy, Bob Wachs, John Landis and virtually every member of the Paramount studio hierarchy before and after the major management shake-up of 1984. The message I wanted to send Paramount was that I clearly intended to find out if the mass exodus from the studio's upper ranks after Charles Bluhdorn died and Martin Davis took over had any effect at all on the decision to dump *King for a Day* and resurrect it under new management as *Coming to America*. Former Paramount chairman Michael Eisner, former Paramount president Barry Diller, former Paramount vice-president Dawn Steel and former Paramount production chief Jeff Katzenberg were all on my witness list, as was Ned Tanen, the Paramount production chief who originally told Bernheim and Buchwald that their services were no longer desired.

More than anything else, however, I wanted Paramount to know Art was taking Martin Davis's musical challenge—"Sue Me"—in dead earnest. I wound up the letter with a hyperbolic flourish and a few bald threats, but no *Guys and Dolls* lyricism. I didn't ship it over to Paramount accompanied with a bottle of champagne either:

> Up to this point, Paramount's attitude about our clients' claims has been cavalier and outrageous. Paramount's position that Eddie Murphy originated the story of "Coming To America" is ludicrous. I can assure you that a Los Angeles jury will be equally outraged by Paramount's brazen misappropriation of Art Buchwald's original idea. The showcase trial will be a welcomed opportunity for the creative community to reaffirm the enforceability of contracts with studios and to deter such conduct in the future.
>
> Art Buchwald and Alain Bernheim have personally suffered serious financial damage, as well as injury to their reputations and their ability to continue developing their careers in the entertainment industry as a direct result of Paramount's wrongful conduct. Although the precise amount of such damage has yet to be determined, we estimate actual damages at $5 million and our clients would settle all of their claims with Paramount for that amount. We await your response.

I gave Paramount a week to reply.

In the middle of that week, reporter Jill Abramson at the *Wall Street Journal* called out of the blue to tell me that a copy of my letter had found its way to the *Journal*. I knew that any chance that Paramount might cave in and meet my clients' demands would evaporate if she printed its contents for the *Journal*'s 1.8 million subscribers.

I had a lot of experience handling the press in high-profile cases with heavy media attention, and I knew when to talk—and when not to. I also knew better than to ask a reporter not to print the story, but I had no intention of cooperating either. I gave her a "no comment," hung up the phone and began to sweat.

Next day the phone rang at 6 A.M. It was my sister Mary Eileen calling from New York.

"Have you seen the article, Pierce?" she began.

"Mary Eileen, what are you talking about?"

I love my oldest sister dearly, but I was standing in the bedroom dripping wet from the shower.

"The article in the *Wall Street Journal* that I just faxed to you five minutes ago. Art Buchwald and Eddie Murphy. Your lawsuit. It's a terrific story," she said.

I thanked her and darted to the fax machine.

The case of *Art Buchwald v. Paramount Pictures* was all over the front page. In the coveted center column, under a headline that read "Art Buchwald Says Eddie Murphy Stole His Idea for a Movie," Jill Abramson had written:

> Eddie Murphy and Art Buchwald have one thing in common, possibly two things.
>
> The Hollywood superstar and the Washington columnist are both very funny fellows. But did they think up the same movie?
>
> More precisely, did Mr. Murphy steal Mr. Buchwald's idea for the 1988 summer hit "Coming to America," which starred Mr. Murphy as an African prince who lands in the U.S.A. and takes a wife.
>
> Mr. Murphy got credit for the story on which the hugely successful Paramount film was based. Mr. Buchwald maintains it actually was based on a story of his. The quarrel, whispered about in gossip columns, is now to become a lawsuit, filed today in Los Angeles County Court. The funny men aren't laughing much about it, although Mr. Buchwald talks a good-humored line. Mr. Murphy isn't talking at all.
>
> Mr. Buchwald has hired a Los Angeles lawyer, Pierce O'Donnell, who contends that "Coming to America" is in fact based on Mr. Buchwald's story, "King for a Day," which the Paramount Pictures Corp. unit of Gulf & Western Inc. optioned from him in 1983. Mr. Buchwald told Paramount to fork over at least $5 million to settle the matter or he'd sue. The 63-year-old Mr. Buchwald, in an interview, says that a 9-page letter from his lawyer was delivered to Paramount by "stealth bomber."
>
> Mr. Buchwald isn't suing the 27-year-old Mr. Murphy. His pockets may be deep, but it's more amusing to sue a corporation. "I want to sue Paramount, a big conglomerate that eats up little people like me," Mr. Buchwald says. "I have nothing against Eddie Murphy."

Paramount, Kulzick and Murphy took my course: no comment. But Murphy's lawyer/manager, Robert Wachs, did have something to say.

"This is between Mr. Buchwald and Paramount. Eddie has nothing to do with it. I know that Eddie Murphy wrote that story."

Oh, Art, I thought, the fax shaking between my wet fingers. Oh, frank, candid, open Art Buchwald, whose very nature is such that he simply blurts out his feelings when asked. I wanted to ring him up and tell him that a nice "no comment" would have sufficed. Why not leave the poker-playing to your lawyer?

It wasn't until months later that I began to appreciate that shoot-from-the-lip Art Buchwald was in fact a far better poker player than I when it came to assessing Paramount's intentions. The joker had Paramount's number from day one.

I read on:

Art's own newspaper, the Washington *Post*, called *Coming to America* a "fizzled fable," but it still set opening-day box office records and grossed more than $100 million in U.S. ticket sales alone, Abramson reported. If the Murphy movie hadn't made that kind of money, she said, it would be doubtful that Buchwald would ever want to claim authorship.

> The two might have made a beautiful movie together. Alas, it was not to be . . . Mr. Buchwald's dreams of hitting the Hollywood jackpot were dashed.
>
> As for Mr. Buchwald, he stewed all summer as "Coming to America" climbed the box-office charts. He resisted going to see the movie but finally succumbed.
>
> "It did not show off Eddie Murphy at his best," Mr. Buchwald says, ever the critic.
>
> Then he switches gears: "For legal purposes, I thought it was the greatest movie ever made."

Robert Wachs had also switched gears by the time he talked with Aljean Harmetz of the New York *Times*. When the veteran Hollywood journalist did her follow-up story to the *Journal*'s, Wachs had a lot more to say than simply that the story for *Coming to America* was invented by his client.

He lobbed the first of many insults, telling Harmetz that Buchwald was just one of the many who wanted a piece of Eddie Murphy's moneymaking talent:

"It's like Zabar's. You better take a number and get in line. There's one suit by a Canadian fellow and a Prince Johnny who says he's Nigerian royalty. A Los Angeles lawyer accused me of stealing the story and I don't even get a credit. But the best one is in a federal court in Memphis. The guy said he submitted a story about a cannibal who comes to America to Richard Pryor, and Richard Pryor must know Eddie and passed the story on. I think I ought to throw a cocktail party for all these people."

Paramount wasted no time answering. A one-page reply was hand-delivered to me in exactly one week.

> Dear Mr. O'Donnell:
>
> We have reviewed your letter of November 10, 1988, with our clients. We cannot discuss settlement in the range you suggest.
>
> As you undoubtedly know, there have been previous settlement discussions when your clients were represented by other counsel. Even the highest prior demand made by your clients bears no relationship at all to your present position.
>
> Moreover, we have learned that your letter of November 10, 1988, was provided to various members of the media, including the "Wall Street Journal" prior to the date which your letter set for a response. This is an outrageous breach of the

standards which govern settlement proposals and discussions. There can be no settlement now or in the future under these conditions.

If this matter is to proceed to suit, we will notice and expect the usual discovery priority for the depositions of plaintiffs Art Buchwald and Alain Bernheim.

Needless to say, our clients do not believe that they have misconducted themselves in any way whatsoever and are convinced that they will prevail should you proceed.

Very truly yours,
Kenneth Kulzick

I expected the first part of the letter. It would take a miracle for Paramount to come this far and capitulate at $5 million, regardless of how good our case might be. Paramount was posturing just like any defendant who receives a strident letter hurling accusations of high crimes and misdemeanors. And, of course, my $5 million figure was merely the opening bid since the clients would accept at that time less than one tenth of that figure in a quick settlement.

What disturbed me was the part about the *Journal* article.

From the very beginning, there had been leaks and gossip, some of it traceable back to Art and Alain themselves and some to Murphy's people. Column items here and there had been popping up throughout the summer—the obvious result of loose cocktail party talk or luncheon chitchat. But this new development had stunned me.

Not surprisingly, the settlement deadline passed without Paramount budging. So, as the *Wall Street Journal* reported we would, on the Monday of Thanksgiving week, November 21, 1988, we filed a thirty-three-page complaint against Paramount, charging a litany of misdeeds: breach of contract, tortious denial of existence of contract, breach of good faith and fair dealing, breach of fiduciary duty, common law fraud, constructive fraud, negligent misrepresentation, conversion, constructive trust and negligence. Thirteen causes of action in all—a smorgasbord of legal theories to describe what I believed was a callous, calculated act of corporate cover-up of literary theft.

With Art's and Alain's contracts attached as exhibits, the entire suit measured an inch thick and weighed in at half a pound.

The war had begun.

And the media smelled blood.

In the wake of the front-page *Wall Street Journal* article and the filing of the complaint, the world press corps decided that this was a Big Story. All three networks, CNN, national radio networks and local radio and TV stations around the country broadcast the news. Articles appeared in almost every newspaper, *Variety*, *Hollywood Reporter*, *Time*, *Newsweek*. European, Australian and Japanese reporters based in Los Angeles all filed stories. Most of the stories were variations on the same theme: Art Buchwald, the Pulitzer Prize-winning columnist and author, was the little guy up against the powerful behemoth.

This was heady publicity, but Art was not lulled by the media blitz.

The day after Thanksgiving, Buchwald appeared on CNN's popular "Larry King Live!" interview program.

"You made front pages, *Wall Street Journal.* You're a story," King began.

"I was a media star for about—you know, Andy Warhol said fifteen minutes. I was good for about twelve," said Art.

"You filed a major lawsuit against a major film company," King persisted. "*Time* magazine came to take pictures of you. We notice you're going to be in *Time* on Monday. You're big. How do you like being a story?"

"I don't mind it if it doesn't last too long," Art answered. "You know, like twenty-four hours or forty-eight hours. It's a lot of fun. But you don't want to go on any longer than that."

Thirty-six months later, Buchwald would be back on "Larry King Live!" discussing the case again . . . and it still would not be over.

8

The Prince
and the Pundit

From this arises the question whether it is better to be loved rather than feared, or feared rather than loved. It might perhaps be answered that we should wish to be both: but since love and fear can hardly exist together, if we must choose between them, it is far safer to be feared than loved.

NICCOLO MACHIAVELLI, *The Prince*

ON THE WALL outside the spacious CEO's office that overlooks Central Park on the forty-second floor of Manhattan's Gulf & Western Building, a visitor can't help noticing a framed *New Yorker* cartoon. A gray-suited executive presides at his oversized desk. To his left is a tiny version of himself dressed as a devil. To his right is a corresponding diminutive angel resembling the corporate chief. Whose advice does he take? It's anybody's guess.

Inside the wood-paneled suite sat the real-life executive who admittedly identified with his cartoon counterpart on the wall. Martin S. Davis, chairman and chief executive officer of Gulf & Western Industries, Inc., had occupied the office at 15 Columbus Circle for most of the 1980s by the time we crossed paths. The man caught between his own devils and angels was one of the shrewdest and best-compensated businessmen in America, as well he should have been. In the space of two decades, Gulf & Western—perhaps best known as the parent of Paramount Pictures Corporation—had risen to become one of the nation's largest conglomerates.

"There's good in all of us, and bad in all of us," the sixty-one-year-old Davis conceded a year earlier to a *Fortune* magazine reporter. "Everybody can be a devil. Everybody can be an angel. Everybody. Even me."

Especially him, some would say.

He was one of the most powerful corporate figures in America. Consistently ranked near the top of the Fortune 500, Gulf & Western was a behemoth loaded with far more assets than a movie studio. Davis controlled Simon & Schuster/Prentice Hall, the nation's largest book publisher; Madison Square Garden and its cable network; a chain of motion picture theaters; the New York Knicks and the Rangers; Associates First Capital Corporation . . .

And, of course, Hollywood's most profitable motion picture studio. In addition to a 55-acre lot with 32 sound stages, Paramount had a library of films and TV shows ranging from *Top Gun* and *The Godfather* to "Happy Days" and "Mork and Mindy." During 1988, Gulf & Western's gross revenues topped $5.1 billion. A third of its $750 million operating income came from Paramount's operations alone.

For his efforts, Davis earned one of the fattest paychecks in the land. He consistently ranked among the highest-paid chief executives of any public company. Before 1989 was over, his earnings as reported to the Securities and Exchange Commission would come to $11,635,000. In 1990, a recessionary year, his annual income dipped to a mere $11.3 million, according to *Forbes* magazine.

Davis dined at the White House, traveled around the world in the corporation's sleek Gulfstream jet and hobnobbed with the likes of Bob and Larry Tisch, Pete Rozelle and Donald Trump. He once gave Trump a copy of Adolf Hitler's *Mein Kampf* as a gift.

Another one of his influential friends was Art Buchwald. They first met through one of Davis's charities and had known each other for years. Marty loved being with Art. (Art could call him Marty and get away with it.) What might appear to be an odd pairing made perfect sense upon closer scrutiny. Both came from the fringes of New York's blue-collar suburbs and both had skyrocketed, through their own shrewd natural talents, to the very top of their professions. They traveled in the same tight, privileged New York circles of ranking business, legal, media, sports and political heavyweights. Their mutual friends included New York Giants football great and ABC-TV's "Monday Night Football" announcer Frank Gifford, Motion Picture Association of America president Jack Valenti and Lazard Frères mega-dealmakers Ira Harris and Felix Rohatyn.

Art's lawsuit came as no surprise to Davis. Buchwald himself had mentioned his unhappiness with Paramount at a dinner party earlier in the year. At first Davis thought that the consummate jokester was kidding. Art told him he wasn't, but gave Davis the impression that he didn't want him intervening.

"Don't bother yourself, Marty," Art told him. "The lawyers will work it out."

Martin Davis was no stranger to lawyers, messy lawsuits or public contro-versy. In fact, it could be fairly said that Davis owed his present position atop the Gulf & Western Building to a masterful ability to capitalize on the prob-lems of others and play hardball. To some, he was a conniving opportunist: the devil incarnate. To others, he was a guardian angel.

But friends and foes alike would agree on one thing: Martin S. Davis was a clever fellow—and a survivor.

Born on February 5, 1927, he grew up in the Bronx, where his Polish immi-grant father was a real estate broker. At sixteen, he dropped out of high school, lied about his age and joined the Army. As soon as his true age was discovered, he was discharged. At eighteen, he reenlisted and served two years in military counterintelligence at the very outset of the Cold War. His skills as an investigator would later come in handy in the business world.

In 1947, he again left the military—this time, with an honorable discharge —and went to work as an office boy in the New York branch of Samuel Goldwyn Productions. Like Buchwald, who started in the Paramount mail room before the war, Davis launched his career at the lowest rung of the show business ladder.

He was a quick study. Seeing promise in the hustling, tough-minded young apprentice, his superiors gradually allowed him to read scripts, negotiate deals with writers and producers, handle publicity and tour with one of the com-pany's stars.

"The motion picture business was probably the greatest testing ground in business," he told an interviewer years later. "You got thrown into everything, including finance and production."

While he occasionally worked for the legendary Samuel Goldwyn himself during his eight-year tenure at the studio, Davis's closest mentor was studio president James Mulvey.

"He'd call me into his office and say, 'This is how you do a deal.' Then he'd send me out to do my own and yell at me when I blew it."

In 1955, Davis jumped to the failing Allied Artists Picture Corporation. Hollywood's premiere manufacturer of B movies, Allied had been home to Bela Lugosi and the Bowery Boys in its heyday, but with the exception of a handful of larger-scale productions in the early fifties, including *Friendly Per-suasion*, the studio had already shifted its focus to the wave of the future when Davis arrived: television. By 1958, Davis had moved back to the wave of the past: Paramount Pictures.

Paramount was a publicly owned studio awash in red ink and over-the-hill management when Davis came aboard. Any ordinary gambler would have wagered that Paramount's best days were behind it. A calculating man would have seen a big upside opportunity, however. Martin Davis went to work in the sales and marketing department.

He soared up the corporate ladder. After less than two years, he was chief of advertising and publicity. Two more years and he was promoted to vice-presi-dent for distribution. He also became official spokesman for all corporate matters and served a brief stint as executive assistant to studio president George Weltner, whom he succeeded in 1967. For the rest of the decade Davis served as Paramount's chief operating officer.

Davis and his team hardly set the film world on fire. In his first dozen years at Paramount, the studio placed only four films among the annual top five box office hits: *Psycho* (1960), *The Carpetbaggers* (1964), *The Odd Couple* (1968) and *Romeo and Juliet* (1968). By contrast, over the next dozen years—after Davis relinquished the reins of the studio—Paramount would enjoy the most profitable decade in its sixty-year history. Six films placed among the biggest successes of the 1970s: *Love Story* (1970), *The Godfather* (1972), *King Kong* (1976), *Saturday Night Fever* (1977), *Grease* (1978) and *Star Trek* (1979). In 1980, the studio cleaned up with *Airplane*, and a year later it launched the Indiana Jones series with the wildly successful *Raiders of the Lost Ark*.

In the seven years that followed, after Davis withdrew to New York and completely washed his hands of the Hollywood production and marketing decisions, Paramount experienced its golden age of profitable pictures. Thirteen movies alone accounted for nearly $900 million in domestic theatrical rentals alone during the 1980s. They included *An Officer and a Gentleman* (1982), *Terms of Endearment* (1983), *Trading Places* (1983), *Indiana Jones and the Temple of Doom* (1984), *Beverly Hills Cop* (1984), *Top Gun* (1986), *Crocodile Dundee* (1986), *Star Trek IV* (1986), *Beverly Hills Cop II* (1987), *Fatal Attraction* (1987), *The Untouchables* (1987), *Crocodile Dundee II* (1988) and, of course, *Coming to America*.

Whatever knack for picking and promoting movies Davis may have lacked, he knew how to win friends and influence the right people. His big chance had come in 1966, when Paramount was one of the weakest motion picture studios. Mired in mediocrity, its four highest officers had a collective age of 287 years. At the dawning of the Age of Aquarius, two dissident directors had launched a hostile takeover that promised to be swift and successful. What the two men, Ernest H. Martin and Herbert J. Siegel, did not foresee was Martin Davis riding to the rescue of incumbent management.

Quickly filling the leadership vacuum, Davis devised the sly defense of eliminating cumulative voting for directors and soliciting friendly shareholders. He galvanized the aging executive team and orchestrated a public relations campaign. With the confidence of a battle-tested general, the proxy-fight rookie also found a white knight: thirty-nine-year-old Charles G. Bluhdorn, the visionary, Viennese-born chairman of Gulf & Western Industries, Inc.

In 1966, Gulf & Western was just a nondescript Michigan-based auto parts supplier. But in the space of less than ten years under Bluhdorn, Davis and president and cofounder David N. (Jim) Judelson, it would grow from a company with an almost worthless contract to supply rear bumpers for Studebakers to one of the nation's first bona fide conglomerates.

Fearing an embarrassing and costly defeat, the dissidents led by Siegel and Martin dropped their threatened proxy fight, resigned from the board and sold their 143,000 Paramount shares (about 9 percent of the outstanding stock) to Gulf & Western at a premium of almost $10 per share over the going market rate. They walked away with $11.8 million. Within a year, Gulf & Western acquired all of the remaining Paramount shares for $130 million and made the studio a G&W subsidiary. Bluhdorn and Davis then relocated headquarters to the new building bearing the Gulf & Western name at the intersection of Central Park West and Broadway on Manhattan's Upper West Side.

Martin Davis didn't worry about such fiduciary niceties as paying "greenmail" to save entrenched management or disclosing confidential financial information about a public company to a potential investor like Bluhdorn. He had only one objective: to win. Years later he would admit that he solicited Bluhdorn and revealed details to him about Paramount's value in order to strike a deal.

"You didn't have all that government supervision you have today," Davis rationalized.

Bluhdorn didn't waste any time rewarding the impressive young man for his extraordinary efforts. In less than a year after he engineered Bluhdorn's takeover, Davis was elected to the board and executive committee of Paramount and rose to head the studio. Only forty, Davis was one of the film industry's youngest chief executives.

Davis immediately tackled the challenging task of revitalizing the moribund studio, focusing on its international distribution network, syndication of feature films, studio operations and that growing cash cow, television. A year after the Paramount deal, Gulf & Western bought Desilu Productions ("I Love Lucy") for $20 million and went into the TV programming production business.

For three years, Davis kicked corporate butt, slashed overhead, fired dozens of executives and support staff, and positioned the studio to compete in the 1970s. Bluhdorn was impressed with Davis's efforts to turn the dying studio around. It was in these early days that the legendary bad guy at Gulf & Western, long considered one of the country's toughest bosses, developed his reputation as one demanding son of a bitch who did not suffer "dummies, incompetents and people who do not step up to the plate.

"Weak people have a problem, with themselves as well as with me," he said. "I don't work well with incompetents."

Only three years after Bluhdorn captured Paramount, he again promoted Davis, making him his right-hand man and installing him as senior vicepresident responsible for acquiring new companies to boost the profitability of the fast-growing conglomerate. A young producer named Stanley Jaffe (*Goodbye, Columbus*) became head of the studio. By then, Gulf & Western owned a hodgepodge of over a hundred businesses in such diverse commodities as rice, sugar, cigars, zinc, financial services, apparel, bedding, bumpers and, of course, movies. Gulf & Western's voracious appetite was satirized in Mel

Brooks's 1976 comedy *Silent Movie* as "Engulf & Devour." *(Silent Movie* was produced by Twentieth Century Fox, not Paramount.)

Davis conceded that he was Bluhdorn's "hatchet man"—the guy who handled the tough, distasteful jobs of negotiating with greedy investment bankers and firing ineffectual managers. Charlie knew better than anyone the ruthless efficiency of his behind-the-scenes strongman and once gave him a photograph of Mount Rushmore with Davis's face superimposed over Theodore Roosevelt's. Davis was "the Elmer's Glue of the Bluhdorn era," remembers Donald Oresman, a former Wall Street lawyer, Davis confidant and executive vice-president, general counsel and director of Gulf & Western. "Marty handled all the interface with the banks, the lawyers, the press and Washington."

Marty also saved Charlie Bluhdorn from prison.

In 1975, the Securities and Exchange Commission kicked off an intensive investigation of massive violations of federal law, including Bluhdorn's alleged receipt of personal loans from G&W's banks, perjury, conflicts of interest, false annual financial statements, questionable tax practices, tax dodging, illegal foreign payments and cheating the Dominican Republic out of $38 million in profits from Bluhdorn's sugar trading. Some of the most serious charges involved Paramount Pictures during the period when Davis was running the studio.

Charlie turned to Davis to lead the defense.

Among the primary targets of the SEC probe were Paramount's accounting and tax practices during the Davis regime in the late 1960s. Motion picture studios are supposed to be creative about making movies, not about filing tax returns and preparing financial statements. While Paramount was usually losing at the box office during Davis's tour of duty, it was making money for G&W. One former Gulf & Western director told the New York *Times:* "I was aware they were playing with profits and losses."

The SEC believed that its strongest case of financial irregularities involved a complex 1969 deal concerning Paramount. In essence, near the end of the June 30, 1969 fiscal year for the studio and its parent, it was clear to company officials that production cost overruns on two Paramount movies would cause a significant loss in G&W's yearly earnings because the parent and subsidiary had consolidated financial statements. Not wanting to show the loss, the company, according to one former G&W director, "cooked up" a phony transaction to generate profits. According to numerous witnesses, including ex-G&W officials, the company gave a failing conglomerate called Commonwealth United Corporation $12 million in cash and a 50 percent participation in the future profits of *Darling Lili,* starring Julie Andrews. In exchange, G&W received an assortment of Commonwealth United stock, debentures, warrants and a note with a face value of more than $30 million. It was the first step in a maze of Byzantine real estate and stock deals involving fugitive Italian financier Michele Sindona, Paramount's Marathon Studio in New York, and overvalued land in California, Florida, Martinique and Italy. The movie bombed.

Not only was Paramount suspected of falsifying its financial statements, the company was the focus of intensive Internal Revenue Service scrutiny for tax cheating. One highly irregular transaction—again while Davis was in charge—involved creating a Canadian subsidiary, Paramount Television Sales. Founded in the late 1960s for the purpose of licensing Paramount films to television, the subsidiary did most of its business with U.S. stations. So why locate in Canada? Simple, according to former G&W officials: by operating what was essentially a U.S. business in a foreign country, the company delayed or avoided altogether the paying of millions in U.S. tax dollars.

The IRS eventually did get around to scrutinizing G&W and tossed in another charge against the Bluhdorn/Davis regime: hiding evidence.

Late one night in July 1968, while Davis was still presiding over Paramount Studios, company officials moved all of Paramount's tax records from the Gulf & Western Building in Manhattan to newly established tax offices in Stamford, Connecticut. As one former company executive admitted, the operation was carried out under cover of darkness for obvious reasons: the very next morning, IRS auditors were scheduled to pore over Paramount's books. Moving everything across the state line not only delayed the audit; it increased the odds that the IRS would fail to detect irregularities at home and overseas because Connecticut agents were less sophisticated than their colleagues in Manhattan, had no prior familiarity with Paramount's books, and were less likely to find fault with motion picture studio accounting practices.

As senior tax official J. Blake Lowe told New York *Times* reporter Seymour Hersh, Gulf & Western's tax dealings were "a game. There are issues that the IRS does not come upon. They may strike gold; they may not."

And the last people ever let in on the "game" were the company's shareholders. One former company executive told the New York *Times*, "We had big tax problems, but never told anybody about them."

Trying his hand at the old game of intimidation, Davis complained to senior executives at the *Times* that Pulitzer Prize-winner Hersh was intimidating former G&W employees and maligning the company during his four-month investigation. When Hersh's editors told Davis to pound sand, Davis shifted gears. He tried bullying the paper with thinly veiled threats of litigation. Davis issued a statement, published prominently alongside one of Hersh's articles:

> The allegations in the *New York Times* story about Gulf & Western are riddled with falsehoods. These falsehoods will be dealt with at an appropriate time and in an appropriate forum.

Given the evidence of widespread illegalities emanating from the company's senior officers, it came as no surprise that Gulf & Western never dealt with any of the "falsehoods," in or out of the courtroom.

Davis also professed to be disillusioned with the legal system.

"I found the system blatantly unfair and seriously flawed," he complained. Davis spent most of the 1970s extricating Bluhdorn and Paramount's parent company from the mire of the tax and stock scandal that G&W insiders ominously called "the cancer." It was a titanic struggle, fought on many fronts and in many battles . . . a seven-year war of attrition with only one clear winner: Martin Davis. The ultimate measure of Davis's total victory was what didn't happen: no indictments, no securities fraud civil penalties and no removal of Bluhdorn from power. When armistice was finally reached with the government in 1981, Gulf & Western signed a wrist-slapping consent decree and agreed to pay a token reparation to the Dominican Republic of $39 million for social and economic development programs.

Marty Davis did not like bad press. Though he did like trumpeting his triumphs and the ever expanding Paramount bottom line, he did not like reading about his mistakes or his ruthless, imperious manner. In his opinion, reporters wrote caustic stories at his expense just so they could sell newspapers.

It was ironic, then, to say the least, that he counted among his closest friends the premiere newspaper satirist of the latter half of the twentieth century.

Art Buchwald's fears about a dulling of the national funnybone proved to be premature, chiefly thanks to George Bush's choice for a running mate. But it wasn't just Dan Quayle who saved his sense of humor, Buchwald told the guests at the Variety Club charity dinner in Davis's honor at the Waldorf-Astoria on January 28, 1989, two months after the *Wall Street Journal* story broke. Davis's movie studio got some of the credit too. So did Davis himself, for being absurd enough to ask Art to speak at this function.

"Ladies and gentlemen of the jury!" Buchwald hollered from the podium, following emcee Frank Gifford's introduction. "This is indeed a fantastic occasion, a sellout crowd of the rich and famous, dressed to their teeth, excited beyond measure to be in the same room with Martin Davis.

"Why do so many people come out to pay tribute to Martin? The reason is that every table in this room was bought by a senior vice-president of Gulf & Western. With his own money. If anyone here knows of a G&W executive who failed to buy a table, please advise him not to bother to come to work tomorrow.

"What makes Martin Davis a superb man of the year is that he not only lends his name to charitable events, but he actively participates in collecting the money. He is one of the most persuasive charity fund collectors in the business."

Art lowered his voice confidentially and drew the audience in with a patented Buchwald shaggy dog story about a husband and wife, Mr. and Mrs. Rappaport, who went on a cruise in the South Pacific.

"The ship sank during a typhoon and Rappaport and his wife were washed ashore on a nameless island. Rappaport said to his wife, 'Is my will in order?' And Mrs. Rappaport said, 'Yes.'

" 'Are the children provided for?'

" 'Yes, they are,' Mrs. Rappaport said.

" 'What about the table for the Variety Club dinner?'

"And Mrs. Rappaport said, 'We took one.'

" 'Did you pay cash or pledge?'

" 'I pledged,' she replied.

" 'Thank God,' Rappaport yelled. 'Martin Davis will find us.' "

As the room broke into a roar, Art glanced at his host, sitting at the head table just a few feet from the podium. Martin, too, was doubled over with laughter. Art cleared his throat in a false signal to the audience that he was now going to get serious.

"My role tonight is to heap praise on Martin Davis," he said. "Now this happens to be a conflict of interest. The fact of the matter is, I am suing Paramount Pictures, and one of the companies that Martin owns is Paramount. So how, you may ask, did I get to this dinner? Well, the lawsuit is nothing more than an honest disagreement between good friends. I say Paramount screwed me. And they say they didn't."

The audience was off and laughing once again. Art let it die down a little before he leaned back into the microphone.

"What happened is that, after I announced that I was going to sue Paramount, I got a message saying that Martin wished to talk to me. I said: 'Did he want to settle?' So I called back. It turned out Martin did not want to settle at all. He told me that he wanted me to make a speech at the Variety Club dinner. I said, 'But I am suing you.' He said, 'One thing doesn't have anything to do with the other.' Then I said, 'I would love to, Marty, but I have to speak in New Orleans that night.' The next morning I found a dead horse at the end of my bed. I then called Martin and said, 'Screw New Orleans.' "

There were men and women in the audience who had been directly involved in the production of the first two *Godfather* movies for Paramount. They were the ones laughing the loudest.

"You may all be wondering how I arrived at the settlement figure I did in a lawsuit. I was sitting with my lawyer at the Four Seasons restaurant and I said to him, 'How much should we sue for?' And my lawyer looked down at the menu at the Dover sole and he said, 'How about $5.5 million?'

"So here I am at the Waldorf-Astoria. Only in America would a plaintiff pay tribute to a defendant. And I am proud to be here at the Waldorf with one of the most powerful men in America today.

"The reason we honor him tonight is because Martin, although a big guy, has always been for the little fellow. As a matter of fact, this crowd would have been three times as large tonight if every person Martin Davis helped could have gotten weekend furloughs. Martin and I go back a long way. We both worked for Paramount Pictures at 1501 Broadway in New York.

"I remember those days well. Every afternoon we would sit around the mail room chewing the fat, and I'd say:

" 'Martin, what are you going to do when you grow up?'

"He said, 'I'm going to become chairman of Gulf & Western, and then I am going to sell off Wickes & Company, Florida citrus, G&W's sugar interest in the Dominican Republic, the auto parts division, the cement companies, the movie theaters, the railroads, and the rain forest in Brazil.'

"I said, 'That's fantastic. What will you keep?'

"And he replied, 'Eddie Murphy.'

"And then he came to me and said, 'What are you going to do when you grow up?'

"And I said, 'I am going to sue you.'

"Well, the rest is history. Martin Davis has led Gulf & Western into the world of financing, grabbing, dropping, running, throwing, kicking and screaming, into the Fortune 500. He has been described by acquaintances as tough and lean: a CEO that watches every nickel of G&W's money.

"But whatever you say about Martin Davis, he has not forgotten where he came from. Every night he goes down to the Paramount mail room to count how many boys are working there, and orders the controller to cut it in half. . . .

"Martin, it's a lovely evening. I know you didn't understand anything I said tonight, but your wife Louella will explain it to you when you go home. You are a rich man, Martin Davis. Rich in family, rich in friends, and just plain rich. Martin, I don't know who will win our suit, but if I lose, I hope you will give me back my job in the mail room in Paramount, and if I win, I want to assure you that you are always welcome to ride on my Gulf & Western airplane."

Martin Davis applauded and laughed a strained laugh along with everyone else in the room. If he had any good-humored references to Buchwald's speech, however, he kept them to himself when he went to the podium a few moments later to receive an award for his Variety Club work.

The following week, he wrote Buchwald, thanking him for helping raise $1 million at the dinner. Marty observed that "no plaintiff has ever honored a defendant with such eloquence and wit—even in America!" He signed off "In Friendship."

On February 7, 1989, Buchwald replied:

Dear Martin:

I am delighted that we raised a lot of money the other night.

I have a great idea for a movie but I didn't get a chance to talk to you about it at the dinner. It's only a treatment and I am sure that everyone at Paramount will be very excited when they hear the details. At the moment it is in a vault in the Bank of England, and only my lawyer and myself have the combination. If Frank Mancuso wants to go to London, he can read it in the vault.

Best regards,
Art

Part Two

— — — — — — — —

Dress Rehearsal

9

Smug Lawyers and Smoking Guns

SHORTLY BEFORE his speech at the Waldorf, Art sent me a bombshell.

It was a four-year-old letter that novelist Jim Harrison had written to Robert Wachs, pitching a movie, and Wachs's reply. The way it got to Art dispelled any doubts that I might have had about the role of chance in the affairs of men.

Rummaging through some old papers during the summer of 1988, Harrison, the Michigan-based author of a half dozen novels and novella collections, had come across his letters to and from Wachs. In 1967, Harrison met Bill and Rose Styron, and he remembered Bill remarking once that he knew the Buchwalds quite well. The Buchwalds and Styrons are neighbors on Martha's Vineyard.

So one day, shortly after Art's appearance on the Larry King show in late November 1988, Harrison called Rose Styron for Art's address in Washington. In light of all the denials that Paramount and Eddie Murphy had been making about Murphy ever having seen *King for a Day* or any other treatment that Buchwald had written, Harrison thought his correspondence with Wachs might prove helpful to Art.

He was right.

On November 28, 1988, Harrison had sent a five-page packet to Art. He ended the transmittal letter with a word of warning that said in effect that he had been back and forth to Hollywood for years, and that at least half the population were scoundrels. But, Harrison concluded, Art probably already knew that.

Art forwarded the letters to me with his own brief cover letter:

Dear Pierce:

I think that this is the first smoking gun ever sent by Federal Express. It is interesting because Bob Wachs keeps insisting he has never heard of us or the treatment.

Cheers,
Art

Cheers, indeed!

"You got it? What do you think?" Art asked in his call to me an hour after the envelope arrived at my office. The excitement in his voice was unmistakable.

"Smoking gun is an understatement," I said. "This is dynamite . . . goddam dynamite, Art."

In 1981, Wachs was an entertainment lawyer in Manhattan, earning a comfortable enough living drawing up contracts and lawyer letters for aspiring actors, writers and other show business types. One of those he had taken on as a client was Bob Dattila, whose small literary agency managed a then struggling young writer named Jim Harrison.

By 1984, Harrison was in between advances on his books (*Wolf, The Farmer, Dalva*) and needed some cash. He was also trying to break into the more lucrative, if less soul-edifying, field of screenwriting. At Dattila's suggestion, he decided to pitch Wachs, who had struck it rich in California with Eddie Murphy.

After he had sold Paramount Pictures on Murphy and his young client had become a star with *48 HRS.* and *Trading Places*, Wachs set up Eddie Murphy Productions on the studio lot. He was always looking around for suitable material to develop into the next Eddie Murphy blockbuster. It was to Wachs, at Paramount, that Harrison, then living in the backwoods of northern Michigan, addressed a letter on September 7, 1984:

Dear Bob,

Long time no see as they say up here. I got the idea for this little treatment at my remote cabin in the Michigan forest, of all places. I think it shows a lot of promise and is closely aligned with Murphy's talents. One of the main items is that it's so available to both the comic and social satire. I would tend to play the last scene straight because everyone would be happy that Murphy is the new Lion King of this country. I am on the verge of receiving a full credit on a film to be shot in Brazil— Lorimar/Orion Pictures with Sonia Braga. I would also like to do something new and this idea seems to fit the bill. Please call as if I don't do this I have several other choices and am trying to line up my year's work.

Yrs.,
Jim Harrison

The treatment itself had no title. It was just one and a half single-spaced typewritten pages, written on a simple letterhead with Harrison's address and the notation, "re: Eddie Murphy" at the top of the first page. The story itself was nearly as terse as Buchwald's *King for a Day* and described Harrison's vision of the next big Eddie Murphy comedy—Eddie in the dual role of a senatorial aide and an African prince:

We begin with Winston (Eddie Murphy) working as an aide to a powerful southern Senator. Someone on the order of the feudal Leander Perez. Winston is a classy, intelligent recent college graduate but no more than a show black for the Senator. In fact Winston is so insignificant that his office deep in the basement doesn't even have a window or an air vent. Many secretaries visit him in this dungeon because he is hip and attractive. One day he is called up to the Senator's office for a secret meeting with the Senator and the most important black mobster in the south, who is not at all impressed that the Senator has a black aide. The mobster leaves behind a half million dollars in a briefcase. Winston has been so humiliated by the Senator that he breaks and tells the Senator he sucks shit through a dirty sock. The Senator in a fit of apoplexy runs from the office to find someone to punish Winston. Winston switches briefcases and splits for Dulles International Airport.

On the way to Dulles, Winston stops for a suitable disguise, buying some shades and a full length sable coat off a pimp. At Dulles he purchases a first class Air France ticket to Ethiopia. He is escorted to the first class lounge where he meets an arriving black who bears a striking resemblance to him. The black is the son of the Lion King of Somalia and is on his way to spend a year at the University of Texas in Austin. The son of the Lion King, however, does not want to go to Austin. He wants to meet a girlfriend in Paris. He fingers Winston's sable coat with extreme envy. In the far corner of the lounge Winston sees the henchman of the black mobster and the Senator's aide enter along with the pimp. Winston ducks and takes the son of the Lion King in the bathroom where they exchange identities and clothes, including a necklace of lion's claws and teeth.

CUT TO: Winston boarding a Texas flight.

CUT TO: The son of the Lion King completely demolishing the henchman, aide, and pimp and boarding a plane to Paris.

In Austin, Winston is met by several dozen members of the African Student League including some white professors, some members of the State Department and the University President. One of the group is a beautiful young black reporter (say Rae Dawn Chong). She is a bit cynical when Winston says that the future Lion King cannot talk but must meditate for seven more days. Winston is whisked away to a rather lavish apartment that has been set up for him, including a young fag cook. During these seven days of privacy Winston reads up on his role not knowing that the reporter is spying on him from a nearby roof. She has also tapped his phone and confronts him with a tape of a phone conversation to his mother. At first he merely bribes her amply to help her family, but then she begins to enjoy the whole idea of the deceit.

Scenes would include: Winston dressed up in Lion robes to break his meditation-fast, Winston speaking to a group of sorority girls whom he insists wear white sheets and bow like Muslims as he wanders around, Winston giving a benediction at a University of Texas football game, Winston living a bit too lavishly and signing leases to some Arabs to drill for oil in his country.

The word of his behavior gets back to his father and Winston and the reporter are captured in the middle of the night and delivered to a private 747.

We CUT TO: A big African village where thousands are mourning the death of the Lion King. After the funeral in a vast gorgeous hall Winston and reporter are installed as the new King and Queen of the country.

Wachs wasted no time in replying. Three days later, Harrison received the following letter on the stationery of Eddie Murphy Productions, Television & Tours, Inc.:

Dear Jim:
  It's good to hear from you. Many thanks for the treatment.
  Unfortunately, there is a project already under development at Paramount for Eddie entitled KING FOR A DAY, based on an unpublished Art Buchwald story, which is fairly close to your story line, hence I really can't give you a go-ahead on this one.
  Thanks for thinking of us. I hope to see you soon.
  Best wishes.
  Sincerely,
  Robert D. Wachs

My first impulse was to drive over to the hallowed gates of Paramount and simply ram the Wachs letter right down the throats of Josh Wattles and the other stonewalling executives who had been piously denying liability and claiming that Art's story had never even been intended for an Eddie Murphy movie. But I resisted.

I had big plans at trial for that document and Bob Wachs.

Instead, I told Art, the wisest strategy would be to just keep mum about Harrison's correspondence with Murphy's manager, especially in light of Paramount's response to my letter that had been leaked to the *Wall Street Journal*. As long as the studio was not in a settling mood, we had no reason to show them more of our cards. For the moment, Harrison's rejected tale about Winston and the Lion King would remain our ace in the hole.

After I hung up the phone I called the troops together, trying not to look too much like the cat who swallowed the canary.

Marsha, Zazi, Dennis and I sat around, role-playing Wachs's cross-examination and conjuring up how he would try to squirm out of his devastating admissions in the reply letter to Jim Harrison. It was a moment worth savoring: our first break, proving that Eddie Murphy's own manager knew about Buchwald's story years before Eddie's sudden inspiration to write *The Quest*.

When I was growing up, I loved to watch Perry Mason. Every week on CBS, Perry would snatch victory from the jaws of impending defeat by destroying the chief prosecution witness in a dazzling display of cross-examination or by producing a missing witness or having Della Street or Paul Drake race into the courtroom at the last minute with a key piece of evidence. You were never sure how, but you could count on Raymond Burr winning the case right there in the courtroom during the last ten minutes of the show.

Not long after I joined Edward Bennett Williams in 1975, I learned how real lawyers win their cases. While Perry was terrific to watch on TV, his sixty-minute victories on some studio sound stage bore little relationship to the real world.

What prime-time audiences never saw were the countless hours of preparation and investigation that are the indispensable raw ingredients of a trial's success. Ed Williams was fond of saying that victory was "90 percent perspiration before trial and only 10 percent inspiration in the courtroom. By the time my witnesses testify, they can repeat Shakespeare backwards."

In the weeks following Art's Variety Club dinner speech at the Waldorf-Astoria, I developed a much better appreciation of what an uphill battle we had on our hands. Winning the case would take a lot of sweat. The Harrison-Wachs letters would go a long way toward leveling the playing field, even before we got into Paramount's files on *Coming to America* and started taking witness depositions. But they established only that Wachs was intimately aware of Buchwald's story. Eddie's own knowledge was still the big question mark.

In every case after the complaint is filed and the defendant files an answer denying all liability, the parties engage in a protracted period of document searching that is euphemistically called "discovery." A more accurate description would be "trial by Xerox." Buchwald told me that he knew his lawsuit was serious when he got his first photocopying bill from Kaye, Scholer.

Our discovery timetable provided for a little less than a year to make our case. In that time we had to complete what I estimated would be a dozen or more sworn depositions, and each side was supposed to give the other all relevant documents relating to the case.

Theoretically, each side knows all the evidence before trial in order to assess the strengths and weaknesses of its case, thereby leading to informed decisions and settlement. In practice, however, discovery is time-consuming, expensive and rarely provides all the answers for either side before trial. Most lawyers waste months and money taking unnecessary depositions and searching for documents that are never used at trial.

Still, the system does seem to work. Over 95 percent of all civil cases are settled or dismissed before trial, and in Hollywood that percentage is even higher. Out of two dozen significant cases filed against Paramount during the decade prior to our suit, not one went to trial; they either settled out of court or were found to have too little merit to proceed to trial.

Perry Mason wasn't my only video addiction in the sixties. Another favorite show I grew up with was "Dragnet." Who could forget Sergeant Joe Friday's familiar admonition to a witness: "Just the facts, ma'am"?

That's what preparing for a trial is all about: ferreting out just the facts that make a difference from the literally millions of facts that don't count. The worst that my mentor Ed Williams could ever say about a lawyer was that he had "an instinct for the capillaries." Those with instincts for the jugular had a sixth sense for the relevant facts that ultimately won lawsuits.

Williams also taught me that creative trial lawyers are limited only by the availability of relevant facts. They aren't hired to ascertain the objective truth. More often than not, the truth is relative anyway, not to mention elusive. Trial lawyers are hired to be zealous advocates for their clients.

Rarely do we know what really happened:

Did the victim attack the defendant before he shot him?

Did the senior corporate executives know that the product was defective when they told consumers that it was safe?

Did Eddie Murphy learn about Art Buchwald's story before he came up with the idea for *Coming to America*? Who could say? Certainly not I. My clients believed he did and Eddie wasn't talking.

Even if they know what happened, protagonists rarely confess their culpability and eyewitnesses seldom show up miraculously outside of anyone's (except Perry Mason's) courtroom. It would be nice if everyone carried a camcorder, but even a videotape is suspect in court. One of the first defenses laid out in the notorious Rodney King battery case, in which four Los Angeles police officers were clandestinely videotaped beating the hell out of a hand-cuffed motorist, was that King had provoked the officers *before* the camcorder was turned on.

Given this customary lack of eyewitness testimony or confessions, the legal system long ago had to resort to means other than direct evidence. The alternative was so-called "circumstantial evidence." Contrary to popular misconception, circumstantial evidence has the same dignity and validity in a courtroom as direct evidence. To come to grips with what really happened, the judge and jury evaluate such evidence as a defendant's motive to kill, memos to the top brass discussing safety problems with a product, or documents showing that Eddie and his managers knew about Buchwald's story.

From such evidence, the jury can draw reasonable inferences about what really happened. Thus, a defendant's fingerprints on a glass at the murder scene are circumstantial evidence that he was there. Of course, lawyer-turned-author Scott Turow showed us in his bestselling novel *Presumed Innocent* that a conclusion of guilt does not necessarily follow from such incriminating circumstantial evidence.

Based on what Alain had told me and my interviews of former Paramount executives, I knew that the key to proving my case was twofold. First, I had to reconstruct the paper trail chronicling the development of *King for a Day* and, later, *Coming to America*. Second, I would have to confront Paramount, its executives and producers, Wachs, and Eddie Murphy himself with this documentary evidence in pretrial depositions.

The first step, then, was to secure access to all of the files at Paramount and Eddie Murphy Productions. Under the rules of discovery, I had a right to examine and copy all of them. Inspecting those business records became the first order of business. So, in the first months of 1989, Zazi and I prepared a

"Request for Production of Documents" in which we asked for anything remotely relevant to the case.

Before Paramount allowed us to inspect and copy the documents, it insisted
that we sign a confidentiality agreement. Studios are big on confidentiality.
I'd learned that in the "Rockford Files" case and from Danny Arnold's protracted battle over "Barney Miller" profits. Studios don't want anyone to
know anything that might be useful in upsetting their tidy arrangement. So,
when Universal settles a nasty accounting dispute with my client NBC and a
star like James Garner reportedly for over $14 million or Columbia lays $50
million on Danny Arnold to keep from going to court, the studios do everything they can to keep this information from the public.

For weeks we negotiated the scope of the confidentiality agreement with
Ken Kulzick. He wanted it broad and all-encompassing; we insisted that it be
narrow and full of escape hatches. Eventually we did what lawyers always do:
we compromised. Under the agreement, signed in mid-March 1989, Paramount had to give us documents revealing business information about persons who were not parties to the litigation such as "actor contracts, director
contracts, producer contracts, executive contracts, and financial analysis."
The studio could stamp CONFIDENTIAL on those items they deemed inappropriate for the public's eyes, however.

I wasn't overjoyed with this accommodation, but it suited our primary
objective: access to the documents that I hoped would unravel the story of
how Paramount used Buchwald's story to make *Coming to America.*

And, perhaps, more smoking guns like the letter Bob Wachs wrote Jim
Harrison in the late summer of 1984.

Shortly after we signed the confidentiality agreement, I got a telephone call
from Ken Kulzick that was music to my ears:

"Why don't you just send your paralegal down and he can take whatever he
needs?"

The files—hundreds of them—were loaded into boxes and stacked up in a
spare conference room at Kulzick's office. I had a hunch that Kulzick's laissez-
faire attitude about the documents meant that it was just so big a job that
neither he nor Tony Liebig wanted to spend the money to screen the files
before they turned them over to us.

Armed with only a portable copying machine, Dennis Landry became a
litigation archaeologist on a dig through a million pages of documents that
would eventually give an unprecedented glimpse of the real Hollywood. He
read every page of the million pages of documents and some of them were
dreadful. In the name of research, poor Dennis had to plod through hundreds
of convoluted interoffice memos and dozens of the worst screenplays ever
written. One story cast Eddie in the role of a dog and another, authored by
rock musician Frank Zappa, envisioned the comedian as a negroid spider.

"Here it is," wrote former "Saturday Night Live" actor Tim Kazurinsky in
his own failed movie pitch, titled *Spanish Fly*, which he addressed to Bob

Wachs back in 1985. "Eddie gets to be a cowboy, shoot a lot of guns, fuck pretty women, stand up for black rights, save the President of the United States, die a hero and get the Medal of Honor.

"I think it would be great for Eddie to die a hero," Kazurinsky continued. "Everyone in the country would cry for him. And the next time they see him in a movie, they'll be worried that he'll get killed because they've seen him die before. It increases the fear and jeopardy."

And *that* was one of the better stories.

Dennis also came across memos that we couldn't use in our own case, but which provided a glimpse into the remarkable pressure constantly on Murphy.

One memo, written by Murphy's uncle and production aide, Ray Murphy, detailed phone threats that Murphy had received since the release of *Coming to America*. Prince Johnny Ousseni-Bellow, the producer-actor who claimed to be a Nigerian of royal descent, falsely accused Murphy of homosexuality, according to this memo. Further, it went on, Prince Johnny threatened to expose Murphy in the tabloid press if he did not cut him in on profits from *Coming to America*.

Explosive material such as the Prince Johnny memo led Landry to believe that the files he was wading through in the offices of Liebig and Kulzick had not been sanitized. There was still a chance that someone had gone through and cherry-picked all the most damning memos. With the Harrison letters, however, Landry had a litmus test. If the Harrison-Wachs correspondence didn't turn up in the files, it was likely that Paramount was holding out on us.

Several weeks later, when Dennis came across the correspondence at the bottom of the umpteenth box of aging Paramount papers in the windowless room down the hall from Ken Kulzick's office, we knew that Paramount had hidden no cards up its sleeves during that first round.

Landry smiled triumphantly when he came into my office with the news. While the studio's lawyers were still proclaiming publicly that Murphy knew nothing about *King for a Day*, Dennis was stamping "Exhibit 1332, 1333 and 1334" on Harrison's letter, his treatment and Wachs's reply. With several thousand pages of the best documents catalogued and analyzed, we were ready for the moment of truth in every lawsuit—testimony under oath.

And Art Buchwald was the first to raise his right hand.

10

The Art
of Deposition

— — — — — — — — — —

FOR THE FIRST FEW MONTHS after we filed suit, Art basked in the limelight, enjoying his new role as the avenging angel for Hollywood's downtrodden. Mike Wallace, Art's pal and neighbor on Martha's Vineyard, congratulated him for "suing the bastards." Former New York Mayor John Lindsay wrote him, calling the lawsuit "a tremendous idea."

In late April 1989, the serious business of Buchwald's lawsuit began when he was scheduled to face Paramount's lawyer. Art was remarkably nervous about going through the deposition. Five years earlier, he might have eased the anxiety by lighting up a cigar, but he had given it up for his health. All that remained of his once trademark tobacco habit was a ring resembling a gold cigar band that he wore around his ring finger like a wedding band. Ann had a matching ring.

The night before the first of three sessions in the last two weeks of April, Art, Ann and I had dinner together at Washington's Jockey Club. We talked about how curious it was that, in more than forty years of writing thousands of newspaper columns, not once had Art been hauled into court by any one of his targets, nor had he found occasion to sue anyone before Paramount.

He *had* figured into a Supreme Court decision once, but that was only because the late Justice William O. Douglas was a loyal reader.

"One of the things I am the proudest of is that I was cited in a Supreme Court decision by Justice Douglas in the Pabst Blue Ribbon merger case," Art told Ken Kulzick early in the morning of his first day of interrogation. "I had written a column at that time about mergers and, instead of handing in a dissenting opinion, Justice Douglas handed in my column as the opinion, which made me very proud.

"I ran into Justice Douglas about three months later and I thanked him for it and said, 'You made me a big man' and he said, 'I am doing one on pornography. Got any columns?' "

Art seemed to tell these stories to ease tension. It was a revelation to me that one of the highest-paid public speakers in the land could be uptight over a deposition. As an after-dinner speaker, Buchwald commanded $20,000 a night to poke fun at corporation bigwigs and powerful politicians. In front of a couple of attorneys and a court reporter, however, he was nervous . . . at first.

It helped a bit that we were holding the deposition sessions in my law firm's Washington office. I'd warned Art that this was a sworn interrogation, just as if he were on the witness stand, and that Kulzick might try to trip him up or get him to contradict himself. So Art went in prepared.

To his credit, Ken also tried to make it easy for Art, though he did so in a typically patronizing way.

". . . All of us have taken off our jackets. This is not an inquisition proceeding," he said for the record as we were getting under way.

As usual in such proceedings, the first half hour or so consisted of an abbreviated version of "This Is Your Life" with a rundown on age, education, profession, military service, etc. In Art's case, however, this usually boring bit of pro forma Q&A proved entertaining—and even surprising.

Born in Mount Vernon, New York, on October 20, 1925, Art lost his mother when he was an infant. His father moved him and his sisters to Queens in New York City and hired two German nurses to raise them. When he was five and a half, Art was placed in a Hebrew orphanage. Even now, he didn't blame his father. Raising a son and three daughters alone in the midst of the Great Depression would tax even the most dedicated parent, he told Kulzick.

"My father was never really far away. He was with us, but he just couldn't handle it," Buchwald said.

It was his difficult childhood, in fact, that gave Art the sense of the absurd that both saved him and served him well in his later years. In a profile that CBS reporter Mike Wallace did for "60 Minutes" during the late seventies, Buchwald told the correspondent what it was like, suddenly finding himself living in an orphanage.

"What am I doing in this place? Who are these people? I'm different than everybody else. What happened to me? And if you say that at six or seven or eight years old, then you have to cope with it," Art told Wallace. "My way of coping with it was to make a joke out of everything."

Art went to public schools in Queens, not more than a dozen miles from Roosevelt, where Eddie Murphy would be going to school thirty years later. After years in the orphanage or in foster homes, a teenage Buchwald moved back in with his father and three sisters—Edith, Alice and Doris—in 1940. They took an apartment together in Forest Hills where Art attended high school and got his first taste of journalism: he wrote a monthly radio column for the Forest Hills High School newspaper, *The Beacon.*

"During this time, this high school period, did you have any employment other than your employment as a radio columnist?" asked Kulzick.

"Yes, sir," said Buchwald, the beginnings of a smile crinkling the corners of his eyes.

"Where was that?" asked Kulzick.

"I worked for Paramount Pictures," he said.

Every night he took the train into Paramount's New York headquarters at 1501 Broadway and worked from 4 P.M. to 8 P.M. in the mailroom. He earned $8.00 a week plus two passes to the Paramount Theater.

"I was looking for a job after school and I went to the personnel manager of Paramount—I forget what floor it was—and I saw his name was O'Connell on the door. So I went in and I said, 'Father Murphy sent me. He thought you could give me a job. . . .'

"He said, 'Oh, I will do anything for Father Murphy.' I just had to assume there was a Father Murphy and he hired me and every time I saw him after that, he said, 'How is Father Murphy?' And I said, 'Just fine.'"

"It started you on your track towards Catholicism?" Kulzick asked.

"Yes. Then I went off to war, I got cigarettes from Paramount and letters to cheer me up."

In October 1942, Buchwald quit high school on an impulse and ran away to Greensboro, North Carolina, to join the Marines.

"It had to do with a girl and a weekend and the desperation that I had to join or else," he explained cryptically.

"That's a future movie treatment," I said.

After basic training, the Marine Corps sent him to Southern California to the fledgling El Toro Marine Air Base amid the orange groves south of Los Angeles. Art joined a fighter squadron after training as an ordnance man and transferred to Hawaii where he spent the next sixteen months cleaning guns, loading ammunition and flying missions in the South Pacific.

He didn't give up writing though. He edited his outfit's newspaper—a mimeographed sheet called the *U-Man Comedy* after the F4U fighter planes that the squadron flew.

He made sergeant and was reassigned to a stateside Marine training base at Cherry Point, North Carolina, as the war wound down, and again he found a way to finagle his way into writing instead of doing drudge work. He became the base publicist for Cherry Point's football team.

"It was to get out of what they had me doing at Cherry Point," he said. "They had us clearing out brush with [a sergeant who had been] a SingSing guard."

Following his discharge in 1945, Art was asked to join the Marine reserves.

"They wanted me to get my teeth filled before they took me and I refused.

The outfit I was trying to join, the guy wouldn't let me in because I had cavities. About eight months later the entire outfit was sent over to Korea, so I was blessed," he said.

After the war he returned briefly to Paramount's New York headquarters where he thought his mail-room experience and his status as a returning hero might land him a job.

"When I came back from the war, I knew all the big shots and I was walking down the hall at Paramount and I ran into Barney Balaban, who was the president and chairman of the board. And he asked me what I was doing and I said I was in the air wing of the Marine Corps, and he said, 'Oh, well, come in. I want to talk to you.'

"I went in and I sat down and he said, 'I am thinking of buying a private plane. Could you advise me what plane I should get?' "

It remains unrecorded just what Buchwald told Barney Balaban he could go flying in, but Art did not try to further his writing career at Paramount. Instead, he returned to Los Angeles and went to the University of Southern California to see about finishing up his high school diploma at night school. But it turned out that he was part of a mob of several thousand other veterans with the same idea, all anxious to enroll in college on the GI Bill.

Art got lost in the shuffle, signed up for several university classes and finished an entire year before anyone in the administration figured out that he hadn't graduated from high school.

"It didn't matter to me and apparently it didn't matter to them, though they said if I want a degree, I might have to take some more courses," he recalled. "I wasn't interested in a degree, so we got along fine."

What he was interested in was writing, so he took classes in playwriting, Shakespeare, history, and creative writing.

"I just found what I wanted, I took it and since I really didn't give a damn about the diploma, I found courses that were much better," he recalled.

For three years, Art was a college student. USC claims him as an alumnus, and Art is still a big booster of the Trojan football team, but he never graduated and has no idea what his grade transcript looks like.

Outside the classroom, he wrote a column for the *Daily Trojan* and was managing editor of the campus humor magazine, *Wampus*. It was there he met a young hustler named David Wolper whom he hired as the magazine's business manager. Buchwald also put together a comedy stage show called *No Time Atoll*, based on the atomic bomb and his South Sea war adventures.

"The plot was about this native island where these natives were happy, and the Navy has been assigned to do an atomic experiment and they take this island. So then the thing is, how do they keep the Navy from taking the island? It was really a satire based on Bikini at that time."

No Time Atoll was such a fine first stage effort that Art employed his good friend Wolper to publicize it.

"We crashed the Academy Awards with a gorilla," Art recalled. "We rented a gorilla suit and . . . a limo and we drove up to the Academy Awards and got out with the gorilla, who wore a sign that said, 'If you think this is good, you should see *No Time Atoll.'* That was a Wolper stunt."

Like Buchwald, Wolper never got show business out of his blood. He went on to produce the landmark television mini-series "Roots" as well as the opening and closing ceremonies of the 1984 Los Angeles Olympics.

But Art was destined to find his fortune beyond Hollywood and Southern California. By 1948 he was ready to move on and he found the means in a one-time $250 bonus that his native New York paid to its returning overseas veterans. He used the money to buy a ticket to Paris and move into a flat at 24 Rue du Boccador.

He'd had enough of school for a while, but he had to stay enrolled in order to collect his veteran's education benefits. So, as Kulzick discovered, Art paid someone to go to class for him.

"Did you, in fact, bribe a girl to take attendance for you in the Alliance Française French class and never show up in class yourself?" Kulzick asked.

"We gave her a thousand francs, but I wouldn't call it a bribe," he said, shifting in his chair like a grammar school kid being interrogated by the principal. "It was a gift for helping us win the war in France."

Even though it was cheap to live in France in that Marshall Plan era, Buchwald couldn't survive on his GI student benefits alone. He hired on as a tipster or "legman" for *Variety*'s Paris correspondent, a seventy-year-old Frenchman about town named Maxim de Beix. Art got no by-line at first. Maxim took all the credit. But the wide-eyed, twenty-three-year-old American didn't mind. His status as Maxim's emissary got him entree into the Lido, the Ritz and the glitziest levels of show business.

"I was running all around town, feeding him stuff," he remembered. "I would go to MGM's offices, 20th Century's offices, cocktail parties. He gave me entry into all of Paris."

Soon Art was writing his own *Variety* dispatches about the rich and celebrated. By 1954 he had left *Variety* to become restaurant critic, night-life gossip columnist, film reviewer and all-around show biz gadfly for the international edition of the New York *Herald Tribune.*

Art and Ann were married in 1952 in London, and for the next ten years the Buchwalds were the toast of Paris. Whenever Darryl Zanuck or Ingrid Bergman or Jimmy Stewart or almost any other celebrated name from Hollywood came to France, Buchwald found them and made them fodder for his column.

When Danny Arnold arrived in Paris in the late 1950s, there was a message for him to call Art Buchwald. Danny had never met him, but he called anyway. Art welcomed him to Paris, took him to dinner and even had him write a guest column for the *Tribune*—something about the inferiority complex American dogs had developed after Russian dogs became the first to go into outer space. Art and Danny became fast friends for life, yet to this day Danny still doesn't know how Buchwald knew he was in town, and Buchwald will not tell him.

It was during the Paris years that the Buchwald persona as well as his column developed a loyal following. Here was the little Jewish wise guy from Queens, crashing the coronation of Queen Elizabeth II and sharing a 4,000-franc luncheon with the Aga Khan. When he toured Khrushchev's Russia, he posed for pictures in a chauffeur-driven Chrysler Imperial with a capitalistic stogie stuck between his teeth.

He also got his first exposure to the sad insanity of Africa—a rich continent that seemed eternally destined to be overpopulated, undercapitalized and ruled by avaricious absentee European colonialists or equally avaricious, brutal tribal chieftains. It was the kind of harsh, wacky world that suited perfectly Buchwald's sense of the absurd.

"I was getting sick and tired of Ernest Hemingway and Robert Ruark, who were writing about their exploits as hunters in Africa, so I did a spoof of a safari of Hemingway and Ruark, for *Collier's* magazine. I spent two weeks down in the Congo, which was then run by the Belgians. . . .

"I went to Ruanda-Urundi . . . and I met the King of the Watusis who was about six foot three," Art recalled. "He received us in his home. We expected to be received in a little thatched roof place, you know. It turned out to be a place that looked like a house in Great Neck. . . . He had two Studebakers in his garage. I think in the back of my mind at that time I said to myself, 'I have to do something with this.' "

When he wasn't out hustling stories, he was sitting in one of the city's celebrated sidewalk cafes with his good friend Alain Bernheim, an agent with several years' experience in the movie business. It was from their observation post along the Champs Élysées that the two of them first noticed the regular pilgrimages of African royalty who came to the French capital to pay their respects to French President Charles de Gaulle.

Art's first dollars-and-cents exposure to Hollywood began with a story tip that *Newsweek*'s Paris correspondent, Ben Bradlee, gave him in 1956 when Bradlee's own editors told him they were not interested in the idea. Frank Frigenti, a small-time mafioso who used newspaper clippings about his felonies as a résumé, told Bradlee a sensational tale of how Mafia figures were being deported from the United States back to their native Italy. There, they set up narcotics and white slavery networks that preyed on the unsuspecting citizens of Naples. Bradlee wanted nothing to do with Frigenti, who demanded $100 to tell his story. Art offered him a $20 bill and Frigenti spilled his guts: names, places, dates.

When Art got to Naples, however, he found a different story. The mafiosi to whom Frigenti had directed him took him on a crook's tour of the city where he learned that times were so tough that once big-time New York hoods had to survive by short-changing tourists and selling counterfeit name-brand pens out of back alleys. The only mobster with any real money seemed to be deported New York godfather Lucky Luciano, who lived in a penthouse financed by the tribute he still received from his minions back in Brooklyn.

Luciano bought dinner for Buchwald and told him a $100 coral necklace

Art had purchased for his wife in a Naples store was worthless. When Art complained about being fleeced, Luciano told him:

"What you complaining about? These wops do that to me every day."

Art admitted to Kulzick that he might have taken some bit of poetic license in remembering the notorious mobster as having used the word "wops," but all the rest of the story, he said, was true.

Luciano was enough of an inspiration for Buchwald to write a series of stories about his Italian misadventures for the *Herald Tribune* and, later, his first novel, based loosely on the Lucky Luciano story and published in 1959: *A Gift from the Boys*.

"I did the series about these deported gangsters and then the thought occurred to me: what if Cary Grant was Luciano and he was sent to his hometown and he could hardly speak Italian and he was put under the pressures of a Sicilian town? What if? And that is what inspired me to write the story."

Cary Grant read *A Gift from the Boys* while it was still in galleys. He liked it and told Buchwald during one of his Parisian stopovers that he wanted to play the lead. The comic novel revolved around a deported Luciano character who receives a woman as a present from his henchmen back in the States.

But by the time legendary agent Irving "Swifty" Lazar sold the film rights to Columbia for $50,000, both Art and Cary Grant were out of the picture. Buchwald was about to get his first taste of the so-called "collaborative" process in Hollywood that can twist and turn a book, story or even a simple idea into something the original writer never envisioned.

"I must say this very strongly. As soon as they bought my book, Stanley Donen [the director] would not discuss anything with me about the book or any of my ideas," said Art. "It was like I didn't write it. And from then on, Stanley was working with a guy named Arnold Schulman. They produced a script which Cary read and said, 'I am not going to do this.' It wasn't anywhere near my story."

After the movie, retitled *Surprise Package*, came out to less than glowing reviews, the episode was still not over for Buchwald. He was approached by a producer who wanted to turn *A Gift from the Boys* into a stage musical.

So he trekked up to the offices of Columbia executive Leo Jaffe to see about getting the production rights back.

"He was very warm to me," Art recalled. "He said, 'Come on up.' I came up and we were in a room like this and he threw his arms around me and he said, 'How are you?' and I said 'Fine.' I said, 'I have a favor to ask you.' He said 'What is it?' I said, 'I would like to work out something so we can get the movie rights back for *A Gift from the Boys*.'"

The box office failure of *Surprise Package* was apparently a little too tender an issue with Jaffe.

"His face went red and then it went white and then it went blue," Art remembered. "And then he said, 'You stole $7 million from me!' And I said, 'I didn't steal anything from you.'"

But Jaffe was not appeased.

" 'You and Harry Kurnitz and Stanley Donen and Yul Brynner! You all are a bunch of thieves! You stole!' " Art remembered him screaming.

"He had been waiting, I think about two or three years, for somebody to explode on and he exploded on me. End of story. I didn't get the rights."

Art put an index finger to his lips and arched his brows, his mouth forming a wicked grin as he thought about retrieving the production rights one more time.

"I might be able to get them back, come to think of it," he told Kulzick. "Paramount might want to make a movie."

Art didn't abandon his on-again, off-again flirtation with Hollywood, even after he returned to the United States in 1962 and settled along the Potomac. By then, he was thirty-five and earning $50,000 a year for his column and other writings. After fourteen years in Paris, he believed he had grown too comfortable. As a humorist, he felt he had to be bruised and battered a bit in order to produce good work.

"You don't have to worry about getting too comfortable or happy in America," Buchwald told an interviewer a quarter of a century later.

What lumps he might take on the letters-to-the-editor page were not reflected in his personal life. Ann and he were comfortable enough to afford a five-bedroom home on a fenced-in compound located in the upscale Wesley Heights section of northwest Washington. The Buchwalds had three adopted children and, perhaps because of his own rough upbringing, wanted the very best for them.

He found himself switching the emphasis of his subject matter from Parisian show biz to Washington politics. Instead of Rock Hudson or Liz Taylor, he was poking fun at Lyndon Johnson and Henry Kissinger. As a result, his journalism changed too. He wasn't writing about marquee airheads whose foibles and foolishness rarely affected anyone beyond their small circle of self-important friends. He was dealing with heads of state and politicians whose bonehead moves and self-aggrandizing maneuvering affected thousands, sometimes millions, of lives.

What he began doing with words, Art explained, was no different from what Paul Conrad or Garry Trudeau or Jeff McNally do on the op-ed pages of America's newspapers.

"I consider myself a political cartoonist in words and what I am doing with a column of 600 words is drawing something," he said. "So, in effect, it is as if you said to Herblock, 'Is his nose exactly the way you drew it?' It is the same way with my words. They are not going to be exactly the way they should be."

Buchwald described the humor in his daily newspaper columns as having "a core of anger, or at least annoyance."

"I don't consider myself an angry man, but I do get upset about stupidity in government, about people lying, about hypocrisy," he said. "We have it in all the government establishments [and] business."

Still, he remained enamored of show business in general and the movies in particular.

Shortly after moving back from Paris, he collaborated with New York *Times* columnist Russell Baker on a script about Nikita Khrushchev's son coming to America.

And, in the late sixties, Art wrote a column about Henry Kissinger that Swifty Lazar once again turned into cash during a transcontinental plane ride.

"I did a column about the five Henry Kissingers: that there couldn't be one Henry Kissinger doing all these things, there had to be five of them. Irving got on the airplane and he sat next to Dick Zanuck, and Zanuck said, 'Got anything for me?' And Irving looked down at the column and said, 'How about this?' So Zanuck bought the column on the plane before he landed and I think they spent a lot of money developing it."

Twentieth Century Fox gave Lazar $10,000 for the rights. He kept his 10 percent agent's fee and mailed the rest to Art.

At the time, Alain Bernheim was Art's agent, and he did not appreciate Lazar's interloping. As I later learned, Alain's experience was not isolated. Lazar has long been described as "everybody's other agent."

"He is nothing if not persistent," Kulzick volunteered.

"Lazar just goes from thing to thing," said Art. "He would come in here and sell us—the four of us—for a movie."

"Maybe he could sell this lawsuit," I added.

After several years with Lazar, Art switched to the William Morris Agency because of its worldwide reach and its century-old reputation as an all-encompassing talent agency. He remembered well his first meeting with Larry Kalcheim, the William Morris agent who took Art on as a client. Kalcheim may have been less crass than Lazar, Art soon learned, but he was still a salesman in the Swifty tradition.

Art was a little worried that his work might get lost in a big multi-national agency like William Morris and that he might not get the kind of hands-on representation that he wanted. One of the first things Kalcheim wanted to do was allay Buchwald's fears and show him how much personal attention his work was going to get.

"Mr. Kalcheim called me one day in Washington and said, 'I want you to come to New York. We have a new guy to handle movie rights and I want you to meet him.' "

Art flew to New York, went to Kalcheim's office and listened to him describe all of the wonderful plans the agency had for his columns.

"He picked up the phone and he said, 'George, come on down. I've got Art here with me.' And he came down and Kalcheim said, 'Now, George, I want you to take Art's columns and find ways that we can sell them to the movies. Each one to be a movie thing.' And Larry turned to me and he said, 'George is the best man in America to do this sort of thing.' And the guy said, 'My name isn't George.' "

I laughed. So did Ken and the court reporter. Art was relaxing, taking charge.

Several years passed, he told us, and another dozen bestselling collections of his columns were published before Buchwald's next, and penultimate, sortie into Hollywood. It began yet again as a column—this one published in 1973 and entitled: "I Was a Beard for Errol Flynn and Found God."

Kulzick wanted to know what Art meant by "beard." It was a colloquial term, according to Art, essential to romance, adultery and show business.

"If there are two of us going out with a lady and we don't want anybody to know that she is with me, then he (the other guy) would be my beard," explained Art. "This is sort of a Hollywood term. Everyone was a beard. There was a third party and that person is the beard, so that people don't start whispering about you."

Art rewrote the column as another comedy treatment and began optioning it through Hollywood agents during the mid-seventies. Though it was optioned five or six times at $2,000 to $2,500 an option, it was never made into a film. Even as we sat there in my Washington office in the spring of 1989, yet another would-be producer had expressed an interest in optioning the column, Art said.

"This is about ten years old and people have been taking options on it and there is a guy right now who wants another option. We think he is wacko. . . . The last I heard is that there is an Arab sheik who wants to put up the money for this film," he said.

"You are not at all fearful of becoming another Salman Rushdie because of the title?" asked Kulzick.

Art grinned at the comparison of his smart-aleck column to Rushdie's notorious *Satanic Verses*. Hollywood, he explained, would take care of any potential threats from fanatic Moslems.

"No. I will tell you, by the time Hollywood got finished with anything that I did, they wouldn't know it had anything to do with me. That title, 'I Was a Beard for Errol Flynn and Found God' will probably be changed to 'Shove It.'"

In the Hollywood of the 1980s, with its gabardine agents and Armani-clad development executives, Art learned that movie deals tended to open and close in somebody's sumptuous office. The only real difference between a studio deal and an independent producer's deal was whether the office space was owned or rented. The rest of the process was as sterile as a ten-minute pitch session.

But, in Art's estimation, conceiving of a movie ought not to be so cut and dried. He remembered sitting by the Seine with Alain and shmoozing about making movies.

"The way I see this business is, there're three guys in a cafe and they don't know what to do, so they say, 'Let's make a movie,' and somebody says, 'I have an idea. I got a book or I have something.' And all of a sudden that is how things start. There are no appointments at the office."

That was essentially how *It's a Crude, Crude World* originated.

When his friend Alain had moved back to Hollywood to try making his fortune as a producer instead of an agent, one of his first calls was to his old pal Buchwald and the message was clear: remember the days they had dreamed about making movies together? Well, if Art could come up with a salable idea, Alain would try to make the dream reality.

"I play a game with myself all the time of what if: What if this happened? What if that happened? I think it is very helpful for the column. But at that point in time I was just concerned—more concerned with the column. I have had said to me over the years, when the column appeared, 'Gee, that will make a great movie.' I've heard that 100 times."

One day in January 1982, Art got to thinking about Alain's promise and played his "what if" game with some columns he'd written several years earlier.

"I was looking back and apparently I have written a lot of columns about heads of state coming to the White House. They give them an ashtray and the President gives them a dozen F-18 airplanes. The state visit is so standard in this town."

Art recalled for Kulzick the incident when President Jimmy Carter and the Shah of Iran were on the south lawn of the White House and were overcome with tears from tear gas intended for 10,000 protesting Iranian students. "That is the incident that probably inspired me to start thinking what would happen if someone got overthrown while in the United States."

Alain told him to write it up in a few pages. In the meantime, Bernheim told another Parisian friend, director Louis Malle, about the idea and he, too, was intrigued. They both believed they might be able to interest playwright John Guare in drafting the screenplay.

Alain suggested that he and Art and Louis get together while Buchwald and Malle were both in New York and discuss it. One day, over lunch at the Pierre Hotel, the trio made movies together the way Alain and Art used to do at the sidewalk cafes of Paris.

"We are talking about this great idea for a movie: about an oil sheik who comes to the United States, and all he wants is tanks and guns. And he is a despot and he is a real rotter. Then he gets overthrown and he winds up in the ghetto. That is the story that I think I told Mr. Malle."

They also talked about who would play the lead—a black African king—in the event they ever got Guare to draft a screenplay. Richard Pryor was a possibility, once he finished his work on *Superman III*, which was then wrapping up production. So was Bill Cosby or Garrett Morris. Once, years later, Buchwald even thought about Whoopi Goldberg for the role.

Another strong contender was a hot young comic who had recently risen to the top on NBC's "Saturday Night Live." Unfortunately, Bernheim told his two associates, Eddie Murphy had been signed to an exclusive contract with Paramount Pictures and was already making a movie called *48 HRS.*

But casting was all pipedreams at that point anyway. The first thing Art had to do was get the story written.

On March 29, Art sent Bernheim and Malle his eight-page story, about an African dictator whose oil-rich country is overthrown while he is on a state visit to Washington. *It's a Crude, Crude World* seemed perfect for the OPEC eighties. The title came from a melding of crude oil and the title of Stanley Kramer's madcap 1962 comedy, *It's a Mad, Mad, Mad, Mad World.*

Malle and Bernheim asked Art to reduce the story to fewer pages and optioned the revised treatment for $10,000. Art copyrighted the treatment while Alain registered *It's a Crude, Crude World* with the Writers Guild. Then he began peddling it around Hollywood.

MGM/UA production head David Begelman, late of Columbia Pictures, was enthusiastic and immediately became Bernheim's "rabbi" on the project in the spring of 1982 when he heard of Malle's interest in directing it. The scandal of Begelman's conviction had seemed to die down but, in the summer of 1982, *Wall Street Journal* reporter David McClintick's book *Indecent Exposure* hit the stores and Begelman's troubles began all over again. In July he was fired by MGM/UA's chairman and chief stockholder, Kirk Kerkorian.

Kulzick seemed especially concerned about Buchwald and Bernheim getting involved with a man like Begelman, a convicted felon. But, in Art's estimation, morality never seemed to get in the way of the Hollywood moguls he'd seen squiring young starlets around Paris on company funds in the old days. Why should Begelman's misdeeds cloud his professional expertise?

"Did you ever hear the comment made by Sid Luft that Begelman gave fresh and literal pungency to the term 'star fucker'?" Kulzick asked Art.

"I have seen that phrase," Art said with a shrug.

"What does that mean to you?"

"I guess Begelman bedded down a lot of women."

"Are you aware that the charge was made against him by the husband of Judy Garland?"

"Yeah. It didn't bother me at the time."

Kulzick wouldn't let up. He seemed determined to create some kind of special relationship between Begelman and Buchwald where none existed. He pointed out that one of Begelman's embezzlements involved a $25,000 check that he wrote to a French restaurateur named Pierre Groleau and suggested that Buchwald might have gotten to know Begelman through Groleau.

"Have you ever played tennis with Pierre Groleau?" Kulzick wanted to know.

"I think I may have played once with him. He was a good tennis player, he was."

Art turned to me.

"Did you ever play with him?"

No, I told him.

"A terrific tennis player," said Art.

"In playing tennis with Mr. Groleau, did he ever advise you of the strange and wondrous embezzlement in which his name was used by Mr. Begelman?" Kulzick demanded.

Art knit his brow quizzically and cocked his head in wonder at Kulzick.

"Did he ever advise me?"

"Of what had occurred regarding Mr. Begelman," Kulzick said insistently.

"No. To my knowledge, all we did was play tennis."

"He never said anything like—"

It was my turn to get sarcastic.

"Like, 'Love, 40, Begelman is a crook'?" I said.

"Like, for example, during the breaks, when he was complimenting you on your excellent serve, that he was being called upon to give testimony in a criminal matter involving Mr. Begelman?"

Up to that point, I hadn't intervened much in Kulzick's questioning. We'd already been through a couple of half-day sessions and the interrogation seemed relevant and worth pursuing. Even when Ken got tough about dates, incidents and contract points, I avoided interfering.

But the Groleau grilling marked something of a turning point in the deposition. Even when Art and I both made light of his bizarre digging for some sort of back-court conspiracy between a French restaurateur, my client and a deposed studio head, Kulzick wouldn't let up.

"When is the last time that you played tennis with Mr. Groleau?" he demanded.

"I have no idea," Art said. He shrugged dramatically. "I mean, it is just—it is one of the blanks of my life."

Kulzick went from the Groleau tennis match to a whole series of equally unrelated questions: Had Art been present at a seminar in Ojai Valley in 1979 in which producer David Susskind and Chicago *Tribune* TV critic Gary Deeb got into an argument? Had he ever had any conversations of substance with director Martin Ritt? Had he ever watched Bill Moyers interview the late Joseph Campbell about his book *The Power of Myth* on PBS?

Throughout the proceedings, I had to keep steering Ken back to his own line of questioning.

During the second day's lunch break, two of my partners, Ken Feinberg and Jason Shrinsky, took Art and me to lunch. On the way back, Feinberg paused in front of our office building and said:

"Art, someday there'll be an historic marker on this building that says 'Art Buchwald was deposed here.'"

"Like hell there will," Art shot back. "At the pace Kulzick's going, the plaque will say 'Art Buchwald slept here.'"

By the third day, it looked to me like Kulzick was running out of steam and grabbing at straws like some desperate trial attorney who knows he's losing and hopes to hit on the right question by just asking any question. His style had the ferocity of a Southern ceiling fan and the directness of the Mississippi River. I was about to intervene when the silver-haired, grandfatherly Kulzick veered back on course and began asking again how Art's treatment went from *It's a Crude, Crude World* to *King for a Day.*

Like Louis Malle, Begelman thought *It's a Crude, Crude World* ought to be boiled down from eight pages to two and a half, Art said. That was good enough for Buchwald. Whatever Begelman might do in the bedroom or boardroom, the beleaguered film executive knew about selling movie ideas.

So Art went back to the typewriter to refine the last version he'd done for Malle and Bernheim.

By the time he finally got the ultra-short version of the treatment just right near the end of the summer of 1982, Louis Malle was out of the project and Begelman—now himself an independent producer—had lost interest. Malle told Bernheim he still wanted to do the movie but he had to finish a quirky caper film that he was committed to make from a screenplay John Guare had just finished for him. It was to be called *Atlantic City* and would star Susan Sarandon and the venerable Burt Lancaster.

Louis parted ways amicably with Bernheim and Buchwald, however, and even made a call to Paramount chairman Barry Diller to clear the way for a pitch session. He wished them well at their next stop: Paramount Pictures.

Diller's young lieutenant Jeffrey Katzenberg liked the idea. It was perfect for Eddie Murphy and the studio was looking for material to give their bright new star if his *48 HRS.* turned out to be the hit Katzenberg predicted it would be when it was released over Christmas. The thirty-two-year-old Paramount production chief wanted to give *It's a Crude, Crude World* a different name, though. He coined *King for a Day*, according to Art, and the name stuck.

By the following February, Eddie Murphy and *48 HRS.* were both hits. Eddie was already working on his second film. And Jeff Katzenberg was scrambling for scripts to offer his newest star.

Alain signed his own producer agreement with the studio in February. The following month, he sent Art's contract on to Washington to be signed.

"His exact words were, 'I am sending it to you,' " Art told Kulzick.

"Did Mr. Bernheim . . . suggest that it might be desirable for you to read it?" Ken asked.

"No, because I told him I wouldn't," said Art, a defiant smile beginning to play across his lips.

"You said that categorically?" Ken said, leaning forward like a bird dog that has finally found the scent.

"Facetiously. Tongue in cheek," Art told him. "I said, 'Do you think I am crazy? I have to read all of that for the kind of money involved?' I must admit, the kind of person I am and the fact I am not involved with Hollywood [does not make me] interested in deals: . . . you know: 'You are going to get *this* and you are going to get *that* and sign *here!*' "

Ken looked slightly disappointed. He had an opponent who hadn't read his contract, but for all the right and rational reasons.

"It was something for me that was completed, just as if I had completed an article for *Collier's* magazine. Therefore, I don't want to give any impression at all that I was in on all the mechanics of this thing. I wasn't. I was a guy who sold my script to Mr. Bernheim who made a deal with Paramount. I got very little money for it."

Art couldn't tell whether Kulzick was brooding or bewildered, so he leaned forward and offered to elaborate his position.

"I am concerned with saving the world, from Afghanistan to Cuba," said Art, again with his tongue planted in his cheek. "I say that facetiously. What I am really saying is, I have a column to write and I consider that my main occupation."

Hollywood, deal making and option contracts were the least of his concerns. He signed it, shipped it back to Alain and forgot about it until several months later.

"Believe it or not, I am not as commercial as one might think," he said. "I will not do anything that will hurt my career or my column."

King for a Day went into development. The next time Art was even peripherally involved was six months later, when the first draft of a screenplay by Tab Murphy arrived in his office. Alain's cover note said it wasn't too good and Art did little more than leaf through it.

On October 13, 1983, he signed the first of three six-month extensions on the Paramount option so that Alain could switch screenwriters and try for a second script. Each time he signed an extension, Paramount sent him a check for $2,500. This time the studio hired seasoned writer-director Francis Veber, a Bernheim pal from his Paris days.

Veber was a heavyweight. In addition to creating and directing the French comedy hit *La Cage Aux Folles* and its sequel, Veber had a track record as a director-writer of European comedies dating back two decades. It took little to persuade Katzenberg, another big Veber fan, but it did take several more weeks of wooing before Veber agreed to a deal worth $300,000 for writing a script. In addition to drafting a script, Veber also agreed to direct, and for the first time Art thought the studio might be genuinely serious.

"That made me feel happy because I figured if Paramount was going to put that kind of money in a project, they were going to make the movie," said Art.

"Have you not heard of the vast sums of money that are spent on movies that are not made?" Kulzick asked.

"I have heard of that," said Art, "but I was assuming that the combination of Eddie Murphy and Veber and large sums of money would guarantee that the movie was made." But while Veber was working on a draft of *King for a Day,* to the apparent approval of the studio's hierarchy, a complete turnover had taken place in the highest ranks. Barry Diller, Michael Eisner and Jeff Katzenberg were out. Frank Mancuso and Ned Tanen were in.

And Eddie Murphy, now more powerful than ever, had made it clear through his chief lieutenant, Bob Wachs, that he was not interested in a comedy about an African despot cast adrift in Washington. In late March 1985, Tanen gave Bernheim the bad news: *King for a Day* was in turnaround. The producer had a year to find some other studio to make the movie and repay Paramount's investment or the scripts that the studio had underwritten during development became Paramount's property. After Alain's abortive attempt to turn *King for a Day* into a French film, Veber finally lost heart and dropped out of the project.

It took another year, but Alain found a home for *King for a Day* at Warner Bros., and yet another team of writers tackled yet another rewrite. This time, it was retitled *Me and the King.*

Then, in the late summer of 1987, the first word began leaking out of Paramount that Eddie Murphy was making a comedy about a black African prince who ends up in the ghetto. Warner Bros. didn't say anything about *Me and the King* right away, but as early as September, Alain and Art were already seeing the handwriting on the wall. From where they sat, it looked very much as though Paramount had stolen their story. Art made a point of telling producer Paul Maslansky what he thought in a letter he wrote in the fall of 1987, in which he coined his own term for the theft.

"Do you think that that is an appropriate name: 'Murphygate scandal'?" Kulzick asked heatedly.

"Yes, I do," Art said.

"Do you think Eddie Murphy is guilty of any misconduct of any kind with regard to *Coming to America*?"

Art gave the question some thought. I probably would have just blurted out, "You're damn right!" but my client, who tended to clown around about most things, was showing impressive restraint.

"I cannot make a judgment right now. But maybe at the end of the trial I will know," he said in measured tones.

"Do you think it is appropriate to call something a 'Murphygate scandal' ahead of time, when there has been no trial?" Kulzick persisted.

Art sighed so hard over Kulzick's utter lack of any sense of humor that it came out sounding more like a shudder.

"Murphygate is not—Murphygate scandal has nothing to do with real life," he said in exasperation. "It is two guys writing to each other on a piece of paper. And it wasn't published to my knowledge."

At that point, Ken went into a mini-lecture on the legal definition of "published" and how all it took was one third party to see the letter for it to be published in the eyes of a court. How Art managed to maintain his composure in the face of Kulzick's pedantics astounded me. But it was the very absurdity of Kulzick's little diatribe that seemed to calm him.

Art wasn't angry. He was amused.

"We are not going to finish Mr. Buchwald today," Kulzick said.

"That is because you wasted all morning on irrelevant testimony," I answered.

"Counsel, you can make disparaging remarks all day . . ." Kulzick said heatedly.

Kulzick wanted Art to see *Coming to America* again so that he would be able to answer his questions about specific comparisons between Art's *King for a Day* treatment and the finished Eddie Murphy comedy. Art, Ken, the court reporter and I would reconvene in Kulzick's hotel room where *Coming to America* was then showing on Spectravision. Art and I told him to forget it. No sideshow, thank you.

"It would be my preference that the next deposition include a viewing," said Kulzick. "If counsel refuses and if the witness refuses, the record will so note. . . ."

Even Art was getting weary of Kulzick. He'd already seen the movie once, which was once too often.

"That doesn't make sense, but I will go see the movie," Art said finally. "I stay at hotels that show that movie all the time, so it is no problem for me to see it again. I almost get sick when I look at it, but I'll go ahead."

"All right. Anything else?" I asked.

"I would hope to finish in less than a day but, with the viewing, a day," Ken said, loading up his papers to go.

Art had one final observation to make. It was notable for its lack of sarcasm or quips or other Buchwaldisms. It was eloquent, unwavering and straight from the gut.

"I am just talking about the idea," he said firmly. "The idea which is mine —I consider mine—that Paramount lifted."

For the first time I saw Art redden a bit, his eyes narrowing in anger behind his horn-rim glasses.

"The idea was mine. It was optioned by Paramount. Paramount spent a lot of money on it. They had it for some time and then they said they weren't going to make it. And they made it. That is what I am saying. I won't have to see the movie to tell you that because I will tell you the same thing after I see the movie as I do now."

He left no doubt about his conclusion: Paramount and Eddie Murphy had teamed up to rip him off.

There was more—some quibbles over when we might meet again and where. But, basically, Ken Kulzick's deposition of Art Buchwald was over.

The next time Art Buchwald met with Paramount's attorneys, Ken Kulzick would be off the case.

11

Development Hell

—— —— —— —— —— —— —— —— —— ——

HOWEVER BLEAK Art Buchwald's childhood and adolescence may have been, Alain Bernheim's was worse. Art was merely abandoned by his father. Alain spent his formative years being chased across France by Nazis. Such were the stories he told us in preparation for his May 3, 1989 deposition by Paramount's lawyers in Los Angeles.

In further contrast to Art, Alain was a nervous wreck. Zazi Pope, Dennis Landry and I spent four days readying him for his confrontation with Ken Kulzick's partner, Tony Liebig—nearly twice as much time as we usually spent with a client. In the course of poring over the documents that Landry had dredged up from Paramount's files and fine-tuning the chronology of events that culminated in the release of *Coming to America*, I got to know Bernheim even better than I had before . . . and learn why he was the alternately timorous and bold soul that he was.

Born in Paris on October 5, 1922, Bernheim graduated from the lycée just before France's entry into World War II. He was trying to continue his studies in drama and the fledgling art of filmmaking in the late 1930s, but every time he enrolled in a school, the Germans would push a little farther into France. After the fall of Paris, he left for Le Mans. When Le Mans fell, he took up his studies 200 miles to the south in Périgueux, the heart of the Bordeaux wine country. As the Nazis moved farther south, so did he. Bernheim checked out of one school and into another—this time, in Marseilles. By the end of 1941, it was clear that even that Mediterranean seaport was not safe for a Frenchman, particularly a Frenchman of Jewish ancestry.

So, naturally, Alain Bernheim moved again. This time, to Hollywood.

His older brother Michel, who had already established a career in France as a screen director, had not been as lucky at escaping the Nazis. He was one of the first Frenchmen sent to a POW camp, but he managed a spectacular escape within months of his capture. He wrote a seven-page account of his exploits for *Life* magazine, and Twentieth Century Fox decided to turn the magazine story into a motion picture. The studio flew Michel to Hollywood to adapt the story for the screen and Alain tagged along. The younger Bernheim found work dubbing dialogue for the French versions of American films but soon tuned into the deal making that—even then—was the very lifeblood of Hollywood.

Perhaps it was because his education was eternally interrupted by the very real possibility of a one-way train ride to Dachau that Alain Bernheim was infused with the quiet anxiety and understated fury that led him to his life's work. Agenting and producing are both occupations, after all, that require a high tolerance for abuse and constant interruption. Whatever the lure, Alain was hooked on the movies within months of his arrival in Southern California in 1942.

Before he and his older brother left for America, Bernheim had volunteered for the French Army, but they weren't ready for him. While he was working in Hollywood, waiting to be called to serve his country, he tried one last time to finish his education.

"During that time I went to USC," he recalled, twisting his fingers together like braids while Tony Liebig scribbled notes on a yellow legal pad as we sat through the morning interrogation in a claustrophobic conference room at his Wilshire Boulevard offices.

"But I wanted to live the American college life and I wanted to become a cameraman in order to have a specialty in the Army," he continued. "It didn't help much."

"They still made you a paratrooper?" I asked.

"They still made me a private with a broom," Bernheim said, chuckling nervously.

"You went back and you were in the army with your broom?" asked Liebig, staring at him steadily through half-lidded eyes.

"I went back and I was in the French Army from '43 to '46."

If Tony Liebig was impressed by Bernheim's tales of his tough early life, his rocky college years and his military service, he didn't show it. While his partner Kulzick was overly patronizing and polite, Liebig was abrupt and impolitic in his interviewing technique. Alain Bernheim, with his thick French accent and his rambling conversational style of answering questions, clearly bored Liebig. Paramount's apathetic defense attorney couldn't seem to zip through the interview fast enough. From the outset, Liebig treated the case like routine copyright infringement, not a breach of contract case. He thought

King for a Day was all about plagiarism, and he never wavered from that supposition through two days of questioning.

Liebig crossed and recrossed his legs, sighing frequently and audibly. Wading through the details of Bernheim's early Hollywood days as a Famous Artists agent during the late forties and early fifties; his repatriation as a Parisian literary agent during the late fifties and sixties; his return to Hollywood at the end of the seventies—all clearly pained Liebig.

Tony didn't nod off, but he gave the distinct impression of a man who anticipated an early lunch. His ears didn't prick up until an hour into the deposition, when Bernheim described his first American film, *Buddy, Buddy*, and the fine art of packaging.

When Bernheim first returned to Beverly Hills in 1979, he linked up initially with Lorimar, which had just hit it big with "Dallas." Lorimar wanted to branch into feature films, and Bernheim had the solution: remake French hits. The idea has since caught on with several U.S. comedies (*Cousins, Dangerous Liaisons, Three Men and a Baby*). But in 1979 the notion of churning out English remakes of French originals was a novel concept with about as much appeal to most studio executives as turning Brie or Camembert into American cheese.

Bernheim's first attempt to persuade Lorimar was with a French film called *L'Emmerdeur* which translates roughly into *The Pain in the Ass*. While still an agent in Paris, he had helped director Édouard Molinaro produce the comedy from a screenplay by Francis Veber. The story involved an impatient hitman who can't carry out a job because of interference from a whiny, middle-aged businessman who keeps trying to commit suicide.

"I called David Picker, who was running Lorimar in those days, and asked him to come and see the film . . . and unfortunately we made three appointments and he never showed up. And then the fourth time he sent me his assistant. I felt that somehow the interest was not great when she walked out after twenty minutes.

"I had a problem working with David Picker because his span of attention was about twenty-nine seconds on a good day," said Bernheim.

He tried several other projects on Lorimar: *The Face of a Hero*, which began as a "Playhouse 90" presentation on television, starring Jack Lemmon; *The Creator*, a novel by Jeremy Levin; and Art Buchwald's *The Beard*. None of them caught on.

He returned to *L'Emmerdeur*.

"I felt it was a property that could be adapted to the American market," he explained. "I then showed the film to Jack Lemmon and Walter Matthau with the help of William Morris . . . and they both loved it. And they said to me, 'Who do you think we should get to direct it?' And I said, 'My wish is Billy Wilder.'

"And they said, 'Tell you what: we never commit to any script until we see a screenplay.' And they said, 'If we can get Billy, we'll commit to it now.'

"And we talked to Billy and he said he would do it. Therefore, I had a full package. I had a director, Billy Wilder—you know his credits—and two major actors and MGM was delighted to green-light the picture because there was a cast."

Unfortunately, Matthau and Lemmon probably should have trusted their instincts and waited for a finished script. Film critic Richard Combs called the resulting bomb "the saddest episode in Wilder's career."

During the early eighties, before Bernheim and Buchwald and Louis Malle dreamed up the original plot for *King for a Day*, Bernheim was not idle. He signed an exclusive two-year development deal with MGM, which remained undaunted by the disappointing 1981 release of *Buddy, Buddy*. In addition to producing *Yes, Giorgio* for MGM (1982) and *Racing With the Moon* for Paramount (1983), he had a half dozen other projects in various stages of development, including a TV miniseries based on the life of Pablo Picasso.

Bernheim also had an oral commitment from Louis Malle to direct and a nod from MGM production chief David Begelman to move ahead on a story written by Art Buchwald. *Voilà!* Alain Bernheim had a sure-fire package.

Eddie Murphy and Paramount were about to lead him into development hell.

"All good stories should be able to be told in one-liners. If you can't, you are in trouble," Bernheim said.

The story of *King for a Day* boiled down to "a king who leaves his native land and, once he's in America, is deposed and reduced to a civilian and what happens to him from there on," he told Tony Liebig.

That was the basic synopsis Bernheim laid out for Jeffrey Katzenberg at Paramount in the fall of 1983, when his package began to fall apart. After Begelman left MGM and Louis Malle had left the project, he took *King for a Day* to the same studio backing *Racing With the Moon*, Bernheim told us.

Tony Liebig was not satisfied with the explanation.

"Tell me what you told Jeff Katzenberg during that first meeting," Liebig said suddenly, putting his pencil down. "Pretend I'm Katzenberg. I'm at my big emperor desk and you are making your best pitch to the mogul here."

Bernheim held his hands up in surprise. He looked at me for help and I nodded for him to go ahead.

"I told him that I had a story by Art Buchwald," he said. "That alone attracts a lot of attention because he is a writer. And I thought also it would fit one of their actors that they have under contract, Mr. Murphy. And he listened to the story and he said, 'I like it. Let me think about it.' They don't commit immediately."

Bernheim left the treatment with Katzenberg, waited a couple of weeks and called him back, he said. Katzenberg approved the start of script development and turned to his creative team, headed by David Kirkpatrick, to come up with a screenwriter.

Twenty-five-year-old Tab Murphy was the first.

•   •   •   •   •

While Eddie Murphy was a budding millionaire following the success of his first two seasons on "Saturday Night Live," Tab Murphy was selling potato chips and dog food out of a North Hollywood convenience store.

In my own investigation, I had learned that Tab had dropped out of the University of Southern California film school during the summer of 1982 and ended up clerking at a 7-Eleven store in North Hollywood to support himself so that he could write the Great American Screenplay in his spare time. Like thousands before him, once he had just the right story with just the right characters down on paper, he was going to take Hollywood by storm.

Tab, a thin, soft-spoken Seattle native, is four years older than the "Saturday Night Live" whiz kid. All the two had in common, however, was their surname. Tab was a suburban middle-class white kid who doubted his talent at every step of the way while Eddie was a big-city middle-class black kid who absolutely *knew* he was going to be a star back in grammar school.

Tab Murphy's break turned out to be a young executive at Paramount who stopped at the 7-Eleven for coffee or a newspaper on the way to the studio each morning. Tom Wright took pity on the enthusiastic kid with his passionate talk about writing for the movies. Wright worked in production with Kirkpatrick and, through David, had Jeff Katzenberg's ear. It was Kirkpatrick who was the studio's direct liaison with Eddie Murphy. Wright asked to see the script Tab had started at USC and liked it well enough to show it around. The consensus among his associates at Paramount was favorable and the first question that came back was: "Does Tab have an agent?"

Of course he didn't. But by month's end he did, thanks to his new mentor from Paramount. A gruff, fast talker named Peter Turner who worked in the literary department of William Morris in Beverly Hills read the script. It was good. The scenes demonstrated that Tab understood not only structure but also the delicate juxtaposition of poetry and action, dialogue that exposed character, and other principles taught in screenwriting classes all over America . . . but rarely understood by any of the students.

Tab Murphy had what agents loved to call "potential" when talking to studio executives.

It was that potential, along with the "spec" script that he had written on breaks at the 7-Eleven, that landed Tab Murphy his first development deal at about the same time that Eddie Murphy was making his screen debut in *48 HRS.* His first project for Paramount was an action comedy about a black detective, set in a 1930s Harlem nightclub that Tab titled *The Black Mask.* Paramount paid him WGA minimum: $35,000. It took him just three weeks to write and Kirkpatrick, among others, knew exactly who ought to star in it.

But, in the meantime, something else had come along that needed a fast, talented young hustler to crank out a quick script. Would a former 7-Eleven clerk give up his day job for $2,500 above the WGA minimum and a chance to draft a screenplay for Eddie Murphy, based on an Art Buchwald story?

Silly question.

Tab Murphy, Alain Bernheim and the three or four Paramount executives shepherding the project along for Katzenberg began regularly meeting together. Almost immediately problems developed, according to Tab. Alain wanted to stick to Art's story while Katzenberg wanted Eddie to play twins: a good twin who sits on the throne and a bad twin who overthrows his brother while he is on a state visit to the United States.

Alain's memory of events during the summer of 1983 was very clear:

"I talked to Tab, and I said, 'Listen, do not give me a twin brother story because I will not do it.' And he said, 'No, no, I won't. We don't need it. I won't.'"

Under Tony Liebig's questioning, Alain remembered sitting down with his young screenwriter in an office out of earshot of Kirkpatrick or Wright or any of the other Paramount development types who were giving Tab mixed messages. It was his film, Alain explained. His name would go on the credits as producer. He wanted it written a particular way.

"One of the main suggestions [was] that the king should be maybe not so likable at first and, during the course of the arc of the film, he becomes a likable character, which we wanted to do," said Bernheim.

Tab dutifully took notes and set to writing. The script might have turned out all right in spite of the studio's meddling if Alain's mother hadn't fallen seriously ill. While Tab toiled to please Bernheim and the studio, Alain flew to Paris.

"While I was in France, I kept in touch with Tab Murphy at least once a week on the phone to see what progress he was making. What he was telling me sounded quite good and I encouraged him and we discussed certain things that he was doing and that was the best we could do, because my mother passed away in August and I then had to stay on to organize my family affairs.

"I returned to New York the end of September or the first of October, I'm not sure. William Morris sent me Tab Murphy's screenplay which I was eager and anxious to read. And when I sat down and read it, I realized that that was not the script I wanted."

Tab took the blame for attempting to please two different bosses and coming up with a compromise that satisfied neither. Just before Thanksgiving, Paramount politely told him his services were no longer needed. He joined the unemployment line and didn't work as a screenwriter again for over a year.

Most projects die after the first script fails, but Buchwald's story was different. After Tab Murphy's abortive attempt at turning *King for a Day* into a screenplay, Katzenberg still loved the idea, and he wasn't willing to give up yet. The next screenwriting guinea pig, Bernheim told Liebig, was Francis Veber. Veber was no 7-Eleven clerk on his first assignment as a screenwriter. Bernheim believed that if he were given a chance to write and direct something from scratch, and not simply remake his own French hits in English, the French comedy writer would be able to bridge the language gap using the unique international idiom of laughter.

Bernheim tried matchmaking his Buchwald story with the proven screenwriting talent of Veber after the Tab Murphy disaster. His only hope was that Katzenberg had a longer attention span and a wider, more sophisticated taste in comedy than some of the other production executives he'd run into in Hollywood.

Bernheim was pleasantly surprised. Katzenberg was ready to dole out far more than the WGA minimum to a man of Veber's proven talents.

"I remember he was to get $300,000 to write a screenplay . . . and another $100,000 for the second draft and $1 million if he also directed the movie," Bernheim recalled under Liebig's questioning.

The way Veber's version of *King for a Day* was to be written turned out to be risky, Bernheim said as we resumed the following morning. Veber would write in French, try out a scene on Bernheim, and then Veber's assistant, Sandy Whitelaw, would translate it into English.

"You can't really translate a movie from French to English," Veber said several years later. "It remains a French movie if you translate it."

Language was not the only barrier. Veber and Bernheim were also handicapped by their lack of access to Eddie Murphy. Katzenberg and Kirkpatrick made it clear to them up front that they watched over their new star carefully and that the writer-director and producer would meet with him in good time, but not in the early stages of screenwriting. Besides, Murphy was in the middle of filming an action comedy called *Beverly Hills Cop* for Paramount and couldn't take time out for script consulting.

Despite the absence of Eddie, studio executives still tried to do with Veber what they had done with Tab Murphy: impose their vision upon his. Veber was called into David Kirkpatrick's office shortly after signing with Paramount and told how the movie would open: feature shots of a lavish, opulent palace with heavy emphasis on Eddie Murphy's being surrounded by beautiful, half-naked native women.

"He seemed to be in a trance and it was like he was talking as an interior designer, not a script consultant or an executive," Veber later recalled.

Veber took a prompt dislike to Kirkpatrick.

At one point, Bernheim took his new collaborator to Washington, to meet with Buchwald and Washington *Post* columnist Courtland Milloy for a guided tour of the ghetto. Even if they couldn't meet with Murphy, Veber reasoned, his script could at least have the proper scenic atmosphere.

Veber insisted on staying at the Ritz Carlton. Since he looked like the key to getting *King for a Day* made, Bernheim humored him, but he did draw the line at luxuriating through the seedy side of Washington in a rented limo.

"We didn't want to go through the ghetto, so to speak, with a limo and chauffeur," Alain recalled.

Despite the obstacles, Veber persevered with *King for a Day* in part because he considered the worshipful Katzenberg a genuine guardian angel among Paramount's corporate elite. Throughout most of 1984, Veber and Bernheim met periodically and exchanged ideas on the project, even though both were deeply immersed in their other projects. Together, they hammered out a script.

However, Paramount now began the massive executive power shift that would remove Katzenberg as a buffer between Veber and Kirkpatrick and turn Paramount's development schedule topsy-turvy. Martin Davis installed Paramount distribution chief Frank Mancuso in the chairman's slot and, to head production at the studio, Mancuso hired former Universal Studios production chief Ned Tanen. At about the same time, family tragedy again overtook Alain Bernheim. His brother Michel, whom he had left in charge of his Paris office, suddenly died.

"My brother passed away and I left very promptly," he said. "I stayed on for family reasons, but primarily to work with Francis [Veber] since I was still there."

On November 1, 1984, Bernheim took a copy of the script to screenwriter Larry Gelbart, one of the creators of the hit TV series "M*A*S*H."

"Gelbart is now considered the number one American comedy writer for films, anyway, and he happened to be a friend of mine," Bernheim explained. "I had worked with him when we both were living in London. We were going to produce pictures together and I also was his agent for a short while."

Veber didn't have his usual retinue of fellow actors and writers to rely on for feedback. *King for a Day*, after all, was not a remake; it was an American original—albeit written first in French and translated into English. To see whether the laughs translated as well, Bernheim asked Gelbart to read *King for a Day* and give him his feedback.

"And then we had lunch," Bernheim remembered. "Francis wasn't here. I think he was in Palm Springs." Alain was encouraged because Gelbart liked the draft.

Veber was already in the final throes of rewriting—in cushy surroundings, of course.

"He thought the only way was to lock himself up in a bungalow with a swimming pool in Palm Springs and a tennis court and to finish it," said Bernheim.

Armed with Gelbart's specific suggestions for improvement of Veber's draft, Bernheim drove the hundred miles from Hollywood to Palm Springs and spent two days helping Veber put the finishing touches on the screenplay.

"And a couple of weeks later we got the script, had it mimeographed and I gave it to Kirkpatrick and to Ned Tanen to read."

"So by the time there was Veber's script, Katzenberg was sayonara. Done," said Liebig.

"That's correct," Alain answered. "I would say because he had a very close relationship with Veber that he had a curiosity. After all, this is something he started."

"Did Mr. Katzenberg ever tell you what it was about the idea that Eddie Murphy liked?" Tony asked.

"I was not that greedy," said Alain, shrugging his shoulders and holding his hands out in supplication. "The fact that he liked it, the fact that Eddie Murphy—there was nothing for him to specify. He must have told him what it was about."

"He could have said, 'I like it because there are pretty girls in it,' " Liebig offered.

"There were none," Alain said, adding, "but I know what you are saying."

Liebig read from Alain's appointments diary that he kept at the time:

" 'November 26, '84: Kirkpatrick invites Bernheim and Veber to party at the Hard Rock Cafe after opening of 'Beverly Hills Cop' in order to meet Murphy. However the crowds are so intense that it is impossible to meet Murphy.' Is that consistent with your recollection?"

Alain nodded.

"It is," he said.

"So up until then neither you nor Veber actually met Murphy?" Liebig asked.

"Right," Alain answered.

"You never did meet him, did you?"

"I never did," said Alain. "It is a Catch 22. Ned [Tanen] said, 'Do the work and we'll show it to Murphy.' I said, 'It is a useless process because, until we meet with him—he is such a creative man anyway; his input, how he would visualize a certain thing in the script . . . there is no way to do it.' Ned agreed that we could go and meet with him."

Bernheim called to set up a meeting at Murphy's New Jersey estate, which was then located in the exclusive community of Alpine, about an hour away from midtown Manhattan.

"We made a date soon after that and the day or two before we were to leave —we had tickets already—we were told that Murphy would not be there. He had left with his lady friend for Jamaica."

The next opportunity Veber and Bernheim would have to meet with their star was during a break in press interviews, after he returned from the Caribbean, they were told.

"And we did not think that was very practical because meeting someone in between publicity interviews is hardly the way I think one can be constructive for a movie," said Alain. "I said either we can spend a day together away from this or he can come to Paris and spend a day just to have his input. And that never happened."

The new head of production was not particularly helpful either. Tanen told Bernheim, "Our procedure is not to show it to Eddie . . . until we are 100 percent happy with the script," Alain recalled.

Bernheim tried being conciliatory, telling Tanen that he understood the studio's position. But he also pointed out that King for a Day was not just any ordinary spec script: it was tailor-made for Eddie Murphy "and a tailor at one point has to try to get a fitting and we were unable to get that fitting appointment."

"Well, do you remember anything he could have said other than, 'It is not all there'?" Liebig said, beginning to bully Bernheim a bit. "That is the most general meaningless thing I ever heard. That can mean it is 90 percent ready or it is a pile of crap to throw away."

There was Tanen's phone conversation with Veber, Bernheim remembered.

"What did Mr. Veber tell you that Tanen said on the phone call?" Liebig asked.

"It was in French and I don't think I want to translate the words. He was very upset," said Bernheim.

"Translate it freely," said Liebig.

Alain looked to me for help. I shut my eyes and nodded. Alain swallowed, trying to preserve his gentlemanly demeanor. Then he began:

" 'I have never been treated like this. I delivered a first draft I intend to do more work on. I had some constructive thinking, not just saying it has to be approved . . .' "

Alain stopped, clenching his jaws, his face reddening.

"I mean, he was so upset, he practically hung up on Ned, I think. He said, 'I have always been able to do things on my second draft, and in France we work differently, and there is no reason for him to talk to me this way!' He said, 'Fuck him!' He said . . . I'm sorry." Alain broke off, shaking his head; he could go no further.

Bernheim feared the rift between Tanen and Veber was irreparable. For the second time in two years, he worked frantically to save his project while he watched events over which he had no control slowly choke the life out of *King for a Day*. Tanen and Kirkpatrick wanted more work on the Eddie Murphy character and Veber was forbidden to even meet Eddie Murphy. Veber made a halfhearted try at a rewrite but hadn't gotten far into it when the project was terminated at Paramount.

Before Tanen called Bernheim with the news that the studio had decided to drop *King for a Day* from its development schedule at the end of February 1985, Paramount had already invested close to $500,000 in the Veber and Tab Murphy scripts. Still, he felt as though it was time to cut Paramount's losses and get on with other Eddie Murphy projects because *King for a Day* was not jelling right. Veber was as infuriated as Bernheim was crestfallen.

Alain gave it one last shot. He quit dealing with studio middlemen and went directly to Eddie Murphy Productions. Tamara Rawitt, a former Paramount publicist, had recently been installed as Murphy's personal development chief and, in March 1985, Alain finally got her to read Veber's script. She told him "that she loved the script and she was going to give it to Bob Wachs and try to get Eddie to read it, but she did say 'try,' " recalled Bernheim.

A few days later Bernheim's phone rang.

"I got a call from Bob Wachs," said Alain.

"What did he say?" Liebig asked.

"He said, 'Al . . .' "

"He said what?"

"He said, 'Al,' which is funny. 'Al, I read the script. It needs work.' It is one of those conversations you don't forget. 'Al, I read the script. It needs work.'

"And I answered, 'I agree with you, it needs work. And I wish you would tell me what kind of work or have your associate tell me and we'll proceed to do it.'

"And he said, 'It needs work,' and after that he hung up on me. He didn't pursue it any further, and that was the last time I talked to Mr. Wachs."

Even Tony seemed mildly amused by this typical Hollywood brush-off.

"He said, 'Al, it needs work.' Did he know who he was talking about?" Liebig asked.

"I assume no," said Bernheim. "There was nothing else we could do. I felt we were going in circles."

"You could have gotten one of those airplanes with the banner that said, 'Eddie, read my script,'" I suggested.

Alain smiled but he didn't laugh.

King for a Day was officially in turnaround—the Hollywood equivalent of putting a major leaguer on waivers. Paramount's contract gave Bernheim one year to find a new home for his project. He began making the rounds. But buying the Veber and Tab Murphy scripts back from Paramount for half a million dollars was a steep proposition. Without Eddie Murphy in it, the turnaround cost seemed prohibitive.

Alain tried MGM. They were interested until they heard the price. The top end that a studio seemed willing to pay for the Veber script was $200,000 without Eddie Murphy cast in the lead.

At one point Bernheim went back to Tanen with the proposition that he and Veber would pay Paramount $50,000 to release the script for a French version of the film, but the studio didn't think $50,000 was enough.

Paramount's option on Art's original story had long since lapsed, however, and Bernheim owed no turnaround premium on either *It's a Crude, Crude World* or the pared-down version that Art had written in the summer of 1983. So, the following year, he took the project to Warner Bros., where he had been working with *Police Academy* producer Paul Maslansky on *National Parks*, a comedy about New York delinquents working in the great outdoors.

"He and I were going to coproduce the picture together, his company and mine, for Warner Brothers," said Alain.

The studio thought that, with the right story, Bernheim and Maslansky might be able to discover "the new Eddie Murphy." They did not have an Eddie Murphy budget to work with, however. The movie, now titled *Me and the King*, was to cost $6–8 million.

Bernheim's plan was to star Lenny Henry, a popular British comic who was unknown to American audiences but who liked the idea. With the right script, the entire cost of *Me and the King* promised to be less than Eddie Murphy's up-front acting fee. After a weak script by Matt Robinson ("Cosby Show"), a second writer, Allan Katz, started writing a new screenplay for *Me and the King.* Then storm clouds once again began moving over Bernheim's project.

"Paul Maslansky called me in Paris to say that he saw something in *Variety* or one of the trade publications that Murphy was preparing a picture about a king going from Africa to America," Bernheim said.

Alain flew back to the United States and asked Ned Tanen to lunch. There, following Tanen's angry tirade over Bernheim's suggestion that *Coming to America* and *King for a Day* might be intertwined, the Paramount production chief assured Bernheim that his Warner Bros. project and the new Eddie Murphy movie were totally unrelated.

Tanen also told Bernheim that Art Buchwald was "a has-been."

By the following January, the *Me and the King* script was not quite where Bernheim and Maslansky wanted it, but that turned out to be a moot point anyway. Paramount's plans to release an Eddie Murphy comedy that summer about an African prince looking for love in Queens, titled *Coming to America,* was just too similar to *Me and the King.*

Warner Bros. pulled the plug, and Bernheim said he had been robbed.

"I did actually mention it to a couple of people to see their reaction because you don't spend four years of your life in getting, you know, at a dead end," he said.

"You were quoted in *Newsweek* saying, 'It is not the same story, but it is the same arc.' Is that a correct quotation?" Tony Liebig asked.

Yes, said Alain, it was.

Liebig clucked his tongue and planted his elbows on the edge of the table, his eyes twitching like those of a Siamese cat waiting for the mouse to emerge from its hole. He had a copy of our complaint in front of him.

"An allegation of fraud is a very serious allegation," Liebig began.

"He didn't make it," I said, leaping to Alain's defense.

"I'm sure he doesn't want to contradict your allegations," Tony said.

"He's not a lawyer," I answered. "I think we're wasting time."

"I want to be on the same wavelength here," Liebig persisted, ignoring me and directing his questions at Bernheim. "The eighth cause of action alleged in your behalf by your lawyer against Paramount is for something called common law fraud and deceit."

"It is taking from somebody, something that belongs to them, very simple," Bernheim said.

"Lying and cheating, okay? The complaint filed at the courthouse on your behalf is a contention that Paramount has not only taken these things, but they lied and cheated along the way," Liebig said in a tone dripping with accusation.

"Well, that's what it says." Alain shrugged. "When I realized they were not interested—Paramount that is—in *King for a Day* and thereafter prepared another film called *Coming to America,* which was, in our opinion, based upon the Buchwald story, that's what I believe is meant by fraud."

Liebig stroked his chin.

"So basically it seems to me when Ned Tanen, in March 1985, told you they lost interest in it, he was lying?"

"Either that or he didn't remember," Alain said. "I don't know why he told me not to worry and then I see the movie and there it is."

But Tony clearly was unsatisfied with Alain's explanation. He wanted him to understand just how serious a charge fraud can be, and he had no intention of letting Bernheim off the hook. When the questioning became antagonistic, I stepped in.

"You're badgering the witness, Tony."

"You may think so, but I want to know if he is seriously alleging fraud here," said Liebig.

"Yes, he is," I answered for Alain.

"You are alleging these guys consciously lied to you?" Liebig persisted, ignoring me and aiming his question directly at Alain.

"Yes, on numerous times," I again answered.

"Let the witness talk," Liebig snapped.

"He's read it twice now," I said.

"Are you aware of the fact?" Liebig asked again.

"Yes," Alain finally answered in a hoarse but furious whisper.

As soon as we were alone in the lobby outside of Liebig & Kulzick's suite, I gave Bernheim a bear hug. Liebig had tried to rattle him, but he failed.

As we started for the elevator, the court reporter who had taken the deposition for the past two days called out to Alain.

"Mr. Bernheim! May I have a word with you?"

The thin, owlish-looking man had an interesting proposition for Bernheim. Once, when he first started his profession, the court reporter had taken a long, confidential deposition for one Howard Hughes. He still had his notes from that deposition. Perhaps Alain would be interested in using his Hollywood connections to pull together a movie deal based upon the reporter's notes?

The elevator doors sprang open. Before Alain could answer, I pulled him inside.

12

Enigma
on the Bench

"WHAT'S ART BUCHWALD complaining about, Mr. O'Donnell?"

I was startled by the sharp tone of Judge Harvey A. Schneider's opening remarks to me and my associate Zazi Pope. It was an informal status conference in his chambers on May 11, 1989—our first face-to-face meeting with the man who held our future in his hands. Paramount's lawyer, Tony Liebig, was also there.

Five months had passed since we filed suit, and the newly elected Los Angeles County Superior Court judge who, through luck of the draw, had been assigned to our case wanted to discuss how we planned to proceed.

"Well, your honor," I began slowly, to gain a precious second or two.

The fact was we had been proceeding for some time: informally interviewing potential witnesses, researching cases, and gathering information like so much rope that we hoped to finally tie together into a hangman's noose for Paramount. Bernheim was a regular one-man surveillance team, collecting bits of Murphy gossip and Paramount buzzings during his frequent lunch and dinner dates among the industry illuminati. And whenever Buchwald heard any back-channel rumblings in New York or Washington about Paramount's next move, he was on the phone to me in a flash.

By the time we met with Judge Schneider, Marsha, Zazi and Dennis Landry had already mastered the Paramount documents and the studio's lawyers had already deposed both of my clients—Art in Washington and Alain in Hollywood. Up to this moment, I felt pretty good about the progress that we had made. While settlement had not yet been broached, I remained confident that by the end of discovery, if my case held up, Paramount would finally come to the negotiating table for an out-of-court resolution.

Now I looked squarely into the eyes of a man with a thousand cases on his docket and little patience with anyone who presented any obstacles to trying them. I gathered my thoughts as best I could, trying to maintain that composure under fire that is supposed to differentiate a trial lawyer from other mere mortals.

"Mr. Buchwald wrote a story for an Eddie Murphy movie for Paramount," I began. "And we claim that they later used it to make *Coming to America* without his permission and in breach of his contract with Paramount. They claim that Eddie Murphy came up with the story independently, and we say that the movie is based upon Buchwald's original treatment."

Harvey Schneider was a total stranger to me and almost everyone else in the main downtown Los Angeles County Superior Courthouse, but in less than thirty seconds of repartee, I knew he was no ordinary judge.

"I don't know why Buchwald would want to be associated with *that* movie," the stern, mustachioed, fifty-one-year-old jurist fired back without missing a beat.

"Look, your honor, as Mr. Buchwald has said, '*Coming to America* is not *War and Peace*, but Eddie Murphy isn't Tolstoy either.' The movie was a big box office hit. My clients want what is due them under their contracts."

Swinging quickly around to Ken Kulzick's ruddy-complected, sixty-year-old law partner, Schneider asked, "What's Paramount say about this, Mr. Liebig?"

My fellow lawyers around the courthouse had been unanimous in their assessment of this new man on the bench. I was told, over and over, that Harvey Schneider was unbiased and evenhanded, even if he did seem brusque. Judge Schneider was, indeed, impartial. He caught Liebig just as off guard as he had caught me. Liebig recovered and quickly assumed the requisite air of superiority of a studio lawyer whose client had remained sinless for three quarters of a century.

"This case has no merit," Liebig replied. "It's just like two other lawsuits that have been filed recently against my client. Plaintiffs in those cases claim they originated the movie too.

"Mr. Buchwald wrote a two-and-one-half-page story that has nothing to do with *Coming to America*," he continued. "Paramount dropped Buchwald's project years before starting *Coming to America*. And Eddie Murphy wrote the story himself. We expect to get rid of this frivolous case on motion."

Schneider rubbed his chin.

"Well, we'll see," he responded, his voice betraying a faint hint of skepticism about Liebig's assumption that this case wouldn't make it past the first hearing.

I was sorely tempted to take a cheap shot at Tony. A decade earlier, Liebig had defended McDonald's against a federal copyright lawsuit brought by the creators of the "H. R. Pufnstuf" children's television show, Sid and Marty Krofft.

In 1973, Needham, Harper & Steers had steered McDonald's toward the Kroffts, whose life-size puppets inspired Mayor McCheese, the Hamburgler and other McDonaldland characters. Before the campaign got off the ground, the Kroffts were cut out of the project. They sued, claiming that the hamburger conglomerate and its advertising agency had ripped off their characters for their "McDonaldland" television commercials, and Liebig lost . . . big. The Kroffts won $50,000 for copyright infringement and appealed for more.

The case, Sid & Marty Krofft Television v. McDonald's Corporation, was upheld in the 9th Circuit four years later and sent back to the trial court for a reassessment of damages. The Kroffts finally won well over $1 million.

Ironically, I planned to use the case in my opening brief, if I ever got Buchwald v. Paramount to trial. James Tierney, the Kroffts' lawyer during their 1977 jury trial, had led us to believe that Liebig was as overconfident then as he was that morning in Judge Schneider's chambers. I resisted the temptation to remind Tony that similar motions for dismissal that he had made in the Krofft case had failed. I would wait. The Irish have a saying: "Don't get mad; get even."

As Judge Schneider proceeded to discuss the routine issues of discovery deadlines and pretrial scheduling, I studied his dour face, thick black mustache and clean-shaven head. Schneider bore a faint resemblance to the silent film comic Ben Turpin. But he was no comedian, though he was capable of trenchant wit. "I wish they'd go to the British system," he had recently told an interviewer from the local legal newspaper, the Los Angeles Daily Journal. "The wigs would be very helpful to me." He could snarl like a Doberman pinscher and scowl like a substitute teacher on the first day of school.

He intrigued me.

Harvey Schneider was one of the newest state court trial judges in Los Angeles. His path to the bench had been anything but orthodox. In fact, he picked the hardest way possible: he ran against a sitting judge when her term expired . . . and won.

Born in Lincoln, Nebraska, Schneider grew up in Los Angeles. He graduated from UCLA in 1958 with a finance degree and served in the Navy as a public information officer. He was too young for the Korean War and too old for Vietnam. Balancing his local school allegiances, he then enrolled in law school at UCLA's crosstown rival and finished near the top of his class at USC Law School. His contemporaries included my good friend Howard Weitzman, who achieved national fame as the attorney who got automaker John DeLorean acquitted of cocaine trafficking and bankruptcy fraud in back-to-back federal trials.

"Harvey has a brilliant legal mind," Howard told me when I called to get some background on our judge. "He was also sort of a loner in law school. He had a family and had to work, so he didn't have a lot of time to hang out and shoot the breeze."

Howard and other friends told me that Schneider practiced criminal and civil law after he graduated, mostly as a solo practitioner. I also had my staff do a computer search of all published decisions in which he participated, as either a lawyer or a judge. The printout for Schneider showed that he handled such diverse matters as protecting First Amendment rights of alleged pornographers; upholding insurance coverage for policyholders; defending a disciplined doctor and a company accused of misappropriating a trade secret; securing a condominium conversion for real estate developers; and appeals of convicted murderers, child molesters and marijuana users. His appellate track record alone was impressive: in twenty-three reported California decisions between 1966 and 1987, he won the majority of his appeals.

One case caught my attention. Three years before becoming a judge, Schneider represented the distributor of a film called *Pink Champagne*. The film's producer sued for breach of contract, claiming he had not been paid his minimum guarantee of $130,000. One of the issues was the proper method of allocating production and distribution expenses in calculating the minimum guarantee. While he had represented a film distributor like Paramount, I was not concerned about Judge Schneider's impartiality. In fact, I thought that his familiarity with some of the Byzantine aspects of motion picture accounting might help down the road.

Reputed to have a 200 IQ, Schneider developed a reputation as one of the smartest litigators in town. He never joined a big firm. He either practiced solo or with no more than one or two other lawyers. He was widely respected as a "lawyer's lawyer"—the person other lawyers hired to write winning briefs or handle oral argument in tough cases.

Only three years out of law school, he had the heady experience of winning a landmark search-and-seizure case before the United States Supreme Court, *Katz v. United States.*

"How do you top it?" Schneider asked a reporter profiling him shortly after taking office. "You can't."

His next case brought him crashing back to earth. He defended a traffic citation in a Los Angeles Municipal Court.

"It keeps you humble," he said.

Harvey Schneider had long aspired to become a judge. But he was a liberal Democrat, a volunteer attorney for the American Civil Liberties Union, and a champion of the underdog: not the credentials for appointment to the federal bench during the Nixon/Ford years or to the state court during the eight-year governorship of Ronald Reagan.

"Getting appointed requires political clout, which I apparently did not have," said the straight-talking Schneider.

But in 1976 he was the best-qualified candidate for appointment as a federal magistrate—a judicial officer hired by the other federal judges in Los Angeles to handle routine pretrial criminal procedures and bail hearings.

Schneider quickly impressed the judges and lawyers in the monolithic old U. S. District Courthouse on Spring Street in downtown L.A. Within a short time he was handling complicated civil matters usually reserved for the life-tenured federal judges themselves. After three years as a magistrate, Schneider returned to private practice because he had "three kids and the oldest was threatening to go to college."

With his kids' schooling nearly over, Schneider was able for the first time in ten years to think again about his first love—becoming a judge. But his prospects for an appointment remained bleak. The problem was still Ronald Reagan—now President Reagan—and his ideological kinsman, California Governor George Deukmejian. Yet Harvey Schneider was determined to be a judge.

In a move that defied conventional wisdom that sitting judges had a near lock on reelection, he filed against an incumbent, Judge Roberta Ralph, who was running for a third six-year term. She seemed invincible.

Early on, he got a lucky break. The Los Angeles County Bar Association's Judicial Evaluation Committee rated Judge Ralph only "Qualified" and bestowed its highest fitness rating, "Well Qualified," on Schneider.

Nevertheless, Schneider was the decided underdog. Judge Ralph, who was generally well regarded, had been endorsed by forty-two fellow jurists. Incumbents invariably won, and few people cared about judicial elections. Worst of all, despite Schneider's higher bar rating, the coveted Los Angeles *Times* editorial endorsement—the most frequently relied-upon source of information for voters in deciding on low-profile judicial races—went to his opponent.

Schneider campaigned hard but unconventionally. He never criticized Judge Ralph. Taking the high road in the strong belief that it is improper to criticize a judge, he instead talked about why he believed that he would be a good judge. On the eve of the election, he told the *Times*'s Ken Reich: "It's unseemly for a professional to say terrible things about a sitting judge. . . . We must dignify the position, if not the occupant. . . . I don't see why a highly competent attorney cannot run on his own qualifications without slinging mud. . . . There are certain things that I will not do [to win]."

Schneider's adamant refusal to criticize Judge Ralph prompted the media to dub him the "mystery" challenger and drove Roberta Ralph to distraction. "If there's some big thing he thinks I've done wrong, he has a duty to say what it is," she protested days before the election. But Schneider stubbornly held his high ground, keeping to himself why he singled out Judge Ralph from the 110 judges he could have opposed.

He also raised a lot of the mother's milk of politics from friends, clients, and fellow lawyers so that he could send campaign mailers to the registered voters in Los Angeles County. He may have been a Democrat and a political neophyte, but he knew how to spend his money wisely. For example, he gave $10,000 to a "Non-Partisan Candidate Evaluation Council" to get his name on a slate card of candidates that was mailed to 780,000 Republican households in Los Angeles County.

On June 7, 1988, on the eve of the release of *Coming to America* and just as settlement talks between Paramount Pictures and Buchwald and Bernheim broke down, making a lawsuit seem inevitable, Harvey Schneider won, garnering 571,129 votes—a respectable 56 percent margin. He was the only winner among three challengers of Superior Court incumbents.

In court, Judge Schneider proved to be a stickler for protocol. When one of the first attorneys to appear in his courtroom questioned a witness while he had a cough drop in his mouth, Schneider let the lawyer know that he was displeased—even though the lawyer had a cold at the time.

This judge did not suffer fools gladly.

While he was a tough taskmaster in the courtroom, he was a dedicated, kindly teacher outside. Not long after he took the bench he decided to do something about the poor quality of lawyering in his courtroom. On his own, he organized an evening program for practicing lawyers to learn how to conduct themselves in court—everything from how to address the judge to how to get an exhibit in evidence. His lectures were sprinkled with flashes of humor and morsels of wisdom. "Schneider on Schneider" got rave reviews from both old hands and youngsters who had just passed the bar.

And now the new Superior Court judge was beginning to shape the course of events that would determine the fate of *Buchwald v. Paramount*. When it was filed, our case had been randomly assigned to another judge. Three months later, it was reassigned to Judge Schneider and designated for so-called "fast track" processing—the result of a fairly recent reform in which one out of every two cases has tight deadlines and speedier processing in an effort to unclog dockets. Under the old system, civil cases in Los Angeles County often had a four- to five-year waiting period between the filing of a lawsuit and trial. To our pleasant surprise, Judge Schneider concluded the status conference by ordering that we would go to trial in *seven* months, on December 11, 1989—just a little over a year after we had filed suit.

As Schneider announced his order, I thought I saw Tony Liebig choke. The studios were notorious for fighting a courtroom war of attrition in cases such as ours. Paramount would not be happy about going to court on such short notice.

Our business concluded, Judge Schneider dismissed us. He was not one for a lot of idle chitchat and turned his attention to another of the thousand cases on his docket. On the surface, he appeared to treat this like any other case on the assembly line of justice. But I was not fooled. Despite his abrupt questioning and apparent matter-of-fact handling of the conference, something told me that Judge Schneider understood this was not going to be an ordinary case.

He was too nonchalant.

As Zazi and I walked down the hallway, she turned to me and gleefully said: "Do you believe it? Tony must be going nuts. The last thing Paramount wants is a speedy trial."

"Yes," I replied, only half paying attention to my colleague's running commentary about our good fortune in getting to trial so fast. I was distracted, still pondering this enigmatic judge who had minutes ago joined the growing cast of characters in *Buchwald v. Paramount*. Harvey Schneider was gutsy, brilliant, cool, formal—and totally unpredictable. That could be terrific. Or terrible.

13

Deposing the Director

___ ___ ___ ___ ___ ___ ___ ___ ___

AFTER PARAMOUNT had finished grilling Art and Alain, it was my turn to go on the offensive. In June, I started with the director of *Coming to America*. How John Landis got involved in *The Zamunda Project*—the name the two screenwriters Blaustein and Sheffield coined for the movie that would eventually become *Coming to America*—was what I hoped to find out by deposing Landis.

If there is a general impression of what a Hollywood director looks like, John Landis fits it. With an unflinching stare and straightforward manner, Landis could be mistaken for a younger, slimmer Francis Ford Coppola, down to his horn-rim glasses and Hemingwayesque beard. Directors usually aspire to be Orson Welles "Renaissance men," excelling in every aspect of filmmaking. In truth, their reputations almost always rest on one particular kind of movie.

There are musical directors (Bob Fosse, Vincente Minnelli, Busby Berkeley) and saga directors (Cecil B. DeMille, David Lean, Richard Attenborough). There are thriller directors (Alfred Hitchcock, Carol Reed, Brian DePalma) and fantasy directors (George Lucas, Steven Spielberg, Joe Dante). And there are action/comedy directors, like John Landis, the man Eddie Murphy hand-picked to direct *Coming to America*.

Landis had tried his hand at other genres—notably his bizarre 1981 horror film, *An American Werewolf in London*—but he always came back to sophisti-cated slapstick. His best-known movies were among the most profitable comedies of all time: *National Lampoon's Animal House, The Blues Brothers* and *Trading Places,* the Paramount production in which he first met Eddie Murphy.

He'd had a run of sophomoric but profitable stinkers in the mid-eighties, with forgettable titles such as *Spies Like Us* and *Three Amigos.* And, of course, there was also the matter of *The Twilight Zone.*

When Marsha Durko and I met him at his Universal Studios office in June 1989, I knew enough about the short, impeccably dressed thirty-nine-year-old to tiptoe around certain sensitive, and still very notorious, issues. More than a year had passed since he had been acquitted in the *Twilight Zone* manslaughter case. When a helicopter hovered too close to the ground during the filming of a war scene on the set, the aircraft crashed and veteran actor Vic Morrow and two Vietnamese-American children were killed instantly.

The subsequent public outcry brought about changes in California's child labor laws and far stricter enforcement policies about the safety of child actors. The furor also brought about the indictment of John Landis for manslaughter. In a lengthy, highly charged trial, it was shown that Landis had, indeed, ordered the helicopter to move in close over the actors so that he would be able to film a hair-raising sequence in which a soldier rescues the two children during a Vietnam firefight. After a marathon ten-month trial, the jury found that Landis had not acted with callous and criminal disregard for the safety of the victims. It was a tragic accident and nothing more, the jury ruled.

Despite his acquittal, Landis briefly became something of a Hollywood pariah. So the movie industry was mildly shocked when Paramount hired him to direct *Coming to America,* Eddie Murphy's next big comedy following the thunderous success of *Beverly Hills Cop II.*

Landis might have lived down the widespread public rancor over the innocent verdict if he hadn't made a major public relations gaffe a year after the trial. To show his appreciation for his acquittal, he offered a private screening to the seven men and five women of the *Twilight Zone* jury. The movie, of course, was *Coming to America.* When the media found out about it, they had a field day. In addition to directing the lackluster *Coming to America,* they insinuated, Landis paid off an old debt to the jurors by squiring them to an exclusive screening of the much-awaited next Eddie Murphy film.

A few days after the screening, the Los Angeles *Herald-Examiner* reported that "the jurors' verdict on the movie wasn't recorded, but the *Hollywood Reporter* pronounces it a decided bomb and said Landis' work on it was 'cloying and flat.' One gets the impression that he'd thrown in the towel before the first shot."

Associated Press picked up the story of the jurors' private screening and spread it across the land as the latest example of Hollywood pandering. It didn't matter that a year had passed since Landis was found innocent. Newspapers everywhere used the screening as a partial justification for savaging *Coming to America,* even before it was released.

The critics may not have liked it, but the ticket-buying public did. By the end of 1988, *Coming to America* was second only to *Who Framed Roger Rabbit?* as the highest-grossing picture of the year.

But the success of *Coming to America* did little to help Landis. A cloud from his highly publicized manslaughter trial still hung over his personal life and his career a year later.

On a smoggy, overcast June 13 in 1989, any lapses of judgment Landis may have experienced during or after the filming of *The Twilight Zone* were still wide-open wounds to him. I vowed that none of my questions would have anything remotely to do with the *Twilight Zone* case. I had another "accident" on my mind.

Like Eddie Murphy, Landis maintained that he knew what he wanted to be as far back as grammar school. They both talked a mile a minute and had razor-sharp memories. And they both oozed the kind of remarkable self-confidence that can slip all too easily into breathtaking arrogance.

The two had a lot more in common. They were both bored with school, loved TV and grew up middle class. And, like Murphy, Landis lost his father when he was still a small boy.

Born in Chicago, he moved with his family to Los Angeles when he was four months old. His father was an interior decorator who died when John was five. His mother was remarried to a municipal worker and continued the work of raising a son who was a confirmed film buff before his tenth birthday.

My first minor shock about the cool, sharp-eyed sophisticate who had worked with some of the biggest names in Hollywood came within minutes of settling down with him and his attorney, Joel Behr, to talk about Landis's early background. Tony Liebig was there for Paramount, but it was Behr who was looking out for Landis.

"Briefly, give me your educational background. Any college or postcollege you may have had," I began.

"I did not go to college," Landis answered.

"Okay. Do you have a high school degree?" I asked.

"No, I do not," he said.

"Okay," I said, trying not to look too dumbfounded. "How far did you get in high school?"

"Tenth grade," he said.

I was floored. According to his *Coming to America* contract, Landis was to receive 10 percent of the gross receipts of the movie after advertising and negative costs had been met. Even without a calculator handy, I was certain that had to mean millions beyond his $2 million up-front fee for directing. And that was for just one hit movie. My father quit school after the tenth grade too and went on to become a very successful merchant, but he hadn't earned that much in his entire lifetime. Once again, Hollywood had shattered a myth from my Jesuit-influenced background: if you want to succeed, stay in school.

Instead of wasting his time in college prep classes, Landis landed a job as a mailboy at Twentieth Century Fox. Through the contacts he made there, he was hired on the production crew of *Kelly's Heroes*, a clone of the World War II adventure film *The Dirty Dozen*, starring Clint Eastwood and Donald Sutherland.

MGM filmed on location in Yugoslavia. Landis was only nineteen, but he was getting a firsthand taste of what it meant to be "in the business." He was a "schlepper": a kind of production assistant who does everything from making coffee to delivering telegrams. After production wrapped, he stayed on in Europe where employers—particularly in the film business—are less interested in college degrees than in whether someone is capable of getting a job done. He continued working on over seventy productions during the next year or so. By the time he returned to the United States, he was no longer schlepping. Landis had done everything from coaching dialogue for foreign actors to stunt work.

Hollywood was in a slump when he returned in 1971. Fans weren't flocking to the theaters and studios were not hiring. So Landis made his own movie: a horror-film parody shot in twelve days on a budget of $60,000 that he raised from friends and relatives.

Schlock was released in 1972. Landis not only produced it; he directed and starred in it too. Just over an hour long, it became a cult classic, winning sci-fi and comedy awards in Europe and the United States for its wacky portrayal of an ape man responsible for a series of "banana killings."

Landis continued to write and work as a stunt man during the mid-seventies, but it wasn't until five years later that he was asked to direct another low-budget comedy. He made *Kentucky Fried Movie* in twenty-three days, using members of a Los Angeles-based comedy ensemble called the Kentucky Fried Theater. The 78-minute-long lampoon of TV commercials, soft-core porn and Bruce Lee movies, a sleeper hit when it was released in 1977, is one of the most financially successful features ever made without the help of a studio. The writers—Jim Abrams, David Zucker, and Jerry Zucker—went on to write and direct the hilarious satire on fifties disaster films, *Airplane!*

Landis was poised for success. For the first time, the studios began to take an interest in this twenty-seven-year-old high school dropout. Sean Daniels, one of Universal Studio chief Ned Tanen's army of young development executives, called Landis after seeing the movie. He needed a youthful director with a strong comedy sense and an equally strong budgetary sense who could make a film starring a bright new "Saturday Night Live" comic named John Belushi.

Screenwriters Doug Kenney, Chris Miller and Harold Ramis already had a script. Landis reworked it with the trio for several months and then took the company to Eugene, Oregon, where he filmed the entire production on location at a fraternity house just off the University of Oregon campus. *Animal House*, completed in thirty-six days, became the comedy smash of 1978 and made John Belushi a box office star. Until Eddie Murphy migrated to Hollywood and made some comedy history of his own, *Animal House* held the record for being the most financially successful comedy of all time.

I decided to start with Landis's story association with Eddie Murphy.

"Prior to your directing Eddie Murphy in *Trading Places*, had you ever had any professional involvement with him before?" I asked Landis.

"I had never heard of him," he fired back.

"And never met him, I take it?"

"No."

When I laid Art's original treatment for *King for a Day* in front of him, Landis denied ever having seen it nor did he profess to know that Buchwald had anything remotely to do with the genesis of *Coming to America* until he read about it in the *Wall Street Journal*. Even though he said he knew nothing of Buchwald's treatment until he read about it in the *Journal*, Landis said he was not surprised that someone was suing Paramount over *Coming to America*. Whenever a picture made money suits were filed. Shortly after the *Journal* story appeared, he spoke with Barry Blaustein and David Sheffield, the writing partners who produced the *Coming to America* shooting script, and told them:

"Every movie I ever made that made over $100 million, there were lawsuits."

That's when I brought out a nine-page letter that Jeff Katzenberg wrote to him while he was in London during the summer of 1983. Dated July 1, the letter laid out thirteen film projects that Paramount's production chief wanted Landis to consider directing. One of them was *King for a Day*, which Katzenberg described as "a highly stylized political satire inspired by Art Buchwald.

"The movie is intended for Eddie Murphy, who is familiar with the idea and likes it very much," Katzenberg wrote. "If necessary, however, I believe any one of several comedy stars could be excellent in the role. The writer is Tab Murphy, who has proved in another project that he has a terrific sense for Eddie Murphy's style. We expect a first draft in about four weeks."

Landis did not doubt that he got the letter, but he did not remember ever reading it. When he did leaf through it, he expressed genuine shock . . . but not over *King for a Day*.

"I'm horrified," he said when he set aside the letter. "It shows I was offered *Beverly Hills Cop*. I can't believe it."

It was no wonder Paramount had been falling all over itself to lure Landis back to direct another film in 1983. *Trading Places* had just opened when Landis received the project list from Katzenberg and the Eddie Murphy-Dan Aykroyd comedy was already receiving dynamite reviews. The New York *Times*'s Vincent Canby dubbed it "the funniest American movie comedy of the year" and proclaimed Eddie Murphy "the brightest young comic actor to hit Hollywood in a decade." For his part, Landis was being compared to Paramount's comedy writing and directing genius of the thirties and forties, Preston Sturges.

The reviews were heady enough, but when the box office grosses started to show up each Monday morning in *Variety* with *Trading Places* at the top of the heap, John Landis was once again in a position to pick and choose whatever project he wanted to do next.

Landis picked *Tropical Trash*.

"I think it had to do with some kind of work farm, like a jail work farm," Landis said.

"And a breakout and everybody starts following and looking for the treasure?" I continued.

"Is that what happens?" he asked.

Yes, according to the progress report documents I had been able to get from Paramount. *Tropical Trash* was trashed in short order. It was a great idea, said Landis, but, like so many great ideas that come through Hollywood, it resulted in a terrible script and Landis finally passed on it.

But even following that snafu, John Landis was still hot in 1983. Movie ideas by the score passed over his desk. By fall, he estimated he had seen 300 to 400. *King for a Day* could have been one of them and he would not have known it, he told me.

According to three different confidential interoffice memos I'd gotten from Paramount, *King for a Day* was, indeed, one of those ideas and apparently near the top of the heap. One memo from David Kirkpatrick, dated July 9, 1983, listed *King for a Day* and four other films as possible Landis projects. A month later, a second memo showed that three of the original projects had been abandoned. Only *King for a Day* and a project entitled *Falling in Love* were still being considered by Katzenberg on the new "Possible Landis Projects" list.

On November 23, Ricardo Mestres, a young development executive in training, sent a much longer list to Katzenberg which included a number of movies that did get made, but not by John Landis. In addition to *Beverly Hills Cop*, Paramount wanted Landis to make *Young Sherlock Holmes*, *The Jetsons* and *Mannequin*.

Also on the list—again—was *King for a Day* which, Mestres noted, Katzenberg had discussed with Landis with "apparent warm response."

Landis's only response to me about the internal Paramount memos was a shrug and a mischievous envy that I had been able to rifle through confidential middle management memoranda.

"It's great. I love to see the executive files on this stuff."

One thing I wanted Landis to tell me more about was his relationship with Murphy. According to several fan magazine stories that had been published since the release of *Coming to America*, Murphy and Landis were not speaking to each other. Murphy blamed their falling out on an altercation they'd had on the set. Supposedly the fight had racial overtones, but Murphy wouldn't elaborate. For his part, Landis wouldn't say anything at all.

"Did you and he have a falling out?" I asked.

"Did we have a falling out? Probably," Landis answered.

When I persisted, trying to get to the bottom of the feud, I saw Landis get fidgety for the first time. It was obvious to me that he was not going to answer, but I had to try anyway just to satisfy myself that what he told me about Eddie and the origins of *Coming to America* wasn't tainted with some sort of grudge to even a score with the actor. Landis admitted to "personality conflicts" but nothing more.

After a half dozen questions, Behr jumped in.

"If you prefer not to answer . . ." he started to tell his client.

"I prefer not to answer the question," Landis said, taking the cue with relief.

"I will ask Mr. Murphy about it," I said.

"I'd be interested to hear what he says," Landis shot back.

Murphy was scheduled for a deposition later in the year. After a comment I'd heard the comic make a few weeks earlier during one of his periodic TV appearances on old pal Arsenio Hall's talk show, I had to admit I was looking forward to hearing what Murphy had to say too.

Landis "has a better chance of working again with Vic Morrow than he does with me," Murphy told the late night TV audience.

Whatever had happened between the two biggest names (and profit participants) of *Coming to America* while it was being filmed, it had clearly been a bitter clash. But enemies or not, Landis still had immense respect for Murphy's talent. He characterized Murphy as "a brilliant performer" and told me about one of his dream projects, before Murphy had vowed never to work with him again.

"I wanted to do [a project] with him and Robin Williams where they each played fifteen characters that had nothing to do with the plot," he said. In one scene, he planned to have Murphy and Williams eating at a Chinese restaurant. Each of them, in Chinese makeup, would also portray the entire staff of the restaurant. With the makeup artist he used in *Coming to America* to turn Murphy and Hall into a whole retinue of barbershop characters, Landis said he knew he could pull it off.

Landis also thought Murphy would be terrific in drag. He tried to coax him to put on a dress for *Coming to America*, but Murphy refused. Arsenio Hall did it, however, and turned in a very funny cameo as one of Prince Akeem's prospective dates, Landis said.

Still, Landis avoided trashing Murphy. He dodged my questions about the pampering and star treatment that Murphy got while on the set.

When I asked him about Eddie's entourage of a half dozen or more friends, relatives and hangers-on who appeared to pad the production budget as "production assistants," Landis acted as though he did not know what I meant. Finally, Behr and Liebig both objected to my question as "irrelevant."

So I made a speech.

"I think the relevance of this is painfully obvious, but we'll wait for the trial to see," I said. "In fact, I will tell you right now, we expect to prove at trial that one of the reasons Paramount Pictures didn't give Mr. Buchwald the credit and pay my clients some money that was due is that Eddie Murphy was the principal, major star at Paramount Pictures, and they would do virtually *anything* to keep this man happy, including allowing him to be surrounded by an uncommonly large number of people, which I will characterize as an entourage."

I was ready to launch into the actual making of *Coming to America* when Landis asked for a short break. I looked at my watch. We'd been at it well over an hour and I hadn't even noticed. Even though I hadn't mined any nuggets of evidence from Landis's testimony, I had to admit that I hadn't had as much fun in a deposition since the "Rockford Files" case. Landis, too, had loosened up.

No sooner were we settled back in Landis's office than he snapped his fingers and began spouting off his memory of the first time Eddie Murphy pitched the *Coming to America* project to him, way back on June 29, 1987.

"It was Richie Rich," Landis said, coming out of left field with an answer to a question that hadn't even been asked. "Remember the comic book? That's what I thought it was. It's Richie Rich because he had all these *toys!* He was a very rich guy and had a lot of toys."

It took some quizzical looks and a couple more questions from me as well as John's own attorney to figure out what Landis was talking about. When he's inspired or suddenly remembers something that has escaped him, Landis has a tendency to blurt out what's on his mind and let coherence be damned. As an attorney, I liked that very much.

What he was telling us, with the aid of his 1987 *New Yorker* desk calendar, was that Murphy called him in Boston one month to the day after his acquittal in the *Twilight Zone* trial with an idea for a movie.

"It dealt a great deal with the wealth of the prince and he had all these elaborate toys," Landis enthused. "He had dough, this Richie Rich, that is."

Landis was caught a little off balance, but he listened. A pitch from Eddie Murphy was as good as gold. Normally, everyone else was trying to pitch Eddie Murphy, so when he chose to pitch you, you listened, Landis explained.

Still, Landis knew enough about the business to demand more than an idea from a bankable star. He wanted a script to look at before he would commit to Eddie, Prince Akeem, Richie Rich or anybody else. Landis agreed to put off vacation and fly back to Hollywood for a full-blown session with Eddie and the Paramount brass to see if a script could be drafted.

One month later he and his agent, Mike Marcus, were in Ned Tanen's office on the Paramount lot. Paramount chairman Frank Mancuso was also there, as was Eddie's manager/mentor Bob Wachs and three people Landis hadn't met before: Arsenio Hall, Barry Blaustein and David Sheffield. Hall, Blaustein and Sheffield were introduced as the coauthors of the story that Eddie pitched. Arsenio contributed no more than a brief scene featuring a preacher, according to Landis, but he still got a $30,000 writing fee and, until Landis intervened, was listed with Murphy on the film's credits as the author of the story upon which *Coming to America* was based.

Landis identified the story with one word: Cinderella. Prince Charming Akeem blows into Queens and sweeps Cinderella out of the fast food business and onto the royal throne of Zamunda.

But Paramount didn't care about Landis's story analysis.

"The two major concerns of the meeting were how quickly could a picture like this be made and what did I think it would cost," Landis said. Mancuso and Tanen wanted something in the can in time for the lucrative opening weekend of the summer season in 1988. Despite the urgency, Landis held firm: no discussion of cost or production time or commitment until he had a script in hand.

"How the hell are you going to figure out what something costs without a screenplay?" he asked them.

With that, Landis left for vacation. St. Martin in the Caribbean first. Then Barcelona. Then Egypt.

By the time he landed in Jerusalem two months later, in late September, a package had arrived for him at his hotel. It was a script, written by Blaustein and Sheffield and titled *The Quest*.

Landis had problems with the script. The word "nigger" was generously sprinkled throughout the first draft. There were also many more of the kind of obscenities that characterize Murphy's stage act than are appropriate for a lighthearted comedy. Landis ordered most of them out. If the story was going to work as a warm Cinderella tale, it couldn't be swimming in "niggers" and "motherfuckers."

Mainly, though, he hated the title.

"Why didn't you like the title?" I asked him.

"Do you like the title *The Quest*?" he asked me right back.

"No. But I don't like *Coming to America* either," I said.

Landis snorted derisively.

"Shows what you know about the motion picture business. I thought the title had nothing to do with the story at all. Eddie's take on the title was it was his quest for the right woman. I felt that it sounded like a western. There used to be a western series, 'Quest.'"

And those who didn't think *The Quest* was a western might get another false idea: that Eddie was on a medieval quest for the Holy Grail.

Paramount disagreed, however. When the studio's legal department ordered research done on the title to see whether the studio could legally call the project *The Quest*, Landis wrote a stinging rebuke to studio executives Richard Marks and Ralph Kamon. Not only was he forbidding the use of the name *The Quest*, Landis told every executive from Tanen on down, "from now on NOTHING will be done regarding our production without first discussing it with" Landis or his staff.

Landis's manifesto set the tone for constant bickering with studio management throughout the production of *Coming to America*. Kamon advised David Nicksay, the studio liaison on *The Quest*, that Landis was just blowing off steam, but he also warned that he had to be straightened out about who was in charge or there would be trouble ahead.

"He's just telling the company who's 'boss' and I think he should be told otherwise," Kamon said.

Paramount business affairs chief Greg Gelfan was a bit more huffy. A studio is the employer and the director is the employee, he reasoned. Landis was way out of line, telling Paramount what it could or could not name its next Eddie Murphy movie.

"It is wholly unacceptable to have any director or producer dictating a proclamation like this to a studio!" he said.

Landis prevailed. While the movie was in production, he renamed it *The Zamunda Project* after a phony African country that Blaustein and Sheffield had come up with as a joke while they were writing. Several months later, when they were in the middle of postproduction, Paramount asked Landis and his assistant, George Folsey, to put together a trailer the studio's distribution department could show at a Las Vegas convention of the nation's theater owners. The trailer opened with an announcer saying: "Eddie Murphy is coming to America this summer."

Though the film was still being shot and reedited, Landis and Folsey had a print made of what they had produced thus far and flew to Nevada to show it to exhibitors. They arrived half an hour late to the preview with a print that was still wet, but the response from that crucial audience of men and women who operate the nation's theaters was resoundingly positive.

When Paramount distribution executive Barry Reardon heard the opening line about Eddie Murphy coming to America, he fell in love with it and decreed that *The Zamunda Project* be rechristened *Coming to America*. This time, Paramount prevailed.

"I said, 'I hate that *Coming to America*,' but I was overruled," Landis said.

Studio executives had no right or reason to dabble in any aspect of the making of the movie itself, Landis believed. He fought to control the film's publicity, in part out of fear that the media might use the film as an excuse to reopen old wounds surrounding *The Twilight Zone*. Ned Tanen was sympathetic and granted that request, but it was followed with more. When Landis asked for a screen credit as large as Murphy's, he was turned down. The most Tanen would go was letters larger than anyone else's except Eddie Murphy's.

The contract Landis had finally signed to do the movie also gave the director broad rights over approval of publicity stills and trailers for the film as well as the final cut of the film. He knew from past experience that promises from studio executives not to interfere in the filmmaking process were empty unless they were on paper.

For example, Nicksay had his own ideas about the script after reading Blaustein and Sheffield's first draft. He wanted the king of Zamunda, played by James Earl Jones, to be overwhelmingly nice in addition to being all-powerful. Dialogue about having his subjects hanged or dragged behind horses should come out.

"I recall his concerns about the king being Idi Amin," Landis recalled.

When studio executives who were used to the language of business memos decided that they were creative, there was usually trouble ahead, according to Landis.

Nicksay wanted Prince Akeem to advance quickly from janitor to cashier at McDowell's Restaurant so he could "interface" with characters from the neighborhood and show how bright he was, for example. Nicksay also wanted Semmi to lose all his money in a floating crap game so he'd have to send home to Zamunda for more. And he had the terrific idea that Clarence the barber, whom Eddie portrayed in addition to the prince, should be sent back to Zamunda as the royal hairdresser.

While some of Nicksay's ideas found their way into the shooting script, many were sidestepped or scrapped before the first camera rolled. Landis smiled in satisfaction at being able to outmaneuver Nicksay and most of the other studio's top bananas. In fact, the only creative battle he almost lost during filming was to Tanen.

"Ned was very distressed that I didn't want to shoot the Michael Jackson/Prince thing," Landis remembered. "He spent a great deal of time trying to get me to shoot it."

The scene, which was eventually hacked from the movie before it was totally filmed, involved Akeem and Semmi walking down a New York street and encountering Prince and Michael Jackson in an elaborate dance sequence. But actually shooting Murphy and Hall on the streets of Brooklyn got to be downright frightening, Landis said. When Eddie and Arsenio showed up, the crowds were so large and loud that shooting was nearly impossible. Back in Los Angeles, when Landis was planning to shoot the rest of the scene with the two pop singers on a sound stage, he just abandoned it altogether as expensive, time-consuming and superfluous to the plot.

"The whole dance with Prince and Michael Jackson I didn't shoot," he said. "We were prepared to shoot it and I abandoned it a week before shooting because I knew I would end up cutting it out."

Tanen, who generally tried to stay above the fray and not involve himself in the day-to-day production chores, was apoplectic about losing the chance to feature the four biggest black pop icons in America on the same splice of celluloid. Again and again he personally tried to intercede and get Landis to include the sequence in *Coming to America*.

Again and again Landis pointed to his contract which, he told Paramount's production managers, gave him final say-so on what went in the movie and what stayed out. Because of the very time and cost factors that Mancuso and Tanen seemed so intent upon enforcing during their very first meeting with Landis, the Prince/Jackson scene had to go. Landis could not finish the film in time to meet the summer release date, he told Tanen.

"Ned was very unhappy about that," Landis said with a sly smile.

Ned, as I would soon learn, was very unhappy about a lot of things.

. . . . .

It was early afternoon when I finished with Landis. Liebig asked no questions at all. I figured that meant Landis was cooperating with Paramount. If they needed him to speak glowingly about the studio, Landis could always take the witness stand during trial. But Liebig seemed sure there would never be a trial—he and Kulzick would get the case thrown out of court.

As I started to leave, Landis asked me when the trial was scheduled. After I told him, he volunteered a final point:

"If I were you, I wouldn't count on Eddie showing up at trial."

"Why's that, John?" I asked.

"He has a history of not showing," said Landis. "I remember one case where he was sued by a former manager. He testified for one full day and enjoyed himself, but refused to return the second day to complete cross-examination. His lawyer pleaded and argued, but Eddie refused to go back to court. His lawyer had to settle and pay a lot more money than any jury would have awarded."

"Thank you, John," I said as Marsha and I walked toward the door. "That's the most important thing you told me today. See you in court."

14

The Mellow Mogul

I DIDN'T HAVE TO GO to Paramount's former production chief for answers to my *Coming to America* questions. Ned Tanen came to me.

Perhaps it was because he had more time on his hands in June 1989. Six months earlier, Tanen had surprised the industry by announcing his resignation as president of the motion picture group of Paramount Pictures Corporation. After four years as the top movie executive at the studio, he pleaded exhaustion.

It was the second time in a decade that he had quit the top spot of a major motion picture studio.

Six years earlier, Tanen had left Universal Pictures after spending twenty-nine years in one capacity or another at Universal or its parent company, MCA. Then, it wasn't exhaustion that made him quit. It was more like mid-life crisis. He was fifty-one, his second marriage had just evaporated, he felt as though he was losing touch with his teenagers, and a longtime friend and fellow Universal executive, Verna Fields, had recently died after a long illness.

But there were other reasons too, he told a reporter for the *Wall Street Journal* at the time:

"It's a job that just eventually wears you down. You're constantly dealing with overpriced actors who aren't remotely worth what they're asking, out-of-control directors with inflated opinions of themselves and quixotic unions that don't face current realities."

He went where all ex-studio execs go: into independent production. Two years later, after his Channel Productions produced a string of independent hits including *Sixteen Candles* and *The Breakfast Club*, Paramount offered him a four-year contract to take the helm of the studio, and he accepted.

I was beginning to understand the approach-avoidance conflict that is the very soul of the movie business. There was something eternally enticing about the power and prestige of making movies, even if it was a killing, thankless business about 90 percent of the time.

Ned Tanen was a living example of that conflict. He hated the egomaniacal actors, directors and producers. But he loved making movies. Reportedly, it was Tanen who inspired the warm but ruthless mogul character in David Mamet's satirical Broadway play about Hollywood, *Speed-The-Plow*. But he was widely respected for acting decisively and—with the exception of the gaffe of passing on *Star Wars*, letting it go to Fox—for having generally sound movie judgment. When he left Paramount as production chief, he was earning about $2.5 million from salary, bonuses and stock options.

Now, after stepping down as president of Paramount Pictures, he was a consultant to the studio. He still had an office on the lot and pulled down a hefty $1-million-a-year salary, but without the pressure he both hated and loved.

When Tanen walked into my conference room on June 22, he was not the hostile witness I expected. I faced a mellow, well-dressed, fifty-seven-year-old gentleman whose unassuming manner and dry, often cynical sense of humor seemed to belie the widely held notion that studio heads are the very epitome of arrogance. Tanned and athletic-looking, he immediately struck me as someone who was not easily rattled or confused. A witness like this could make—or break—my case.

I wanted to know first from the man at the top during the making of *Coming to America* how he got on with the other principals: Paramount chairman Frank Mancuso, John Landis, Arsenio Hall, Blaustein and Sheffield and especially Eddie Murphy.

"Mr. Mancuso described Eddie Murphy in the *Wall Street Journal* a couple of weeks ago as 'Our Kellogg's Corn Flakes,'" I began. "Do you agree with that assessment of the importance of Eddie Murphy to Paramount Pictures?"

"We'll never finish paying for that comment," Tanen quipped. "Well, he's extremely important—I mean, there's no way to overemphasize his importance. His movies have all been successful, which is unheard of. . . ."

Why? I wanted to know. Why was Eddie Murphy this phenomenal box office draw?

"A rebelliousness that attracts people. An ability to say things that you wish you could say. He's someone who is in charge of his own life—and I'm talking about the portrayal, not the person. He doesn't need anything from anyone. He's a persona who is really an off-center character, but very likable, very identifiable.

"And what's most amazing, he totally crosses all color lines and all ethnic lines internationally, not just American, which is unheard of. I'm always amazed by the international aspect of it because American black actors have never ever made it internationally, and so much of that appeal is based on verbalization, and yet it doesn't seem to make any difference. There is an attractiveness to him as a bad boy—a quality that really seems to come across."

I hung on words like "portrayal" and "persona." I got the definite impression that, much as he appreciated and admired the universality of Paramount's bread and butter—or, rather, its corn flakes—star, Ned Tanen saw a different and perhaps less appealing human being behind the mask that Eddie Murphy wears for the world.

"When did you first meet Eddie Murphy?"

"It was accidental," Tanen said. "I met him walking down a hall at Paramount. I introduced myself, had some general conversation for perhaps forty-five seconds. That was it."

What was remarkable to me about this otherwise unremarkable first meeting was that Tanen had been at the studio's helm for eight months before it happened. In the old days, that would have been comparable to Clark Gable ignoring Louis B. Mayer for half a year before running into him in the halls of MGM one day by accident, giving him a minute of his time and then going on about his business. It simply never would have happened.

But Hollywood had changed. Stars had the power in the eighties.

It wasn't that Murphy was uncordial. It was just that he acted as though he had better things to do with his time. In his entire four-year tenure at Paramount, Tanen told me, he spoke with Murphy on the telephone no more than three or four times and met with him face to face no more than four or five times.

"Did you ever have lunch with him?" I asked.

"No."

Breakfast?

"No."

Dinner?

"No."

Perrier?

"No."

When Tanen did see his single biggest, highest-paid and most bankable star, Murphy was never alone. He always had an entourage of several hangers-on with him.

How many?

"I couldn't even guess," Tanen said. "I remember there were a lot of them."

Bernheim had told me Tanen referred sarcastically to Eddie as "King Murphy" at times. Tanen denied it, but without conviction.

As with his other spoiled children, Tanen only seemed to hear from them when they weren't getting their way.

He remembered Murphy summoning him to the set during filming of

Golden Child when an indignant Eddie was fighting with director Michael Ritchie over whether or not he got the girl.

"Something about his relationship with the girl in the movie and was it to be a sexual relationship or not," Tanen recalled. "And he had heard that Paramount did not want it to be and he was very upset about that. And he presumed I *was* Paramount. He wanted a clarification from me. And we just talked about it."

Eddie wanted Tanen to let his character, a social worker named Chandler Jarrell, sleep with a mysterious Tibetan woman, played by Charlotte Lewis. Eddie had boiled the problem down to overt miscegenation. Eddie was black. Lewis was white, made up to appear to be an oriental. It didn't matter that the story was an Indiana Jones-type adventure romp and had little to do with any romantic liaisons. Eddie wanted to sleep with the girl and thought that race might be playing a role in Ritchie's refusal to let him do so.

Murphy, of course, got his way, but nobody—critics or fans—seemed to care much. What everyone did agree upon after the film's release was that it was perhaps the worst film Murphy had ever made. The plot was contrived, the acting weak, the scenes tossed together like a Waldorf salad.

In inverse proportion to the times he heard from Murphy, Tanen seemed to be on the phone constantly with his manager, Bob Wachs.

"It was made clear to me early in the game by Mr. Wachs and Mr. Tienken that it would be better if I dealt through them, which was perfectly fine with me," Tanen said.

By the time *Coming to America* was first conceived, Richie Tienken was no longer Eddie's comanager and had been replaced by Mark Lipsky, a business manager who had handled Eddie's finances during the early "Saturday Night Live" days back in New York. A CPA with Rochlin, Lipsky, Goodkin, Stoler & Co., the Hartford-born Lipsky was the silent partner in Eddie Murphy Productions who left his firm in 1982 to hitch his fortunes to Eddie's rising star. Lipsky kept the books and let Wachs do the talking . . . something Wachs did a lot.

"He is an attorney, which he never stops telling you," Tanen said. When Eddie wasn't with his entourage, the comic was with Wachs. Eddie saw Wachs as a guiding light, while the rest of the world—including Tanen—saw Wachs as Rasputin.

Tanen wanted to go off the record to talk about Wachs, but I couldn't let him. The picture he painted was that of a man very nearly as intoxicated on power and blown up with his own ego as the star he represented and I wanted to hear about it, first hand, from someone who had to deal with him on an almost daily basis.

"When I first came to Paramount, one of my first conversations with Mr. Wachs was about Eddie Murphy's *Raw*," Tanen recalled. "I thought it was at a difficult stage in Murphy's career for him to be doing something that was that—what is the proper word?"

"Vulgar?" I offered.

"Your word, not mine," Tanen said, still trying to play the diplomat.

"Pick your word, please. I'm not trying to put words in your mouth," I said.

Tanen thought a moment.

"Vulgar," he said.

Wachs didn't want to hear any studio advice about Eddie's career because he, Wachs, was running that end of things. Eddie Murphy Productions would go ahead and shoot the concert movie anyway, whether Tanen thought it was good for Murphy's image or not.

It took a bit longer than Wachs would have liked, but the two-hour theatrical version of Eddie's foul-mouthed stand-up routine did eventually get made and, when released in 1987, it became the most successful concert film ever produced.

"What's the old saying, 'No accounting for taste'?" I said.

Tanen laughed. From off in the corner of the room, Paramount's own attorney chimed in with a Latin translation of my platitude.

"*De gustibus non est disputandum*," said Ken Kulzick.

And when Murphy made a bomb like *The Golden Child*, it cleared $60 million and made the top ten list for the year.

"Prior to your arrival at Paramount, had you ever worked on a movie where an actor was paid $4.2 million, guaranteed, for starring in it?" I asked Tanen, in reference to *Beverly Hills Cop*.

Tanen sat and thought for several moments.

"I can't recall. I'm trying to think of the—there had been movies I had done with Paul Newman and Robert Redford and, yes, Barbra Streisand, yes, there had been other people that had gotten that kind of money," he said finally.

"So Murphy, by late 1984, had already risen to the status of a Streisand, Redford and Newman in terms of the amount of money he could command for a picture?"

"Yes sir," said Tanen.

Still, to Tanen, it was worth it just to have a movie under way with Murphy, because the general rule was that Wachs—and, by extension, Murphy—never seemed to read a script he thought was good enough.

"Do you recall ever sending a script to Bob Wachs in four years that he liked?" I asked.

"No."

Paramount spent millions developing dozens of scripts for their biggest star, but one by one they were all eventually shelved.

When Tanen first took over in 1984, two scripts seemed to have the best shot at being rewritten into something that Wachs and Murphy liked: *King for a Day* and *Hell of an Angel*, a story about a no-account New York street hustler who is killed, tries to get into heaven and gets one more chance to make good on earth.

But Wachs didn't like *Hell of an Angel* and, when he didn't like the script, according to Tanen, Murphy didn't either—probably in part because Murphy never got to see it.

"With the demise of *Hell of an Angel* and then the demise of *King for a Day*, there were no major projects in development for Eddie Murphy at that point?" I asked.

"That's true. It's very difficult to find material for a major star, male or female."

It was at that point, in 1987, that Eddie Murphy had his inspiration.

"Eddie Murphy called me and asked me if I could come to his office on the lot, which I did," Tanen remembered. "He was with two or three of his people. Bob Wachs . . . I think Mark Lipsky may have been there and I believe Arsenio Hall.

"And he told me that he had written forty pages of a screenplay—I remember forty because he was specific about the number of pages—on an idea. And he proceeded to tell me the idea for the movie.

"He told me that he had been working on a project by himself about a prince of a mythical kingdom—he wasn't specific about where he was from—who was a very pampered, isolated young man who, with one good friend, who I presume was going to be Arsenio Hall, was going to go to New York in an attempt to find a bride. He couldn't relate all of the adventures, but he started to act out the script.

"And it was extraordinarily funny. And he proceeded to act out as far as he had gone, as I recall. Then gave me, if I remember this correctly, gave me the pages and asked me to call him after I had read them."

Tanen shifted in his seat, knitting his brow.

"Understand something," he said suddenly. "My major reaction to this was his sitting in a room, acting out what he was going to do. It wasn't really as much as what was on the page."

Eddie Murphy, who had snubbed or sidestepped Tanen most of the three years that he had been employed as head of the studio, had Paramount's production boss in stitches in one and a half minutes. Such were his powers of timing, mimicry and improvisation.

"Did you think it was funny or did you think it was funny because he was a big star? I'm just curious," I asked.

"Unfortunately or fortunately, that has never been my problem. Otherwise, I'd have a better relationship with Eddie Murphy. . . . I thought it was very funny. I remember he was playing this very innocent kind of character, which was very interesting given the fact that Mr. Murphy's screen persona is not innocent at all. And then he would enter these other characters who showed up in the movie, two of whom were black barbers. Old black barbers. One who was an old white Jewish man. And he started acting those characters out. And . . ."

Tanen began giggling out loud at the memory.

"I'm sorry," he apologized. "It's funny."

I zeroed in on the script—the forty pages that Eddie handed him. What had become of them? What did they say?

But Tanen didn't know. In fact, as I continued my mild grilling, he began to wonder whether he had actually seen the pages. It was clear that he had not seen the two-page treatment that Eddie said that he dictated to a secretary, copyrighted on August 31 and submitted to the studio the following February. For his two-page treatment, Murphy was paid $400,000.

When I asked him about *The Quest*, Tanen thought I was asking about the working title of *The Golden Child*. I smiled to myself, remembering Landis's wise remark about the original title of *Coming to America*. Even the head of the studio remembered it as some half-baked adventure, not a love story about a prince looking for a princess.

I showed Tanen a copy of a July 1987 *Newsday* article that announced that Paramount and Murphy were going ahead with *The Quest* project. He shrugged it off. By July 1987 he was too busy trying to persuade Landis to direct the movie to read the newspapers.

"He is the kind of director who could get in and get it made, get it made on a schedule and deliver the picture and not spend an inordinate amount of time . . . in postproduction and in preproduction," Tanen said.

One of Tanen's biggest problems, even before the script was written, had to do with where the movie would be made. Worried about runaway costs, from location shooting in Brooklyn, he wanted Prince Akeem coming to Los Angeles. Landis wanted him coming to New York.

"We felt we would have somewhat better control of the movie if we kept it closer to home. . . . I don't think Eddie had any position. I don't think he particularly cared one way or the other. John Landis was adamant. He made it a deal point. If these shots were not done in New York, then he didn't want to be involved with the movie. So we let that one go. Most of the movie was, in fact, shot in L.A. The interiors, the mythical kingdom, were built on the sound stages, but the New York street scenes were done in New York in the middle of January."

Landis was a good director and generally got his way, but he was also a pain to work with, according to Tanen, because he saw himself as more than just merely a good director.

But Tanen was not overly impressed with the final product that Landis delivered. "I thought it was a bit overblown. John is a very talented man, but he tends to excess and since he's made three or four movies with me, I'm an authority and I've found that parts of it were excessive."

Such as?

"The whole palace sequence at the opening was so ornate and rich. . . . There was a dance sequence in it that reminded me of a 1930s Betty Grable musical that went on and on to no end and to no purpose, with many more extras than we really needed."

At that point, I decided to put myself in the shoes of one of those average Joes who plunk down as much as $7.00 to see a first-run movie. It occurred to me that even I wasn't all that clear on just where my $7.00 went when I took my wife or kids to the movies.

Tanen gave me an introductory course in box office economics. The first thing I learned was that half the money stays in the box office. The studio gets the other half and immediately takes its profit, which it calls a distribution fee. On *Coming to America*, the studio's domestic distribution fee was 30 percent.

I did some quick calculations on my pocket calculator and came up with $1.05 of each $7.00 ticket as Paramount's share. That left about $2.45 from each ticket sold to pay for the movie, advertising, John Landis, Eddie Murphy and miscellaneous. As net profit participants, Blaustein and Sheffield, the two men who actually wrote the movie, fell in the miscellaneous category, along with Art and Alain . . . if we managed to make their contract stick.

"Knowing the contracts that were negotiated for profit participations for *Coming to America*, would you expect *Coming to America* to enter net profits?" I asked.

"No," said Tanen.

"At any point?" I asked.

"Not in reality," he told me. Someday, perhaps, a long ways off. But not any time soon. "This was a very, very expensive movie," he added.

After draining off large percentages for Paramount, Murphy and Landis, the constant interest that the studio charges on all aspects of the production and distribution of the movie gobbles up any additional revenue before it can ever be used to reduce any red ink. It was what I referred to as the Pac-Man effect.

"I would never want to define when a movie is close to being in profits," Tanen said. "I've been on both sides of the desk."

The actual production cost for *Coming to America*—the so-called negative cost—was about $36 million, according to Tanen. But the profit participation statement that Landis had given me showed a negative cost of $50,127,544. Tanen said that much of the $14 million difference was probably overhead, charged off to Murphy and his Eddie Murphy Productions. I couldn't believe anyone—not even a star of Murphy's stature—could get away with sticking a studio with that kind of an overhead bill on a movie that took all of three months to shoot. Tanen pointed out that $8 million of the Eddie Murphy overhead was his enormous acting fee but that, yes, the rest was, in fact, mostly the freight the studio agreed to pay just to keep Eddie and his entourage happy.

"Murphy's overhead is all of their office overhead, their entire staff, the write-offs of projects that do not go forward. You've seen some of that paperwork. It can average anywhere from $2 million to $5 million a movie with Murphy, and has."

One memo I turned up during discovery showed that Eddie's relationship with the studio was often that of a Visa customer with a virtually unlimited credit line to his bank. The only difference seemed to be that somebody else always seemed to pay the principal and interest charges.

In October, three months before shooting began, Eddie received a $1.75

million advance from Paramount which the studio immediately charged to the budget of the movie. For his part, Landis wanted it made clear that his own profits from the movie would not be affected by any interest or overhead charges assessed on Eddie's advance.

I had obtained a sterling example of just how convoluted and absolutely indecipherable studio accounting policy really could be from an interoffice memo Paramount's business affairs chief, Greg Gelfan, sent to Tanen, explaining how this Murphy/Landis cash conflict was to be resolved. I handed Tanen Gelfan's memo and a bewildered expression crept over his face as he read:

> If the Eddie Murphy overhead charge to the picture is less than $2.45 million (i.e., less than the cap we agreed to), then that portion of the $1.75 million advance equal to the difference between the amount of overhead charged to the picture and $2.45 million will be treated as additional overhead except that it will not bear Paramount Pictures Corporation overhead.
>
> Remember this is only for the purpose of computing actual breakeven in the John Landis deal. For all other participants, the $1.75 million advance to Eddie Murphy and whatever the actual amount of Murphy overhead is, will be part of the negative cost without any limitation.

Tanen, a man with thirty years in the entertainment business, looked up at me quizzically.

"Confusing to me," he said simply.

I looked up at the ceiling.

"Thank you, God," I said. "I thought it was my pea brain."

I suggested that it might mean that Gelfan had put a maximum cap on the amount of overhead Murphy could charge to *Coming to America* and that amount was $2.45 million.

"That's what it appears to say," Tanen said, handing the memo back to me.

I offered to hire three Jesuit scholars to examine it so that we could try to unravel its meaning before trial.

Tanen's version of his fateful luncheon with Alain at the Paramount commissary that November afternoon in 1987 was remarkably similar to Bernheim's. There were significant details that gave his account a subtly different turn, however.

It was the first time, for instance, that Tanen had ever even dreamed that there might be any similarity between *King for a Day* and *Coming to America*.

"I suppose it crossed my mind when Alain Bernheim confronted me at lunch and kind of baldly said between the salad and the fish, 'Gee, aren't these projects somewhat similar?' That was the first time it ever really occurred to me.

"I never even thought of it as being a similar thing, 'cause the main thing with Murphy's project was that he was dealing with . . . a very, very naive young man who was coming to find a bride in America. . . ."

The only time Tanen had ever thought about the defunct *King for a Day* project was when Alain tried setting it up as a French production after Paramount had put it into turnaround. Alain had returned to Tanen, asking for some monetary help, but Tanen told him that the company couldn't give him any relief.

Bernheim's suggestion at lunch that Murphy might have stolen his story came like a bombshell.

"I was shocked when he brought it up because we had just been talking about all kinds of other things. French movies that he was going to look at for us that maybe we could get involved with at Paramount. Nothing to do with Murphy. General social conversation.

"And suddenly he dropped on me, in the midst of the lunch, a statement about 'Isn't this project very similar to *King for a Day?*' or 'Isn't it really the same story or a similar story?'"

Tanen immediately felt that Bernheim had asked him to lunch in order to set him up. His face flushed, his jaw tightened and his emotional response flashed from betrayal to anger in a nanosecond.

"What do you mean, 'set up'?" I probed.

"To allow him to present a position that had never even occurred to me. I was so shocked when he first said it, I didn't even answer. I thought, He's setting me up. . . . I was very angry and really I must say, unfortunately, I lost my temper, became very angry with him. I raised my voice, which I don't do very often. I became more than a little agitated."

He wasn't sure that Bernheim had brought it up on a lawyer's suggestion, in order to find grounds for a lawsuit, but he immediately suspected it.

"It was so bald, so lacking in subtlety, and so unlike him," Tanen remembered.

Coming to America had nothing to do with Bernheim's project, Tanen fairly shouted at him across the table. He also told him that if Eddie Murphy hadn't been black, he wouldn't have even brought it up.

"What did you mean by that?" I asked.

Tanen felt obliged to give me a little background buildup to the touchy subject of movie racism before answering my question.

"There had been movies like *Roman Holiday* and *Prince and the Pauper.* Movies about royalty. Because Eddie Murphy is a black actor . . ."

He trailed off for a moment, collecting his thoughts, then talked about the basic story differences between *King for a Day* and *Coming to America.*

"One is about a really despotic, ugly—I don't want to exaggerate it, but shades of an Idi Amin-ish character coming to America. The other is about a twenty-year-old naive boy looking to get out of his country, out from under his father's thumb."

The stories, he suggested, could not be any more different. But because Murphy is black the stories suddenly seem similar. If Dustin Hoffman had been the naive prince coming to America, nobody would have thought the story of the despot in Washington, D.C. was the same story, Tanen said.

"It's about our society," Tanen said wearily. "I don't know, maybe because Murphy is black anything he is cast for takes on overtones."

Tanen's flashpoint anger with Bernheim dissipated almost as soon as it happened. Within moments, he was embarrassed.

"I'm really sorry. I shouldn't blow up at you," he apologized to Bernheim. *King for a Day* had been a nightmare for everybody involved, he told him.

But, he added, *King for a Day* was not *Coming to America*.

The idea of someone hiding his identity and going someplace else has been done repeatedly. Most movies have been done over and over in different guises, Tanen said. His own one-liner description of *Coming to America*, in fact, was a reverse *Roman Holiday*—the 1953 romantic comedy in which newspaper reporter Gregory Peck falls in love with Princess Audrey Hepburn, who is posing as a commoner.

But I had read *The Quest*—and, by now, I was sure Tanen had not. I had also read all of the scripts that had been spun by Tab Murphy, Veber and the Warner Bros. screenwriters out of Art's original story. The question was not whether Art's two and one half pages, written back in 1982, had any direct resemblance to Eddie's two pages dictated five years later to an Eddie Murphy Productions secretary. The question was: did Art's work and Alain's subsequent script development influence Murphy to make his own movie?

"Let's assume the idea that Eddie Murphy had for *The Quest* first came from his exposure to Art Buchwald's *King for a Day*."

Under those circumstances, I asked Tanen, wouldn't it be proper to say that *Coming to America* was based upon *King for a Day*?

Tanen thought long and hard before he answered.

"Yes, it would seem to be," he finally answered. "If that is the case, it would seem to be."

Tanen had finally given me a hypothetical chain of events, leading from Buchwald's crude, crude world to Murphy's Zamundan paradise. Now it was up to me to find the missing link.

15

Dopey and Mickey

HOLLYWOOD is not a great place for job security—at least if you are a high-ranking studio executive whose tenure is often subject to fickle public taste in movies. The only consolation is that a fired studio boss usually lands on his feet—either at another studio, his own production company or a talent agency. It is one big happy Club—reserved almost exclusively for white males.

A case in point is the changing of the guard—some would say Tuesday Night Massacre—at Paramount in September 1984 while Francis Veber was finishing up his first draft of *King for a Day*. The trouble began twenty months earlier when Gulf & Western's chairman and chief executive officer, Charlie Bluhdorn, died of a heart attack while flying back from Casa de Campo, the company's estate in the Dominican Republic. It was a blow to the triumvirate of Barry Diller, Michael Eisner and Jeffrey Katzenberg which ran Paramount studios—and ran it very well under the laissez-faire management style of Bluhdorn and his watchdog, Art Barron.

In a swift succession battle, Martin Davis, Bluhdorn's hatchet man, proved the superior infighter and won control, beating out two higher-ranking G&W execs. Davis made Diller a vital ally with promises that he would not make changes at the studio. Davis also garnered the key vote of Charlie's widow, Yvette, with assurances that she would retain her husband's perks. Davis rewarded Diller by interfering with his stewardship over the studio. And for her loyalty, Mrs. Bluhdorn was stripped of her promised perks and thrown out of Casa de Campo in the Dominican Republic.

It didn't take long for Davis to let it be known that he was interested in increasing Paramount's already engorged bottom line. When Barry Diller first took over as chairman in 1974, the lackluster studio's earnings stood at $40 million. For seven years straight, the studio had a string of box office hits and made $100 million or more annually. By 1984, studio profits had increased to $145 million, but that was still not enough to satisfy Davis.

Davis was unhappy with the favorable press that Diller and company attracted and with the big bonuses paid to Diller, Eisner and a small number of their closest lieutenants. The brewing confrontation came to a head when Davis ordered Diller to fire Eisner, and Diller refused. Convinced that Davis would lower the boom on him, Diller quit before he could be axed, defecting in early September 1984 to head up Fox. Everyone assumed that Diller's understudy—the bright, charismatic Eisner, whose contract guaranteed him Diller's job—would ascend to the studio throne.

Everyone except Martin Davis.

Davis summoned Eisner and Katzenberg to New York for a late Tuesday night meeting to discuss succession. As they spoke in Davis's penthouse suite atop the Gulf & Western Building, the presses of the *Wall Street Journal* were spitting out the next day's edition announcing that Frank Mancuso, the head of marketing and distribution and Eisner's subordinate, would be named head of the studio. Davis didn't bother to tell Eisner to his face.

The next day Eisner took matters into his own hands, demanding his $1.55 million bonus and announcing his resignation. Eisner and the new owners at Disney had already been talking, and Diller wanted him at Fox. But Eisner wanted to make his own mark, and when Disney offered the chairmanship of the entire company, he jumped at the opportunity. And to run the film operations, Eisner immediately tapped Katzenberg, who turned down Davis's offer to take Eisner's job at Paramount.

So, in that single month of September 1984, Paramount lost most of its leadership. And in a short time Eisner and Katzenberg were joined at Disney by thirty other senior Paramount execs—nearly half of the studio's top management packed up their Rolodexes and standard form contracts and drove the ten miles to Walt Disney Studios in Burbank.

A few years later, the Paramount alumni association at Disney was joined by David Kirkpatrick, who had been recruited by Katzenberg to be president of production of Walt Disney Pictures and Touchstone Pictures.

My next two witnesses were Katzenberg and Kirkpatrick. And it was in the Animation Building on the Disney lot, at the corner of Dopey Avenue and Mickey Drive, that I took two depositions that would greatly influence the outcome of the case.

Although Jeffrey Katzenberg, the smiling dark-haired chairman of Walt Disney Studios, greeted me warmly in the palatial digs that he occupies inside the halls of Disney, he made it subtly clear at the outset that he was going to attempt to control the interview, beginning with setting a time limit. He had an important meeting. We would be allowed no more than two hours in his presence.

It didn't help that our court reporter showed up late, unaware that we would be doing the questioning on the lot of the fifty-year-old Disney studios in Burbank. Katzenberg seemed to have a subtle psychological advantage. Nonetheless, this thirty-eight-year-old smooth-talking transplanted Manhattanite with a vague resemblance to Jerry Lewis in black-frame eyeglasses was cordial, gracious and given to wit that verged on sarcasm.

Disney staff lawyer Richard Clair sat in on the questioning, as did Ken Kulzick, pinch-hitting for Liebig while Tony was on vacation. Before anyone switched on a tape recorder or the court reporter set up her dictation machine, Katzenberg was brimming with small-talk civility. He chatted with Ken and me about the success of *Who Framed Roger Rabbit?*, the latest Disney movies and the new MGM/Disney theme park that would be opening shortly in Florida.

Once formal questioning began, we got through the preliminaries easily: he was a New York University dropout who first worked for Mayor John Lindsay and then started as a gofer for New York-based independent producer David Picker, went on to be an agent for a while and eventually apprenticed himself to then Paramount chairman Barry Diller in 1975. He graduated to production vice-president in 1978, senior vice-president in 1980 and president of production in 1982. When Paramount president Michael Eisner defected to Disney in 1984, Katzenberg was right behind him. Chairman Eisner named Katzenberg studio president at the tender age of thirty-four.

But after he had finished reciting his *bona fides*, I found myself questioning a far more evasive Jeffrey Katzenberg, particularly in regard to his years with Eddie Murphy at Paramount.

"When you decided that you liked a project and wanted to put it into development, say for a script, whose approval did you need?" I began.

"I don't know," he said quickly. "I mean . . . when I say I don't know, you're asking . . . you're dealing in areas that are . . . have, at least for me, historically been highly undefined. So every project, you know, was a matter of judgment, depending on people's availability. And I can't answer that question for you here today."

I took a deep breath. I could see that Mr. Katzenberg was going to be a tough nut.

"Okay," I said.

But he was already off on another nervous stream-of-consciousness explanation of why he felt he could not answer the simplest and most straightforward question.

"I mean I just . . . we don't . . . we don't . . . have never believed in defining those . . . since I worked for Michael Eisner for, you know, twelve or fourteen years, I've always had an understanding with him that, you know . . . I don't know. I don't . . . it's not defined."

Katzenberg was unable to tell me who it was he reported to or who reported to him or how a movie got off the ground or exactly how a studio operated. He didn't remember whether or not Eddie Murphy, Paramount's biggest star, had an office on the studio lot, and he disputed whether it was accurate to call Murphy a star in the first place back in 1983. How did you define star? he asked. By the number of times his studio contract was renegotiated? By his status as a cover story for *People?*

Later on in the session, he recanted.

"Eddie Murphy is someone whom we dealt with believing he was the biggest star, comedy star, in the world, irrespective of his color."

I had stacks of documents from Paramount that laid out—often in Katzenberg's own handwriting—how he oversaw the step-by-step development of Art Buchwald's original story into scripts clearly earmarked for an Eddie Murphy picture. Yet I couldn't even get Katzenberg to admit that he might have had a hand in committing the original money paid to Buchwald and Bernheim to develop *It's a Crude, Crude World.* He recalled nothing about the story or the scripts, blaming the passage of time for his memory lapse.

Nor could he even remember coming up with and authorizing the name change to *King for a Day* which both internal Paramount memos and other Paramount personnel at the time ascribed to Katzenberg.

He scratched his head, shrugged his shoulder and crossed his arms.

"But if that's a good thing, you can blame me," he conceded, giving me a big, toothsome grin.

The affable Mr. Katzenberg was clearly going to try to dodge every question I fired at him. Any nuggets I would get from him I would have to extract like one of his glinting teeth. At one point, our court reporter even interrupted the dialogue in an effort to get the studio president to answer my questions more directly.

"Excuse me," she said. "Can I have a yes or a no?"

"Sure. Yes. Okay. Sorry," said Katzenberg.

"You had a habit of liking to write notes on memos and send back directives or inquiries or asking for follow-up. Do you recall that was your practice?" I asked.

"No," he said flatly. "I'm . . . again, I would just say I am one who avoided paper over the years. So I'm not a big note writer."

Fortunately, I had a folder full of interoffice memoranda that directly contradicted him. I laid the top document—a biweekly status report on Paramount film projects from April 1983—in front of him.

"There is a series of notations that you've made. Comments. I think that's your handwriting, is it not?"

He read it over quickly.

"Uh-huh," he said.

"That was your practice at the time, was it not, to make notations and fire them off to David Kirkpatrick or Ricardo Mestres?"

"Well, I mean . . . I don't know whether that was my general practice. Certainly with the Eddie Murphy business in some ongoing things, yeah. I just . . . I just . . . I'm trying to categorize. I don't write lots of notes so that is one that I did do."

As I pulled more and more memos, reports and letters out of my bag of tricks, each one addressed to or from Jeff Katzenberg and most bearing comments and questions in Katzenberg's handwriting, I noticed a subtle change in Katzenberg's attitude. His nervous "uh-huh" responses and his flat-out denials gave way to a standard reply.

"Great," he would say, his eyes widening with each new sheet of paper I showed him to "refresh" his recollection.

It was my turn to offer up a quip and a huge grin.

"Paramount opened up their doors, Mr. Katzenberg. We drove in with a truck and we took everything in sight," I said.

"They're generous guys," he said.

Later on, after reviewing dozens of pages, Katzenberg gave me a pleading look and held out his hands in a mock entreaty.

"Think about all these poor trees that you butchered for this."

Katzenberg's sarcasm didn't impress me as much as his cynicism. When he was caught in what appeared to be an obvious lie, he managed to carry on blithely as though nothing untoward had happened.

He told me he didn't remember Tab Murphy or anything that he had ever written. When I handed him a letter he'd written to John Landis in 1983, singing the screenwriter's praises, he didn't blanch, even as I read his own words back to him:

" 'The writer is Tab Murphy, who has proven in another project that he has a terrific sense for Eddie Murphy's style.' Do you remember what the basis was for that statement?"

"No," he said, accompanying his one-word standard answer with his by now cloying grin.

Later on, when I asked him about his reaction to reading the Tab Murphy script, he tried turning the tables on me.

"Well, did I read it? I'm going to start asking you questions here," he said.

"We believe that you did read it," I said.

"Is that supposition or is that fact?" he demanded.

"It's a reasonable inference," I shot back.

"I see. Based on . . . ?"

"Based on the circumstances of the situation," I said, nodding my approval at his amateur interrogation technique. "Very good."

"Okay," he said, slapping his hands down on the arms of his chair and sitting forward triumphantly. "I rest my case."

I turned to Katzenberg's lawyer.

"Your witness," I said.

"Case closed," he said over a room full of laughter.

When we got around to Francis Veber's involvement, Katzenberg had a partial memory restoration. He admitted that it was "probably" his decision that the French director-writer be paid $300,000 to write a completely new script.

By the time Paramount sent Bernheim into turnaround with *King for a Day* in 1985, the studio had spent over $400,000 on the project. There were many reasons why a studio nixes a project, according to Katzenberg.

"We could get tired of the idea. He [Eddie] could get tired of the idea. Somewhere else the idea could have gotten made by someone. We could never have gotten a good script on it."

Katzenberg didn't know which reason—or reasons—led to the demise of *King for a Day* at Paramount, but he did make one major concession to me regarding the development process—a concession I would rely upon again and again over the coming months.

"Paramount, in developing [Buchwald's] original material, had the right to do almost anything they wanted with it," I said, paraphrasing Art's contract. "They could adapt it, use it, dramatize, rearrange, vary, alter, fold, spindle, mutilate, tear, whatever. Contractually, Paramount had the right. Were you familiar with that?"

"No," he said, "but it sounds reasonable."

"Why does it sound reasonable?"

"I'm being sarcastic," he said, getting off the hook as best he could by calling any question about contracts a "legal question" best left to attorneys to interpret.

I knew the day I took the case way back in the fall that one of my biggest obstacles would be the fact that Art's original treatment bore little resemblance to *Coming to America*. Getting a judge and a jury to understand the studio development process and how someone's idea can be twisted and revised into something completely different would be a tough assignment.

But I sensed that, in the obdurate Mr. Katzenberg, I had a golden opportunity to show how the twist-and-revise process works.

"You had in development a motion picture called *Joy of Sex* while you were there. Do you recall that?" I asked.

"Oh, boy, do I," he said.

Paramount in fact produced the comedy about a dying woman who wants to get bedded down at least once before going to her grave, but *Joy of Sex* was DOA at theaters in the spring of 1984. Katzenberg couldn't even remember the story line, but this time I couldn't blame him.

"I think that's one of those things that you just sort of block out of your mind and erase. Want it to go away," he said contemptuously.

"Do you remember that popular book that came out in the seventies called *Joy of Sex*?" I asked.

"Yes. I wasn't allowed to read it, but I do remember it," he said.

Paramount's ill-fated sex comedy had nothing whatsoever to do with the bestselling sex manual by Dr. Alex Comfort, but Paramount might well have optioned the book just to use the title of a bestseller, I suggested.

Not likely, according to Katzenberg.

"It is uncommon," he said.

"But it happens, doesn't it?" I persisted.

"It's a stretch," he said.

That's when I asked about a Woody Allen movie—*Everything You Wanted to Know About Sex but Were Afraid to Ask.*

"Did that picture have any bearing on the book, other than the title?" I asked.

"I have no idea. I didn't even know it was based on a book or the title came from a book," said Katzenberg of the number one bestselling book of 1970.

Right, I said to myself.

As for the movie *Coming to America,* Katzenberg's memory was even worse than his memory of his Paramount days in the early eighties. He remembered seeing it, but nothing much beyond that. He didn't remember it opening in an African kingdom or the spoiled Prince Akeem character or the time the young prince and his sidekick, Semmi, spent in the New York ghetto or that Akeem fell in love with a beautiful black American woman whom he took back to Africa to be his bride.

And he certainly did not recall the remark he made to one of his former colleagues at Paramount after a screening of *Coming to America.*

"Do you recall stating to Mr. Kirkpatrick words to the effect, 'Who are they kidding? That's *King for a Day.* I cannot believe this'?"

"No," Katzenberg said.

In seventeen years of practicing law, I had come across few witnesses who had a poorer memory for events, people, names or detail than Jeff Katzenberg.

"Based on our overview for the first hour, I'm able to eliminate 90 percent of the documents because of your terminal amnesia," I told him as we neared the bottom of the pile of documents I had brought along to refresh his memory.

"There you go," he said, chuckling.

"Note that I said that in a joking manner," I added.

"Note that I smiled when you said it," Katzenberg said, flexing his eyebrows at me like Groucho Marx.

It was a week later when I stepped into David Kirkpatrick's office, right down the hall from Katzenberg's suite. If his boss's manner was garrulous yet evasive, Kirkpatrick's was businesslike and—as near as I could tell—disarmingly frank. He also more closely resembled my preconceived notion of what a somber-looking film executive ought to look like.

The Pittsburgh native whom Ned Tanen had called "Paramount's link to Eddie Murphy" was prematurely balding and bespectacled, giving Kirkpatrick the appearance of a man far older than his thirty-seven years.

But appearances can be deceiving. The truth was that Kirkpatrick, whom

Katzenberg had named president of production for Walt Disney's Touchstone film division just two months earlier, was one of the new generation of mini-moguls brought along in the late seventies and early eighties by Tanen's predecessor at Paramount, Barry Diller. Along with Dawn Steel, Larry Mark, Ricardo Mestres, John Fiedler and Jeffrey Katzenberg, Kirkpatrick was part of the Paramount creative staff—one of the so-called under-thirty "Killer Dillers" whom then Paramount chairman Diller had hired to take on the rest of the film industry with fresh ideas, street-fighting tactics and an eye to serving the burgeoning youth market.

Kirkpatrick might have looked more like a bank manager than a movie executive, but he had a reputation for being as glib, clever and nearly as manipulative as Katzenberg. Among the Killer Dillers, his nickname was "Davey the K." The one thing he had in common with his peers in the highly specialized field of movie development was a fierce devotion to the eternal hope of melding talent, story, camera and money into blockbusters.

After graduating from the California Institute of the Arts in 1974, Kirkpatrick went to work for the low-budget godfather to dozens of young filmmakers, Roger Corman. Dennis Hopper, Robert Towne, Peter Fonda, Jonathan Demme and Jack Nicholson, among others, all understudied to the man who will go down in film history as producer of such grade Z movies as *Attack of the Crab Monsters* and *She Gods of Shark Reef*. What he learned about the high art of filmmaking at CalArts, Kirkpatrick unlearned at Corman University. The chief lesson was beguilingly simple: If a movie costs too much to make and doesn't pack 'em in at the theater, you're out of business.

For Corman, Kirkpatrick wrote *The Great Texas Dynamite Chase*, which Corman's New World Pictures produced as *Dynamite Women*. On the strength of that credit, Kirkpatrick moved on to Warner Bros. and Fox and Universal, where he wrote three more screenplays—none of them produced—as well as scripts for the "Hardy Boys" and "Nancy Drew" television series. Paramount production president Don Simpson gave Kirkpatrick his first break as a development executive in 1977 when he offered him a job as a story analyst.

"About how many screenplays do you think you've read in your career in the entertainment industry?" I asked.

"I would say approximately 6,000 screenplays."

"And treatments? How many of those do you think you've read, approximately?"

"Five hundred," he answered. And only one had ever been optioned in his ten years at Paramount—Art Buchwald's *King for a Day*.

I sat up straighter. What I had in Kirkpatrick was more than Eddie Murphy's rabbi at Paramount. I had an expert who would be able to help me prove my "based upon" argument before I ever got into court.

"Do you understand the dispute in this case deals essentially with whether or not *Coming to America* is based upon *King for a Day*?" I asked.

"Yes."

It wasn't the first such dispute in which Kirkpatrick had been involved. A couple of years earlier, none other than Bob Wachs and Eddie Murphy had fought two successful novelists over the story credit on *Beverly Hills Cop II*. Dan Jenkins and Bud Shrake, who had been commissioned by Paramount to write the original screenplay, charged Wachs with hijacking their original story and passing it on to two other screenwriters, Larry Ferguson and Warren Skaaren, to rewrite into another script.

The dispute was settled the way virtually all such credit disputes are settled in Hollywood: in secrecy by an arbitration board of the Writers Guild. Kirkpatrick testified on behalf of Wachs and Murphy at the arbitration proceeding and the pair eventually prevailed. Shrake and Jenkins might have been bitter about the outcome, but if their story had any influence on the comedian and his manager, the three Guild arbiters didn't believe it. Story credit went to Murphy and Wachs, along with a larger stake in the $153 million that fans paid at the box office to see the second Axel Foley saga.

" 'Based upon' encompasses all sorts of original material that have some sense of essential tangential connection with the movie or screenplay," said Kirkpatrick. "For instance, 'based upon' could be a record album. 'Based upon' could be an old Greek myth. Whereas 'story,' to me, has a more professional connotation where a screenwriter was hired to write an original treatment that became part of the screenplay and movie and is also more of a Writers Guild term as it relates to arbitration."

I could hardly believe my ears. Could this straight-talking witness really be one of the chief lieutenants of the amnesiac and quibbler working just down the hall behind the door labeled "Studio Chairman"?

Kirkpatrick became Paramount's main channel to Eddie Murphy in 1984, with the departure of production vice-president Richard Fischoff. When Kirkpatrick took over, he learned that one of his main responsibilities was to make sure that Eddie did a movie every other year.

So he pitched movie ideas to his finicky star. Constantly.

One of the projects Paramount had on tap for its new star in 1983 was a remake of a Jerry Lewis comedy, *The Nutty Professor*. Almost as soon as Kirkpatrick proposed it, there was opposition, but from a completely unexpected direction.

"We tried to buy it from . . . Jerry Lewis. And Jerry Lewis insisted on starring in it so we dropped it."

"He wanted to star in it again?" I asked incredulously.

"He wanted to star in it again, so we weren't able to pursue it."

"Call it *The Double Nutty Professor*," quipped Ken Kulzick.

There was also *50/50* or *Soldiers of Misfortune*, in which Kirkpatrick planned to costar Murphy with Sylvester Stallone. The two also proposed acting together in another project called *Boys*. Ultimately, neither movie was made, not because they weren't good but because it was financially impossible to have two megastars in the same movie. Their combined acting fees and profit-sharing deals would ultimately have made even an enormous box office hit unprofitable for the studio.

Murphy was also considered for *Star Trek IV*, but Kirkpatrick nixed the idea after he'd read the script. He concluded that there was no part for Eddie and manufacturing one would only hurt both Murphy and Paramount's *Star Trek* franchise.

It was not easy to pitch Eddie. To begin with, he was not always available.

"He lived in New Jersey and he worked on his own rules as to when he felt it was appropriate to return phone calls," said Kirkpatrick.

When he could get Eddie to sit still for a pitch session, usually at a restaurant during one of Murphy's infrequent Southern California visits, Kirkpatrick had a further problem: Eddie's attention span.

"I used to call them the 'M-E-G-O meetings.' "

"M-E-G-O?" I asked.

" 'My eyes glaze over.' We would sit at restaurants and pitch him ten or twelve ideas and he would just sit there and sort of nod his head and listen."

Some of the pitches, like the idea of playing an old man who becomes young again or playing opposite a child, like Emmanuel Lewis, appealed to Murphy. But most put Eddie into a trance, like the idea of acting as a black astronaut or a black man in Washington. Kirkpatrick suggested he be a black detective or a black member of royalty or a black pilot in a project called *Black Bird* about the first black squadron to fly across the United States. He proposed *Black Sheep* about a black CIA agent.

"We were always looking for an annuity project for Eddie where he could play a character every couple of years which ultimately became, in a sense, Axel Foley. But the area of spy espionage is a good franchise, so we were looking for a franchise character that Eddie could play over time."

The annuity character came about quite by accident, as it turned out. Murphy was the last-minute substitute for the lead in *Beverly Hills Cop*—something I had heard before from Tanen and others. When Stallone decided to pull out, the movie was already in preproduction, so the studio simply dropped Eddie into the Axel Foley role.

Almost anything that came along with a black character—and many, like *Beverly Hills Cop*, which didn't specify race—were tossed Murphy's way. If it bore the word "black" anywhere in the pitch, Eddie was the man who wound up with it whether it was any good or not.

One project Kirkpatrick did not pitch to Eddie was called *Uriah*, about a disillusioned record producer who turns an African witch doctor into America's newest singing sensation—a kind of latter-day Little Richard.

"Boy, I don't think we ever had the balls to give that to Eddie. We were just getting to know him."

There were some things, like the suggestion of playing a gay rocker like Little Richard, that Murphy would not even consider. Kirkpatrick had tried selling Murphy on a *Some Like It Hot* turn as a man dressed as a woman in a property called *Sob Sisters*, but Murphy was adamant and angry at the suggestion that he go before the cameras in drag. Kirkpatrick was learning how to tailor pitches to the whims and insecurities of his star—what Kirkpatrick referred to as "a sales job."

Murphy got more finicky and reclusive as his Paramount power base grew. M-E-G-O meetings were bad enough, but getting him to read something was virtually impossible.

"Eddie wasn't terribly responsive to the development process, so he wouldn't want to read a draft and comment on it and then have it go back and have rewrites. Basically our experience with Eddie was, 'Here's the script. We'd like you to commit to it.' "

But Kirkpatrick—like Tanen and everyone else at Paramount—spent most of his time talking with Wachs.

"About how many times approximately do you think in 1983 you spoke on the phone to Mr. Wachs?"

"Three phone calls a day, 360—a thousand times," he said.

Unlike Murphy, Wachs always had an opinion. Most of the time he simply hated everything and didn't even show it to his client. Although he might have hated everyone else's work, Wachs was indefatigable when it came to his own ideas.

"Okay, Mr. Kirkpatrick, what do you think of this?" I asked, reading from a memo written on an Eddie Murphy Productions letterhead. "A movie, comedy-adventure film, wherein the illegitimate son of an African despot wins the freedom of his country by winning a bet with the ruler wherein the young man wins championships in running, tennis and boxing. Do you remember being pitched that idea by Bob Wachs?"

No, he didn't.

Wachs and Murphy also came up with *Fountain of Youth.* Two aging con men, portrayed by Eddie and Joe Piscopo, discover Ponce de Leon's fountain in south Florida. The guys quench their thirst, regain their youth and then the hijinks begin. Like most Murphy film projects, it was a good premise that never went anywhere.

Whether it was his early training at the knee of Roger Corman or simply an acquired cynicism from being a Killer Diller for so very long, Kirkpatrick didn't even consider taste when Wachs came to him with the concert movie project. It was a movie Eddie was willing to make, it was easy to do and it would satisfy his at-least-one-picture-a-year mandate. He approved *Raw* without comment.

From David Kirkpatrick's point of view, *King for a Day* was the right project at the right time for Eddie Murphy back in 1983. Everything about the basic concept, down to the style of comedy for which Paramount was known throughout the industry, was just right.

"Half of Paramount's comedies are fish-out-of-water," he said. "So we responded to the fish-out-of-water aspect of a sophisticated black entity coming to the States and realizing America through different eyes. The other aspect we liked had to do with giving Eddie Murphy, who was a star under contract, a sophisticated quality as opposed to a black street kid."

After two hits in which he portrayed a black street kid railing against honky white capitalists all the time, Eddie wanted a change.

"In our M-E-G-O meetings with him we had talked about the African prince idea, but nothing more than that. Other than an English-bred—possibly for Eddie—kind of character who came to America and didn't just have to go up against the white capitalist pigs, but could go up against America in general. . . .

"While we never got into specific story attitudes . . . we did talk . . . about this kind of character, particularly one which was ultimately used in *Trading Places.*"

In the last two reels, the Murphy character masquerades as an African "buha-buha" in a turban, Kirkpatrick said.

At that point, Buchwald's treatment with its own buha-buha character in the Washington ghetto passed over Kirkpatrick's desk. It was "maybe a little too politically satirical, but something to work with," he recalled.

Kirkpatrick was still working under production vice-president Richard Fischoff then, but he was already champing at the bit to rise in the fast-moving, heady world of studio politics. The way to do that was to get successful movies made and "to maximize Eddie as a star." Kirkpatrick moved quickly to match the Buchwald buha-buha story with a screenwriter.

Kirkpatrick found Tab Murphy in the spring of 1983.

"He was cheap, it was a so-so idea, and he could write a script, and so we took a shot at it," Kirkpatrick said.

So Tab Murphy got his big break.

By October, however, it was apparent that Kirkpatrick's 7-Eleven find did not have the touch. As usual, Wachs hated it but, in this case, so did everyone else . . . including the author.

The script was rejected and Kirkpatrick was back to square one. Katzenberg told him to go with Bernheim's choice for a screenwriter: Francis Veber.

At one low point during Veber's ordeal, when Veber complained about his mistreatment, Katzenberg ordered Kirkpatrick to call Veber on the phone and "tell him you love him." Kirkpatrick referred to the order as a "talent relationship mission." Smiling, he wove his fingers together and told me it was still his mission in his new capacity as Touchstone president at Disney. Soothing stars and writers and directors is all part of the "selling process," according to Kirkpatrick. What that meant to me was telling people what they wanted to hear . . . not necessarily the truth.

In early 1984, in another memo written to the top Paramount brass, Kirkpatrick sang the praises of Veber's latest rewrite of *King for a Day* as a project with tremendous potential—an excellent candidate for summer release in 1985.

"There's a little sales job there," Kirkpatrick said.

In terms of?

"Presenting it."

Optimism?

"Yeah."

"Okay. Sales job is common in your business?" I asked.

"We sell all day long to everyone we deal with," Kirkpatrick said.

And everyone sells right back.

When Kirkpatrick was promoted to production vice-president in 1984, Bob Wachs sent him a clock as a congratulatory gift. It was yet another "sales job," according to Kirkpatrick, deserving of a return sales job. Kirkpatrick sent Wachs a thank you note.

"Whether I continue to work in the industry or end up getting kicked out of it, I know I will always cherish this wonderful gift," he wrote to Wachs. "You have been a good friend and a great partner to me and I truly appreciate it. . . ."

"Had Wachs been a good friend and great partner to you?" I asked Kirkpatrick.

"This was a sell job," he said flatly. "I got a promotion and he sent me a clock."

By the following January, after the unprecedented performance at the box office of *Beverly Hills Cop*, Kirkpatrick wrote Wachs again to sing Eddie's praises. His client had knocked 'em dead at the box office again. Kirkpatrick also wanted to suggest to Wachs that *Hell of an Angel* and *King for a Day* be considered as the two strongest prospects at Paramount to become the next big Eddie Murphy film, perhaps for Christmas release in 1985.

Here again, I learned, Kirkpatrick was selling.

"This is a sell job, just want to preface it by saying that," Kirkpatrick said when he put the memo down on the conference table. "Again, a sales job to them to get them enthused. Eddie had just come off a major movie . . . so we wanted to make sure that they knew things were going to be happening."

"To the unschooled reader, is there any way I can tell, when you're writing a memo, when it's a sales job or when it's sort of just normal?" I asked.

"You have to ask me," he said.

"Okay. Otherwise I can't tell, right?"

"You can't," he said.

"I have to trust you, right?"

"You do."

I asked Kirkpatrick about Ned Tanen's claim that Alain Bernheim's suggestion of a connection between *King for a Day* and Eddie's new movie was so preposterous that it did not merit investigation.

"If you were still at Paramount in the fall of 1987 and someone like Alain Bernheim came to you and said, 'This thing, *The Quest* or *Coming to America*, may implicate my deal and Buchwald's deal,' what would you have done?"

"I'd have investigated it further." He explained that Paramount's files contained a copy of Art's treatment, detailed synopses—called "coverages"—of the Tab Murphy and Francis Veber scripts, and every draft of the screenplays themselves—all of which were readily accessible to anyone who wanted to review them. In addition, Paramount's legal department had the originals of Alain's and Art's contracts, and the studio's movie division alone had over a dozen lawyers.

Earlier in his deposition, Kirkpatrick had jolted me with a claim that he didn't remember our telephone conversation back in September. He'd said then that he'd told Josh Wattles in late 1987, after Tanen's lunch with Bernheim, that Buchwald and Bernheim were going to sue Paramount. He'd also related Jeff Katzenberg's remark at a movie theater about the striking similarity between Buchwald's story and *Coming to America.*

I had not yet asked *the* question about the several times he told Eddie about Buchwald's concept. Would he forget that too?

As the deposition continued, Kirkpatrick testified that as the studio's liaison with Eddie Murphy, he regularly informed Wachs, Richie Tienkin—Eddie's former manager who left in early 1987—and Murphy about a project before it got under way. (I had listed Tienkin as a potential deposition witness, but we had been unable to find him. I made a note to redouble our efforts.) Wachs and Hildy Gottlieb, Eddie's ICM agent, were periodically sent the biweekly status reports on Eddie Murphy projects that included *King for a Day*, and Wachs was sent Art's treatment in June 1983.

"Was it your experience that Wachs kept Eddie Murphy informed or abreast of information that you were passing on to Wachs about the status of projects?"

"Yes."

This was encouraging, and now I was ready to pop the question. I showed Kirkpatrick Katzenberg's letter to John Landis, dated July 1, 1983. I suspected that Kirkpatrick had drafted the letter and asked him directly.

"Most likely, but I don't recall."

I read to him the following sentence in the letter: "The movie is intended for Eddie Murphy who is familiar with the idea and likes it very much."

"Now, how many times had you spoken prior to July 1, 1983, with Eddie Murphy about the *King for a Day* project? Do you recall?"

"Once," Kirkpatrick answered.

"Okay. Do you remember when that was?"

"It was in the spring of 1983 at a restaurant called—it's no longer there. It's Ma Maison."

Besides himself, the other diners were Murphy, Wachs, Katzenberg and possibly one or two of Eddie's friends. Katzenberg had about twelve projects that he briefly pitched to Eddie over dinner. I asked Kirkpatrick to recount the discussion about *King for a Day*.

". . . This was basically a get-together in which we were discussing the kinds of things that we had in development for him. We didn't go into any great detail because Eddie was in one of his M-E-G-O moods. To say that he liked it very much is a bit of a sales job, but Eddie did seem to respond to it just in, you know, sort of, you know, in short strokes. There were a lot of things that we went over at that time."

This didn't give me enough to argue that Eddie knew the concept and liked it. So I went back for more.

"Do you remember what his response was in particular about *King for a Day?*"

"The specific, no, but I know that he was responsive to it."

"Positively responsive?"

"Yeah."

". . . So he was familiar with the idea by July 1, 1983, is that fair to say?"

"The truth was that he was receptive to it, and the interpretation for a sales job for John Landis was probably a little misrepresentational."

I now had one definite communication of Art's idea to Eddie well before Paramount claimed that Eddie conceived *The Quest*. But I wanted more—I wanted Kirkpatrick to relate the other occasions on which he had told Eddie about the *King for a Day* project. And he recalled all three: once after the Tab Murphy rewrite to tell Eddie that Francis Veber had been hired; a second, to tell him about Kirkpatrick's idea to bring a child into the *King for a Day* story so that Eddie could act opposite a kid as O'Neal had done in *Paper Moon* and Chaplin in *The Kid*; and a third, to inform him that the project was being dropped.

Kirkpatrick had broken the case wide open. If I could nail down what appeared from the documents to be Wachs's extensive knowledge of the Buchwald project and scripts, I would have a shot at defeating any defense that Eddie independently created the story for *Coming to America*. And then Paramount and we would be on a level playing field at trial where the battle would be over whether the movie was in fact based upon Buchwald's treatment.

I had one more question for Kirkpatrick. . . .

"By the way, did you like *Coming to America?*" I asked.

"Do I have to answer this?"

"No, you don't. I'll withdraw the question. It's not my purpose to embarrass you."

"Okay."

"Or to cause any tension in friendships."

"I appreciate that."

"But you can tell me off the record later."

We both laughed and called it a day.

"I think I could write a book about Paramount and how they develop a movie," I said.

16

The Gatekeeper

THE DEPOSITIONS of Robert Wachs and Eddie Murphy were next, scheduled for the first two weeks of October. But nailing down a firm date—especially for Murphy's deposition—had been a monumental struggle. Paramount was not eager to have its superstar subjected to testimony under oath.

During the summer, every time we had tried to arrange mutually convenient dates, Marsha Durko and Zazi Pope had been told that Eddie was either in preproduction, production or postproduction on his next Paramount movie under his five-picture deal, *Harlem Nights*. By mid-September, after twenty telephone calls to Liebig & Kulzick, we still had no firm commitment. Finally, on my advice, Zazi gave Ken Kulzick an ultimatum: "Either you agree to dates or we'll hand your fellows an invitation from the Superior Court to appear for a date that we select."

The threat worked, and I was promptly put in touch with Bob Wachs. We quickly worked out a schedule. But I had more on my mind.

"You know, Bob," I began, "this whole thing is crazy. I can't believe that Paramount is going to make Eddie sit through three days of deposition in a case in which he is not even a party. I have heard how much he enjoys being asked questions by lawyers."

I knew that tensions had developed in the relationship between Paramount and Eddie over creative issues. My sources told me that Paramount had not yet settled with us because Eddie insisted that it was his story and wanted the studio to defend his honor. If Eddie told the studio to make peace with us, I reasoned, the case would settle.

"Well, what would it take to get rid of this thing?" Wachs asked.

"Around a million bucks," I told him. "That's hardly a lot of dough for Paramount, especially since Fireman's Fund is on the hook for some or all of it."

My $1 million figure had more than a nice ring to it. Art and Alain were not vindictive and had always been willing to settle for a fair amount. By September, Kaye, Scholer had run up about $400,000 in legal fees based on our normal hourly rates. So a $1 million recovery would yield the lawyers 40 percent or $400,000 and give the clients $600,000—more than double what they had been willing to take before Kaye, Scholer took over a year earlier.

A $1 million settlement would not be a home run for my law firm. By getting paid only the value of our time, we would not receive any premium for having done a good job and having taken the risk of a contingent fee. Typically, a contingent fee lawyer wants to recover a multiple of what he would get paid on a standard hourly rate basis because some of his contingent fee cases pay nothing and the winners subsidize the losers. Nevertheless, I wanted to settle for a solid economic reason: to avoid the escalating legal fees that would inevitably result from three more months of pretrial preparation and the trial itself.

And then there was the problem of the incredibly shrinking pot of gold at the end of the rainbow. Ned Tanen had shaken my conviction that *Coming to America* would generate any net profits. If he was right, a victory at trial might result in obtaining only the $265,000 in guaranteed compensation under my clients' contracts. The lawyers' share would be a little over $100,000—a fraction of our investment of time in the case—and the clients would get only $165,000—a number close to Paramount's original settlement offer. It would be an unsatisfactory result for clients and counsel, especially since I was growing more confident that I could prove at trial that Paramount had misappropriated Art's story to make the movie.

"Have there been any settlement talks?" Bob wanted to know.

"Not since last summer before I got in the case. Paramount was livid about the *Wall Street Journal* article and refused to talk."

"Yeah, well, we weren't too thrilled with it either."

I decided to ignore that sore subject—sore for Paramount, Murphy and me —and get to the point.

"What I was thinking, Bob, was that you might be willing to play a friend-of-the-court role and get the ball rolling."

"Well, as you know, this is a beef between Art and Paramount," Wachs replied. "But I'll be happy to see what I can do. I'll get back to you."

But it was all to no avail. On the eve of his own deposition, Bob told me that he had spoken several times with Richard Zimbert and his protégé Joshua Wattles, but the bottom line was that Paramount wasn't interested in talking settlement. The studio was going to ride it out. And its lawyers had assured them that the case would never get to trial because Judge Schneider would grant the motion for summary judgment that they had filed a few days after I finished Kirkpatrick's deposition.

But before Paramount got a decision on its motion, Wachs and Murphy would have to testify under oath.

I had no reason to believe that Wachs would deliberately lie to me. I did have every reason to believe that he would duck the truth instantly if he thought that it would threaten—in even the most insignificant way—the interests of Eddie Murphy.

He was born the year before World War II began, but the Harvard-educated Wachs was clearly a man ahead of his time . . . a man custom-tailored for Hollywood.

"I met him outside of the Beverly Hills Hotel, this real earnest guy in Ray Bans and Nikes," recalled one film actor who encountered Wachs during the lawyer's first few years in Hollywood, in the early eighties. "He introduced himself as Bob 'Eddie-Murphy's-Manager' Wachs, like 'Eddie-Murphy's-Manager' was his middle name."

"From everything I know about him now, Bob's exactly the same way he was before he met Eddie and went to the West Coast," said a longtime New York acquaintance. "If you're not powerful, you're eccentric. So Bob Wachs was eccentric. Now he's whatever he used to be plus $10-million-plus clout in the entertainment industry."

Another former client is less charitable in his assessment of Bob Wachs after he met and massaged Eddie Murphy into a superstar.

"He was a really straight-up, honest, hardworking guy when he was with Paul, Weiss, Rifkind in New York. He was scrupulous, diligent, toiled from 8 A.M. to midnight, killing himself. Amateur Freudians would say he had some insecurities. That's why he drove himself like he did. He was trying to find the right client.

"He probably gave very good service to Eddie, but he got obsessed with him. He got sycophantic, especially after a few drinks. He got to be a bore about it. What good is all the money and power if everybody thinks you're an ass-kissing prick?"

As Eddie's manager, Wachs was protective to the point of obsession of his biggest and (until he took on Arsenio Hall in 1986) his only client. What began as a mother-hen role overseeing the interests of his then teenager client in the early eighties had by the end of the decade developed into a controlling, often sneering domination of Murphy's professional life and career direction. Nobody saw or talked with Eddie Murphy about his acting, singing or comedy unless they went through Bob Wachs first.

At watering holes like the Polo Lounge in Beverly Hills or Elaine's on Manhattan's Upper East Side, Wachs never tired of telling and retelling the story of his discovery of Eddie Murphy. According to one comedy writer who watched Wachs and Murphy rise meteorically, the tales Wachs has allowed the media to perpetuate over the years—of the struggling young comic Bob Wachs discovered, overnight, on the Comic Strip's "amateur night"—are largely apocryphal.

"Eddie had a TV show before he ever even hung out at the Comic Strip," said the writer. "He wasn't around to hang out with other comedians. He already had a bit part on 'Saturday Night Live' in 1981.

"Bob is contentious. He used to argue for the sport of it all the time. He used to bait this one comedian just for argument's sake. If you're arguing movies and points and stuff, he'd take the other side just to argue."

In far plainer terms, another longtime Wachs associate summed up the latest *Coming to America* adversary I was about to face in the late summer of 1989.

"There are those people who help their friends up the ladder when they are successful and there are those who don't. Bob falls into that second category."

During Bob Wachs's deposition in my Century City office on the first Monday of October 1989, Paramount had yet another lawyer on the case.

Lionel "Lon" Sobel is a respected law professor at Loyola Law School, where he teaches copyright, trademark and entertainment law. He is also the editor and publisher of a highly influential specialty newsletter called the *Entertainment Law Reporter*. Occasionally, he farms out his expertise as a consultant, though he hasn't practiced law full time since 1982. When Ken Kulzick asked the diminutive law professor, with his distinctive shock of prematurely gray hair and dimpled cheeks, to join Paramount's team, Sobel quickly agreed.

Believing that he had a sage for a client, Bob Wachs decided to represent himself.

Wachs—with his blow-dried sandy hair, open shirt and slight paunch—came off initially as humble. But that quickly changed.

"You're what? The president of Eddie Murphy Productions?" I asked him.

"I'm not really," he said modestly. "I don't have any title. There's only one title: chairman. And you know who has that."

Though there might be only one chairman of the board, I quickly discovered that just about everybody around owned a chunk of him. Wachs and his partner, accountant-manager Mark Lipsky, each earned 5 percent of Eddie Murphy's income. As a former manager, Richie Tienken also received a percentage of Eddie's income.

"How about International Creative Management?" I asked. "What's their arrangement with Mr. Murphy?"

"They have a percentage, I believe equal to 10 percent of the first $10 million of cash and contingent compensation on a project, and 5 percent thereafter. . . ."

Despite the nibbling away at his income, Murphy was anything but poor, and Wachs took much of the credit for that.

"Why did Eddie Murphy agree to an overall deal originally with Paramount and then continue to stay under that umbrella? Do you know?" I asked.

"Of course I know," Wachs began, hesitating briefly to cast me a quizzical look. "Seems to be an unusual question," he observed. Then he continued. "I was the architect of that idea. To me it was a no-loss proposition because if you made movies under a multi-picture deal that were successful, the door was always open to come in and say, 'I've brought success. I want to increase my fee.'

"If you had bombs, your fee was still pay-or-play and you were guaranteed. Also, his very first contract gave him a $1 million advance against a movie to be determined. Now the studios never do that. The only thing studios do, as you know, is pay you the day you work.

"This was a very unusual kind of deal. And as the business guardian of a very young man, I felt I had a burden to find for him a formula that would guarantee his financial future . . . which I think the original deal proves, followed by the later deal in June, all bears out. So at the time and even until last year, I think it has been the proper way to guarantee success."

"Do you know anybody in the industry who gets $8 million a picture against 15 percent of adjusted gross?" I asked.

Wachs shrugged and rubbed his chin—a sure sign I was dealing with the evasive side of Bob Wachs.

"Probably. Probably Tom Cruise. Probably Nicholson. It's very rare. Very rare."

I tried again.

"Do you know anybody in the industry who has as favorable a definition of profit participation as Eddie Murphy?"

"Tom Cruise, Nicholson, Clint Eastwood—I'm sure there are a few of those top-level guys," he said. "Bill Murray in certain respects may have a more favorable definition on video. Stallone, of course."

"Eddie Murphy has a very good memory? Is that true?"

"Very good memory," Wachs said, shutting his eyes as he nodded.

"Can you give me any examples of it?"

"He can probably give you any lyric from any theme song of any television program that's ever existed," Wachs said without a hint of sarcasm.

"That's a tremendous retention ability," I said, straight-faced.

"Yeah. He can recite cartoons at length and . . ."

"Movies he's seen? Dialogue?"

"Oh, yeah," Wachs said, nodding more vigorously. "Well, he's also . . . I don't know if it's a function of memory or repetition sometimes. If he sees a movie that he loves, you know, he'll see it a lot."

"Do you know, does he read a lot?" I asked.

"No, I don't think he does, really. I mean, he reads newspapers and magazines, occasionally books. But I wouldn't say he's a voracious reader."

"Does he watch a lot of television?"

"Yes. And movies."

Despite his close business relationship with Murphy, Wachs had always been something of an outsider when it came to the comedian's creative and personal life. Murphy was closer to Tienken than he was to Wachs. Wachs worked the phones. His comanager, Tienken, liked to party.

"You and Tienken shared information with each other as it came along?" I asked.

"We weren't Siamese twins. We led very different lives. I was the day man, he was the night man," Wachs said.

Eddie was more apt to share his feelings with Tienken or someone like Ken Frith, a peer from Roosevelt High School who literally lived with Murphy at his New Jersey estate where the two kicked around ideas for skits, bits and comedy routines.

"I rarely speak to him when we are not together, in the same state," Wachs said.

"And that's been true throughout your relationship?"

"From day one. I have a personal philosophy about it that when you see somebody frequently in a work situation and that work is over, give it a break, you know. You go your way, let them go their way. Absence makes the heart grow fonder."

"How do you keep him advised or apprised of what's going on in terms of various projects?" I asked.

"Pick your shots, pick the mood and pick the timing," Wachs said.

"Is he a person of shifting moods?"

"Very much so. Sometimes he's very quiet. Sometimes he's very outgoing. Sometimes when he is intense about a project he's working on, I will not ask him or bother him with anything, you know. He becomes very tunnel-visioned. And I think it's all about timing with him. Unless you want your head handed to you . . ."

"Eddie controls the mood," Wachs continued. "If Eddie's in a good mood, and if everything is jovial, everything is jovial. If Eddie is not in a good mood, you know, the door is closed."

"Are you as close to him as anybody?"

"In certain areas, yes. In certain areas, no."

One of the "yes" areas was Eddie and Paramount. Murphy's star treatment demands had become so frequent and so outrageous at times that Eddie/Paramount jokes had begun to make the rounds at Hollywood watering holes and inside the hallways of the studio itself. There were one-liners, like: Why was Eddie Murphy late for his first call? Answer: He was raising hell with Paramount because the 30-foot-wide mobile home dressing room he ordered for the shoot turned out to be only 28 feet wide.

"Does Eddie currently enjoy a good relationship with Paramount?" I asked.

"Not particularly," Wachs said, shifting uncomfortably in his chair.

"Why is that?"

"Well, Eddie feels that he is not treated in the first-class manner that a star of his caliber should be treated," Wachs said with absolute ingenuousness.

"And any particulars that he's voiced?"

"All particulars. Everything."

I got up and walked around the room for a moment, scrutinizing Wachs for some sign that he was pulling my leg. His client, after all, made the tabloids on a regular basis for his tantrums on and off the set. Eddie had the clout to order up women during filming the way some lesser actors might ask the studio to send out for a pizza.

But Eddie was never satisfied. I remembered his recent complaints about Paramount in an interview he gave to *Rolling Stone.*

"When he was describing his contract with Paramount he said he had the shittiest deal in town," I said.

"Or the worst," Wachs muttered.

"Do you agree with that?"

"No."

Finally. An honest disagreement with his superstar client.

"Okay. Why not?"

" 'Cause he probably has one of the best deals in town," Wachs said, shrugging off his own disbelief and frustration with Eddie. "I have no answer for why people say what they do."

It wasn't the money. It was what studio veterans like to call "creative control" issues that gave Eddie what he perceived to be Hollywood's shittiest deal.

"They operate to a great degree, and much more in the early days [of Eddie's career], under a big cloak of secrecy," said Wachs.

"Why is that?"

"That was their style. That was their policy." Wachs shrugged. "Never give anybody a script until it's almost perfect, and I mean, they had their policies. Very strange at times."

As a result, Eddie felt typecast as a funny guy who never got the girl—a pattern that Murphy interpreted as inherently racist. By way of example, Wachs pointed to Paramount's duplicity in the development of *The Golden Child.*

"We were never given the script of *Golden Child*," he said. "*Golden Child* was sold by ICM to an independent producer who brought the script to Paramount. Paramount bought it. And that producer was going to Australia to give it to Mel Gibson. So ICM never gave us the script. Paramount never gave us the script. But I uncovered it at ten o'clock at night from New York in a conversation with Kirkpatrick. I described to him what I was looking for as Eddie's next movie and he told me that they had a movie like that, but they had never thought of it for us.

"I told Kirkpatrick I wanted to read that script that night, and point of fact, I did get it and read it that night and the next day. I brought it to Eddie the day after and Eddie committed the day after that to doing *Golden Child.*"

But *Golden Child* was the sixth movie Murphy had made for Paramount. By that time, he had developed enough clout to demand to see a script. Until then, the way Murphy's movies materialized seemed haphazard to an outsider. The oft-told tale of Murphy's last-minute replacement of Sly Stallone on *Beverly Hills Cop* was only one of the catch-as-catch-can castings, according to Wachs.

Murphy's first film, *48 HRS.*, was written for Richard Pryor. The fact that its director, Walter Hill, lived with Eddie's agent, Hildy Gottlieb, might have had something to do with Eddie finally getting the part, Wachs implied.

"And how about *Best Defense?*" I asked.

"That was Katzenberg leaning on Eddie to do a cameo," said Wachs. "It wasn't an Eddie Murphy movie. He only worked two weeks. He had nothing more than a cameo although Paramount then billed it and marketed it as an Eddie Murphy movie. We don't include that as one of our movies."

Following the success of *Beverly Hills Cop*, Murphy didn't want to play a cop or carry a gun. He wanted to vary his roles. The studio couldn't argue with his success, so it budgeted $35 million to make *Coming to America* and even more—a cool $40 million—to make his next feature, *Harlem Nights.*

But Murphy had never had an interest in politics. That's why Wachs maintained he never even considered letting his client see the *King for a Day* scripts.

"We kept saying, 'We're not interested, not interested,' and it was almost as if Kirkpatrick or the studio had to have some kind of show with these people because they were trying to get something from them."

"From whom? Buchwald? Veber? Bernheim?"

"All of them. All of them. That's the nature of Hollywood."

But even if *King for a Day* had not been about politics, Wachs would not have recommended the script to Eddie. The writing was terrible, he said.

The only time Eddie might have even heard about *King for a Day*, according to Wachs, was during a business session following a surprise dinner for Murphy at Ma Maison restaurant. Both Kirkpatrick and Katzenberg were there.

"There was some business done and they would review a list," Wachs recalled. Wachs settled into an obsequious pose, grinning like a studio boss anxious to sell his project to a star.

" 'We have under development blank-to-blank which is about this *King for a Day* about the king that gets overthrown. The CIA wants to replace him or rather reinstate him,' " Wachs blathered, trying to demonstrate how Paramount's brass acted toward Murphy that night. "Such and such . . . uh, 50-50 which is maybe something for you and Mr. Stallone.' And so on. They would give the menu and that was it."

Eddie didn't take it too seriously, Wachs said. It was something he was forced to sit through. That was the first and last time Eddie Murphy had any exposure to *King for a Day*, Wachs asserted. He never expected it to result in a lawsuit.

"I had thought that Paramount might have settled it very early, just based on what I considered to be a friendship between Mr. Davis and Mr. Buchwald," he said.

There was sarcasm in his voice. I ignored it.

"The original deal between Paramount and Eddie Murphy Productions, I believe, required Eddie to submit a certain number of projects which he would be ready, willing and able to act in as a lead actor before a certain date. Do you have a recollection of that?"

"None of those procedures have ever been followed," Wachs said, sighing at my naiveté. "It's not the nature of the relationship."

"Why were they in the agreement? Do you know?"

"That's Paramount's standard form. They've got to protect themselves in case an actor, you know, runs away to Hawaii for three years."

No, Wachs insisted, it wasn't the *King for a Day* scripts or any list of projects Katzenberg may have spouted off to Eddie that finally got the actor interested in an African prince coming to America. It was Eddie's own from-the-gut inspiration.

"Eddie called me one Sunday in the spring and just in a minute-and-a-half or two-minute conversation says, 'I'm real excited. I'm working on this idea I've had for a bunch of years and it's about this young African prince who doesn't want to get involved in this tailor-made marriage by his parents and comes to America to search for real true love.' And he says, 'I'd really like to do it with Arsenio who is my sidekick.' I said, 'Great. Keep working.' It's always nice to hear him get excited about something and get it working. That would be it."

Wachs was certain that Buchwald's story had nothing to do with Eddie's inspiration. Eddie had no exposure to it, and Wachs had only limited knowledge. Wachs did recall that one day in early 1985 Alain Bernheim called and insisted they talk about *King for a Day*.

"He wanted to speak to me about setting up a meeting. . . . But I said, you know, 'I really don't want to meet. Mr. Murphy is not interested in the idea.' "

"Okay," I said. "And how did you know he wasn't interested in the idea?"

Wachs eyeballed the ceiling in exasperation.

"It was not something that interested him, playing a nasty king who gets involved in CIA politics. . . . It might have come about in two words or a look or a sneer or a grunt or 'no way' you know? Just— You know when there's interest in something and when there isn't. And this was not something that he was interested in."

I handed him a letter Katzenberg had sent to NBC Entertainment chief Brandon Tartikoff in late 1984, outlining a dozen or so of the movies that Paramount had planned for Murphy and others in the coming months. One of them was *King for a Day*.

"My opinion is the writer was hyping Brandon Tartikoff to mention as many high-level names as possible," Wachs said after studying the letter.

"Does that mean he wasn't telling the truth?"

"That's correct," Wachs said blandly.

" 'Cause you know an average person reading that letter doesn't know whether he's hyping or telling the truth. Right? And that's the problem I've got."

"Tartikoff understood," Wachs insisted. "That is a piece of publicity. This is a piece of promotion. He's the president of production. He's got to show to NBC that he's got a lot of things in the pipeline, whether or not that's true."

"So you can't tell whether he's hyping or telling the truth?"

"The objective reader in Hollywood would know," said Wachs. "The layman wouldn't know."

Wachs shut his eyes for a moment. The entire time that he dealt with Katzenberg, the young executive was trying to preempt Wachs as Eddie's manager, Wachs said.

"You have to understand the nature of the way these people operate," he said with undisguised contempt. "These people have to operate for themselves with paper among each other to justify their jobs. We don't operate that way. I don't write memos to Eddie. I don't tell Eddie what I did in the course of a day. I don't tell him how many calls I got or answered or made. They have to do all that."

And the worst part, from Wachs's standpoint, was that the studio brass imposed their bureaucratic ways on him. He would tell them Eddie was not interested in doing a political story and memos would go around Paramount saying that Eddie was doing a political story anyway.

"They've been told, and they know that's for their own internal purposes for them to show the boss that they got some things in development," he said.

"Even though?" I prompted.

"Even though he has said, 'I'm not interested.' "

During the filming of *Best Defense* outside of Jerusalem in 1984, Eddie got his first real taste of dealing with the stonewalling attitude of the Paramount "Suits." According to several sources besides Wachs and Eddie himself, the story went like this:

Eddie was bored sitting around the Hilton Hotel. He couldn't get a cheeseburger from room service. It was hot, dusty. He was afraid he'd get mugged by a terrorist if he stepped outside of his hotel. He didn't much care for his manager's wife, but when he went to Israel, he specifically asked Linda Wachs to come along. He told friends that if he was going to get killed he wanted to take her with him.

All in all, living in an Israeli Hilton reminded him of the incipient paranoia of living in New York City. That gave him an idea for a movie. What if New York State seceded from the Union? He wrote it down, enthusing over ways to turn it into an action-packed thriller comedy starring . . .

EDDIE MURPHY.

Paramount didn't like it. In fact, Bob Wachs said later, Paramount didn't like much of anything that Eddie and his manager came up with, before or after the Israel trip. They would much rather have Murphy spend two weeks in the occupied West Bank doing a guest appearance as a tank driver in a bomb like *Best Defense*. To add insult to injury, the studio billed him as the star in order to sell tickets when the real lead was Dudley Moore. Eddie's cameo didn't last ten minutes.

In the meantime, Eddie's movie idea was given the bum's rush back at the studio.

Wachs began submitting his own ideas. He offered up a comedy-adventure about the illegitimate son of an African despot who wins the freedom of his country by winning a bet with the ruler, in which the young man succeeds in winning world championships in track, tennis and boxing.

Paramount wasn't interested.

Murphy and Wachs kept trying, Wachs told Lon Sobel and me.

"You have to be very careful with an actor," he said. "Too much of a repetition of the same thing leads to a one-way street. It can't always be about beating the system or Axel Foley running around with a gun. You have to grow as an actor, try different things.

"When it really came time to focus on something that was right for him— at least what I thought was right for him—nobody understood. À la *Golden Child*. Perfect example. You finish up a tough kind of a movie like *Beverly Hills Cop* with guns and shooting, now all of a sudden comes a softer kind of a character, a social worker who is approached by a magnificent woman who tells a sort of wild, way-out story, but tender, about a kid, a special kid from Tibet who's been stolen; that you, Eddie Murphy, are the chosen one, you know. He doesn't believe any of this. It's preposterous, but it's an interesting fairy tale."

It was a perfect vehicle for Murphy, Wachs said.

"Now, his agent didn't see this and his studio didn't see this. They don't know what they're doing, which is why they've never found anything for him, and to this day they don't find anything for him. You have to understand that Katzenberg had his own vision of how and what Eddie should do and Kirkpatrick was a worker bee."

It was time to get back to other story ideas that Paramount liked and Wachs/Murphy didn't. Ideas like *King for a Day*. I handed Wachs the letter he'd written Jim Harrison four years earlier, in which he insisted that Harrison's idea about a comedy featuring a Lion King coming to America could not be submitted to Paramount because Buchwald's *King for a Day* was "fairly close" and was already in the works for Eddie.

"It was an out," he said, setting the letter aside. "It was a cop-out. I didn't want to hurt a brilliant man's feelings. It was terrible. I couldn't tell him it was terrible. It was easy to say Paramount has something in development. It would make him feel good. Easy way out. 'Development is too close. Can't do the same thing twice.' The man had done brilliant work in the past. This was horrible. It looked like trash. Lion Kings and, you know, I don't know. It was almost unreadable."

I picked the letter up and read from it.

"What does 'fairly close' mean to you? Those words, 'fairly close'?"

Wachs shrugged.

"That an ordinary person would find that any two items had more similarities than dissimilarities."

"But you didn't pick *Me, Myself and I* or *Falling Angel*; you picked *King for a Day* to ease him out. As you say: to be nice," I told him with a big grin.

He squirmed.

"Well, if there's something about going to Somalia, he was not going to know what Art Buchwald's story was. He wasn't going to know what *King for a Day* was or was not about. It's an easy way out. I wanted to get out real fast. I mean, you have no idea! In a million years this could never be given to Eddie Murphy. It's terrible. Probably a lot of things in here Eddie would consider racist anyway."

Coming to America came about as the result of Eddie's breakup with Lisa Figueroa, Wachs claimed.

"At the beginning of '85, he had a very, very bad experience with his fiancée," Wachs said. "They broke up and he was very much affected by, you know: 'Did she ever love me or did she love me 'cause of who I am' and 'who I've become or what I could give her financially?' and all the rest."

Wachs had noticed that Eddie was distancing himself during the filming of *Raw*. He was isolated, disillusioned, insecure about who was truly his friend and who was not his friend. While he and his crew were on tour for *Raw*, he wrote down his idea about a naive African prince coming to America in the pages of his cousin Ray Murphy, Jr.'s notebook.

The Quest was "about life in an ivory tower and, you know, to some degree being insulated from the real everyday world and not knowing who among your friends really cares about you and who doesn't care about you," said Wachs. The story was about how someone knows when somebody wants something from him, as opposed to just liking him for what he is.

"And all the more with women," he continued. "How do you really know? If I'm Eddie Murphy and make all this money and have all this fame and what not, how do I know that a woman really cares about me or what she can get from me?"

Richard Pryor had advised him to trust no one, but Murphy didn't want to spend the rest of his life like that. Still, he had examples in his own life of people using or attempting to use him.

"He's had multiple instances with women where he's raised this, as well as with men, you know. Where he's seen people attempt to stab him in the back."

There was a bit from *Raw* about Eddie traveling to Africa in search of a naked African woman mounted on a zebra that reflected that bitterness, Wachs said.

"Um Foo Foo is her name. He goes to meet some woman who runs nude through the jungle so she'll have no pockets, 'cause if she has pockets she'll want to put things in the pockets. Then the piece continues about how he brings her back to the United States."

And the incidents in his life that reflected an unhappiness and a mistrust of women didn't end there. Murphy regularly raised the question: Why would a woman love me—for who I am or for what she can get from me?

John Landis clearly loved Eddie for what he could get out of him: a good performance. But there had been a power shift since the pair worked together on *Trading Places*. Eddie was no longer the tender young comic trying to get a foothold in Hollywood. It was Landis who was now slipping. When *The Quest* became *Coming to America* and Murphy approved Landis as director, sparks began flying between the two major egos—and profit participants—almost from the moment that the first cameras rolled.

"Landis and Eddie Murphy have had a falling out. Is that correct?" I prodded.

Wachs shifted himself uncomfortably in his chair and became a lawyer once again, carefully selecting his words at first.

"Landis did not treat Eddie in an appropriate manner. . . . Landis interfered in matters of Eddie's personal life that really were none of John's concern and I think John held a grudge against Eddie for not being supportive of John during the *Twilight Zone* case. . . ."

I waited for Wachs to continue with something a bit more specific about what he meant about Landis interfering in Eddie's personal life. What he meant, as it turned out, was that Landis kept Eddie from scoring with his leading lady.

"He attempted to interfere with a young lady who was going to be in the movie with Eddie when Eddie had asked her out to dinner," Wachs continued. "He said to her, 'Oh, don't go out with him. He's really no good with women. And stay away. You will regret it.'

"What happened simply was the leading lady was cast, Shari Headley, and she was excited and happy and Eddie said, 'Great, let's get to know each other. Let's have dinner tonight.'

"And Eddie went back to his office and Landis said to her, 'Oh, you don't go out with him, you know. He just treats all women alike. And you're special.' And Arsenio overheard this and told Eddie.

"And Eddie said, 'I'm not talking to this guy. What the hell is it his business?' That was one of four episodes."

The old *Twilight Zone* wounds reopened on the set of *Coming to America* too, according to Wachs. Landis pulled out all the stops to get his starpower friends and acquaintances to visit the Los Angeles courtroom where he stood trial. Eddie Murphy was one of those who failed to show up.

"You're no good!" Wachs remembered Landis yelling at Eddie on the *Coming to America* set. "Everybody else came down and helped me. Why didn't you?"

By the time the movie was in its final shooting at a set of the Zamundan palace that had been built in Simi Valley on the northeast outskirts of Los Angeles, Landis and Murphy had taken their feud to new heights. Eddie wanted to shoot the Simi Valley sequences early so he could leave by Friday afternoon.

"Landis seemed to be shooting everybody in the world but Eddie and just leaving Eddie to sit out in a hot trailer," said Wachs. "And finally it looked to Eddie that it was quite intentional."

Neither Landis, Murphy nor Paramount had much to kick about when the box office receipts started rolling in. As of August 1989, Eddie Murphy had earned about $16 million from *Coming to America*. Landis's adjusted gross cut was also in the millions. Paramount, of course, cleaned up.

"At one point I had guessed that Eddie would receive about $750,000 from videos, which is his 15 percent of rentals from videos. They don't pay a great royalty. They pay 20 percent and throw that into the gross."

But even Eddie Murphy was not exempt from Hollywood accounting. Personally, he earned a fortune because his contract called for a percentage of the gross. But his production company had the standard Paramount net profit deal and, unlike Murphy himself, the company earned nothing from *Coming to America*.

"It's in the hole and it gets more in the hole with every statement," Wachs said.

17

Panda Bear

— — — — — — — — — — — —

"BY THE TIME he did *Coming to America*, Eddie's whole life was different," recalled comedian Louie Anderson to a colleague of mine. Anderson had acted the part of a fast food restaurant clerk in Eddie Murphy's hit comedy. "That whole experience changed me too. I saw what it would be like to be him. It wouldn't be easy. Entertainers in general have big egos. They want to be the biggest.

"But what I saw that week we shot in New York changed my goals. Eddie was mobbed. He had no autonomy at all. He had nowhere to go. What happens is you're stripped of your self. You're stripped of your own identity. Part of having that entourage of his is having a secure group of people whom you can trust. I mean, Eddie's really not that much different from Elvis. He *had* to create his own world."

It is an artificial world in which the clock stops for a time and all indulgences are accommodated. I came to appreciate that, long after my first research into the Eddie Murphy mystique on my plane ride to New Orleans in August 1988. For more than a year since then, I had been following Eddie Murphy's skyrocketing career. I had taken special note of the subtle psychological changes in the young comic's behavior since he had become a star.

On the eve of our first meeting—a scheduled two-day deposition beginning October 12, 1989—I was already steeled for a tough session with a wary, hard-nosed screen comic who was cynical well beyond his years. I didn't believe for a moment Bob Wachs's characterization of his client as "the same person basically as the day I met him . . . just a little richer."

Louie Anderson wasn't the only cast member who had seen a change in Eddie during the filming of *Coming to America.*

"Murphy was quiet but polite to me," Dennis McDougal was told by actress Billi Gordon, who played a Zamundan palace dancer in the opening scenes of the movie. "He always had his boys around, but I imagine it was very difficult for him because people are always trying to get at him."

By the time he made *Coming to America*, Eddie Murphy trusted very few people he knew and almost no one he met for the first time. He rarely let his guard down.

Another actor in *Coming to America* recalled for my colleague that Murphy spent most of his time in his trailer or away from the rest of the cast. The only time he remembered Murphy and costar Arsenio Hall cutting up was when heavyweight champ Mike Tyson came on the set. It was one of the few times during the production that Murphy seemed to forget he was the star and let loose. The strutting and jiving that went on among Murphy, Hall and Tyson was more reminiscent of schoolyard hijinks than a conversation among three grown men.

"He made out like he was boxing with Tyson and joked around about how he was gonna knock him out," recalled the cast member. "Both he and Arsenio acted like little kids."

And having the heavyweight champion of the world paying homage to you —instead of the other way around—can be very heady stuff. In Louie Anderson's estimation, that kind of popularity can lead to a self-destructive egotism and, ultimately, to professional and personal disaster.

"It scared me to watch what was happening to Eddie," recalled Anderson. "I don't want that happening to me. I just decided then and there to check on myself and see to it that I never took this thing that seriously. I now work only for a purpose and a goal. It's much better to be number ten than number one. There are a lot more number tens around than number ones for a lot longer. The best line I've ever heard about a show business career came from another stand-up:

"It's not a fifty-yard dash. It's a marathon."

At twenty-seven, the Eddie Murphy I faced in mid-October was just as much a "fish out of water" as many of the characters he portrayed in his best-known comedies. The world of lawyers, lawsuits and depositions was not part of his day-to-day reality. He was an entertainer and now a filmmaker. And he was running late, tied up in day and night postproduction of *Harlem Nights*. All of his movies had always been made on a tight schedule, and the latest picture under his Paramount umbrella deal was supposed to be released in a little over a month.

I sat patiently in my conference room waiting for the star's arrival. Suddenly, without any warning, a streaking figure literally leaped into the room.

With his legs spread open like scissors, this intruder announced his arrival with a loud "Dah-dah!"

It was Eddie Murphy.

Dressed in black pants and an open black silk shirt that exposed his chest hair and a gold necklace, Eddie gave me his patented, ear-to-ear smile. It was certainly the most entertaining start of a deposition in my career. And it was also the best bargain ever since I had been able to command Eddie's presence for two days of deposition for only the $35 that accompanied the subpoena— a real steal when you figure that he earns $35 about every ten seconds when he is making a movie.

After a good laugh at the witness's hijinks, there followed handshakes, and introductions of Eddie, Lon Sobel and Bob Wachs to Suzanne Tragert and another associate, Barry Fiedel. The court reporter, Terri Sauer, administered the oath to Edward Regan Murphy.

"Good afternoon, Mr. Murphy," I began.

"Hello," he said in a surprisingly soft voice. He was polite but wary. And nervous. I quickly realized that he had made his grand entrance not to impress us but to calm himself down.

For the first few minutes, all I could get out of the world's top box office attraction were terse "yes" and "no" answers to my questions that I was certain had been coached by Bob Wachs, who sat paternally at his side. Murphy had given depositions before. He knew the less said under oath the better.

Eddie the conglomerate had a wide array of companies, I discovered during the slow first hour of questioning. Each company represented a different aspect of show business and each was owned only in part by Eddie Murphy. His Eddie Murphy Productions, for example, was only half Eddie Murphy's. Comanagers Mark Lipsky and Bob Wachs each owned 25 percent of the company that produced Murphy's movies.

"At Eddie Murphy Productions, Mark and Bob are vice-presidents of the company," he said.

Wachs shook his head.

"We don't have any titles," he said.

Murphy drilled him with a look. Then he spoke matter-of-factly to me, as if Wachs wasn't in the room.

"They're vice-presidents of the company. I'm president," he said.

Wachs shrugged and laughed nervously.

"I guess we're v.p.s," he said.

"Did you just make him a vice-president?" I asked Eddie, pointing a pen at Wachs.

"Yes," Murphy said imperiously.

"Want a notary? We'll get a notary," I joked.

Richie Tienken had also been a "vice-president" once, but the owner/operator of the Comic Strip, where Eddie got his start, had a falling out with Murphy. It was not an amicable parting, Eddie told me. After Eddie fired him, Tienken threatened suit. They settled out of court, with Murphy never revealing the terms of the settlement.

The rest of the Eddie Murphy Productions staff was living testimonial to Murphy's distrust of strangers and the reason for the nepotism. Several of Eddie's relatives—half brother, uncle, and cousins—had key positions in his production company. But I wasn't as interested in who ran Eddie Murphy Productions as in how much it was worth.

"Eddie Murphy Productions got 14.5 net profit points for *Coming to America*. Does that sound right to you?"

"Yes."

"Do you expect to see any net profits from that?"

"I think we may have seen money, yes."

Wachs shook his head

"Unh-uh."

"No? The company hasn't made any money?" asked Eddie.

"Um-hum," Wachs grunted. Eddie grinned his famous toothy grin.

"I made money."

"Oh yeah?" I asked in mock incredulity.

"I thought it was the company," Murphy explained.

"You got about $16 million. Right?"

"I made some money," he repeated.

"Good. Even if you have to give a lot of it away to charity, there's still some left over. Right?"

He didn't answer. I guess I wasn't funny.

Eddie owned 50 percent of Eddie Murphy Television, Inc. The rest was divided up among Lipsky, Wachs and Eddie's producer pals from his schooldays, Mark McClafferty, Clint Smith and Mark Cory.

"My favorite of all your companies is Panda Bear Enterprises, Inc.," I said. "What's that? . . . Would you mind ending the mystery of where the name came from?"

Eddie gave me a sheepish grin.

"When I was a kid, I wanted to own— This is embarrassing," he said, burying his face beneath his arm. He cleared his throat and continued.

"I thought the Playboy Club was really cool. I thought the Playboy bunny thing was cool. I wanted to own a club called Panda Bear. It was a corny idea that kind of dribbled over when I was nineteen. I still had aspirations of owning a Panda Bear one day. So I called my company that."

When I asked him about any college education, he started to loosen up.

"I did about three weeks at Nassau Community College and—"

"Bob told us about that last week," I interjected.

"And—"

"Was it a good three weeks?"

"Yeah, solid foundation," Eddie laughed.

I had read everything I could find about Eddie. As the deposition progressed, I began to understand something about this movie star. Just beneath the aloof, hard-bitten image he began nurturing after the release of *Beverly Hills Cop*, Eddie Murphy was a minnow who had suddenly found himself in a tankful of Hollywood sharks. With each passing year, he seemed to tell more and more interviewers in the articles that I had read, he trusted fewer and fewer people. It was no wonder that he began surrounding himself with high school chums like Kenneth "Fruitie" Frith and family members and studying the life of Elvis Presley for clues on how to live within the restraints of super-stardom.

Eddie was a member of the Writers Guild but not a disciplined writer. "I have no discipline whatsoever. If I did, I'd be really quick." Instead, Eddie was "an inspirational writer"—when the spirit moved or he had a deadline, he wrote.

"I'm a reader but I hate reading. I can read very well, but I hate doing it," Murphy told me.

"Do you read novels?"

"No. Bizarre novels, like about people's lives. Stuff like that, about Elvis Presley's life."

"You've had a fascination with Elvis for years?"

"Yes," he said.

At one point during the filming of *The Golden Child*, he even consulted a psychic about the solipsistic lifestyle of Elvis. I slapped the top of a stack of Eddie Murphy movie development projects, memos and scripts that Landry had turned up during discovery.

"There's some story idea in this pile of paper here about an Elvis movie. Do you recall that?" I asked.

"That was going to be part of *A Piece of My Mind*," he said.

A Piece of My Mind was the name of Eddie's 1985 comedy concert tour that he had originally planned to turn into a movie. What he envisioned was a traveling movie, like the Beatles' *A Hard Day's Night*. Half of the movie would be stand-up comedy routines and the other half would be scripted vignettes, written by himself and one of the first friends he made upon coming to Hollywood, Keenan Ivory Wayans.

What emerged from that tour instead was *Raw*—the biggest-grossing live concert movie of all time. The only Murphy/Wayans vignette that survived was an opening sequence in which a grade school Eddie Murphy entertains his elders during a Thanksgiving dinner by telling jokes about defecating monkeys. In terms of taste, that was the high point of the movie.

"*Raw* was originally going to be good," Murphy suggested.

"Did you like *Raw*?" I asked.

"No."

"The way it came out?"

"No."

He squirmed in his seat and looked at Wachs for a clue as to what to say next.

"I don't know," he said finally. "I was in a bad frame of mind when I did it."

"What don't you like about it?" I asked.

"I was a little hostile in the movie. . . . I just regret how hostile I—I was. And I regret the suit I had on," he laughed, rolling his eyes. Eddie, I was learning, didn't like to stay serious for too long.

"Now we got to the truth," I said, trying again to loosen up the witness. "He didn't like his wardrobe. You know, with colorization and all this technology, they could probably put a different suit on you."

"No," he said, holding his hands up and shaking his head to show me that I wasn't getting his drift.

"It's like in *Beverly Hills Cop*, there's a scene where my character is walking down the street and these guys walk by in these leather suits and I laugh at them? And I look at *Raw* and I think: I have become those guys I was laughing at!"

For all of his public chutzpah, I was beginning to learn that the private Murphy was enormously self-conscious and self-critical. During his first couple of years in Hollywood he tried his hand at developing his own movies. One of the first he called *America 1990*—the one with the overtly political messages that he conceived in Israel while bored to death shooting *Best Defense*. This didn't seem to me to be a guy who hated political themes in movies—a claim made by Wachs to prove that Eddie was never interested in *King for a Day*.

"All I know, it's about a guy, a Vietnam veteran who couldn't get a job, hooked up with a couple other ones, went and tried to take over the National Guard in different states. . . . It was stupid. I was twenty, twenty-one years old."

Later in his testimony, Eddie read the first paragraph of his treatment for *America 1990*: it "isn't that bad. . . ."

"It isn't bad at all," I reassured him. "It gets a little weird in some places."

"That's the comedy," Eddie wanted me to know.

He had other ideas.

"There was something I was going to do called *Soul, Soul, Soul*. It was to be an experiment in self-indulgence. I was going to take these soul singer characters, build a fictitious background on them and do like—follow their career, very much like the movie *Spinal Tap*. Follow their career from the forties until now, and myself and a friend, Clint Smith, would play the other guy."

But it would have taken a year to put together and Eddie had limited patience. He didn't stop trying to come up with his own movie project, though. One that had persisted to this day in various stages of development was *Satan's Key*.

"I read the book Dante's *Inferno* and kind of adapted Dante's *Inferno* to, like, a movie," he said.

"Do you remember what the sign over the gates of hell in Dante's *Inferno* said?" I asked.

"No."

I glanced at a bored Bob Wachs to see if he was paying attention. He wasn't.

" 'Abandon hope, all ye who enter here,' " I said.

"Yes." Eddie nodded, grinning a knowing grin.

"That's what they have in lawyers' offices," I said. "Somebody would say the courthouse, but . . ."

Eddie grinned, Wachs scowled at me, and I moved on to another Eddie project that never made it to the screen: *The Butterscotch Kid.*

"It's about a show in the fifties," Eddie said, pitching the story the way he would in a production meeting. "Vaudeville was kind of going out of style. Vaudeville shows. This is a vaudeville show and, to get audiences in, the manager of the show raffles off a car every night to get people to come to the show. And what happens is one of the dancers that he used to go out with that worked in another show, rival show, has a kid. She's claiming she's his girlfriend. She wants him to take the kid across the country to the kid's father's house because she's got a show in Paris. And he's like saying, 'I can't do that! I can't take a kid across the country!' And she kind of leaves him in the hotel room and stuck with this kid. Sort of *Paper Moon*-ish."

As he described his project, Eddie came to life, his eyes radiating a magnetism that was irresistible. Thank God I had decided not to videotape his deposition. Television was *his* medium. If Eddie didn't show up at trial, as Landis had speculated, I didn't want the jury to see Eddie on a big screen. Instead, without a video, Paramount would be forced to read Eddie's testimony from the cold transcript—a well-known way of putting juries to sleep.

In reviewing the list of projects that had been suggested for Eddie, I noticed one called *The Kid.*

"That's a remake of a Charlie Chaplin movie," Eddie explained. "Couldn't get the rights. . . . It was an idea that I had."

"And you couldn't get the rights from the family?"

"No one does Charlie Chaplin movies over again."

That's what I thought, too, until the trial of *Buchwald v. Paramount.*

Murphy's version of how he came to author the story for *Coming to America* seemed to me to be as fantastic as the plot of *America 1990,* as fanciful as *The Butterscotch Kid* and as long a time in coming as *Satan's Key.* It was not that it could not have happened the way he told it. It just seemed to me that I was getting only part of the story.

To begin with, Eddie told me, he came up with the idea for *The Quest* while he was on the *Piece of My Mind* tour in 1985—after Paramount abandoned its two-year development of *King for a Day.*

"I wrote the idea down in the back of my cousin Ray Murphy, Jr.'s appointment book," he said.

The book had since disappeared, Eddie confirmed.

Nonetheless, Eddie remembered very clearly the inspiration for *The Quest.*

"What happened was I had just broke up with my girlfriend," he said.

It was a traumatic breakup. Lisa Figueroa, the young Adelphi College medical student who had been with Murphy for two years, had a final falling out with him while the two were together in London. According to those who watched the romance blossom and then sour, Lisa's intoxication with the trappings of fame and fortune got the best of her. One close associate recalled that she freely spent Eddie's money for jewelry and humiliated Murphy's friends by ordering them to hold her furs for her.

By the time they split, she was announcing to the world that she was Eddie Murphy's fiancée. Eddie remained silent about the straw that broke the camel's back. But after he had cut her off, there was no repairing the rift.

For days following the split, Lisa called Eddie's home phone and left plaintive messages on his machine, begging him to take her back. In a touch of cruelty that shocked even Eddie's closest friends, Murphy put Lisa's sobbing pleas on the answering message of his telephone so that anyone who called his private number when he was out heard Lisa crying:

"Please, Eddie! Please! I love you, Eddie! Take me back!"

He left the message on the phone for several months, during which he brooded over his own broken heart and began to think about translating his pain into a movie. He came up with a story about a young African prince who was so rich and powerful that he could never be sure whether a woman truly loved him or his money.

"Kind of like the old cliché thing about, 'Once you get to a certain level of success, it's hard to find somebody to love you just for you,'" he explained to me. "I thought doing a movie about me would be kind of like boring. So you take it and magnify my situation a hundred times, which took me back to Africa and made me a lot richer."

"It was a fairly traumatic breakup for you, wasn't it?" I asked sympathetically.

"Yeah. Yes. To think about it, *Raw* and *The Quest*—*Raw* and *Coming to America* both—the core of both of those things is my breakup with this girl."

Eddie sat back in the chair, lost in thought until he caught me staring at him.

"I just realized how it affected my work," he added by way of explanation.

I asked him how the chief love interest in *Coming to America*, Lisa McDowell played by actress Shari Headley, had come to get her name.

"Anybody in your life that influenced you there?" I asked.

"No one in particular, I guess, but she's based on the ideal of the person that I, you know, was looking for," he said.

When I showed him a copy of the two-page typewritten story that was submitted to the Writers Guild under his by-line in order to secure story credit for *The Quest*, Murphy explained a genesis that went from Lisa Figueroa to the back of the tour bus where he first jotted down the idea in cousin Ray's appointment book to story sessions with his production people months later.

"What happened was maybe six, seven months later, sitting around trying to come up with another movie to do, someone said, 'What about that idea?' I said, 'Yes,' and sat down and wrote this one day," Murphy said, dangling the sheets with his thumb and forefinger.

"Then that went in a drawer for another six, seven months. Then we were sitting around still trying to figure out something to do. Someone said, 'What about those pages you wrote?' I said, 'Yeah,' and we got some writers," Murphy said.

"Good thing you didn't write the Bill of Rights," I said. "You would only be on the Fourth Amendment by now."

Eddie shivered and wrapped his arms around himself, as though he were Prince Akeem sitting on a Brooklyn stoop in the dead of winter.

"It's cold in here."

I smiled in mock malevolence.

"We will turn down the heat."

"No, don't do that," Eddie said with feigned fear, giggling as the questioning became more informal. Eddie was relaxing. That would make my job easier.

Of all his movies, *48 HRS.* was his favorite, Eddie unequivocally told me. It was no accident that it was also his first.

"It's like the first time you paint a picture. You've never been criticized. So you just paint," he said.

From that point on, an actor tries to grow—sometimes with diminishing returns. And an actor tries to do other things. In Eddie's case, an actor tries to do everything.

"*Coming to America* was supposed to be the movie where I wrote and directed and acted and starred and played five guys and all that stuff," he said. "That was the movie I was going to do everything. I had originally planned to do the music on *Coming to America* too and what happened was they said, 'Are you crazy?' "

"So you've done pretty much all the major functions on a motion picture, haven't you?"

"Yeah, I guess so."

"You haven't written the musical score yet, have you?"

"It's coming, though. I just put a recording studio in my house. So that's coming."

Murphy did do some of the writing for *Coming to America*, though ultimately neither Arsenio Hall nor he took credit for their writing efforts. Originally, Keenan Ivory Wayans was supposed to play Eddie's sidekick in the movie. But, when Wayans couldn't do it, the actor/creator of TV's "In Living Color" comedy series suggested that Eddie substitute a mutual friend in the role of Semmi.

"How long have you known Arsenio Hall?"

"Maybe about eight years."

"How did you meet him?"

"We were both misquoted in a newspaper about something I had said about comedians. Then he said something like a rebuttal as to what I had said. They were trying to pit us against each other, which they're always trying to do. And he was a friend of Keenan's, and Keenan said, 'Oh, no. He's not like that at all.' So I met him. He's a really good guy. We had a lot in common, became good friends. We've been close friends for about three years."

During the summer of 1988, Hall joined Murphy in several improvisational sessions that they taped for screenwriters Barry Blaustein and David Sheffield. It was during those cut-up sessions over the course of a week at the Mayflower Hotel and the Gulf & Western Building in Manhattan that the pair created the array of characters that they portrayed in the movie's barbershop scenes. The two screenwriters turned the mishmash of improvised exchanges between Eddie and Arsenio into a story line, but Eddie still felt as though most of the movie's writing belonged to him.

The kind of hollow feeling that Art Buchwald had described to me a year earlier, after he'd first seen *Coming to America*, was similar to Murphy's own feelings when he saw the movie screened for the first time. He picked out the jokes and bits that he knew Arsenio and he had authored, but for which Blaustein and Sheffield had received screen credit.

"You'd sit in the movie theater and see a joke you wrote get this huge laugh and then it says 'screenplay by' these two guys and you're sitting there going, That's my fucking joke! So after that, you felt bad," Murphy remembered.

Yet when I asked him to identify who conceived forty-three different scenes in the movie, Eddie took sole credit for only nine of them. For the majority, he gave credit to Blaustein and Sheffield, including two that were strikingly similar to scenes from Tab Murphy's script—passing off the name of a famous hamburger chain and the use of the mop handle to foil the robbery at McDowell's.

A lot of what Murphy was beginning to tell me sounded like something I had recently read. *Rolling Stone* magazine had just published an extensive Q & A with Paramount's biggest star and most of it came off sounding bitter and petulant. The growing dissatisfaction and sense of betrayal that preceded every breakup—personal and professional—that Eddie Murphy had ever experienced in his young life came across clearly in the interview. It seemed to me that Paramount might soon be facing the same fate as Lisa Figueroa and Eddie's ex-manager Richie Tienken. Eddie felt used and abused.

"I read the *Rolling Stone* interview," I said.

"Oh, Jesus!" he cried out.

"In the course of that interview you told the reporter that you had 'the shittiest deal in town,' or words to that effect. Do you recall that in describing your Paramount deal?"

"Yes," he answered, before I even had the question half out of my mouth. "I've been pretty successful in terms of my movies. I haven't had a movie that has not been successful yet, and there are actors who get paid more than me. So I got a shitty deal," he said. And he wasn't kidding.

Stallone earned more money than Murphy. So did Schwarzenegger and maybe even two or three others: Nicholson, Cruise, possibly Dustin Hoffman. Yet they had all starred in box office clunkers at one time or another and the closest that Eddie had come to starring in a bomb was *The Golden Child,* which pulled in a mere $60 million at the box office and finished eighth among the top-grossing films of 1986.

If Eddie felt self-righteous about the way he was treated by the studio, he believed he had a right to be. Paramount executives used his name to make deals and sell movie ideas he had never heard of, he said.

I told him about Jeff Katzenberg's letter to NBC's Brandon Tartikoff in late 1983.

"That's pretty shitty to say I'm going to star in a movie that I knew nothing about, just to sell it. Yeah, that's pretty shitty," he said, growing angrier by the minute.

"If I wanted to quote you with sort of a cleaner version of what you said, what would you say about that conduct?" I asked.

Eddie thought for a minute, then snapped back with a smile that broke the tension.

"That's pretty crappy?" he said.

Then Eddie got more serious.

"Especially sitting here now, you know, 'cause it makes me look like I'm lying, you know, 'cause I didn't know anything about that."

At one point, the studio planned to team Eddie up with TV child actor Emmanuel Lewis, who starred in the Paramount-produced sitcom "Webster."

"They're both on the lot. They're both black. We can make all this money. That's probably what happened, you know," Murphy explained.

"Elementary, my dear Watson?" I asked.

"It's something studios do," he said.

Almost from the first day Paramount signed the comic to his first five-picture deal, the studio had its agenda for Murphy. The studio's executives listened to Eddie's ideas, but they rarely heard them.

"I've never had an experience where I pitched an idea to the studio and they didn't like it."

"Amazing, isn't it?" I said.

"You know, there's two ways to look at that. I don't think they're being—I don't think they, like, patronize me."

"I was going to ask that."

"Because movies that wound up being—*Beverly Hills Cop II* and *Coming to America,* like, they wind up being successful movies. You can look and say, 'Everything you pitch they like,' but the movies are successful. Maybe they were good ideas. I would like to think more on that."

What really happened was that Paramount cajoled him into doing their projects and Bob Wachs cajoled him into doing his projects, but Eddie's own personal projects were generally shunted aside.

"I've pretty much had to develop my own stuff the last three, four years, and before that, there were scripts that I just like happened upon," he said. "I don't think we've taken a script from A to Z in development. I don't think [Paramount] ever [said], 'Here's an idea for a movie, and we got these writers and we're going to put them on it.' And then it turns into a picture. That's never happened."

Initially, Paramount provided its young star with movies that Richard Pryor either turned down or couldn't make.

"Hand-me-down parts" Eddie called them. He repaid his early debt to Pryor by hiring him to play the part of his gangster foster father in *Harlem Nights.*

"It's pretty good, it's a pretty good [movie], real good for Richard," Eddie assured me.

"Did you see *See No Evil, Hear No Evil?*" I asked.

"Yes. I'm under oath?" Eddie asked, flexing his neck muscles.

"I'll withdraw the question," I volunteered, sparing Eddie from commenting on an earlier performance of his friend whose work he had just told me he admired "a great deal."

"Did you collaborate with anybody on the writing of *Harlem Nights?*" I asked.

"No. We had a problem. When I was trying to work my scam out, I was in production. I had to rewrite a scene. I had to rewrite like two or three scenes and I was producing and I was directing and I was acting and I didn't have time to rewrite a scene. So we called a writer in, like another guy I used to work with on 'Saturday Night Live,' and he did some stuff for me. He worked two or three scenes up for me."

But the "Saturday Night Live" writer didn't get screen credit. Everything on *Harlem Nights,* from production to direction to writing, belonged to Eddie Murphy.

"Do you enjoy the writing of movies?" I asked.

"I don't enjoy any of the work involved with it. That's why I think I have no discipline. I think I enjoy most seeing the movie," he said.

He did like sitting in the director's chair.

"I like—I like—I like being in charge more, but I don't like the responsibility, if that makes any sense," Eddie said.

Murphy had made enough money to last him a lifetime. What he sought in *Harlem Nights* was creative control—the right to make his own movie portraying himself and his friends in exactly the way he wanted to portray them with little or no input from the studio.

"There's this big thing about blacks in Hollywood, that they try to hide their sexuality. A lot of blacks feel [the studios] don't want blacks to be portrayed as sexual on film," he said.

Eddie remembered a love scene he did for *The Golden Child* that the studio brass fought and fought.

"I thought that it was necessary to show a sexual side to the character. I think there was a weirdness about it because the studio felt like it was a PG

movie and wanted to go PG. You know, 'There's not that much cursing. A love
scene might get an R rating.' It was that kind of thing. We ultimately shot
this timid, ridiculous love scene that didn't wind up in the movie, which I
could have told them wouldn't . . . but I think just to cool me off they shot
it."

"It got edited away?" I asked.

"If there was ever, in fact, film in that camera."

The Paramount publicists touted the reunion of Eddie Murphy and John
Landis as a reprise of their huge success *Trading Places*. It would be a big-
budget extravaganza; Eddie would get 15 percent of the gross receipts and
Landis would earn 10 percent of the gross after certain adjustments. It all
sounded so wonderful.

To hear Eddie tell it, however, the story of the filming of *Coming to America* was the nightmarish story of the war between Murphy and Landis—the
War of the Grosses.

Eddie respected John as a professional and gave him his due, but Eddie's
final assessment of the director he first met on the set of *Trading Places* was
highly negative: "he's just a real bad guy."

What Eddie described as "an ego clash" on the set of *Coming to America*
had little to do with proving my case against Paramount but a lot to do with
why the movie was so disappointing.

"There's a scene with Don Ameche and Ralph Bellamy doing a throwback
to *Trading Places*," Murphy recalled, during the shooting on *Coming to America*.

"The bums on the street?" I asked.

Eddie nodded.

"It was all Landis' idea, all Landis' idea. I thought that was a great idea. I
really wish it wasn't *his* idea. Wish I had come up with that one, 'cause I
thought it was a great idea."

"Think about it," I mischievously suggested as Bob Wachs swallowed hard.
"Maybe you did come up with it."

"No, it was Landis."

The trouble between Murphy and Landis started even before a script was
prepared. It was all tied to the *Twilight Zone* manslaughter trial, as Landis had
implied obliquely during his own deposition three months earlier.

"What happened was he wanted a lot of people in the show business
community to come down and sit down in court and show like public support," Murphy said.

"Solidarity?" I suggested.

"Like, 'We're in this business. We don't feel he did anything wrong.' And
that kind of thing."

Eddie had a movie coming out at the time of the trial and didn't want his
presence in the courtroom damaging his picture at the box office. But, more

than that, he said, was the feeling that Landis might not be innocent of manslaughter.

"It was like I was caught between a rock and a hard place. I considered John a friend, but I didn't—I didn't go. I didn't feel like he was innocent. I was like, you know, You were directing the movie. That was my personal thing. I would never say that to him. That's what my feelings were. So I was like, Hey, if you get acquitted, I'm happy for you. But I'm not coming down and sitting down, you know, 'cause some kids died. That was the way I felt.

"He always resented the fact—I didn't know this. He had resented the fact that I didn't come down and sit with him in the courtroom, and when I got in touch with John to do the movie, he brought it up. And he said, 'I didn't talk to you. Where were you at? They almost sent me to jail.' I was thinking: You weren't going to go to jail. And he said, 'They almost sent me to jail.'"

This rocky start should have been a signal of trouble ahead, Murphy said. He remembered a story Landis loved to tell about his direction of Michael Jackson's "Thriller" video. It, too, foreshadowed trouble.

"His favorite story to me is how he tells Michael Jackson 'Fuck you.' You know: 'No one else will tell Michael "Fuck you" but I'll tell him "Fuck you."'"

"So he says, 'Everybody is afraid of you, Eddie, but I'll tell you "Fuck you."' He's one of those guys trying to tell you, you know, 'Eddie, I'm the director. You work for me.'"

"Kind of macho?" I asked.

"A power freak. And I had little problems with his wife 'cause his wife was kind of like a prima donna."

Five years had passed since their successful collaboration on *Trading Places*. But Eddie was not a star then. Landis was. Ironically, their professional fortunes had reversed in a mild replay of the *Trading Places* plot.

As *Coming to America* got under way in the winter of 1988, John Landis was treating Eddie as if it were 1983.

"John approached the project like . . . I was still the twenty-two-year-old that he worked with in *Trading Places* and he was still this hot-shot director, you know, rather than this guy who just went through this big trial and had like four flop movies in a row," Murphy stated, his eyes betraying his rising anger. Paramount didn't want to pay John his $2 million fee and 10 percent of the adjusted gross, but Eddie wanted him to direct.

"I was like, You got to pay him. I was in this guy's corner after all this stuff."

Landis repaid Eddie's loyalty with contempt.

In front of the cast and crew during the early shooting, Landis told his assistants not to be afraid to order Eddie around.

"So I went and I grabbed him from behind and I said to one of my guys, 'What happens to a guy who's not afraid of me?'" remembered Murphy. "Fruitie says, 'They get fucked up.' We were kind of playing.

"John reached down and tried to grab my private parts, and I cut his wind off and he realized I was serious. He started crying and said, 'Eddie,' and ran out of the room."

Later the same day, Landis visited Murphy in his trailer.

"I thought he was going to talk about the picture and he went on and on about 'You didn't come down to my trial and the only reason I did this movie is because I knew I would get paid a lot of money for it. I have no respect for you as an actor and you fucked me over as a friend.'

"And he just went into this big, long thing about how he had no respect for me and didn't feel I'm talented, how he doesn't like me. This was like in the middle of production! This was like out of nowhere! What it boiled down to: he had harbored all this stuff, 'cause I didn't come down for his trial."

Once again, Eddie Murphy felt betrayed by someone he had considered a true friend. And once again, his cynicism hardened.

"This guy has sat at my table and smiled in my face and been trying to play my buddy," Eddie said. "And all this time he's been like, 'I don't like this guy. I'm just doing this 'cause I have to do it.' You know?"

The day Shari Headley and Allison Dean were cast as the sisters Lisa and Patrice McDowell was the day that Eddie finally broke off any remaining cordiality with Landis.

"The day they got the parts in the picture, I wanted to take them out to dinner. You know, 'Let's all go out.' I didn't know either of the actresses, so I said, 'Let's all go out to dinner.'

"But John caught up to the girl in the hallway and was telling her, 'Don't go out with him. He's going to fuck you if you go out with him and it will fuck the movie up. Stay away from him. He's going to fuck you if you go out with him.'

"And I walked up at the time and heard John say, 'Eddie's going to fuck you if you go out with him.' And I was like: What the fuck are you doing?"

The cold war turned hot. Eddie resorted to sending spies to Landis's staff meetings to find out what the director was saying about him behind his back.

"I remember once the subject of Paula Abdul's background came up. The choreographer goes, 'Paula Abdul, what is she?' And John said, 'Oh, she's a nigger,' " Eddie testified. At least, that's what his spies told him Landis had said.

Eddie remembered the day Mike Tyson came to the set, but he remembered it as far more tense and telling of Landis's hypocrisy than others did.

"Mike came by and . . . he wanted to take a picture with the director 'cause he knew him from some movie, I guess," Eddie began.

"Probably *Animal House*," I offered.

"John had this look on his face. And I was like—"

Eddie paused to shake his head in disgust and disbelief.

"I said, 'Look at that. Look at that "I-have-to-stand-by-this-nigger" look on his face.' And he said, 'That's what I do for a living.' That kind of shit. That kind of stuff."

From Eddie's point of view, Landis was a screamer. He insulted and insinuated as the weeks of production rolled forward. And it was all in the family, according to Eddie. He remembered being half an hour late for a still photo session with Lord Snowden once, and Landis's wife, Deborah Nadoolman, dressed him down in front of the former husband of Princess Margaret.

Nadoolman, head costumer for *Coming to America,* ranted and raved with as much venom as her husband, Murphy complained.

" 'What does he think he is, a real prince?' " Eddie shrieked in a parody of Nadoolman's pique.

The last confrontation between director and star took place in California, when the final scenes in the Zamundan rain forest were being filmed. Eddie complained that Landis was spending too much time, film and effort on an unfunny scene.

"They were getting on my nerves and I made a suggestion as to something I thought would be funny," said Eddie. "And Landis goes, 'That wouldn't be funny.' And I told him, it would be funny and he goes, 'It wouldn't be funny.'

"So I said, 'John, I mean, say you don't want to shoot it. Don't say it won't be funny. I know when something is funny. That's what I do for a living.' And he said, 'Well, I have final cut.' "

A miffed Eddie excused himself and returned to his trailer. When an assistant director came to the trailer with orders from Landis to return to the set, Murphy ordered his lieutenants to fire Landis's underling. In an escalating show of directorial force, Landis said he would quit if the assistant director remained fired.

"And that's the last confrontation," said Eddie. "The first assistant director later came and apologized. It was an unpleasant time."

Murphy seemed oddly concerned that Landis might know about the back-biting that Murphy had given him, both in his *Rolling Stone* interview and on his friend Arsenio Hall's late night talk show. Though Eddie was not nearly so specific or vitriolic on TV or in the magazine about his feud with Landis as he had been during the deposition, he seemed genuinely distressed that Landis might get wind of his public diatribes against him.

"Did you depose him? Did he say he heard it?" Eddie wanted to know. "It's the kind of thing you wouldn't want somebody you didn't like to hear."

I waited until Eddie was real loose before I started cherry-picking what I needed for trial about what he knew about *King for a Day.* My approach here was low key: a little bit of testimony here, a little there, all of it adding up to the mosaic that I wanted to piece together for the jury.

When Eddie was talking about writing down ideas and script material for *The Quest,* he told me that he had been unable to find his original notes. But he didn't have to consult them. "I have a pretty good memory with stuff I've written, pretty good memory with stuff I've seen, really good memory."

"In fact, people have said you have almost like a photographic memory," I suggested.

"Almost. Like if I like something, like if I go to a movie and I see a movie and I really like it, I can like come back—"

"Or read something that you like?" I interrupted.

"Yeah."

"That's a gift, isn't it?"

"I guess so, yeah. . . . I'm terrible at math. I can remember everything except six times nine."

Eddie was very close to Katzenberg. He admired him as "a smart studio executive, and he's been pretty honest with me. Plays tennis well."

"Do you play tennis well?" I asked.

"No. Jeff's pretty good though. We play tennis and stuff and talk show business. He's a good guy. He's the only studio executive that I've become like friends with."

"Would you like to work with him someday?"

"Yeah, I guess so."

"I want you to think carefully about the answer to this next question because Mr. Buchwald is going to read this. He asked me to ask this question. Had you ever heard of Art Buchwald before this lawsuit?"

Eddie didn't hesitate in answering:

"Yeah. He is a—like a political satirist."

"Right. He writes a newspaper column—"

"Yeah."

"—that comes out in about five, six hundred newspapers around the country. You have read him?"

"Yeah. I've seen his stuff sometimes."

". . . You like his work?"

"Some of it, yeah."

Eddie was adamant that he "never read *King for a Day*"—either the treatment or any scripts—and he never heard of Tab Murphy or Francis Veber or a part being written for Emmanuel Lewis in *King for a Day*. And he knew nothing about the progress of script development or Paramount touting *King for a Day* as an excellent candidate for a summer 1985 release. But he readily acknowledged someone at Paramount in 1982 or 1983 told him about *King for a Day* on one occasion. While Eddie did not remember the Ma Maison setting or who told him, he recalled correctly the gist of what he was told.

" 'It's a story about a guy this, that'—"

"Do you remember what they said about the story?"

"I just know it was about some African guy."

"Did they tell you about an African guy that comes to America?"

"I don't remember. All I remember is about an African guy who—loses power in Africa. That's what I remember."

"And ends up in the streets?" I asked.

"Of Washington," Eddie answered.

"Right. In the ghetto?"

"Yeah."

"You remember them telling you that?" I pressed.

"Yes."

Eddie also admitted what Wachs had denied: Paramount was developing

King for a Day specifically for him. But he did not recall talking with Kirkpatrick four times about the project. Yet he had "a very vague recollection, maybe, of Jeff going into this *King for a Day* thing. 'You'd be great in it.' . . . He liked the idea of it, I guess, 'cause I remember."

I was feeling mighty relieved as Eddie calmly searched his recollection. Katzenberg may not have recalled, but Eddie did. And that's what counted most.

I handed Art's treatment to Eddie. "It's interesting," he said after reading it. A few minutes later, when I asked him what he thought was the basis for Katzenberg telling Landis that Eddie was familiar with and liked *King for a Day*, Eddie replied:

"Most it could have been was Jeff telling me the idea and me saying it sounds like a good idea."

"You're not denying you may have responded positively to it to Mr. Katzenberg?" I asked, my tone firmer for that one question than any other for the two days of the deposition.

"May have. It reads like a good idea."

I wanted no ambiguity about this critical testimony. Sometimes you are willing to accept an ambiguous answer, thinking that it is too risky to follow up for clarification and that you will argue your interpretation of the answer to the jury at trial. But my judgment call was to probe the outer limits of Eddie's recollection and court disaster.

"That you were familiar with the idea is a factually correct statement—familiar with the idea for *King for a Day*?" I asked.

"I'm saying—I'm saying that Jeff may have said to me, 'I got this idea about this African king who loses all his money in New York, blah, blah, or in D.C.' And I say, 'Hey, that's a good idea. Let me see a script. Sounds like a good idea.' That may have happened."

". . . From which he could infer you liked it?"

"Yeah, I guess so."

". . . That would be an accurate statement at the time, that you were familiar with the idea and you liked it?"

"Yeah. I thought it was a good idea. . . . I think the idea of a twin brother who was born a couple of minutes later and is mad—mad because he was out of it two minutes early was very funny."

That testimony—"I thought it was a good idea"—scored a 15 on a scale of 10. Most trial lawyers would have gotten out while the getting was good. But something told me there was another nugget to mine, deeper in the recesses of this remarkable young man's psyche. So I decided to ask a question that, before the deposition began, I had been sure Eddie would duck. But that was no longer my instinct as I went for an answer that could appreciably improve our odds of winning the case.

"Do you know whether anything you learned about *King for a Day* before you did *The Quest* may have subconsciously influenced your thinking about *The Quest*?"

"Was my subconscious triggered by something I heard from *King for a Day?*"

"Possible, yes," I said. "Do you know for a fact whether it was or not?"

"I don't know what triggers my subconscious."

"That's my point," I observed. "Okay. So you really can't tell, can you?"

"No."

I knew that I had scored big points on this line of questioning, and so did Eddie. Wachs looked pale.

The second day of the deposition, Eddie, noticeably fatigued from marathon editing and mixing sessions for *Harlem Nights*, lapsed back into a more subdued pose. His answers were, again for a while, more simple yeses and noes. It was obvious to me that, following our first session, Wachs had coached his client not to be so forthcoming.

For me, the second day was devoted to cleanup. I was still high from the gold that I had extracted the first day. One of the things that I wanted Eddie to do was to elaborate in his own words whether he knew anything more about Paramount's two-year development of Buchwald's story for him.

"I must admit, Mr. Murphy, that first of all I think you're telling the truth. Okay. I want to make that perfectly clear. But it's hard for me to understand. There's page after page of documents here—and I won't waste your time showing you; you'll have to accept my representation—where Paramount's saying, 'This is a great one for Eddie. This is one of the top two. This is going to be next summer's release.' Yet you're testifying you were totally in the dark about this?" I asked.

"Yeah," said Eddie.

"And that much of what I've been telling you is somewhat of an eye opener?"

Eddie nodded. I sighed.

"A lot of shareholder money has been used to write all these scripts that you say you knew nothing about," I said.

But a lot of shareholder money had been spent developing other dead-end projects that Eddie did know about. One of them was based on a whim from Eddie's video youth, when he wanted to transubstantiate from planet to planet just like Captain Kirk, Mr. Spock and Dr. Scott.

"I think they started writing something that I didn't like and they changed back to—to the whales and the girl in the aquarium or something," Eddie said, recalling the development of the script for the fourth film in the *Star Trek* series.

"What happened was, see, I had always wanted to be—I'm a Trekkie and I wanted to be in *Star Trek*. I wanted to beam up, all that stuff with the phaser. So I said I wanted to do a *Star Trek*. The producers of the movie thought, 'Great. We'll bring them down to Eddie's environment. Take, like *Star Trek* into like this jive environment.' That's not what I wanted so it was, like the Trekkies dealing with this guy on earth and it was, like, 'No, no, no! I want to go to space! I want to get beamed up!' I wanted to be in space with the guys. And it never happened."

"Lost opportunity?" I said.

"There will be other *Star Treks*," said Eddie.

This episode reminded me once again that I was questioning a man/child whose stage discipline might be impeccable, but whose self-restraint in other areas of his life was questionable. He never had to think about the bottom line and yet he had disdain bordering on contempt for those who did—the "Suits" at Paramount, as he was fond of calling them.

At twenty-seven, Eddie Murphy was still a kid. There was more than a little irony in the fact that he was about to become a proud father. Toward the end of the deposition, I planted a seed in Eddie's mind when I learned he would soon be a father. In the guise of asking innocuous questions about his schedule, I told him that he didn't have to show up at trial.

"The trial for this case is set for December 11. It may or may not go then, but do you expect to be in California at that period of time?"

"No, I'll be in New York. . . . The trial isn't in California, is it?"

"Yeah, here in Los Angeles," I informed him. "Well, we have your deposition. That's why I took it. I didn't know whether you'd be here or not. You see, the deposition has a twofold purpose: one is to find out what people know. The second is if somebody is not available, beyond the subpoena power, because you live in New Jersey, then at least I can read portions of it to the jury."

Eddie was relieved.

"Okay. Great. 'Cause in December I got a kid coming and I have my first Christmas with my baby in December."

"Congratulations," I offered.

"Yeah. I'm happy about that."

"When's the baby due?"

"November 23."

"Terrific."

"I hope it's a girl." Eddie beamed.

We were getting close to wrapping up. Eddie Murphy was everything and nothing at all like what I had expected. If he seemed hard or arrogant or mean-spirited to outsiders, it was because they were just that: outsiders.

Here was a young man whose first real romance had left him so scarred that he distrusted even the woman who was bearing him his first child. Within another two years, he would father a second child by another woman and again refuse to marry, despite his pledge to support both mother and child.

Eddie had felt similarly betrayed by former friends and business associates who had tried to turn the Eddie Murphy phenomenon to their own ends. When he was still fresh to fame during his first season on "Saturday Night Live," the show's chief writer Herb Sargent arranged to have Harry Belafonte pay Murphy a visit. The legendary singer/actor had also achieved stardom at a tender age, his calypso music of the 1950s peaking the same year that John F.

Kennedy was elected President. Belafonte advised Eddie to beware of syco-phants and to keep his own counsel, according to Sargent. Old friends were often the best friends. It was advice that Eddie apparently took to heart.

I paused to nail down something Eddie had mentioned in passing earlier in the first day of his deposition. He told me that, at the Ma Maison dinner, Paramount gave him retroactively a few net profit points in *48 HRS.*—"mon-key points, they call them."

"By the way, you called net profit participation points yesterday 'monkey points.' What's the origin of that, do you know?" I asked Eddie as I started to pick up my papers.

"Well, it's, like, stupid points."

"Like, you're stupid to take them?"

"Stupid to take the points."

"Won't be any net profits?"

"You sit there with your points going, 'Eeeh, eeh, eeh, eeh, eeh.' "

"Did you get that down, Terri? Imitating a monkey . . . would that be fair to say what you were just doing?"

Eddie sat forward, giving me an impish look.

"Yes."

After months of reading some of the most god-awful scripts and story ideas in Paramount's files, I was convinced that there was a lost opportunity for a truly great comedy if Buchwald and Eddie Murphy could ever have combined their enormous talents. And that's what I told Murphy.

"Maybe we can get you and Buchwald together someday," I said. "But we won't take any monkey points. I learned something from you today. . . . I wish you luck in your career."

18

Rocking the Boat

I DIDN'T HAVE LONG to savor the sweet success of Eddie Murphy's deposition. My trial team was waiting in my office to discuss urgent business. It was less than two months to trial, and we had our hands full.

The most pressing matter was Paramount's pending motion for summary judgment. The showdown was scheduled for hearing in about two weeks, and we had only a few days to file our final papers in opposition. It was do-or-die time for us. If Paramount prevailed, we would be out of court, our only option being to pursue an uncertain appeal that could take a year or more to resolve. And even if we staved off dismissal, Judge Schneider could still make rulings on the relevant legal standards that could place insuperable barriers in the way of proving our case.

"How are we looking, Marsha?" I asked as we started the meeting.

We had held regular team meetings throughout the case. There we brainstormed, formulated strategy and worked out assignments and scheduling. On all my cases, every team member is kept informed of all developments by receiving copies of all pleadings, correspondence and exhibits and participates actively in the team meetings. That way they can substitute for one another and contribute meaningfully to our collective decision making.

"We're in pretty good shape," Marsha answered. "As you know, while you've been hammering away at Wachs and Murphy, Zazi, Suzanne and I have been focusing on drafting the pleadings and taking the depositions that the court gave us the extra time to take. And Dennis has been killing himself completing the trial exhibit list and getting the depositions ready to file with the court. It's a tight schedule."

"Did we get anything out of the depositions?" I asked.

"You bet," Zazi answered. "Alexandra Denman, the former Paramount in-house lawyer who drafted the Buchwald agreement, totally supports our theory that, once Paramount's option lapsed, the studio could not use Art's treatment without making a new deal with him."

In moving for summary judgment, Paramount had made one argument that was breathtakingly audacious: They could use Art's material even after their option lapsed.

This position defied common sense—why would any creator give an original idea to a studio if the studio could wait until a day after the option lapsed and then use it without compensating or crediting the creator? It also ran squarely counter to industry custom and practice—Roger Davis and David Rintels were infuriated by Paramount's outrageous attempt to obtain a judicial seal of approval of literary theft. And, as we pointed out in our opposing memorandum, it was not what the contract said: Alexandra Denman testified in late September that, once Paramount's option lapsed on May 1, 1985, all rights in the story reverted to Buchwald. She also admitted that the Tab Murphy and Veber scripts, while legally owned by Paramount, were "sterile" without the underlying story rights on which they were based. In her deposition, Denman's former boss at Paramount, Helene Hahn, also refuted Paramount's cynical interpretation of the boilerplate language in the studio's standard form of agreement.

"What about Paramount's federal preemption argument?" I asked.

"We have that one slam dunked," the gung-ho rookie, Suzanne Tragert, confidently asserted.

"I hope you're right, my friend," I said, "since that assumption has been a cornerstone of our strategy from day one."

Paramount had paired its expired option argument with a radical constitutional law argument. The studio contended that our state court breach-of-contract action was legally barred because federal copyright law was supreme and preempted the right of states like California to allow plaintiffs like Buchwald to enforce private contracts with studios for payment of money for use of ideas that would otherwise not be copyrightable because of their alleged lack of novelty. We thought that Congress, in enacting the comprehensive copyright reform laws of 1976, had not intended to preempt state law and that a state contract enforcement suit and a federal copyright suit were readily distinguishable: the former had one element missing in the latter—the defendant's voluntary promise to pay for an idea (even if it is not copyrightable) that induces the plaintiff to disclose his never-before-published idea.

"How does it look on fiduciary duty?" I wanted to know.

"Pierce, we have the better argument on the law because the parties had unequal bargaining positions and the law presumes a confidential relationship when Art gives them his treatment," Marsha told me. "But I'm worried about whether we can prove a breach of fiduciary duty if all that Paramount did was breach Art's contract and not engage in stonewalling and cover-up tactics. We still don't have a smoking gun, and discovery will be cut off in another three weeks."

"Have we found Richie Tienkin yet?" I asked.

"No," Zazi answered. "I immediately followed up on your instruction to increase our efforts to find him. Our New York office hired a good private investigator, and we think we know where he lives in New Jersey. But the stakeouts of his home and the Comic Strip in Manhattan have yielded nothing. No one knows where he is. It's almost as if he's dropped off the face of the earth. It's spooky."

"Keep trying for another two weeks," I instructed Zazi. "I smell a rat here. Richie gets a big severance settlement with Eddie—probably in seven figures. It's all hush-hush. And then he disappears. Puff!"

"I have to admit that Zazi, Suzanne and I might have been wrong about something," Marsha volunteered.

Referring to a decision that I had made a month earlier, she said, "Paramount has filed a weak opposition to our cross-motion for summary adjudication. I think we have a chance."

After Paramount filed its motion for summary judgment, I had concluded that it was likely we would defeat the studio's bid to deprive us of a trial. All I had to do was show that some material facts were disputed, and that could be done on the issue of similarity between Art's treatment and the movie alone.

I devised a plan that was deceptively simple: try to knock out all of Paramount's defenses about how the contract should be interpreted and get the judge to agree with our interpretation, thereby leaving for trial only the factual issue of whether *Coming to America* was in fact based upon Buchwald's treatment. In particular, I wanted the Court to rule that Paramount's use of Buchwald's material more than two years after the expiration of the option constituted a late exercise of the option contract that Buchwald could waive and then claim a breach for not paying him.

A victory on our cross-motion would be a major blow to Paramount and force it to settle with us, I argued in our fierce internal debates. My colleagues, in turn, thought my strategy was too risky since the judge might disagree with our interpretation and leave us mortally wounded as we went into trial. I reasoned it was better to know now, and not as the trial was ending, what Judge Schneider was thinking about such critical issues. After seriously considering my cocounsels' opinions, I stuck with my decision.

Judge Schneider had a typically full calendar set for 8:30 A.M. on October 30, 1989. He went through routine items like a hot knife through butter. At 8:53 A.M. our matter was called.

"No. 13, *Buchwald*," Judge Schneider announced to a nearly empty courtroom. He had put our matter toward the end of his calendar.

"Let me tell you how I stand," the judge began after Tony Liebig and I entered our appearances. "As both of you know, in ruling on a motion for summary judgment, I'm going to address the defendant's motion first. Since the defendant went for the whole ball of wax, a motion for summary judgment, all I'm required to do is find an issue of fact and the motion for summary judgment must be denied. There are issues of fact with respect to a number of issues."

I breathed easier at counsel table as I looked back at my three beaming colleagues in the first spectator row. Each one had her right thumb up in the air. We were going to trial.

In opposing Paramount's attempts to throw out our breach-of-fiduciary-duty claim, we had argued in our papers that powerful studios like Paramount prepare standard form—boilerplate—contracts for optioning properties like Art's treatment, but they do not negotiate the terms. This issue had caught Judge Schneider's attention. Little did I suspect then how significant his interest in this subject would later become.

Nor was Judge Schneider persuaded by Paramount's preemption argument that Liebig had confidently claimed at a hearing two months earlier would totally dispose of the case. As good as I was feeling about staving off Paramount's attack, however, my stomach was in knots waiting for the ruling on my motion. I didn't have to wait a moment longer.

"With respect to plaintiffs' motion for summary adjudication concerning three issues . . . my inclination is to grant all three of the motions for summary adjudication."

I shut my eyes and slowly nodded my head in agreement as the judge elaborated on his reasoning. In essence, he accepted my interpretation of Art's and Alain's contracts. First, he ruled, "the argument that the option had lapsed is defeated by the cases that indicate that the person who gave the option can waive a defect in the exercise of the option." Judge Schneider agreed with us that Buchwald could treat the use of his treatment in making *Coming to America* as an implied exercise of the option and waive the tardiness of the exercise.

Second, Paramount was required to pay Buchwald if it made a movie based upon his treatment. "That's what the contract says on its face. I don't quite understand the argument to the contrary."

Finally, as for Alain's contract, it was clear to Judge Schneider that Paramount "was obligated to pay Bernheim under the terms of the contract if Paramount produced the movie" based on Buchwald's treatment.

It was a total wipeout of all of Paramount's technical defenses, leaving for trial only the issue whether *Coming to America* was in fact based upon *King for a Day*—an issue that the judge several times stressed "I am specifically not deciding." Liebig was furious. Kulzick and he had bet the ranch on getting our case thrown out of court, and now they were being forced to go to trial.

My team and I retired to the public cafeteria on the top floor of the courthouse to celebrate and do an immediate post-mortem about the implications of our victory. As I made my way to the coffee urn, I ran into my predecessor, Howard King. He was thrilled to hear our good news. And, he speculated, this devastating setback would finally get Paramount to focus on the case and negotiate a reasonable settlement.

Howard was half right. Our clean sweep of the motions did get Paramount's attention, but it didn't drive them to the bargaining table.

Instead, they fired their lawyers.

Following their failure to get the case tossed out of court, Liebig & Kulzick were quietly replaced by the blue-chip Los Angeles firm of O'Melveny & Myers. Technically, it was only an "association of cocounsel," but Tony Liebig and Ken Kulzick never appeared again in any proceeding. By mid-November the only Liebig & Kulzick lawyer left on the case was genial Loyola Law School professor Lon Sobel, an expert on intellectual property who had some familiarity with the record but not a lot of trial experience. Changing trial lawyers a month before trial is a serious vote of no confidence in the incumbents—and a monumental undertaking for the successors.

I learned of the replacement as Zazi and I waited outside Judge Schneider's courtroom for our November 16 conference with the judge to discuss the status of the case three weeks before trial. Lon Sobel was coming down the hall with a lawyer whom I knew from another civil case in which we were representing codefendants in a securities fraud suit. It was Robert Draper, a bearded O'Melveny litigation partner who resembled David Niven in a goatee. I immediately guessed what was happening: Paramount was bringing in its main outside lawyers—and one of the nation's oldest and most respected law firms—to defend my "frivolous" case.

"Bob, how nice to see you," I said to Draper as we shook hands. "What brings you to the courthouse? I thought you big-firm lawyers tried to stay out of court."

"I looked at my calendar and realized that I had nothing else to do on December 11," the thin, dark-haired and bearded Draper retorted. "Anyway, as you say, I need the experience, and I'm sure that I can learn something from you, Pierce."

We had a good laugh and went into Judge Schneider's chambers.

Bob Draper had a reputation as a bright, tough and tenacious advocate. One of my partners had tangled with him for several years in a hard-fought case. When I asked about Draper, I was told to beware of "the honey badger." This cryptic reference was to a small African badgerlike carnivore that is fond of honey and neutralizes much larger animals by biting off their testicles. The mere sight of a honey badger sends elephants and lions scurrying.

"Your honor, I think we are looking at a trial that should last only a couple of days," Draper informed the judge and me. "There are really only two pieces of evidence that the jury has to consider—Buchwald's two-page treatment and the movie."

Draper made a little ceremony of taking each out of his briefcase and offering them to the judge.

"I don't know why we need expert witnesses to decide whether the one is based on the other," continued Draper as he tried to dominate the discussion. "Just read the treatment and watch the videocassette. An opening statement, a closing argument and a few jury instructions. That's it. I can't imagine how the trial could possibly take the two weeks estimated by Mr. O'Donnell, unless the Court is going to let him put on all ten of the expert witnesses that he has designated."

"That's a good point," Judge Schneider agreed. "There's no way, Mr. O'Donnell, that I'm going to allow you to parade all those expert witnesses before the jury. I know what you are trying to do, but you can do it with a lot fewer experts."

"How about six?" I asked.

"How about two?" Judge Schneider replied.

"How about a compromise, four?" I suggested.

"Okay, but let me tell you something else that I've been thinking about. I'm not sure that I'm going to allow any experts for either side to testify about the ultimate issue of whether the movie is 'based upon' the treatment—whatever 'based upon' may mean. It strikes me that such testimony would usurp the jury's function here. I haven't done a lot of research on the issue."

"Your honor, this is an important issue," I told him. "I have predicated my trial strategy on the assumption that I could put on experts to help the jury through the esoteric world of motion picture development. And we are about to begin depositions of expert witnesses in the next week or so. I need to know where we stand on this critical issue."

"I agree, your honor," Draper added.

"All right," Judge Schneider concurred. "Let's brief the issue and I'll get you a ruling quickly."

"Your honor, there is one other issue that needs your attention sooner than later," Draper said. "This will be a jury trial, and my client is concerned about publicity before and during trial that could influence the jurors. I think we need a gag order that would prohibit counsel and their clients from discussing the case with the media."

"I'm not big on sweeping gag orders, particularly in civil cases," Judge Schneider said, "but if you two can stipulate to something, I will not oppose it."

This was a tough call for me. On the one hand, I did not intend to try my case in the media. I wanted to persuade nine out of twelve jurors that Paramount breached my clients' contracts and then maliciously denied their contract rights. Yet I knew that the threat of the public spotlight on Paramount's practices could be a powerful incentive to settle the case. So far, I had refrained from talking to the press after the initial flurry of coverage when we filed suit, and I had not yet done anything to stimulate articles or television reporting. But if Paramount did not settle, I did not want the studio's misconduct to be largely ignored, especially since Art had sued to expose Paramount's misappropriation of his story and to deter such rip-offs in the future.

I made a snap judgment.

"Your honor, I don't have any problem with a carefully drawn order that deals only with comments by counsel and the parties on the trial while it is in progress and during the days leading up to trial. That is what the code of professional responsibility requires of us, and that is fine. However, my clients will not agree to any order that will limit media coverage of the trial."

"I'm glad that you mentioned that. I have received requests from television stations and networks to televise the trial. I have looked at the guidelines and concluded that I will allow a single pool camera to tape the proceedings and then feed the material to everyone else. I expect counsel to behave like professionals and not be influenced by the presence of the camera."

I went straight from the courthouse to Los Angeles International Airport and Ireland, my ancestral homeland that I had visited a half dozen times in the prior ten years. For the next six days I would walk along the wind-swept sea cliffs and country back roads of picturesque Ballybunion, County Kerry, in remote southwest Ireland. Each afternoon I would accompany my dear friend and former law partner, Michael Flaherty, as he golfed on the legendary Ballybunion course. At night I would make small talk at one of the twenty-five pubs in this coastal town of only a few thousand people or play cards with Mike's local cronies.

As the most important trial of my career drew near, I needed some space, some precious time alone—free of phones, faxes and Fed Ex—to gather my thoughts about how I was going to present my case. Discovery was concluded, I had taken the key depositions and read the others, and I had virtually memorized all the exhibits from using them so often in the depositions. It was now time to reflect, and the place for that was almost halfway around the world.

Every morning at Mike's home overlooking the Atlantic, I would be up before sunrise, outlining on a legal pad my ideas for opening statement, closing argument and structure of my case. A trial lawyer's craft demands mastery of all the elements essential for a successful motion picture—writing, directing, producing and acting. As I blocked out cross-examinations, made "To Do" lists, and bounced ideas off my quick, tough-minded host, I was putting the final touches on my shooting script for *Buchwald v. Paramount*, scheduled to open in less than three weeks.

Rested and ready for trial, I returned to Los Angeles to celebrate Thanksgiving with Connie, Meghan and Brendan. Across town, Robert Draper had a drumstick in one hand and Art Buchwald's deposition in another. He was playing catch-up and, as I would soon discover, the honey badger was playing for keeps.

·   ·   ·   ·

In late 1989, the Los Angeles branch of Kaye, Scholer, Fierman, Hays & Handler occupied two floors of the Fox Plaza Building in Century City. It is a famous address because it houses the offices of former President Ronald Reagan and billionaire oilman Marvin Davis—and it is the high-rise that served as the target of movie bad guy Alan Rickman and his gang of terrorists in the Bruce Willis action-fantasy film *Die Hard*. The same summer that *Coming to America* was raking in $128 million at the domestic box office for Paramount, *Die Hard* took in a tidy $80 million for Twentieth Century Fox, our next-door neighbor in Century City.

Up on the twenty-first floor, my conference room occupied the southwest corner. From there, I could see Santa Catalina Island, the Palos Verdes Peninsula and the Santa Monica Mountains on a clear day. From my office, I looked down on the headquarters of Twentieth Century Fox. Fortunately, I had no view of the Hollywood sign. I was beginning to think of "Hollywood" as a dirty, expensive word.

It was November 30, 1989, and a year had passed since I filed Art and Alain's $5 million lawsuit against Paramount. Trial was eleven days away. In addition to the depositions of Landis, Tanen, Katzenberg, Kirkpatrick, Wachs and Murphy, we had deposed another twenty witnesses, including Arsenio Hall, Ricardo Mestres, and Bruce Berman. The trial team and I were busy subpoenaing two dozen witnesses, finishing our trial brief, jury instructions and final pretrial motions and attending to the myriad of tasks that must be accomplished in the last, feverish days before a trial. I was more than ever convinced that Eddie Murphy had used Buchwald's story as the basis for *Coming to America* and that the studio had connived to cover up for its biggest star. Whether we could prove that to a jury was something else.

The studio wouldn't budge from its position. We settled on their terms or not at all, and their terms were still only $100,000—take it or leave it. My firm had already invested nearly eight times that amount in pretrial preparation, and we would rack up another several hundred thousand dollars of time before the trial was over. A settlement of $100,000 would barely cover my clients' costs for depositions, photocopying, travel and the other expenses that are part of the burden of litigation. The prospects for settlement were dim.

Celine Quarroz, my ever patient and ultra-efficient assistant, looked up from her desk as I started to walk into my office.

"Mr. McDougal is waiting for you in your office," she told me in her lilting French-Canadian accent.

Burrowed into one corner of the sofa inside my conference room was Dennis McDougal, a harried-looking forty-one-year-old man in a rumpled beige business suit who simultaneously spoke a mile a minute into a telephone, drained his coffee cup, scratched notes down on a legal pad and fiddled with a pocket tape recorder. He looked disheveled but focused.

"Ah. Gotta go. Call you later," he said when he saw me. He dropped the receiver back in its cradle and stood up like a shot, reaching across the table to shake my hand.

I'd first met McDougal almost a year earlier, shortly after the lawsuit was filed. He wrote about the entertainment business for the Los Angeles *Times*, but not like any reporter I'd ever encountered before.

When the rest of the media were praising Michael Jackson, Lionel Richie and Harry Belafonte for producing the mega-hit record "We Are the World" to feed African famine victims, McDougal kept asking where the money went. When outraged parents demanded that Congress outlaw indecent TV and radio programming, McDougal reminded his readers that banning an occasional "fuck" or "shit" from the public airwaves was a first step toward erasing the words "Congress shall make no law . . ." from the First Amendment. And when the powers of Hollywood lined up behind former Paramount Pictures chief Robert Evans in an effort to keep the producer's name out of the papers during the so-called "Cotton Club" murder case, McDougal was digging into Evans's past and writing about his cocaine addiction, womanizing and ruthless, imperious method of operating in Hollywood.

McDougal covered the stars, but he was definitely not starstruck. He asked uncomfortable questions and he would not go away.

The first time he called me about the Buchwald case was in November 1988. All he wanted to know then was whether or not I was serious.

"What do you mean? Of course I'm serious! We sued, didn't we?" I told him.

"So have a lot of other people," he countered. "But when the studios start playing hardball, they always settle out of court. Fold their tent and go home."

McDougal and I thrust and parried for a while until I reminded him who the plaintiff was in our case. Most writers and actors settle because they're afraid of being blackballed by the studios. Buchwald didn't give a damn whether he was blackballed or not. He had nothing to lose by going all the way.

"That's why I figured you were serious," said McDougal. "That's why I want to cover this case like a blanket. This could be the one that finally breaks open the studio's books."

A handful of greedy men with often questionable talent ran the movie business like a private emirate, he said. They were members of a loosely knit club who moved in and out of studio hierarchies, made mega-bomb movies and still bounced back, never seeming to lose a paycheck in the process. They held all the power, scratched each other's backs and operated the industry at the expense of others, hiding their lucrative dealings behind a cloak of accounting and contractual secrecy that rarely saw the antiseptic light of a public trial.

This Hollywood executives club surfaced as a group from time to time: during Hollywood charity dinners, labor negotiations with the guilds, Beverly Hills bar mitzvahs, Motion Picture Association of America meetings and celebrity funerals. Most of the time, however, the studio cabal remained an informal network with one overriding credo: Don't rock the boat.

All of that was popular knowledge in the film business, but no writer or producer or actor or director had been able to break the system's grip for almost a century because everyone who made movies was genuinely afraid of the old Hollywood adage: if you buck the system, you'll never work in this town again.

"Buchwald never worked there in the first place," I told McDougal. "He's already told me he'll sign a nondisclosure statement with Paramount when hell freezes over."

I could almost hear McDougal grinning over the telephone. I invited him to a charity dinner at which Art was going to be the featured speaker. I told McDougal that, before the dinner, he could meet the man who was taking on Hollywood and judge for himself. This would be a one-on-one session, I assured him.

If McDougal wasn't convinced after hearing Buchwald's scathing attack on Hollywood in the interview that night in early January 1989, he was a week later when Art dropped him a thank you note for writing a *Times* article about his speech:

"That was a wonderful story you wrote and when we win, I will give you the first ride on Paramount's private jet."

Since then, McDougal had been calling me at least once a month to check on the status of the case. Each time, I told him that there was nothing new to report. In truth, McDougal would have had a field day with the deposition transcripts, but I did not want a repeat disaster like we had with the *Wall Street Journal* leak before we filed suit. I was still holding out a faint hope that we could get Paramount to settle, and I did not want to anger them again by trying my case in the newspaper.

Not yet, at least.

As time went by, the case did not settle, and I forced the elusive Eddie Murphy to sit for a two-day deposition. Even the cynical Mr. McDougal was convinced that we were, indeed, serious. This was one case the studio system was unlikely to stifle through cloak and dagger settlement or intimidation. We were going to rock the boat, and McDougal wanted on board, even if it was just to observe.

He had come to my office that November morning to get an off-the-record, pretrial briefing of how I intended to argue the case. For the next hour, I lectured while he took notes. I told him about *Desny v. Wilder* and *Krofft v. McDonald's*, *Fink v. Goodson-Todman* and *Buchwald v. Paramount*. Perhaps most important of all, I told him that the depositions that we had taken in our case were being lodged with the court. What that meant, I said, was that the material—including nonconfidential exhibits such as the correspondence between Jim Harrison and Bob Wachs—would be public record. An enterprising reporter who leafed through those exhibits might find some explosive material, I suggested.

I liked McDougal. He did not say that he disbelieved me, but I could tell that he would check out everything I had told him. He trusted me no more or less than he trusted Paramount's lawyers, but he also knew a news story when he heard one. And he had just heard one.

As I walked him back to the elevators, Judge Jerry Pacht entered our suite. I shook his hand. It hadn't occurred to me until that moment that having a *Times* reporter present just before a pretrial discovery session might be indelicate. McDougal apparently saw my eyes darting in panic. He could have stood by, waiting to be introduced, but he just smiled and flashed me the peace sign, stepping quickly to the elevators himself.

Jerry Pacht had spent more than half a generation on the bench in Los Angeles, earning a reputation as one of the most liberal judges in California. A short, Jewish Democrat with a deep baritone voice and a penchant for ribald jokes, he probably made his biggest media splash just a few years after Governor Edmund G. "Pat" Brown appointed him to the bench in 1966, when he ruled that black radical Angela Davis could retain her job as a philosophy professor at UCLA, despite her membership in the Communist Party. Jerry survived an unsuccessful recall movement over that decision.

In November 1989, however, Jerry was sixty-seven and already several years retired from the bench. He still handled civil cases by appointment of the court or agreement of the parties as a so-called "rent-a-judge," receiving more for one hour of private judging ($350) than he had for an entire day as a public judge. Judge Schneider had appointed Jerry to serve as a discovery referee to decide what further documents Paramount must release before trial. Pacht was a good choice—he had been a story analyst for MGM back in the 1940s before he turned to law, his law firm had represented the Writers Guild and he had presided as a judge over numerous entertainment industry cases.

A few weeks earlier, we had filed a motion to compel Paramount to divulge information about various matters, including details about the profit and loss picture for *Coming to America* to help us prove our damages; the use of "based upon" in other studio agreements to shed light on Paramount's interpretation of the term; and the gross receipts that Paramount had received on Eddie Murphy films to show that Eddie was the studio's biggest star and someone it had to keep happy, even when it meant cheating other people like my clients. Paramount claimed that this evidence was either irrelevant, burdensome to produce or premature because we had not yet established liability.

Zazi, who had been coordinating discovery, handled the hearing before Judge Pacht.

"Should the plaintiffs be limited to information about net profits and therefore subject to motion picture creative accounting?" Pacht asked Zazi and Robert Draper early in the hearing. Pacht had been raised in Hollywood, and he knew how studios managed to lose money when it came time to share profits with their net profit participants. He ruled that we were entitled to a formal net profit statement and details about "how gross gets to net. I realize that may turn into a twenty-week trial, but that's not my problem." And production of this financial information, he further ordered, would be subject only to the existing confidentiality order in place since March and would not be conditioned on Paramount's ridiculous request that the public be excluded from the courtroom during trial when we presented this evidence to the jury.

As for other Paramount literary option contracts, the judge denied our request, but he had some free advice for the parties.

"Someone at some point must define the words 'based upon.' If the parties don't, the Court will in jury instructions. I suggest that the parties define it and not leave it to a judge outside the industry, although I understand everybody is happy with Judge Schneider. That's good. I have heard nothing but good about him."

"He is excellent," Zazi quickly agreed.

"He needs to be educated a little bit but—" Draper asserted.

"Sure, sure," the savvy jurist replied with a knowing grin. "You've got to defendant-ize him a little bit."

Judge Pacht's initial inclination was to deny our request for information about Paramount's gross receipts from Murphy's movies.

"I don't think that you will wind up with a juror in this town who is over three years old that doesn't know Murphy is a big shot and a star, and you could always argue that what they did they did because of Murphy's posture . . . unless Zazi can persuade me to the contrary."

Zazi did just that. Off and on for over an hour, my tenacious colleague stuck to her guns, skillfully combining her mastery of the record and law, not to mention her considerable charm, to move the veteran judge. In the course of the lively exchange, Judge Pacht gave a primer on Hollywood accounting:

"You are going to battle them if you win and say, 'Those are illegitimate accounting procedures and you are loading up negative costs, loading up distribution fees, loading up a whole lot of things, and trying to charge us 20 percent of Paramount's overhead.' That is the usual argument. Why will you be any better off if you require them to tell you what their [accounting] theory is than you would be after you prove they stole your story?"

Draper was not happy that we already had the details of Eddie Murphy's five-picture overall deal with Paramount, including his now $9 million per picture against 15 percent of the gross receipts. Bob was worried about what I would do with that information in front of a jury that Judge Pacht noted would be "twelve postal clerks . . . who will be awed by that kind of thing."

"Eddie Murphy goes on, I can't remember, the Arsenio Hall show for an interview and says he has the shittiest deal in town," Draper groused. "He only makes $9 million a picture. He's not my favorite part of the case."

"He's been reading baseball players' contracts," Judge Pacht quipped.

"Or first-year associates'," Zazi added, referring to the fact that students straight out of law school were paid more than $80,000 per year at major law firms like Kaye, Scholer. As a third-year associate, Zazi made more money than a Superior Court judge like Harvey Schneider. Zazi was worth every penny we paid her, but shockingly low judicial salaries are a sad commentary on society's misplaced priorities.

Zazi finally won over the judge, and he ordered that Paramount produce the gross receipts from Eddie Murphy's pictures. But he would not order Paramount to produce other net profit definitions because only Buchwald's and Bernheim's contracts were relevant.

His comments on net profit contracts were sobering:

"I think how it is defined again may have something to do with the muscle that the respective contracting parties have. If you are a newcomer and you just buy a net deal, look out. I don't know, Mr. Buchwald is not a newcomer in many fields, but I don't know if he is a newcomer in this field."

Judge Pacht deferred requiring Paramount to produce detailed fees and cost information for the picture. Earlier that day, Judge Schneider had agreed to bifurcate the case for trial. The jury would first decide the issue of liability, and if we won, the judge himself, assisted by some expert referee, would oversee what we lawyers call an "accounting" to calculate our share, if any, of the net profits for *Coming to America.*

In the course of the discussion of accounting issues, Draper argued that Alain had negotiated the net profit deals for Art and himself, that he "was a well-known and experienced producer" and that the agents for Art and Alain, the William Morris Agency, "have been in the industry 200,000 years and negotiated a good many deals and they weren't babes in the woods."

I wasn't sure what he was driving at, but I would learn a few months later.

The judge urged Zazi to back off on detailed accounting information at this point, wryly noting that he would prefer to see Paramount take the money it would spend for lawyers and accountants to gather the data and "add [it] to the settlement offer." And, he further observed, what would get Paramount to settle would not be an order compelling production of accounting information but "sitting here knowing Art Buchwald will charm the pants off everybody in that courtroom. But you made your point and you can take the transcript back to Pierce and you can say, 'Your friend Jerry Pacht is a royal pain in the butt. Why is he your friend?' "

A week later I received a letter from Bob Draper enclosing a net profit statement for *Coming to America* as of September 23, 1989. According to Paramount's arithmetic, the movie had earned $122,409,123 in gross receipts for the studio but remained $17,969,780 in the hole.

I had been hearing tales of creative accounting all the way back to the "Rockford Files" days. I'd had a healthy dose of studio flimflamming during the Danny Arnold case against Columbia Pictures. But even I was left breathless by this down-to-the-dollar fiction that *Coming to America* was *still in the red!*

Following the industry rule of thumb that fifty cents of every dollar goes to theater owners and that the reported studio gross represents only half what a movie actually earns, the five pages that I held in my shaking fingers meant that *Coming to America* had already earned almost $250 million . . . and still had an $18 million "net loss."

"How the hell can that be?" I shouted out loud.

My office door cracked and Zazi stuck her head inside.

While I was still howling, she brought into my office another gift from Bob Draper. This was a stipulation regarding communication with the media that Draper wanted me to sign, restricting attorneys and the parties for both sides to "expressions of general optimism" to the press and nothing else. We couldn't comment on witness testimony. We couldn't comment on money matters. And we couldn't comment on any of the evidence offered at trial, period.

Zazi and I exchanged looks. She shrugged, and I grabbed my pen. I had agreed to this gag order in Judge Schneider's chambers. As I signed, I wondered whether McDougal had found those depositions and exhibits while they were still public records.

19

Stars Always Win

THE LAST FEW DAYS before any trial are hectic, chaotic and perilous. In this pressure cooker, a trial lawyer must guard against mistakes that can send a case into a death spiral.

In an ordinary case, the tasks that have to be accomplished in the waning days of pretrial preparation include expert witness depositions, jury instructions, finalizing trial briefs and witness and exhibit lists, motions *in limine* to limit or preclude some of your adversary's evidence and arguments, witness preparation, and fine-tuning your opening statement and closing argument. In our case, I had the added challenges of defending Art in his fourth deposition session on the eve of trial, a mandatory settlement conference, deciding whether to waive a jury trial, threats on my professional career, an eleventh-hour attack on my integrity, a major setback in my trial strategy, and the failure of the Writers Guild of America to support our cause.

I will never forget the first fourteen days of December 1989, when our hopes for victory flickered but our resolve never wavered.

Bob Draper had indigestion after he read the three volumes of Art's deposition over the Thanksgiving holiday. Pleading befuddlement at Ken Kulzick's rambling, uninspired examination of my client and reminding us of our promise to make Art available, Bob insisted on another stab at Buchwald before we went to trial. I had no choice but to agree.

So, on December 5, 1989, Art Buchwald raised his right hand again. This time the questioning took place in my Los Angeles offices with Lon Sobel—the only remaining member of the original Paramount defense team—sitting next to Draper. Art was obligated to attend the mandatory settlement conference two days later, and we piggybacked his deposition onto that trip.

In the heady days following his initial deposition, Art wrote me one of his many hilarious letters. After teasing me for getting him to sign a routine waiver of conflict of interest because one of my New York partners did some tax work for Gulf & Western, Art wrote, ". . . it doesn't bother me because I am going into the witness protection program anyway." After his first encounter with Draper, I thought that just might be a good idea.

"Mr. Buchwald, I have a few questions," Draper began. "I've read your deposition carefully . . . and I have read all the exhibits that have been used before, and I have no intention of duplicating the stuff that's been done before. But I do have some follow-up questions of a fairly limited nature that I need to cover. So please don't feel like I'm starting into a long regurgitation of your 400-plus pages."

"Yeah," Art interrupted, cutting off Draper's long-winded introduction with a nod that he understood.

"Five hundred pages," I corrected him.

"Who's counting?" Draper said.

"You didn't have to sit there," I said, remembering Kulzick's folksy how's-the-wife, how's-the-kids interview style.

Draper smiled. He asked Art for videotapes of his 1988 appearance on "Larry King Live" and "Person to Person" on CBS way back in the sixties. We got him Larry King but I wasn't so sure we were going to be as successful with the old Edward R. Murrow interview show. I offered a copy of Martin Davis's rendition of "Sue Me" as a consolation prize.

"We know we don't have the bottle of Dom Perignon that Mr. Davis sent to Mr. Buchwald. I'm told that's been consumed," I said with a smile.

"That's the worst news I've had all day," Draper said wryly.

We all laughed, including Art and Lon Sobel. Then Draper got down to business. *King for a Day* wasn't the only thing Buchwald had sold to Hollywood, he pointed out. There had been several projects and, to date, only one had made it to the screen: his novel, *A Gift From the Boys,* which was turned into the bomb *Surprise Package.*

"Subsequent to that, did anyone call you and say, 'Mr. Buchwald, I'd like to use you or have you write something for a movie'?" Draper asked.

"A lot of times," Art answered.

And didn't Buchwald currently have another movie treatment floating around Hollywood? Draper wanted to know. A treatment called *The Beard?*

"It's over," Art said. "Finished. I'm not interested anymore. I'm not interested in selling it. I'm not interested in it being made. It's finished."

"Mr. Buchwald, I'm not offering to buy it," Draper said soothingly. "I'm just trying to ask you a couple questions."

I didn't know why Art was so flummoxed over the question, but I knew enough to jump in and help him.

"He's answered your question," I said. "He's not actively pursuing it any-more."

"I heard him, Mr. O'Donnell," Draper said.

"I'm interpreting," I offered, shrugging.

"Well, you might start training for trial because I don't think you could do that at trial," Draper said icily. Then, in the same breath, he smiled thinly at a bewildered Art Buchwald and said: "We're friends."

I wanted to tell Art that nothing could be further from the truth but a quick glance from him told me that he already understood that fact.

"I write a lot," Art said quickly, a note of irritation in his voice. "I've written 7,000 articles over a period of forty years."

At the moment he wrote something, Art said, he always thought it was brilliant. Upon inspection a while later, it often lost its sheen. When it did, he kissed it off and moved on to something else. That was what happened with *The Beard*, he told Draper.

"The last person that claimed to be interested was an Arab sheik in Lon-don, and he wanted it for his wife," Buchwald said. He was not interested in having his name attached to a movie that was to be produced just so it could be shown to the neighborhood harem.

Art continued spieling off projects he'd sold or planned to sell to Holly-wood, ending with his own explanation of how he created story ideas. He stored information in his imagination over a period of years, as if it were a computer data bank, he said, synthesizing ideas from all that collected infor-mation in his subconscious.

"You file all this stuff away and then, six years later, you do a story on lawyers," he said. "And this scene—I may write this scene. I may not even remember who it was or where it was, but that's all subconscious. That's how a writer works."

"And that memory bank . . . goes back to the time you were in Paris?" Draper asked.

"Goes to the time when you were a little kid," Buchwald answered. "That's all a writer really has, if you want the truth, is his memory bank."

Draper then read a portion of Art's *King for a Day* contract to him.

"It says: 'The work is original with author; that neither the work nor any part thereof are taken from or based upon any other material or any motion picture.' You see that?" Draper asked

"Yes, sir," Buchwald nodded.

What was Draper after? I wondered.

"Did anyone ever tell you that if any part of the creative spark for your treatment was based upon any other motion picture or other material, that you would be in violation of the warranty in your contract?" Draper said.

"No, nobody told me that," Art said, his eyes widening.

Again, Art was on top of what was happening as soon as I was. Barely restraining his anger, he reached for a glass of water, swallowing without taking his eyes off Draper.

"I'd like to just say that I wrote the thing," he said as emphatically as he could. "It was mine, all mine. I've never, ever in forty years ever been accused of using somebody else's stuff. And I pride myself on the fact I will not take even an idea that's in the mail from somebody because I'm afraid it doesn't belong to me."

Draper sniffed, bending over his yellow legal pad and scribbling away.

"You'd never take somebody else's column and write it as if it were your own?" he asked.

"Never," said Art, gripping the arms of his chair. "I've never been accused, ever, of it and I've never had any problem with anybody ever accusing me of saying that a piece of material of mine was theirs."

"In Paris, did you go to motion pictures?" Draper asked.

"Yeah. I was even a critic."

There it was again. Art and Paris and movies. What was the fascination with Paris? Draper had something up his sleeve.

Art felt he owed an explanation—the fatal impulse of every honest witness facing a hostile attorney who has attacked him where he lives. I had to hand it to Draper. He was getting a full "confession" from Art Buchwald.

"I don't know how many story ideas there are in the world," Art said. "There are supposed to be seven, eight. I don't know exactly how many there are: boy meets girl, boy leaves girl, and all movies seem to be something to do with that. I go to the movies. So I'm sure I saw something like that. . . . The reason why I didn't even pay attention to that clause is I *know* it was my material and I wrote it!"

Draper put down his pen and reached in a folder for a carefully folded newspaper clipping. It was an article, written by Dennis McDougal, from the Los Angeles *Times*, dated Monday, January 16, 1989. Draper read Art's own words back to him, about the backing Alain and Art were getting from Hollywood writers as a result of their lawsuit:

" 'One of the reasons we're getting a lot of sympathy from the writers is because they're disturbed with this new thing where producers give story credit to the star of the picture,' Buchwald said."

Draper wanted to know whether our expert witnesses "were upset about the fact that studios [were] giving picture credit to people like Eddie Murphy."

"Other people too." Art shrugged. "Other writers."

"You've gotten quite a bit of publicity about this case, have you not?" Draper inquired.

"Yes."

"Have you enjoyed that?"

"Up to a point," Art answered. "I don't want to be known as a litigator. I want to be known as a writer. . . . And now I'm getting tired of it."

"Now, is it true that in your contacts with the press you've portrayed yourself as the little guy going against the big guy, Paramount?" Draper asked.

"That's absolutely correct," said Art. "That's absolutely correct. Doesn't it fit?"

"Are you taking my deposition or am I taking yours?" Draper wondered. "Do you like Eddie Murphy's movies in general?"

"Yeah."

At one point Draper asked how long Art had been a member of the Writers Guild.

"Were you a member in 1983?" he asked.

"Was I? Can I ask my counsel that?" Art asked.

"Sure. He testifies on everything else. He ought to know that," Draper hissed.

We had been at it for close to an hour, and Art was showing the effects of Draper's tease and taunt questioning. He was delivering more "yes" and "no" answers and a lot fewer full-blown explanations.

Draper began stuffing his papers back into his briefcase, marking the end of the deposition. Sobel followed suit, and Art seemed to relax for the first time in nearly an hour. He picked up the glass of water and finished it off just as Draper fired off one last question.

"Is there a definition of plagiarism you feel comfortable with in terms of your own understanding?" he asked.

"I'll give you mine and I don't have any dictionary basis for it," Art said. "Somebody who takes and claims it as his own when it doesn't belong to him. Theft. I think plagiarism is theft."

Screen credits are everything in Hollywood.

Guilds strike over them. Grown men and women fight over them. Careers are made or broken over them.

When *Coming to America* was screened for the first time, comedy writers Barry Blaustein and David Sheffield got screenplay credit. Eddie Murphy was credited with originating the story. But those credits didn't just happen. They were discussed and divvied up like marbles.

Long ago, the Writers Guild secured from the studios and production companies through collective bargaining the exclusive right to devise and administer an arbitration process to settle disputes over writing credits. If more than one person claimed screenplay or story credit, their claims were turned over to three anonymous Guild members who examined screenplays, treatments, outlines, stories and the resulting movie. They then decided who deserved screen credit.

In the case of *Coming to America*, both Arsenio Hall and John Landis said they had contributed to the movie, but neither of them got credit. Eddie Murphy said he contributed to the screenplay, but he was given only story credit. Art Buchwald was now claiming that he deserved the "story by" credit, but it was much too late for his name to ever show up on the screen.

It was not too late, however, for four seasoned Writers Guild veterans to belatedly go through a quasi-arbitration process and decide, for the Buchwald legal team, whether or not the movie was based upon Art's original story. That is precisely what we asked Lynn Roth, David Rintels, Edmund North and Danny Arnold to do during their expert witness depositions over seven days in early December.

But we almost didn't have experts.

It wasn't for lack of volunteers willing to lend their support to what they believed was a watershed test of judicial protection of creator's rights. In addition to Arnold, North, Rintels and Roth, our original list given to the Court included some of Hollywood's other top writers and directors—legendary Billy Wilder, Mel Shavelson, David Shaw, Jack Rose and Paul Monash. Among them, they had directed, written, and/or produced more than 225 feature films, television series, and/or specials over the past quarter century. Two (Shavelson and Rintels) were former Writers Guild presidents. *Daily Variety* called them "star witnesses." While the going rate for your basic expert witness was $250 an hour, this array of volunteer talent was priceless.

When Judge Schneider ordered me to pare my list down to four experts, Zazi and I decided to go with Arnold, North, Rintels and Roth because they represented a cross-section of Hollywood writers—movies and television, old and young, male and female—that we thought would impress a jury. Then Judge Schneider knocked us for a loop.

On December 1, just a few days before Paramount was about to grill our four experts, the judge ruled that he would not allow experts to make comparisons of the similarities between Art's treatment and *Coming to America*. Such testimony, he reasoned, would usurp the jury's function as the sole determiner of the facts. The only topic on which he would allow expert testimony would be the meaning of "based upon" in the motion picture industry since the term was not defined in Buchwald's contract.

We were devastated. Not only were our months of hard work spent recruiting, educating and prepping the experts totally wasted, we were left in the lurch. I had built an important part of our presentation on the similarities between the two works around the testimony of our four experts, each one emphasizing a different aspect of our proof about theme, characters, story and setting. What the hell was I going to do now?

Maybe I could repackage my expert testimony and have them talk to the jury about the nature of the creative process in filmmaking. After all, it took a huge leap of faith for twelve laymen, unschooled in the motion picture business, to accept that a two-and-a-half-page treatment could be the basis for a 120-page screenplay. While I couldn't ask my experts to comment on the similarities, I could have them help the jury understand the evidence and how Art's story evolved into Eddie's story and then into Paramount's movie. It was at least worth a try.

Zazi met with each of the experts and reoriented them about their new tasks. Dennis Landry revamped the exhibit list, and Marsha, Suzanne and I revised our witness interrogation outlines to incorporate more testimony about similarities and the meaning of "based upon." If I couldn't get my experts to testify about how the two properties resembled each other, then I would extract damaging admissions from Paramount's former executives. Within a matter of only a few days, the revised edition of our case was ready to go. And as it turned out, Judge Schneider had done us a favor.

Ed North, who won an Oscar for writing *Patton* in 1970 and had written twenty-six screenplays, went first. After an hour of small talk with Bob Draper during which North described his twenty-one-year tenure on the Guild's Screen Credits Committee and delivered dozens of "yes" or "no" answers about Guild arbitration and his fifty-five years in the screenwriting business, the sagacious old storyteller told a simple anecdote. It was drawn from his own personal experience at Twentieth Century Fox in the early 1950s, when he came upon a science fiction story that he could easily have stolen and called his own.

"Some years ago I wrote a screenplay for a project called *The Day the Earth Stood Still*," he said. "I was given a short story by a man named Harry Bates and I used only, I think, elements of the first two pages of his story. And those pages told of a spaceship landing on the Mall in Washington and out of the spaceship came a spaceman and a huge robot. That was all I used.

"I proceeded to do a screenplay, which meant that I had to create a series of characters, I had to develop a story, a full . . . story line, and do a screenplay from that. In spite of the fact that Mr. Bates contributed only the slight amount of material that I described, he got a 'based upon his story' credit. And I think he was entitled to it.

"And I think the two instances here, the story of *The Day the Earth Stood Still* and the story of *Coming to America*, are almost identical in their content."

Draper spent much of the rest of the deposition trying to undermine North's simple comparison of Harry Bates with Art Buchwald, but North would not back down. At one point, Ed was able to express his opinion that, if Paramount had properly submitted Buchwald's treatment and the Tab Murphy/Veber scripts as part of the Guild's screen credit determinations for *Coming to America*, Buchwald should have been given a "based upon" credit because his treatment was the source material for the screenplay.

Draper also asked a series of hypothetical questions about a satirical movie involving a king from a mythical country who comes to America, is deposed as a result of a revolution in his country, takes a suite in a fancy hotel, has a romance and is forced to take a menial job. Coupled with the questions Draper had asked Art about his days as a Paris movie critic and Art's definition of plagiarism, I was starting to get an uneasy feeling as the countdown to trial continued. What I couldn't figure out was from what movie Draper was going to allege that Art plagiarized.

Like Ed North, Danny Arnold had a story to tell about a comedy he wrote in 1960 which was based on an article by Marion Hargrove in *True* magazine about a schooner.

"Hargrove wrote a factual account of a particular situation that occurred as part of history during World War II," he said. "That article was optioned by a second writer who then created a story, using that boat as the center of the fiction. . . . That was the basis of the motion picture."

The movie, starring Jack Lemmon, was titled *The Wackiest Ship in the Army*. It turned out to be a hit and Marion Hargrove got the "based upon" credit, even though his *True* magazine story bore little resemblance to the finished film. Retold on the witness stand, I thought, both North's story and Danny Arnold's story would damage Paramount's case.

Arnold had another story to tell. Lon Sobel asked him if he had ever been the victim of a studio rip-off like the kind Buchwald was alleging. Danny's answer gave an insight into how endemic plagiarism is in Hollywood.

"Before I left Screen Gems in 1964, I had an idea to do a television series, a western series based on the exploits of a black gunfighter, a character that came out of the Civil War who had moved out West to find a new life for himself. . . . Lazarus Benjamin was the name of the character. But I found it very difficult to get a show on the air with a black protagonist in those days.

"So I suggested to Jackie Cooper, who was then head of Screen Gems, that I would split the character. I would make it essentially a partnership between a black gunfighter and a white gunfighter who meet in a particular town where they are in a confrontational situation, where neither can beat the other. . . . And the two of them join up because they mistrust each other, and no one wants to turn his back on the other. So the two of them wind up in a grudging partnership. . . . I couldn't get that done either. Then I left the studio. And two years later, a series went on the air starring Otis Green and Don Murray. . . . And [Screen Gems] did a series based on the relationship of a black gunfighter and a white gunfighter, and it was exactly my story.

"What happened was they hired a writer who was a friend of mine to do the pilot. And when they told him the concept, he said, 'Wait a minute. That is Danny Arnold's story.' They claimed that it was not, that they had given me the story. So he went ahead and wrote the pilot, and they put the series on the air. They did it badly, I'm afraid, and it only lasted one season. But I sued them."

"What was the outcome of that lawsuit?" asked a spellbound Sobel.

"They settled the lawsuit," Danny answered.

One of the industry's most respected dramatic writers, whose many credits included *The Defenders* for CBS, *Clarence Darrow*, *Gideon's Trumpet*, *Sakharov* and *Day One*, David Rintels gave us his deposition on December 7. Like our other experts, Rintels also saw Art Buchwald behind every frame of *Coming to America*—the connection between the two was "as clear and direct a link as there is between me and my father and grandfather." While Danny Arnold expressed his anger sardonically, David was simply furious.

"My sense of outrage was that I had known that Art and Alain had been working for a long time on a project with Paramount for Eddie Murphy," Rintels told Lon Sobel. "I knew from Alain. I saw him often enough to know that he was working on a script with one fellow that didn't work out, so he went and got Francis Veber to do it. I knew that he had his heart and soul invested in this, that he cared deeply about it, that this was a breakthrough project for him. Terribly important."

That Paramount would option the story, dump it and then make substantially the same movie was nothing short of rape, according to Rintels.

As outraged as David was, he managed to preserve some of his sharp wit. He watched *Coming to America* on an airplane flight once, he told Sobel.

"Tell me of your reaction, if you're able to recall it, as you sat in the plane and watched *Coming to America*."

"I walked out."

Lynn Roth, who brought the critically acclaimed series "Paper Chase" to television, was the last of our experts to be cross-examined. Almost immediately after beginning her deposition, she pointed out that Paramount didn't even have the legal power to determine whether Eddie or Art wrote the story that was the basis for *Coming to America*. In their union contracts, all of the studios had given sole credit authority over to the Guild.

"Paramount is a signatory to the Writers Guild, so the Writers Guild would say Paramount has no power to determine any kind of credit whatsoever," she said.

Lynn was a logical choice as an expert, and her testimony on December 11 was riveting. A terrific writer, she had great presence. She also knew how the other half lived because she had done a two-year stint as Twentieth Century Fox's comedy development head and served for a while as a production executive at Lorimar. But, at forty, she had spent most of her adult life writing for a living and she too knew what a city of barracuda Los Angeles can be. The first script she ever wrote for TV, in fact, was stolen from her.

"My very first experience as a writer was on 'All in the Family,' the first episode I ever wrote. But the cowriter, a man . . . to whom I pitched the idea, went and sold it to Norman Lear at 'All in the Family,' and did not give me credit for it," she testified. "And then once Norman Lear found out, they compensated me and gave me another assignment. That was my reward [and] my initiation."

Idea theft was pandemic in Hollywood, she told Lon Sobel, and, in her judgment, *Coming to America* was a perfect example.

"I believe that Mr. Buchwald created the initial spark for *King for a Day*," Lynn testified. "More than a spark. . . . Spark isn't big enough a word for me."

"So you would not describe Art Buchwald's treatment as a spark for *Coming to America?*" Sobel asked.

"I would—I would put it more as a fire," Lynn replied.

Our four experts exceeded my highest expectations. With trial just a little more than one week off, I was riding high. But I knew that it would be a mistake to put on four experts. First, it would be overkill and could turn off the jury—and certainly Judge Schneider, who had qualms about any expert testimony at all. Second, it would give Paramount a chance to use the experts to contradict each other. Finally, I wanted to try a lean case in which I hammered home repeatedly the best evidence and left out extraneous issues.

It was an agonizing decision because I was confident that any one of the four would be brilliant. Eventually, I chose Danny Arnold. Of the four, he had the most extensive and varied experience with comedy writing in movies and television. His "Barney Miller" television series was a classic with which most jurors would be familiar. In addition, the judge wanted to hear expert testimony about the meaning of "based upon" in the motion picture industry, and I thought that Arnold and Schneider would hit it off. Danny had been a plaintiff and testified in the famous "Family Hour" litigation in 1976 challenging on First Amendment grounds the television networks' decision to limit the type of evening programming that they would broadcast before children's bedtime, and the federal judge who ruled in favor of the plaintiffs was very taken with Danny.

Finally, as I told Danny a few days before trial began, he had gotten me into this mess, and he had to get me out.

The support of all these distinguished writers and former Writers Guild presidents and directors was gratifying. What was disappointing, however, was the failure of the Writers Guild of America West itself to support us. At David Rintels' urging and with the assistance of former Guild president John Furia, Jr., I wrote on December 11 a five-page letter to Brian Walton, the union's executive director, requesting that the Guild, before trial began at the end of the week, "take maximum action under the Basic Agreement to rectify Paramount's failure to give Buchwald notice of tentative writing credits as required by Paragraph 11 of Schedule A and to accord him a 'Story By' credit as required by Paragraph 2 of Schedule A." While it was too late to get Paramount to put Art's name on 2,000 prints of the movie and tens of thousands of videocassettes, the Guild had the power to punish Paramount. More importantly, as I told Walton in my letter, "the active, public support of the Writers Guild before trial begins would greatly aid our cause." We had few public allies, and we needed the moral support of Art's own Guild. "In our view," I concluded in my impassioned plea to Walton, "writers are at war over a fundamental principle, and the Guild cannot remain neutral."

The Guild would in fact remain neutral, Brian Walton told me the next day. He viewed this as a dispute between two Guild members—Murphy and Buchwald—and the Guild would not take sides. The excuse was phony. It was Paramount that we had sued and Paramount that we claimed had flagrantly violated the contract between the Guild and the studio requiring that Buchwald be allowed to participate in the credit arbitration process *before* the movie was released. And as for taking sides, the Guild took sides every time it adjudicated a disputed credit.

What was the real reason that Brian Walton wouldn't help us in our battle against Paramount? I was to find out six months later—and it would scare the hell out of me.

.   .   .   .   .

The mandatory settlement conference took place in Judge R. William Schoettler, Jr.'s chambers on Friday, December 8. Judge Schoettler had been a mediator for a year and a half. He loved being known in the downtown courthouse as the "Settlement Don." In many respects, the fifty-one-year-old jurist's job was far tougher than that of a trial judge because he was the first and last arbiter two warring sides saw before they actually wound up facing each other in court.

"The hardest people with whom to reach a settlement are those who feel a strong sense of personal injustice has been done them," he once told a reporter for the *Daily Journal*. "They want not only their day in court but also their pound of flesh."

I had appeared once before at a settlement conference with this tall, handsome judge who liked to wear cowboy boots and seemed to enjoy playing a Solomonic role in settling complex civil matters. One of his favorite tactics was always insisting on having everyone on hand: plaintiffs, defendants and the lawyers who would try the case. In the "Rockford Files" case earlier in March, he ordered the MCA/Universal chief executive officer Sid Sheinberg, plaintiff James Garner and John Agoglia, executive vice-president for my client, NBC, to be present all day. He would call everybody into his eighth-floor chambers early in the morning to find out what both sides wanted and then begin calling in each side, one at a time, for alternating fifteen- to twenty-minute sessions. In the "Rockford Files" case, he kept everyone there all day long and narrowed the gap between the parties to the point that the case was settled a few weeks later.

Art was apprehensive. Being in a courthouse was a new experience for him. I assured him that this would be painless, but not to be too surprised if Paramount refused to cave in to our initial demand for $5 million. We would be prepared to drop to $3.5 million—perhaps as low as $3 million. But the studio would horse-trade clear up until the last moment.

Alain was anxious. I soothed him too. The last thing any studio wanted was to have to open its books in a public court proceeding, I assured him. That was our ultimate hammer.

Flanked by Zazi, we all shuffled into Judge Schoettler's chambers. I settled Alain and Art into their seats and shook hands all around, sizing up the opposition. Paramount's highly respected charmer, Richard Zimbert, was there, glad-handing around the table as fast as I was.

Zimbert was much more than a lawyer for Paramount. He was former business affairs head and executive vice-president and assistant to chairman Frank Mancuso. He was the quiet, well-coiffed bureaucrat behind the Bronson Avenue gates of Paramount Pictures—the ultimate "Suit." He wielded power smoothly, subtly and effectively—and he was a survivor.

Zimbert was the Wizard of Oz on major business and legal issues. With a fifteen-year tenure in the studio's inner circle, he was the closest thing Paramount had to an institutional memory. When it came to negotiating with the guilds, devising litigation strategy, drafting the standard net profit definition, or settling sensitive accounting disputes with profit participants, Zimbert *was* Paramount. It was no accident that he was the one who showed up as Paramount's official voice at the eve-of-trial settlement conference.

He knew that Paramount had problems on liability for breach of contract. Publicly, he remained a loyal soldier. Privately, however, he had been grumbling since the day we filed suit against Paramount the previous year. As far back as Christmastime of 1988, he had told Robert Goldberg, one of Hollywood's top accountants, that the studio would end up paying millions for a case that it could have settled for next to nothing in the summer of 1988.

"I've got to admire the way you've handled this case so far, Pierce," Zimbert said, vigorously shaking my hand just before we entered Judge Schoettler's chambers. "I've read all the depositions and pleadings. You'll probably win the contract claim."

But he made it clear that his admiration had its limits. He warned me that he would never accept our claim that Paramount had any fiduciary duty to Buchwald or Bernheim. "All you had was a contract relationship with us. Period. I'll go to my grave believing that Paramount is not a fiduciary to people with whom we merely contract for services."

As Zimbert spoke to me, I noticed that Bob Draper was being charmed by Art a few seats away. Draper was a hell of a lot tougher lawyer than Ken Kulzick, but even he couldn't resist Buchwald's easygoing, friendly way of dealing with people.

Judge Schoettler was little comfort to Art and Alain when it was our turn to sit alone with him while Paramount waited out in the hallway. He bluntly pointed out the facts of life. While Buchwald might be a world-famous writer —and Schoettler was clearly an admirer—Eddie Murphy would be the star if the case went to trial before a Los Angeles jury in a few days.

"Stars always win in Los Angeles courts," he said.

I immediately flashed back to Schoettler unsuccessfully trying to broker a settlement in the "Rockford Files" case. He was pretty clearly star-struck in that one too. At one point, he asked Garner whether he could get him tickets to the Oscars. He was joking, of course.

But this time, this bright, savvy judge was dead serious. He pointed out two vastly different jury trials in downtown L.A. where the stars had shone: Carol Burnett's libel suit against the *National Enquirer* and Valerie Harper's $1.6 million damage award against Lorimar Television for wrongfully firing her.

In Burnett's case, her impassioned performance on the witness stand cost the tabloid $3 million for a story that falsely accused the actress of getting drunk at a Washington restaurant and spilling her drink on Henry Kissinger. In the Harper case, the jury didn't stop with the cash award. They also gave the actress a chunk of any profits that came out of future syndication of her sitcom, "Valerie," which had subsequently been renamed "The Hogan Family" after Harper's character was killed off and replaced by actress Sandy Duncan. The defendants in both cases had solid legal arguments, but legal niceties meant little to the working men and women who sat in the jury box and got to hear a real live TV star personally plead her case.

"Imagine what the appeal will be when Eddie Murphy takes the stand," Schoettler suggested.

While we brooded on Schoettler's sobering observations outside the courtroom, Paramount's team spent its first session alone with Schoettler, offering its one and only concession. The studio offered to go ahead and make good on the original contract. We would get $265,000. But any hope of net profits was a pipe dream. When Judge Schoettler called us in to hear Paramount's offer, he reported that Zimbert claimed that expenses were so high on *Coming to America* that there were no net profits.

"From what Paramount tells me, the movie is likely to earn net profits maybe, Mr. O'Donnell, in your children's or their children's lifetimes, if ever," Judge Schoettler said. What was more, Zimbert had demanded a private, confidential arbitration, and not a public trial, to resolve any dispute if we wanted to challenge Paramount's figures.

Despite Judge Schoettler's considerable skill at shuttle diplomacy, several more sessions in and out of his chambers proved to be an exercise in futility. The parties were divided by a Grand Canyon of philosophical differences—not to mention $3.5 million. Art and Alain dismissed out of hand any non-public resolution of the looming net profits battle, and Paramount thought that we had taken leave of our senses by demanding millions of dollars in reparations. Worse yet, the cavalier way in which Paramount assumed that we would jump at its concession of liability but would be willing to go home empty-handed—while the studio, Murphy and Landis pocketed at least $100 million in profits—spoke volumes about its lack of sincerity. Paramount was playing games, we all quickly concluded.

It was time to make good on my threat a year earlier to stage a showcase trial and teach the bastards a lesson.

"See you in court," I announced to the waiting reporters outside Judge Schoettler's courtroom as Art, Alain, Zazi and I made our way to the fifth floor. We had an appointment with another judge.

"Well, gentlemen and lady," Judge Schneider said as Draper, Zazi and I appeared before him just before he took his noon recess. "Does this mean what I think it means?" he asked us.

"Yes, your honor," I answered. "We're going to trial."

"Okay. Let's see. Today is Friday, and I have three or four more days in this jury trial. I'll keep you posted, but I think we look good for the middle of next week. I'll tell you what. Why don't you come in on Thursday to take care of our housekeeping issues? We'll pick a jury on Friday."

Not if I had anything to say about it.

The morning had not been totally wasted. We *had* learned one valuable piece of information from Judge Schoettler—something that had worried me from the very first day that I started thinking about taking the case.

"We can't have a jury trial, Pierce," Zazi said to Art, Alain and me at lunch at Jimmy's restaurant in Beverly Hills an hour after we left the courthouse.

"I know. I know," I said. "If they put Eddie on the stand, we could get eaten alive. Everyone's star-struck in this town. The juries—even the judges."

"Does that mean that Judge Schneider would be our jury?" Art asked.

"That's right. Judge and jury all rolled into one," I answered. "I'm not convinced that Eddie is going to show, but we should assume that he will and that he will levitate the jury. Even if I knew for a fact that Eddie'll stay home, I would still be thinking very seriously about recommending waiver of the jury. With the experts out of the case on the similarities issue, we have a tougher job ahead trying to persuade twelve postal clerks, as Judge Pacht said, that Art's short story is the basis of the movie. It is not intuitively obvious, and a jury verdict against us would not likely be overturned by the judge or appellate court. By the same token, if we win before a judge, we have a much better chance of holding onto our victory than if we won before a jury."

"From seeing Judge Schneider in court, I've been very impressed with him," Alain offered. "I have a good feeling about him."

"He is sharp as a tack, hardworking, and no nonsense," I added. "I was extraordinarily impressed with his handling of the summary judgment motions, and even his ruling against us on the experts is principled and well reasoned. I think he'll give us a fair shake."

"I might add that I don't see Judge Schneider being overwhelmed by Eddie Murphy—or anyone else," Zazi said. "He strikes me as oblivious to those kinds of influence."

"It seems to me that we have made a decision," Art said.

That was the way that we made all of our decisions. While Art and Alain respected my judgment and left tactical matters to Kaye, Scholer, we had agreed from the outset that all three of us had to concur on all strategy issues. It was a modus operandi that served us well throughout the case and contributed to the amazing fact that we never once had any serious disputes about how the case should be prosecuted.

Two days later and three days before the trial, we filed a notice waiving trial by jury—and held our breath. If Paramount insisted on a jury trial, we were stuck with a jury. To my amazement, Draper told Zazi the next day that Paramount was also going to waive the jury. At the time, I speculated that either Eddie wasn't going to appear or Draper felt uncomfortable about pleading his case before a jury.

My decision to waive a jury surprised a lot of people—including Paramount. Anyone who knew me realized that this was a counterintuitive move. I believe passionately that juries possess a collective wisdom that leads them to reach the correct result in the vast majority of cases. Usually not awed by privilege or power, juries are one of the last bastions of true democracy in a polarized society. And my courtroom style played better in front of juries than judges.

Yet I waived a jury trial. When all was said and done, I did it for one reason: Harvey Schneider.

As we left Jimmy's, we ran into Ned Tanen at a table near the exit. He was charming and friendly, just the way I remembered him from his deposition six months earlier. He complimented Art on his speech at Marty Davis's dinner in January and told us that our trial subpoena was jeopardizing his trip to Africa. And he told Alain that it had been much too long since they had lunch together.

As a matter of routine procedure, we had served subpoenas in late November on over twenty potential trial witnesses, including Jeffrey Katzenberg. Typically, after receiving the subpoena, the witness or his attorney calls to work out scheduling arrangements. Not long before trial, I got a call from Rick Clair at Disney while Zazi was in my office. Clair called to talk about Katzenberg's subpoena—he wanted me to withdraw it.

"Rick, I can't do that," I told him. "Jeff is an important witness for us."

"Look, Pierce, Jeff's schedule is crazy, and he is needed here at the company."

"Rick, I would like to accommodate Jeff. I'm not trying to bust his chops, but I need him."

"You don't need him. You took his deposition. He doesn't recall anything."

"I remember, Rick. Believe me, I remember his terminal amnesia."

"Then why do you need him?" Clair pressed.

"I have my reasons."

"Well, what are they?" Clair asked.

"I'm afraid I can't tell you my trial strategy. I need him."

"You can read his deposition at trial," Clair noted.

"No, I can't. He is a resident of Los Angeles County, so I can't read his deposition. He's legally available."

"Look, Pierce, we have been very impressed with your lawyering skills. You wouldn't want to do anything to hurt that favorable impression here at Disney."

"Thank you, Rick, I appreciate your kind words. But I still want Jeff."

"You're a very stubborn Irishman, O'Donnell. You're going to need expert witnesses, friends, around this town in your cases in the years ahead. Don't count on getting them."

"You'll have to do better than that, Rick," I calmly noted.

"You're just doing this for publicity, that's all."

"Have a nice day," I said and hung up.

Zazi had listened to my end of the conversation, and she knew something was terribly wrong. I repeated the entire conversation to her and then said, "Get me Jeff Katzenberg's trial examination outline. He's going to be very busy, all right. Testifying in Department 52—twice as long as I had originally planned."

On Monday, December 11, the Los Angeles *Times* broke a story previewing the trial which was now just three days away. The article was picked up by the wire services and published coast to coast. It was the first comprehensive public disclosure of what we had learned in a year of discovery.

I read the opening paragraph out loud to my wife Connie over morning coffee.

> "In a trial that promises to give the public a rare glimpse into the highest levels of Hollywood wheeling and dealing, humorist Art Buchwald and producer Alain Bernheim are taking Paramount Pictures to court Thursday, a year after suing the film company for allegedly stealing Buchwald's story concept to make the hit 1988 release 'Coming To America,' starring Eddie Murphy."

The lengthy story by Dennis McDougal on the first page of the Calendar Section then detailed the history of the case. It also included references to Jeffrey Katzenberg's 1983 letters to both John Landis and Brandon Tartikoff in which the then production chief at Paramount enthused over *King for a Day* as the next big Eddie Murphy movie. And, if there remained any doubt that Eddie Murphy knew all about *King for a Day*, the article also included references to the 1984 exchange of letters between Bob Wachs and Jim Harrison. The smoking gun that Dennis Landry had found buried in a Paramount file box eight months earlier had finally been fired in the largest-circulation daily newspaper in America.

Dennis McDougal had found the depositions and attached exhibits in the courthouse.

"There is a God," I said, putting the paper down on the breakfast table and breathing deep.

"Of course there is, silly," Connie said. "But is She on *your* side?"

Paramount had refused to return McDougal's calls as he was writing the blockbuster story, but its lawyers had a comment. The next day, Draper filed an innocuous-sounding "Memorandum Re Pre-Trial Publicity." The contents, however, were hardly harmless.

Draper accused Kaye, Scholer of willfully violating the gag agreement. He alleged that a lawyer from their side had seen McDougal "in a meeting with Mr. O'Donnell on November 30, 1989" when Judge Pacht was in our offices for the discovery hearing. Draper also charged that the two Katzenberg letters and Wachs correspondence highlighted by McDougal had not been publicly filed at the courthouse but were attached as exhibits to the plaintiffs' confidential settlement memorandum that I had filed with Judge Schoettler the previous week. Therefore, Draper concluded, "the only way that McDougal could have obtained these documents . . . would have been if the Confidential Settlement Statement was given to Mr. McDougal by plaintiffs' attorneys on December 8, 1989, the exact day upon which they signed the Stipulation Re Communications with the News Media."

Draper's attack on my integrity was devastating. I had just waived a jury and agreed to have Judge Schneider decide the case. The judge did not know me or my reputation, but he did have on his desk allegations which, if believed, indicated that my word could not be trusted. For a trial lawyer whose credibility is his stock in trade, it could be a mortal blow.

The charge was absolutely false. No one at Kaye, Scholer had given McDougal any documents or violated in any way the gag stipulation. I had met with McDougal and given him a briefing, over a week before the agreement was signed, but that was not prohibited by the pact. I was not quoted in McDougal's article—either by name or as a source—and his article twice mentioned that my clients and I would not comment. Everything I had told McDougal was an accurate, factual account of the record.

Worse yet, I also told Judge Schneider in a formal response filed the next day, the charge was predicated on a demonstrably erroneous assumption that the three explosive documents were not part of the court record.

> In truth, each of the documents quoted by Mr. McDougal is part of the public file in this case—and has been for over one month! Indisputably, the presence of these exhibits in the public court record could not have escaped the notice of anyone who, as Paramount's counsel has represented to the Court, in fact "reviewed the files in this case." Worse yet, we have learned that Robert Draper . . . was told by Mr. McDougal—*before* he filed his Memorandum Re Pre-Trial Publicity with its vicious allegations—that the reporter obtained the documents from the court records. . . .
>
> The time has come for the Court to put a stop to the war that Paramount has declared on Plaintiffs' counsel. Character assassination is no substitute for truth and justice. And if Paramount thinks that it can intimidate Plaintiffs and their counsel, it has, once again, sorely misjudged its opponents.

The same day that Paramount filed its baseless assault on my integrity Bob Wachs sent a letter on Eddie Murphy Productions stationery to George Cotliar, managing editor of the Los Angeles *Times*, complaining that he had been misrepresented in McDougal's article. Apparently relying on Draper, Wachs claimed that the Harrison correspondence was not public record and demanded a retraction. The paper refused and heard nothing more from Wachs.

For the next two days I drilled my witnesses, including Buchwald. I couldn't get them to recite Shakespeare backward the way Edward Bennett Williams used to say he could, but at least I prepared them about what *not* to say.

"This will be a war fought as much in front of the TV cameras as it will be in front of a judge," I told them, feeling very much like Vince Lombardi, the legendary head coach of the Green Bay Packers and Washington Redskins.

I was especially tough on Art. His performance under Draper's stiletto questioning concerned me. I did not want him losing his cool on the witness stand when Draper baited him with the plagiarism rap. Until Eddie Murphy showed up, I told him, Art would be the star everyone would be clamoring to quote. His sound bites had to be crisp, witty and on point.

"For instance, you say in your deposition that Alain and you were 'screwed' by Paramount," I told him. "Don't say that on the stand or in the hallway when the cameras are on you. Let me suggest that you tell them you were 'shafted.'

"You can get away with 'screwed' in the New York *Post*, but conservative papers like the *Times* or TV news will edit it out."

Art nodded. He understood well enough since his column ran in many family newspapers. Besides, he said, whatever you called it—screwed, shafted or diddled—in the end it was the same thing.

"Paramount fucked us," he said.

"*Don't* say that for the cameras," I begged.

The day before trial, Buchwald was home in bed sick. He had a bad cold, and he sounded terrible on the phone. I also suspected that he may have had a case of pretrial jitters.

Bernheim was not sick, but he was anxious. For seven years Alain's experience with Art's project had been nothing but a cruel cycle of rising expectations followed by crushing disappointment. If it was within my power, I promised him, that would all end in a few weeks. All he had to do was stay cool and be himself on the witness stand.

Paramount remained placid. Far above Columbus Circle in New York City, Martin Davis—apparently unconcerned about his former friend's $5 million lawsuit on the other side of the country—began preparing an annual report on another profitable year for his conglomerate and its cash cow Paramount Pictures.

Eddie Murphy was at home in New Jersey, celebrating the birth of his first child.

And, in Hollywood, the curtain was about to rise on *Buchwald v. Paramount.* Rehearsals were over. The trial would be live, televised and bruising. And the outcome was uncertain.

Part Three

— — — — — — — — — —

Lights, Camera, Action!

20

Promises, Promises

―――――――――――

"BUCHWALD V. PARAMOUNT. Counsel, please state appearances for the record," said Judge Harvey Schneider.

I glanced at the large institutional clock mounted on the east wall of Department 52 of the downtown Los Angeles Superior Courthouse. It was 9:45 A.M., December 15, 1989—nearly eighteen months since that first fateful phone call from Danny Arnold.

Schneider's tiny fifth-floor courtroom was packed, mostly with members of the press and Paramount brass. Chairman Frank Mancuso was there. So were Joshua Wattles and the studio's general counsel, Robert Pisano, a former O'Melveny & Myers litigation partner who had hired his former law firm at the last minute to defend Paramount.

The first scene of *Buchwald v. Paramount* was about to begin. After nearly thirteen months of taking twenty-five depositions and reviewing hundreds of thousands of pages of documents, we were ready. I had compressed my case into one large black notebook in which I kept my outlines for witness examination, opening statement and closing argument.

"Pierce O'Donnell, Zazi Pope, Suzanne Tragert and Marsha Durko for plaintiffs, your honor," I heard myself say in what I hoped was a firm, self-confident voice.

The thin, bearded attorney who had recently become my sworn adversary on behalf of Paramount Pictures stood up from the left side of the counsel table and made his own introductions.

"Robert Draper, Lionel Sobel and Steven Warren for defendants," said Draper in his distinctive nasal twang. "And may I introduce Frank Mancuso, who is the chairman and chief executive of Paramount Pictures."

Already the celebrity appeal of the trial was being laid before Schneider and the assembled press. I couldn't let Draper upstage me.

"May I likewise introduce Alain Bernheim, your honor, one of the plaintiffs in this case. Mr. Buchwald is nursing a cold and will be here Monday morning," I said.

Draper shot me an icy glance, then smiled.

"May I introduce Elizabeth Loper, your honor, who is my executive producer," he said with a flourish, indicating his paralegal who stood guard over a stack of defense exhibits at Paramount's end of the counsel table.

Schneider shuddered at the opening histrionics.

"The introductions now completed? All right," he said. "Mr. O'Donnell, you may begin your opening statement."

I then proceeded to promise Schneider, and the assembled press, "the anatomy of a movie" in a very important case for "the creative arts community in Hollywood." It was my goal, I told an impassive Schneider, "to teach Paramount and others like it a memorable lesson and to deter them from ever mistreating creative people like this again."

The evidence would take us through the creative process of filmmaking, from inspiration to box office, using the saga of *King for a Day* as our case study. Art and Alain themselves would tell how their movie for Eddie Murphy was nursed along by Paramount for three years to the tune of close to $500,000, dumped, and resurrected a year later at Warner Bros.

But they would also hear how, two years later, Eddie Murphy—the world's biggest box office star whose movies have grossed over one billion dollars—supposedly experienced an independent inspiration during a bus ride through middle America following the breakup with his girlfriend. The same movie idea, according to Paramount, descended upon the brokenhearted comedian, who then made his own version of an African prince in the United States: *Coming to America.*

And the Buchwald/Bernheim project was, again, unceremoniously dumped —this time, by Warner Bros., which was uncomfortable with the "uncanny and striking resemblance" between Buchwald's story and Eddie's new movie.

"As Jeff Katzenberg will testify this morning, once you've had exposure to someone else's idea, you really can't unscramble the egg," I pointed out. "You can't sort out where you learned something. There *is* someone who could have independently created *Coming to America*, but that man or woman is not here and will not testify."

I glanced around to see if ears had perked up to hear just who that man or woman could have been. They had. Even the placid Frank Mancuso leaned forward a little in his chair. Who? Arsenio Hall? Eddie Murphy? John Landis?

"There could have been a weather observer at the North Pole between 1983 and 1988, incommunicado. And in our modern society that means three things: no phone, no fax, and no Federal Express. *That* person could be an independent creator of *Coming to America.*

"But not Eddie Murphy, who was on the Paramount lot during this period of time and fully exposed, as was his staff, to . . . *King for a Day.* As a matter of biology, and law, the evidence will show you simply cannot have an immaculate conception after you have been pregnant."

After outlining the overwhelming similarities of both works, I told Schneider that the evidence would show that Buchwald's *King for a Day* and Paramount's *Coming to America* were "as close as any fraternal twins born of the same parents. The evidence is overwhelming that Art Buchwald's story inspired *Coming to America.*"

Buchwald's reputation was worth repeating, even though I knew everyone in the courtroom understood that I was not representing some amateur off the street. Lawyers are given to hyperbole, but there was no need in Art's case: a Pulitzer Prize winner, author of over thirty books, playwright, novelist, humorist, raconteur and internationally renowned newspaper columnist.

"Sadly, the evidence shows in this case, your honor, that even a towering literary figure like Art Buchwald is easy prey to an unscrupulous major motion picture studio," I concluded.

What Buchwald sold Paramount was an idea, I acknowledged, but ideas were the lifeblood of Hollywood. Paramount itself conceded that point in a philosophy paper Katzenberg wrote and distributed to the studio's inner circle in June 1982.

"This document reveals what that collective wisdom thought was the most successful ingredient for moviemaking, your honor. Quote: 'Idea is King and material is Queen.' What a good idea! Paramount wrote it down for us. Here it is."

I waved the Katzenberg memo toward Draper like a red flag at a bull before continuing my reading.

"Quote: 'Essence lies in the way it is new, unique, different, or in some way imaginative and exciting. A compelling idea may not be strictly original, but it will seem different and engaging for its time.'"

Art's idea was so terrific that the studio sank half a million dollars into it over a two-year period, I reminded the Court.

But there was someone more important to Paramount than Buchwald or Bernheim—or virtually anyone else who ever had the least thing to do with making a motion picture, I said.

"Mr. Mancuso told the *Wall Street Journal* a few months ago that Eddie Murphy is Paramount's Kellogg's Corn Flakes," I said. "But the evidence will also show, I respectfully submit, that Eddie Murphy is more than the corn flakes kid at Paramount Studios. Eddie calls the shots. Whatever Eddie wants, Eddie gets.

"If he wants Paramount to put its name on vulgar concert movies like *Raw*, okay, Eddie.

"If he wants a scene shot his way, he summons the president of the studio, Ned Tanen, to the set. Okay, Eddie.

"And if he tells the president of the studio, Ned Tanen, that he's conceived a movie idea strikingly similar to Buchwald's original idea, okay, Eddie.

"And, as the evidence will show, too bad, Buchwald and Bernheim."

I looked over my shoulder at Frank Mancuso, sitting quietly behind the railing that separated spectators from the judge and attorneys. If looks could kill, I was a dead man.

For the next several minutes, I held up document after document that Landry had dug up on his first fishing expedition, showing Paramount's complicity in knowing full well that *King for a Day* was being molded into two screenplays specifically for Eddie Murphy: Katzenberg's 1983 letters to both John Landis and Brandon Tartikoff, extolling the virtues of the Buchwald story; internal memos showing the progress of script development and, of course, the correspondence between Jim Harrison and Bob Wachs in the fall of 1984.

"I'm not sure the defense anymore is what did Eddie know and when did he know it, but rather when did he forget it," I said sarcastically.

I knew the press would leap on the next morsels. *Coming to America* would gross over $400 million, the studio had already collected over $50 million in distribution fees, and Eddie Murphy's cut would be $22 million, I said. Even so, the movie would remain forever unprofitable because studio accounting practices ate up everything with expenses. When I quoted from Murphy's deposition testimony about someone having to be crazy to accept "monkey points," I heard a couple of the journalists behind me laugh out loud.

The opening scene of *Buchwald v. Paramount* was coming in at under a quarter of an hour. I had worked hard to compress my opening statement and distill our case to its essence. One of the great mistakes that trial lawyers make in their openings is to promise more than they can deliver in the trial. Your opponent will crucify you in closing argument if you fail to make good on your promises.

For that reason, I cautiously limited my promises about what the evidence would show to exhibits that I was confident would be admitted into evidence and admissions that I had obtained in depositions. If I proved more, as I expected I would, it would enhance my credibility. For now, however, less was better.

I launched into my climax.

"Your honor, the case here, I believe, is clear and compelling. . . . I know as an experienced trial lawyer that I have quite a bit of convincing to do." After all, I told Schneider, Paramount was one of the original film studios and, given the kind of conduct that I had alleged, its prominence alone would be a tough obstacle to overcome.

"But I'm happy that we're in this courtroom, your honor, where reason and logic and the evidence will prevail. And we are happy to submit the cause of the plaintiffs in this case to your honor. Thank you."

I sat down. Zazi squeezed my right arm. Judge Schneider was still inscrutable.

Behind me, seats squeaked as reporters and others in the audience readjusted themselves for the next scene. The faint sound of pencil lead racing across two dozen notebooks could be heard as Bob Draper helped his paralegal set up an overhead projector and scoot a couple of aluminum easels out onto the courtroom floor. Paramount was mounting a major production. As everyone settled back down, Draper began.

"Your honor, you asked yesterday for a copy of *Coming to America*. I have a copy for you I'd like to give to the clerk," he said, holding up a videocassette of the movie.

"Hand it to the clerk, please," Schneider said.

"So that there won't be any charge of undue influence, it's $19.99," Draper said smugly.

Schneider did not seem amused.

"There still won't be any net profits, your honor," I interjected.

The judge didn't laugh, but the gallery behind me did. I heard pencils scribbling madly, jotting down this opening parry and thrust for the news reports that would be written later that day. Draper was undaunted and, in fact, buoyed up by what he saw as a real street fight. He made it clear, right away, that this was a grudge match between him and me.

"The plaintiffs' position, as I understand it in this case, is that Paramount is a venal corporation that loves to rip off people like Mr. Bernheim and Mr. Buchwald. Mr. Buchwald has testified that Mr. O'Donnell loves to sue movie studios. He has said that both under oath and on the large number of talk shows in which he publicized this lawsuit."

Draper fumbled with the projector, finally hitting the switch that displayed a list of Eddie Murphy's hit movies and their release dates on a screen set up on one side of the courtroom. Murphy was in high gear by 1985, when Paramount dumped *King for a Day*, he pointed out. Why would the studio, "desperate for ideas," dump a good idea? he asked rhetorically. Just to spite Buchwald and Bernheim?

"The idea that Paramount would go out intentionally in 1985 or at any other time and attempt to affirmatively harm these people just doesn't make any sense, particularly if they had the wonderful idea that was going to make tons of money for whoever picked it up. It makes no sense," he said.

The real reason Paramount ditched *King for a Day* was that it tried three times to come up with a workable script and failed. Buchwald's idea, Draper told the court, "just wouldn't write."

"You indicated you want to read those scripts," Draper told Schneider. "I wish you the best of luck. I wish you Godspeed. You're going to find that exactly what I'm saying is true."

At that point, Draper got personal, going after Buchwald's reputation as a writer. Addressing the absent humorist as "this brilliant columnist," Paramount's lawyer pointed out that Art had written three movie treatments in his career—all failures. *The Gift* lost Stanley Donen and Columbia $7 million, he said. *The Beard* had been ricocheting around Hollywood for ten years without getting made into a film. And a wacky comedy sketch he wrote back in the fifties about a movie star marrying the prince of Monaco was deep-sixed when it turned out that Grace Kelly actually *did* marry Prince Rainier.

"Now, I don't think that he sued at that time, but also Mr. O'Donnell was not his lawyer at that time," Draper said. The honey badger was in good form —Art couldn't write and his lawyer was a bum.

As for *King for a Day*, it simply bore no resemblance to *Coming to America*. Tanen was on the money when he concluded after the Paramount commissary lunch with Bernheim that "any contention that the two are similar, are based upon any similar material, is absolutely ridiculous.

"The similarity is that a black African prince comes to America," Draper said, shrugging. "And I don't know Eddie Murphy is going to play—if he's to play a prince, he's not exactly going to play a *French* prince. The idea that somehow Eddie Murphy, this bad Eddie Murphy, this dumb Eddie Murphy is such a force at Paramount that it's an incentive for them to be un-nice to Mr. Buchwald and Mr. Bernheim and not pay them $250,000, I don't think stands up," he said.

And why would Paramount want to cheat Art Buchwald out of his $50,000 —especially when his personal friend Martin Davis is "the top guy . . . in New York. He's the whole conglomerate.

"It sounds, when my friend Mr. O'Donnell says it, like such a greedy, venal thing for Eddie Murphy to get pure gross profits. On the same movie, John Landis got 10 percent pure gross profits. And you will hear testimony that it is standard in the industry for people like Eddie Murphy to get pure gross profits because they make the movie. That's the way the movie business works. You take a look at what's making the money for you.

"What I'm trying to point out is that Mr. O'Donnell, who loves to sue movie studios, is leading Mr. Buchwald and all the other creative people in the industry—actors, directors, producers, writers and studio people—down a primrose path that would destroy the industry. They don't really believe that Eddie Murphy ripped them off. That's not their case," he said.

Then the hard-nosed Draper pulled an emotional about-face.

"I'm new to this case," he said in a palms-up appeal. "Mr. O'Donnell refers to me when he wants to make a point about me as Paramount's 'new lawyer.' I am Paramount's new lawyer. I got into the case when my friend, Bob Pisano, my former partner and now general counsel of Paramount, called me when I was at a baseball tournament in Phoenix. I was playing actually, believe it or not. And he said, 'I've got a two- or three-day case that has about six documents and two depositions. Can you try it?' I said, 'Sure, Bob, I trust you.' "

I smiled at Zazi. She grinned back, slightly raising her clenched fist off the counsel table at this small triumph. Whether he meant to do so or not,

Draper was publicly acknowledging that this third-rate literary theft—that he and the puffed-up Paramount lawyers figured to blow off like so much dust—had risen up to bite a big chunk out of their collective rear end.

Draper told the court he read from my deposition of Eddie Murphy while eating Thanksgiving dinner.

"Mr. O'Donnell says, 'Well, can you tell me that you didn't have anything in your subconscious you didn't know about?' And Eddie says, 'I can't tell you what's in my subconscious.'

"And when I was taking a bite of turkey in one hand and reading the deposition, I said, 'This is getting a little weird.'

"What they are claiming, I think the evidence will show, is that Eddie didn't intentionally rip them off, as Mr. O'Donnell says. Eddie didn't want to rip them off but in his subconscious, he ripped them off," Draper concluded.

Again I glanced at Zazi. This time she shrugged. Farther down the counsel table, Marsha and Suzanne looked equally puzzled. Draper seemed to be rambling. He even invoked one expert whose deposition I had never taken: he had his twelve-year-old daughter compare *King for a Day* and *Coming to America*, he told the court. She saw what even he hadn't seen.

"She not only said she didn't think they were similar, she said that the reason was the character doesn't change" in *Coming to America*, Draper explained. "Eddie Murphy is the same in scene one as he is in scene two and the whole movie. The whole treatment by Buchwald is about a character change."

I dimly recalled that my professors back in my undergraduate days at Georgetown drummed it into my head that even the early Greek playwrights recognized that characters had to change between Act One and Act Three. Good ones became bad, bad ones became good. If you had no change, you had no story. What Draper and his daughter seemed to be saying, however, was that Eddie Murphy didn't have to change.

Draper called his "executive producer" into play, having her set up charts on the easels that he used to walk Judge Schneider through Paramount's version of the two stories, *King for a Day* and *Coming to America*. He pointed out the many differences and the few similarities, including the fast-food restaurant scene in Tab Murphy's initial script where the African king finally takes a job during his sojourn in the Washington ghetto.

"There is a scene in *Coming to America* where Mr. Murphy goes to work for McDowell's and it's a rip-off from McDonald's," said Draper. "And he goes there not because he has to work. He is there because he's fallen in love with a woman that looks very much like your reporter."

Judge Schneider blinked. Draper's gaze fell on Mary Malone, the attractive young court reporter, who bore little resemblance to Shari Headley beyond the fact that she was young, pretty and black. Malone smiled and looked away, embarrassed.

"I'm married. Not for long," said Draper.

Zazi leaned over and whispered in my ear:

"What the hell was *that* all about?"

Draper barreled on, oblivious to Schneider's consternation, Malone's confusion or the tittering among the audience.

Then he went for the jugular.

"And it's interesting to me that in a case where Mr. Buchwald, or Mr. Buchwald's lawyers, contend that Eddie Murphy ripped off Art Buchwald, that the evidence will show more strongly, if that were the case, that Mr. Buchwald ripped off Charlie Chaplin."

I rocked forward in my seat, Draper's words—"Buchwald ripped off Charlie Chaplin"—reverberating in my mind. Draper might just as well have hit me in the face with his Thanksgiving turkey. Art's worst nightmare had come true. The case had taken an ugly turn. From that moment on, we had to win two lawsuits—the one we had filed against Paramount a year earlier, and the one the studio had just "filed" against Art Buchwald.

Draper instructed his paralegal to peel off the charts on the easels, exposing side-by-side synopses of the stories for *King for a Day* and a little-known 1957 comedy made by Charlie Chaplin, *A King in New York*. Draper took full credit for his pièce de résistance. I wrote down his words verbatim for future reference:

"The charts I've put up for you about *A King in New York* and *A Crude, Crude World* and *The Quest* are my representations to you as to what I believe you will see when you watch those two movies and you read Mr. Buchwald's treatments."

Chaplin was sixty-eight when he made *A King in New York*. He had been living in England for nearly a decade, an exile from the United States where he had incurred the wrath of Senator Joseph McCarthy by insisting upon an open mind toward socialism.

A King in New York was an uneven political satire about a deposed European monarch, played by a white-haired Chaplin, who visits the United States during the McCarthy era. The finger pointing and false accusations about the king's political leanings formed the backdrop for the plot—a send-up of the Communist hysteria of the day. But the king did have a comic love interest of sorts in a sultry TV advertising pitchwoman.

During his Paris years with the *Herald Tribune*, Art had written a column about *A King in New York*. Draper found it and proceeded to lay out a claim that Art had stolen Chaplin's idea. He was trying to turn the case into a plagiarism suit, regardless of the contract. If the rules had allowed for an objection in the middle of opening arguments, I would have hollered out loud at that point.

But Draper went on. If Eddie Murphy could subconsciously "steal" Art's idea, why couldn't Buchwald subconsciously "steal" Charlie Chaplin's?

Eddie Murphy would testify as to how he came up with the idea for *Coming to America*, Draper said. Eddie did not always write his ideas down. Not everybody did. Draper himself didn't, except when the idea was really, really important.

"Mr. O'Donnell made a point about paternity. I thought that was quite a nice analysis, to be honest," he said. "My notes say 'Paternal case would take a blood test.' What that means, in my shorthand, is if this *were* a paternity case, what we need is a blood test to determine who was the father of this movie."

Jeff Katzenberg would testify, Draper promised, that if such a test were adopted he'd have to go out of business. He could not have a conversation. He could not enter into an option agreement. That would be the result of this test.

Draper was asking Judge Schneider to swallow the hyperbole that these two Hollywood outsiders were about to wreck an industry—"they are leading the creative community down a path that is destructive of the creative process.

". . . When you look at the contract, when you look at the treatment, when you look at the scripts, when you look at all the evidence that's coming in, keep in mind, your honor, what industry we're talking about," he said. "And keep in mind that the contract must be interpreted, reasonably, in the context of the industry that it's entered into in order for the contract to be properly interpreted. Now, I'm finished. I look forward—when it comes time, not just to state the evidence but actually present our argument—to talking with you about this more. But I appreciate your indulgence."

Schneider sighed deeply and glanced at the clock.

"All right," he said wearily. "We'll be in recess till five after eleven."

21

The Great
Embellisher

THE FICTION that Jeff Katzenberg bandied about town was that he never talked to the press. The fact was that he talked all the time to the media if it served his purposes. He manipulated reporters as well as, or better than, nearly anyone in Hollywood. When he showed up December 15 as our first witness, dressed in a form-fitting light blue business suit, he was all smiles.

He took his place among the reporters and made nervous small talk but seemed always aware of his station. He was a studio executive—perhaps *the* studio executive of the future.

The Fox Entertainment News camera, maintaining silent vigil, scanned the scene, picking out famous faces for the nightly news. As pool camera, the Fox crew would furnish tape to other broadcasters in much the same way that a wire service like Associated Press supplies stories to hundreds of newspapers. More than anyone else in the courtroom, Katzenberg—as he adjusted his silk tie for the camera before stepping to the witness stand and taking the oath— seemed to be conscious of the global reach of *Buchwald v. Paramount* in the Video Age.

"You started out right away as a young fellow in the motion picture business or the entertainment business?" I began.

"Pretty much," Katzenberg answered.

"What did you do?"

"I worked for an independent producer for a short period of time, and I was an agent for about twenty-five minutes. And about 1973, I guess, went to work as an assistant to the chairman of Paramount," Katzenberg told me through his ever present smile.

"Were you about twenty-two years old then, is that right?"

"Yes."

Katzenberg was a veteran at the tender age of thirty-eight.

"Since you've been at Disney, what are some of the successful movies that Disney released?"

"*Roger Rabbit. Blaze.* Opened two days ago. *Little Mermaid.* Opened a few weeks before that," he said directly into the lens of the Fox camera.

"We're going to charge you a camera fee here," I remarked.

"I hope so. Now playing at a theater near you," he replied with an easy laugh.

When the interrogation shifted to Buchwald's *King for a Day*, Jeff began to have memory trouble again. I gave him a letter Alain had written to International Creative Management agent Sam Cohn on December 3, 1982, reiterating Bernheim's conversation with Katzenberg about Paramount's plans for *King for a Day.*

"Have you had a chance to review that document?"

"Yes, I have," Katzenberg said, never for a moment letting his bright, white smile vanish before the TV camera.

"Does that help refresh your recollection?"

"No, not at all," he said.

"Do you have any reason to believe that that conversation didn't occur?"

"I have no reason to believe it did occur," he said with a small, self-assured shrug. "The fact that a third party who was not in the room recounts to somebody that [the conversation] occurred, I don't have any recollection of it."

What the hell was going on here? I tried again.

"Did you believe that Buchwald's movie concept would be a terrific multi-star vehicle?"

"I don't recall."

"You don't remember ever saying that it was an excellent idea?"

"I may have."

He smiled benignly at me and flashed his winning smile directly over my shoulder at the TV camera again. After his deposition performance, I had thought that Katzenberg's lawyers would get him to stop the "I don't recall" routine about letters, memos and notes that he had written about *King for a Day.*

Suddenly, McDougal's words about the Hollywood executives club flashed through my mind. They might seem like competitors, but studio brass were interchangeable. When outsiders threatened their comfortable arrangement, they circled the wagons. Their only true loyalty was to one another. I had almost made the mistake of forgetting that Katzenberg was a pro who was not above convenient memory lapses if he thought it would somehow save his stand-up-guy image within the industry.

And I also suspected by now another reason why Disney's studio chairman was being so evasive: Katzenberg was wooing Eddie to come to Disney when his five-picture deal with Paramount terminated. No matter what happened, it would never be said that his courtroom testimony gave any comfort to Eddie's accusers. Once I realized what Jeff was up to, I decided to accentuate his recalcitrance so that Judge Schneider could see for himself the arrogance that I believed epitomizes top studio bosses. In that way, rather than helping Paramount and Eddie, Katzenberg would become a star witness for the plaintiffs.

Whenever Katzenberg strayed from the record, I impeached him by reading from his deposition or the exhibits. It was pure gold, and Judge Schneider took notes every time I mined another nugget. Katzenberg was powerless to do anything about it.

"And do you recall that on July 1, 1983, you wrote a letter to John Landis describing, among other things, *King for a Day?*"

"You're going to show it to me, so—"

"You're right again, Mr. Katzenberg," I said.

I handed over the list of "exciting" movie projects Katzenberg had mailed to John Landis, including one titled *King for a Day* which Katzenberg himself had earlier said he intended to use as a "star vehicle" for Eddie Murphy. Murphy was "familiar" with Buchwald's story and liked it, Katzenberg enthused in his letter to Landis.

This was one of the key letters that I had shown him in his deposition and McDougal had quoted in his article a few days before trial started.

I asked him point-blank whether this was "an accurate and truthful statement" about Eddie liking Buchwald's story.

"I'm not sure."

I then asked him why he was not sure that his statement in the letter to Landis was accurate and truthful. I deliberately violated the cardinal rule about not asking a witness on cross-examination a "why" question. This was the exception to the rule, however. I knew why, and I wanted the witness to squirm on the witness stand as I rubbed his nose in his evasiveness.

After giving this now familiar exhibit a quick once-over, Katzenberg cleared his throat and carefully framed a rehearsed response.

"Well, I think that, as with some other documents that you've put before me in the last couple of months, I'm in a business of selling," he said. "And in the interest of interesting someone else in a project, you make it as enticing as you can for their consideration. So, I would say to you, it's possible that this is exactly accurate. It is also possible that I've embellished it."

"Does that mean it wasn't true?" I asked.

"As I said to you, I don't know," Katzenberg said, losing his toothsome smile for the first time that morning. "I'm saying to you there is a—it is possible that it is not 100 percent accurate. . . ."

"What do you mean by 'embellished'?" I asked.

"Make something appealing. Interesting."

"Does that mean you can make a false statement?"

Katzenberg fidgeted with his tie and shifted his weight around in the witness chair.

"You can—I don't think a false statement is necessarily—I don't think that the issue is black or white. These are subjective judgments and they are subjective opinions about what embellishment means," he said.

"Was it subjective when you wrote it on July 1, 1983, to say that Eddie Murphy was familiar with the Buchwald idea?" I asked.

"I don't have a specific recollection of having—of how accurate this was six or seven years ago when I said it," he said. "It may have been. It may not have been."

"My question, sir, was: did you consider, when you wrote the words 'familiar with the idea,' that that was a subjective judgment . . . that he was familiar with it?"

Katzenberg's smile returned, but it was muted.

"Could be," he said.

But Judge Schneider was not appeased. The skeptical jurist wasn't even certain that Katzenberg had written the letter.

"Well, have we established that he wrote the words?" he asked me. "Or that he wrote the letter? I don't know that he wrote the words yet, do I?"

Apparently thinking that he was about to be rescued, Katzenberg was grinning again.

"You sent the letter, did you not, sir?" I asked.

"Yes, I did."

"And you read the letter before you sent it?"

"Yes."

"And you believed it was accurate at the time you wrote it?"

"For the purposes of which I was sending it, yes."

"Which was to hype John Landis?" I asked.

"Yes," Katzenberg answered.

From the defense side of the counsel table, Draper was not taking kindly to the media intrusion in the courtroom. Katzenberg was playing to the camera and hurting Paramount's case. And while I might have been prevented from talking to the press about the case outside the courtroom, I was free to get our message across by asking tough, embarrassing questions inside the courtroom. Draper knew what I was doing but was powerless to stop it.

When I asked Judge Schneider to read from Katzenberg's deposition about the Landis letter, Draper could contain his frustration no longer.

"I'd like to read. I'd like to get on camera!" he exclaimed.

"Gentlemen, let's just try our case, please," Schneider said.

Once I had extracted the truth from Katzenberg that the Landis letter did, indeed, contain references to a Murphy/Buchwald link, I went on to the equally damaging Tartikoff letter.

" 'Dear Brandon,' " I read. " 'Michael [Eisner] just charged in my office and told me that I have ten minutes to give you, in writing, the entire future of Paramount Pictures.' Was that a little bit of an overstatement?" I asked.

"No, Michael does that all the time," Katzenberg said.

"Still?"

"Absolutely—not with Paramount," he corrected himself.

Then something truly extraordinary happened—a lucky break that I could never have imagined would fall in my lap on the first day of trial.

At one point during my examination, Draper interrupted me to ask for a chambers conference. This struck me as odd since there was no jury to worry about hearing whatever he wanted to say, and I was not engaging in any inappropriate conduct in my interrogation of Katzenberg.

I soon learned why Draper didn't want anyone in the courtroom to hear what he had to say to Judge Schneider.

"Your honor, I have a special request to ask," Draper began as Schneider, still wearing his black robe, stood by the side of his desk. I watched from the sidelines, leaning against the bookcase as the scene unfolded.

"The courtroom as you know is packed with reporters," Draper continued. "When we break, they will descend upon Mr. Katzenberg as he leaves through the courtroom doors that lead to the fifth-floor hallway. Mr. Katzenberg's lawyer has asked me to ask the Court if Mr. Katzenberg could be allowed to leave by the back door near the witness stand. I understand that there is an interior hallway that would lead from your chambers to an exit that would allow Mr. Katzenberg to avoid the press."

I looked at Judge Schneider as Draper spoke, a frown moving across his face like a dark cloud.

"Let me see if I understand," Schneider began. "You want me to help Mr. Katzenberg sneak out the back way through my chambers so that he doesn't have to face the media. Is that what you're saying?"

Draper, apparently oblivious to the damning message he was delivering, replied, "Well, I guess that's one way of interpreting the request."

"It's the only valid interpretation, isn't it, Mr. Draper?" The judge gave Draper a cold, hard stare. "Let me think about it. I want to consult with a colleague of mine."

When I arrived back at counsel table, I leaned over to Zazi and Suzanne and whispered cryptically: "We don't have to worry any more about the judge appreciating the type of people we are dealing with here."

Back on the witness stand later in the day, Katzenberg claimed that the letter he sent to Brandon Tartikoff just before Christmas, 1983, was just as much an "embellished" Paramount communiqué as the one he had sent to Landis the previous summer. He still could not bring himself to use the word "lied."

"If [the John Landis letter] was a sales document in its intent, this is that squared," Katzenberg announced to the courtroom after scanning what he had written six years earlier to the president of NBC.

"Even more hyping sales?" I asked.

"Yes."

"What are you trying to sell Tartikoff?" I asked.

"What I'm selling him is the new schedule of production out of Disney—not Disney, excuse me, out of Paramount," Katzenberg said, catching his faux pas with a self-conscious grin.

"Hype letter, I guess, is that a fair description of it?" I asked.

Katzenberg cleared his throat.

"Sales document, we refer to it as."

Regardless of what they were called, the Tartikoff and Landis letters established, at the very beginning of the trial, the link between Murphy and Buchwald that I wanted Schneider to hear. The next step was to show that Katzenberg, who had already admitted to professional "embellishing," was equally capable of embellishment in other aspects of his professional life.

"How many telephone calls do you make a day?"

"It varies. It's reported that it's two hundred."

"How many scripts do you read in a week?"

"About a dozen."

"Let me ask a question," Schneider interrupted. "Does that twelve scripts a week relate to a period of time at Paramount?"

"For the fifteen years I've been—I've always done that," Katzenberg said, looking up to his right at the judge. Schneider nodded, stroking his chin.

Reading again from Katzenberg's July deposition, I tried to show Schneider that the Disney executive's memory of *King for a Day* and how it may have evolved into *Coming to America* was hazy at best. His comprehension of the hundreds of movie projects on his mind at any one time was broad . . . but not very deep.

Draper objected.

"I don't see the relevance," he said. "We're talking about six or seven years after the fact."

"That's my point," I said. "He gave deposition testimony that he is not able to differentiate when he's read a treatment and then he's read a screenplay, and then he's seen a motion picture. And that's a very important part of plaintiffs' case . . . about Eddie Murphy and the independent creation defense."

Draper shot me a self-confident look.

"Actually, it's an important part of ours," he said. "I'll withdraw the objection."

Up on the witness stand, Katzenberg fidgeted. He hadn't a clue as to what Draper and I were sparring over.

"And that's not accurate as to what I believe I said," the befuddled Disney executive blurted out, drawing snickers from the courtroom spectators.

"Well, outside of that we seem to have nothing but agreement," Schneider said wryly. "Go ahead."

Nailing an embellisher of Katzenberg's stature was going to be harder than I anticipated. I rephrased and reframed my line of questioning.

"If I wanted to know at any given time what Paramount knew about development . . . for *King for a Day*, the best place to look would be in the files where there might be written material such as a treatment or screenplay, is that correct?" I asked.

"Not solely," he said.

"Where else would we look?"

"To a large degree, inside the heads of the creative executives," Katzenberg said.

Bingo! In other words, inside the minds of studio executives with convenient memories! I hoped that Harvey Schneider was paying close attention.

I was about to ask another question along the same lines, but decided against it. "Quit while you're ahead," I said to myself. After a few more questions, I sat. Draper stood.

"Mr. Katzenberg, my name is Bob Draper and I represent Paramount Pictures. A competitor of yours, right?"

"Yes, it is."

"And are you willing to reveal all the projects you have under development?" Draper asked.

"I'd prefer not to but I may be compelled to," Katzenberg replied.

"I don't think so," Schneider interjected.

Draper rehashed Katzenberg's reluctant answers about the list of movie projects he had outlined in the Landis and Tartikoff letters. Despite Katzenberg's "optimistic" language, at least 75 percent of those projects on the list had never been made.

The handful that were made generally flopped at the box office—like the 1985 sci-fi comedy *The Explorers*.

"Was it what you might call in the movie industry a dismal failure?" Draper asked.

"No. Didn't work," Katzenberg said.

"I'll go with that. Have you been involved with any dismal failures?" he asked.

"Not in my life," Katzenberg insisted. "Never saw a movie I didn't like."

"Do you believe that Eddie Murphy is a comedic genius?" he asked.

"Yes," said Katzenberg.

"Do you believe that Eddie Murphy has a talent to write a successful motion picture?" Draper asked.

"Yes," said Katzenberg.

That should have been enough, but Draper wanted to drive home his point like a bullet.

"Is it correct that if someone had pitched the Bible to you as a movie and they said John Landis will direct and Eddie Murphy will star, you would have said, 'Let's go'?"

Katzenberg looked amused for the first time since Draper had begun cross-examination.

"No," he said.

"I guess I went too far," Draper said.

"Yes," Katzenberg said, nodding.

"While you were at Paramount, did you ever observe that Paramount stole an idea from a prior work and then just copied it in subsequent motion pictures?" Draper asked.

"Not that I have knowledge of."

If there had been any doubt up to this point as to Draper's basic strategy, he now spelled it out in deadly serious, apocalyptic tones for both Judge Schneider and the television audiences that would be watching his performance all over America that night. Draper began to ask Katzenberg questions about what would happen if the Court were to agree with the plaintiffs' supposed argument that once a studio optioned material for development it could not produce any other motion picture that was similar without fear of being sued. The point being that, should Buchwald prevail, no studio would ever be able to contract with a writer again without fear of being sued.

I repeatedly objected that this line of questioning was irrelevant.

Draper replied with an offer of proof: "I believe that the testimony of this witness would be that no motion picture company could operate under that standard and that it would be destructive of the entire creative process." Absolute chaos would reign in the movie industry, he warned.

Schneider wasted no time puncturing his balloon.

"Whether that would or would not be disruptive of the creative process is an interesting issue," Judge Schneider said. "That may be the next case that we'll have to decide. But I don't think we do have to decide it in this case."

Draper remained undaunted. He paced a bit in front of the witness, who was now looking attentive but bemused.

"I want to describe an idea for a movie and see if you can guess the movie," Draper said. "Cop in an inner city. Lives in a rough-and-tumble world. Because of a violent crime, he goes to another social world in which he's a fish out of water. You got it? That idea?"

"Yes," Katzenberg nodded.

"Have I just described *Beverly Hills Cop?*"

"Yes."

"Have I also just described *Witness?*" Draper asked.

"Yes," Katzenberg replied.

"Who produced those pictures?" Draper demanded.

"Paramount," Katzenberg said.

Draper held his head high, as if to say "The same idea can spawn two radically different movies. Therefore, I rest my case."

But the case was far from over.

. . . . .

"You were asked questions about Eddie Murphy's writing talents by Mr. Draper. . . . Have you seen *Harlem Nights?*" I asked Katzenberg when I once again had the floor for redirect examination.

"Yes," Katzenberg said.

"And Eddie Murphy wrote that, right?"

"I believe he did."

"Well, let me tell you, he has the following credits on that, does he not? Story by?"

"I don't know."

"Screenplay by?"

"I think so, yes."

"Directed by?"

"Yes."

"Acted by?"

"Yes."

"And produced by?"

"Right."

"Okay. In fact, all those credits are all up on the screen at the beginning of the movie, aren't they?"

"Yes."

"And you were aware of the savage, critical reviews of the writing of *Harlem Nights?*" I began.

Draper was on his feet.

"Objection, your honor."

"It's cross-examination, your honor," I protested.

Schneider blinked at both of us, stroking his chin.

"What's your objection?" he asked Draper.

"Ambiguous," Draper shot back.

Schneider looked back at me. He had a better objection.

"Well, what relevance does this have?" he demanded.

The fact that *Harlem Nights* was one of the worst movies to crawl out of Hollywood in the past several years, I wanted to tell the Court. The fact that the creative genius behind every frame was none other than the so-called creator of *Coming to America*, Edward Regan Murphy. But I caught myself.

It was clear that Judge Schneider did not want to hear any attacks on Eddie Murphy. I realized that, in the heat of battle, I had started to stray from my own strategy not to disparage Murphy. It was just so hard to sit there and listen to all that hyperbole. Talented, Eddie is. A "creative genius" who originated *Coming to America*, hell no!

"This is 1989," Schneider reminded me.

"I understand that. I understand that, your honor—"

"Shouldn't I focus on the relevant time period involved in the lawsuit?"

"Yes," I conceded with a sigh, thankful for Draper's objection that spared me. "I'll move on. Thank you, your honor."

. . . . .

When the first day of trial in the matter of *Buchwald v. Paramount* had come to an end, two dozen men and women of the press corps shuffled out of Department 52 and lay in wait outside the double doors for the witnesses and their lawyers to emerge. It was a daily ritual my team and I would repeat for two weeks.

But this first day, they would be sorely disappointed. Reluctantly, Judge Schneider had granted Katzenberg's request. So Jeffrey Katzenberg managed to dodge the media by escaping through Judge Schneider's chambers and out a side door, twenty yards away from the klieg lights, tape recorders and reporters' notebooks poised for his exit. It would be the last time that a studio got any special treatment from Harvey Schneider.

Months later, during another chambers conference, I reminded Judge Schneider about the day that Disney's studio chief sneaked out the back door through his chambers.

"Yes, I remember. What was *that* all about?" Schneider asked.

I had no doubt that he knew very well what it was all about.

22

Fairy Tales

"YOUR HONOR, the defense calls Arsenio Hall," announced Bob Draper.

Hall finished signing the last of his autographs for courtroom fans, including Judge Harvey Schneider's bailiff. Then the six-foot-tall talk show host with the diamond stud in his left ear lobe and the trademark box-cut hairstyle looked up at the bench. Ordinarily, the plaintiffs first put on their witnesses and then the defendant puts on its defense. But Draper had asked me for an accommodation to allow Hall to testify out of turn because of scheduling problems. It was a routine professional courtesy, and I readily agreed.

"Sir, please step forward, stand behind the reporter, face the clerk and raise your right hand," said Judge Schneider.

It was day two of *Buchwald v. Paramount* and Eddie Murphy's "Black Pack" pal stepped to the witness stand, solemnly swearing to tell the truth, so help him God. In his loose-fitting black coat and checkered open-neck shirt, Hall was a genuine contrast to the bland attorneys and most of the spectators in the courtroom, clad in their business suits, ties and uniforms. The only thing around Hall's neck was a simple silver cross that swung like a pendulum when he leaned forward to speak into the microphone.

"This is all very exciting. I do a talk show every night. But this is all very exciting to me," Hall gushed.

"Well, you can get my autograph afterward," Draper said.

Hall began his testimony by talking about his relationship with Eddie Murphy.

"I am an only child and he is like the brother that I never had," he said. "We're very close."

"Would you lie for Eddie Murphy in court?" asked Draper.

"Excuse me?"

"Would you lie for Eddie Murphy in court because you're so close?"

Hall paused for maximum effect and then answered.

"No, absolutely not."

It was a position from which this thirty-four-year-old son of an itinerant Baptist preacher and a Cleveland housewife refused to waver during nearly two hours of tough courtroom interrogation.

From a cold, career point of view, Hall really didn't need his close relationship to Murphy anymore. He had recently signed his own two-year, $3 million TV/movie deal with Paramount. On the third Monday of December 1989 he was already a bona fide superstar in his own right. On the witness stand or in the studio, however, he never forgot who had given him his big show business breaks.

In many respects, Eddie Murphy's self-described "best friend" was a direct contrast to Murphy, beginning with Hall's own difficult rise within the entertainment business.

His first job after graduating from Kent State University was selling advertising for a department store. In 1979, when the nineteen-year-old Roosevelt junior college dropout Eddie Murphy was working the Comic Strip in preparation for his "Saturday Night Live" audition, his future best buddy Arsenio Hall was working a similar comedy club in the Chicago suburb of Rosemont. Unlike Eddie, Arsenio went unnoticed.

Singer Nancy Wilson finally gave Hall his first break. He impressed her enough as emcee of a 1980 Christmas show in which she sang in Chicago that she financed Hall's first trip to Los Angeles. He polished his stand-up routine at the Roxy Theater on Sunset Boulevard and got his second big break as the opening act for Aretha Franklin. Then Tom Jones, Patti Labelle, Tina Turner, Wayne Newton and Neil Sedaka soon began hiring him to open for them during road trips.

But, as he testified in Judge Schneider's courtroom this December morning years later, breaking into show business was not for the fainthearted, even with the series of lucky breaks Hall got during the early eighties.

"I did everything from episodes of a 'Twilight Zone' to sketch situations on cable and commercials for Tab and Levi's . . . everything from co-hosting movie macabre with Elvira to being the guy on the radio that says 'available on A&M records and tapes,'" Hall said. "I mean, everything to make ends meet, you know."

Arsenio played second banana to Canadian comic actor Alan Thicke on his short-lived talk show "Thicke of the Night" during the 1984 TV season. That led to a co-hosting gig on Paramount Television's syndicated "Solid Gold" hit song countdown show and—perhaps his biggest break of all—substituting for Joan Rivers as host of Fox Broadcasting's "The Late Show" during the final days of that 1987 late night talk program.

Following a much-publicized dispute between Rivers and Fox, "The Late Show" was canceled. But Hall's career was skyrocketing, fueled by the same national TV exposure and attendant critical acclaim that first launched Murphy's star in 1981.

And once he had the spotlight, he basked in it. His testimony was that of a man who understood diplomacy and deference, but he remained totally in control of the moment.

"Mr. Hall, are you under contract with Paramount?" Draper asked.

"Yes, I am," Hall said.

"And since when have you been under contract with Paramount?"

"Probably late '87."

"How long have you known Eddie Murphy?"

"About a decade."

"Is Eddie Murphy dumb?"

"No."

"Do you consider Eddie Murphy honest?"

"He's brutally honest sometimes."

"You knew him in the period 1983 through 1985?"

"Yeah."

"And did you discuss any specific projects that he had going during that period of time with him?"

"We often had discussions about all the things he was working on," Hall said.

"Did you ever remember discussing with Mr. Murphy a project called A Crude, Crude World or sometimes called King for a Day?"

"No."

In addition to swearing that he never heard of Buchwald's project out of Eddie's mouth, he testified at length about how Eddie first told him about his ideas for The Quest and how Eddie and he wrote the movie—with a little help from Blaustein and Sheffield. In their deposition, the two screenwriters had painted a different picture: they wrote the script with a little help from Eddie and Arsenio. Even among friends, creative credit can be terribly divisive.

Coming to America, Hall insisted, was "a black fairy tale" that "was just beautiful and the prince gets the girl. . . ."

Right, I thought. Just don't tell my wife Connie that I took Brendan and Meghan to see a "fairy tale" that opens with the hero having his penis washed by a half-naked woman and uses profanity as a substitute for character development.

Draper then triggered Hall to fire the first volley on the race issue.

"You're black?" Draper earnestly asked.

"Correct."

"Did you see it as a positive that the story that you and Eddie were pitching would portray blacks in a positive way?"

"Well, yeah, we definitely wanted to do that because it's kind of our responsibility," Hall answered in his most sincere voice. "Nobody else is going to do it, and that's why we wanted to have a major hand in writing it so that it won't be another story of black people written by a white person."

That's why they hired Barry Blaustein and David Sheffield, two white persons, to write the screenplay, I thought to myself. Then, a few minutes later, Draper floored me with a major gaffe that irritated his own witness. Speaking of Blaustein and Sheffield, Draper asked:

"They were two white boys, white men."

"Yeah, yeah."

"Sorry to use the term boys," Draper apologized.

"Not a good term," Arsenio scolded, drilling Draper with a critical look through his prescription sunglasses.

"Not a good term either way," Draper meekly noted. "Now, I'm white. You noticed that," Draper continued in a feeble stab at humor. "And so it may be hard for me to get into your head and ask this question. But you mentioned before that . . . Africans are portrayed in movies made in this town, or had been historically, in the Tarzan concept. And was there any aspect of your idea that you were pitching that was an attempt to kind of reverse that—if you will excuse the expression—stereotype?"

Hall sat forward in his seat when he wanted to make a point. His arms dangled in front of him as he leaned into the microphone, revealing that his broad shoulders were actually thick pads sewn into the shoulders of his coat. He talked with his hands and spoke attentively but quickly, like a kid competing in a spelling bee.

"That was—that was very important," he began. "And I'm only speaking for myself, but as a kid growing up in Cleveland, I never knew that there were skyscrapers in Africa and there was wealth. And I never knew about the mines of Africa and the kings of Africa.

"I really only knew about the guys—and this may sound funny—but I only knew about the guys that helped Tarzan and helped people who were on hunting expeditions. And they all were natives. I never knew about the riches and the wealth and the dignity of Africa. Through our research and our writing, that's what we wanted to put down."

Coming to America was about "positive attitudes," Hall maintained. By the time he had finished his eloquent description, the often crude and uneven comedy that millions saw in the movie theater sounded more like some rich and enduring public statement designed to raise social awareness, on a par with Gentleman's Agreement or To Kill a Mockingbird.

"There are racial divisions in our society which you're aware of, are there not? There are some racial problems?" Draper said.

"Oh, yeah."

"Was it part of the concept of *Coming to America* that this was a bridge, a gap filler?"

"Yeah, in a sense. That wasn't the most important thing we were going after in this, but it was very, very important for us to make these people universal and make it something for everyone."

Throughout his testimony, Hall never forgot his humility. The fledgling actor—whose only previous film appearance was as a stand-up comedian in John Landis's poorly received, 1987 sci-fi spoof *Amazon Women on the Moon* —almost didn't take the role of Semmi, even when Eddie offered it to him, he said.

"I didn't know whether I wanted to be caught between Eddie Murphy and James Earl Jones, which is what eventually happened," Hall explained.

What was more, the fictive roles the two best pals portrayed on the screen were directly reflective of their roles in real life, according to Hall.

"See, you have to understand: I was raised by his parents in Africa and I wasn't even—I wasn't really rich," he said of the Semmi character. "[Prince Akeem] was rich. And we wanted to portray me as kind of being the jerk who loved to spend money that's not even mine. And live high on the hog. And Eddie, who's rich . . . it is his money and his dad's wealth. Being very humble and wanting to pretty much hide from wealth. To be loved for himself.

"The other thing you have to understand about this idea was, you got two guys who are successful in real life. And he's a lot more successful than me. But regardless, it's relative. And you experience a thing in this town of wanting to put that away and hide that and get somebody to just appreciate you and deal with you for the person that you are. And in a sense, this script kind of came out of our own real-life experiences."

Coming to America was also designed to be a "face lift" for Eddie as an actor.

"Instead of the wisecracking Axel Foley-type character that people knew him as, this showed him soft, sensitive, nonmaterialistic," said Hall. "It made a gentleman out of him. He was kind of the perfect man in this movie and any woman would love this guy. It was totally different for his image."

He could get away with demanding such a role.

" 'By this point, if Eddie had cut wind, Paramount would want to make it into a movie,' " Draper read from Hall's own deposition. "Can you give us the context of that comment?" he asked.

"Basically, it's probably a statement of low self-esteem on my own part," Hall said with embarrassment. When he said it, Hall testified, he was assuming that he wasn't important to the making of *Coming to America*. What was important was Paramount wanting to see another Eddie Murphy movie made, he said.

Hall then told about his role in his granting sole screenwriting credit to Blaustein and Sheffield. When John Landis asked him to give up his claim, Hall readily agreed.

"These writers could use the money they could make by sharing the writer's credit alone," he recalled Landis telling him. "They both have kids and all that kind of stuff.

"And Landis said, 'Why don't you give them the writer credit? Let them have it solely.' And I said, 'I'm cool with that. Did you talk to Eddie?' And he said, 'I already did this morning and he said that's fine.' So, basically, that's how they ended up with it."

He didn't mind giving credit to Blaustein and Sheffield, he said. He felt as though his act of charity may have launched a couple of comedy writing careers.

Eddie could be as magnanimous as the next guy, he said.

"The man doesn't have the ego that people might think he has, and he obviously doesn't need the money," Hall said. "He's a very generous man."

Nevertheless, Hall's contribution to the creation of *Coming to America* was anything but negligible. He originated the Bon'Do stick fighting scene between Semmi and Prince Akeem during the first few minutes of the movie, and created the characters of both the jive-talking barbers and the neighborhood preacher in *Coming to America*.

"Did it ever occur to you during the time that you were going through the creative process that you have described with Eddie Murphy in creating *Coming to America*, that it was really amazing because Eddie was really too dumb to have thought all this stuff up by himself?" Draper asked.

I stood and raised my hand. Draper had gone too far.

"Objection, your honor," I said. "It's an impermissible question. It's argumentative."

"I'll sustain the objection," Schneider said.

"We're not alleging in this case at all that Eddie Murphy is anything but an intelligent human being, your honor," I added before sitting back down.

But Draper wouldn't give up. He was determined to bait us on the issue of Murphy's intelligence.

"He's your best friend?" he asked.

"Yes," Hall answered.

"Do you give him your phone number?"

"Yeah, my home number, yeah."

"How many times do you have to give it to him again?"

I was on my feet again.

"Same objection, your honor," I nearly shouted.

"Sustained."

That was enough for Draper. He had us primed and, he hoped, flustered. By the time he handed the witness over to Zazi Pope for cross-examination, Bob had made his argument that our suit was an insult to both Arsenio Hall's and Eddie Murphy's intelligence and creativity. We had to exorcise any such notion, and it was imperative that we clip Hall's angel wings.

A red ribbon in her hair, Zazi took over the podium to begin her first trial test since graduation from Harvard Law School only a little more than two years earlier. For the next thirty minutes she methodically but sweetly snipped away, pointing out contradiction after contradiction between Hall's testimony in his deposition and in the courtroom that morning.

"Mr. Hall, you told Mr. Draper that you and Eddie Murphy discussed projects he was working on," she said with an ingenuous smile. "But [during your deposition] you told me that you and Eddie Murphy almost never discussed projects."

Draper objected to a lack of foundation for her question. Zazi answered by reading the first of several passages from Hall's November 1 deposition.

"As close as we are as friends, I always found it a bad idea to mix business and pleasure," Hall had told Zazi in our conference room six weeks earlier. "Because I have seen Eddie constantly bombarded by people who want to know him because of his business and because of what he can do for an artist, I always avoid conversation about anything that can bring financial gain or Hollywood business."

As she read his own words back to him, Hall—the man who rarely let a week go by without capitalizing on his friendship with Eddie Murphy either by referring to him or having Murphy do a rare TV appearance on "The Arsenio Hall Show"—wriggled uncomfortably in his seat.

"The television show that you're currently doing is syndicated by Paramount, is it not?" Zazi asked.

"Correct," Hall answered.

"And you've got lots of offices on the Paramount lot?"

"No, but I'm trying to get more. . . . I just have the office that I work out of and my production trailer where we put the show together," he said.

If Arsenio had been briefed by Draper before court about the *quid pro quo* connection that Buchwald's lawyers would try to make between his loyalty to Paramount and his favorable testimony, he didn't show it. He spoke with pride about his—and Paramount's—talk show and the accommodations the studio made for him on his three-picture movie deal.

"I'm not really a motion picture star," he said. "I'm a stand-up comic and a talk show host. And they chase me around the lot trying to get me to do movies. But that's really not—I have no acting experience *per se*. . . ."

"Isn't it correct that Paramount agreed to count your brief cameo role in *Harlem Nights* as a picture for the purpose of your multi-picture deal?" Zazi asked.

"That's what Paramount wanted to do," Hall said, his hands flying up in an "ah shucks" gesture as he spoke. "You have to understand, I'm doing a talk show all day long. They wanted me to leave my talk show every evening at 7 P.M. and work until 5 A.M. and I didn't want to work all night long. But they really wanted me to play this part, and that was the offer they made to me."

Hall's hands were flailing and his answers sounded like alibis. Zazi did not relent. She asked Hall whether Murphy first mentioned his plan to portray an African king or prince as early as 1985.

"When he mentioned it to me then, it was the conversation about using this guy, Keenan [Wayans], and maybe doing that together. But we had talked before that about playing royalty," Hall said with a shrug.

"In fact, Mr. Hall, when Eddie first mentioned that idea to you in '85, he mentioned a *king* coming to America, isn't that right?" Zazi persisted.

"No. I think it was the king's son," Hall said.

Zazi grinned ear to ear and turned to the judge.

"May I read from the—" she began.

"I mean, he becomes a king, you know, I guess at some point," Hall interrupted nervously. "But I think it was a prince."

Hall was losing his cool and beginning to make the mistake that many first-time witnesses make when they answer a hostile question or address an apparent contradiction in their testimony: he talked too much. From that point forward, Arsenio Hall was a guest on the "Zazi Pope Show"—and was talking.

"If Eddie Murphy wanted to break wind, they were going to accept it as a film?" Zazi asked.

"See, that's kind of—that's kind of a joke, you know," Hall said. But he didn't stop with a simple answer to the question. He made us very happy. He made a speech.

"Paramount, Gulf & Western, obviously are very bright companies," he elaborated. "And I've seen them turn Eddie down many times. As a matter of fact, this recent project that we did together [Harlem Nights] isn't the first time we've wanted to do something and seen Paramount say no.

"The break wind thing is a joke. It's a joke that a lot of people who know him use a lot because it's just to say that he's so talented. I did a sketch on my show with a guy named David Nicksay, who used to be an executive at Paramount. I was pitching him movies as a character. And his running tag was, 'Is Eddie in it?' It's kind of just a joke, kind of a compliment to his talent."

But Zazi was more interested in the limits to Eddie Murphy's talent. That's where she led the garrulous Arsenio Hall next.

"Now it's true, is it not, Mr. Hall, that Eddie Murphy never showed you anything he had written for *The Quest*, which became *Coming to America*, until the pitch meeting. Correct?" she asked.

"A little before that pitch meeting," Hall said.

Again, he could not let a simple answer suffice. He remembered seeing a legal pad lying around before the pitch meeting and perhaps the conversations he and Eddie had about *The Quest* were being scribbled down, he guessed.

But, Zazi persisted, he had never actually seen anything Murphy had written about *The Quest* until they all pitched Ned Tanen on it during the summer of '87?

"No, I did not, ma'am," Hall said sullenly.

Still, the plot outline that was eventually transcribed and used as the basis of the Blaustein/Sheffield script came from the Eddie/Arsenio story sessions, Hall maintained. The parody of McDonald's restaurant was a good example of a running joke that was pure Murphy and Hall.

"We had a lot of jokes initially about, 'Well, isn't your sandwich just like . . . McDonald's?' And Eddie says, 'No. See? Mine don't have no sesame seeds. See? Theirs has sesame seeds on the bun.'"

McDowell, the restaurant owner portrayed in the movie by actor John Amos, was "a guy who had kind of really just knocked off McDonald's," said Hall, adding, "And it came from those sessions and mostly me and Eddie."

"Are you aware, Mr. Hall, that exactly the scenes that you have just described appear almost verbatim in a screenplay by Tab Murphy based on Mr. Buchwald's *King for a Day?*" Zazi asked.

Draper shot out of his chair.

"Object just on relevance," he said angrily. "The scene that Ms. Pope described is a scene developed not by Mr. Buchwald but by Paramount under its contracts. And under its contract, it owns that scene."

Zazi smiled at me. Paramount's own lawyer had just admitted, on the record, that one of the running jokes in *Coming to America*—the McDonald's parody—came from a script the studio had developed from Buchwald's original story.

Zazi picked up the fumble and ran with it, pointing out that both Blaustein and Sheffield had also testified in deposition that the fast food idea was part of the original pitch to Ned Tanen—before it was incorporated into Eddie's *The Quest* story treatment.

In Hall's deposition, the talk show host claimed he had also come up with the idea of planting a sign in the middle of the African jungle, advertising the construction of a McDowell's fast food restaurant.

"I thought it would be funny in the woods of Africa to see one of those 'coming soon' signs," he said.

Though the "coming soon" sign didn't make it into the final film, it did find its way into Eddie's "original" treatment.

"Isn't it a fact, Mr. Hall, that this story synopsis couldn't have been written before your involvement in the project in the summer of 1987 because of the fact that it contains some of your ideas?" Zazi asked, waving a copy of the two-page *The Quest* that Eddie had supposedly dictated to a secretary without any input from other sources—least of all, Buchwald's *King for a Day.*

"Logically, yes," Hall said.

"Isn't it true that this description is in fact a synopsis written with ideas from all four of the people who contributed to the story, *Coming to America?*" she persisted.

"Yeah," Hall said. "I assume there are probably some things here that might have come from Blaustein and Sheffield. But I don't know that for a fact. I never saw this document. I just know it definitely contains some things that at some point I had to have said to Eddie."

Then Zazi went for the kill.

"According to your manager, Mr. Wachs . . . this was the story that Eddie Murphy gave him in May of '87. In fact, a lot of the ideas were contributed after May of '87, isn't that correct?"

Hall fidgeted and, once again, talked too much.

"At some point Eddie had spoken to Bob Wachs and Bob Wachs's assistant, Marilyn, about all the ideas," he said. "And someone physically typed it up and they put them all together, rewrote it or whatever, turned it in. So that it—there could technically be a treatment or whatever. I honestly never saw this document and don't know when they did that and all that kind of stuff."

In other words, *The Quest* was *not* an Eddie Murphy original. I beamed with pride as Zazi took it one last step, planting the fact in the judge's mind that Art Buchwald was writing about African kings years before Murphy or Hall ever did.

"Are you aware that Art Buchwald was writing articles about African kings as early as 1954?" she asked.

"That was before I was born," Hall said.

When Bob Draper took his turn for redirect examination, the first thing he did was give Arsenio an opportunity to demonstrate that his relationship to Murphy was not mercenary.

"Obviously being someone's best friend, you're always around," Hall said. "I'm just saying I never had these kinds of conversations like, 'I could be one of the sergeants in *Cop II*, uh-huh,' you know. I didn't want to get into it like that, you know."

"Did you observe, being a friend of Eddie, that a lot of people tried to take advantage of him by saying, 'Hey, I could be a cop in *Beverly Hills II*,' or something like that?" Draper asked.

"Most of the people around you want something except the ones that were there before you made it," Hall said.

In an apparent attempt to show the bad judgment exercised by Blaustein and Sheffield, Draper asked whether they weren't responsible for originally trying to write a king patterned after the bloodthirsty Ugandan ruler, Idi Amin.

"I'm not sure who it came from," Hall said. "It might have even made it into one of the earlier scripts. But there was something where the king was supposed to be more of an Idi Amin-type guy.

"Eddie and I were playing polo," he continued, recalling one of the Idi Amin-inspired scenes. "And we were losing. It was us against some other guys in the palace and the king stood up and said, 'If one more person scores against my son, off with their heads,' or something like that.

"It is supposed to be a love story. We didn't want any type of hard edge on the king or his family. We wanted the prince to be a sweet loving guy, naturally, because, like I said, we were trying to make Eddie this lovable, wonderful character. We were also very, very set on making the James Earl Jones character strong and proud but fair, honest and a kind man."

"He allowed his son to go to America because his son kind of lied to him a little bit. His son told him he was going to sow wild oats," Draper said.

"Objection, your honor," I interjected. "I think this movie speaks for itself."

"I've seen the movie, gentlemen," Schneider said.

"Oh, okay," said Draper, turning back to Hall. "Was Eddie Murphy a fish out of water in *Beverly Hills Cop?*"

Zazi objected and the judge sustained again.

"I saw that movie too," he explained.

"Is there one you haven't seen, your honor?" asked Draper.

"Not very many," deadpanned Schneider.

Draper turned his attention back to Hall.

"Were there any . . . ," he began, shooting Judge Schneider a look. He waved away his own question. "Forget it. You've seen the movie."

Draper shifted strategy. Trying to maintain that the movie was all Eddie's idea was a losing proposition.

"Eddie has an Uncle Ray and Uncle Ray is chief of security," said Hall. "He watches his house when he's not around and all that kind of stuff. And he went with us into the city to meet Blaustein and Sheffield at the Gulf & Western office building in Manhattan. He was sitting in the corner and . . ."

"Did he appear to be asleep?" Draper interrupted.

"He was nodding off, yeah. He was in and out, but that's how security people are. It's a decoy," said Hall. "He just sat up and said, 'You know, I think it would be great if they got back to Africa and there was the girl from America.' That's a perfect Uncle Ray if you knew him."

"Do you know him, your honor? I'll stop right here."

"I haven't seen *that* movie," said Schneider.

"Coming soon," I interjected.

"Mr. Hall, thank you very much. I wish you Godspeed and good luck getting out," Draper said.

His testimony over, Hall did in fact have trouble extricating himself from the courthouse. A horde of reporters followed him and his entourage down five flights of stairs to a waiting limousine. On the way, he angrily maintained that he had, indeed, told the truth in the courtroom. If Buchwald was so bad off financially that he felt he had to sue, Hall told reporters, "I'll loan him the money."

"I'm a kid from Cleveland," he told a television news reporter in a stunned but angry voice, thumbing back up toward the courtroom. "I didn't know this kind of thing went on."

Then he excused himself and headed back to Paramount where he had another performance to tape. But his attacks on Art Buchwald and his lawsuit made the evening news and were reported on radio stations around the country. Paramount may not have drawn blood in the courtroom, but it hurt us in the court of public opinion.

It would be the last time.

23

"Our Kellogg's Corn Flakes"

———— —— —— —— —— —— —— —— ——

"CALL YOUR NEXT WITNESS, Mr. O'Donnell."

"Mr. Frank Mancuso."

Like other studio heads, the chairman of Paramount Pictures was not used to public scrutiny. The graying hair, parted low on the left side of his head and hanging over his ears in unkempt tufts, hadn't been cut in weeks. The dark circles under both eyes and the hunched shoulders welcomed comparisons to a beleaguered Richard Nixon at the height of Watergate. He drummed his fingertips against each other with the studied cadence that suggested Captain Queeg clicking his steel ball bearings.

Besides the high-profile nature of the trial and gavel-to-gavel TV coverage, Mancuso's nervousness may have been attributable to the fact that he had no idea what to expect from me. In a move that defied conventional wisdom, I intentionally had not taken his deposition. I wanted to take advantage of the element of surprise and not give his lawyers and him any advance notice of what I would ask him. I also suspected that Mancuso would come across as evasive.

I was right.

His answers were as terse as Arsenio's had been long-winded.

"You know Eddie Murphy, do you not?" I asked.

"Yes, I do."

"You're a professional colleague of his?"

"That's correct."

"Are you a personal friend too?"

"Yes, I believe so."

"Socialize with him?"

"On occasion."

"And at Paramount Pictures, I understand you became the chairman in like October, November 1984?

"September 7 of '84."

"And you replaced whom?

"Barry Diller."

"He went to Fox at that time?"

"Yes."

"And as I understand it, you were promoted over Michael Eisner, is that correct?"

"I was made chairman."

When it came to the damning documents, showing that Paramount planned Buchwald's story for Eddie Murphy as early as 1983, Mancuso was equally brusque and noncommittal. On the witness stand, Jeff Katzenberg had admitted that he embellished his words and arguments as a matter of business routine. But Frank Mancuso, who had spent twenty-seven years at Paramount climbing his way from temporary double feature booker in Buffalo to head of distribution before Martin Davis elevated him to the chairmanship of the studio, was above such things. Preferring to think of himself as a godfather to the 3,000 employees who worked on his 56-acre lot, he constantly referred to Paramount as his "family." At Christmas, he lit the huge tree on the Paramount back lot for the employees' party. He was rightfully proud of having the first studio in Hollywood that provided free child care for every working mother on the lot, from secretaries to stars. Mancuso had the reputation in Hollywood of being a man whose word was as good as his bond.

Mancuso would not embellish à la Katzenberg. But he did admit to enthusing a bit much on occasion.

"This is anticipation and, I guess, enthusiasm," the soft-spoken former Paramount distribution chief said of Katzenberg's so-called "sales document" letters to Landis and Tartikoff.

"You have to be very enthusiastic to be in the production department because of the nature of the business," he said. "So it's always approached with great enthusiasm."

"Can you tell me where the dividing line is between optimism and lack of candor?" I asked.

Draper objected, naturally, and Judge Schneider sustained the objection. I was determined to press the point about the highly subjective line between enthusiasm and bald-faced lying. So I rephrased the question.

"Did you hear [that] Mr. Katzenberg characterized this letter as, perhaps in part, an embellishment in the writing to Mr. Tartikoff?

"Yes, I did."

"Do you agree this is an embellishment?"

"I think I've just described it as one which is more enthusiasm. I think you have to be very enthusiastic in our business. I think it's more enthusiasm than it is embellishment, hopefully," Mancuso said, shifting his weight around in the hot seat and trying to undo some of the damage from Katzenberg's testimony.

"Does the enthusiasm in your business have to have a basis in reality?" I followed up.

"Objection! Argumentative!" Draper said.

"I'll overrule the objection," Schneider said calmly.

Mancuso sighed, arching his thick, black brows.

"Any project or anything that you undertake, there has to be a kind of objective goal or an attempt to achieve something," he said. "So, when you say reality, I mean it has to have some foundation in what it is you're attempting to do."

What the hell did that mean? I asked myself, casting a puzzled look at Suzanne and Zazi. The fact was, Mancuso's initials, F.M., showed up on virtually every internal memo that had anything to do with the development of *King for a Day*, indicating that the studio chairman, along with a dozen other Paramount executives, had read and signed off on its progress.

"Your initial F.M. is on there, is it not?" I asked, pointing to a Paramount "Flash!" or Preliminary Deal Summary that is regularly distributed like a newsletter throughout the studio whenever a development deal has been finalized or revised.

"Yes, it is," he said.

The "Flash!" was about a new Eddie Murphy comedy, based on a Buchwald story. To deny that he knew anything at all about *King for a Day* was disingenuous at best.

"Were you aware that, in the summer or fall of 1983, Paramount was considering engaging John Landis to direct the Art Buchwald-inspired movie *King for a Day?*" I asked.

"I heard that the other day," Mancuso said.

"The first time you ever heard it?"

"Yes."

Mancuso was distancing himself. It wasn't anything I hadn't expected. As top man, he could follow the example of Ronald Reagan during the Iran-Contra scandal or Nixon during Watergate, and simply shrug his shoulders. He had nothing to do with it. The worst that anyone could say of him was that he ought to have kept better control of his underlings.

"You have to understand my particular position in the company is one where you support enthusiastically the enthusiasm of the creative production executives and development executives," he said. "But I tend to try to deal more with what *really* is happening."

What really was happening was "tentpole" philosophy and watching the bottom line.

"Tentpole" theory had developed into Mancuso's favorite movie marketing philosophy, even though he did not invent the concept. It was his predecessors at Paramount, Michael Eisner and Barry Diller, who first began developing blockbuster films whose profits could support all of the studio's smaller and/or riskier releases. These blockbusters were "tentpoles" that held up the big top for the rest of the studio, despite the inevitable flops and "critical successes" that happened at every studio.

At Paramount, *Beverly Hills Cop I* and *II*, were tent poles. So were the Indiana Jones series, the *Star Trek* movies and techno-adventure hits like *Top Gun*. And every Eddie Murphy feature, of course, was seen by the studio as a potential tent pole.

The other way of looking at tentpole philosophy was almost Marxist: winners paid for losers. If you were the producer of a winner, paying for a slate of turkeys somehow didn't seem especially fair.

Mancuso was nervous. His throat was dry, so we paused while the bailiff got him some water in a paper cup.

Enthusiasm, he maintained, was contagious, especially if it came from Eddie Murphy. Eddie's enthusiasm over *King for a Day* may have been nil, but he fairly bubbled over with effervescence when he decided to do *Coming to America*.

"He was incredibly enthusiastic," Mancuso said.

One of the prime reasons for calling Mancuso was to wrest an admission that he had been involved in the decision to dump *King for a Day* in 1985 and resurrect it as *Coming to America* two years later. What I got was a studio head making the amazing argument on the witness stand that he knew little or nothing about *King for a Day* being developed in the first place for his major box office star. And yet, when it was dumped after the studio spent nearly $500,000 on it, Mancuso would have *had* to know about it, according to his testimony.

"You personally approved, after your takeover, did you not, sir, a decision whether to shelve any script?"

"I just didn't want any kind of massive turnaround," he explained.

When a new chief takes over, his own pet projects usually replace those developed under the old regime. Such purges, according to Mancuso, were fiscally irresponsible. At a cost of a half million dollars for two fully developed scripts, I could understand why.

"It was something that was on my mind at the time," he said. "I don't know whether I was personally approving every one, but it was sure part of what was important to me at that time."

It was especially important if it involved Eddie Murphy.

I wanted Judge Schneider to learn the details of how Paramount had lavished one terrific movie deal after another on Eddie. I had his contracts, but they had been given to me under the confidentiality agreement governing discovery. It was time to let the cat out of the bag.

As I started to ask Mancuso about Eddie's first contract back in 1982,

Draper objected, and we had a heated sidebar conference with the judge out of earshot of the audience. I had prepared an exhibit summarizing the evolution of the key terms over a seven-year period, including Eddie's base compensation for acting and his contingent compensation arrangement. The judge had it in front of him, digesting the information as Draper went on and on about the irrelevance of all this material. After Draper finished, I told the judge that it was relevant to my tort claim because it showed that Paramount had been very accommodating to Murphy and we believed the studio had been similarly accommodating when it denied credit to Buchwald for originating the idea for *Coming to America*. The judge agreed and that was how I was able to introduce into evidence—and reveal to the eager press—that Eddie Murphy's current deal gave him $8 million per picture against 15 percent of the gross receipts.

"Do you recall telling the *Wall Street Journal* in an article on June 6, 1989, that Eddie Murphy is 'our Kellogg's corn flakes'?" I asked.

"I have a vague recollection," said Mancuso. "What I referred to was that he was as well known as Kellogg's corn flakes is."

"And so you don't deny making that quote?"

"No."

Mancuso shied away from one interpretation of his Kellogg's corn flakes quote: namely, that Eddie's popularity would cost the studio a lot of money at renegotiation time. The most popular movie star in the world, according to a leading survey, Eddie was the studio's bestselling and most profitable product. I introduced into evidence financial data furnished by the studio that showed Eddie's movies had put over $1 billion in gross receipts into Paramount's coffers.

"Are you aware that Eddie Murphy is not happy with his five-picture deal with Paramount?"

Mancuso looked as though he had been slapped.

"No."

When I started to ask him if he had read Eddie's *Rolling Stone* interview, Draper objected on the ground that what Eddie said to the magazine was inadmissible hearsay. Generally, lawyers cannot offer at trial out-of-court statements of persons who are not available to be cross-examined in court about the statements. Admission of such hearsay would violate the objecting party's right to confront such persons and have the trier-of-fact (here Judge Schneider) evaluate their credibility. Prepared for Draper's objection, I asked to approach the bench for a sidebar conference to argue this legal point. I pointed out to Judge Schneider that I was not offering Eddie's statement about the "shittiest deal in town" for the truth of the matter but rather to show his agitated state of mind and the tension in his relationship with Paramount.

Judge Schneider overruled the objection, and Suzanne Tragert handed up the *Rolling Stone* interview with Eddie. Without reading a word from it, I handed it to Mancuso and asked:

"Isn't that what he says in this interview?"

Mancuso's eyes twitched back and forth over the copy. He admitted that he'd read it before.

"This is nothing more than having an opportunity to negotiate," he said. "Since 1982, I have negotiated with this gentleman three or four times. And just like a good baseball player, it's a negotiation. We are always in negotiations with Eddie."

"Each time he's come back for more money, you've given it to him, right?" I asked.

Mancuso squirmed. He would not answer this question with his usual "yes" or "no." Whatever he said Eddie would undoubtedly read in the next morning's newspaper.

"We try to accommodate him. He's very important to Paramount. He's a very big box office star, so he has certain worth and we try to recognize what that is."

I had no more questions. I had accomplished what I set out to do with Paramount's chairman, and I could see that the judge was getting impatient because the witness claimed to know so little.

Now it was Draper's turn. To begin with, he established that Mancuso received between 200 and 400 memos, letters and other documents on his desk every day. Mancuso was a busy man.

But not too busy for Eddie Murphy.

"Mr. O'Donnell asked you . . . about the amount of money you paid to Eddie Murphy," Draper said. "Does Paramount pay Mr. Murphy that money because it's an equal opportunity employer?"

No, said Mancuso, "because he's a valuable, creative talent who has a tremendous following."

Draper then scored a point when he elicited from Mancuso the fact that Eddie Murphy's back-end compensation under his gross deal would not have been in the least bit affected if Paramount had in fact paid Buchwald and Bernheim their combined 19 percent of net profits.

"When you were being asked the question about Mr. Murphy's renegotiations, by the way: do you do that for your lawyers too?"

Draper finally got a chuckle from the audience, but Mancuso only managed a smile before Draper withdrew the question.

Draper was convinced that we were bringing out Eddie's huge salary in court for devious reasons and said as much to Judge Schneider.

"I think, your honor, that they are trying to put a big number up on the board to . . . imply that Eddie Murphy is so important to Paramount that, somehow, we'll do something to Mr. Buchwald and Mr. Bernheim. . . ."

Draper got Mancuso—who gushed with pride about his twenty-seven years at Paramount which had "been my life along with my own family"—to deny vehemently that Paramount would in any way attempt to injure my clients to pacify Murphy.

"They are both very nice people. . . . We don't operate that way."

Paramount could not survive if it treated the creative community in the callous way that we were alleging it had treated Buchwald and Bernheim, Mancuso asserted. Paramount's relationship with talent is "the life blood of the company. Creative relationships, whether they be writers, directors, producers or actors, are the most important thing we have going. Without them, you don't have film or television. And therefore we're always cognizant of the importance of a relationship and how we handle a relationship."

Then Mancuso waxed eloquent about why it was a seller's market for great movie ideas and how "very competitive" the movie business really was. I let him go for a while, but finally, when Draper asked Mancuso whether Paramount would turn down a project for development "if it thought it was just a dynamite, sure-win deal," that was enough.

"Objection, your honor. We've gone down the road of speculation into pure conjecture, I think."

"I'll sustain the objection."

Draper proceeded to get Mancuso to agree that Paramount was in business to make a profit. To no one's surprise, Mancuso added that the talent was also trying to get a piece of the profit pie.

"All the talent is working in a way to produce the most for their talent. Whether it be a writer, producer, actor, director . . . They all want to maximize."

Including, he implied, Art and Alain.

"You don't get many free stories," said Draper.

"No, we don't. We don't get *any* free stories. . . . We obviously would like to retain as much of the profitability as possible. We have reluctantly given away what we have to give away."

Draper sat down. I had one last shot at Mancuso. Earlier I hadn't been able to pin him down on a single dollar detail about the profitability of *Coming to America*. So I took another tack in my redirect examination.

Since I couldn't get him to admit that the "profit you report to the shareholders may be different than the profit you report to the profit participants," I asked about the negative cost of the film. Mancuso put it at approximately $40 million, even after I showed him John Landis's profit participation statement, which put the cost closer to $52 million. When I asked about Paramount's distribution fee, he wouldn't even confirm that the norm for a feature is 30 percent for domestic receipts.

"Before you became chairman of the board, you were involved actively with distribution with Paramount, weren't you, sir?"

"Correct."

"So you know what a distribution fee is, don't you?"

"I don't think you understand what it was I was doing back then," Mancuso said, dodging the question one more time.

I lost my temper. I couldn't resist one more little shot.

"Do you know what you're doing now?"

"Objection. Argumentative," said Draper. Judge Schneider quite properly sustained the objection to my intemperate comment. I silently counted backward from 10 to regain my cool.

"Do you know what a distribution fee is, Mr. Mancuso?"

"Yes."

"What is it?"

"A fee that Paramount gets for distributing the movie."

When I asked him whether 30 percent was the standard Paramount distribution fee for domestic receipts, Mancuso—the studio's former head of distribution and marketing—professed that he didn't know what the standard is.

To my delight, his evasiveness had created the impression that it's easier to nail Jell-O to the wall of the courtroom than to get a straight answer from Paramount.

I decided to drive the point home with one more question.

"Has *Coming to America* been profitable by any definition for Paramount Pictures Corporation?"

"Pardon? . . . I assume it's been profitable, yes," he said.

"Do you know how profitable?"

Mancuso shook his head.

"No, I don't."

He smiled, confident that there was no way that I could easily prove otherwise.

Mancuso was right on one count. It wouldn't be easy.

24

Show Time

BUCHWALD, my star witness, had sufficiently recovered from a bad cold to fly into Los Angeles on Sunday for final preparation so that he could take the stand Monday afternoon. I needed Art a day earlier than expected because a couple of appearances by the next celebrities in line to testify Monday had been canceled at the last minute.

John Landis was directing Disney's 35th Anniversary Special for TV, and the studio estimated that each day he took off from the project would cost the company $50,000. Disney's amiable TV legal affairs vice-president Larry Kaplan begged off sending Landis to the trial at all. Leafing through his deposition, I concluded that he did not have much to offer on the issue of whether or not Paramount had breached Buchwald's contract. It would have been nice to extract from the witness stand more details on his 10 percent adjusted gross profit deal with Paramount, but his profit participation statement would be introduced into evidence.

I excused Landis—to the chagrin of the reporters who were eager to chronicle Landis's first court appearance since his *Twilight Zone* acquittal.

As for Eddie Murphy, Draper had explained to the hungry press out in the corridor following Arsenio Hall's testimony that Hall's best pal would be staying out of state and out of reach of a subpoena during the holidays. It was the media's fault, he told them, not Eddie's. "*He* wouldn't add to the circus atmosphere," he told a couple dozen reporters in the corridor outside Department 52, his voice dripping with contempt. "The crush and bellow would add to the circus atmosphere. I would like this to be a trial, not a circus."

Besides, he explained, an "odd person" had been roaming the hallways of the courthouse. Proud new papa Eddie Murphy wasn't going to take any chances with his life and safety by showing up for a media circus in such a public place.

The *Times*'s Dennis McDougal, who had been covering the county courthouse for years, had seen his share of strange folk in the corridors, but rarely the threatening kind of person that Draper implied Eddie Murphy might risk encountering. After a dozen years as an investigative reporter in the entertainment industry, McDougal had a sixth sense for phony excuses. He called courthouse security to ferret out further details about the strange man stalking Eddie Murphy. If the man could be found, he might have a story to tell. What McDougal discovered, however, was that nobody from Paramount, O'Melveny & Myers or Eddie Murphy Productions had registered any complaint about a strange man roaming the hallways. That's what he printed in the *Times* and an embarrassed Draper took some ribbing over it the following day when a wire service reporter suggested that Draper himself might have been the "odd person" in the hallway.

Though Eddie was a no show, Buchwald was there. It was show time. The celebrity atmosphere was enhanced by the appearance of longtime compatriot Billy Wilder, who had come to watch the proceedings and cheer on Buchwald. The wizened genius whose classics included *Some Like It Hot, Sunset Boulevard* and *Stalag 17* made it clear to the same media hounds who had scared off Eddie Murphy that Art and Alain were not Don Quixote and Sancho Panza, tilting at windmills. Theirs was an all too routine case of creative people who get fleeced by the studio money men. The only difference was that they had the courage to take on the system.

"There's no great friendship between writers and the front office," Wilder told the TV cameras.

Wilder's appearance was not accidental. He had consulted with us on trial strategy and been one of the nine top Hollywood writers we had recruited to testify. Zazi and I had invited him to come to the trial. I told him that his presence during Art's testimony would be a dramatic show of solidarity that would be widely reported in the media. I was right: almost every newspaper, television and radio story about that day of trial featured Billy's appearance to support Art.

Before taking the stand, Buchwald told the reporters in the hallway that he had a solemn message for Hollywood producers.

"They better not do *anything* without first talking to me," he said.

Art left them laughing but promised to get serious on the witness stand.

With his horn-rims slightly askew and his delivery always deadpan, sixty-four-year-old Buchwald looked like an intellectual Archie Bunker in a gray suit. I knew he was nervous and still drained from his weekend illness, but no one else in the courtroom did. He might have been no stranger to talking before the television cameras, but this was his first time doing so under oath. You could have fooled me. He talked like a man who was born to be a witness.

I spent the first few minutes asking Art familiar biographical information. I didn't want to take for granted that Judge Schneider knew the details of Art's pedigree, and I wanted to relax my client.

When Art testified that his peers awarded him the coveted Pulitzer Prize for commentary in 1982, I asked him, "Is there any honorarium that comes with it?"

"You get $1,000, but you don't have to go to a lunch or dinner."

When I noted that Art had received a lot of honorary degrees from Jesuit universities like my alma mater Georgetown, he quipped, "Yeah, they passed me around."

Art loved recounting the tale of how he and director Cy Howard pitched Charlie Feldman back in the late fifties on a sure-fire comedy called *Long Live Lillie.*

"I went down to Monaco, which was my beat in those days, and there was an American priest there called Father Tucker. Father Tucker was from Philadelphia," said Art.

"And he gave me an interview about Prince Rainier. He was the prince's confessor. He said, 'Here I've got this prince and if anything happens to him, we are going to lose the country to France. And he's scuba diving and he's flying airplanes.' He let me write this all down.

"And I said, 'What do you want to do?' He said, 'I gotta get him married.' I said, 'Who you got in mind?' So he said, 'Grace Kelly.' I said, 'Well, has the prince even met her?' He said, 'Met her once.'

"So the title of my article is, 'If Grace Kelly Only Cared.' And the thrust of it was that Grace Kelly doesn't know that the whole country of Monaco is going to revert to France if she doesn't marry Rainier. So Charlie Feldman, the producer, read this and he says, 'This would make a heck of a movie. We'll hire an American movie actress. Not a well-known one. She is unknown and we'll take her into Monaco. We'll make the guy more like Ali Khan than we will Rainier.' So I went to work. Feldman put me to work at a nice salary with Cy Howard and we worked on this.

"And we set it in a film festival. We were doing good. We had that thing worked out. And one day I was in the office at the *Herald Tribune* and a guy says, 'You better look at the ticker.' And I went to the ticker and it says, 'Mr. and Mrs. Kelly announce the engagement of their daughter to Prince Rainier.' And that was the end of the thing."

Reality made *Long Live Lillie* Art's first and, as it turned out, only attempt at a full-fledged film script. It was an exercise in instant obsolescence.

Art's description of the creative process for ideas for his newspaper column and stories and how he stored all experiences in the data bank in his head yielded a sneak preview of two of his next columns:

"This week . . . I have an East German coming to me because East Germany's in the news, and the East German comes to me and he says now that they are going to have capitalism in East Germany, he wants to start a business. What should he go into? So, I suggest savings and loan. And the whole column has to do with him getting in the savings and loan business. And first he has to find five senators who will help him. And so it's a satire on the savings and loan and East Germany."

Judge Schneider was listening intently, his hand over his mouth to cover up the big smile on his face.

"Is it true that your column appears regularly in Russia?" I asked.

"Not regularly, but they like to steal it," he said.

"Do they pay you for it?" I asked.

"No, they don't pay me."

I shot Judge Schneider a glance. I didn't want another Draper objection to interrupt the flow of Art's testimony, so I didn't draw the analogy of Paramount studios and the new free market Russia. But I had little doubt that the judge had figured it out all on his own.

Art told the story of how A *Gift From the Boys* became the disappointing *Surprise Package* and how the long, futile attempt to make *The Beard* into a movie wound up in a sheik's tent. By the time he got to *King for a Day*, Buchwald was more than a little cynical about Hollywood.

I took Art through his conception of *It's a Crude, Crude World*, the meetings with Louis Malle and Bernheim, the option deal with Malle and Bernheim and then with Paramount, and his reaction when he learned from Alain that Paramount wanted to develop his treatment.

"I was delighted. . . . Eddie Murphy was a very, very big star, and I was very excited that the movie would be made. . . . I was very impressed with *Trading Places*. I thought he was terrific—and I've seen him on 'Saturday Night Live.' I thought he was good."

Consistent with my trial strategy, Art was taking the high road when it came to Eddie. Paramount was another matter. Lying in his sickbed, Art had gone ballistic when I told him about Draper's Charlie Chaplin plagiarism charge in his opening statement. My client was even more livid when he learned that the media had played up the allegation. I had never heard him so angry about "those bastards" in the year and a half we had been together. Paramount's smear was what got Art out of bed so quickly to testify.

He grew more comfortable and relaxed, mixing the serious and humorous as we spent the first afternoon of his testimony completing the chronology of events leading up to Paramount's abandonment of *King for a Day* in 1985. But he wasn't the only person in the courtroom with a razor-sharp sense of humor. Judge Schneider's wit became increasingly evident as Draper and I sparred over objections to questions and exhibits.

During Mancuso's testimony, I had tried unsuccessfully to introduce into evidence a *Daily Variety* column by Army Archerd from early February 1984 about Francis Veber writing *King for a Day* for Paramount. I made another run at it with Buchwald, who said he was "thrilled" when he read the story sent to him by Alain. I offered the exhibit, Draper objected, and the judge told me that "it appears to be hearsay and I'll sustain the objection."

"Even if it made him excited?" I asked, pointing to Art.

"Even if it did that and more," Judge Schneider fired back to the amusement of everyone in the courtroom.

At the very end of the day I asked Art if he had learned about Paramount dropping his project, and Draper started to object.

"I think he's also about to ask for hearsay," my opponent suggested.

"I think we're going to take our afternoon recess now," Judge Schneider replied.

"And I will frame an unobjectionable question," I offered.

"You may," Judge Schneider said. "You will have all night to think about it."

"It's a daunting challenge in this courtroom, your honor," I said. Already, after only two days of trial, I was certain that I had made the right decision to allow this man to decide our fate. While I had no inkling of how he was leaning, he was soaking up the evidence like a parched sponge and making consistent and correct rulings on objections.

That evening, Art, Alain and Zazi went to dinner, and I went home to my study and computer to prepare for the next day. Trials are grueling—that's why I had completed a six-week, intensive Pritikin program and lost forty pounds just before the trial began. I needed all the stamina I could muster.

A typical court day produces about six or seven hours of testimony. For every hour of courtroom testimony, I spend another hour the night and early morning beforehand in final preparation for the day ahead, reviewing the outline of questions, checking the depositions for impeachment of the witness and rethinking what I want to accomplish with the witness in light of what has already happened at trial.

I rolled a flat-bed trolley brimming with charts, briefs and boxes of Paramount documents through the door of Judge Schneider's courtroom the next morning, December 19. The chances that I'd use even a tenth of those thousands of pages during trial were remote, but I had to be ready for any surprise. Yet the sheer volume spelled out for the TV cameras the unmistakable message that we were serious about this lawsuit. The trolley was as much for effect as it was for convenience in transporting the exhibits.

The effect on Harvey Schneider was comparable to a migraine, however. He had already stayed up half the night reading scripts alongside new briefs from both Paramount and our side. When he saw the double doors open and heard the trolley wheels squealing with the weight of the exhibits as it rolled into his courtroom, Schneider shuddered.

I didn't have a lot more for Art's direct examination. But I had one thing that I wanted to communicate loud and clear to Judge Schneider.

"Why did you file this lawsuit, Mr. Buchwald?" I asked.

"First, I'd like to say it's very hard for a so-called humorist to be taken seriously when he does something seriously," said Art. "I consider this a very serious matter. I feel my property was stolen, invaded, raped—whatever you want to call it. I was very upset by it and I didn't know what to do about it."

You always try to end on a high note. I sat down.

Art looked far more rested and chipper than he had the day before. He still wore that wide-eyed, hangdog pout that had become something of a Buchwald trademark. But his body language spoke something else. Draper's rough, hard-edged style during Art's brief deposition two weeks earlier left Art twice shy. He crossed his arms and left them that way throughout most of Draper's cross-examination.

"Marty Davis is a good friend of yours?" Draper asked.

"He was."

"He was?"

"He's not as good as he used to be," said Art to a chorus of laughter.

"Well, when did he stop being a good friend?" asked Draper.

"When I felt I had been shafted by Paramount," Buchwald said.

"And when you filed your lawsuit?"

"No," Art replied, his eyes never leaving Draper's. "I felt I was shafted before I filed suit. I mean, you have to feel bad before you file a lawsuit."

A titter rippled through the courtroom. Even Schneider smiled, though he quickly hid it. Draper allowed himself a smile too, but he was clearly not amused. As I had predicted, that evening and the next morning the media broadcast around the globe Art's testimony that he had been "shafted" by Paramount.

Draper was off to a terrible start. He stood at the podium at the right side of the counsel table where both he and I did most of our witness questioning. Politely annoyed at the giggles, he gripped the podium with both hands and started again.

He asked Art the meaning of "based upon" in his Paramount contract.

"Objection, your honor," I said. It is my practice to object sparingly and only when it makes a difference. But the last thing I wanted was Art Buchwald or Alain Bernheim being grilled about a legal definition that even Judge Schneider had not yet figured out. "There's no foundation established that this witness is qualified to give the answer. It calls for a legal conclusion."

"Sustained," the judge said without hesitation.

Draper then asked Art for a definition of the word "original." I smelled trouble and again objected. We were drifting into Paramount's plagiarism charge—that Art lied when he told Paramount in his contract that his story was "original." This time, the judge overruled my objection because the question called only for Art's understanding of its meaning. But Draper couldn't have liked what he heard when the judge was ruling on my objection: Schneider ominously implied that he agreed with a brief that I had recently filed in which I excoriated Paramount for the Charlie Chaplin sneak attack on Art's integrity. "Well," he said, "we are going to have to talk about this original business because I have now read the plaintiffs' points and authorities, and we're going to have to talk about that issue."

" 'Original' is something that you wrote without help from anybody else, with your own little fingers," Art said confidently.

"And did you write your treatment that's at issue in this lawsuit all by yourself, without any help from anybody else?" Draper asked.

"Yes," Buchwald answered in a firm voice.

Draper was setting my client up for the kill. Art's uneven performance in his last deposition session made me apprehensive. I could have objected every thirty seconds and risked incurring Schneider's wrath the way Draper had, but that would have been counterproductive. Art had to defend himself.

My concerns proved unfounded.

Art deftly deflected Draper's questions about how much Malle or Bernheim may have contributed to his treatment. When Draper tried to get Art to admit on the stand that he knew the contract his agent, Sterling Lord, had negotiated for him was "a standard contract in the motion picture industry," Art answered with the skill of a veteran trial lawyer:

"I haven't seen it. I don't know if it is standard or not."

"Were you proud to be on the front page of the *Wall Street Journal* in connection with this suit?" Draper asked, trying to show that Art's suit was a lark.

"Oh, yes, I was," Art began and then caught himself. "I don't know if the word's proud. I was very pleased with it, that the *Wall Street Journal*, which to me is a very—it's like the Vatican—would deign to put our little suit on the front page. I was pleased with that."

Art was a good student. I had coached him to give a complete answer to Draper's questions, even if he sought to cut Art off. This vexed Draper and blunted the effectiveness of his cross-examination. Once Art got into an explanation, he often held the floor for several minutes. After recounting every detail of the "Sue Me" incident with Marty Davis, Buchwald sat back in his chair spent and out of breath.

"Do you think you've been fully responsive to my question now? I don't want to cut you off," said Draper.

"What's the question?" Buchwald asked.

"I don't remember," said Draper.

"Are we going to soon get to the lawsuit?" Schneider said impatiently.

"I'd like to, your honor," Draper said.

"I'd really like you to do that, too," Schneider said.

Every question that Art answered led toward a snare. All I could do was hope that Art remembered well the traps that I had warned him Paramount's lawyers would try to set for him—and the zingers that we had discussed he would use in self-defense.

The biggest potential pitfall of all revolved around Charlie Chaplin's last starring role and a sneak preview that Buchwald had written about the 1957 movie, *A King in New York*, when he was covering the entertainment industry for the *Herald Tribune* in Paris. Draper had dug up a photocopy of the column, synopsized it on a large poster he displayed for the court and asked Art to explain how it had come about.

"That was way, way back," Buchwald said. "And my recollection is that I was then writing a column from Paris for the *Herald Tribune*. Charlie Chaplin was very big news at the time, and he had made this movie and people were very interested in it.

"He was banned in the United States because of his Communist background, they said. And I got to see it somehow. I don't remember exactly. I think someone let me see it before it got into the theater. And I wrote an article."

Art's explanation of his writing process could now be used against him. I could see it coming when Draper read Art's own thumbnail sketch of the plot for A *King in New York* from his column written thirty-two years earlier:

" 'The story is of a European king who gets booted out of his own country and arrives in America hoping to sell an atomic energy idea.' "

I could see in Art's eyes that he, too, knew what Draper was doing. He was accusing Art of plagiarizing Chaplin. He was twisting Art's explanation of how his so-called mental "data bank" of experiences operated and using it against him.

When Draper tried to enter the *Herald Tribune* column into evidence, I objected, long and loud. Besides my overarching objection to any plagiarism argument, this piece of evidence had never been produced in discovery or included in Paramount's trial exhibits given to us days before the trial, and I had never read the column. My voice rising, I told the judge that I found it offensive that Draper was allowed to trot out the Big Lie in front of the court and world press.

Fortunately, Judge Schneider seemed to know what was going on, and he calmed me down.

"We are dealing here with adults who have thick skins," he said. "I suspect Mr. Buchwald has, I'm sure, taken criticism as I'm sure all of the rest of us have. So I'm sure he'll be able to bear up under it."

Art explained patiently that his ideas came from experience, not movie reviews.

"I think you have to understand something about writing," he said. "You can mull on one idea for one month, two months, a year before you sit down and write it. The fact that you write it in one week doesn't mean that you put one week's labor into it."

Nevertheless, Draper relentlessly rubbed Buchwald's nose in the Chaplin column. He suggested repeatedly that Art might have subliminally stored A *King in New York* in his "data bank," only to bring it out twenty-five years later as *King for a Day*. Art looked less pugnacious than just plain hurt.

If I could have called for a "time out" to tell Art that it was all right, I would have done so. But this was a different kind of game and I was a different kind of coach.

But Buchwald was also a different kind of player.

When Draper had exhausted the A *King in New York* argument, he switched to an attack on Buchwald's public posture as Hollywood underdog.

"Has this litigation given you an opportunity to appear on the talk shows and portray yourself as the little guy being abused by Paramount, the big guy?" asked Draper.

"Yes," Art answered.

"Another Art Buchwald original treatment," Draper said, suggesting that the columnist stole that posture too—from the biblical story of David and Goliath.

I was sick of Draper's smart-ass questioning, so I objected to this "impermissible line of questioning." Schneider agreed and cut Draper off.

Later, on redirect, I asked Art if he had been seeking publicity for his lawsuit. No, he answered, but "it's fascinating, something that I didn't expect when I was going to sue. . . . And all of a sudden, the entire media in this country decided this was a news story. . . . After that, I was called by television stations and I was interviewed by newspapers. I never called them."

Art paused, then hammered home the last sentence in his answer.

"To be honest with you, I did not feel unhappy about some of the publicity because I felt it was a way of getting my story out on *Coming to America*."

Art appeared on several talk shows. One that had driven Paramount crazy the previous year was Larry King's Cable News Network program, "Larry King Live!" A couple of weeks before the trial started, Art had gone on the show again. This time, he tossed even more barbs at the studio and took a few shots at the second-rate quality of *Coming to America* as well. Draper wanted to read the talk show's transcript into the court record.

"May I read, your honor?" Draper asked.

"Sure," Buchwald told him before Schneider had a chance to answer.

"*You're* not 'your honor,' " Draper said. He pointed to the bench where Schneider sat with his chin in his hands. "*He's* 'your honor.' "

"Nice of you both to notice," said Schneider.

"I did notice, your honor," Draper said defensively.

Art shrugged his shoulders and smirked. The Chaplin plagiarism charge hadn't completely disarmed his instinct for the jocular.

Draper read from the transcript of Larry King's interview of his buddy Buchwald:

"I think it was a stinker," Art said.

"Some critics asked why you'd want to be associated with that film," King said.

"Only because I have a piece of the profits," Buchwald had answered. "And this picture will eventually make $400 million. So while in a sense we've suffered a lot of agony and pain, we should share in the profits."

"I see. So you didn't like the movie?" King asked.

"Oh, I loved the movie because I knew I was going to share in it," Art answered.

Draper wanted to know what Buchwald meant by those statements.

"I knew it made a lot of money and my idea about the movie is we were going to get some of that," Buchwald said.

"Do you still think that the movie was a real stinker?" Draper asked.

"*Coming to America* was in the middle. It really wasn't a question of a stinker or not a stinker," Buchwald said.

Draper put one leg up on the podium and rocked back and forth. This was where he would show just how mercenary this David on the Potomac really was when it came to challenging the Goliaths out in Hollywood. Buchwald was a hypocrite. He could tell Larry King's audience that he thought very little of the movie but still wanted a cut of the profits.

What he got instead was a patented Buchwald zinger.

"As you got closer to the concept that maybe you would get some money out of the movie, did you decide that it was a terrific, great movie after all? It wasn't a real stinker?" Draper asked.

"Worse than that," Art said with a sigh that rumbled all the way to the back of the courtroom. "I found out there wasn't *any* money involved. So *that* disturbed me greatly."

At the end of his second day on the witness stand, Draper had not laid a glove on Buchwald. In fact, Art had mugged his examiner. I was reminded of the comment of Art's best buddy, Edward Bennett Williams, when his beloved Redskins were losing by five touchdowns in the second quarter to their archrival Dallas Cowboys: "If this were a fight, they would stop it."

25

The Suits

AS EDDIE MURPHY tooled around the Paramount lot in his golf cart, the studio executives would wave at him as they moved from office to office, meeting to meeting, deal to deal. These were "the Suits."

They might be the kind of people Eddie got on well with, like Jeff Katzenberg or David Kirkpatrick. Or they might be the higher-ups Eddie had little patience or love for, like Frank Mancuso or Ned Tanen. But the one thing they all had in common, it seemed, was that they spent most of their waking hours in matching slacks and coats, tasteful silk ties and well-starched dress shirts, generally with their initials embroidered on the sleeves.

The fourth and fifth days of *Buchwald v. Paramount* were Suits Days, beginning with the executive in charge of Eddie at Paramount, David Kirkpatrick. His particular outfit was navy blue with a conservative blue patterned tie and a crisp white shirt. Peering out at the world through thick, round glasses and speaking with a ponderous, halting voice, he could have been an accountant or a college instructor.

Instead, Kirkpatrick was one of Hollywood's top studio executives. He left Paramount in 1986 and presided over the debacle of Weintraub Entertainment Group, a short-lived production company created by Jerry Weintraub which produced such turkeys as *Troop Beverly Hills* and left millions of dollars of debt in the wake of its bankruptcy. Kirkpatrick himself was personally responsible for the neutron bomb *My Stepmother Is an Alien*.

At the moment, he was president of Touchstone Pictures, the Disney diamond mine that had given America such comic jewels as *Down and Out in Beverly Hills* and *Ruthless People*. What I expected from the man the other Suits called "Davey the K" was a primer on Hollywood storytelling for the benefit of Judge Schneider—and a little more candor than I had got from either Katzenberg or Mancuso.

"You have an understanding of what 'based upon' means in the entertainment industry?" I asked him, once he had settled into the witness box and given his résumé. He answered after a moment's deliberation.

"That there exists some underlying antecedents that triggered the realization of the story in a screenplay," he said.

I smiled, pleased he was remaining faithful to his deposition testimony. In fact, over the course of the two days of his testimony—the longest in the trial—Kirkpatrick not only testified consistently with his prior sworn testimony, he answered truthfully questions that I had not asked him but were prompted by new matters raised by Draper. On any number of those occasions, Kirkpatrick could have hurt me because I had no deposition passage or exhibit to impeach him if I got a bad answer. To his eternal credit, however, he was the honest broker of the facts that I had hoped he would be. Although I called him as a "hostile witness" so that I could ask him leading questions in the nature of cross-examination, his testimony was in fact so helpful to our case and the rapport between us so good that news accounts of the trial a year later were still remarking about the fact that this member of the Club had "testified for Buchwald and Bernheim."

At all times, Davey the K remained placid. His face was as smooth as an egg, from his mustache to his high, tonsured hairline. Even when he wrinkled his forehead in thought, only one simple V of flesh appeared above his eyes. It was difficult to discern what might be going through David Kirkpatrick's mind.

It was clear by his answers, however, that he understood better than anyone who had thus far occupied the witness chair the complexities of creating and then telling a story that can be translated into a movie. Kirkpatrick's testimony, more than anyone else's, gave the judge and public the rare glimpse I had promised into the high-stakes world of moviemaking. Kirkpatrick may have never been a successful screenwriter himself, but he knew from top to bottom the anatomy of a movie.

Like Buchwald, Kirkpatrick recognized that every story is, to some degree, a retelling of one of a handful of archetypal tales, dating back as far as Adam and Eve.

"In the lexicon of literature, you could find, within the thirty-six plot points that there exist in the world, a lot of material that's interrelated," Kirkpatrick said. "But if you don't have that chain which says 'this has been sparked by this,' then you can't really say it [that one story is based on another]," he said.

Kirkpatrick walked Judge Schneider through a series of definitions: concepts; treatments; the difference between adaptations and original screen-plays; and the stories that they are based upon.

When we got to the definition of "coverage," Kirkpatrick rested his elbows on the arms of his chair and rested his chin in his hands. Thousands of screenplays were reduced to executive skim sheets, he said.

"These coverages are kept on file for a number of years in the story depart-ment at Paramount, are they not, sir?"

"Forever," Kirkpatrick said.

"Forever. That's pretty long," I said.

Kirkpatrick grinned his thin, professorial smile.

"Forever in the history of the movie business isn't too long," he said.

It was a mind-boggling irony worth noting: the same studio that would pay hundreds of thousands of dollars to develop a story premise into a full screen-play paid thousands more to maintain a full-time staff of readers whose job it was to synopsize the screenplays back into single-page story premises. For some executives, however, even the one-sheet coverages were too long. Pro-posed movies had to be reduced to even less, as was the case with Kirkpat-rick's boss, Jeff Katzenberg, who liked his movie concepts boiled down to hand-held notes.

Holding up a card Dennis Landry had found in the Paramount files with *King for a Day* listed among the entries, Kirkpatrick said:

"This is a Jeff Katzenberg crib sheet which was a small card, which could have been used in maybe apprising any number of people about the status of Eddie Murphy projects."

"A card he could keep in the breast pocket?" I asked.

"That he would hold in his hand and just go through," Kirkpatrick said.

Under Katzenberg, memos became the lifeblood of Paramount Pictures. When he moved over to Disney, Katzenberg took his memo obsession with him, according to Kirkpatrick.

"Mr. Katzenberg had a habit of writing handwritten notes on typed memo-randa and directing them with inquiries to various members of the creative group," I said.

"A paper-driven company," Kirkpatrick said.

"Is Disney a paper-driven company?"

"It is," he said.

I showed him one of Katzenberg's scribbled notes on the edge of one of his memos.

"There's something about 'Francis Veber is going to write,' or something?" I asked.

"It says, 'Get him writing!' " Kirkpatrick read.

Kirkpatrick unconsciously pulled his lower lip up and over his fuzzy blond upper lip. He left it there for several seconds, ruminating with a blank look on his face like a victim of a petit mal seizure. Then he smiled again, correcting his former assessment of Katzenberg's Paramount as a paper-driven company.

"It was a noodge-driven company," he said.

Katzenberg noodged Kirkpatrick into overseeing Eddie Murphy's career shortly after the young comic arrived at Paramount. Though he never let on to Eddie about it, Kirkpatrick was not too wild about the prospect. Eddie was actually *too* popular and many of Paramount's best writers shied away from the "Eddie Murphy sweepstakes," Kirkpatrick said.

"What was the Eddie Murphy sweepstakes?" I asked.

"We had a lot of projects at the time in development for Eddie Murphy," he said. "A writer, when he enters an assignment, wants to have a betting chance that the movie is ultimately going to get made. And with, I think at the time, approximately ten to twelve projects in development for Eddie, they weren't sure that this was worth a shot."

One of those projects was Tab Murphy's version of *King for a Day* and, according to Kirkpatrick, it had problems.

"It was too political," Kirkpatrick said. "It had no real third act. There were a lot of problems with the nature of the treatment of blacks. . . . We had creative problems with it."

"That's a polite way of saying it didn't work?" I asked.

"Yeah, I suppose."

I walked Kirkpatrick through the laundry list of top Hollywood writers who were next considered for the *King for a Day* project:

- TV's "Soap" creator Susan Harris;
- Former "Saturday Night Live" regular Tim Kazurinsky and his partner Denise Declue;
- *Trading Places* and *Twins* screenwriters Herschel Weingrod and Timothy Harris;
- "M*A*S*H" 's Larry Gelbart;
- Teen comedy writer Jim Kouf and director David Greenwalt;
- *Howard the Duck* authors Willard Huyck and Gloria Katz.

Blaustein and Sheffield were also considered for *King for a Day*. And the studio's early list of directors for the Buchwald/Murphy project included some of Hollywood's biggest names—Richard Benjamin, Sidney Lumet, Paul Brickman, and, of course, John Landis.

Throughout both my examination and Draper's cross, Harvey Schneider showed keen interest in everything Kirkpatrick said. When Draper asked one of his unfocused questions, Schneider was johnny-on-the-spot to clarify.

"Do you understand the question?" Schneider asked Kirkpatrick after Draper asked a particularly convoluted question.

"Sort of, yeah."

"Well, sort of answer it," said the judge to the amusement of the spectator gallery, which had thinned out after Art's testimony.

The list depicting *Hell of an Angel* and *King for a Day* as the two top Paramount projects for Eddie Murphy in 1984 was yet another sales job, according to Kirkpatrick. But a sales job driven by a slightly different motivation.

"To clarify this memo, I believe Mr. Tanen had just come into the company. I was an executive who wanted to keep my job and I was also in charge of the Eddie Murphy account."

This time Kirkpatrick wasn't just trying to get a network executive like Brandon Tartikoff or a director like Landis to buy into a project. Now Kirkpatrick was acting out of self-preservation in the wake of the Diller-Eisner-Katzenberg mass resignations when he wrote: "*King for a Day* is intended for Eddie Murphy who's familiar with the idea and likes it very much."

" 'Likes it very much' may be overselling," Kirkpatrick said.

"Was it the nature of your business to be as optimistic as you could about the project you were in charge of?" Draper later asked the witness.

"It depends on who you're talking with," Kirkpatrick answered.

Overselling or not, Kirkpatrick under my questioning unequivocally testified—while Judge Schneider took careful notes—that Wachs and Eddie himself knew more than enough about *King for a Day* to defeat any defense of independent creation. In fact, Kirkpatrick admitted, Buchwald's story was the "catalyst" for beginning development of the concept of a member of African royalty coming to America and ending up a fish out of water.

Draper's examination of Kirkpatrick was surprisingly brief—a little over an hour—and predictable. He got the witness to repeat some of his deposition testimony that was favorable to Paramount:

- To be "based upon," the antecedent had to be of "a significant story nature"—something more than a one-sentence concept and closer to the three-act structure of the movie itself.
- The only time that Paramount talked to Eddie himself about the "essence of" Buchwald's story was at the Ma Maison dinner, but Eddie was in one of his M-E-G-O moods—"very inattentive" and largely unresponsive.
- Kirkpatrick never gave directly to Eddie either the Tab Murphy or Veber scripts.
- Wachs told Kirkpatrick that he read only fifteen pages at most of Veber's screenplay, and "he was very unflattering about it."

Draper did elicit one surprise revelation from Kirkpatrick. Buchwald's was not the first *King for a Day* on the Paramount lot.

A comedy writer named Charlie Peters, who had written *Her Alibi* and worked on Disney's wildly successful French remake, *Three Men and a Baby*, had submitted a script to Paramount through his agent, Marty Kahn, two years before Buchwald's original two-and-a-half-page story, *It's a Crude, Crude World*, wound its way to Jeff Katzenberg's desk. Peters's script was titled *King for a Day*.

"It was a story of a fifty-ish mercenary who had previously deposed a black ruler in the Caribbean and had been hired by that same ruler now to go back and have another coup in the Caribbean, is that right?" Draper asked.

"Yes," said Kirkpatrick.

"One of the characters that was . . . a vile, disgusting Idi Amin-like Sonomi. That was the current ruler at the start of the story, correct?"

"Right," said Kirkpatrick.

The aging mercenary, Simon Blakely, orchestrates a countercoup to take
back a Caribbean island for the ruthless dictator. Sonomi cements his power
by importing a nuclear device, disguised as a military statue, and a disgusted
Simon Blakely engineers yet another coup, taking the island back for the first
ruler. During the interim between the time Sonomi is in power and the
reentry of the other ruler, Blakely himself is "king for a day" on the small
island paradise.

"And this was a script submitted for consideration for Eddie Murphy?"
Draper asked.

"Yes," said Kirkpatrick, but he didn't know if Eddie had ever read the
script.

Like all the rest of the scripts that went through the Paramount story mill,
Peters's *King for a Day* wound up reduced to a page of coverage in the story
department's files. There it remained when Katzenberg just happened coincidentally to come up with the new name for *It's a Crude, Crude World* in early
1983.

On the whole, Draper failed to score with Kirkpatrick for several reasons.
The witness was honest and not malleable, his deposition was a fait accompli,
and with a series of strategic objections, I succeeded in blocking potentially
damaging testimony. For example, when Draper tried to get Kirkpatrick to
testify indirectly whether *Coming to America* was based upon *King for a Day*, I
successfully objected, ironically citing the judge's pretrial ruling limiting the
scope of expert testimony—a result that had been urged by Draper.

Judge Schneider had his own questions too—in fact, more of this witness
than any other. After Draper and I had postured back and forth, extracting
what we wanted from Kirkpatrick for the court record, Schneider first asked
him the meaning of theme, concept and plot and then got down to the heart
of the matter: where does a story really begin?

"A character in action is a story," Kirkpatrick said. "So his actions are
triggered by his heart, his motivations."

"Do you equate heart with motivation?" asked Schneider.

"Yeah."

Francis Veber's version of *King for a Day* was to be based upon Jeff
Katzenberg's interpretation of Buchwald's original story, as executed by Tab
Murphy. By then, according to our next witness, that story had been folded,
spindled and mutilated in Paramount story meetings so that it bore little
resemblance to Buchwald's original.

Ricardo Angelo Mestres III, who teamed with Kirkpatrick to steer *King for a
Day* through development, remembered it sounding something like this:

"A story about a black king from an island in the Pacific who had a twin
brother on the far side of the island who had been banished because of his

misbehavior. This king went to Washington, D.C., to enter into negotiations with the U.S. government and/or U.S. companies for drilling rights which would result in vast fortunes coming to the island. And while he was in Washington, his bad brother from the other side of the island executed a coup d'état, took control and suddenly the visiting king—who had been treated with all of the dignity of royalty, especially in terms of his value as a source of oil—was basically rejected. Thrown out on the street, penniless, without any idea of how to survive in the U.S. And the story was how he banded together with a group of other characters from the Washington, D.C., area, eventually to return to the island, reclaim his throne, banish the bad brother and regain his authority."

Mestres, a bona fide whiz kid among the Suits, was able to spiel the story instantly in his testimony, even though six years had passed. It was seared in his memory from having pitched it over and over to writers, he said, trying to get one of them to write it for the studio.

In late 1983, when he was trying to find someone to turn the mélange of Katzenberg-Buchwald-Bernheim-Murphy (Tab) ideas into a viable screenplay, Mestres was already rising extraordinarily quickly in an industry that anoints and catapults people to positions of immense power and prestige long before their thirtieth birthdays.

The twenty-three-year-old Harvard graduate went from Cambridge to Hollywood in the summer of 1981, hired by then Paramount production chief Don Simpson. His only experience: working summers as a production assistant on made-for-television features. But Hollywood agreed with him.

In 1982 he was promoted to executive director of production. In 1984 he became vice-president of production for Paramount's motion picture group. It was through Simpson, by then an independent producer with his partner Jerry Bruckheimer, that Mestres went on to achieve a major early triumph in his skyrocketing career: Paramount production executive on a Simpson/Bruckheimer movie called *Beverly Hills Cop*. By his twenty-sixth birthday, Mestres was credited with shepherding a major hit to the screen.

In 1985 he moved over to Disney as vice-president of production and one year later his old bosses at Paramount, Katzenberg and Eisner, promoted him to senior vice-president of motion picture production. By the time he appeared in Department 52 to testify as the sixth witness on the afternoon of the fourth day of *Buchwald v. Paramount*, Mestres was head of his own division at Disney: Hollywood Pictures. One writer described him as "the original corporate ninja warrior." He had just turned thirty-one years old.

Mestres was as representative of the New Hollywood executive as Eddie Murphy was of the New Hollywood actor. Though they differed in education, upbringing and culture (Mestres's parents are of Cuban descent), both men radiated an ambivalent cynicism that seemed unwarranted by their years. They were bright young men—perhaps the best the country had to offer in many respects. Mestres had earned a reputation for fairness and decency. But I still couldn't help wondering what either Murphy or he would do if they were faced with some moral choice about grabbing the next golden opportunity to achieve even more success, regardless of the consequences to others.

Mestres's dark blue suit, white shirt and blue and white striped tie were perfectly coordinated with his piercing blue eyes. His answers were crisp yeses and noes, with only the rarest Mancuso or Katzenberg refrain of "I don't remember." The confident New York City native did remember the Katzenberg memo about successful filmmaking. After all, he wrote it.

The so-called Katzenberg "Philosophy Paper" ran on for several pages, but in classic story department style, Mestres was able to boil it down to a one-liner suitable for a Katzenberg crib sheet:

"Idea is King; material is Queen."

This high-concept one-liner, championed by Katzenberg first at Paramount and later at Disney, would become a keystone to our attack on the studio. Buchwald had the idea, after all. And the idea in this case was, quite literally, King. As Mestres wrote in the Philosophy Paper, every iota of script material that followed from Buchwald's story would, by Paramount's own definition, be Queen.

"In your view, concept is preeminent?" I asked.

"Yes."

"And it was also your view that the idea was what was powering the entire process and, ultimately, the success of the movie?"

"Yes."

"Is there a difference between concept and idea?" Judge Schneider wanted to know.

"No," Mestres replied.

During his Paramount tenure, Mestres was also the executive in charge of regularly reviewing projects being developed for Eddie Murphy. It was his practice to assign each of them a grade, as though he were a teaching assistant evaluating term papers. They got an A, B or C, depending upon how hot and viable they were.

And high on Mestres's A list, I pointed out to the Court, was *King for a Day*.

Mestres repeated without hesitation his favorable deposition testimony that severely impeached his Disney boss's testimony:

- The internal Paramount June 1983 memo—summarizing the first story meeting with Tab Murphy, Bernheim, Katzenberg, Kirkpatrick and Mestres and showing the changes in Buchwald's story early in the development process, including Eddie playing at least two characters—was accurate.
- When Katzenberg met with Eddie and Eddie was enthusiastic about a project, Katzenberg would then aggressively push development of that project, and Katzenberg wanted "a full court press" on *King for a Day* in early April 1983—right around the time of the now storied Ma Maison dinner.
- Katzenberg loved Buchwald's movie concept and told Mestres that

The Buchwald legal team: from left, Zazi Pope, Marsha Durko, Dennis Landry, Pierce O'Donnell, and Suzanne Tragert. MICHAEL JACOBS

Eddie Murphy's manager, Robert Wachs. CELEBRITY PHOTO AGENCY

Paramount Pictures chairman Frank Mancuso, sitting beside Paramount attorney Lon Sobel. WIDE WORLD

Eddie Murphy, flanked by Arsenio Hall, accepting the 15th Annual People's Choice Best Actor award for his work in *Coming to America*. WIDE WORLD

Ned Tanen in 1980, four years before he took over the reins as production chief at Paramount Pictures. WIDE WORLD

Art Buchwald and Alain Bernheim in the front row of Department 52, Los Angeles Superior Court. SUSAN WERNER

The adversaries: Paramount's Charles Diamond and Pierce O'Donnell face reporters. SUSAN WERNER

Disney's Jeffrey Katzenberg. CELEBRITY PHOTO AGENCY

John Landis, director of *Coming to America*, and his wife Deborah Nadoolman
CELEBRITY PHOTO AGENCY

Pierce O'Donnell and Art Buchwald leaving court. SUSAN WERNER

Los Angeles Superior Court Judge Harvey A. Schneider.
LEO JARZOMB

O'Melveny & Myers attorney Robert Draper, counsel for Paramount.

King for a Day "would be a fantastic vehicle" and was "ideally suited" for Eddie Murphy.

Draper had no questions, so before thirty minutes had passed the adroit, unruffled New Hollywood ninja warrior was excused. Head held high, he walked out through the front door. On his way out, he did make one stop at the front row of spectator seats in the courtroom to whisper a hello, good luck and Godspeed to a representative of the Old Hollywood who had recently signed a production development deal with Disney. Mestres thoughtfully wanted him to know that he was in good hands—that Disney would treat him right.

"Take care of yourself," Mestres whispered, clapping the man on the shoulder.

"I will. Thanks," said Alain Bernheim.

Bruce Berman was also New Hollywood. Chubby, ruddy-complected and six years older than Mestres, the Warner Bros. production chief had the same black, coiffed hair, blue suit, white shirt and blue tie that the Disney executives sported.

Berman was something of a late-blooming yuppie, given the right-out-of-school rise of such peers as Katzenberg and Kirkpatrick. He didn't break into show biz until he was twenty-six—the same age as Mestres when he supervised *Beverly Hills Cop.* Berman hired on as an assistant to a hot young lawyer named Peter Guber who worked in the film division of Casablanca Records. Universal, then under the leadership of Ned Tanen, lured him away a year later with an offer to make Berman vice-president of production. Then, after Tanen retired, he moved over to Warner Bros. in 1983, first as a vice-president and later as president of theatrical film production for Warner Bros. chief executive officer Bob Daly and chief operating officer Terry Semel.

Just the day before, the courtroom had been packed with reporters, spectators and fans, crowding in to catch a glimpse of Arsenio or Art or, maybe, Eddie Murphy himself. But by the time Berman—one of the two or three dozen most powerful executives in Hollywood—took his oath late on Wednesday afternoon, there were no more than a half dozen people in the audience, including the studio's high-powered general counsel John Schulman, who stood guard in the first row. As in politics, the truly powerful in the entertainment industry seem to remain anonymous, mostly because the media and, by extension, the public let them.

An admirer of Buchwald's books and columns, Berman recounted for the court how Alain teamed up with *Police Academy* creator Paul Maslansky in 1986 and brought *King for a Day* to Warner's movie-by-committee management.

"I believe that when Paul came to me . . . that Paul and Alain told me that Paramount was abandoning their project and that's why I didn't feel a conflict," he said.

Assured that Paramount had dumped the idea, Berman signed them up with an option deal for Art and a development deal for the two producers that was almost identical to the deal that Alain had at Paramount. As he told Draper under cross-examination, signing production development deals with a proven talent like Maslansky was almost routine.

"It wasn't unusual to spend about $200,000 to $250,000 on a development project at Warner's, was it? A development project that didn't get made?"

"Not unusual," said Berman, pushing his tortoise-shell glasses up on his nose.

"How many development projects did you have in the . . . let's say 1985, '86, '87 time frame, approximately?"

"Approximately 200, 250," said Berman.

"And if I wanted to go to the movie theater and see those, where would I go?" Draper asked.

"Most of them did not make it to the theater," said Berman.

Neither did the Bernheim/Maslansky project, despite two different scripts by two different screenwriters. Matt Robinson's *Me and the King*, written during hiatuses from his head writer position on the Cosby show, was not up to Berman's expectations and its successor, *King Jomo*, by Allan Katz, also left something to be desired. Then, near the end of 1987, the trade press began reporting leaks from Paramount about a winter shooting in Brooklyn for a big Eddie Murphy summer blockbuster called *Coming to America*. On January 20, 1988, Berman wrote his regrets to Bernheim, telling him that Paramount's new movie—starring Eddie as a fish out of water in urban America—was too close for comfort to Buchwald's story.

Berman had never considered trying to make changes to the Buchwald movie at Warner Bros. to avoid conflicting with *Coming to America*. Paramount's project had a premise that was "directly competitive" with his movie's premise—and with the biggest movie star in the world to boot. So he liked *King for a Day* for what it was about.

"And you didn't want to change *King for a Day*, the Buchwald movie story, and make it into a quiz show or something like that?" I asked him.

"No, I didn't," he quickly answered.

"Because that wasn't the premise you had purchased from Mr. Buchwald, was it?"

"It wasn't."

My final questions to Berman were important to establish that Paramount's movie had destroyed my clients' chances of making their movie anywhere— strong evidence for punitive damages and the accompanying message to all of the studios that they couldn't steal a writer's idea and call it their own without paying for it. Berman had told me that he had not decided to abandon Buchwald's project before he learned of Murphy's new movie.

"Would you have ordered Katz to revise the script if you had not learned about the new Eddie Murphy movie?" I asked.

But Judge Schneider, sustaining Draper's objection, would have no part of any such speculation. So I settled for second best.

"Before you learned about that, had you decided not to have Mr. Katz do the revisions?"

"I don't think I did."

Like the other Suits, Ned Tanen was a company man. Unlike Katzenberg, however, he was far more candid, more relaxed and more secure in himself when he took the witness stand on Thursday afternoon, December 21, Day Five of the trial. This was the dangerous witness that I had to handle like a lion trainer.

"We're in the business to make money, not art," he had once bluntly told an interviewer.

At fifty-eight, roughly two thirds of his life had been devoted to the entertainment business—twenty-nine years alone at Universal/MCA. Now he was a consultant at Paramount.

"What do you do as a consultant?" I asked.

"Look at some of the screenplays they are interested in producing. Perhaps make comments on them," he said. "Suggest screenplay changes. Suggest casting ideas, perhaps directors. Look at the movies that they produced. Offer some editing suggestions and also good will and welfare. I've been dealing with them on some European matters that aren't really directly related to motion picture production. Things of that nature."

In other words, he did pretty much what he wanted to do. And, reportedly, he earned $1 million a year for his trouble.

The fact was, Ned Stone Tanen's instincts had not waned with age. Here was the man who green-lighted a project way back in 1986, based on an obscure deep-sea submarine thriller by an untried novelist, that would become Paramount's biggest hit during the first half of 1990. Tanen read the book on a transatlantic flight and was ready to make a deal when his plane set down in New York. The author was Tom Clancy and the book was *The Hunt for Red October.*

Tanen was also the first to admit that he was imperfect. He was the man who turned down *Star Wars,* after all.

"This business has a way of teaching you some humility," he said. "And it's one thing to mention the successes. There's another list that isn't quite so successful."

Generally, Tanen could still spot a hit. Not every suit could. That was at least one of the reasons that he was not a great believer in making movies by committee.

"The creative executives at a studio can make comments and contributions that result in changes in the original movie idea as it is being written?" I asked.

"They can suggest and you try not to make it an open forum," Tanen explained. "You're trying to keep it down to a limited number of people involved in a project."

"You hopefully don't hold an election," I noted, and he readily agreed.

With his thinning black hair and low growl of a voice, Tanen represented a link between the Old and New Hollywoods. In both eras, the stories worth putting up on the screen were harder to come by than most people knew. So a terrific movie idea like Buchwald's was a valuable commodity.

I had decided to use Tanen as the judge's guide through the world of filmmaking in hopes of persuading him that it was common for an idea to evolve from an abbreviated outline to a complete screenplay and to go through wrenching changes. So, near the very beginning of his testimony, Tanen and I took Harvey Schneider on a ten-minute tour of the creative gauntlet that even a terrific idea has to endure from conception to finished movie. Walking away from the podium and my outline, I engaged in more of a dialogue than a cross-examination with Tanen about the many people who can and often do change the direction of a story—writers, studio executives, director, the star, the film editor—and the variety of reasons why a story can be changed, including budget accommodations, change of locale, casting changes, MPAA ratings and audience survey results.

As we did our number, Judge Schneider took notes. At one point I asked Tanen whether "in the course of the writing by the screenwriters, the original story or movie idea can also undergo changes and modifications." When he answered, "Yes, sir," the judge asked the court reporter to read back that question and answer so that he could write it down verbatim.

It often took several years to shepherd a story to the screen. *American Graffiti* was such a film, according to Tanen. And *Coal Miner's Daughter*, another of his triumphs during his years at Universal, had a nearly five-year gestation period.

"If one screenplay out of fifteen or eighteen is ever made into a movie, it's par for the course at a major company," he said. "It's basically a development business and most of the projects you develop do not get made."

"These are the rules," he testified. "These are the rules you play by."

Winners paid for losers, according to Tanen. That was how it had to be in such a risky, speculative and incredibly expensive business. If the studios didn't take the biggest chunk of change from an *E.T.* or a *Godfather*, he had told *Screen International* columnist Chris Brown way back at the very beginning of the Greed Decade, other movies might not get developed at all.

While not conceding that he thought *Coming to America* owed any creative debt to *King for a Day*, Tanen was not contentious. What he had to say on the stand was basically what he had said during his deposition six months earlier. And that was not always flattering—as in the case of John Landis, whose expensive ways on the set plagued Tanen as far back as *The Blues Brothers* at Universal. Instead of high-priced African dance production numbers that contributed little to the plot, Landis staged expensive multi-vehicle car crashes that contributed even less.

"What is a production value?" Judge Schneider asked.

"Production values, your honor: dance sequences, ceremonial sequences, the huge number of extras, overbuilt sets, overblown, overproduced," Tanen said, twisting in his seat and directly addressing Schneider. "This is a subjective reaction but it was mine. I thought the best parts of the movie were Eddie, Arsenio, and the idea of his fairy tale romance in America. And playing those other characters."

Landis had made creative contributions to Coming to America, however, Tanen acknowledged.

"You hold him in high regard? Mr. Landis?" I asked.

"I hold him in regard," Tanen said wryly.

The point I was driving at was that everyone involved in the development process changed the original story. Whether influenced by Suits or director or budget or the Motion Picture Association of America's rating board, a movie as conceived and its final form were often two different animals.

As Draper discovered when he posed a hypothetical question about the development process, there were limits to the lengths to which a studio would go in altering an original story. Not many limits, but some.

"Have you ever had a situation where you start off with a movie that's, say, about Jack the Ripper and as a result of the changes in the process, you end up with a Doris Day comedy?"

"I've developed hundreds if not thousands of screenplays," Tanen said. "I've never had that happen."

By now, Ned Tanen was comfortable on the stand. "Everyone's in two businesses," he said at one point. "Their own and the movie business."

He compulsively took off and replaced a pair of aviator-style reading glasses but otherwise remained relaxed but attentive. His mouth curled up on the right side of his face in a half smile when he was amused.

It was time to get down to dollars and cents with Ned Tanen. The first item of business was the amount of money that Paramount poured into King for a Day. According to Paramount's accounting, the three abandoned screenplays the studio developed from Buchwald's story cost about $418,000.

"Carrying and interest cost: that was another $69,000?" I asked.

"Development is a very expensive business," Tanen said.

But not even remotely as expensive as the care and feeding of Eddie Murphy.

"Would you explain to us what 'above the line' means in Paramount motion picture accounting?" I asked.

" 'Above the line' generally means the creative ingredients: the writers, director, producer, actors, principal actors, secondary actors," Tanen said.

The "above the line" acting costs for Coming to America totaled $8,960,000, according to the accounting memoranda Paramount had turned over to us before trial. I laid the figures in front of Tanen and the judge.

"Eddie Murphy's advance was $8 million for Coming to America, was it not?" I said. "We can infer from this number that the rest of the cast cost $960,000?"

"Well, the principals," Tanen said, peering at the figures through his aviators. "That would not be day players and the other people."

I heard a collective gasp from the press behind me and the sounds of dozens of pencils scratching across paper—the disparity between stars and other actors had rarely before been spelled out in such stark figures. More important, Judge Schneider took note, asking Tanen and me to point out the line on the budget to which we were referring. No question about it, I thought to myself, his honor is getting very interested in the numbers. That could only bode well for us.

And $8 million was only Eddie's acting fee. That didn't include his 15 percent share of gross profits and $5 million of "overhead" charged to the picture.

"Eddie Murphy is a major movie star and Eddie Murphy gets what the market will bear. And that's what the market will bear," Tanen said with a shrug, his disgust with runaway star salaries barely disguised.

Even with that hunk sliced out of the Coming to America revenue pie before one foot of film was ever shot, Paramount was still willing to close the deal because company officials like Tanen knew the studio would come out ahead.

"It's my understanding that Paramount was willing to take an unusually small share of net profits as opposed to what it usually takes, in connection with Coming to America," I said.

"Yes, sir," Tanen answered.

Regardless of whether the movie ever earned net profits, Paramount would still get its 35 percent average distribution fee as soon as the first dollar of gross receipts rolled in—just as Eddie Murphy would get his 15 percent. Essentially, they were partners in the same accounting game. Murphy and Paramount were first in line.

John Landis was second, with a 10 percent adjusted gross deal. Under Landis's contract, Paramount's accountants calculated the director's slice of the pie as if Paramount were charging only a 20 percent distribution fee to Coming to America, instead of the 35 percent charged to net profit participants. He wouldn't earn the multiple millions that Eddie and the studio would, but Landis would bank at least several million dollars in back-end pay long before any of the net profit participants, including the producers and writers, ever saw a dime.

Clout was everything, an exasperated Ned Tanen agreed.

"Yes, yes, certain people can negotiate different deals, yes, of course," he said.

Alain Bernheim was not one of them. The deal he got for King for a Day was the deal virtually every good packaging producer in Hollywood gets—monkey points, take it or leave it. And the day in November 1987, when Tanen agreed to have lunch with Bernheim at the Paramount commissary,

Alain felt as though he had not only taken it; he had *been* taken as well. He told Tanen as much and the studio chief quickly got the message, Tanen told Draper on cross-examination.

"I felt that it was an attempt to get some money, because *King for a Day* was a project that, it seemed to me, was pretty dead," Tanen said. "It was almost a last-ditch effort to try to get some money. And I also felt angry about it because . . . if Eddie Murphy hadn't been the principal . . . this would not have been brought up."

"Did you feel Mr. Bernheim was setting you up at this luncheon?" Draper asked.

"I thought he really was trying to ask me, indirectly, and somewhat uncomfortably, for some money," Tanen said.

"Why didn't you run out to the lawyers and say, 'Let's fine-tooth-comb . . . the contracts'?" Draper asked.

"Because it would never have occurred to me that these two properties had that much in common."

This testimony was even more sincere and cogent than when he had talked about it in his deposition. Alain's claim about the similarity between *King for a Day* and *Coming to America* was "ridiculous," but he felt "affection and friendship" for Bernheim, and respected Buchwald "enormously." As he testified, I started to believe him, to accept that the similarity between Art's treatment and Eddie's story never crossed his mind until Alain confronted him. When Tanen finished testifying on this subject, I knew we were finished on our tort claim. While I had lots of evidence that we had taken a year to develop about why the movie was based upon Art's story, I had no impeaching evidence to show that Tanen or other Paramount officials talked about the similarities and chose to ignore my client's contract rights. This was one time when I could have used another smoking gun from Federal Express.

"You testified that you thought it would be tough for *Coming to America* to get to net profits," Draper said. "Why is that?"

"It's a very, very expensive movie," Tanen said. "And gross participants make it an even more expensive movie. The advertising on this movie was enormous. The expenditure to distribute this movie was enormous. This was not a small production. It was a big, big venture."

King for a Day, on the other hand, was "an interesting idea and a very, very bad screenplay," Tanen said. "In Texas, they say, 'That dog don't hunt.' And this script didn't write. It just didn't. It just wasn't good. It was not a good screenplay. For all the conversation about it, it didn't seem to be going anywhere."

After his run-in with Bernheim, Tanen had sat down with the two screenplays: Veber's version of *King for a Day* and *Coming to America*. If it hadn't been for Eddie Murphy, he told Draper, he didn't think the two scripts would ever have been linked.

"I didn't see it the same. It was apples and oranges to me," he said.

Would it have made any difference if it had been written for, say, Dustin Hoffman instead of Eddie Murphy?

"I am hard pressed to find what those two stories have to do with each other. And if it weren't for Eddie Murphy, I don't think we'd be sitting here. If it were Dustin Hoffman, I don't think we'd be sitting here."

I was livid as Draper sat down. Turning in my chair, I started to speak before I reached the podium for my redirect examination. Draper's comparison between Hoffman and Murphy struck me as something more than just an arbitrary comparison of two big-name actors. One, after all, was black. The other was white.

"You went through a very long and interesting comparison," I said to Tanen. "If it were Dustin Hoffman and not Eddie Murphy, you didn't think this claim would be made," I began. By now, I was leaning forward on the podium, eyeball to eyeball with the witness. The courtroom was absolutely still.

"You're not suggesting that the plaintiffs in this case are racists, are you, sir?"

Tanen paused in shock at the suggestion, then answered quickly and with an edge of incredulity in his voice.

"I'm not suggesting that," Tanen said.

I stared at Draper. He nervously rustled through some papers and would not look me in the eye.

26

Not in Those Words

ON DECEMBER 21, I called Robert Wachs to the stand as a hostile witness. The bushy-browed lawyer was still Eddie Murphy's overseer, mentor and general factotum. More recently, he had taken on a second star client in Arsenio Hall, and he had grown even more powerful, more haughty and more confident that he had Hollywood by the tail.

"Do you recall being told by Jeff Katzenberg in 1983 that Paramount was so excited about Buchwald's *King for a Day* movie project that Paramount was going to put on a full court press to get a script and get the movie into development?" I asked of the man who owned 5 percent of Eddie Murphy's income.

"I don't remember that it was treated any differently than any of a dozen projects they had under development," Wachs said.

"All of which were under a full court press?" I asked.

"I don't know," he said peevishly. "I don't work for Paramount."

Wachs's mission on the witness stand seemed to be to minimize Eddie's and his knowledge about *King for a Day* as well as Paramount's extensive development of Buchwald's story for any Eddie Murphy movie. My mission was to impeach his testimony, and I had plenty of ammunition for the task at hand—his own deposition testimony along with the letters and memos he had written or received between 1983 and 1985. The 1984 Jim Harrison correspondence was the pièce de résistance.

Wachs, touchy and tired-looking, turned out to be an evasive performer on the stand. The bags beneath his eyes were deep and dark.

"Did anyone at Paramount ever tell you in the period 1983 to 1985 that Paramount was developing a motion picture called *King for a Day* for Eddie Murphy to star in the lead role?"

"Not in those words, no." Murphy was only one of many possibilities, he insisted. "They never develop one movie for one star," he said. "They never mentioned Eddie specifically."

"Never told you that it was being developed specifically for Eddie?" I asked.

"No, they never did."

In light of the parade of witnesses and cascade of documents that conclusively proved that *King for a Day* was being developed for one and only one person—King Eddie—and that Wachs had been sent dozens of those exhibits, Wachs's testimony was incredible—and a gift.

Wachs testified that during the first three months Eddie and he were in the movie business together, he asked the Suits about foreign exploitation of *48 HRS.* and why Paramount used a different film poster for foreign than for domestic distribution. When he and Eddie went to Philadelphia for *Trading Places*, they discussed the hotels the studio put them up in, how cold it was and how long they'd have to remain in Philadelphia before the movie wrapped. They discussed "what the dailies were like and how it was going and where we were going to set up offices in New York," Wachs said. "And what would our modus operandi be for finding projects. That's sort of the first three months of 1983, when we were just setting up offices."

They did not discuss *King for a Day*.

Wachs did remember a big welcome party the studio threw for Murphy in August 1983, but that was all he could remember.

"And do you recall who were some of the celebrities who attended that party?" I asked.

"You mean other than Mr. Wachs?" Draper injected.

"Indeed," I said.

"No, I don't, sir," Wachs said. In fact, the guest list for his twenty-two-year-old client's soiree read like a Who's Who of Hollywood: Richard Pryor, Johnny Carson, Burt Reynolds, Sylvester Stallone, Bill Cosby, Michael Jackson and Prince, among many others.

Wachs had no trouble recalling Murphy's response to *Beverly Hills Cop*.

"That was committed to in twenty-four hours from the time we first got the script," said Wachs.

"And so Eddie didn't have a hard time making up his mind to do something when he liked it?"

"None whatsoever."

Beverly Hills Cop was a completed, well-developed script. It seemed perfectly suited to Murphy at the time. The difference between the quick commitment to that movie and Eddie's utter ignorance of the fact that *King for a*

Day was being developed for him at the same time was a matter of studio policy, according to Wachs.

"Until Mr. Katzenberg and company left, their technique was to hone a project until, in their minds, it was almost a shooting script, before they would present it to the star," he said. "They wanted to take their best shot."

Wachs did not remember any partial screenplay or early draft of one of the *King for a Day* scripts falling into Eddie Murphy's hands. He himself could not remember much about the Buchwald story or any of the screen treatments that evolved from it.

But Wachs's memory returned in full force when we got to Exhibit 54: the Jim Harrison correspondence. With two months to develop a line of defense since he was first confronted with this bombshell in his deposition, his recollections were particularly sharp with regard to Harrison's movie treatment. Judge Schneider listened intently as I went after Wachs.

Wachs first told me that he had cursorily read Harrison's treatment—only a paragraph or two but enough to tell him that he didn't like it.

"I think I stopped at 'pimp,' " he said, sniffing like a man recovering from a bad cold.

"Stopped at what?" Judge Schneider asked.

" 'Pimp,' " Wachs told him.

"Where does that appear?" the judge asked, leafing through the exhibit. Wachs donned his black horn rims and read aloud from the story description.

" 'On the way to Dulles, Winston stops for a suitable disguise. Buying some shades and a full length sable coat off a pimp at Dulles, he purchases a ticket to Ethiopia.' "

Wachs set the treatment down, crossing his arms to emphasize his disgust.

"That was it for me," he said, deep creases emphasizing his frown. I nearly laughed out loud at his offended sensibilities.

"By reading the first paragraph and up to the word 'pimp' in the second paragraph, you knew that the treatment by Harrison bore enough of a resemblance to Buchwald's story to blow him off. Is that correct?" I asked, standing only a few feet from him and pointing to a huge blowup of his letter and the treatment mounted on several tripods in the empty jury box.

Wachs suddenly sat forward, concerned. He didn't want his brush-off of a former friend and client to be characterized in court record as a *cynical* brush-off. Just a brush-off.

"No, no," he said, his voice rising. "The story had to do with politics and it wasn't very good. He had been a client of mine. I respected his writing. This was a poor piece of work and I just wanted to respond to it the day I got it and be done with it."

There was an inflection at the end of each of his sentences, and he held his horn-rim glasses in his right hand like a prop. I had seized Wachs's attention. He widened his piercing blue eyes as though he were offended each time I asked a question.

"Was there something in the first paragraph and/or the first two sentences of the second paragraph that brought to your mind the Buchwald *King for a Day* treatment?"

"Something to do with Washington, D.C., senators, and Ethiopia," he said. "And a whole concept of Eddie Murphy walking around like a pimp."

Judge Schneider jumped into the hunt. He didn't understand Wachs's convoluted answer and wanted clarification. After Wachs gave a further explanation of his reaction to Harrison's treatment, the judge asked a question that told me he knew exactly what was going on here.

"Does that also mean that there was, in your mind, some similarity or at least minimal similarity that caused you to believe that there was something at Paramount that was being done along this line? Is that what you're saying?"

Looking up at the imposing figure in a black robe, Wachs replied, "I knew that the Buchwald story was about the CIA and politics. I knew that. That was a two-sentence pitch."

"It was both inappropriate for Murphy and it resembled something that you were aware was ongoing?" Schneider summarized.

"Yes, sir," Wachs meekly answered.

"Why did you pick Buchwald's *King for a Day* story to be the reason or excuse for letting down Mr. Harrison?" I asked as I went in for the kill.

"I'm sure that it was probably something that Jimmy'd heard of and he could relate to the fact that Paramount was developing a story by a well-known columnist," said Wachs.

I wasn't about to let him off the hook that easily. There was Wachs's line in the brush-off letter that utterly nixed Harrison's allegedly distasteful "pimp" story as a Murphy movie because it was "fairly close" to *King for a Day*.

"What did you mean by the use of the words 'fairly close'?"

Wachs shrugged and ran his fingers through his thinning blond pompadour.

"It was a device to tell him please don't continue sending me this kind of stuff," he said. "And certainly don't send me anything that related to pimps in Ethiopia. And I've never heard from him since."

Having set him up, I then read for five minutes from his deposition ten weeks earlier. That testimony contradicted his studied courtroom recounting of the reasons for picking Buchwald's story for the kiss-off out of an infinite number of other excuses that could never be investigated by a guy in the Michigan backwoods. And it also supplied a definition of what he meant when he told Harrison that Buchwald's story that Paramount had in development for Eddie was "fairly close to your story line."

"What does 'fairly close' mean to you?" I had asked in his deposition, which I was now reading to Judge Schneider.

"That an ordinary person would find any two items had more similarities than dissimilarities," Wachs had answered.

Mission accomplished. Wachs had admitted that he was keenly aware in September 1984 that Paramount had a Buchwald story in development *specifically for Eddie*, and Wachs clearly knew more about Buchwald's story than what could be told in a two-sentence pitch. And on the issue of similarty, if Harrison's treatment had more similarities to Art's treatment than dissimilarities, then *King for a Day* and *Coming to America* were overwhelmingly similar.

One of the hundreds of newspaper and magazine articles about Murphy that Landry had dug up during the course of research was a column published in New York in February 1984, wrapped around a mug shot of Eddie Murphy and a headline that read LOOK WHAT'S IN BUCHWALD'S WASTEBASKET. It seemed to belie any doubt that *King for a Day* was a major Buchwald project being developed by Paramount for Eddie Murphy in late 1983 and early 1984.

But Judge Schneider had already made it clear that he was not interested in reading any more exhibits. He had already been through a half dozen scripts, two dozen depositions and enough case law to make a second-year law student gag. Schneider propped his chin up against his right hand, curling his fingers around his cheek. He sighed deeply when he saw me waving around yet another piece of paper he would have to study.

"Your honor, I'm not going to offer it," I said.

"I'm proud of you," Schneider said, blinking through his square half-lens reading glasses.

That Bob Wachs would be offended by the word "pimp" struck me as the absolute height of absurdity. I was fairly certain the hypocrisy must have been transparent to Judge Schneider too. Wachs, the man who gave the world *Raw*, had no aversion to adolescent jokes laced with obscenities. I had no problem getting his double standard into the court record.

"You said in your view *Coming to America* is a sweet, romantic comedy," I said.

"There's profanity," Wachs conceded.

"It's audible on the screen," I said. "The 'F' word is used several times. . . . It's some pretty raw stuff."

Wachs shot me a "So what?" look.

"And there's some other off-color gags and gimmicks that are going on, sexual matters, in that movie too," I pressed further. "Are there not, sir?"

Draper came to the rescue with an objection.

"I'm going to sustain the objection," said Schneider. "I've seen the movie." This was a golden example of a trial lawyer not caring whether the question was answered. The judge gave the answer.

I continued to skewer Wachs with inconsistent testimony from his deposition and, confronted with the glut of documents sent to him over two years, he was forced to admit that:

- Eddie has a very good memory.
- Wachs and Kirkpatrick had a close working relationship and Kirkpatrick sent him regular reports about the progress of *King for a Day*.
- In 1983, Paramount executives told him that they "were high on the concept" and that it might be good for Eddie.
- Wachs received a *King for a Day* script in March 1985.

- During the same period that *King for a Day* was in development at Paramount, Blaustein and Sheffield were writing another script for Eddie.
- Eddie was interested in movies with a political theme in 1984 as evidenced by the outline for *America 1990* that he wrote and submitted to Paramount.
- The supposed story that Eddie submitted for his story credit was really a summary of the screenplay.

Sometimes I had to get firm with Wachs when he got evasive.

"There came a point, did there not, sir, when Paramount executives told you that they wanted to develop a movie starring Eddie Murphy based on an Art Buchwald story which had the working title *King for a Day?*"

"It was mentioned in a menu listing about ten or twelve other projects."

"So the answer to the question is yes, they did tell you about it?"

"Yes."

It was time to drive a wedge between the paternalistic Mr. Wachs and the young talent he appeared to regard as a commodity.

"It's a fact, is it not, that Eddie Murphy is not satisfied with his current overall deal with Paramount?"

"I think that's correct," conceded Wachs.

"But you believe that he probably has one of the best movie star motion picture deals in town, right?"

Wachs hunkered down in his seat.

"I think on an exclusive multi-picture situation, I think he's got a fine deal," he said, sticking his chin out like a prize fighter.

True enough insofar as his salary and gross points were concerned. But Eddie's *net* profit deal remained as pathetic as anybody else's in Hollywood.

"With each of the net profit participation statements that Eddie Murphy Productions has received from Paramount in connection with *Coming to America*, the . . . loss has gotten higher, has it not, with each statement?" I asked.

Draper objected.

"Your honor, I object to the question on relevance," said Draper. "If we were to get to the next stage, that would be an issue."

I held my tongue. It would indeed become an issue if and when we got to the next stage. *The* issue, in fact.

The most regularly punctual member of the Buchwald team was not Zazi or Suzanne Tragert or even I. It was Alain Bernheim. Arriving each day ahead of everyone and patiently waiting for his chance to be the first one in Department 52 and usually accompanied by his son Daniel, he took his place in the first seat of the front row, right side of the courtroom. Alain acted as if he had always belonged there. In his daily uniform—blue suit, white shirt and blue and white striped tie—he could have been one of the Suits if he had a different face.

Bags beneath his eyes and remnants of his strawberry blond hair combed straight back on his naked scalp, Bernheim looks a little like a short, slightly potbellied Charles de Gaulle, down to his ruddy pippin cheeks. There is a sad seriousness to his brooding frown and his forehead is a sea of wrinkles. But when he smiles, the creases that run along both sides of his mouth are miraculously transformed into laugh lines. Alain Bernheim does not wear his heart on his sleeve—he wears it on his face, masking nothing from the outside world.

I used Alain to chronicle the development of *King for a Day*, introducing documents detailing the uninterrupted evolution of the chief character from Buchwald's mean-spirited king to Murphy's sweet prince. Bernheim came across as very believable and decent. Even the pool television cameraman, who had seen all of the witnesses through his lens during the two-week trial, remarked that Bernheim was the most credible man on the stand. His performance was all the more remarkable since he had nearly lost his voice the day before he took the stand.

Alain testified that he made his deal with Veber the old-fashioned way: while chatting over cocktails at a social gathering. He remembered their exchange during a party in the autumn of 1983, shortly before Tab Murphy turned in his first and only abortive draft of *King for a Day*.

"My God, you're lucky to do a picture with Eddie Murphy," Veber had told him between sips of wine.

"Well, I think I am," said Bernheim.

"What is it about?"

Alain gave him a thumbnail sketch of Buchwald's original *It's a Crude, Crude World* story and Veber acted like a Frenchman who had just heard the plot line for the next Jerry Lewis movie.

"Nobody has ever given me such a good premise to work on!" Veber told him.

"Well, would you like—if the occasion occurs—would you work on this?" Alain asked.

"In a minute," said Veber.

After he had signed Veber and got a first draft out of him, Alain gave the completed screenplay to Larry Gelbart, he testified. The cocreator of TV's "M*A*S*H" was one of the first to offer suggestions on the Veber version of *King for a Day*, and I wanted to emphasize to Judge Schneider that Gelbart was anything but a lightweight reader.

"He has a play on Broadway right now?" I asked.

"Yes," said Bernheim.

"I understand it's getting good reviews, is that correct?"

Bernheim nodded.

"I'm sure Mr. Gelbart will appreciate all this," Schneider said.

"Why don't we go see it?" said Draper.

In fact, *City of Angels* had been getting rave reviews and would go on to receive several Tony awards, including one for Gelbart's script. Ironically, there were disturbing parallels between Gelbart's fiction and what happened to Art and Alain in real life.

The plot of *City of Angels* revolves around a screenwriter whose original angst-filled detective story is massaged, manipulated, revised and ravaged by Hollywood producers into a farcical feel-good movie. One of the songs from the show, sung by an obsequious two-faced studio executive, is about the methods that producers use to manipulate talented writers into compromising their talent. In the play, instead of being honest and saying that he doesn't like the screenplay, the executive keeps singing to his writer that the screenplay "needs work."

Bernheim recalled for the court a similar refrain from Ned Tanen when the Paramount chief read Veber's second version of *King for a Day* back in 1985. Tanen professed to like the screenplay even though the French director-writer never got the opportunity to even shake hands with Eddie Murphy.

"He felt it needed some more work but he liked a lot of it," Bernheim remembered.

"What did Mr. Tanen tell you?" I asked.

"He said it needs more work. That Francis should do another draft. Should I tell you what I said?"

"Please," I prompted.

"I told him then that it was impossible after a year and a half," Bernheim said. "Having done two drafts, we were told that Eddie likes it but we never had met him. It's very difficult for a tailor to make a suit if he never meets his customer."

The day was growing short and Schneider was growing weary.

"We'll be in recess until nine-thirty Tuesday," he ordered.

"Tuesday, your honor," I said.

"Merry Christmas, your honor," said Draper.

"Thank you," said Schneider.

I shuddered. Christmas was only four days off. Like everyone else in Department 52, I had neglected my Christmas shopping. I'd left the role of Santa to Connie and the elves and still hadn't been to the stores to pick up her gift.

For me and everyone else in the room, the Buchwald case had become an obsession. When Schneider called an end to the day's proceedings, it was like waking from a dream.

Usually we went away for the holidays: upstate New York to visit my folks or New Orleans to see Connie's mother and family. If nothing else, we'd take off to the snow, either in the Sierras or the Rockies, and enjoy the kind of white Christmas that never came to Southern California except on a motion picture sound stage.

But this Christmas would be different: it would be spent at home. While Brendan and Meghan emptied their stockings, Daddy would be rereading daily transcripts by an open fire and hoping St. Nick left him a verdict against Paramount Pictures beneath the Christmas tree.

But my Christmas present would have to wait.

On Tuesday, the day after Christmas, the trial was winding down, but Draper, refreshed from a weekend with his own family, was ready to destroy my own Christmas wish as soon as Bernheim was back on the stand.

"And would it be correct to say that the majority of your income, since you came to the United States in 1978, has been derived not from movies that have been released, but from movies which have not been released?" he asked.

"I think it's half and half," Bernheim said uncomfortably.

"You're a beneficiary of the motion picture system in which properties are optioned," Draper accused. "The motion picture companies try to develop a movie and spend money, even though they don't ultimately make those movies."

Bernheim blew up.

"Do you know how much producers get?" Bernheim said, his indignity finally pouring out into the courtroom. He sat forward in his seat, angry.

"No," Draper answered, his voice mirroring his disinterest.

Alain sputtered, meaning to put into the public record just how little of the Hollywood largesse falls into the hands of writers and struggling independent producers like himself who actually create the words that actors like Murphy, Stallone and other actors mouth for millions. His protest was cut short by the cold steel of Draper's voice.

"Are you a beneficiary of the system, sir?" he insisted.

"Yes," Bernheim said with a defeated sigh, sitting back in his chair.

"Did you tell Mr. Buchwald that net points were simply monkey points?" Draper asked.

"No, that's not my language," said Alain.

"Mr. Buchwald is your best friend, is he not?"

"Certainly one of my best. Yes, a very close friend."

"And you wouldn't want to do something that would harm your close friend?"

"Never. He's a great human being."

But Draper wasn't interested in Bernheim's opinion of Art Buchwald. He wanted to know about the Bernheim/Buchwald contract with Paramount.

"I'm a producer, not a negotiator," said Bernheim.

"You didn't put in a provision or ask for any provision . . . limiting what Mr. Murphy got?"

"No," said Bernheim. "I'm not important enough to do that."

The point Draper seemed to be driving at was that Bernheim would have done anything—even sacrifice the amount of money that his close friend Buchwald would receive under the contract—in order to secure Eddie Murphy for the lead role in the movie.

"Would you have been happy with Sylvester Stallone in your movie?" Draper asked.

"I don't understand," said Alain. "What's he got to do with a black king?

No. No way. Eddie Murphy or Cosby or Pryor. I mean, not Stallone or Dustin Hoffman. It's a different movie!"

"You had movies that you were pitching around to people in the industry, right?" Draper asked.

"Yes, I have to."

"And would you have been happier or would you have liked Sylvester Stallone to be in one of those movies?"

The crinkles returned to the edges of Alain Bernheim's sad gallic eyes and a smile turned up the corners of his mouth.

"Off the record?"

"Yes?" said Draper.

"Not particularly."

"Why not?"

"I'm not a fan of his work," Alain replied to the amusement of everyone.

"Oh. I guess I picked the wrong person. Are you a fan of anybody other than Eddie Murphy?" Draper asked.

"Oh, yes."

But it was the story—not the star—that carried a film for two hours inside a darkened movie theater, Bernheim insisted. The finest actor in the world can't act without a story. And character equals story: a character who begins as one kind of person at the start of the movie and ends as a changed person.

"Character has to have an arc," explained Bernheim. "Starts here and finishes totally different."

But Draper challenged Buchwald's story on grounds that the chief character was a crass boor.

"Do you think he started totally wonderful?" Draper asked.

"Yes. In both the two-page treatment and in the Veber script, he's fun-loving, kind. He was wonderful. He was fun to be with. He was not a despot. Not Idi Amin, I can tell you that."

"Just one of the guys?"

"One of the royalty guys," said Bernheim.

"Do you recall saying in your deposition that the story was not amour?" he asked.

"It was not what?" asked Alain. Draper's French accent left something to be desired.

"Amour. That it was not amour. Amour is—however you say it in French—amour means love, doesn't it?"

"Oh, I'm familiar with that, but—"

"Actually me too. Although not lately."

Ha! Maybe Draper's Christmas wasn't as terrific as I had thought. But his senses were sharp enough to go to the heart of the contractual dilemma that I had always dreaded.

"You've mentioned the term 'turnaround.' Can you just tell us briefly what turnaround is?" Draper asked.

"Turnaround is when a studio gives the producer the right to take the project he started at the studio elsewhere to another studio, to have it, hopefully, made there," Bernheim said, his right elbow resting on the arm of the witness chair.

"And in your deal, the turnaround right you had was a one-year right?"

"Yes."

"You didn't need any permission from Paramount to take Art Buchwald's eight-page treatment or two-and-one-half-page treatment?"

"I did not."

He did need Paramount's permission to use the scripts developed from the original story, however, and that was the point that Draper went back to again and again. Under the turnaround precept, Bernheim was not permitted, unless Paramount agreed, to use scenes from either the Veber or the Tab Murphy script at Warner Bros.—including the fast-food restaurant scene which parodied the Burger King restaurant chain.

"There was a scene in the Tab Murphy script where there is a take-off on Burger King. It was Burger Basket. Do you recall that?" asked Draper.

"Does Paramount own Burger King?" Alain asked, bristling. "I don't think a scene with Burger King is owned by anybody. That should be public domain, shouldn't it?"

Draper didn't answer. He let Alain's outrage hang in the air for a few seconds and blinked at the judge as if to say, "You decide." Schneider decided to excuse the witness and go to lunch.

The men and women of the press corps had thinned out drastically since the pre-Christmas rush to cover Arsenio Hall and Art Buchwald. But this particular afternoon, the day after Christmas, they had returned in droves. The word had got out that Eddie Murphy's confidential deposition was about to be made public and everyone from the Associated Press to the South Bay *Daily Breeze* wanted a copy.

"Your honor, over the lunch break I put together the two Eddie Murphy volumes," Draper said. "For some reason that I can't understand, there's interest from the people behind me about this. None of them have exactly offered money, but nobody has actually said they wouldn't pay me. But anyway, we have twenty-five copies for the press."

Draper's feeble stab at humor drew a sigh from Harvey Schneider. From behind the bar, chairs squeaked where reporters were poised to launch themselves toward Draper's stack of edited Eddie Murphy depositions—the prime fodder for that afternoon's news stories.

"Maybe we should assign an exhibit number to the Murphy deposition," said Schneider. "I'll tell you what I'll do. So that you won't fight over whose it is, I'll make it Court's exhibit number one," he said.

Then I called my final witness.

Danny Arnold wore a suit as blue and crisp as any worn by the Paramount executives, but with a blue silk kerchief in the coat pocket and a blue and white polka dot tie around his neck. His fashion statement seemed to be: I can be dapper without being crass or cloying. His hair was as thin and sandy as Bob Wachs's and he wore it in a pompadour off to the right of his scalp. Beyond that, comparisons between the two faded.

"My first job was as an apprentice in the sound effects department at Columbia Pictures in 1944," he said. "Swept out cutting rooms, emptied film bins, et cetera. . . . I went through film librarian, sound effects editor and then film editor."

He even did a little acting during his early post-World War II career in Hollywood—for Paramount Pictures. But his place, he concluded after a few years, was behind the cameras, developing stories and creating characters. He'd done it for over a generation and he knew as well as anyone how it was done. That's why I had winnowed down our list of expert witnesses from ten of the best storytellers in Hollywood to one and Danny was it.

One thing he had learned after years of writing and rewriting screenplays was that Hollywood told stories unlike any place else on earth.

"You're doing a specific motion picture for a specific actor, which is really the basis on which Hollywood worked for many, many years," he said. "Pictures were written for personalities, much more than from original stories. . . . You would write a Clark Gable movie, for example."

Or an Eddie Murphy movie.

Regardless of the Gables or Murphys around whom the studio system had always revolved, some things always remained the same, according to Danny. Stories always start with an idea or concept and a theme. From that point forward, things snowball and the final movie is often difficult to trace back to the original idea.

"An idea and a concept and a theme start to feed on each other," he said. "It's very hard to peel them apart. It's like trying to separate cellophane." As he testified, Danny often talked directly to Judge Schneider, who listened intently and shaded his eyes with his right hand.

In fact, writing ceases to be an easily dissected scientific kind of process and takes on something of a mystical character after you've done it for a while, according to Arnold.

"If you have done a fairly good job with character relationships, they start to take on a life of their own," he said. "Happens to almost every writer."

That doesn't mean that reality doesn't regularly rear its ugly head. If the film character who has taken on a life of his own demands that he walk through a scene in Rio, surrounded by a hoard of extras, the studio front office will not be amused, Danny related.

"You would like to go to South America but you can't afford it. Or you would like to have 3,000 extras in a scene. Well, you can't afford it. So you change the nature of the scene so you don't need that many," he said.

When it was Draper's turn to ask questions, Danny played the straight man. When Draper told him that we had picked him from among ten expert witnesses to take the witness stand, Danny told him he was flattered.

"Do you realize you were one of four finalists?"

"Even better," Danny said.

But did he also know that they had their depositions taken too?

"No, I had no idea," Danny said.

"You thought you were the Lone Ranger?"

Danny put on a hangdog expression.

"I really believe I'm disappointed," he said.

Draper had already been through the depositions of Lynn Roth, David Rintels and Ed North, plucking out their definitions of story, plot, character, "based upon" and other writers' terms in an effort to use our own expert witnesses' testimony against us. When they used the word "original" to describe Art's story, Draper became the amateur etymologist and asked what "original" meant. He seemed determined to hang the plagiarist label around Art's neck like a scarlet letter and he didn't care how he did it, even if he had to use his own wife to prove his point.

"If my wife were here, she'd tell you that I wake up almost religiously at four o'clock and go into the bathroom and start writing things down," Draper said. "Now, you wouldn't think I would give her a 'based upon' credit for closing argument in this case, would you?"

"I don't know your relationship with your wife," said Danny, provoking smirks around the courtroom.

Draper seemed less interested in Danny's expertise than he was in discrediting him. But Draper picked the wrong fight. The man who told off network executives, studio heads and powerful talent agents when he thought they were wrong—and still worked in this town—did not rattle easily. If anything, he was the rattler, turning the tables with ease on an outmatched Robert Draper.

"I used to go to the movies for, I think it was five cents, but other people have told me it must have been a quarter," said Draper. "Every Saturday, I would see a movie and it would have a cowboy. And the cowboy would meet a horse and then he would meet a woman and usually, to my disgust, he would kiss the woman but not kiss the horse. Generally. He would then fall in love and take her back to the ranch. Is that a theme?"

Danny blinked at me. Later in the day, after it was all over, he asked me if Paramount got its lawyers from a different galaxy. For the moment, he just shrugged and tried to answer a wacky question with a straight answer.

"No," he said.

"What is it?" Draper asked.

"Well, I think it's just another way of presenting a love story," Danny said.

Draper stroked his chin and decided to try again.

"If you kissed the horse, would it become unique?" Draper asked.

Danny smiled his patented "gotcha" smile.

"Not anymore," he said.

The courtroom burst into laughter and I thought Judge Schneider was going to have to use his gavel for the first time during the trial. But he was laughing too.

If Danny Arnold hadn't gotten to Draper, Schneider did. On this, the seventh day of testimony in a long and difficult trial, Harvey Schneider was still as sharp and attentive as he had been the first day. When Draper was trying to make a point about the star quality of the *Crocodile Dundee* movies that had made millions for Paramount, he tried and failed to pronounce Paul Hogan's costar's name correctly.

"And Linda Kozwolski . . ." said Draper.

"Kozlowski," Schneider corrected.

"You're a closet movie buff, your honor," said Draper.

"Not in the closet," Schneider corrected again.

"I haven't mentioned a movie yet that you haven't seen," Draper said, still marveling at Schneider's knowledge of film lore.

"Kozlowski," Schneider repeated for the court reporter.

"Koz-low-ski," said Draper. "I'm not good with these French names."

Danny Arnold stepped down from the witness stand and the room grew quiet, save for the shuffling of papers. There would be a last-minute attempt to put documents into evidence, but as far as testimony went, the trial of *Buchwald v. Paramount* was now history. Danny Arnold had been the last witness. Paramount called no more witnesses in its defense.

Now it was Harvey Schneider's turn to talk.

"A lot of testimony about the motion picture industry has been interesting and we'll all remember it fondly as we grow older," he began. "But some of it, it seems to me, was not entirely germane. . . .

"There are three key provisions of the agreement that we ought to focus on. There may be others but none of these will come as any shock. They are, of course, 'based upon,' 'work' and 'original.'

"My request is that you folks, among other things, focus on these kinds of questions:

"What did Paramount buy under its agreement with Buchwald?

"What does 'based upon' mean and does that definition come about from a contract, cases, experts or some or all of the above?

"How much of Buchwald's work had to be used in order to give rise to a 'based upon' liability? Idea? Concept? Theme? Plot? Story? Characters? All of the above? Some of the above?

"Next, do we consider Buchwald's treatment and *Coming to America* only or do we consider the evolution of Buchwald's treatment and *Coming to America?*

"Next, is there anything inconsistent about saying that *Coming to America* possessed a good deal of Eddie Murphy's original ideas and still saying Buchwald is entitled to 'based upon' payment, based upon the use of his work?

"If Paramount made a movie based upon Buchwald's work, however that term is defined, does it make any difference that Murphy did not intentionally use Buchwald's material?

"What's the evidence that *Coming to America* is based upon Buchwald's treatment, whatever 'based upon' means? What's the evidence that Buchwald's work was not original? Why can't an original work be based upon something else? Even if that were true, the thing that comes immediately to mind is *West Side Story*,which is obviously based upon *Romeo and Juliet.* But no one would seriously contend that it's not original."

Draper and I and our cocounsel were madly scribbling down every word, knowing that the questions were the first insight into the judge's thinking about the outcome of the case. Harvey Schneider was giving us an outline to follow, just as surely as if we were first-year law students in Professor Kingsfield's law school classes in *Paper Chase.*

"I'm not saying that those are the only issues or even the right issues, but those are the things that are running around in my mind now," said Schneider. "And since, as it were, I am the house to which this scenario is being played, we should at least address some of the issues that I'm thinking about. There are probably others. I didn't mean this to be an exhaustive list. But those are the things that I am thinking about. I thought maybe I would focus you. Hopefully, it has been helpful."

27

The Final Day

THE CLOCK in the study read 10 A.M. It was Wednesday, December 27, 1989, the next day after the end of testimony in *Buchwald v. Paramount* and I sat, bleary-eyed, hunched over my computer screen. I couldn't sleep, so I'd tumbled out of bed at 2 A.M., made some coffee and started to prepare a new final argument in light of the judge's specific questions.

I knew I had already lost on the punitive damage claim. Judge Schneider said he'd put our tort claims "off to the side for a little bit." That meant our stonewalling charges were out the window. While I still believed that Paramount had engaged in high-level cover-up, I couldn't prove it.

The judge's ten final questions were the only ones worth addressing. His final lecture to Draper and me was his way of saying, "You or your adversary are in trouble on a point here. Better persuade me." The essence of the case was still up for grabs: Paramount's breach of Art and Alain's contracts. We had to win on breach or the case was over.

The phone rang, shattering my concentration.

"Yes?" I snapped into the receiver.

"Pierce, is that you?"

At first I almost didn't recognize Art's voice. It was low and flat. Something was wrong. He sounded far away, as though he were calling on a bad line from Beijing, not Washington.

"Art! Good morning! Or, I guess for you, good afternoon."

"I just got off the phone with a reporter," he said. "She told me a story just went over the AP wire . . . or was it UPI? I don't remember. But it says Paramount is going to sue me for breach of contract because I plagiarized from Charlie Chaplin when I wrote *King for a Day*. It also says that the judge ruled yesterday that they could do that. I'm very upset. Can they do that?"

I started to answer, but Art jumped in, his voice cracking.

"Paramount is trying to destroy my reputation! They're making me pay for suing them! They don't care anymore whether they win or not. They're going to take me down with them. It's all over. If I win, I lose."

I had never heard Art so down. In the early 1980s, he had a rough bout with depression. He'd written and spoken openly about it. A living hell, he'd called it. But hearing it welling up in his voice over a transcontinental telephone call told me just how much of a living hell.

"I knew it, Pierce. I knew it," he said. "Those bastards have stolen from me again. But this time, I'll never get it back. Never. I've worked for forty years as a writer. I have never, *ever*, never been accused of stealing someone else's work. I have always written my own material. God, why did I do this?"

I knew that, if Art really felt this down, we had to get out now. Thursday was not going to be nice for him. Draper would play up the plagiarism accusation. The wire service story was just an early warning shot.

I had one chance at turning him around.

"Art, you have every right to be pissed off," I began. "Paramount's behavior is outrageous. But it's because they're desperate. They know you're going to whip their ass tomorrow. They're pulling out all the stops. You have 'em on the ropes, Art. One more day, and it's all over."

Buchwald was not convinced.

"It's all over for Alain, you and the other lawyers, but it's not all over for me," he said. "It's just beginning. I'm the one who'll have that plagiarist rap hung on him. You get to go on to another case. For the rest of my life, I'm the plagiarist."

The sympathetic approach wasn't working. I decided to get tough.

"Art, that's bullshit! You're no plagiarist. You *know* it. I know it. And I'll bet my eyeteeth the judge knows it too."

The only reason Judge Schneider allowed Chaplin's *King of New York* in evidence was because he didn't want any legal errors, I said.

"What do you mean?" Art asked.

"A good judge wants a clean record, free of reversible error if there's an appeal. My guess is he's letting the film in to blunt any claim of error by Paramount on appeal. But then he'll just ignore it."

"Does that mean he'll reject the plagiarism argument?"

"I think so," I said. "You can never be certain. But I like most of the questions Schneider's asking. He's fair. I think he'll see the whole Charlie Chaplin thing as a smear campaign."

"I hope so, Pierce. I hope so."

Art's voice was getting stronger.

"I'm going to make you a promise," I said. "I'm taking off the gloves on this Chaplin crap. Don't worry any more about it. Just hold on for another twenty-four hours."

There was a deafening pause. Art was still thinking about what to do. I held my breath.

"Okay, Pierce," Art said finally. "We've gone this far together. I'll trust your judgment. I hope you're right. God, do I hope you're right."

So did I.

The following morning there were no vacant seats in Department 52. Reporters, lawyers and spectators sat on the courtroom floor, spilling out into the hallway where those who could not get a spot inside watched on the pool camera's TV monitor. A simple breach-of-contract suit had escalated into a titanic battle over the rights of creative people, and the world watched. My clients were no longer just Art and Alain, but every writer or producer who had ever been or would be cheated in Hollywood.

The next hour would be the most important in my career. Regardless of what I had accomplished before now or what I did in the future, I would always be the lawyer who won—or lost—the *Buchwald* case. I looked back at Alain in the front row surrounded by his Margie, Daniel and Nicki. He shot back the same trustful gaze that I had seen seventeen months earlier when we strolled on the beach in Del Mar.

When the bailiff called everyone to order and Harvey Schneider swept into the courtroom, I looked up at the now familiar impassive face, mustache and bald head. I spread my three-ring binder of argument notes on the podium.

I was ready.

"Mr. O'Donnell," Judge Schneider said, nodding slightly.

"Victor Hugo once said, 'Greater than the march of mighty armies is an idea whose time has come.' In answer to the first question the Court posed, What did Paramount buy under its agreement with Buchwald? I submit to you that it bought a great idea . . . conceived by a great writer and humorist. It was original in every sense of the word. Far more than a creative spark, it ignited a fire that lasted for five years and raged in two studios. . . .

"Hollywood makes movies but not without ideas. And at a minimum, what Paramount Pictures purchased was the idea—or the synonymous term, concept—for a major motion picture starring Eddie Murphy."

I hadn't been speaking for a full minute before Judge Schneider interrupted.

"Is it your view that if the concept or idea—which I agree the witnesses seem to say are synonymous terms—if that was utilized in *Coming to America*, is that enough?"

Of course it was, I told him. Neither Eddie Murphy nor Paramount came up with "a $400 million idea" before Buchwald gave them his special and unique concept.

"All the witnesses [testified] that it was the catalyst, it was the starting point, it was the springboard for this concept . . . that is *Coming to America.*"

Furthermore, the contract that Paramount's own legal department drew up made the studio liable. Paramount's boilerplate language put the label "author's work" on Buchwald's story and "author's work" in the contract left no doubt that the studio meant anything and everything that ever stemmed from the two-and-a-half-page "original story and concept" that Buchwald had typed out under the title *It's a Crude, Crude World* back in 1982.

According to the standard terms of Paramount's own contract, Buchwald had sold the studio "prior, present, and future versions, adaptations, and translations" of *King for a Day*, including any story that evolved from it that contained "theme, story, plot, characters . . . and each and every part or all thereof."

But my case was based on more than just a shred of Art's original plot or character or theme surviving in the final script of *Coming to America.*

"I do not stand on just the sniveling little 'any part thereof,' " I said. Paramount "used all of it," not just a piece of Art's underlying theme. "And they used it handsomely and to their great financial benefit."

Both Paramount and Buchwald knew *King for a Day* was going to be developed for one person: Eddie Murphy. Proving that *Coming to America* was based upon Art's story required a clear understanding of the studio's development process. I was certain Schneider understood that process by now, but he continued firing questions at me, putting me through my paces in proving it all over again.

"From day one, they were already considering changes, making changes— significant changes that would be propelled forward for five years into *Coming to America.*"

"So I take it," Judge Schneider broke in again, "your position is that . . . it's the evolution of the character that is significant, not simply a comparison between Buchwald's original treatment and *Coming to America?*"

Again, the judge was pressing, relentlessly forcing me to commit.

"Both are important," I responded unhesitatingly. "For example, we're not talking about a sixty-year-old, white-haired Caucasian king who lived somewhere in a white community in Europe and comes to the United States and has experiences. We're talking about a distinct, unique character—an African king, young, playful, coming to America, having experiences. That character was molded and shaped for one person, Eddie Murphy.

"And when he ended up on the silver screen in the summer of 1988, he had been transformed somewhat. But the essence, the important part, of Buchwald's character was there. . . . I do not hang my hat on the fact that there is a little snippet here, a little snippet there," I continued, gesturing with my left hand and then my right and holding my thumb and index finger near each other. "It was wholesale, it was in gross, and it was used in *Coming to America.*"

I had a major point to convey to the judge. Since the day Draper had entered the case, he and I had fought about how much similarity I needed to show to establish "based upon." I had advocated merely "some similarities," while his test resembled the stringent copyright test of "substantial similarity" which I had tried to avoid by filing a breach-of-contract case in the first place. Ironically, as things turned out, I thought that my case was so strong that I could meet the tougher test. And I wanted the judge to say that he applied it so that I could blunt another Paramount argument on appeal.

"I don't stand here to say *some* similarities. I'm saying under any test, even the one that's been submitted by Paramount. And I submit to you there is overwhelming proof, not just a preponderance of the evidence, that *Coming to America* owes its origin to Buchwald's original story and concept."

"Is there any particular definition for 'based upon' that you're offering?" Judge Schneider wanted to know.

After months of poring over dictionaries, contracts and depositions, Marsha, Zazi, Suzanne, Dennis Landry and I had hammered out a definition. I recited it like a schoolboy.

"One work is based upon the other if it has been the inspiration for the later work, and if there has been use," I said. "But in a nutshell, it's inspiration *and* use. I don't have a case unless there's been use."

The Buchwald treatment and Veber and Tab Murphy scripts bore thirty-five points of similarity with the final *Coming to America* script, and we knew Paramount had access to everything: treatment, story-meeting notes and scripts. For example, Tab Murphy's scene depicting the African king working in a menial hamburger stand job might have coincidentally and independently occurred to the four credited authors of *Coming to America*, I said. But was that plausible when you added the foiling of a robbery with a mop handle?

"I don't have to have a videotape of Eddie Murphy and Arsenio Hall and Blaustein and Sheffield in a hotel room saying, 'Hey, see what . . . Tab Murphy wrote here?' " I said. "I've learned after forty-two years of life to be very skeptical about such coincidences. And there's thirty-four other points of similarity."

If it was coincidence and Eddie really had independently created the story, Schneider asked, did that mean we lost our case?

"Well, that's not the evidence," I said anxiously. "But that's a hypothetical?"

"It is," the judge responded.

I stalled.

"Because Paramount is pregnant," I started, delaying to process the pointed question and frame a precise answer. "They've got Blaustein and Sheffield. They've got Tanen still."

An impatient Schneider screwed up his face and glared at me.

"What's the answer to my question?"

"The answer to your question is: if it's totally, absolutely, purely independent . . . I might lose. But that's not the evidence here, your honor."

"I'm not suggesting it's the evidence," he said. "I'm trying to crystallize the issue."

A slight smile played over Judge Schneider's face. He was testing me and, for the moment, it was a standoff. I breathed a sigh of relief and returned to the evidence.

Judges routinely claim that they read everything given to them during a trial, but few do. Schneider was exceptional: a "hot bench" in trial lawyers' jargon. I wondered if he'd already drafted his final decision and was just waiting for Draper and me to deliver nuances—or fatal admissions—so he could fill in the blanks.

"In Hollywood, I doubt you could have such uniform opinion on any other subject except that Art Buchwald had a tremendous idea," I said. "This is a very blasé town. Everybody at Paramount goes gaga over *King for a Day*, and the reason they were gaga is, as Danny Arnold says, it's a unique concept. It's original. Not in the sense that Art Buchwald said, 'I typed it with my own little fingers.' It is unique. It doesn't have antecedents like *Phantom of the Opera* or *Romeo and Juliet*. It is special. It's the creative product of the fertile mind of one of our age's great humorists and writers.

"Paramount liked it so much that they dispensed with their historic practice of wanting a script. They grabbed it. They optioned it. Katzenberg gave the baby its name two months before he optioned it: *King for a Day*. And they spent a half a million dollars. That's not chump change, even by Hollywood standards."

As for Bob Wachs's claim that *King for a Day* was a "running joke" for two years, I simply noted that, while Paramount may have developed lots of projects for Eddie Murphy, how many of them cost $500,000? Wachs, I said in a parenthetical shot, was "the Pinocchio of this case. If you credit his testimony, then they didn't let a lot of people in on the running joke."

But Schneider was less interested in how much Paramount paid to develop *King for a Day* than he was in the subject of character motivation. Paramount and Wachs had kept coming back to the fact that Prince Akeem was motivated by a search for true love while Art's king was motivated by true greed. What about that? Schneider wanted to know.

"I think it's a nit in the final analysis," I said.

Art's contract never mentioned motive in its definition of the author's "work," I said. It mentioned theme. It mentioned story. It mentioned plot. But not motive. On the stand, Danny Arnold called motivation "a story development that comes later in the process." The important thing was a unique character. The situation and the motive could, and usually did, change from script to script. And even if the motive was different in the two works, "that would not be such a dissimilarity as to have us fail the 'based upon' test."

How did I draw the line? the Court asked, posing the central question in the case: How much similarity is enough?

In the final analysis, any one single element did not determine whether *Coming to America* was based upon Art's story. It was a gut issue, I said, like the late Supreme Court Justice Potter Stewart's famous test for obscenity. In a landmark pornography case, Stewart summed up the way he determined the difference between art and obscenity with a one-liner: "I know it when I see it."

Harvey Schneider seemed unconvinced that deciding "based upon" was quite as visceral a task as Justice Stewart's highly subjective and suspect method for separating art from smut. For starters, five years of script development muddied the waters. How much of the first story had to be in the second in order for the second to be based upon the first?

The way studios develop a story from original spark to final script meant that, over the years, a kind of pattern evolved with each part of the final story sprouting along the way, according to Schneider's logic.

"It's a continuum," he said. And somewhere along that continuum, the original story's value to the final product is fixed, he reasoned.

"We have to decide where along the continuum," he said.

I saw my opening and jumped in with both feet.

"The fact that they make changes is implicit and it's part of the understanding of 'based upon,' " I argued. "Buchwald didn't give them a 120-page script or even a 40-page treatment."

"In fact," the judge interjected, "the contract contemplated change."

"Clearly contemplates change," I agreed, my head nodding in unison with my words.

Under the "rights granted" section of Buchwald's contract, Paramount got everything.

"It says you can fold, spindle, mutilate, change, transform, adapt, transmogrify my original story and concept in your unfettered discretion, but you've got to pay me. That's what it says. I don't think it's asking too much that a major studio which drafted the contract should be required to honor its contract," I said. "Their contract forms the bedrock of a relationship."

It was Paramount's standard contract, designed to deny the writer any future claim on the rights to his work. "The flip side or equitable counterpoint to that broad grant of rights is a broad grant of protection to creators like Buchwald. . . .

"Here's an idea," I said, summing up Art's attitude as he signed on the dotted line. "You like it? You gonna run with it? You gonna change it? You gonna develop a motion picture out of it? Fine. I'm not going to write it. I'm not going to have that videotape there, videotaping how you do it. I'm not going to ask for all the drafts. But at the end, if it hits the silver screen, send me a check.

"That's what Buchwald bargained for. That's what every writer bargains for in the process, your honor," I said.

I was still faced with Paramount's claim that it indisputably owned the Tab Murphy and Francis Veber scripts and had the right to bowdlerize them—and the Court could not use them to bridge the gap between Art's treatment and the final script. If we lost on this point, our chances for victory were dim.

But scripts are like any offspring. They simply wouldn't exist if there weren't parents, I argued.

"The concept of 'based upon' connotes relationship, time, and change," I said. The Court should look at "the genetic composition of the Buchwald treatment and then see how it evolved because of its environmental influences—writers, studio executives, directors, audience surveys, and the lead actor's predilections about his portrayal. At the end, you can see that there has been a transformation of the original literary property."

I returned to the thirty-five points of similarity between the movie and all the material that had been written by Art, Veber and Tab Murphy.

"Some of these thirty-five points obviously could be coincidence. And I'm not saying that they literally sat down and copied all thirty-five aspects. But when you get to thirty-five and you realize the variety of choices that writers have, the mind begins to boggle—somewhere between fifteen and twenty in my case—over these similarities."

"Is there anything inconsistent with finding a great deal of creativity by Murphy on *Coming to America* and still finding 'based upon'?" the judge then asked.

I had gone out of my way not to criticize Eddie. Whenever Draper had tried to suggest that we were demeaning Eddie's intelligence or integrity, I was all over him like a fire extinguisher. I wanted to signal to Schneider that he could strike a defensible compromise that would allow us to win but not at Eddie's expense.

"They are not inconsistent at all. . . . We didn't sue Eddie Murphy," I said. "I've never disparaged his talent nor have my clients. He's a creative young man. Whether he's an accomplished screenwriter and story creator remains to be determined. But that's not the issue in this case."

Eddie borrowed from the original inspiration and came up with a story. He collaborated with Blaustein, Sheffield and Arsenio Hall and turned it into a screenplay, I conceded. Murphy and the screenwriters got credit. Why shouldn't Buchwald, as the original inspiration, also get credit?

"It is not a zero sum game," I said. "Eddie Murphy does not have to be denied his story credit in order for Buchwald to prevail on his contract claim that *Coming to America* is based upon his *King for a Day* . . . I think there's room for both, your honor."

Long ago I had decided not to argue that Buchwald was entitled to "story by" credit. Not enough of his treatment survived in the final movie to satisfy even the Writers Guild on that point. In suggesting that the judge could spread around the three credits, I had done my best to take the high road. It would soon be up to Solomon to decide whether or not to split the baby.

Eddie Murphy may have come up with a fine love story, but he didn't do it on his own, I said. Eddie, Wachs and Paramount had been exposed to Art's story. They were "irradiated with Buchwald's treatment and the scripts, and there is no decontaminating them.

"If you're going to have an independent creation, you can't be a little bit pregnant. You have to have total lack of knowledge."

Eddie Murphy had knowledge of *King for a Day*—maybe a lot or maybe just a little. But his imagination was pregnant. And Art Buchwald was the father.

I pointed to the precedent of "My Sweet Lord."

The composer of the Motown hit "He's So Fine" had successfully sued former Beatle George Harrison for misappropriating his song as the basis for the Harrison hit. Once Harrison admitted that he'd heard "He's So Fine" before, the court ruled Harrison had been influenced enough to duplicate the melody in "My Sweet Lord." He had to pay damages to the owners of the "He's So Fine" copyright. In Buchwald's case, Eddie had admitted in his deposition that he could not say his own subconscious had not been influenced by the Buchwald story.

Schneider rubbed his chin thoughtfully.

"Let me give you a hypothetical," he said, smiling. "Let's assume there is this fellow named Bernstein who comes up with an idea for developing a musical about a Puerto Rican girl who fell in love with a boy with gang roots, and it has a tragic ending. And Bill Shakespeare comes along a little bit later and sees the play and decides, 'Gee, that sounds like something I wrote.'

"And so he sues him. And I'm a judge for *Shakespeare v. Bernstein*. And I have Mr. Bernstein on the stand. He says, 'Well, I've heard there is a Shakespeare but I didn't like his stuff, never understood that kind of writing, and I didn't base any of my material on *Romeo and Juliet*.' And I believe him. What's the result?"

Maybe Shakespeare sued because *West Side Story* tickets were going for $50 a pop, I said. "So there was money in it—perhaps unlike my case as it may turn out," I deadpanned.

But *Romeo and Juliet* and its theme of star-crossed lovers were public domain. Bernstein could use anything he wanted.

"I want to forget about public domain issues," Judge Schneider said, once again not letting me off the hook with even an artful dodge. Can there be an independent creation by Bernstein even if I find access and similarity to Shakespeare's work?

I squirmed but had to admit that, without a contract like Buchwald's, Shakespeare might not have had a case if there was in fact independent creation. The judge had boxed me in a corner. It was quite possible that he was at that place in his own mind: Eddie was like Leonard Bernstein. He had exposure to, but he was not influenced by, Buchwald's story. That wasn't the law, but I had to answer his question, without making any fatal concessions.

"I think I would have to look and see how much of *Romeo and Juliet* actually got into *West Side Story*—an analysis I didn't have time to do, your honor," I said.

"So, are you now coming to the point that if there is a lot of that in it—

even though Bernstein never heard of [*Romeo and Juliet*]—it may still be 'based upon'?"

Schneider wanted an answer. Judges do not appreciate lawyers who refuse to answer their questions.

"I guess, under that circumstance, you'd be sustained in finding for Mr. Bernstein," I finally answered, to Harvey Schneider's obvious satisfaction.

But if Bernstein's exposure to *Romeo and Juliet* had any influence on him, even if it only "tickled his subconscious," it should be enough to give the Bard of Avon a piece of *West Side Story*, I argued. And that result would be all the more compelled if Bernstein had given Shakespeare the kind of contract that Paramount gave the Pundit on the Potomac.

"So, as in many cases, evidence is important," Judge Schneider noted, stating an article of faith of every trial lawyer.

I looked at the clock. My time was almost up.

I still had one piece of unfinished business and a promise to keep: What was the evidence that Art Buchwald's story was not original—that he ripped off Charlie Chaplin?

With a rising voice, I read to the judge from the side of the box in which the videocassette version of *A King in New York* was sold.

" 'It's a political satire on the McCarthy era about moronic American movies, about advertising, a modern utopia.' It has nothing to do with the concept, the story, the characters—anything having to do with *King for a Day*," I insisted.

Chaplin's film about a rich, exiled Caucasian king was hardly the inspiration for a film about a black African king in the American ghetto, I told Judge Schneider. Several years before Buchwald had even seen the Chaplin movie during his Paris days, the humorist had written a column about a seven-foot-tall Watusi king who drove a Studebaker and had an expensive modern home. *That* was the kind of king Art portrayed in *King for a Day*.

Draper's chart, purporting to show how Chaplin's story and Buchwald's were the same, was outrageous, blatant character assassination, I said. To accuse Art Buchwald of plagiarism was an abomination.

"I submit to your honor it's an intentional act by Paramount Pictures to hurt Art Buchwald. No fair-minded human being could see, could watch, could experience—even in a stupor—Charlie Chaplin's movie and conclude that there is any resemblance. . . ."

I leaned forward, fire in my eyes.

"I submit to you that, if there is one thing in this case that cries out for a punitive damages award by this Court, it's a lie broadcast around the world now twice, your honor . . . about Buchwald plagiarizing Charlie Chaplin.

"That is a *desperate* act of a *desperate* defendant!"

I paused, apologizing for raising my voice. But I wasn't finished.

"Your honor, that's not just dirty pool, that's *scurrilous* conduct by a defendant who should be sanctioned in this case. Art Buchwald does not have to have his well-deserved reputation tarnished in a California court by this defendant merely so it might be able to win a lawsuit.

"The fact remains that this is a damnable lie!

"Your honor, if you would do one thing in this case, for Art Buchwald and writers like him who have the guts to stand up to Paramount Pictures . . . I would ask that you proclaim that it is a damnable lie. And that there is not a shred of evidence in this record to support any finding, much less an argument by counsel, that Art Buchwald is a plagiarist.

"Art Buchwald is one of the great writers of our time. And I submit to you, whatever happens in this case, let's keep his good name intact. Thank you."

After a fifteen-minute recess, Draper began his closing argument. He made it clear at the outset that he was taking off the gloves.

"Mr. O'Donnell has called me the 'H' word and the 'B' word and the 'damned liar' word right in front of my family," Draper said furiously, pointing to his wife and daughter, who sat in the audience with Paramount's Josh Wattles and A. Robert Pisano.

Draper accused me of deceptively playing a "word game" with my plot summaries of *King for a Day* and *Coming to America*. His own plot summaries of *King for a Day* and Chaplin's *A King in New York*, on the other hand, merely compared plot points between the two movies, to hear him tell it.

"And as I'll show you in a minute, you can make that same comparison with any movie that was ever made," he said. "You can come up with a list."

But Draper didn't dwell long on what was similar or dissimilar about any of the stories. He was much more interested in black and white issues.

"Now, of course, Eddie Murphy's *black*," Draper said. "And Eddie Murphy's a megastar and Eddie Murphy makes a lot of money. But Eddie Murphy has some feelings too. And he's not a Pulitzer Prize winner like Mr. Buchwald and he's not *white* like Mr. Buchwald and he's not an attorney. Not an establishment person like Mr. Buchwald. But I don't really think that Mr. Buchwald is submitting this treatment that's in evidence for his next Pulitzer Prize. In fact, the meanest thing I could do to Mr. Buchwald is . . . distribute it to the press."

Eddie was the victim of racial prejudice, according to Draper. Normally, trial lawyers aren't supposed to object during closing argument. But this was too much: Draper was out of control. I was on the edge of my seat, poised to stand, when Harvey Schneider saved me the trouble.

"I don't perceive this to be a case about race, Mr. Draper," the judge said in a stern voice as he leaned forward in his chair.

"I'm sorry, your honor, but I disagree," said Draper. "But I will abide by your feelings. You do perceive it to be a case about contracts. I know that."

"I understand contracts," an unamused Schneider said.

Draper apparently had calmed down a bit as he pointed to some large blowups he had made, listing the judge's ten questions and highlighting points and exhibits that he wanted to use in his argument. But as soon as he began speaking, he seemed anxious and muddled.

"These are the documents or exhibits I plan to use during opening statement—I'm sorry, closing statement or closing argument. I'm a little confused here," he said with a nervous laugh.

He eventually got to the first issue: what Paramount was buying from Buchwald. But when he said that Buchwald's contract required that his story be "original, not . . . in the public domain," Judge Schneider interrupted him.

"What's the evidence they didn't get that?" he asked.

"I think that—I think the evidence is that, under any fair standard of law, the evidence is that they *did* get that. . . ."

"I want to see if I understand," the judge interjected. "Are you telling me that you *concede* that [Paramount] got an original work?"

"Yes, sir. Under any fair standard of the law, okay? And it is not based upon the Charlie Chaplin movie under any fair standard of the law and . . . the totality was not in the public domain under any fair standard of the law. And so why do you have—"

A skeptical Schneider interrupted once again, giving Draper another chance to correct what appeared to be a damning admission.

"There must be a 'but' there somewhere," Schneider said.

Draper finally explained what he was driving at. The way I had defined the term "based upon," Draper claimed, *West Side Story* would be based upon *Romeo and Juliet* simply because the two stories had common themes. So, too, would *King for a Day* be based upon *A King in New York*, he reasoned. But when Draper tried to suggest that I had said Paramount breached Art's contract if it used only one of Buchwald's ideas in making *Coming to America*, Judge Schneider immediately corrected him.

"I don't perceive that to be the plaintiff's position," Schneider said. Instead of letting Draper attack my definition of "based upon," Schneider asked him to come up with one of his own.

"I'm asking the definition because I have a contract that says somebody has to be paid some money if something else is based upon it," he said. "And I'm trying with a fairly substantial amount of vigor to figure out what 'based upon' means."

Draper responded that it didn't matter whether a little or a lot of Buchwald's treatment was used in *Coming to America*, but he didn't answer the judge's question.

"Hear my question to you," Schneider said, hunching over the bench and peering straight ahead, like a linebacker. "I agree with what you've said—that both extremes are inappropriate positions. A little element is not going to be 'based upon' and I'm confident that every single thing doesn't have to be the same in order for there to be 'based upon.'

"What is *your* position for me in determining where along—here's the word again—the continuum one makes the decision?"

Draper tried not to look unsettled.

"I think substantial or significant similarity has to be the standard and I can give you words that—"

"Of what?" Schneider interrupted.

"The two works," Draper replied.

But the judge wouldn't let up. Substantial similarity of what? Of theme? Plot? Character? Everything?

After watching him squeeze me on the definition of "based upon," Draper should have seen it coming. Schneider wasn't about to let Draper off the hook until he gave him a precise definition.

"Substantial or significant similarity as to their elements," Draper said, still hedging.

He still would not define "based upon"—a dangerous move with a judge who demanded crisp, clear definitions.

Instead, Draper tried to switch gears and argue that Eddie Murphy planned to portray a black African prince long before Paramount ever optioned *King for a Day*.

"But you'd have to concede that Paramount had nothing substantial along the lines or they would have never paid Buchwald for the idea, is that right?" Judge Schneider asked.

Again, Draper would not give a "yes" or "no" answer. But if Schneider insisted that Art's story was the starting point in the creative process, Draper told him, he could not include the Tab Murphy or Veber scripts along his "continuum." The scripts were Paramount property. They had been bought and paid for.

"That's a different issue," said Schneider.

"It's an issue of what the 'work' is," Draper said. "It's an issue of what 'based upon' means."

"Do I correctly understand your position, then, that unless the movie that is ultimately made by Paramount is, for all practical purposes, the same as the Buchwald treatment, that it cannot be 'based upon'?" Judge Schneider inquired.

Draper still would not define "based upon." The judge's frown grew deeper.

"What Paramount bought was the uniqueness of the Buchwald treatment," said Draper. "There was a uniqueness in the Buchwald treatment. I wouldn't talk too much about it because I think it would be embarrassing to Mr. Buchwald to talk about what there was. But there was a uniqueness in the Buchwald treatment and there were generic ideas: black African prince."

Schneider finally grew tired of Draper's semantic hopscotch and began cross-examining him like a drill sergeant.

"What were you buying from Mr. Buchwald?" he snapped.

"The original treatment. The combination, okay? The whole thing," Draper answered.

"And in order for it to be 'based upon,' the film had to come out substantially like the treatment?" the judge asked again.

"Well, no, it had to have some material, nonpublic, nongeneric, non-—well, those are the words—elements to it," stammered Draper.

Draper tried to prove that my test for "based upon" was too elastic by arguing that *Valley Girls* would be based upon *West Side Story* and *Romeo and Juliet.* Art's ideas were too generic for protection, he insisted. But the judge didn't buy it.

"Isn't there a difference? If we were talking about a noncontract case, you would have to have an awful lot of those characteristics in order to find 'based upon.' But this is a contract case, isn't it?"

Buchwald's contract doomed him, Draper asserted, because it says that Paramount owned whatever was adapted from it. And without the intermediate work product of Tab Murphy and Veber, we had no evolution of our character from an Idi Amin to sweet prince. Worse yet, none of the four scripts based on Buchwald's treatment ever "got close to what the basic spine of *The Quest* is about."

Then Draper lost it.

"And so I think . . . not for purposes of the dissection that they want to do. There are bare breasts in this scene and bare breasts in this scene. Well, I've even bare breasts at home."

I stared at Marsha and Zazi. Were we watching a man having a nervous breakdown on the courtroom floor?

"That's not the point," Draper said, catching himself and resuming some semblance of composure. "The point is, look at the spine of the work. *The Quest* is about a man who is pampered. Whose parents have put him up to a marriage with a beautiful girl . . ."

Then, once again, Draper drifted off into the ozone.

"Beautiful woman. Actually prettier than Shari Headley as Arsenio Hall— Maybe not prettier than Shari Headley, but he doesn't want that kind of trained woman. He wants a *real* woman and a *real* love and that's why he comes to America and that's why he goes to Queens, et cetera, et cetera, et cetera."

When he finally got back on track, Draper summed up his definition of "based upon" with a question: "Are the two things about the same thing?"

Schneider sighed.

"I don't see anything to put my hands on and say, 'This is how I make this decision,'" he said. "I have experts who give me all kinds of definitions of what 'based upon' means. I have lawyers who tell me the same. How am I supposed to approach this task?"

"Well, how about a quote?" Draper offered.

"That's always helpful," the judge responded.

Quoting from a twenty-year-old California case involving the origins of the "Sea Hunt" television series, Draper concluded that Paramount did not have to pay unless it made "a substantial use . . . of the idea or literary property." Trivial or minor use didn't count.

Judge Schneider still wanted a definition from Draper. He zeroed in on the difference between "substantial" and "trivial": if the use of any single element was substantial, would that be enough for *Coming to America* to be based upon *King for a Day?*

"Themes, story, plot, characters; is that what you're saying?" Draper asked.

"Yes," Schneider replied.

"Yes," Draper answered. "Not playing the word game, but yes. As those terms, I think, should be interpreted under the case law and under the experts' testimony."

I sat up straight, my eyes glued to the judge. Had he appreciated what Draper had just said? My ears were still twitching. If I had heard right, Draper had just blown the case for Paramount.

"So, if the theme were the same . . ." Schneider began.

"Theme were the same . . ." Draper repeated.

". . . or substantially similar or similar, according to you that would be enough?" Schneider asked.

"That would be enough."

"And if the story was the same, that would be enough?"

"As I define it, yes," Draper again agreed.

"And if the plot were the same, that would be enough?"

"Definitely," Draper acknowledged.

Same with the characters, Draper conceded.

Thanks to Harvey Schneider's deft cross-examination, Paramount had finally admitted that substantial use of Buchwald's theme, story, plot or main character in *Coming to America* was enough to prove our case. If the judge found that *Coming to America* was substantially based upon even *one* element of *King for a Day*, the studio would have to pay.

To my further surprise, Draper also accepted the view that "inspired by" and "based upon" meant the same thing. He embraced David Kirkpatrick's testimony that antecedents—the scripts that the studio bought before it came up with a final shooting script of its own—were enough to claim a "based upon" credit if they were the stimulus.

But he still hadn't given up. In what seemed to me an almost hysterical tone, Draper railed against his own concession that mere use of substantial aspects of Buchwald's theme would be enough to establish liability.

"But to say 'black African prince coming to America,' and then *that's* one of the barkers that's among the four hundred [dogs] in Paramount's dead files, and nobody else in the world can ever make a movie?"

It was grossly unfair, he concluded.

Draper was scoring points. If he could persuade Judge Schneider that our definition of "based upon" would have a chilling effect on creativity in motion picture development, he might yet make a comeback. This was one of his best arguments, and he was making it effectively.

But the judge still wanted to know whether Paramount now agreed that its contract meant it had to pay for use of Buchwald's theme.

"I don't think so, your honor. . . . You could take six different ideas, all of them in public domain, all of them nonoriginal, and package them in a certain way and give them to Paramount, okay? Now, if Paramount later makes *Valley Girls* and what you have presented to Paramount was *West Side Story*, it doesn't make any sense to say that [*Valley Girls*] is 'based upon' [*West Side Story*] because there is some similarity that some lawyer can argue."

The judge still wanted to know why he couldn't look at his continuum: the progression from *King for a Day* treatment to the Veber/Murphy scripts and then to *Coming to America*. Draper gave Schneider his marching orders:

"What you ought to do is watch the movie and read the treatment. And be a reasonable man."

"That's it?" Judge Schneider asked. That was like telling a pilot to fly from Los Angeles to New York in the fog without navigation charts. But that's what Draper told Harvey Schneider to do: figure it out himself the best he could.

The Veber, Tab Murphy and even the two *Me and the King* scripts at Warner Bros. "never came close to *Coming to America* or *The Quest*," said Draper. "There is . . . a grand canyon between the last *King for a Day* script and *The Quest*. A grand canyon."

When they created the story for *Coming to America*, Eddie Murphy and Arsenio Hall were inspired by girlfriends, family, childhood experiences, but not by Buchwald's treatment, Draper pleaded.

"I have no doubt that a great deal of creativity was and could have been involved in *Coming to America* on behalf of Murphy and Hall and Blaustein and Sheffield," Schneider said. But that did not resolve the separate issue of whether *King for a Day* was the basis for *Coming to America*, he maintained.

Josh Wattles winced as the judge spoke. The in-house Paramount lawyer who had originally dismissed Buchwald's claim as unmeritorious sat with his arms crossed in the spectator gallery, growing more uncomfortable with each passing of the minute hand on the wall clock.

Draper cleared his throat.

"The evidence in this case is that, as a twenty-one-year-old having a dinner at Ma Maison, Eddie Murphy was pitched this idea along with ten others. When Mr. O'Donnell showed him the treatment, he said, 'I never saw it.' "

I couldn't believe what Draper had just admitted: although Murphy had *scant* access, he *did* have access, along with several other stories Katzenberg pitched him at Ma Maison.

"And I think you remember, and maybe this is—" Draper stumbled around, apparently realizing his own blunder. "I have a lot more I'd like to say, but I guess your eyes are glazing over, and you may have other things to do, I know."

If Eddie Murphy had wanted to appear in court, Draper might not be squirming. He might have been able to evoke the same amnesiac statements from Murphy on the stand that he had elicited from Wachs, Mancuso and Katzenberg. How ironic, I thought. Paramount went to trial to prove to Eddie that it really cared about him, but Eddie apparently didn't care enough about Paramount to show up.

Draper made reference to Murphy's absence. When Eddie was deposed, he talked about wanting to be in a *Star Trek* so he could get beamed up, Draper said.

"If I could have beamed him up and beamed him down, you would have been looking at him," he told Schneider.

But Draper was not Captain Kirk, he pointed out, and Eddie remained in New Jersey. All Draper had was what I had: Eddie's deposition. And in it Eddie claimed to be unfamiliar with the development of Buchwald's treatment—a claim I told Murphy I believed *at the time.*

"I think he, Mr. O'Donnell, is telling the truth," Draper said with an amazed inflection that implied that, most of the time, I did not tell the truth.

"I don't think that I have to find anybody to be a liar in this case," said Judge Schneider.

"Well, you might tell the world that Mr. Buchwald shouldn't call Mr. Murphy a liar and that would be a helpful thing," Draper snapped.

Schneider sighed deeply.

"Each of you are asking me to do things about making nice for the other. I'm not sure it's my role. But I don't think I have to find Murphy to be a liar. I don't think I have to find Buchwald to be a liar in order to reach a result in this case."

The one thing Schneider did need to find was whether Eddie Murphy had enough access to Buchwald's story, Draper said.

"Is access an issue when there is knowledge?" the judge asked.

"What knowledge?" a stunned Draper wanted to know.

"He knew about the concept. So did Art Buchwald know about the Charlie Chaplin movie. But there is . . . *no evidence* to support the proposition that . . . Buchwald's treatment was based upon A *King in New York* that I've seen other than he saw the movie and reviewed it."

"What evidence is there that Eddie Murphy's treatment—movie is based upon *King for a Day?*" Draper asked. "He saw it once. He was pitched it once."

"Four times, according to Kirkpatrick," said Schneider.

"If you read the transcript . . . Look at Kirkpatrick's transcript," Draper insisted, shaking his head in disbelief.

Judge Schneider had read the transcript.

Paramount "talked to him about it four times," he said flatly.

By now Draper had rambled way beyond his allotted one hour. The judge had indulged him, but his patience wore thin as Draper continued to ricochet from one argument to another.

"I don't know if you've ever broken up with a girlfriend, and I guess we are not going to get into that," Draper said.

"Probably not," the judge assured him as the audience laughed.

"But let me ask you this, let me ask you this question," Draper went on, one eye on the clock. "Mr. Murphy described in somewhat vivid detail—and,

I thought, painful detail—his breakup with Lisa Figueroa and how that formed the basis for his story and his treatment.

"And I just ask you one question: do you remember what the name of the woman in *Coming to America* was?" Draper asked the judge. "I know it's not your favorite movie, but do you remember what her name was?"

"Lisa," the judge answered.

"Lisa. Thank you, your honor."

Draper looked around at the audience dramatically, as though expecting a gasp but getting only a shrug. He gathered his papers and sat down. The courtroom fell into silence.

"All right," Schneider said. "Gentlemen, the case will now stand submitted. I have homework to do, obviously. I want to thank everybody for a professional presentation and you ought to be hearing from me relatively soon."

With one arm around Connie and the other around Alain, I walked out into the glare of TV camera lights. Expressing optimism only, I dodged most of the questions and refused to predict the judge's decision. The case was over. The gag order was moot. But for once I did not have anything in particular I wanted to say.

But there was someone with whom I wanted to talk.

For all his clowning around, Art Buchwald was not a man who was easily or visibly moved. He kept his strongest emotions to himself. But even over a transcontinental telephone line the day after closing argument, I could feel the quaver in his voice.

We had sent overnight to Art a tape recording of the closing arguments. In response to my impassioned plea, the judge had exorcised Paramount's false charge that Art had plagiarized Charlie Chaplin. When we spoke the next day, Art thanked me from the bottom of his heart for my vigorous defense of his integrity—a thank you forever etched on my heart. And when Ann came on the phone to express her own appreciation, she remarked that Ed Williams had to be smiling too.

It was over. No more depositions, briefs, cross-examinations or arguments. There was nothing more to do.

Except to wait for Harvey Schneider's decision.

28

"Pay Buchwald, Studio Told"

ON THE DAY before New Year's, the skies were blue and the air was clear. It was what Los Angelenos call "Chamber of Commerce weather": sunny, warm, and no pollution. I was sitting by the pool, wading through the Sunday New York *Times*, when Buchwald called.

"What ya doing, counselor, now that you're not going into court every day?" he asked. The familiar bounce was back in his voice. It was the old Art.

"I'm catching up on what's been happening in the world the past two weeks," I replied.

"You notice we invaded Panama?" Art asked.

"I heard something about it, Art."

"Bush did it as a favor for Marty Davis: to get our case off the front pages of the newspapers," Art deadpanned.

Then he asked to read me something.

"Sure, what is it?" I asked.

"It's my statement for the press. You told me that the judge could hand down his decision any day now, and I want to be ready."

In the year and a half I'd known him, Art had never written anything in advance for the media. He was one of the most natural ad-libbers I'd ever met. He always said just the right thing. He was a one-man public relations firm for our cause.

"Why're you drafting it in advance?" I asked.

"If we win, I'll know what to say, Pierce. That'll be easy and fun. But if we lose, I want to be sure I say the right thing. I know myself: I'll be angry and I could say some things that I might regret. Let me read it to you, okay?"

Art delivered a speech thanking his lawyers, complimenting the judge for a fair trial, and explaining why he had sued in the first place: he believed that he had been violated and he wanted to stand up for his rights so that it would not happen to other, less-well-known writers in the future. He underscored what Schneider had already acknowledged in the courtroom: Paramount had falsely accused him of plagiarism and racism. The quaver was back as he spoke, but his voice was strong.

It was a beautiful concession speech.

He never had to deliver that speech.

A week later, Harvey Schneider announced his tentative decision. Zazi got the news from a newspaper reporter calling from the county courthouse shortly after the judge released his decision at 8:30 A.M. on January 8, 1990. A few minutes later, my car phone buzzed.

"We won! We won! We won!" Zazi screamed, as I fell uncharacteristically silent for a few seconds. "Pierce, did you hear what I said?"

I heard.

"Do you have the opinion yet?" I asked.

"No, but the verdict is already out on the wire. The decision is thirty-four pages long. I've sent a messenger to pick it up."

"Great," I told her. "Call Art. Alain is in Mexico, but Celine has his phone number. See if you can reach him. I'll be in by eleven o'clock. Get the team together and schedule a press conference in our main conference room for 1 P.M. And, by the way, Zazi . . . congratulations!"

When I arrived at Kaye, Scholer's offices in Century City, every lawyer and staff person I met hugged, high-fived or kissed me. There were already phone messages from fifteen reporters, ranging from AP and UPI to a radio station in Montreal and a Japanese television network. The American networks had interrupted their morning programming for a news bulletin.

In my own office, Marsha, Zazi, Suzanne, Dennis and I had our own private celebration. We'd beaten formidable odds, I told them. I went around the conference table, spending a minute or two stressing each person's special contribution to our victory. And then I gave my personal assessment,

"Savor this moment," I enjoined them. "A year ago, everyone said we were crazy and would be annihilated. Well, we proved them wrong. The good guys beat a studio."

When we settled down enough to study Schneider's statement of tentative decision, I noted that it wasn't the least bit tentative.[1] The judge laid full blame for breaching the contract on Paramount. But he also wanted to leave no doubt regarding what the case was *not* about.

"It is *not* about whether Art Buchwald or Eddie Murphy is more creative. It

---

[1] Judge Schneider's Statement of Decision is reproduced in full in Appendix A.

is clear to the Court that each of these men is a creative genius in his own field and each is an uniquely American institution. This case is also not about whether Eddie Murphy made substantial contributions to the film 'Coming To America.' The Court is convinced that he did. Finally, this case is *not* about whether Eddie Murphy 'stole' Art Buchwald's concept 'King For A Day.' Rather, this case is primarily a breach of contract case between Buchwald and Paramount (not Murphy) which must be decided by reference to the agreement between the parties and the rules of contract construction, as well as the principles of law enunciated in the applicable legal authorities."

Unfortunately, most reporters never understood the difference between plagiarism and breach of contract. Long after the decision was handed down, newspapers and television were still incorrectly reporting that Murphy "stole" Buchwald's story.

Schneider turned to the linchpin of his decision—the meaning of "based upon."

"Because the term is not defined in the contract, it was the Court's hope that the term had a specific meaning in the entertainment industry and that the experts who testified would so indicate," Schneider wrote.

But nobody could agree. Finding no consensus among the experts, Schneider went to the California appellate decisions, looking for "a road map through the 'based upon' mine field." He recited from the 1970 case in which Goodson-Todman Productions made the "Branded" television series based on Harry Julian Fink's treatment, a 1955 dispute involving the origin of TV's "Sea Hunt" and another breach-of-contract case involving producer Sol Lesser's use of author Ilse Weitzenkorn's *Tarzan in the Land of Eternal Youth* in Lesser's 1953 RKO movie, *Tarzan's Magic Fountain.*

"Although both works included the same characters in Africa being involved in a mythical Fountain of Youth, the moral of each was entirely different," Schneider wrote. "Specifically, the moral of plaintiff's work was that eternal youth was not a blessing. The moral of defendant's work was that eternal youth was a reward for good."

In spite of that, the Court decided in writer Weitzenkorn's favor. She had a contract with Lesser and Lesser had to pay.

So what was the definition for "based upon"?

Schneider had finally answered his own question. Paramount had to pay Buchwald if *Coming to America* was based upon "a material element of or was inspired by Buchwald's treatment."

Of course, he could still find that the movie's inspiration was Eddie Murphy's muse, not Art Buchwald's. But the next nine pages of his decision brimmed with "compelling evidence of similarity," culled from 2,000 pages of sworn testimony and hundreds of exhibits.

"[T]hese similarities alone, given the language of the contract involved in this case and the law that liability in a contract case can arise even if a non-substantial element is copied, might well be sufficient to impose contract liability on Paramount," Schneider wrote. "The fact is, however, that other compelling evidence of similarity exists."

The Burger Basket scene from Tab Murphy's script was particularly damning.

"In the original script written by Tab Murphy that was indisputably based upon Buchwald's treatment, the king ends up as an employee of a fast food restaurant where he ultimately foils a robbery attempt by use of a mop. In 'Coming To America' the prince is also employed by a fast food restaurant and foils a robbery attempt by use of a mop. These similar 'gimmicks' provide compelling evidence that the evolution of plaintiffs' idea provided an inspiration for 'Coming To America.'"

(Those three sentences were enough to send Paramount's envoys scrambling when Tab Murphy's lawyer, Don Zachary, called within a few weeks of our victory. The studio promised Murphy $100,000 if he would sign a release form and forget about pursuing a claim. The young screenwriter, who had finally begun to hit his stride in Hollywood, took the money and agreed not to sue or disclose how much he was paid. Unlike Buchwald, Tab *did* have to work in this town again, and refusing to play ball with the studios was still not a prudent thing to do. He took the money and shut up. The irony that Tab Murphy had money in his pocket from our efforts—and Art and Alain had nothing—was not lost on my clients or me.)

Jim Harrison's story treatment, in which Eddie Murphy was to play a Southern senator's aide who ultimately becomes the king of Somalia, was likewise "significant with respect to the similarity issue," according to Schneider. Bob Wachs dismissed Harrison's story because he already had an African king story: Buchwald's *King for a Day*.

"I think that we should send some Dom Perignon to Rose Styron for giving Art's address to Jim Harrison," I said when I read that portion of the decision.

"I think we should send a bottle to Bob Wachs," said Suzanne.

Finally, Schneider etched in stone his opinion that Art Buchwald did not plagiarize from Charlie Chaplin.

"It is true that Buchwald testified that he saw 'A King in New York' in Paris in the 1950s and wrote a column concerning his review of the movie after seeing it. Besides these facts, there is not a scintilla of evidence that Buchwald's treatment was in any way based on 'A King in New York.'"

"Besides the fact that the movie involves a king who comes to America, there is not the slightest resemblance between 'A King in New York' and 'King For A Day,'" he wrote. "In Chaplin's movie, the king is an elderly Caucasian who is already married and deposed by the time he comes to America. Although he loses his fortune, he spends the entire movie living in luxury at the Ritz Hotel. Moreover, and most significantly, the movie is a satirical look at the McCarthy era and the American mentality during that period of time."

But our victory wasn't total.

As I had expected, Judge Schneider rejected our claim for punitive damages. We believed we'd been victims of classic stonewalling, but Schneider ruled that we lacked evidence—the mother's milk of lawsuits. He was unable to "conclude that Paramount's conduct was in bad faith, let alone fraudulent, oppressive or malicious."

Tanen had denied he knew of any connection between *King for a Day* and *Coming to America* and that was enough to toss bad faith out the window. We had no witnesses who could testify that Paramount, Eddie Murphy or Eddie's people engaged in a cover-up.

No punitive damages meant even more work for Team Buchwald. We wanted $5 million and wound up with zip. The case was still a long way from over.

Celine burst into the room, pausing for dramatic effect in the doorway before holding up the newspaper she held hidden behind her back. The inch-high banner headline across the entire top of the front page of the midday edition of the Los Angeles *Times* told the whole story:

PAY BUCHWALD, STUDIO TOLD

The accompanying article by Dennis McDougal trumpeted our victory and highlighted the significant portions of Judge Schneider's opinion, but it also emphasized our unfinished business:

> Schneider did not specify a dollar amount for damages, so it was not immediately clear how much money Buchwald and Bernheim stand to collect for their role in the film. . . .
>
> The 1983 contract between the studio, Buchwald and Bernheim calls for them to receive 19% of the net earnings of any movie that resulted from Buchwald's story treatment. Paramount officials maintain, though, that the movie has not yet earned any net profits.

There were broad grins all around my conference table as Zazi, Suzanne, Marsha and Dennis Landry skimmed McDougal's story. It took the sixty-four-year-old nebbish of D.C. to put our heady victory in perspective. Reached at his pigeonhole of an office in Washington, Buchwald told McDougal he was delighted but never wanted to go through the ordeal again. It was an important decision for Hollywood's downtrodden creative talent but meant little in the grand scheme of things, he said.

"This may help writers a bit," Buchwald said, "but it doesn't change Noriega's position, I'll tell you that."

While my confreres were laughing, I was already brooding over how we were going to parry the obvious ploy Paramount would try next: the 19 percent net profit interest was worthless. Draper gleefully told reporters, "There *are* no net profits. Basically, they spent $1 million to get $250,000."

It was true that our attorneys' fees had topped the seven-figure mark, and it was true that, combined, Art's contract and Alain's contract guaranteed them a grand total of about $250,000 in up-front money. But I still didn't believe Paramount's bravado that a movie that would eventually gross over $400 million—the twentieth-highest-grossing film of the past decade—had not generated a nickel in net profits—and probably never would.

"What's the matter, Pierce? We won! We won!" said Marsha.

The banner headline of the *Times* had made the circuit and landed back in front of me. I must have stared blankly at it a second too long.

"You all right?" asked Zazi.

I shook the anxiety out of my face and grinned ear to ear.

"You bet I am," I said, hitting the table with my fist. "To hell with Draper and Paramount and their claim that our victory is only Pyrrhic. We'll deal with them tomorrow. Right now, we've got a press conference to stage. Now let's get ready."

After my colleagues had left the office, I glanced one more time at McDougal's article. *Buchwald v. Paramount* now entered a second "accounting phase," he wrote, and possibly "an engrossing legal voyage through the mysterious straits of studio bookkeeping . . . and an extraordinary public accounting of the expenses of a blockbuster film." This stage of the case "could last as long as a week," and might produce some provocative documents detailing how books are kept for a single picture.

McDougal was right on all counts except one. Instead of "week," he should have written "over two years."

Part Four

Working
Without a Net

29

Pyrrhic Victory

———— —— —— —— —— —— —— —— ——

THE MEDIA around the world agreed: it was a landmark victory for writers, and Art Buchwald was a genuine folk hero.

When Peter Jennings anointed him ABC "World News Tonight" 's Person of the Week during the second week of January 1990, Art Buchwald joined the ranks of presidents and pontiffs—the very personalities he had been satirizing for forty years.

"Art Buchwald took on a big guy—Paramount Pictures—and won," Jennings said. "In Hollywood that's a victory for all screenwriters, the men and women that the late Jack Warner once called 'schnooks with typewriters.'

"Art Buchwald's decision to challenge the system really could result in a victory for other creative people. And, after all, they're the ones who make us laugh and cry—not the accountants."

Alain Bernheim was also accorded hero status in Hollywood circles. He was elevated to one of the best tables at Le Dome, a chic restaurant in West Hollywood favored by such power brokers as Creative Artists Agency chairman Michael Ovitz, Carolco chairman Mario Kassar and superagent Swifty Lazar. Directors and writers whom Alain knew only socially or hadn't seen in years called to talk about projects. Everywhere he went, motion picture people congratulated him for his courage in risking his career to vindicate the rights of producers and writers.

My life changed overnight too. Right up to the decision, the betting was heavily against us. The conventional wisdom in the Hollywood community was that we had embarked on a noble but quixotic mission that would end in defeat. Eddie Murphy and Paramount were just too powerful to buck.

But America loves an underdog. So, when we won, I became a dragon slayer who revels in taking on the big boys (*Forbes* dubbed me "the new Perry Mason"). All this attention was flattering and heady, but I went about my business the same way I had before January 8, 1990, with one noteworthy exception: I told BBC interviewer Clive James I could finally make reservations at Spago's.

But there was a downside. The international publicity and Art's deadpan announcement on national television that his lawyer worked for "free" attracted to my door an army of kooks who claimed they had written the original material that had been the basis for virtually every successful movie of the last half century. And they wanted me to represent them—free of charge.

My all-time favorite was the RayOVac man. He wrote to me with the news that the CIA had implanted a special battery in his brain that allowed him to receive messages telepathically from outer space. During the past twenty years, extraterrestrial signals he'd heard from deep space inspired him to come up with the original ideas for *Star Trek*, *E.T.*, *Star Wars* and *Close Encounters of the Third Kind*. Then, he explained, Gene Roddenberry, Steven Spielberg and George Lucas came along and sucked the ideas right out of his brain. So, did he have a case? he wanted to know.

Another classic was a young man in his early thirties who called to tell me one year after the fiftieth anniversary of the release of *Gone With the Wind* that he, not Margaret Mitchell, had originated the story for the film.

Then there was the woman from Alabama who wrote with the news that she, not Eddie Murphy, had crafted the original story for *Harlem Nights*. She had more to tell me, she wrote, but her telephone had recently been disconnected, and she needed cash to restore her phone service. If I would send her a check for $38, she would call me and tell me all about her case.

All in all, I received over 150 calls or letters from people claiming authorship of successful films—so many in fact that I had to set up a separate filing system to keep track of them. Zazi, Marsha, Suzanne or I responded to every single inquiry, whether it was a crackpot or a legitimate-looking claim.

The most disturbing thing was that we found roughly 10 percent of the 150 cases had potential merit. Their stories had got into the hands of an agent, producer or writer connected with a movie that bore striking similarities to their material. Perhaps their ideas really had been stolen, but fear of studio reprisal, coupled with a paucity of lawyers willing to invest $1 million to pursue a case that might be worth only low five figures left them with nothing. They had to lick their wounds and get on with their lives.

Idea theft is a cancer in Hollywood far more prevalent than anyone is willing to admit. The temptation to steal someone else's story or script is overwhelming for too many producers, studio and network creative executives and writers. And in an industry where original movie ideas are the coin of the realm, idea theft is grand larceny.

I didn't take any of the 150 cases. None of the writers had a contract like Buchwald's nor could they afford to pay by the hour. Even if I wanted to make a *pro bono* career out of attacking story piracy, I couldn't. I had my hands full with *Buchwald v. Paramount*.

The ink was barely dry on Harvey Schneider's final decision when Bob Draper was taken off the case. But he didn't exit quietly or graciously.

For days after the January 8 tentative decision, Draper disparaged our victory as "hollow," noting smugly that the movie was $18 million in the red and probably would never earn a dime of net profits.

"Mr. O'Donnell spent $1 million to get $265,000," he taunted over and over to the media.

In reality, it was even worse than Draper had guessed. Just a few days after Judge Schneider's decision, I had our accounting staff run a computer printout of the fees and costs. Buchwald's and Bernheim's expenses for everything from transcripts to photocopying totaled more than $200,000. Kaye, Scholer had invested $1,100,000 in the case beyond that.

Regrettably, law is not exclusively a noble profession. It is also a business. Our joy over whipping a major studio was muted by the sobering fact that my clients and the firm might not earn a penny out of the case. Worse, Art and Alain might be out several hundred thousand dollars in costs, and Kaye, Scholer might wind up several million dollars in the hole. I was not looking forward to my appointment in February with the firm's billing committee to discuss the financial implications of the case.

Still, my partners were thrilled with our stunning win. Our senior statesman in Kaye, Scholer's New York office, former Senator Abraham Ribicoff, sent me a personal note, congratulating our team on kicking the stuffing out of Paramount. For a law firm that had opened its Los Angeles office only two years earlier, the case was also a boon for attracting clients and recruiting top young lawyers.

Theoretically, getting enough money to fairly compensate our clients and the firm was not impossible. Paramount's seven-year-old contracts with Buchwald and Bernheim did provide that, in addition to their $265,000 up-front fee, the pair could eventually earn between 19.5 percent and 40 percent of the net profits.

Even the most thorough audit would not make up for my initial bad judgment call. When I persuaded Kaye, Scholer to take the case, I had estimated $25 million in net profits. If Paramount was right, I was off by $43 million. And 19 percent (or 40 percent) of a net loss was nothing—nothing for the clients or their lawyers. We had already invested $1.1 million in legal fees, and the case wasn't half over.

I kept a stiff upper lip for the public. While I struggled to solve the mystery of the missing $18 million and find a winning strategy, Art and I mounted a media offensive to draw attention to the absurdity of Paramount's claim that *Coming to America* would never pay net profits.

At his post-victory press conference in Washington, Art said:

"Paramount has informed us that so far the picture has not made any money. It's in the red. And if you believe this, I have some wonderful S&Ls that I'd like to sell you."

Forbes magazine weighed in with a mid-February feature article: "Profits? What Profits?" Author Dana Wechsler captured one of the emerging themes in our media blitz: "According to industry insiders, the studios have, over the years, devised a definition of net profits that guarantees that profit participants will rarely receive anything substantial, no matter how successful the film."

An editorial in the Los Angeles *Times* two days after the ruling, entitled "Casting a Net for the Bottom Line," skewered Paramount and the other studios:

"The only thing funnier than an Art Buchwald column is Hollywood arithmetic. Doubtless that is something that the Pulitzer Prize–winning satirist will discover for himself during the next phase of his lawsuit against Paramount Pictures Corp."

The harder Paramount tried to make the public understand that "net profits" and studio profits were not the same, the more people laughed. Our mighty adversary was snakebitten.

Humiliated by its trouncing, Paramount got its back up and defiantly refused to compromise. "There's no possibility of settlement," a petulant Draper announced the day of the ruling. "Absolutely not. We have no incentive to settle this case."

Speaking before the same TV cameras that Draper had faced, I told reporters, "Our accountants will leave no stone unturned. We will audit all the studio's records—budgets, contracts, profit statements—right down to the nails and the paint for the sets. I will be like a heat-seeking missile looking for profits."

After rendering his tentative decision, Judge Schneider announced that the trial would move into a second phase on January 24, 1990, to determine how much Buchwald and Bernheim would get. Draper told the world that a special master, probably with an extensive background in accounting and auditing motion picture ledgers, would be appointed to go over Paramount's books and tell Judge Schneider if, in fact, any profits did exist. They didn't, Draper said with a confident smile.

Paramount asked the court to forbid the special master to consider any terms other than those in the contract. The studio's strategy was clear: get the case away from Schneider and give it to a technician who would corroborate in secrecy the studio's version of the numbers without questioning whether they were legal or fair. This was exactly what Paramount had offered at the eve-of-trial settlement conference.

As I was getting more and more depressed about our prospects in the accounting phase, we got a lucky break. The Los Angeles *Times* sent its outside counsel and First Amendment specialist, Rex Heinke of Gibson, Dunn & Crutcher, head to head with Draper the same week that the judge handed down his tentative decision. Pleading a First Amendment right to know, the *Times* asked Schneider to unseal seventeen exhibits that Paramount had successfully kept under wraps during the trial.

Most of the information had come out during the trial anyway—including the dollar amounts *Coming to America* earned for Eddie Murphy, John Landis and Paramount. So why not make the documents public? Schneider asked Draper.

"Trade secrets," Draper told the judge.

Revealing any of the contracts, profit participation statements or other documents would give rival studios a glimpse into how Paramount put a successful motion picture together, Draper argued. Schneider agreed that four of the documents dealing with the actual negotiating of contracts might reveal tactics and *that* could be construed as a trade secret. But most of the documents were just contracts and payment schedules showing how money was divvied up before and after the movie was made.

To Draper's horror, Schneider ordered most of the documents unsealed, including Eddie Murphy's contract with Paramount Pictures. As the trial moved into Phase II, Schneider said, the rest of the sealed documents might be revealed to the public too. Out in the hallway after the hearing, Draper fumed that Judge Schneider was wrong and that Paramount would immediately petition a three-judge state appeals court to overturn the decision.

But the die was cast. It was only a matter of time before the press would devour the documents. It was true that most of the shocking information, such as Eddie's 15 percent gross deal, had already come out during the trial. Paramount's reluctance to reveal the obvious only gave that information new life in the eyes of the media, however. The contracts and profit participation statements became forbidden fruit.

The irony was delicious. I couldn't believe how badly a studio owned by Paramount Communications Inc. was handling communications with the public and press.

By the morning of the January 24 hearing, Bob Draper was subdued. Fighting a war of quiet containment, he tried hurrying past the special master issue, but Judge Schneider stopped him cold.

The judge had no objection to an expert entertainment accountant helping him sort through some of the "drudge work." But the UCLA finance major had developed a taste for Hollywood accounting himself during the trial. Draper seemed to turn a few shades paler as Schneider, agreeing with our proposal, outlined how he planned to roll up his own sleeves and dig in when the *Coming to America* balance sheets and ledgers began to come out of the studio's files and over his desk.

Rather than having the books investigated "in the dark recesses of someone's office," Schneider declared, Phase II of *Buchwald v. Paramount* would be a public proceeding.

The judge wanted to know if either side was in a settling mood.

"Absolutely not!" barked Draper.

"We're always willing to talk, but it takes two to tango," I told the judge.

Draper's swan song wasn't quite finished. Scanning the final version of Schneider's January 8 decision, he wanted to make sure he correctly understood the judge's finding about tort damages. It was true, was it not, that neither Buchwald nor Bernheim had any further right to collect punitive damages from the studio and that Mr. O'Donnell could not collect attorney's fees?

Perhaps Draper asked the question too matter-of-factly or perhaps the judge had heard him gloat once too often on the evening news. Giving us both the eye for a couple of heartbeats, Harvey Schneider dropped a live grenade in Draper's lap.

"I can certainly imagine a scenario that might bring back tort liability if the damages/accounting phase went a certain way," he said in measured tones. "For example, if there was tremendous skulduggery with respect to the financial and accounting issues, there might well be tort liability."

My heart leaped as Draper's jaw fell. The door was *not* closed on punitive damages! The fat lady had *not* sung. I didn't know it at the time, but she was more than two years away from even showing up at the stadium. There was still a long way to go before *Buchwald v. Paramount* was anywhere near being wrapped up. All I knew was that I had some ray of hope to deliver to my partners in New York when I flew back to brief them on the future course of the case.

By the close of the January 24 hearing, Draper's crowing in the media had apparently grown too shrill even for Paramount. He sent a letter to the judge the following day declaring that he was no longer attorney of record for Paramount. The studio stayed with the same law firm, but the man Paramount selected from among O'Melveny & Myers' 165 partners to take them into Phase II was not Bob Draper. He was Charles P. Diamond.

Where Bob Draper was abrasive and hard-nosed, Chuck Diamond was smooth, easy and confident. Bob was bearded and brooding; Chuck was clean-shaven and glib. At forty-one, Diamond was only five years younger than Draper. But Chuck, trim, healthy and tan, could have passed for ten years younger.

If Bob always looked a little rumpled, even in his best navy-blue blazer, Chuck showed up for court in a different form-fitting suit every day. His shirts were crisp and creased, his ties a tad more colorful than the dutiful drab that could be expected of most O'Melveny & Myers partners.

Led by former Deputy Secretary of State Warren Christopher, O'Melveny has offices in five American cities as well as London, Tokyo and Brussels. The blue-chip Los Angeles law firm fights hard for its clients and tries to fit the right lawyer to each case. They'd already made one mistake on *Buchwald v. Paramount*. They weren't going to make another.

Diamond certainly had a flair for high-profile cases. In the past, he had argued on behalf of *USA Today*, in a First Amendment battle over use of the name "New Kids on the Block" with the singing group of the same name. And he'd represented the Calnev Pipeline Co., which had wanted to resume operations in a leveled San Bernardino neighborhood where one of its pipelines had exploded in the spring of 1989, killing two people. Diamond had shown himself to be a master at media damage control, deflecting citizen outrage toward government officials and away from the pipeline company. He was obviously the right man for *Buchwald v. Paramount*. He anticipated questions and prepared his answers and always returned phone calls and explained his side of things thoroughly while minimizing the opposition's arguments.

James Clark, a friend of Connie's and mine from Georgetown undergraduate days, had gone to law school with Chuck and served with him on the law review at New York University. In a congratulatory phone call, after we won, Jim gave me an earful of what was in store for me. A star litigator himself at O'Melveny & Myers's rival, Gibson, Dunn & Crutcher, Jim knew Diamond's reputation as creamy smooth and dangerous. He was smart, diplomatic and unrelenting. He played for keeps and, unlike Draper, he slipped the knife in before you ever had a chance to cry foul.

If imitation is the highest form of flattery, Diamond flattered me from his very first day in the case. His media strategy was uncomfortably similar to my own. Rather than sitting back and issuing bland "no comments," he launched a media counteroffensive. The first hundred days, he seemed to be everywhere. If Art Buchwald appeared on the Michael Jackson radio show on KABC in Los Angeles, Diamond was immediately on the phone for an equal time interview. He courted the press, patiently explaining why my inflammatory charges were false and why it was fair for the studio to reap huge distribution fees, hefty overhead and higher than prime rate interest. My newest adversary —Paramount's fourth lead counsel in a little over a year—was confident, crisp and effective.

Just as Paramount was beefing up, I had to pare down. A surge of new business left our Los Angeles office with a serious staffing shortage on litigation. I could no longer afford the luxury of four lawyers and Dennis Landry on *Buchwald*. I didn't relish streamlining my winning team at the very moment we faced our greatest threat, but I was the head of the office and could not hoard lawyers when other cases were understaffed.

I put my most experienced lawyer, Marsha, and my most junior colleague, Suzanne, on other cases. That left Zazi, Dennis and me to battle Paramount's significantly expanded "A Team": Diamond, another O'Melveny & Myers partner named Charles Reed, senior associate Robert Schwartz, outside consultant Lon Sobel and Paramount's in-house team of Richard Zimbert and Joshua Wattles, plus the rest of Paramount's legal department.

We were outnumbered, on the defensive, and still wandering in the desert searching for a viable legal strategy.

It was a prescription for disaster.

In late November, just before the Phase I trial began, I was having breakfast with a friend. A Pasadena investment banker who specialized in mergers and acquisitions in the $50 million to $200 million range, Jack Whitehead is a fellow member of the Economic Round Table: a professional and business-men's group that meets regularly for breakfast at the California Club in down-town Los Angeles. I assumed that I was admitted into this pillar of the old boy network in part because I was a token Democrat among a group of heavy-hitting Establishment power brokers whose political persuasion was almost exclusively Republican. Jack is a San Marino Brahmin in his late fifties with a wide circle of influential acquaintants as I found out one morning before the trial in December.

"They're going to beat you," he teased me.

"Excuse me?"

"Paramount's going to beat you. That's what they're all saying back in New York, at headquarters."

"You know people back there?"

"Sure. And they're all convinced back there that they're going to beat the pants off of you," he said.

"They're calling the shots from New York?"

"No. Leaving it all up to Mancuso and the lawyers here in L.A. But they don't seem very worried. Say, you know, we ought to go to breakfast some-time," he said.

"We *are* at breakfast," I pointed out, gesturing to a roomful of four dozen of the most powerful men in Los Angeles.

"No, just one on one, Pierce. Just you and me."

Jack attended the trial for a while, but it wasn't until two months later that we spoke again about his contacts back in New York.

"Do you have any interest in settling?" he asked one day in February.

"If the price is right," I said. "Why? You know somebody at Paramount?"

Jack knew Marty Davis through a mutual friend and that friend had re-cently died. If I wanted him to act as a middleman, he'd discreetly place a call.

"Okay. Tell him $5 million," I said, sticking to the number we had laid at Davis's doorstep from the very outset.

It didn't take long for Jack to call back.

"Davis said he's not interested in talking settlement and, in any case, your numbers are beyond the pale," said Jack. "He's going to let the case take its natural course."

He sounded defiant, said Jack. He sounded like a man who had lost a battle but definitely won a war.

"We could try again. Maybe try a lower figure. It's up to you."

I thanked him but declined. I had made an offer, and Davis had not countered. I was not about to play poker with myself.

A week or two later, I asked my New York partner Michael Malina to call Paramount Communications Inc.'s general counsel, Donald Oresman, as an informal follow-up to Whitehead's feeler. Oresman went back more than a decade with Marty Davis, when he made his move to take over the company following Bluhdorn's death. When Malina called, Oresman, a shrewd poker player in negotiations, immediately asked him how much we wanted. Malina said $5 million and Oresman went ballistic.

"O'Donnell's out there attacking us so he can run for the U. S. Senate when Cranston retires," he said. "I also have it on reliable authority that Buchwald's just using the case to pump it for publicity so he can increase his speaking fee."

No, Oresman wasn't interested at all.

Later that same month, Oresman ran into Peter Fishbein at a dinner. Peter tried to keep the conversation on a light tone. But Oresman wasn't laughing.

For the next ten minutes, he blasted Buchwald and me, just as he had during Malina's phone call. According to Marty Davis's lawyer, I was a "bomb thrower," and Buchwald was a publicity seeker. This was no longer just a lawsuit. This was personal.

30

The Worst of Times

——— —— —— —— —— —— —— —— —— ——

IT WAS NOT the best of times.

We were under siege, and the prospects of holding out were growing dimmer each day. The news was bad on every front. Our accounting advisers were unanimous: an audit of Paramount's books would not reverse an $18 million deficit. A million dollars—maybe two in a stretch—but not $18 million. Art and Alain owned 19.5 percent of nothing. Kaye, Scholer owned 40 percent of that.

Not only had Paramount fielded a new army with a dynamic leader and fresh soldiers against the beleaguered remnants of the Buchwald trial team. Paramount's public relations campaign was in full swing too. Diamond appeared to be spending more time on television and radio than he did at the office. After talking with Diamond, Richard Stevenson of the New York *Times* found it "highly unlikely" that I would find $18 million in bloated or improper costs.

Kirk Pasich, a partner in a rival law firm that represented the Hollywood studios, spelled out our problem in the Los Angeles *Daily Journal*:

"The question that Judge Schneider must resolve is whether Buchwald received that to which he is entitled under the contract. Art Buchwald has won the first round and has been 'king for a day.' In the long run, and absent accounting discrepancies, he is not likely to be king for more than a day."

On the litigation front, expenses were spiraling out of control. Art and Alain would soon be out of pocket an additional $250,000 for transcripts, accountants and experts. Kaye, Scholer's investment would climb at least another $500,000 to finish the accounting phase. It was like being trapped in quicksand: if you struggled, you sank quickly; if you did nothing, you sank slowly. Either way, you sank.

On a personal level, I was beginning to have trouble sleeping and had become increasingly short-tempered and edgy. My appetite was a mood barometer. In the two months before trial, I had lost forty pounds. Three depressing months later, I had gained back all the weight.

More than anything else, I was angry. Preliminary accounting estimates indicated Paramount would reap over $85 million in profits from *Coming to America*. Eddie Murphy would earn over $22 million and John Landis would collect over $6 million. But the two men Harvey Schneider had declared to be the genesis of it all would collect nothing. As days turned into weeks and weeks into months in the first quarter of 1990, I started to believe that the law afforded us no remedy.

In one of his appearances on the Michael Jackson radio show, Chuck Diamond conceded that *Coming to America* was profitable.

"It was a huge success," he said. "No one has ever denied that it's returned handsome profits."

But my clients were never promised profits.

"It's not what we promise any writer, performer or director," he continued. "What we promise is a formula that allows the studio to recover its distribution fees and costs and then split what's left over. It's *net* profits. It's not profits. It's *net* profits, and it's solely a creature of contract.

"The contractual terms of net profits really have little to do after all is said and done [with] whether the studio has lost money or made money. The studio makes money, as I said, on its distribution fee. . . . We're not talking about profits the way accountants talk about profits, and we're not talking about profits the way you and I would."

Paramount maintained two accounting systems: one for itself and another for its net profit participants. They were as different as profits and losses. The first set of books, based on what accountants call generally accepted accounting principles (GAAP), was how Paramount was legally obligated to account to its stockholders, the IRS and the Securities and Exchange Commission.

The other set of books was maintained according to the net profit definition included in Paramount's 53-page, single-spaced standard form contract. Instead of GAAP accounting, Hollywood's wags called this second brand of bookkeeping GAP accounting: revenues rarely bridged the gap between costs and profits.

Two sets of books, two sets of rules—one for winners, the other for losers. Everyone in the motion picture business knew that net profits were not really profits. They were the leftovers after the studio got back all its costs, generously paid its big-name talent and took out a hefty chunk for itself. Little wonder Eddie Murphy called net profits "monkey points" or that David Sheffield testified that he looked forward to receiving his net profit participation financial statements for *Coming to America* because "I enjoy reading good fiction."

Diamond kept telling everyone that net profits really meant "bonus" for participants who contributed to the success of a movie. That sounded nice, but where the hell was Art's and Alain's bonus? After all, *Coming to America* was one of the thirty top-grossing movies of all time.

An invisible hand took hundreds of millions of dollars out of the pockets of the film industry's creative talent every year. Over the fifty years that net profits had been part of the industry's compensation package, billions had been diverted into the studios' coffers. It was the financial "crime" of the century and it looked like Paramount would get away with it again.

In late January, I threw a victory bash at Harry's American Bar at the ABC Entertainment Center in Century City. The whole Team Buchwald was there: Zazi, Marsha, Suzanne, Dennis, Alain, Danny Arnold, Lynn Roth, David Rintels and Ed North. Everyone except our fearless leader, that is.

Buchwald was stuck back East with a conflicting speaking engagement. But he was there in spirit—and on cassette. After I gave a short speech thanking everyone, Zazi surprised me by turning on a tape recorder:

"Greetings," said the familiar voice. "I regret that I am unable to be at your victory dinner tonight. Apparently, 19 percent of the net profits does not cover a tourist ticket to Los Angeles. I wish to say that in all my years of litigation, I have never had a better lawyer than Pierce O'Donnell."

The room erupted with laughter. Everyone knew that this was Art's first and only lawsuit and that I was the only trial lawyer he had ever hired.

"Pierce does not take a case lightly. I recall many a morning being woken up at six o'clock and at the other end of the phone was the cheerful voice of Pierce O'Donnell shouting, 'Kid, we made legal history today! The judge granted us valet parking privileges under the courthouse.' . . .

"Every day was a new triumph for our case and not once did I ever hear Pierce say, 'Will someone please tell me what the hell we're doing here?'

"Thanks to Pierce, I have become a famous man. Warren Beatty gave me his little black book on the bus the other day. Stephanie Powers wants me to play polo with her, and Mike Milken gave me his private telephone number.

"This has been a year's work for all of us. To me it has been very meaning-ful. I was blessed twice. Not only did I win my suit, but everyone in the country knows that I didn't get any money.

"I'm sorry I can't be there, but I know it must be a wonderful thing to be amongst friends. And as far as I'm concerned this thing is not over now. I feel in fifteen years, every year, we will be having a party like this to find what the other side is up to.

"In keeping with Kaye, Scholer's policy, I am faxing this tape to California rather than mailing it. Thank you."

． ． ． ．

While we were gearing up for a full-fledged audit of every line item in the *Coming to America* budget, the Court of Appeals rejected Paramount's attempt to reverse Judge Schneider's order unsealing financial documents in *Buchwald v. Paramount*.

On February 4, the headline in the Sunday Los Angeles *Times* read: MURPHY MOVIE MADE MILLIONS BUT STAYED IN RED, STUDIO LEDGERS SAY. The article by Dennis McDougal flatly stated what had been hinted at for weeks: moviegoers around the globe had already paid more than $350 million to see *Coming to America* and yet the movie remained in the red. The usual suspects were blamed: high production, marketing and distribution costs and contractual obligations to gross profit participants.

But other details came out of the unsealed documents too—details that showed just how outrageously out of hand "star treatment" had got.

Murphy had renegotiated his own contract with Paramount at least four times in eight years. Each time, his asking price to make a movie was higher. He had stopped accepting "monkey points" as part of his compensation as far back as 1984.

His up-front personal salary demand rose from $8 million to $12 million for *Another 48 HRS.* He also received 15 percent of every dollar collected by Paramount, including "film rentals": box office receipts split between Paramount and each individual theater around the world.

According to the studio's own arithmetic, Murphy's 15 percent of the gross had already come to $13,081,711 over and above his base salary of $8 million. The cash spigot had yet to stop flowing, and Eddie Murphy had already taken in more than $21 million.

But the unsealed trial documents showed that Murphy didn't stop there. He cashed in even further. During the filming of *Coming to America*, the comedian received a $5,000-a-week living allowance, $4,920 for a limousine and round-the-clock chauffeur and $3,792 per week for a motor home that had once been customized for Sylvester Stallone, plus a full-time driver to move it from place to place.

The gravy train also included $1,500 per week for Eddie's personal trainer; $650 per week for Eddie's valet; five production assistants for Eddie at $650 per week each; and $1,000 per week for his film stand-in: one Charles Murphy, Jr., who did look a lot like Eddie. After all, he was his brother.

In addition to their salaries, Eddie's entourage of relatives and buddies also got per diem pay, just like their boss. It totaled $50,400 during the two months of filming. The movie also paid their travel expenses: $68,000. In all, the limo service, food, travel, lodging, personal employees and other overhead for the movie came to about $5 million—a $13 million total price tag for the care and feeding of one actor in one movie.

Murphy's insistence that he be allowed to leave the set a couple of days early because he was homesick for New Jersey cost the studio $212,800 in production delays—all of which was charged to the picture's production budget instead of being deducted from Murphy's paycheck.

But it was the "Big Mac attack" that the world remembered. The expense item heard round the world was a $235.33 charge made on Eddie's petty cash account and charged to *Coming to America*. It was for breakfast at McDonald's.

The street headline for the February 6 edition of the New York *Post* screamed: EDDIE'S BIG MCBUCK$. The Washington *Post's* Kim Masters opened with: "Talk about a Big Mac attack . . ." A $235 breakfast at McDonald's raised eyebrows even within the studio.

"Under normal circumstances, it is customary to provide complimentary food and beverages for an actor in his trailer," executive producer Leslie Belzberg wrote Paramount production accountant Frank Bodo in an internal studio memo dated January 19, 1988. "However, as you can see, these petty cash disbursements far exceed what is usually requested."

A Paramount spokesman later explained that the $235.33 was for Egg McMuffins that were passed out to all the members of the film production crew. But when the charge first came under the studio's routine accounting review, it showed up on Murphy's expense account as breakfast for himself and his pals. In any event, the damage had been done, and the $235 Eddie Murphy breakfast became a symbol of Paramount's profligacy.

Paramount's official response that coddling a superstar like Murphy was "standard in the industry" just didn't wash outside of Hollywood. A bemused Buchwald called to say he'd been getting the same response on the East Coast that I was getting in California: where did Murphy get off buying over $200 worth of Egg McMuffins for his buddies and charging it to *Art's* movie?

You did not have to be a CPA to understand that Paramount and all the other studios employed an Alice in Wonderland accounting system for net profit participants. Nothing was as it appeared. The Mad Hatter was the chief financial officer in Hollywood.

- Distribution fee *income* was treated as an *expense* and was not used to reduce the deficit.
- *Expenses*—such as a flat overhead charge of 15 percent of every dollar spent on production—were largely fictional and became *income* for the studio, even though they were treated as actual cash expenditures, thereby enlarging the deficit.
- When Paramount took in box office rentals, it immediately took out its 35 percent distribution fee as if it were accounting on a cash basis, just as an individual taxpayer does in computing his taxes. But when it came to expenses, the studio charged the picture for costs that had not yet been paid. The net effect was to engorge the deficit and make a break-even point more impossible.

In reality, net profits were gross losses. In the coming months, what Paramount routinely described as "income," "expenses" and "profit" would boggle our minds and raise a public outrage heard all the way from the Potomac to Department 52 of Los Angeles Superior Court.

. . . .

Our lineup of experienced film auditors, Phil Hacker, Sid Finger, Jay Shapiro and Ernie Nives, had nearly a century of experience auditing studio books for profit participants like Art and Alain. Over several decades, each had been able to dislodge millions of dollars for their clients by ferreting out unreported income and improper charges on motion pictures and television series. Whenever any one of them called to say they wanted to see the books, studio executives cringed. When I announced that I had recruited all four for a frontal assault on Paramount's books, Paramount's bean counters reached for their calculators and studio lawyers went to work devising ways to make auditing as difficult as possible.

Ernie Nives was our foreign distribution expert. An urbane CPA educated in France and New York, he started auditing movies for Allied Artists in 1954. Over the years, his blue-chip client list included names from every band of the Hollywood spectrum: producers like Otto Preminger and Darryl Zanuck; actors like Clint Eastwood, Gene Wilder, Frank Sinatra, Warren Beatty and Lucille Ball; directors like Stanley Kubrick and Mel Brooks.

Foreign distribution was one of the first places where funny business occurred with regularity in movie accounting. Ernie Nives had caught Paramount at it more than once.

Over the years, studio distribution departments had learned how to squirrel away millions through perfectly legal, if morally suspect, methods of accounting in foreign countries. One classic maneuver dating back to the 1950s involved the sales of film packages in foreign countries. For example, a studio would put together a dozen films and sell them as a unit for $12 million to Japan or Argentina. The package might include one or two big hits: say, a *Sound of Music* or a *Rocky*. But most of the movies would be B grade or lower: *Raging Bimbos from Hell* or *Uncle Doofus Finds a Bug*. The hits would play all over the country, perhaps for months, while *Bimbos* and *Doofus* remained in their reel cans, often still sitting on the delivery dock, unopened.

When it came time to divide up the $12 million, however, each of the dozen films in the package would get an equal portion. Of course, a fair allocation would give a hefty share of the pot to what distribution specialists call "the locomotive"—the film that drives the train of other films and induces the buyer to buy the whole package, even if he doesn't want *Uncle Doofus* and the other junk in the deal. Back at the studio's accounting department, however, *Rocky* or *Sound of Music* would be weighted exactly the same as *Bimbos* or *Doofus*.

For the *Doofus* account, that meant $1 million extra earned off the back of *Rocky*. For the unsuspecting *Rocky* participant, several million dollars in which he should have shared evaporated into the ozone.

Often, the studio's motive for such suspect accounting was the fact that a *Rocky* might have already broken even and be paying net profits, while *Doofus* was hopelessly mired in net losses. So the extra, undeserved $1 million would not take *Doofus* out of a deficit position, but it would prevent the *Rocky* participants from sharing in it, thereby keeping more money in the studio's bank account. Meanwhile, the studio still skimmed a 40 percent foreign distribution fee off the top of the whole $12 million package.

Once again, it was heads the studio won, tails the creative talent lost.

But the biggest problem in tracking dollars beyond our territorial waters was not fraud or sleight of hand. It was knowing the territory. An actor or writer rarely knew the foibles of foreign countries when they signed a contract. Studios *always* knew.

Thus, when a profit participant agreed to the reasonable proposition that he would take no profits in a country like Colombia until all expenses had been met, he would never be told ahead of time that Colombia charged a 30 percent withholding tax on all monies earned at the theater box office. That meant that the studio would get its 40 percent distribution fee up front and pay the 30 percent tax out of whatever was left, leaving only thirty cents on the dollar to pay for everything from prints and advertising to air conditioning in the Bogotá distribution office. As a result, movies that screened in Colombia rarely produced a net profit. Once again, however, the studio got its money off the top. In addition, it took a fat 30 percent foreign tax credit on its corporate income tax return at the end of the year, passing on none of the credit to the profit participants.

Ernie Nives had similar horror stories from many other foreign countries. The studios got their money out of the country, but nobody else connected with the picture ever did. And it was just too expensive in most cases to hire accountants to go overseas to audit the studio's books. After meeting with Ernie, I concluded that I would place primary emphasis on domestic production and distribution activities and leave a foreign audit to another day— assuming we survived that long.

I turned to Phil Hacker, one of the leading auditors of studio books and our anchorman in Los Angeles. I had met Phil in the mid-1980s when he was the expert accountant testifying for a "Barney Miller" profit participant who had sued Danny Arnold for allegedly not paying monies owed to him. Phil was smart and honest. Arnold won the trial, but I remained impressed with Hacker.

I had talked with him before the *Buchwald v. Paramount* trial about working with us. Within days of Judge Schneider's decision, I was on the phone confirming his engagement. The day after I called him, Paramount's lawyers called to hire Hacker. I thanked God I'd gotten there first.

Movie posters for hits ranging from *Moonstruck* to *Jaws* lined the walls of Hacker's Century City offices. They explained in one glance why he ranked among the top two or three film auditors in the country. Each was autographed to Hacker by grateful Hollywood luminaries.

Hacker, a balding man with piercing blue eyes, told me that, since he first began auditing movies full time for a living back in 1970, more and more actors, writers, producers and directors had become financially sophisticated and emboldened about challenging the system. When Paul Newman came to him looking for his fair share out of *Fort Apache: The Bronx*, a modest 1981 hit about a police precinct under siege in the South Bronx, the actor knew exactly where to point in his contract to give Hacker a road map to the hidden profits.

Even the granddaughter of Cecil B. De Mille found the courage to ask Hacker to go back to Paramount nearly forty years after the studio released *The Ten Commandments* and demand her late grandfather's full and up-to-date profit participation in the movie. Similarly, Hacker represented Groucho Marx's estate in trying to extract more profits out of the 1930s comedy *A Night at the Opera.*

"It's sort of like a battle of wits," Hacker told me. "You feel like Robin Hood. You represent very wealthy people like Newman, but you represent people who are up against the monolith-type studio which sometimes becomes very, well . . . shall we say, haughty?"

Hacker had about a 99 percent success rate. His efforts invariably resulted in recovering the cost of the audit and extra money for his client. In two decades of challenging the studios, Hacker—a cautious man by nature who chose his words as precisely as he tabulated figures—never came across anything he felt confident that he could call out-and-out fraud. But the line items had grown so numerous and the income and expense categories so open to imaginative interpretation over the years that, almost invariably, he found interest charged here or food expenses charged there that shouldn't be laid off on a profit participant.

"Like a couple hundred Egg McMuffins?" I asked.

Hacker flashed me his wide, toothsome grin.

And he offered me one caveat before we launched into the tedium of examining 95,000 line items in the accounting records of *Coming to America.* It was advice I would reflect upon many times over the months ahead.

"There are many people I turn away because it just doesn't pay, Pierce. What I mean is, if I found $10 million in audit issues for them, they still might not ever get to profits because the movie has a $20 million deficit. It just wouldn't pay according to the contract. Everything is in the contract. The normal accounting rules don't apply in net profit statements. It's another world."

We had Hacker on the domestic front, and Nives poised for a foreign assault. I still had to pay a visit to The Terminator from Manhattan.

Back in the sixties, both Hacker and Nives got their start apprenticing to a legendary New York accounting firm: Solomon, Finger & Newman. Ben Solomon, the man who *invented* independent movie auditing in the 1930s, had recently died and the mantle of patriarch of independent film auditors passed to his partner: Sidney Finger.

Tall and handsome, Sid resembled Gregory Peck. When I walked into his office the second week in February, he was dressed conservatively in an understated pinstriped suit, white shirt and quiet tie.

What Phil Hacker had been doing for a quarter century, Sid had been doing for almost twice as long: giving the studios the heebie-jeebies every time he phoned to say he was coming over to look at their books.

In the early 1980s, Solomon, Finger & Newman merged with the up and coming national accounting firm of Laventhol & Horwath, which wanted to break into auditing motion picture studios and production companies on behalf of profit participants. By the time I was on the hunt for accounting experts, Sid was semi-retired and serving as adviser for Silver Screen Partners, a collection of syndicated limited partnerships that had successfully invested over a half billion dollars in motion pictures, including most of Disney's hit movies since 1984.

Back in the fall when I was reviewing net profit statements for our settlement conference, I had retained Laventhol & Horwath's chief entertainment auditor, Jay Shapiro, in Los Angeles. It was Shapiro who arranged for me to meet Finger.

Soft-spoken and courtly, Sid was the perfect gentleman. He was thin, with clear gray eyes to match his silver hair. He had Parkinson's disease, but he was not disabled. And the malady heightened, rather than lessened, his dignity.

He offered me coffee and asked about my family and how I had got into entertainment law before we got down to business.

"Mr. Finger—"

"Call me Sid. Please," he insisted.

"Sid, you've seen Paramount's statement for *Coming to America*, my clients' contracts and the summary of the terms of Murphy's and Landis's deals. What do you think?"

He paused, tapping a slender finger thoughtfully on his knee.

"I think that this movie will never break into net profits on its own, and any conventional audit of the books will not find enough unreported income or inappropriate expenses or interest to make up the $18 million deficit," he said.

My heart started to pound. I didn't want to hear this. That's what Phil Hacker, Ernie Nives and Jay Shapiro had told me. I had thought the great Finger could find some *deus ex machina* to rescue us.

"Even if Paramount collects another $100 million in gross receipts?"

"That's right," he said. "Look at what happens to that $100 million. First, some of that $100 million is videocassette income, and only 20 percent of that goes to the picture's account as a 'royalty.' So gross receipts reported on the movie's books will be less than $100 million. Let's say it's $95 million. Paramount takes 35 percent off the top of that for its so-called distribution fee—something that happens only in profit participant accounting, by the way.

"Then Murphy and Landis take 25 percent. That leaves only $40 million. But the $25 million paid to Murphy and Landis is added to the negative cost, so that increases the deficit by $25 million. That means you're $43 million in the red, not $18 million. Then there is the accumulating interest, probably another $4 million."

I held up my hand.

"Whoa! That leaves nothing for Buchwald and Bernheim!" I said. "Nothing now. Nothing ever."

"Regrettably, that's true, especially when you have such high production and distribution costs. Over $75 million, according to Paramount. And then you have huge gross participations paid to Murphy and Landis.

"*Coming to America* could have had worldwide sales of $600 million and studio gross receipts of $300 million, and there still would have been no net profit," he said.

"God, it's over before it even starts," I said softly.

"Yes, the die is cast," he said. "The fault lies in the contracts your clients signed."

"That's what Phil said. He keeps telling me that Paramount and the other studios don't cook the books, they cook the contracts."

"That's right. The studios copy each other, and they rarely negotiate any meaningful changes. What works for Disney works for Universal. The net profits definitions are virtually identical—exact same wording and same result."

"Almost never any net profits," I said.

"In your case, there are six items that your clients' contracts authorize Paramount to do that doom any net profits. You'd find the same six items with almost no variation in the contracts of the other studios."

Item 1 was the 35 percent distribution fee, he said. That $42 million constituted almost pure windfall profit to the studio. A fairer figure would be 15 to 20 percent.

Next, Paramount was allowed to charge 15 percent for overhead on the negative cost, including the gross participations. Originally, overhead covered general and administrative costs, including in-house lawyers, accountants and insurance that couldn't be attributed to a particular movie. But the studio kept collecting the 15 percent overhead charge regardless of how much overhead the picture actually used.

"This is a big profit item," said Finger.

"How big do you think it is?" I asked.

"Probably a $4 to $5 million profit on overhead alone."

Third, the studio still exacted a 10 percent surcharge on all advertising costs, despite the fact that it no longer had an in-house advertising department. That surcharge represented at least $2 to $3 million of the $36 million in distribution costs.

Fourth, the Eddie Murphy overhead of $5 million was claimed as a cost of development.

"It should be part of the studio's overhead for which Paramount is already collecting $8 million," said Finger.

"It sounds like double dipping," I noted.

"That's right. So's the fifth item: interest on negative cost."

Paramount had already taken in $42.3 million on its distribution fee. How did it justify another $6.4 million in interest? Not only was Eddie Murphy a bankable star, box office money came in so quickly that the studio's risk was almost negligible. Nevertheless, the contracts allowed the studio to keep on charging interest until hell froze over.

The sixth big-ticket item built into the contracts was ancillary revenue—especially videocassette money.

"Phil's figures put video gross at $45 million," said Finger. "That's impressive, but Paramount keeps 80 percent of that and pays only 20 percent to the picture's account. It costs the studio maybe 25 percent to produce and distribute the tapes. So their profit is about 55 percent. That's $24 million here. Also, the studio takes its 35 percent distribution fee on the 20 percent royalty that it paid to the picture, so tack on another $3 million plus."

"That doesn't leave much video money for our guys."

"About $3 million out of $45 million. Less than 10 percent trickles down."

I was shell-shocked. I knew generally how the system operated. Ernie, Phil and Jay had schooled me in various aspects of this arcane art, but Sid deftly pulled it together into one giant Excedrin headache.

"Is there anything you would recommend that we do?" I asked.

"Not anything that an accountant can help you with, Pierce. It's going to take more than an audit to get a fair and rational accounting system for net profit participants. Count me in for whatever help I can give you, though."

I rose to leave after my numbing, two-hour tutorial on Hollywood accounting, but Sid asked me to wait while he ducked into another room. A few minutes later, he returned with a document.

"I think that you might find this informative. It summarizes a lot of what we've been talking about this afternoon."

"What is it?" I asked.

"It's a speech I gave back in 1977 at a UCLA conference of entertainment industry people: lawyers, accountants, talent managers, studio executives."

I took it and shook his hand. His grip was firm; his mind razor sharp. He narrowed his eyes and put his arm around my shoulder.

"I wish I had met you forty years ago," he said. "What you are going to try to do is what I have wanted to see happen all my career. I *want* to help you. This may be the only chance that we will ever have to stop this larceny."

I read Sid's speech on the plane back to Los Angeles. Even thirteen years earlier, he had been too much the diplomat and gentleman to accuse the people who drew up the studios' contracts of conning actors, writers, directors and producers out of their rightful share of a film's profits. But he left no doubt that film auditing required a willing suspension of disbelief. Instead of balancing ledgers, he had told his audience, film auditors had to prepare to step through the looking glass into a world of topsy-turvy numbers that would have driven Lewis Carroll bonkers.

"The film auditor's role is occasionally confused with the job of certifying financial statements in accordance with generally accepted auditing standards," he noted.

But the fact is that GAAP simply doesn't exist inside the make-believe borders of Hollywood. All a film auditor can do is make sure that the studio lives up to the letter of its contract.

But instead of ending on a sour note, Sid was optimistic. "The modern, complex distribution agreement, running from 50 to 100 pages, had its genesis in a simpler, more straightforward era when production costs were less, production time shorter, collections faster, foreign theatrical sales and ancillary sales less important, and funding techniques less involved. Then, too, distribution agreements were shorter and probably more equitable. . . . The trend is inexorably to more complicated distribution arrangements reflecting the inevitable introduction of new media technology and the fragmentation of the funding process."

As I flew back to Los Angeles, I couldn't get what I had learned the past month out of my head. They cook their contracts. They cook their contracts. They cook their contracts, I kept saying Hacker's words to myself as if it were a mantra. Then, at 35,000 feet, I picked up the airphone and called Zazi Pope at the office. The connection was fuzzy, but my message was short.

"Just saw Sid Finger. I've been missing the big picture here, Zazi. We're gonna lose if we keep on playing by the studio's rules. They *made* the rules! It's preordained that we lose."

"So what do you have in mind?" Zazi asked.

"Drop everything you're doing and get to the library. I want to know every conceivable legal ground for knocking out Paramount's net profit contract."

"Wow! That's high-stakes poker, Pierce."

"I know. Believe me, I know. But we don't have a choice. The majors have been cooking those contracts for fifty years. I have a hunch they do it together, secretly, standing over the same large pot. You up for dowsing their fire?"

"But how can we sue and win on one part of Art's contract and then turn around and try to invalidate another part? Paramount will have a field day. I can hear Diamond now: 'Pierce O'Donnell must have Alzheimer's. A few months ago, he wrapped his clients in their contracts. Now they can't shed them fast enough. This is a new low for chutzpah.' "

"Maybe. But I don't see any other way out. I can't worry about being consistent when we're teetering on the brink. Unless we find something to latch on to fast, we're history. Hacker and everybody else tells us an audit is hopeless. We have to go for broke or quit. And goddam it, I'm not quitting!"

In late February I was back in New York. I had an appointment I had been postponing for two months but couldn't put off any longer. It was time to meet with Kaye, Scholer's billing committee, affectionately known by some as the Inquisition. Riding herd on over a hundred partners, it is the three-man committee's unenviable task to be the financial cops of the firm by making sure that we take only clients who can pay our fees and get rid of the ones who can't.

In a conference room on the fifteenth floor of 425 Park Avenue, I faced the dreaded troika: Gerry Feller, a senior banking partner; Cliff Hook, our chief financial officer; and Al Capilupi, the firm's controller.

"Congratulations, Pierce, on your great victory," Feller began.

A crusty member of the old school who had not been crazy about opening a Los Angeles office two years earlier, Gerry had become a friend and supporter. His bark was normally bigger than his bite, but today he wanted me to account for the firm's investment in the lawsuit.

"Do you think that the clients and the firm will ever see any money?" he wanted to know.

It was the same straightforward, fair question I'd been asking myself since Ned Tanen first hit me in the solar plexus during his deposition back in mid-1989 when he testified that it was doubtful that *Coming to America* would ever turn a net profit.

"We are about to begin auditing Paramount's books, but our auditors tell us we will not overcome an $18 million deficit. Right now, I'd have to say that our chances are marginal—unless we come up with a knockout strategy in the next few months."

"How much more time will we have to invest?" Cliff Hook asked.

Like myself, Hook is a Jesuit-trained Catholic. A talented financial manager who worked closely with the firm's chairman Peter Fishbein, Cliff had helped Peter increase per-partner profits every year for the past several years. We had become friends, but at the moment he was all business.

"The judge has signaled that he wants to move the case to a prompt conclusion, and Paramount is trying to rush everything to a July 2 trial so that we don't have time to come up with a winning attack," I said, my throat getting drier by the second. "But to answer your question, I'd estimate that the accounting trial will be over by August, and the appeal will take a year. We should be finished with the whole case in late 1991."

"What about future legal fees and costs?" Al Capilupi wanted to know.

Al is a dark-haired, athletic accountant who looks like Central Casting's version of a financial watchdog. A star of the firm's baseball team in the New York Lawyers' League, he had just thrown me a curve.

"We have almost $1.15 million invested now. Assuming the case moves according to schedule, the rest of the trial court and appellate work should cost another $600,000 or so. So, added to the time we already have in the computer, we're looking at a total investment of about $1,750,000."

"And it looks like you're not going to get any damages other than the $265,000 in fixed payments?" Feller asked.

"Right now, you ought to assume that," I replied. "It's a crime, but unless I can find some way to interest our judge in throwing out the contract or finding that Paramount mismanaged the movie's finances, we're going to take gas."

"What about settlement, Pierce?" Cliff asked.

"Everyone I have spoken with, as well as the media, speculate that Paramount will sue for peace because it will not want its books opened for public scrutiny. But their new lawyer has said publicly that the studio must defend its honor against our charges and will, therefore, not settle. Nonetheless, I'm cautiously optimistic that we can maneuver the situation to a point where it will be too painful for Paramount to go forward. We'll be starting the audit in a few weeks, and that may be the magic moment."

I swallowed hard and sweated, my speech still hanging in the air. Smiles broke out around the table.

"Well, settlement or no settlement, we have two clients to represent, re-gardless of the cost," Gerry said. "Go get 'em, tiger."

"Good luck," Cliff and Al said in unison.

My apprehension had been unfounded. The firm was backing me all the way. No recriminations about my original projections about the cost of the case or that Paramount would settle before trial. Art and Alain were Kaye, Scholer's clients, and they would get the same first-class treatment that our fee-paying clients received.

In fact, in the months ahead, the firm would pour even more high-priced resources into the case. In addition to my New York partner Michael Malina, Bruce Margolius and Joel Katcoff joined our team in April.

A criminal lawyer who had assisted my Los Angeles partner Jeff Gordon and me in investigating the brutal murder of LIVE Entertainment chief executive officer Jose Menendez and his wife Kitty in their Beverly Hills mansion, Margolius was perfectly suited for the sleuthing that I wanted done. Bruce, innately skeptical and tough-minded, has a knack for knowing someone who knows someone who could get us the information we needed.

Bruce lives on a ski slope in Park City, Utah, and is connected to our office by the firm's network of computers and a fax machine. When he wasn't writing the Great American Novel or shooting gophers in Montana for relax-ation, my burly, bearded colleague commuted to Los Angeles to battle Para-mount.

Joel Katcoff also commuted to Los Angeles—from New York, where he left behind a newborn child and an understanding wife. For the critical weeks leading up to the mid-May deadline for filing our specific charges against Paramount, Joel helped refine and test our strategy and draft our brief. An Orthodox Jew whose faith never ceased to impress me, Joel left Los Angeles each Friday morning so that he could be home by sundown for the Sabbath. On Sunday afternoon, he'd get on a plane back to Los Angeles.

Bleak as our prospects looked, we still managed to have some fun. Art called regularly with his latest jokes and wry observations about Paramount's ac-counting claims.

"If Paramount makes any more money on *Coming to America*, they're going to declare bankruptcy," he liked to say.

In late March, Paramount released its official accounting, supporting a find-ing of an $18 million net loss for *Coming to America*. The top-line figure, the studio's gross receipts, was $26 million *less* than it had been in December when Bob Draper first gave me a profit participation statement.

The Washington *Post*'s John Richardson interviewed me about it. I suspected that the studio simply hadn't added in its video revenue, but I wasn't going to volunteer that assessment to the press.

"It was good reading because I enjoy good fiction," I told Richardson, paraphrasing *Coming to America* co-screenwriter David Sheffield's deposition testimony. "I have a theory that Frank Mancuso went home to his wife after trial and said, 'Honey, I shrunk the gross.' Inquiring minds want to know—what happened to the $26 million?"

Alain had told me stories about Hollywood hardball. I had seen at first hand Paramount's scorched earth tactics at trial as Draper tried to trash Art's reputation and brand my clients as racists. But I had sued studios for a decade and never personally experienced any foul play.

That all ended at 12:15 P.M. on February 21, 1990.

I was in New York for yet another Sid Finger session. The day before, I had received a message to call Jay Shapiro at his office at Laventhol & Horwath. I had known Jay since the mid-1980s when I started using him as an expert witness in high-profile entertainment cases. An imaginative numbers cruncher, he is an exceptional forensic accountant—a magician with numbers in the courtroom. When I hired him on our team, we agreed that he would have to be Harry Houdini to make an $18 million loss disappear.

The minute Jay picked up the phone I knew there was a problem.

"How are you, Jay?" I said.

"Not very good, Pierce," he said somberly. "I don't know how to tell you this so I will just tell you. The powers on high here have decreed that Laventhol & Horwath cannot do the Paramount audit for Buchwald and Bernheim."

"What are you talking about? The last time we spoke, you told me that your only problem was doing the distribution audit because Murphy and Landis might ask you to do a distribution audit for them. But you said there would be no problem. You pitched heavily for the production and interest calculation audit and suggested that Phil Hacker's outfit do the distribution audit to avoid any appearance of conflict."

"Yes, that's right," Jay replied, his voice tired and cracking. "But things have changed. I was summoned yesterday, and that's why I called you. I met with Ivan Axelrod, who does work for Landis, and Phil Winik, the head of our Western region. I was told that Murphy and Paramount had put a lot of pressure on us to withdraw from handling the Buchwald case."

I listened, not believing what I was hearing. Since October, Art and Alain had already paid Laventhol several thousand dollars. Jay had wanted all of the audit work, but I insisted Phil Hacker and Ernie Nives would share in the massive audit. As the largest accounting firm in the country representing profit participants, Laventhol pushed hard for a prominent role in what the firm knew was shaping up to be the mother of all Hollywood accounting trials. Only two weeks earlier, Jay's partners had been thrilled when *Forbes* mistakenly published an article stating that Laventhol had won the audit contract.

"And it gets worse. They got Sid too."

"What the hell are you talking about?" I asked, my voice rising. "Sid's retired. He can do whatever he wants."

"Not really, Pierce. They've got him tied to the pension plan. Sid was paid a visit in New York yesterday by a Laventhol partner. He was given the same message: 'You're out of *Buchwald v. Paramount*.' "

I was shaking. This had to be a bad dream. Was this Paramount's *Godfather, Part IV*? As I sat there in utter silence, I realized for the first time what a threat *Buchwald v. Paramount* really posed, not only to Paramount, but to the entire Hollywood studio establishment. We were getting too close for comfort. Someone had put a contract out on two of my key experts.

Collecting myself, I weighed in to find out what had happened and who had muscled whom.

"Okay, Jay, tell me what really happened."

"Eddie is an important client of our New York office," Shapiro explained calmly. "Eddie is beside himself about the lawsuit in general, about the loss of the lawsuit and about the embarrassing disclosures of his financial arrangements with Paramount and his lavish deal."

"That's great," I fired back. "He's upset because he's been shown to be a hog. What the hell does he expect?"

"And Landis is a very important client of Ivan Axelrod in our Century City office, and his lawyer, Joel Behr, has been good to us over the years," Jay said. I detected no conviction in his voice.

"I've not exactly been a stranger to Laventhol & Horwath over the years, Jay. Your firm and I go back a long way."

"Don't think I didn't make those arguments, Pierce. They fell on deaf ears. The firm has made a decision that Murphy and Landis are more important than Buchwald and you. I don't agree with the decision but that's the way it is."

I was still convinced that I wasn't getting the whole story.

"What is this about Paramount?"

"Paramount, at the highest level, has made it known to our firm, at the highest level, that if we continue to represent Buchwald and Bernheim, Paramount will subpoena all of our profit participation audits for other clients on Eddie Murphy movies," said Shapiro. "Paramount has told us that they will try to show that we did not question various items in Eddie Murphy's deal and that we are taking an inconsistently aggressive position in your case. That will expose the firm to malpractice lawsuits from our other clients because we did not challenge items that we plan to challenge for you."

In fifteen years of practice, I had never encountered such a blatant interference with my clients' rights to prosecute a lawsuit. As angry as I was, I had to make sure I had all the information.

"Has Paramount done anything else?" I asked.

"Yes, they have," Shapiro answered slowly. "One of Paramount's business affairs people has approached one of our Los Angeles partners about doing work for Paramount."

That was enough. One way or another, Paramount was going to neutralize Laventhol & Horwath.

"Jay, this is outrageous," I said. "You know it and I know it. I can't believe what I'm hearing. I can't believe that a firm like Laventhol & Horwath, which has made its reputation over the years as the fearless advocate for profit participants, is caving in. I can see a possible conflict of interest in representing Murphy, Landis and my clients in a production audit. But there is absolutely no problem with Sid and you testifying as expert witnesses. Any damages we recover will come from Paramount, not from Murphy or Landis."

"I tried to make that argument but our management committee is adamant, Pierce. No involvement whatsoever."

The high road hadn't worked. It was time for another approach.

"You know, I'm not going to stand for this bullshit! I'm going to blow the lid wide open on this one. Before I'm finished, Laventhol & Horwath will regret that it ever trimmed its sails in order to curry favor with Landis, Murphy and Paramount."

Jay was unflappable. In his characteristic levelheaded fashion, he tried to deflect my heat.

"What the hell good will that do, Pierce? It's not going to change things, and it's only going to make things worse for both you and me."

He was right. I switched tactics.

"I'd like to meet with your management committee to discuss this and to persuade them that Sid and you can serve as expert witnesses. In fact, I'm willing to make this deal: if the Court orders that the audits you have done for other clients on Eddie Murphy movies must be produced to Paramount, I will agree to withdraw you as expert witnesses."

"Well, that's perfectly reasonable. Your suggestion meets the stated concern."

Jay was willing to try this approach, which would give me what I desperately needed—Finger and Shapiro—and still protect Laventhol against potential exposure to former clients.

"I'll tell you what, Jay, I'll be back in Los Angeles on Friday. Talk to your regional head, try out this idea on him and set up an appointment for me to come in next week."

"I'll do what I can," Jay promised.

The next day, February 22, I met with Sid Finger. I wanted to hear Sid's own account of what had happened to him.

"I can't understand what's going on here," he said.

"Yeah, it's really terrible," I said tentatively. "I'm very disappointed in your former partners."

"So am I," said Finger.

One of Laventhol & Horwath's New York partners had paid him a visit. While he had not been forbidden to participate, Finger was told it would be inadvisable for him to do so. He was a retired partner with a pension and it was in the firm's interest not to be involved with *Buchwald v. Paramount.* Sid also told me that he questioned why an expert witness, who was not participating in the audit, would be a problem.

"I was simply told that the firm did not want me involved. Period," Sid said, shaking his head in disbelief.

I outlined my proposed compromise. Without this gentle giant of studio auditing at my side, my waning chances of a win sank below the horizon. Worse yet, a Laventhol withdrawal would have a chilling effect on other accountants. What if Hacker and Nives also quit, leaving me with only a hand-held calculator to audit 95,000 transactions?

"So, what do you say, Sid? Can I count on you?"

The old trooper's eyes sparkled, and he smiled.

"If they don't approve your more than reasonable compromise, I'll testify anyway," said Finger. "You have to stand up for what you believe in or you believe in nothing. I made a commitment to you. I'm going to honor it."

31

Take It
or Leave It

——— ——— ——— ——— ——— ——— ——— ——— ———

"HERE IS THE WRY and astute observer of the Washington scene who has created lately a few headlines himself. Please welcome Art Buchwald."

With that sparse introduction from George Kirgo, president of the Writers Guild of America West, Art bounced onto the stage of the Beverly Hilton Hotel ballroom on the evening of March 18, 1990. Dressed in his best tuxedo, he was given a hero's welcome by the attendees of the 42nd Annual Writers Guild West Awards Banquet.

"Before I begin I would like to announce that all the money raised this evening will be donated to the Lighthouse for the Blind for Paramount accountants," Art began.

Holding a thumb and forefinger together to form a big zero, Art announced, "I'm delighted to be here tonight to share with you the net profits of our victory."

He said that when he was first asked to come to Beverly Hills from his home in Washington to participate, he almost declined for fear of another earthquake. Just a few weeks earlier, Southern California had been rocked by a temblor that measured 5.5 on the Richter scale, he explained.

"I was about to cancel my trip . . . when I heard that Paramount was claiming it was only a 2.2," he said.

"I want to thank my coplaintiff Alain Bernheim, who had a lot more to lose in the suit than I did. Alain not only has to live in this town, but he has to drink the Perrier.

"I also want to thank our lawyers Pierce O'Donnell and Zazi Pope, who fought our good fight. We chose Pierce not because of his spectacular track record in court, but because he was the only one who would take our case for free."

I laughed nervously from my table off to the left of the stage. The last time Art told the world I was a free lawyer, our switchboard lit up with callers from other galaxies.

"I have learned many things from this experience. One is that executives of studios get hurt feelings—just like human beings. In court I heard a Paramount lawyer mutter, 'We're human like everyone else. We have wives and children and have to work for our living, and we believe in God.' If he hadn't mentioned the last thing, I might have given him the benefit of the doubt.

"The judge was fair and justice was served. That means we won. The problem now is that we are entitled to 19 percent of the profits. *Coming to America* has made $350 million but has not shown a profit. This is the part that blows everybody's mind."

The audience went nuts laughing. Art couldn't contain himself either, vigorously nodding his head in disbelief as he looked around the room.

"But I have good news for you tonight. The judge has ordered that tomorrow morning our accountants can look at Paramount's books. We call this part of the suit the Hunt for Red October.

"And November.

"And December.

"And January.

"For many years, many of you out there have taken percentages of net, so-called monkey points. And when there was no net, you were surprised and disappointed. I have good news for you. We're going to put an end to monkey points.

"We are going to make the studios treat your net percentage with the same respect that they treat Eddie Murphy's room service bills."

Then Art turned serious. His infectious smile gone, he looked out at the crowd and delivered what might be called "The Buchwald Manifesto."

"One thing the studios like to do when the heat is on is pay people off on the condition that they promise not to talk about the settlement. I promise you tonight neither Mr. Bernheim nor Mr. O'Donnell nor myself will accept any deal that will muzzle us. We want the world to know where the profits to *Coming to America* really are."

Then the smile returned. He flexed his bushy gray brows à la Groucho and said:

"People ask me if I'm bitter about this experience. I was until Paramount executives explained to me that Paramount is a nonprofit organization."

Art left the audience the way he has left his readers for almost half a century: laughing and thinking.

For fifty years the WGA has always presented the loudest and best-reasoned arguments of any of the entertainment unions in the ongoing struggle for a larger share of studio profits. But the Guild invariably caved in during its tri-annual contract talks with the Association of Motion Picture and Television Producers. Like the Screen Actors Guild and the Directors Guild, the writers walked a fine line and remained at the mercy of the entertainment conglomerates, which could make them very rich or leave them penniless.

The Writers Guild, whose elected leaders had failed to come to Art's aid during the trial, was not high on my list of favorite organizations in town. They really didn't want to get involved. We got strong backing from individual Guild members, like David Rintels, Lynn Roth and Danny Arnold, but the Guild itself turned its back on us. There was too much at stake, and the Guild did not want to alienate Paramount—one of the chief sources of income for its 8,000 members.

Privately, the Guild hierarchy, led by president George Kirgo and executive director Brian Walton, cheered on Buchwald and Bernheim.

Publicly, we were on our own.

It therefore came as a surprise when Walton agreed to a lunch meeting with Art, Alain, Zazi, David Rintels and me at the Beverly Wilshire Hotel on April 30, 1990. A few hours later, the Writers Guild Board would meet to act on my request that the Guild file a friend-of-the-court brief on our behalf. Several WGA leaders, including Rintels, had already agreed to request that the WGA urge Judge Schneider to condemn Paramount. Creative people had been applauding from the sidelines, but none of the guilds had officially endorsed our crusade. If the Writers Guild agreed to file the *amicus curiae* brief, we were confident that the actors and directors guilds would join. This would be an impressive show of support, and we needed every edge we could get.

Walton, a bright lawyer with a cheerful personality and keen survival instincts, had been outside counsel for the Guild. After a divisive strike in 1985, he took over as its executive director. In the ensuing five years, he consolidated his power base. While he was supposed to report to the Board, many knowledgeable insiders felt it was the other way around.

When we won round one in January, Walton had issued the equivalent of a "no comment" to the press. Then, in a March 26, 1990 article, Washington *Post* writer John Richardson quoted Walton as agreeing with Chuck Diamond.

"What 'net profit' really means in Hollywood is 'bonus,'" Walton told Richardson. Net was not profits in the ordinary sense.

Art was incensed.

"What the hell is he doing agreeing with the enemy?" Art yelled at me through the phone on the morning the article appeared. "He's supposed to be the writers' champion, not the studio's flack."

I hoped the lunch would lead to a rapprochement between Walton and Buchwald. But, within minutes of his arrival, Walton tried to impress everyone with how smart, busy and important he was. A perfunctory, "How are you?" sparked a five-minute monologue.

We learned about his many crises; the battles with the studios; his lack of staff; the continuing problems with the Directors Guild; and on and on and on.

Alain listened politely. Art said nothing. He wasn't buying Walton's act. Nor was I, but I wanted something from Walton. I shared the results of our investigation and legal theories with him.

"In a nutshell, Brian, it's not just Paramount's accounting. It's an industry-wide problem. All the contracts are the same: nonnegotiable, one-sided, oppressive. You have a better chance of being hit by lightning on a golf course than getting net profits out of these deals. It's a scam, and we need the Guild's public support. We'll never have a better shot at getting these dinosaurs declared illegal. Paramount was caught red-handed ripping off Art's story. We own the moral high ground. Now we need to win in court."

"What's your theory?" Brian asked.

"Paramount has a fiduciary duty to Art and Alain. And if not that, then at least a duty of utmost good faith and fair dealing that prohibits this kind of lopsided stewardship over the movie's finances. Those are the two that we'd like the Guild to advocate in its brief."

"Sounds reasonable," Brian responded. "I haven't looked at the case law lately. I imagine that the fiduciary claim will be a tough sell, but the studio's good faith obligation seems solid. I'm confident I can get the Board to endorse an *amicus curiae* brief in principle, subject, of course, to approving the brief itself before it's filed."

It appeared to be a done deal. Rintels, a former Guild president and current director who had clashed with Walton, had advised us that if Brian supported the idea it would be rubber-stamped by the Board. If Walton opposed, forget it.

"By the way, any developments on the settlement front?"

"Stonewalling," I said.

"You know, I have a pretty good relationship with the top people over there. If you would like, I think I could set up a high-level settlement meeting with Frank."

"Frank?" Art asked.

"Ah, yes, Frank Mancuso. The head of the studio."

"I know who he is," Art shot back.

"This is only if you'd like me to be an intermediary, but I think I could help," Walton continued. "Despite our antagonistic roles, I know they respect me. I could arrange that meeting. It might be helpful."

I thanked Walton and told him I'd get back to him. When Brian and David were gone, Zazi, Alain, Art and I conducted a post-mortem.

"Do you believe that guy's ego?" Art asked.

"He certainly has a high opinion of himself," Alain said tactfully.

"I should say," Zazi added. "How can he think that we'd trust him to help us when in the same breath he brags about his buddy-buddy relationship with Mancuso and offers to broker a settlement? What a hypocrite!"

"No wonder writers are second-class citizens," I said. "Walton acts like he'd rather be a studio exec than a champion for his union. With leaders like that, they'd be better off without a guild."

"Well, Pierce, I'll tell you one thing: Walton's worried about our suit hurting his relationship with Paramount," said Art. "He wants to be our intermediary with Paramount to further his own personal agenda, not help us. I wouldn't be surprised if he's promised Paramount he can deliver us. We don't need an intermediary. Diamond and Mancuso both have your phone number. I do not want him to represent me in any way at all."

"Nor me," echoed Alain.

"Mark my words," Art said. "Regardless of what happens this evening, that friend-of-the-court brief will never be filed. It will offend Paramount, and that is the last thing that Walton wants to happen."

That night the Guild Board overwhelmingly approved the brief in principle, but Art turned out to be right. We drafted the brief and submitted it to Walton in May. But, by June, Walton's Board and the Board of the Writers Guild East withdrew their support without ever reacting to our draft. No brief was ever filed.

Art then sent Walton a letter, recounting the discussion at the April 30 lunch in which Walton professed enthusiastic support for the friend-of-the-court brief.

> I wonder why, if it didn't fit the Guild's specifications, one or more of the [Guild's] seven lawyers couldn't have consulted with our lawyers before the second Guild Board meeting or drafted an amicus brief themselves. The answer is that the Writers Guild Board, after voting to support us with an amicus brief, decided not to give us one. As far as I'm concerned, it was a cowardly decision which has given aid and comfort to Paramount and brought shame on the Guild Board.

> Alain, Pierce and I will continue to fight our battle. We can no longer count on the Writers Guild to do what is right and honorable. But the rank and file of the Guild still support us and are as disgusted as I am with the Board for breaking its promise to us.

> The tragedy is that our original fight was only with Paramount. By your actions, you have fractured the membership of your Guild. You can't convince us that we were not sold out.

Once again, Art was right.

As word of the Board's double cross spread, the membership revolted. It took another six months, but on January 4, 1991, in a rebuke to Walton and his Board, forty-nine of the Guild's most prominent members—including Julius J. Epstein, Herb Gardner, Larry Gelbart, Hal Kanter, Elaine May, Jack Rose, Mel Shavelson, Neil Simon, Alvin Sargent, Norman Steinberg and Gore Vidal—signed a full-page ad in *Variety*, supporting Buchwald and Bernheim in their fight against Paramount Pictures.

It wasn't an amicus brief, but it was the next best thing.

. . . .

Judge Schneider had granted us only the spring to finish auditing Paramount's books, to complete discovery and to prepare our witnesses. He wanted us back in court no later than the second week in July. For a case that was shaping up as a frontal assault on the way Hollywood had done business for half a century, it wasn't a lot of time.

The audit would be the cornerstone of our attack. I needed to know precisely how money had been spent and whether all income had been reported before I could challenge Paramount's accounting. I told Hacker about the Laventhol incident and said that if he wanted out I would release him. I didn't want him if he wasn't 100 percent committed.

"I don't scare easy," was Phil's one-sentence response.

But Paramount tried.

He and his colleague Barbara Bebe were not allowed to photocopy documents, had to work in a cramped, windowless room in the Clara Bow Building on the lot, were forbidden to ask Paramount employees routine questions, and were not allowed to inspect records in chronological sequence. Instead, they were given a mishmash of boxes of receipts, canceled checks, financial statements, expense reports, computer printouts and microfiche.

A mild-mannered man not easily angered, even Hacker couldn't contain himself.

"I've never seen this before," Phil told me after one of many frustrating days. "Paramount's going out of its way to make our job unpleasant. I've never been treated so badly. It's deliberate harassment."

When Bebe arrived one morning, she was insulted by the guard at the front gate, reduced to tears and barred from the lot. I threatened to go to Judge Schneider, and Diamond apologized, claiming that the guard must have been acting on his own.

At another point, Phil and Barbara couldn't even buy their lunch in the Paramount commissary. Diamond's young associate, Bobby Schwartz, said our accountants would not be permitted to buy even a cup of coffee at the commissary while they were on the lot. Barbara asked to leave the 10-by-12-foot cubicle where she and Hacker conducted their records review to bring a doughnut back from the cafeteria. Schwartz denied permission.

Zazi wrote an angry letter to Diamond, reciting Schwartz's concern "that our accountants might improperly discuss this case with other individuals and for this reason has decided that as long as our accountants are on the lot, they must be confined to the small office Paramount has provided for the document review,"

Buchwald phoned later in the day to assure Zazi and Phil that he would personally have pizza delivered during the coming weeks. I made the most of this latest public relations gaffe by reassuring several reporters that the audit would continue, uninterrupted.

"That is, provided my people don't starve to death," I said.

Diamond quickly rescinded the commissary ban, but the damage had been done. The studio looked like it had something to hide.

What it couldn't hide was the profit-draining items in its net profit statement.

One that sent me up the wall was a charge of $1.7 million for a payment to Eddie Murphy. It wasn't his salary for the movie—that was a separate $8 million. It wasn't a gross participation payment—that was another $10 million. It wasn't a breakfast charge either.

It was a "bonus."

Paramount paid Eddie Murphy a $6.8 million signing bonus when Murphy renegotiated his contract in 1987 and agreed to make five more pictures for the studio. If Paramount had paid the bonus out of its own coffers, we would have had no gripe. But the studio didn't do that. Paramount's front office regarded the bonus as an "advance" and simply tacked it onto the production budgets of the next four Murphy movies, including Coming to America. What that meant was that the already bloated budget for the comedy had been inflated another $1.7 million, making the possibility of Art and Alain ever getting any net profit out of the movie even more remote.

When I screamed about the additional charge, Paramount's bland reply was that people with clout, like an Eddie Murphy, could get away with such demands. They were stars. If it affected the break-even point for Coming to America, that was just tough luck.

With such arbitrary star charges tacked onto the expense side of the movie, the best-case scenario for Coming to America ever moving into the black meant that the movie would have to earn well over $100 million more than it had already earned! In other words, Coming to America—which had already exhausted its worldwide box office potential—would have to earn as much or more than one of the top five grossing motion pictures of all time just to get out of the red. Every questionable expense, including Eddie's signing bonus, only put my clients further behind the eight ball.

I railed against the bonus. I railed against the expense of Murphy's entourage. I railed against Murphy's $1 million expense account. I made the most of the "Big Mac attack" which had become such a cause célèbre that the $235.35 breakfast at McDonald's had been translated into 143 pounds sterling by the British press. One business magazine in the U.K. took to referring to Murphy as "the hideously well-compensated star."

But the contracts with their standard net profits definition were beginning to wear me down. After four months of poring over Paramount financial records, reading the net profit clause until my eyes were sore, and talking to dozens of accountants, talent managers, agents and entertainment lawyers, I had finally come to fully appreciate that the word "profits" really didn't mean the same thing in Hollywood as it did in the real world. There were oodles of different kinds of Hollywood "profits"—gross profits; adjusted gross profits; profits with rolling break-even points and profits with modified rolling break-even points; net profits after recoupment of negative; net after distribution and advertising . . . etc., etc., etc., ad net nauseam.

But the kind of profits my clients were saddled with were "standard net profits" and the bottom line was really bottom of the barrel. It was no exaggeration to say that a security guard at Paramount studios would see *Coming to America* profits before Art and Alain ever did.

To make matters worse, Paramount, confident of a quick kill, turned up the heat in the media. When reporters asked why I would have taken it this far if I didn't think I could win, Chuck Diamond didn't hesitate to offer his own theory.

"I just think that he bet wrong," Diamond said. "I think he bet that Paramount Pictures didn't have the stomach for this fight and it would give him his $5 million to go away. So he's probably wound up in a position where he's way, way in the hole and figures if he keeps making noise that sooner or later Paramount will say, 'Okay, here's X number of dollars. Now shut up and leave us alone.' That's my guess."

But my strategy had backfired, according to Diamond. Instead of badgering Paramount's brass into throwing us a $5 million bone, the shots I had taken at the studio had really hit home. Paramount had to save face.

"The problem is the accusations that he has hurled really go to the core of the studio," Diamond said. "He's got a tiger by the tail. The people who run the studio view themselves, and rightfully so, as honest, straightforward straight shooters. The studio's life blood depends upon having solid foundations in its relationships with the people who write movies and the people who perform in movies and the people who direct movies. You simply cannot turn the cheek when somebody calls you a thief.

"So, he's made this bed. He's going to have to sleep in it. Because we're going to trial."

There was truth in Diamond's pronouncement, and it stung. I had wildly overestimated profits. I had hoped for a quick knockout, followed by a fat, out-of-court settlement. And I had used my ability to shoot from the lip in order to fight the case in the court of public opinion as well as in the courtroom.

I took some moral solace in the knowledge that things had not gone well for Paramount or Murphy since the audit had begun. Murphy's new film, *Harlem Nights*, was raked over the coals by the critics when it was released in the fall. Since then, it had earned a scant $58 million at the box office. By anyone else's standards, that might have been a resounding success. By Eddie Murphy standards, however, it was a bomb—his first ever. Was the magic wearing off? I wondered.

That *Harlem Nights* was the consummate Eddie Murphy movie (he had conceived, written, directed, produced and starred) made the blow even harder to take. Two different East Coast writers came out of the woodwork and sued him for allegedly stealing their stories as the basis for *Harlem Nights*, and Murphy grew even more bitter.

In my estimation, the script seemed 100 percent Eddie Murphy. The 112 pages contained more "bitches," "shittin's," "cocksuckers" and "mother fuckers" than any screenplay I'd ever read in my life. The plot revolved around a group of Harlem gangsters in the 1930s making off with a white gangster's money. The final stage direction —and last line in the script—was a dead giveaway that it *had* to have been written by Eddie Murphy:

"They exchange smiles, get in the car, and head down the highway as we roll credits and go to the mother fuckin' bank."

In real life, Murphy's overriding concern did seem to be visiting his bank often and with ever increasing mounds of cash. A scathing interview that he granted *Playboy* magazine for their February 1990 issue was even more vitriolic about not getting enough money from Paramount than the *Rolling Stone* interview Murphy had given the previous summer. If he cared about the stories his movies told or any obligation that he might feel to entertain and uplift his millions of adoring fans, it certainly wasn't reflected in his interviews.

In fact, Murphy and Paramount seemed made for each other in the spring of 1990. Both were rolling in dough but artistically impoverished. After selling its financial services subsidiary, The Associates, to the Ford Motor Company the previous summer, Paramount had over $3 billion in the bank. But when the Academy of Motion Pictures Arts and Sciences announced Oscar nominations, Paramount got only an embarrassing eight—less than any other leading studio. *Harlem Nights* was nominated for Deborah Nadoolman's costume design, but ultimately lost on Oscar night, along with every other Paramount nominee except the sound effects editors on *Indiana Jones and the Last Crusade*.

Just one week before the Oscars, Eddie's *Harlem Nights* ordeal continued during the 42nd Annual Writers Guild Awards at which Art had made his triumphant speech. The entertainment portion of the dinner featured a parody of the trailer for the hit movie *Field of Dreams*. In it, an Eddie Murphy look-alike kept hearing voices telling him "If you write it, they will come," "If you star in it, they will come" and "If you direct it, they will come." They didn't come, of course, and the tuxedoed writers had a good laugh at the expense of an egocentric star who thought—incorrectly—that he could do everything except the makeup on a major motion picture and, somehow, make it good cinema.

In mid-March, comedian Billy Crystal hosted the annual Oscar show, seen by an estimated one billion television viewers around the globe. With the first words out of his mouth, Crystal demonstrated just how hurtful *Buchwald v. Paramount* had become to the studio. Billy turned to the audience following an opening montage that featured clips from 330 famous motion pictures and said that Paramount Pictures maintained that "not one has yet gone into profit." Before the show was over, our case had been mentioned three times.

The year 1990 was already proving to be a disastrous one for the studio. *The Hunt for Red October* was a big hit (one of the profit participants called me after the movie opened strong the first weekend). But Paramount's big summer and Christmas blockbusters were in trouble. *Days of Thunder*—a Tom Cruise race car movie green-lighted by Ned Tanen while he was still president of the studio and produced by the same team (Don Simpson and Jerry Bruckheimer) who created *Beverly Hills Cop*—was way over budget in Florida.

To make things worse, an unnamed screenwriter was challenging Paramount and screenwriter Robert Towne over Towne's sole screenwriting credit for *Days of Thunder*. In a case that sounded eerily similar to Buchwald's, the writer filed a grievance with the Writers Guild against Paramount, and an arbitration had been scheduled. As with *Coming to America*, the story credit for *Days of Thunder* was eventually awarded to the film's star. Tom Cruise had come up with the story that Towne's script was based upon, according to the studio.

Two Jakes, the long-awaited sequel to *Chinatown*, was another Paramount headache. The studio kept postponing its release date because Jack Nicholson could never get the script, also by Robert Towne, revised to the point where the story worked dramatically.

And negative reports were already filtering back from Rome where Francis Ford Coppola was wrapping up principal photography on Frank Mancuso's personal favorite for a 1990 box office bonanza, *The Godfather III*. The truth was Coppola had a thin story line, no idea how to end it, some terrible casting choices—including his own daughter, Sophia, in a pivotal role—and a runaway production budget that threatened to make the movie one of the costliest ever produced on the planet.

In Los Angeles, Eddie Murphy was reteamed with Nick Nolte for location shooting in *Another 48 HRS*. Murphy turned twenty-nine during production and Frank Mancuso helped throw a surprise birthday party for him on the set. All the good will from Paramount hadn't altered his harsh words about the way he felt he had been exploited by the studio, though. All he wanted to do was finish the picture and get home to New Jersey to spend time with his new daughter, Bria.

Advance word from the set was that *Another 48 HRS*. was *not* another *48 HRS*. It wasn't even *24*. Gone were the Murphy ad libs and the Murphy quips. All that remained was a production budget of about $45 million and the Murphy attitude: he was surly and that's how he came across in the screening room. The buzz on and off the Paramount lot was that the movie would be lucky if it made enough at the box office to cover costs when it was released in early June.

Something odd had happened in the three months that had passed since the trial. I couldn't put my finger on it, but *Buchwald v. Paramount* began to take on aspects of a holy war. The whole was bigger than the sum of the parts. More than money was at stake.

Buchwald v. Paramount represented a cause that every producer and member of the WGA, DGA and SAG felt to be just, but which only the bravest among them would speak about publicly.

This, then, was the real reason that neither Paramount nor my clients could settle out of court. A showdown was inevitable. By early April, I had recruited my experts and learned how the net profit system had originated, evolved and systematically ripped off creative talent for a half century. I still didn't have a legal strategy, but we were getting closer.

My threats had worked with Laventhol & Horwath. Within two weeks of my phone conversation with Jay, the firm changed its mind. I agreed to release Shapiro and Finger as experts if Judge Schneider ever ordered the firm to turn over prior client audits of Paramount films. Hacker and Nives were also available to testify if need be.

Roger Davis, Alain's agent, also agreed to testify. A principled, decent man who spent hours teaching me how the motion picture industry worked, Davis had been the man who negotiated Bernheim's contract back in 1983. Chairman of the executive committee of the William Morris Agency, Roger is a highly respected show business figure who deals at the level of a Lew Wasserman, Frank Mancuso or Michael Eisner. Few people in the industry have his insider's knowledge of how the studios impose net profit deals on all but a few in Hollywood.

But getting top producers or former studio executives to testify was a problem. Many we approached told us they supported our cause but balked when we asked them to testify. Even the heaviest hitters in town were following the Writers Guild's fainthearted example. Privately, they rooted for us. Publicly, they took no stand that might have helped snowball support.

But then we found Max Youngstein and Rudy Petersdorf and gained access to the inner workings of The Club.

Youngstein is bald, wears glasses and sports a goatee and mustache—a colorful, loquacious, bigger-than-life character. Well into his 70s, he has been everything: writer, producer, actor, studio executive, coffee maker, lawyer, salesman, chauffeur, creative consultant and accountant. In a career that has spanned over fifty years, he has been involved in over 500 profit participation deals. Max knows the real Hollywood—the dark side that I wanted the judge to understand was not the idealized "free marketplace" about which Paramount rhapsodized.

A few years before *Buchwald*, Max had consulted with me in a movie tax fraud case. He was an expert on film distribution, particularly "four-walling": the practice of renting a theater for a flat sum and keeping all the box office receipts.

"I'll give you a declaration, but you aren't gonna find many people who will," Youngstein told me. "I got nothing to lose with these bastards. Everybody else who ever wants to make a movie with 'em does, though." He then evoked a legendary name from Hollywood's past.

"Adolf Zukor was five foot tall, loved the good life and surrounded himself with goons," said Max Youngstein, describing the founder of Paramount Pictures in a single sentence.

As Paramount's vice-president for distribution in 1949 and 1950, Youngstein came to know Zukor first hand. Zukor was a bitter man right after the 1948 Paramount consent decree, in which the studio was ordered by the

Supreme Court to sell off Zukor's beloved chain of movie palaces. Max listened to him rail against the government and the Court, predicting ruin for the industry he helped to found now that he and other moguls could only produce and distribute but no longer exhibit motion pictures.

Zukor spoke to Max fondly, almost wistfully, about the golden era of the twenties and thirties. It wasn't golden because of the fine films produced back then, Zukor told him. It was golden because of the firm stranglehold he and a handful of other studio chieftains had on the movies and the public who went to see them.

Zukor loved to tell and retell stories of his "boys" moving into a new town, sizing up the theatrical competition and then building one of his palatial Paramount theaters right across the street for the express purpose of putting the first theater out of business. Sometimes, if patrons persisted in going to the wrong theater, his "boys" would persuade them, gently and otherwise, to buy a ticket to a Paramount picture instead. If, after a few months, the rival theater owner didn't shut down, he might have an accident or his theater might suddenly self-immolate, said Youngstein.

The 1948 consent decree ended all of that and turned the industry upside down.

"In 99 percent of the cases, the creative people who worked for the studios prior to 1951 were employees," he said. "It didn't matter whether they were Clark Gable or some lesser actor or writer or director. They had nothing to say about how the picture was marketed or distributed and there would be constant control of studio employees on every phase of the picture making.

"They were under a seven-year, multiple-picture contract. Nobody received any participation in profits or gross participation."

In the 1950s, the weakened studios found that they had to make more and more compromises to get first-rate talent for their movies. Before the decade was over, all of them followed the lead of the company Youngstein joined after he left Paramount in 1951.

United Artists was founded in 1919 by Mary Pickford, Douglas Fairbanks, D. W. Griffith and Charlie Chaplin in order to cut out the studios' distribution fee and still get their films to the theaters. Even then, the four biggest names of the silent era were convinced that the studios were stealing from them.

By the 1950s, when all four of the original founders had retired or sold their shares in the company, United Artists was still leery of the studios. In fact, United Artists did not regard itself as a studio per se. It didn't own a back lot, and it seldom bought costumes when rentals would do the job. Under Youngstein and his two partners, Arthur Krim and Robert Benjamin, United Artists pioneered profit participation in the early 1950s as a way of luring talent away from other studios. Then they would shoot their films on location or on rented sound stages, cutting their own overhead and passing on part of that savings to the stars they hired. The traditional seven-year studio contract began to disappear.

"We were taking away some of their best creative talent by offering them a better deal," Youngstein said. "Slowly but surely, the other studios began to offer participation in addition to salaries."

Participation contracts went to actors with a proven box office draw, writers with a few Academy Awards, an author with a bestseller or one of the "better" filmmakers.

"By 'better,' I don't mean necessarily creatively, but those who turned out big commercial smashes, or with some consistency," said Youngstein. "Pretty soon, though, the studios started to exercise control. They put in provisions that gave them the ultimate say-so in the way the picture was made."

They also put in provisions that made the studio rich at the expense of the creative person who naively signed on as a profit participant, he said.

"A guy sits down and spends a year writing a screenplay. It has a value. The producer spends weeks—years at times—in finding that screenplay or helping develop it. . . . He sweats out every phase of the daily shooting which may take, between the start of preproduction and the finish of postproduction . . . at least a year. He may be devoting out of his life somewhere between three and four years to a project. That is a risk which can be quantified. A salary and a worth can be placed on that. He is taking a risk that his distribution company knows what the hell it is doing, that it will be honest with him, and that's a big 'if,' " said Youngstein.

Max's assessment was at once fascinating and appalling. After his years at United Artists, he went on to executive positions at Cinerama, Todd-AO, Taft International and the Taylor-Laughlin Company, which independently distributed the "Billy Jack" movies of the early 1970s.

Max had been through the very onset of Hollywood's antitrust violations and watched net profit participation deteriorate from a promise of economic equity to the obvious and well-publicized scam it had become by 1990.

He was ready to talk about it on the record.

"Studios are like a secret club. Their whole raison d'être is to perpetuate the privileged, luxurious lifestyle of a select few white males," said Rudy Petersdorf.

Alain Bernheim had turned me on to Rudy, a lawyer and former Universal Pictures business affairs executive. Alain knew him from the days when Alain represented writers and directors, and Rudy handled the negotiations for his studio. Alain had always been impressed by the fairness and wisdom of this quiet, unassuming gentleman.

I called Rudy at his home in Ojai, California, a serene town above Santa Barbara about a hundred miles from Los Angeles at the base of the Santa Susanna Mountains. Would he be willing to consult on *Buchwald?*

"You bet I would, Mr. O'Donnell. I've been reading about the case in the trades. I like what you are trying to do: to inject some fairness into net profit accounting. I think I can help you."

Zazi and I spent dozens of hours with Rudy in March and April, picking his brain. He was as bald as Harvey Schneider but allowed himself to smile more, now that he was no longer part of the suit-and-tie world of MCA.

"They don't care about the stockholders," said Rudy. "They don't care about the talent. And they don't care about the quality of the movies. They want to perpetuate their power and huge incomes. So when a studio head falls from grace, he never falls far from the trough. He gets an independent production deal or gets hired by another studio. He is still a member of The Club.

"And the standard form contracts are the protection for The Club. They perpetuate a caste system. The talent can only move from one lower caste to a slightly higher caste. A select few get to be gross players, but they are still only talent. They never get into The Club.

"As soon as their box office draw diminishes, they descend back down the caste ladder."

Elliott Gould and Christopher Reeve—even Stallone—were all examples of stars who fell from studio grace. On the female side, whatever happened to Jill Clayburgh or Jennifer Beals?

But The Club was different. The public was unfamiliar with most of their names. They lunched at Morton's and dined in each other's atriums. Their talent was in making money and deals, not movies. David Puttnam, briefly the head of Columbia Pictures, had been a probationary member of The Club, but he failed to measure up and was expelled. Ex-studio chief David Begelman, on the other hand, was never thrown out, even though he was a convicted felon. Paramount's own Robert Evans, convicted of cocaine possession, was another member who still had friends in The Club who took care of him despite his fall from grace.

Rudy said the infamous "rolling break-even point" got its start at Universal in the 1970s while he was still working there. By feeding gross participation payments back into the negative costs of a film, the point at which a picture breaks even and supposedly begins generating net profits is always rolled back. The result was that a film with enough gross participation, like *Coming to America*, would simply never achieve net profits.

Petersdorf said one more thing: whenever one studio makes a change in the contract to disadvantage net profit participants, the other studios always follow suit.

From the flickers of Adolph Zukor to the big-budget extravaganzas of Frank Mancuso, Paramount led the way—vesting real moviemaking power in the hands of a few executives who let others perform the hard work of spinning a screen story while they sat back and reaped the profits. Paramount was right on one count: it *was* a case about money. But they were dead wrong in believing that was all it was about.

It wasn't even about right or wrong, black or white. *Buchwald v. Paramount* was about different world views. I saw Paramount as using their take-it-or-leave-it contracts to cheat talent out of their fair share of profits. Paramount saw itself as a corporation engaged in a risky business in which they put up all the money and took all the risks while writers and their agents cruised the town in their Mercedeses, smoking cigars and generally reveling in the Good Life.

In late March, Paramount released its own "audit" of *Coming to America*. Not surprisingly, the studio's lawyers claimed that, when computed according to the formula in Bernheim's and Buchwald's contracts, the deficit was in fact $18 million as of the end of 1989. After checking virtually every one of the 5,000 expense items, Paramount's accountants did find one instance of an item that should not have been charged to *Coming to America*, said Diamond. A $10,000 expense should have been charged to a different movie, they discovered, and it was reversed.

"On the grand scheme of things, that seems like a drop in the bucket. A molecule in the bucket," said Diamond.

Diamond also did some finessing on the issue of videocassette sales that made it sound as though Paramount was doing everyone a big favor by granting them a 20 percent "royalty" on the gross sales of videocassettes without charging profit participants a dime to manufacture and sell them. In truth, the studios had enjoyed an ever increasing bonanza from home video since the widespread advent of the VCR in the early 1980s. Each year, home video became more and more important—billions of dollars and most of it was not shared with net profit participants.

Incredibly, the studios usually kept 80 percent of the video gross. I conjured up a vision of a minimum-wage employee, sitting in front of a high-speed tape duplicating machine and cranking out a couple hundred videocassettes a day. Some manufacturing expense. For that, Paramount and its retailers kept the lion's share of every dollar consumers spent on the home video version of *Coming to America*.

In 1990, home video often produced more revenue than the box office. But the old 80/20 formula the studios had put into their profit participation contracts ten years earlier, when home video was negligible, still prevailed. Even profit participants with clout like Eddie Murphy could not get a higher royalty on videocassette sales than 20 percent.

It was the videocassette royalties on *Coming to America* that had "grossed up" the original bottom line figure for the movie's gross revenues that Draper had given us the previous November. Diamond explained that gross receipts for *Coming to America* were $125 million, not the $151-million figure Draper had given me. The additional $26 million represented the amount that the studio expected from home video sales but had not yet received. At least for the accounting period ending December 1989, video was not included in actual gross receipts, he said.

That further reduced the possibility of Art and Alain getting any of the net.

At the same time he announced Paramount's own audit results, Diamond reaffirmed that there would be no settlement. Not only did the studio plan to go to trial on Phase II, it would also campaign to dispel my "disinformation" leaks to the media. "We've bent over backward not only to follow the contract, but to do this very carefully and correctly," he said.

I countered with the first public hint that I was going to go for the jugular and not toy around with Big Macs.

"The net profit system in Hollywood," I told Dave Robb of *Variety*, "is fundamentally unfair. We will demonstrate that motion picture accounting is illegal."

During the second phase, I planned to introduce profit statements from another hit Paramount movie, *Fatal Attraction*, to show how the studio systematically drained its biggest hits of all money before any of its profit participants got anything. In an interview with Sam Donaldson for "Prime Time Live," I called it *Fatal Subtraction*.

A studio profit statement for the runaway hit movie, released in September 1987, showed that a little over two years later it had grossed $166 million for the studio. But, unless you had the clout of a Michael Douglas ($8.9 million in profit participation) or producers Stanley Jaffe and Sherry Lansing ($20.1 million) or director Adrian Lyne ($5.5 million), your profit statement would still show a net deficit of $100,000.

Such was the case with Laurence Myers, the British writer and filmmaker whose original short film, *Diversion*, produced in England, was the basis for *Fatal Attraction*. Even without Eddie Murphy sucking the cash out of the coffers, *Fatal Attraction* was a "loser" to anyone strapped with Paramount's standard net profit definition.

But Paramount wasn't the only studio that had a history of inflating expenses. A participation statement I'd obtained for MGM/UA's big 1988 hit, *Rain Man*, showed gross receipts totaling $189 million as of November 1989, but for net profit participants the movie remained $24.3 million in the hole.

Over at Warner Bros., Roman Polanski's *Frantic*, starring Harrison Ford, remained $28.4 million in the red six months after its February 1988 release, despite the fact that it had already taken in more than $26 million in gross receipts.

And so on.

Movies dating all the way back to the beginning of the 1980s had raked in millions for the studios and those select few who could demand that their contracts be rewritten, but nothing for the majority who were forced to accept "monkey points." All the studios did it. All the studios got away with it. And it was ruining Hollywood.

In an interview with the Los Angeles *Times*'s Robert Scheer in the April 1990 issue of *Premiere* magazine, Sean Connery minced few words about Hollywood greed killing the goose that laid the golden egg.

"You should look at the case of Paramount and Art Buchwald because what it's going to reveal, really, is where the industry has taken itself," he said. "Buchwald is going to have to find a battalion of auditors to be able to go back over [*Coming to America*]. . . .

"There have been changes before. For example, there were producers and now there are director-producers, because they want the control. There are actors who want more money than a picture can carry. All it does is make the budgets bigger. I think that here one of the problems is also that the executives who are involved in the making of pictures are farther and farther removed from the reality of producing films. Therefore they have to rely on information that is gathered or presented to them so that going in they know they have to have this amount above the line, this amount below the line, and now they say you cannot make a movie for less than $20 million. Well, there's something wrong."

I began to feel like a moviemaker myself, trying to pull together the elements of *Buchwald v. Paramount*. Here are the stars in Buchwald and Bernheim; here's the producer in Kaye, Scholer; here's the director in Pierce O'Donnell . . .

But my accountants were supposed to be my writers and they told me that they couldn't write the script. So I didn't have a star witness who could come out on the witness stand in a green eyeshade and testify that he juggled the books for twenty years.

That was because there was never any need to juggle the books. The problem was, as Hacker had said so often, in the contract.

"They never negotiate these things," Sid Finger told me during one of my trips to New York to work with him. "It's take it or leave it. Contracts are all the same, all the time."

A little light went on in the back of my head. They're all the same. Based on everything I'd learned, my only chance really was a frontal assault on the industry itself.

Such an idea sounded like a kamikaze attack.

But it was an industry-wide problem, not just unique to Paramount. It involved every studio. And there seemed to be no solution. I couldn't sue every major studio in Hollywood.

Or could I?

32

The Indictment

"SIZE IS ITSELF an earmark of monopoly power," the Supreme Court wrote in *United States v. Paramount Pictures, Inc.*, the 1948 landmark decision that found Paramount and five other studios had monopolized the distribution and exhibition of films in violation of federal antitrust laws. "For size carries with it an opportunity for abuse. And . . . the power created by size was utilized in the past to crush or prevent competition. . . ."

For years, Paramount and the other studios had engaged in a massive conspiracy by fixing prices of theater tickets, block booking (conditioning a theater's right to exhibit a picture upon taking other pictures) and discriminating against small independents in favor of large theater chains. Lamenting "the concentration of economic power in the industry" in a few hands and "their strategic hold on the industry," the Supreme Court condemned the studios for their "marked proclivity for unlawful conduct," "the discriminatory practices and predatory activities in which the defendants have engaged" and their "bald efforts to substitute monopoly for competition." The Supreme Court was particularly struck by "the genius [needed] to conceive the present conspiracy and to execute it with the subtlety which this record reveals. . . ."

By May 1990, I was convinced that what had happened to Alain and Art was not isolated or accidental. They were two of thousands of net profit participants who had been systematically cheated out of their fair share of a bonus for their contributions to the financial success of hundreds of movies.

It was not, as I had originally surmised, an invisible hand that picked their pockets clean. Seven hands were involved—and they were only too visible.

In the forty-two years that had elapsed since *United States v. Paramount*, little had changed to curb the studios' awesome power. Everywhere I turned, I was struck by the conspicuous lack of competition. If anything, the studios' collective "strategic hold on the industry" and "marked proclivity for wrongful conduct" was even greater today.

Controlling over 90 percent of the distribution income, the seven major studios—Paramount, Warner Bros., Universal, Twentieth Century Fox, Disney, Columbia/Tri-Star and MGM/UA—totally dominated the domestic movie market. It was a monopoly that economists called an "oligopoly" because it was maintained by several companies instead of only one. But the effect was the same: near total domination of the development, production and distribution of films.

In the United States of 1990, the studios produced one third of the films exhibited but distributed nearly all of the rest, made by independent production companies such as Carolco (*Rambo* and *Terminator I* and *II*). These so-called "independents" were independent in name only. In truth, their financial fate was dependent on getting a major studio to agree to distribute. Their chances of getting a film made without a distribution agreement with one of the seven majors were slim, bordering on nil. No one would invest or lend money unless a firm distribution commitment was in place and, with few exceptions, the major studios were the only game in town.

For an Alain Bernheim, backing from a major was an absolute necessity. Without it, he could not option properties, attract a star or hire a top director. And without one or more of those elements, he was a producer with nothing to produce. For the Bernheims of the New Hollywood, the studios were not only the only game in town—they also made the rules by which the game was played. So, when the studio told Alain that all he got was a standard net profit deal and that all gross participations would be added to the negative cost of the picture and that 80 percent of the video receipts would be kept by the studio—and whatever else the studio said would be part of the deal, he said, "Where do I sign?"

In reality, it was worse than "take it or leave it." There was nowhere else to go for a better deal. When Bernheim set up *King for a Day* at Warner Bros., the net profit definition was the same one he had at Paramount—and would have been the same at the other five studios.

Dennis Landry had collected dozens of standard form net profit contracts that the seven major studios had used over the past twenty years. He looked for identical language in each contract to see just how much one studio tracked another in drafting its agreements. Landry came up with thirty-five passages that were virtually identical in every contract. His comparative chart showed that Paramount's concept of gross and net, distribution fees and overhead were precisely the same in the business affairs departments at Universal,

Columbia/Tri-Star, MGM/UA, Warner Bros., Disney and Twentieth Century Fox—right down to the percentage point.

Our four-month investigation had uncovered a shocking lack of competition and remarkable similarity in business practices among the studios that comprised the "Holligopoly":

- They conducted their financial affairs in a distinctively similar way.
- Their executives moved freely from one studio to another.
- They had one trade association, the Motion Picture Association of America, that rated all movies and lobbied Congress, the White House and the Federal Trade Commission on matters of common concern to the studios.
- They collectively bargained as one unit with the guilds.
- They had essentially the same financial terms for splitting the box office take with theaters.
- They had historically refused to bargain with the guilds over the terms of the standard net profit definition.
- They refused to negotiate the economic terms of the standard net profit contract with all but a minuscule number of writers, directors, producers and actors—the Brahmins of Hollywood's caste system.
- And, most important of all, they used virtually identical standardized, non-negotiable net profit contracts.

Looking at this indisputable evidence, I asked myself whether this uncanny similarity and anticompetitive market was the result of coincidence or conspiracy. Thanks to my populist tendencies and a healthy distrust of powerful institutions, I opted for the sinister explanation. To accept sheer coincidence as the rationale was like believing in the Tooth Fairy.

These were hardly victimless "crimes." In addition to the diversion of millions—perhaps billions—into the studios' pockets and away from the profit participants, the studios also cheated the public. With this massive concentration of power came higher ticket prices, the stifling of creativity, fewer quality films each year, a narrowing of the opportunities for new filmmakers (particularly women and minorities), and mindless similarity in the films that were made. How else could you explain only one Spike Lee and the squandering of $100 million on the production and distribution of a movie like *Days of Thunder*?

Independent production companies had learned how to live in the shadow of these 800-pound gorillas. They wanted to keep working in this town. So they paid the standardized distribution fees, expenses, overhead, interest and other studio charges just to reap their small slice of the pie.

Members of the Hollywood creative community, unwilling to risk career suicide, meekly did the same. The courts rarely listened to their complaints. When a major star like Paul Newman and a prominent director like George Roy Hill had the guts to file a federal antitrust suit in 1985 alleging price fixing because the studios refused to pay more than their standard 20 percent royalty on video receipts, their case was thrown out on a technicality.

Even the guilds and the unions, usually so effective for their membership in other industries, could make little headway against the studios. That was hardly surprising: after all, too many of their leaders seemed more interested in making friends with influential studio executives than in launching a full-scale assault on business practices that appeared to be robbing their members blind.

Abdicating their responsibility to promote competition and bust monopolies, politicians looked the other way. Since the *Paramount* case, the Justice Department—particularly in the Reagan-Bush era—had fallen into a deep sleep. By 1990, motion picture studios once again owned large and increasing numbers of theaters—backsliding influenced by the benign neglect of a succession of Presidents—Republicans and Democrats alike—who courted studio brass and their stars for political support. Congress was likewise asleep at the switch as monopoly concentration in the motion picture industry intensified after World War II.

No one seemed to be willing to stand up to the studios.

From its beginnings, Hollywood had been a cruel cartel whose edicts were enforced by intimidation. Studios represented a self-perpetuating fiefdom, passing on power, glory and money from generation to generation. While Paramount's founder, Adolf Zukor, used brute physical force to get his way, his successors used brute economic force to exploit the men and women who really made the movies. David McClintick, whose *Indecent Exposure* in 1982 first brought to light the unscrupulous power elite that lorded over the motion picture industry, concluded that "Hollywood is rife with the corruption of power and arrogance. It is the corruption that inevitably pervades a large and glamorous institution when that institution is tightly controlled by a handful of people, and thousands upon thousands are clamoring for entry."

I thought about accusing Paramount and the other studios of price fixing. We had enough evidence to file a complaint. If we won an antitrust case, damages were trebled, and our attorneys' fees would be paid by the defendants.

Antitrust was tempting but impractical. Kaye, Scholer might be one of the preeminent antitrust firms in the country, but we would need the resources of the Justice Department to bust up the motion picture cabal. Even the federal government had only partially succeeded in its own celebrated efforts, dating all the way back to the 1920s. Besides, I had filed a simple breach-of-contract case, and its cost was already spiraling out of control.

How, then, could I use this powerful evidence of a noncompetitive market to knock out the grossly lopsided standard net profit definition? Any fair-minded person would have to admit that it was unconscionable for Paramount to get all the profits from such a hit movie.

Unconscionable.

That was it: contracts class, first year of law school. The Doctrine of Unconscionability:

Under certain circumstances, contract terms that are offered on a nonnegotiable basis and are extremely unreasonable or harsh in their application can be denied enforcement. Zazi and I headed for the law library.

"You know what it's like? It's like one of those Harlem slum contracts thirty years ago, Pierce," said Zazi, plopping down on the couch in my office, next to Suzanne Tragert, who had been conscripted from another case to help with library research on our unconscionability theory.

Phil Hacker's team had been closeted for two months in the claustrophobic office at Paramount where they went over the last of the 95,000 line items on the *Coming to America* books. Zazi looked exhausted and emaciated. I asked her if the pizza Art had been sending in to the Fortress on Melrose had been getting by the studio guard.

"Very funny," she said.

"I know what you mean about the contract," said Suzanne. "It's like Art and Alain are the tenants and Paramount's the landlord. If our clients want a movie on the screen, they have to sign Paramount's contract. It doesn't matter what's *in* the contract. They've just got to sign it, period. That's . . ."

"Unconscionable," I said.

In the "Job Opportunities" classifieds of *Variety*, Paramount Pictures Corporation had a help wanted ad for managers of the studio's accounting department. The people they were looking for, according to the ad, would "oversee a staff of financial analysts with responsibility for timely payments and accuracy of profit participation statements."

"I don't believe it. Let me see that," said Suzanne, grabbing the paper out of my hand. She scanned quickly through the ad and began to giggle.

" 'Paramount employees enjoy the rewards of working for an industry leader whose business is recognizing and rewarding talent!' Oh, my God!" said Zazi.

"Talent named Eddie Murphy maybe," said Suzanne.

"Hey. You got to remember: some talent gets the elevator. Some get the shaft," I said with a shrug.

Zazi had news from the front. Hacker had just finished his audit and was about to draft his preliminary statement, she said. The bottom line was, if we stuck to traditional accounting standards, we were, as we had anticipated, going to get the shaft.

"Phil says, even if the judge upheld all the challenges he could find, it would barely get us to net profits," Zazi said. "And Phil's the best, Pierce."

Hacker had found all kinds of minutiae buried in the film budget that Paramount tried laying off on our clients. They ranged from expenses for Landis promoting his wife in her failed Oscar bid to a $2,500 luggage rental fee for Lord Snowden's photo shoot of Eddie to an $8,838 charge for some globes that were stolen from the set. At one point, Eddie and Arsenio bought $16,814.15 in costumes from wardrobe and charged that back to the movie. Though it appeared that Eddie Murphy Productions may eventually have paid the bill, the charge was typical of the kind of expenses that kept any net profit participant from ever seeing a dime.

"But I'm telling you: it won't add up to much more than $18 million in challenges," said Zazi. "Twenty million at the most—and that includes millions of dollars of aggressive contract interpretation on our part. Judge Schneider's probably not going to grant all of them to us. Even if he did, the interest and the overhead and Eddie's gross deal would still probably eat up the profits and keep us in the red."

I was only half listening. I kept coming back to "unconscionable."

As far back as January, I'd thought about attacking the contract on bad faith grounds. Zazi even did an alternative strategies paper for me, outlining four different ways to attack.

She called Alternative Four "the Global Approach." It meant attacking the landlords in this unconscionable landlord/tenant contract that my clients and half of Hollywood had been suckered into signing at one time or another. It meant attacking *all* of the studios, not just Paramount.

Bruce, Suzanne and another associate, Jennifer Curran, had been busy researching the statutes and precedents since February. The first and best argument they had come up with was that Art and Alain had been victims of what is known in legal parlance as unconscionable "contracts of adhesion." The legal definition of such a pact was "a standardized contract prepared *entirely* by one party to the transaction for the acceptance of the other."

It was also a contract that had unduly harsh, one-sided or oppressive provisions that were offered on a take-it-or-leave-it basis. No bargaining. No negotiation. Just "Sign it or the deal's off."

Among the precedents, Jennifer discovered a 1981 case involving rock concert promoter Bill Graham, who had signed a standard form union contract as a requirement before he could stage a show featuring pop singer Leon Russell. Later, when a dispute arose over the contract, the union stepped in and pointed to a clause that required Graham to submit to mandatory arbitration, overseen by a union officer. It was a kangaroo court and a violation of the right to a fair and impartial decision maker.

Graham fought the union on grounds that he never had any opportunity to bargain the arbitration clause out of the contract. There had been no negotiation before the show. He was simply instructed to sign on the dotted line or there would be no Leon Russell concert. Period.

After a trial and appeal, the California Supreme Court ultimately decided that Graham was right: the arbitration portion of the contract was unnegotiated boilerplate that was simply foisted on him. It was a contract of adhesion. He had no choice. If he hadn't signed it, the show would not have gone on. Despite his admitted clout as a concert promoter and the fact that he had been able to negotiate other terms of the contract, Graham won his case.

Graham's stature in the music industry was important because I knew Paramount would respond with the charge that Art and Alain were big boys—hardly hicks off the bus from Podunk. Worse yet, they were represented by the William Morris Agency, the largest talent agency in the world. They knew who they were dealing with when they signed their contracts, and they would have to abide by the agreements—the same as any sophisticated adult.

But if a Bill Graham could have a take-it-or-leave-it contract forced down his throat, so could an Alain Bernheim, who had no effective choice when Paramount presented him with its standard producer's contract, despite his years of experience in the film industry. If he wanted to make a movie, he had to sign.

Buchwald, of course, had almost no direct experience in dealing with Hollywood. If he'd been asked what an adhesive contract was, Art would probably have shrugged and said that it was one in which the pages stick together.

With both of our clients, we had a plausible case on the unconscionable contracts of adhesion argument—the stand-in for my antitrust claim.

Suzanne delved into our second major attack point: good faith and fair dealing. The shorthand of the argument was in every contracts textbook:

"There is implied in every contract a covenant by each party not to do anything which will deprive the other parties thereto of the benefits of the contract."

Suzanne's "memo" on the subject went into considerably more detail—93 pages of it, citing dozens of contract breach cases dating back decades. In every one of them, one of the two parties in a contract failed that simple test: they did something that deprived the other party of the very benefits to which the contract said they were entitled. In our case, Diamond admitted that net profits were a bonus for contributing to a successful movie, but Paramount had frustrated our clients' realization of net profits by consistently preferring its own interests.

The third component of our battle plan involved fiduciary duty. By our way of reckoning, Paramount had both an obligation to act almost as a trustee of the monies that flowed out of *Coming to America* and into the pockets of the profit participants. Joel Katcoff, who continued to work on the case from our New York office, spelled it out: Paramount's fiduciary duty was one of "*utmost good faith*" to Art and Alain.

Finally, there were several contract interpretation arguments, the gist of which was that Paramount could not charge millions of dollars of items to the picture because the contract did not unambiguously authorize the deduction. For example, Eddie Murphy's $1.7 million bonus was not expressly permitted and did not qualify as a development, production or distribution cost. Another example was the effect of breaching a clause in Alain's contract that required the studio to consult with him before it charged any third-party profit participations to the picture and reduced his 40 percent share to the floor of 17.5 percent in his contract. Paramount of course did not hire Alain to be producer, much less consult with him about Murphy's and Landis's profit shares, but the exclusion of those payments alone would reduce the deficit by $11 million.

If we could nail Paramount on any one or all four of our arguments— contract of adhesion, failure of good faith and fair dealing, breach of fiduciary duty, and contract interpretation—we could hit the studio for substantial damages.

"Bernheim should also be able to recover damages for loss of publicity, reputation and increased future earnings," Jennifer Curran had written in her memo on damages issues. "Buchwald has a decent argument for obtaining damages for loss of screen credit. . . . Tort damages could include damages for emotional distress, loss of reputation and punitive damages."

The tough question was whether a finding of unconscionability would allow Judge Schneider to refuse to enforce the contract, ignore those provisions that made it unconscionable or simply throw out the old contract and rewrite it from scratch. A section of the California Civil Code said that he did, in fact, have that power, but it was rarely used by the courts. But if he found, as we believed, that the net profit definition was permeated with unconscionability because 100 percent of *Coming to America*'s gross went to the studio, Eddie Murphy and John Landis, the Court could invalidate that entire 26-page portion of Paramount's contracts with Art and Alain.

If Judge Schneider threw out the net profit formula, he could give us something other than "monkey points." As Jennifer Curran wrote in her analysis, "Buchwald and Bernheim *may* be able to argue that they were entitled to Paramount's *actual* profits on *Coming to America*." And actual profits meant Paramount's distribution fee, excess overhead, interest and other expenses that exceeded normal distribution and production expenses. Using Hacker's preliminary audit results and adjusting for the items that we believed were unconscionable, Joel Katcoff and I computed a new *Coming to America* financial statement. Our accounting showed that, rather than an $18 million loss, Paramount's actual profit that should be shared with us was $39.8 million, broken down as follows:

	PARAMOUNT	BUCHWALD/BERNHEIM
Income	$125,300,000	$160,600,000
Distribution fees	42,300,000	54,800,000
Distribution expenses	36,200,000	43,100,000
Interest	6,300,000	0
Negative cost	58,500,000	22,900,000
NET PROFIT (LOSS)	($18,000,000)	$39,800,000

Numerically, the difference between these two world views was a whopping $57.8 million. But, in terms of what was in reality a class struggle for power, the difference was that the slaves were mad as hell and were not going to take it anymore—they were revolting. The $57.8 million figure was a symbol of the arrogant power that had historically abused creative talent in Hollywood.

We were ready to go public with the results of our audit and investigation. As the deadline drew closer, I gathered my brain trust. Malina was hooked in by computer from New York. Bruce flew in from Park City, Joel came from New York, and Zazi, Jennifer and Dennis stopped working on all their other cases to devote full time to the final preparation of our report to the judge. For two weeks straight, I sat at the computer in my office drafting and editing our statement of contentions. In the final forty-eight hours, no one slept. It was like a political campaign—the adrenalin was flowing, time was running out, and the camaraderie was invigorating. There was one big difference, however. In our case, only one vote counted.

On Wednesday, May 16, we filed what was officially called a "Preliminary Statement of Contentions Concerning Damages and Accounting Issues." Our full-scale attack on the studio's accounting procedures didn't confine itself to Paramount. It was a 114-page declaration of war against the entire Hollywood studio accounting system as it had evolved over more than half a century. Harry Hurt of *Newsweek* called it an indictment of the studios.

Each studio "exploits . . . ambiguities [in its own standard profit participation contract] to the great financial detriment of profit participants," we asserted. And each studio "abuses its awesome power and unconscionable contract terms to manage the venture by making hidden profits, charging exorbitant interest and utterly destroying any hope of 'net profits' by self-interested acts."

In the words of Julia Phillips, I had no doubt that I'd never eat lunch in this town again. By our estimate, Buchwald and Bernheim's real share of the net ought to have ranged between $6.9 million and $14.6 million. That's what we asked for. Paramount's reaction was swift and predictable.

"You've got to misread the agreement to get to those figures," Bobby Schwartz blustered to the press.

The claims were baseless, and Paramount planned to tell Judge Schneider the same thing, he continued. There was a $58 million gap between what Paramount said the picture earned and what we said it earned. That, too, was bunk, according to Schwartz.

"As for the auditor's claims regarding 'Coming to America' expenses, they're meritless," he said.

Diamond was less hysterical, but just as indignant as Bobby Schwartz.

In his formal 28-page response to our brief, filed with the court four days later, Diamond simply referred to Judge Schneider's own description of the case: "primarily a breach of contract case . . . which must be decided by reference to the agreement between the parties and the rules of contract construction."

And when he met the press, Diamond made it clear that Paramount didn't take us seriously.

"Art Buchwald, having decided that he can't live with his deal with Paramount, is relegated to having to ask the judge to make a new one for him by throwing out the terms that are favorable to Paramount, but keeping the ones that are favorable to Art Buchwald," Diamond said. "Art Buchwald and his attorneys have finally shown their hand, and it is empty."

In effect he was saying, "We're going to blow you out of the water on these legal issues. You're not even going to get to a final accounting."

I was banking on the continued overconfidence of Diamond and Schwartz and fanned the flames with my own prepared statement for the media.

"Paramount's response is old wine in old bottles," I said. "They have not denied our claim that Paramount has reaped over $73 million in hidden profits from 'Coming to America.' The studio is hiding behind its one-sided, grossly unfair contract-of-adhesion which Paramount consistently misinterprets as its excuse for charging tens of millions of dollars in unauthorized and excessive expenses to the motion picture."

But our public posturing was not the real test of which side had the advantage. That came two days later, at 4:20 P.M., in the Kaye, Scholer conference room next to my office.

Judge Schneider was on vacation, but he had received our statement as well as Diamond's response. He wanted a status conference. Immediately. He showed up with a law student extern, but he'd left his robes at home. He wore a sport shirt, slacks and a grim expression.

"I've read the tome," he said, glaring at me and my associate, Doug Lee, on our side of the table. On their side of the table, Chuck Diamond, Bobby Schwartz and Lon Sobel shared satisfied smiles.

I squirmed uncomfortably. Was the judge put off by my inflammatory rhetoric? The length of the document? The request for millions of dollars in damages?

But then Schneider switched to the accounting: were both sides satisfied?

"I have no disputes with the figures, but I do have a problem with the inclusion of certain items in the calculation of net profits, your honor," I said.

Diamond was basically satisfied with the figures, though he didn't like our way of doing the math either. He did quarrel with our use of hypothetical net profits but saved most of his venom for our discovery demands. He told Schneider we were asking for a lot of irrelevant documents about Paramount's outside borrowing habits and its actual studio overhead.

Schneider remained the Great Stone Face. I got the impression he felt like the junior high principal called back from his spring vacation to settle a dispute between a couple of schoolyard incorrigibles. If we couldn't straighten out our difference over which documents were relevant and which weren't, he told us, then he would appoint a discovery referee to straighten them out for us.

But, in the meantime, we had some legal issues to wrestle with, he said as he looked over seven pages of handwritten notes that he had made while reading our statement of contentions.

My ears perked up.

"The legal issues are the covenant of good faith and fair dealing, fiduciary duty, unconscionability and whether the contract was adhesive," he said.

I glanced over at Diamond. He seemed slightly distressed. Sobel sat up in his chair. Schwartz was still beaming, apparently unaware of what this portended.

"We need to talk about whether the gross participation was chargeable to the picture too," Diamond said. "And what the parties intended in Bernheim's deal memo. And the deductibility of hiring another producer."

Schneider held up his hand. He would be glad to take Diamond's brief on those issues, provided the brief didn't run on forever like *other* recent briefs he'd read. He addressed his words to Chuck, but he stared at me.

But the judge's primary interest was unconscionability and all the attendant legal issues that I had raised in my "tome." He wanted those pivotal points straightened out before we did any more auditing. July 9, which had been our target date for resolving the case, was now rescheduled for deciding whether the contract Buchwald and Bernheim had signed was fair and legally binding.

"Lie low on the accounting issues," he warned.

What he wanted was a road map to the end of the case, he explained. We could depose expert witnesses and take evidence, just as we had in Phase I. If possible, he wanted to base his decision on the depositions and avoid a live trial.

But now, he said, there would be more than just a Phase II to *Buchwald v. Paramount.*

"We are now trifurcating the trial," he said. "The second phase will only concern legal issues." He bade us good-bye and left the room to finish his vacation.

I felt a rush. We weren't dead by any means. It would still be a long way to Phase III, but Draper's red ink predictions and Diamond's crowing about our Pyrrhic victory suddenly sounded hollow. My fear that Schneider wouldn't take us seriously dissolved.

I went to work preparing for the depositions that would make or break our claims. It was one thing to issue an indictment, it was another to prove the charges with legally admissible evidence.

But one thing was clear: Paramount had not succeeded in an early knockout. This was going to be a fifteen-round fight.

33

Risky Business

THE SAME WEEK we released our 114-page indictment, Paramount re-released Cecil B. De Mille's 1956 version of *The Ten Commandments*, brought up to 1990 production standards in 70-millimeter Super VistaVision and six-track stereo. Buchwald happened to be in San Diego that week, delivering a speech, when he was cornered by members of the media who wanted a comment on our sensational charges.

"It's hard for me to believe the studio that made *The Ten Commandments* messes with its books," he said with mock solemnity.

Art was trouncing Paramount regularly. One night after he spoke at a testimonial dinner for his old USC compadre David Wolper, Warner Bros. studio chairman Bob Daly told the people at his table, "You've got to be crazy to pick a public fight with *that* guy, don't you?"

I was having fun with the media too. I routinely called Paramount's accounting "fatal subtraction," and my running pun on the surprise Disney hit of the previous summer was *Honey, I Shrunk the Gross.* People were starting to laugh at Paramount and the other studios; it was a crack in the façade.

Art, Alain and I were no longer "quixotic" adventurers, however. No one predicted victory, but the sheer bravura of our "daunting task" (as the Washington *Post*'s John Richardson put it)—our taking on the entire Hollywood studio accounting system—had reinvigorated the case.

The day after we filed our brief, *Variety* reported the deaths of two entertainment giants—Sammy Davis, Jr. and Jim Henson—on the front page. But the biggest story of the day, bannered across the top of the page in a headline blaring "Slice of 'America's' Pie: $15.9 Mil," was *Buchwald v. Paramount.*

Our two-pound statement of contentions attacking Paramount's $18 million deficit claim was so much in demand, we had to send it out for mass photocopying. *People, Time, Newsweek* and all four TV networks stepped up coverage. ABC's "Prime Time Live" ran a special segment on Hollywood accounting centered around our case.

As the significance of our spring offensive sank in at Paramount, publicity became an important weapon in both of our arsenals. The sleeping giant had awakened, and the message from the corporate executive suite was clear: fight the case in the media as well as the courtroom. Paramount came out swinging.

"The studio lives up to its contracts and we're shocked that Buchwald does not intend to do the same," Diamond fumed. "We are confident that Judge Schneider will view this as a very transparent attempt by Buchwald and his lawyers to walk away from the contract that he and his agent negotiated. Before this case is over, Mr. O'Donnell is going to call it *My Left Foot in My Mouth.*"

While Diamond was hammering away at us in the media, his predecessor was keeping busy behind the scenes.

In June, a TV producer named William Derman came to me with a breach-of-contract case he thought I might like to handle on appeal, given my *Buchwald* experience. Several years earlier, he had granted another producer an option on his game show, "Beat the Odds." The option lapsed, but years later a show called "Press Your Luck," which had elements of a "Beat the Odds" clone and was produced by the same people to whom he had sold the original "Beat the Odds" option, aired on television. Derman sued, lost and appealed. When the case was appealed, the justices discussed in their opinion the legal standard for proving breach of contract to pay for an idea: an issue Bob Draper and I sharply debated before Judge Schneider.

When Derman called me, he wanted me to take his case to the California Supreme Court. He dropped off a stack of papers at my office, and I began pawing through them. About midway, I found a three-page letter dated May 19, 1990 from Bob Draper to the Court of Appeal in Los Angeles.

Draper wrote, "I am lead counsel for Paramount Pictures in a case now pending in the Los Angeles Superior Court known as *Buchwald v. Paramount Pictures.*" He urged the justices to publish their recent decision in *Derman v. Carruthers* because "many of the issues in the [Buchwald] case are quite similar to those you have decided in *Derman.*"

If *Derman* were published, the decision would become a binding legal precedent on future cases, and Paramount could use it against us on appeal. There was nothing wrong with that, but sneaking a letter to the Court of Appeal without sending a copy to us was unethical. Under long-established canons of ethics in California and other states, a lawyer can't communicate with a court about a matter affecting his case unless a copy of that communication is sent to the opposing lawyer.

Worse, Draper was influencing the very court in which our case would be heard if Paramount appealed as promised.

Marsha and Suzanne drafted a letter for me, blasting Draper for his appalling conduct—"no more than a thinly veiled attempt to gain an advantage . . . on appeal."

The three-justice panel didn't see enough significance for formal publication, and by the time the Court of Appeal received my letter, the decision to publish or not to publish had shifted to the California Supreme Court. So I wrote to the seven justices, urging them to ignore *Derman* because it was a run-of-the-mill decision that broke no new legal ground. It took another six months but, on November 20, the Supreme Court denied Draper's request.

I remained deeply disturbed by Draper's conduct. I asked myself again: Why was Paramount so hell bent on winning at any cost? Were there any lengths to which the studio would not go to beat us?

In her office, just fifty feet inside the famous Bronson Avenue gates of Paramount Studios, the studio's chief publicist, Deborah Rosen, established a command post from which she tried to track and control public opinion on the case. Her office looked like a secure room inside CIA headquarters at Langley—rows of videotaped newscasts along the walls and file folders stuffed with Buchwald-related clippings. Our every utterance was being monitored by Rosen and Karl Fleming, a former *Newsweek* correspondent and TV newsman hired by Paramount to consult about handling the media. Whenever Art or I appeared on radio or television, a transcript was immediately prepared and transmitted to the top brass in Hollywood and New York. I had my own counterintelligence operation, with a source feeding me the transcripts at the same time that they were distributed around the studio.

Paramount coined a new name for me. Around the Adolph Zukor Building, I was known as "Whiplash" O'Donnell: first, I wanted the judge to uphold Buchwald's and Bernheim's contracts, but now, after I had convinced Schneider to uphold those contracts, I whipped around and wanted him to nullify them!

Buchwald and I were frauds, according to Rosen.

"O'Donnell is chauffeured to work every day by town car," she said. "How's *that* for a crusading shirt-sleeve lawyer who's out to protect the little guy from the big, bad studio?"

I demanded the same star treatment Eddie Murphy did, she said. And Buchwald was anything but a little guy, fighting the Establishment. Buchwald *was* the Establishment, with a capital E, she told Dennis McDougal when he visited her on the lot to get Paramount's side of the story. Buchwald dined with senators and Supreme Court justices and summered on the Vineyard with the hoi-polloi of the East Coast cognoscenti. He was a millionaire several times over—hardly the powerless David tilting with Goliath at Hollywood and Vine.

Rosen was right about a couple of things: Art Buchwald was affluent and knew a lot of important people. Without those resources, he would not have got as far as he had in his war over writers' rights.

"We interrupt our regularly scheduled programming to bring you this ABC News special presentation," the voice on the tape recording announced to the thirty men seated at the long breakfast table in the Fireside Room of the California Club on June 7, 1990. "Your host is Howard Cosell in New York."

"Good morning and welcome to our special broadcast," I said in my best imitation of the former lawyer turned sports announcer. "Today marks the final day of ABC's continuing gavel-to-gavel live television coverage of the historic trial of *Buchwald v. Paramount Pictures Corporation.* We will shortly take you to the courtroom in downtown Los Angeles where the judge will be instructing the jury and the lawyers will be making their closing arguments. At issue is how much money, if any, Paramount must pay the Pulitzer Prize-winning writer Art Buchwald and his producer/partner Alain Bernheim as damages for breaching their 1983 contracts."

It was my turn to be the toastmaster at the Thursday morning gathering of the Economic Round Table. Once a year, each member must deliver an original, one-hour talk on any subject. Over the organization's sixty-year history, the speeches had dealt with everything from artichokes to Zionism.

That June morning, thirty pillars of the Los Angeles establishment served as a jury hearing a mock closing argument of Hollywood's most famous accounting case. During the next hour, I portrayed not only Howard Cosell but also Harvey Schneider, Chuck Diamond and myself. Disappearing behind a screen off to the right of the speaker's podium, I switched from one suit jacket to another or donned a flowing black robe, depending on the role.

It was a tough jury for Buchwald and Bernheim: rock-ribbed conservative businessmen and lawyers who believed in the sanctity of the written contract and instinctively distrusted claims made by plaintiffs against large corporations. To make matters worse, I delivered a blistering attack on our case when I played Diamond.

"Mr. O'Donnell is fond of waving the flag and invoking the American way," I said, miming Diamond in his most sarcastic voice. "What could be more American than keeping your word? A deal is a deal. You signed these contracts. You are big boys. Stop whining!"

The "jury" filled out verdict forms and the answers sent my spirits into orbit: 96 percent said Paramount's accounting was improper, 62 percent believed Paramount acted in bad faith, 69 percent found that the net profit formula was a contract of adhesion, and 59 percent thought the terms unconscionable and unenforceable. All but four of the thirty "jurors" awarded us damages. The low was $2 million. The high was $16 million. The average came in at $7,125,000. At the moment, I would have settled for a lot less.

Ten days later, Jack Whitehead called. He had sat among the "jurors" and he wanted to tell me how impressed he had been and that Martin Davis ought to know just how strong our case was. Jack still thought a deal might be brokered. I told him that I was not optimistic, but I never said never about settlement. The following day, June 19, he called me.

"I just got off the phone with Davis. He remembered me and our conversation from back in February. We spoke for ten to twelve minutes. And let me tell you: this was a totally different Martin Davis."

"What do you mean?"

"He wasn't belligerent or contentious. He was polite. Didn't talk down to me. If anything, Pierce, he was conciliatory."

"And?"

"I told him I didn't know how well informed he was about what was happening in Los Angeles, but that from where I sat there was a chance you might just get Paramount's accounting thrown out of court. If that were the case, I told him, as a businessman, I thought that it made sense to settle."

I was on my feet and pacing like a lion.

"What did he say?"

"He told me he was on top of what was happening and that his lawyers assured him they'd beat you. But I've got to tell you: in the next breath, he asked me what it would take to settle.

"I told him I wasn't negotiating for you, but I believed that the case could be resolved for between $4 and $5 million. That's what you told me when we spoke last about the price for peace, right?"

"That's certainly in the ballpark, Jack. So, did Davis say anything?"

"He didn't reject the suggestion out of hand. Twice he said you should talk with . . . Diamond? Is that right? 'I'm not going to get into it. Have Pierce talk to his counterpart,' were his exact words."

"Anything else?"

"Yes, at the end of the conversation, Davis said, 'I know that Pierce has a big investment and a lot of expense to cover. I hope he wins.' "

"What?"

"That's what he said. When I asked, 'Do you mean that?' Davis answered, 'I hope it comes out well for everybody. Art Buchwald is my friend. I still consider him my friend.' "

On Thursday, June 21, Paramount answered our indictment. I expected their first defense: that the contract was clear and unambiguous and both our clients knew exactly what they were getting when they signed on the dotted line.

Movies are a risky business, Paramount insisted in its second defense. When you signed a contract, you accepted the fact that "winners must pay for losers." If blockbusters did not subsidize the many money-losing movies studios made, the movie industry would not survive.

"More than most industries, the motion picture community has fashioned a complex but universally understood set of rules that reasonably allocate risks, rewards and controls in a business where failures outnumber successes."

I couldn't believe it. The studios were *always* first in line to get their money back from the box office. With the rise of videocassettes and global TV, they were usually the last in line too. Everybody from the net profit participants to the Internal Revenue Service might get stiffed, but the studios always came out smelling like a million dollars—their own and everyone else's.

Sid Finger and Phil Hacker were right. The contract was the problem. Studios offered every writer identically unfair terms. It was impossible to shop a script or movie idea around for a better deal because the system forced writers and producers into take-it-or-leave-it arrangements with studios.

"That's like Ford saying General Motors and Chrysler build cars that blow up sometimes, so Ford should be able to do it too!" Bruce remarked after reading Paramount's brief. "What are they thinking, Pierce? Saying that everybody does it is no defense."

"I agree, but there is a surface appeal to this argument. Paramount has upped the ante," I said.

They were challenging Judge Schneider. They wanted him to think twice before he decided: if he invalidated the standard net profit contract, the financial fate of the motion picture industry might hang in the balance.

"It's a powerful argument. We'd better start doing some homework in the modern economics of the movie business."

The following week, Zazi, Bruce and I spent an entire day locked in Harvey Schneider's jury room with Lon Sobel, Bobby Schwartz and Chuck Diamond, as if we were deciding the verdict in a capital case. The judge wouldn't let us leave until we had all agreed on how to try Phase II. He wanted to hear evidence on the legal issues raised by us—particularly contract of adhesion and unconscionability.

The lawyers couldn't even agree on how to frame the issues, but somehow, by the end of the day, we had hammered out a stipulation. Paramount would offer written declarations from nine experts. We had four of our own: Max Youngstein, Rudy Petersdorf, Roger Davis and Sid Finger. We'd crash through the depositions in the record time of ten days and report back to Schneider on July 9, as promised.

It would be ten days that shook Hollywood.

Art no longer considered Martin Davis a friend.

It was June 26, and I was in New York preparing Sid Finger for his deposition. Art was in town and invited me to meet him for breakfast at the Regency Hotel. When I arrived, hobnobbers clustered around his table, congratulating Buchwald for thrashing Paramount. Even after I sat down, a steady stream of well-wishers made it difficult to carry on a conversation.

Bob Tisch, co-owner of the Regency along with brother and CBS chief Larry, stopped by to say that his son Steve was working in Hollywood and might need my legal services someday.

"You can probably afford his hourly rate," Art groused, raising his eyebrows at the prices on the menu. "Donald Trump couldn't afford to stay in this hotel."

"Yeah, but with all your Paramount money, you will," Tisch fired back.

We ordered, and Art told me about the party he had attended the night before celebrating Helen Gurley Brown's twenty-fifth anniversary as publisher of *Cosmopolitan* magazine.

The guest list included Barbara Walters, Don Johnson, Peter Jennings, Roone Arledge, Beverly Sills, Mike Nichols, Diane Sawyer, Henry Kravis, Jane Pauley, "Swifty" Lazar, Diane von Furstenberg, Felix Rohatyn, Polly Bergen, Robert Wagner, James Woods, Eva Gabor, Merv Griffin, David Frost, Erica Jong, Arthur Liman, Dominick Dunne, William Randolph Hearst III . . .

And Martin Davis.

"Mutual friends kept coming up to each of us, saying that Marty and I should make up and settle the lawsuit, but I don't make scenes at public gatherings like that, Pierce."

"Did you talk with Davis at all?"

"Not until the end of the evening."

Throughout the night, sportscaster Frank Gifford had engaged in shuttle diplomacy, moving from Davis's table to Art's, urging the two feuding friends to reconcile. Art couldn't be bothered. He was seated between two of the most beautiful and richest divorcees in America—Pat Kluge and Ivana Trump.

Patricia Rose Kluge was the attractive actress/model and ex-wife of Metromedia billionaire John Kluge, and, with her picture on the cover of all the tabloids, Ivana Trump's pending split-up with Donald Trump had made her at least as rich and notorious as her financier husband. Art wrote, "Ivana, consider this a prenuptial agreement," on his program and handed it to her just as Gifford leaned over and whispered to him:

"Art, you and Marty have to make up."

Buchwald thanked him for trying to help, but didn't budge. As the evening drew to a close, Davis finally came to Art's table.

"Why are you mad at me?"

"You accused me of being a plagiarist," Art whispered in an attempt to avoid a scene. "That is the worst thing that you could say about me."

"I didn't do that," Davis protested. "The lawyers did."

"Yeah, but they're *your* lawyers."

"I feel terrible about this, Art," he said. "My lawyers have really let me down."

"Your lawyers are jerks," Art told him.

"I'm really getting creamed by all this," Davis continued. "I want to sit down and talk with you. No lawyers, no papers, and no pens. When can we meet?"

Art smiled weakly and put him off with small talk. They might talk once he returned from summering at Martha's Vineyard, he said.

They never did.

And the reason, Art told me over Irish oatmeal and coffee, was that Buchwald no longer wanted to settle.

"We've gone this far, Pierce, and we have kept our dignity. We've always taken the high road. Your attack on Hollywood's cheating has captivated the public. Let's see it through to the end."

"You and Alain are the clients," I said. "Whatever you want. Believe me, I would love to nail these bastards, but Alain and you call the shots on settlement."

"I sued because Paramount wouldn't acknowledge that it used my story. I've been vindicated. I never cared about getting a lot of money. But Kaye, Scholer has a lot invested, and Alain has worked hard for years for almost nothing. If Alain and you want to settle, I'll go along."

"I can't speak for Alain, but Paramount's lawyers know my phone number. If they want to discuss settlement, we should at least meet with them but, for now, it's an academic point. They're not calling."

And they never did.

34

Worlds Apart

— — — — — — — — —

WHILE I WAS HAVING BREAKFAST with Art in New York, Phase II depositions were about to begin on the other side of the country. Over the next ten days a battery of lawyers and thirteen expert witnesses would fill more than two thousand pages of deposition transcript. Every day, we shuttled back and forth between Kaye, Scholer and O'Melveny & Myers to depose each other's witnesses. Our offices were only a few blocks from each other in Century City, even if our perspectives on how Hollywood did business were worlds apart.

Roger Davis, the astute chairman of the William Morris Agency executive committee and the man who negotiated the original *King for a Day* contracts for Art and Alain, was first up on June 26.

Shortly before his deposition, I had asked him if he was worried about either reprisals from Paramount or pressure from within his own agency about getting involved.

"To hell with Paramount and I *am* as much William Morris as anyone else," he said. "This is the right thing to do. Let the chips fall where they may."

For three decades, Davis worked at William Morris headquarters in Beverly Hills and for many of those years he was chief assistant to the legendary head of the William Morris organization, Abe Lastfogel. One of the original Hollywood agents, the cherubic Lastfogel started in the New York office in 1912 as an office boy and worked his way to the top. He pitched directly to the heads of studios, not to underlings, but never missed an opportunity to sell a client. He was credited with resurrecting the career of a fast-fading New Jersey night club singer with a movie role that made the singer a star. The singer's name was Frank Sinatra, the movie was *From Here to Eternity*, and Lastfogel managed the entire episode without having to put a decapitated horse in anyone's bedroom.

Each morning for many years, Lastfogel and Davis would climb in the back of Lastfogel's limousine and drive to a different studio, according to Davis. At noon, they drove to Hillcrest Country Club where Lastfogel always had a table reserved for the one-on-one schmoozing so necessary to the art of agentry. Even now, six years after Lastfogel's death in 1984, Davis spoke with some reverence about learning the fine art of arm twisting from the master.

"My job was to, in effect, carry his briefcase," Davis told Chuck Diamond early in his deposition at O'Melveny & Myers' offices.

In the intervening years, Davis, a lawyer by training, graduated to his own high-priced clientele: Steve McQueen, Kirk Douglas, Barbra Streisand, Elvis Presley, among others.

By 1990, Davis had become one of two men who ran the agency. He knew Hollywood through and through, and he was bluntly honest about how he functioned in the Tinseltown milieu. It was that very expertise and honesty, however, that enabled Diamond to score first in Roger's deposition.

"Mr. Bernheim was coming off two unsuccessful pictures which he had produced or coproduced," Davis gave as his explanation for only getting net profit deals for his two clients on *King for a Day*. "He had nothing but a three-page outline by Mr. Buchwald, who was a personal friend of his, and I had no credentials to go on."

Davis understood Paramount's argument that Bernheim and Buchwald had "made their beds and they should lie in them." He even conceded that, if he had thought it possible, he would have got them a better deal back in 1983. Nevertheless, he was angry at the way Paramount had handled things.

"Bernheim and Buchwald were cheated out of an opportunity to secure greater profits than they secured or greater participation than they secured because in my view, based on what I understood, somebody, whether it was Paramount or Eddie Murphy Productions, had stolen their property and cheated them out of an opportunity to not only make the picture but to improve their compensation," he told Diamond.

Had he known what Paramount had planned for his clients' story, he might have been able to negotiate a better deal, he said. And, in an admission that would have made Abe Lastfogel proud, Davis noted that he still expected his 10 percent agent's fee in the event that Art and Alain won their case. But neither Roger nor I knew how much it would eventually cost the agency to actually earn that fee.

The following day, my troops squared off with O'Melveny's attorneys over wizened, wise and feisty Max Youngstein, one of our key witnesses.

"My daughter wanted me to grow the beard, so I did," he explained to Bobby Schwartz.

During three hours of questioning, his overriding message was that studios made money, either by accident or design. Even movies that bombed at the box office usually made up for the losses in foreign markets, over pay channels like HBO or in the neighborhood video stores. To report any kind of loss on a blockbuster like *Coming to America* was sheer accounting fantasy.

"They run no risk as a company. There is no risk in today's world with all of the ancillary rights and with all of the other sources of income for a picture, unless the studio totally turns out a picture that they have stepped away from and let run amok," he said.

All of the risks are taken by "the guy who sits down and spends a year writing a screenplay" or "the producer who spends weeks—years at times—in finding that screenplay or helping develop it," Youngstein said.

All the rewards, however, go to the studio, according to Youngstein.

"Did Paramount get its investment back on each film it released in 1988?" Schwartz asked.

"I don't know that. Let me look at the books and I'll tell you," Max taunted.

"Not a bad idea," Bruce said under his breath.

Even if Roger Davis had been able to secure a better contract for his clients in the *King for a Day* negotiations, the Byzantine and one-sided process of studio accounting was still wide open to "serious abuse," Youngstein testified.

"The entire contract can be so manipulated by the studio, in so many different ways, that it can literally wipe out any chance of net profit participants receiving any money," he said.

Schwartz asked what he meant by "manipulated."

"It means what it means in the dictionary sense: namely, to use figures in a way that produces dishonest results, inequitable results—thievery."

Schwartz didn't ask for any more definitions.

Zazi, Bruce, Diamond, Sobel and Schwartz met Helene Hahn and Alexandra Denman at Disney for back-to-back depositions the day after Youngstein's testimony. Both are examples of the new breed of professional Hollywood women: rugged, poised and dressed for success. In 1983, it was Hahn who represented Paramount in negotiating the *King for a Day* agreements, and Denman the Paramount lawyer who drafted the contracts in the Paramount legal department.

Denman had been pleasant and helpful when I took her deposition for Phase I back in September 1989. Things had changed in the nine months since we first met, however. Her Phase II declaration supported Paramount's argument that Alain had lost all his rights in *King for a Day* after the expiration of his one-year turnaround agreement in 1986—a position she had not taken in the first round.

Neither Hahn nor Denman remembered anything unusual about the Paramount contracts, which was just what we were hoping to hear. In fact, it was so common, they said, that the contracts and codicils were printed up in advance, including the notorious Exhibit A: the standard net profits definition.

"Paramount had a bunch of Exhibit A's that were kept in legal files and, when one was drafting a contract and an Exhibit A was called for, that's what we put on," said Denman. "I mean, it made no sense for us to do a whole one every time."

During her Paramount tenure, Denman drafted between 50 and 100 contracts and on 60 percent of those, she routinely attached an Exhibit A which always put the contracting talent at the back of the line when it came to collecting any money.

Hahn, who had negotiated over 100 deals in her seven years at Paramount, said the same thing: Exhibit A had become so routine in Hollywood that it was printed up like a handbill and kept handy in filing cabinets whenever a new deal was closed.

"It was a form that was taken out of a drawer and attached to the deal memo when a producer had a net points deal. Is that correct?" Margolius asked.

"Actually, I think it was taken out of a closet, but it was attached," she said.

The following day, the man who invented Exhibit A testified that the forms were not only preprinted, they were bound together in tablet form and ripped out every time a studio lawyer needed one to cinch a deal.

"The original 1975 version of this I drafted," said Richard Zimbert, holding up a copy of Exhibit A with the letters "RZ" printed in one corner. "And forever more it appears . . . they have chosen to keep my initials on it."

The executive vice-president and assistant to the chairman of the board of Paramount Pictures Corporation started practicing entertainment law in Chicago, shortly after he took his bar exam in 1949. He'd worked for Aaron Spelling, ABC and American International Pictures before coming to work for Paramount in the early seventies where he witnessed the birth of the modern net profits deal.

Zimbert is one of the leading legal minds in the motion picture industry, held in a regard bordering on awe among adversaries and allies alike. He learned early that Hollywood is about power and money—who has it, who wants it, and who gets it. In an industry where status equals power, no one knows better than he that money completes the equation.

"Since the movie business comes down to one thing, money, everything in the deal revolves around that," Zimbert wrote in an article published the same year that Art and Alain had signed with Paramount.

Zimbert was as tough and cunning as he was charming and thoughtful. No doubt he reported to Martin Davis and Donald Oresman in New York, but when it came to our case he called the legal shots. He was the company man on the firing line.

According to Zimbert, the Buchwald case was "outrageous," but very much the talk of the industry. Whether in the commissary during the week or at the marina where he kept his boat tied up on weekends, all anyone wanted to talk about was the "unconscionable" Paramount contract, he said.

But it was not unconscionable by Zimbert's measure. The studio set out to make the best deal it could and so had the William Morris Agency.

"Is the producer risking some of his time and labor on the chance that his time and labor might produce a successful movie and that his contingent compensation will be substantial?" Bruce asked him.

"Sometimes, yes," Zimbert answered. "Sometimes they are not risking anything. Sometimes they thank their lucky stars that they are attached to a project that someone else is risking greater elements than they are."

Usually that "someone" was the studio, according to Zimbert. It might take as little as twelve months to actually make a movie, but the gestation period could take years and the studio paid the price. He gave the stage musical *Evita* as an example. In 1982, Paramount paid $1 million for the film rights and still hadn't developed a script to the point that a single frame could be shot.

For nearly four hours, Zimbert walked Bruce, Chuck and Sobel through the intricacies of contract law, provision by provision, as he believed it applied to Buchwald. But Bruce saved the best for last. Zimbert would be Paramount's best witness. He had that inner calm of a man accustomed to winning and the self-confidence to say what was on his mind.

In answer to Bruce's question about profit participants in *Grease* being awarded $600,000 in an accounting arbitration, a smiling Zimbert replied: "I sent a bottle of champagne to the lawyer with a note that said, 'If they had asked me for $600,000, I would have kissed them and given them the check in five minutes.' "

"The last question is . . . how large a check is Paramount prepared to write to Mr. Buchwald and Mr. Bernheim?" Bruce asked Zimbert.

"Let me answer, please," Zimbert said, sitting forward in his chair.

"I'll instruct him not to answer," said Diamond.

"On what grounds?" asked Margolius.

"It's improper discovery," Diamond replied.

"No, it's not," said Margolius.

"May I depose your clients and find out what they are willing to take?" Diamond asked.

Bruce shrugged. "You can ask."

Zimbert never got to answer the question.

The chief reason Paramount offered David Leedy $175 an hour to testify on their behalf was his book: *Motion Picture Distribution—An Accountant's Perspective.* Published in 1980, it had sold only 5,000 copies, but those who bought it presumably were the businessmen and women who tallied the money Hollywood made. It was a book by a bean counter written for bean counters.

The Paramount legal department felt that Leedy was the kind of expert author they needed to justify the logic of studio accounting procedures.

They were wrong.

When he entered our conference room on the first weekend in July, Leedy was comfortable, confident and unexceptional.

"All of the major motion picture studios use essentially the same form of accounting statement when accounting to net participants," Zazi started off.

"The boilerplate agreement? Yes," Leedy said, nodding.

Bobby Schwartz raised his eyebrows at the word "boilerplate." Zazi stifled a smile.

"The *boilerplate* agreement," she repeated. "Do you agree that the *boilerplate* agreement is essentially the same from studio to studio?"

Schwartz objected, but Leedy answered anyway. Distribution fees might vary from studio to studio, but most boilerplate provisions were "well understood" by most people involved in the industry.

Zazi picked up a copy of Leedy's book and casually leafed through it.

"Mr. Leedy, do you recall taking the position in that book that at least certain contractual terms and provisions in the standard profit participation formula are *not* generally understood in the motion picture industry?"

"Yes," he said.

For the next two hours, she went through the book, item by item, pointing out Leedy's own sharp attack on the studio accounting system that he had now been called upon to defend.

On page 42, he called studio overhead "artificial" and warned profit participants to be on the lookout for rebates.

Under a section captioned "Taxes," Leedy advised participants to watch for income taxes that studios sometimes hid among distribution expenses they charged to the movie.

Studios often slap a standard overhead charge on a movie shot on location to milk it for using studio facilities even when it wasn't even shot on the lot, he wrote.

Zazi told me later that she wondered if anyone at Paramount or O'Melveny & Myers had even bothered to read his book. Finally, Leedy managed to say something that he thought was favorable to Paramount.

"A studio is a facilities provider," he said. "They are in the business of providing facilities and equipment, and they have an investment in that equipment and in that facility, and they should be able to make a profit thereon. Unfortunately, my experience in a lot of studios is they don't make a profit."

Maybe Buchwald had been right. Paramount really *was* a nonprofit organization.

I rejoined my colleagues back on the twenty-first floor of the Fox Plaza Building on Monday morning, this time with Paramount's brand-new head of contract accounting as the studio's latest expert witness.

Carmen Desiderio had moved to California only six months earlier. At the same time he was named a vice-president for Paramount Pictures Corporation, the entire accounting department of Paramount's film division also moved to the West Coast, making Paramount the last major studio to concede that the accounting ought to occur on the same coast where the movies were made instead of three thousand miles away in New York.

Desiderio is heavy set and Mediterranean in appearance, complete with bushy black mustache. He had been well coached. In two hours of Bruce Margolius's questioning, the company accountant had little to tell us.

The best Margolius was able to extract from him was an admission that Paramount probably did not lay out $107 million in cash to produce, market and distribute *Coming to America* before receiving its first dollar back from the box office. But Desiderio's close parroting of the company line was not a complete waste of time.

During Bobby Schwartz's cross-examination, Desiderio dropped a bomb.

"For the past fifteen years, Paramount has paid out in excess of $150 million to net profit participants," said Desiderio. A short time later, he handed over a chronological inventory of the films, breaking out the net profits for each film:

1975: *The Longest Yard* ($4,723,000)
1976: *Bad News Bears* ($5,027,000) and *Lifeguard* ($505,000)
1977: *Bad News Bears—Breaking Training* ($1,433,000)
1978: *Foul Play* ($1,999,000), *Grease* ($30,697,000), *Heaven Can Wait* ($715,000), *Looking for Mr. Goodbar* ($929,000) and *One and Only* ($837,000)
1979: *Escape from Alcatraz* ($1,985,000) and *Warriors* ($2,899,000)
1980: *Airplane* ($15,531,000), *American Gigolo* ($2,368,000) and *Little Darlings* ($1,987,000)
1981: *Ordinary People* ($2,831,000)
1982: *An Officer and a Gentleman* ($13,419,000) and *Star Trek II* ($6,011,000)
1983: *Flashdance* ($17,264,000), *Trading Places* ($662,000) and *48 HRS.* ($3,260,000)
1984: *Footloose* ($2,583,000), *Star Trek III* ($4,885,000) and *Terms of Endearment* ($4,989,000)
1985: *Beverly Hills Cop* ($20,555,000) and *Witness* ($1,289,000)
1986: *Top Gun* ($4,481,000)
1987: *Beverly Hills Cop II* ($379,000) and *Star Trek IV* ($258,000)
1988: *Eddie Murphy Raw* ($1,044,000)

For the first time, Paramount was admitting that, while Buchwald and Bernheim might not have earned net profits, others who had signed similar Paramount boilerplate contracts had. In fact, Desiderio certified that twenty-nine Paramount movies in all had generated $153,394,000 in net profits for ninety-four participants since 1975. I pulled out a red pen and circled five of them. They all starred Eddie Murphy.

Diamond believed this new evidence wiped out my charge that net profits were a cruel hoax and a scam perpetrated on the creative community. He was wrong. I had big plans to turn this belated disclosure against Paramount.

Tiny and wrinkled, his face dominated by dark-rimmed eyeglasses, Mel Sattler was a career MCA man—a studio lawyer from the old school. For forty-three years the diminutive lawyer, who was in his seventies, had been negotiating movie deals, including the landmark 1950 arrangement between Universal Pictures and actor James Stewart that launched the modern net profit deal. Stewart agreed to accept 50 percent of the net in lieu of his normal $250,000 salary to star in *Winchester '73*. Sattler agreed, but only after Universal had earned back twice the movie's production costs. The logic, according to Sattler, was that both the studio and Stewart evenly shared the risk, so they would evenly share the profits.

A decade later, however, stars of Stewart's caliber were demanding more and more. What began as an even-risk proposition had become a no-lose bargain for major name actors and a handful of star directors. Their agents negotiated deals that called for a share of net profits *and* an up-front salary.

"The father of the net profit deal, Jimmy Stewart, was soon receiving $250,000 *plus* 10 percent of the gross," Sattler told Bruce.

By the 1980s, the spiraling cost of first-rate actors, directors and even some producers had catapulted to $1 million minimum scale plus as much as 15 percent of gross receipts, according to Sattler. Further, competition for their services from well-heeled independent newcomers like Carolco, Cannon and Weintraub Entertainment Group made their asking price climb ever higher. So, when a studio made a major flop, Sattler explained, it was in big trouble. To heighten the risk even more, only twenty-five movies out of a hundred broke even or actually made any money, he maintained.

"Anything that doesn't recover its negative costs and distribution expenses is a disaster," said Sattler.

Studios created the present-day net profit deal as a means of protecting themselves from such disasters, according to Sattler. By the early 1980s, the phrase "Hollywood accounting" had become an oxymoron. Still, virtually everyone in Hollywood knew net profits often meant no profits, Sattler said.

"There's no secrets in this town."

"And everyone is aware of everybody else's contract?" asked Bruce.

"Just about," Sattler answered.

Art and Alain were by no means the first to cry "Uncle!" According to Sattler, Academy Award-winning writer William Peter Blatty complained that Warner Bros. unfairly siphoned off his profits from the 1973 hit, *The Exorcist*. Actors Sean Connery and Michael Caine similarly objected to their spare net profits for *The Man Who Would Be King*, a 1975 Allied Artists picture.

Ironically, the latter picture centered around the adventures of a pair of greedy drifters.

35

The Tide Turns

IT WAS the Fourth of July.

Most people celebrated with fireworks, watermelon and backyard barbecue. But my team and I observed this holiday in the offices of O'Melveny & Myers. Only a few days remained before our July 9 deadline, and up to now the depositions had been a draw.

Our case was generating its own fireworks in Hollywood, and I was not the only one feeling the heat. While no one said it publicly, the whispering had started: Alain and his buddy Buchwald were doing more than rocking the boat —they were threatening to capsize it. The very thought polarized people.

Not long before our nonstop depositions started, Alain had told me of a meeting where he was talking about a project to Steve Friedman, the head of Kings Road Entertainment (*The Big Easy*). Friedman started hassling Alain about his audacity in challenging his contract after he signed it.

"How the hell can you complain about the contract *after* you realize that the deal doesn't work for you?" Friedman pressed.

"Look, Steve, my lawyer tells us that if the contract was forced on us, we don't have to accept it, and the judge can decide whether it's a fair deal."

"That's a bunch of crap, and you know it. A deal's a deal. If you get away with walking from your deal, where the hell are we going to be? No contract will be safe from endless attacks. I think what you are doing is outrageous and terrible for *our* business."

Even sympathetic observers couldn't understand how we could attack a contract when we weren't claiming any of the conventional grounds for voiding an agreement. For example, we weren't arguing that Paramount had made fraudulent misrepresentations to induce us to sign. Danny Arnold's agent, Jerry Zeitman, and I spent a lot of time together in the summer of 1990 negotiating Danny's deal with Disney.

"Isn't a contract sort of sacred?" Jerry asked one day as we took a break in the Disney commissary. "I mean everybody has agents and lawyers representing them, and we all know that net profits are an iffy proposition."

"Jerry, I don't mean any disrespect—you are a fine agent who fights hard for his clients—but the truth is that for decades many of the agents and lawyers have been conning the talent they represent. They come back to a director and say, 'Hey, Joe, we just got you 10 percent of the net profits. It was a bitch of a negotiation, but we were tough on them and wouldn't budge.' And then the agent takes 10 percent of his guy's fee, and the lawyer hands him a bill for $25,000. For what?"

"For negotiating a deal in which the back end is usually worthless?" Jerry asked.

"That's right. It's a fraud. And we're exposing this net profits charade. Lawyers and agents for the talent should be applauding what we're trying to do for their clients. Instead, they're lining up with the studios, wringing their hands about how we're going to ruin *their* Hollywood."

"I've heard from several good sources that the studios want this case to go away," Jerry told me. "They're mad at Martin Davis for dragging them into the fight by arguing that the net profit formula is necessary for the survival of *all* the studios. What they're most afraid of is that the judge will throw out Paramount's contract and effectively kill theirs too."

"Well, Jerry ol' boy, that's exactly what I'm trying to do."

"You know, my Irish friend, you've got *chutzpah.*"

"I've got no choice."

It felt like a Berlin Wall prisoner exchange.

In one O'Melveny & Myers conference room, Chuck Diamond questioned Rudy Petersdorf, with Zazi there to anchor our defense, while in another conference room down the hall I grilled Paramount's chief financial planner, Mark Badagliacca. During breaks, I shuttled back and forth. Each side would release the other's star witness once the "dueling depos" had concluded.

More than any other witnesses, Mark and Rudy symbolized the fundamental differences between the two sides. Badagliacca was cold, cynical and orthodox—the defender of the status quo. Petersdorf, on the other hand, was passionate, idealistic and bold—the champion of the oppressed.

Balding, bearded, and relaxed, the ruggedly handsome Petersdorf had been asked to testify in net profits disputes for over a decade, supporting writers who had quarreled with coproducer Saul Zaentz over profits from *One Flew Over the Cuckoo's Nest*, and consulting for comics Cheech and Chong in their efforts to get profits from their first movie, *Up in Smoke*. He even testified in the divorce trial of Mr. and Mrs. Robert Chartoff when a question arose over just how much the net profits were worth in a couple of films Chartoff coproduced: *Rocky* and *Rocky II*.

Rudy's twenty-six-page written declaration testimony was powerful support for our contract of adhesion and unconscionability claims. Among its main points:

- "The motion picture studios are steadfast in their refusal to negotiate and modify, in any material or significant respect, the terms and provisions of their net profit participation agreements."
- If writers, producers and other talent "wanted to do business with the studio, they had to accept the studio's standard form profit participation agreement."
- "Paramount's standard form net profit participation contract is in its essential terms identical or virtually identical to the standard form contracts used by other motion picture studios. . . . Thus, creative talent have no choice in terms of obtaining a different and more favorable definition of net profits at another studio."
- The net profit formula as a whole as well as several of its individual components are unconscionable because "the contract is designed, formulated, and, at every turn, construed by the studio in such a way as to preclude, at the studio's whim, the possibility of achieving net profits even if—and indeed especially if—the movie yields a huge box office gross and the studio makes huge profits."
- Particularly unconscionable terms included the 15 percent overhead charge, interest charges, 10 percent advertising overhead charge, charging distribution fees on the 20 percent videocassette royalty and charging the full 25 percent of Murphy's and Landis's participations to the picture.

This was a do or die day for both sides. Rudy's written testimony, if not discredited by his deposition, was sufficiently credible and specific enough for us to prevail on adhesion and unconscionability. Diamond had to break him. Zazi, Bruce and I had therefore spent days woodshedding Rudy with hour after hour of practice cross-examination that anticipated every conceivable line of interrogation from Diamond. The more Rudy perspired in our conference room, the more likely it was that he would be inspired in Diamond's.

Diamond first took Rudy through his impressive professional history.

After working with Capitol Records and Desilu Productions ("I Love Lucy"), Rudy joined Universal Pictures legal department in 1963, then moved into business affairs and ultimately became vice-president for business affairs, reporting to Lew Wasserman.

In 1978, he moved to Warner Bros. in the same capacity, and left there in 1980. Rudy had negotiated hundreds of movie deals for the two studios, though less than half of the movies were ever made. Of those that were produced, perhaps 20 to 25 percent earned net profits. One out of every three wound up being audited by the skeptical profit participants.

As a negotiator for Universal, Petersdorf had faced producers, directors and writers who had been told their picture cost one amount to produce, only to find a much larger amount on the ledger when their profit participation statements showed up in the mail many months later. Like the sticker price of a new automobile, the cost often skyrocketed with studio add-ons.

"That, from a psychological standpoint alone, quite apart from the monetary detriment, is a hard pill to swallow . . . for a net participant who has worked on a film during development, during production, if he's lucky enough to get a go-ahead on the picture, and during postproduction—a period that often involves two or more years," said Petersdorf.

When Diamond tried to get Rudy to admit that "successful pictures" had to pay for losers at Universal, he balked.

"Well, you know, it's a question of defining success, and success for a net profit participant is one thing; success for the studio, however, may be a different thing. And so many pictures were made that were not successful to participants but where the studio did all right. . . ."

"And I assume there was a third category of pictures that were insufficiently successful to make any money for either the studio or the participant?" Diamond asked next.

"I imagine that there were some such pictures. However, even without the ancillary market, which became an important source of revenues in the late 1970s and was even more important in the '80s and now that we are in 1990, there were still sufficient sources of revenue so that an unsuccessful picture at the box office would recover most of the studio's investment from sources such as network television, syndication and foreign. So even pictures which were way down on the list in terms of performance at the box office generated enough money to recover the studio's cash outlay and perhaps even make some money for the studio."

Stung by Petersdorf's refutation of his risky business defense, Diamond tried some damage control.

"But there were instances of pictures that didn't make enough money from both theatrical and other distribution to pay back the studio's cost, isn't that correct?"

"Yes," Rudy admitted, "but I would say they were very few."

In the main, the chances of a net profit participant actually receiving a payment were "problematic, somewhat chancy," Diamond suggested.

Rudy agreed that it was certainly far from guaranteed. But the chances for actually getting net profits had been greater before the early 1980s. Over the past decade, when you started with the standard formula for computing net profits and "when you combined a system of escalating production costs, escalating distribution costs . . . and then when you added on top of that the participation of a gross participant, the amount of money necessary for a film to reach net profits was being pushed back to a point almost impossible to reach." This was the studios' ingenious "rolling breakeven" that pushed net profits further and further beyond the grasp of the disappointed—and angry —profit participant.

Diamond pointed out that Rudy had been a senior business affairs executive at Universal who had forced net profit participants to accept the standard net profit formula but had not disclosed to them the negative effect of the terms on their ability to realize net profits.

"Did you feel like you were committing a fraud?" Diamond wanted to know.

"I felt that the studio was increasing its charges to a net participant and, frankly, I expected the participants to balk at this. But I realized that when the practice was adopted at the other studios the participants just meekly accepted it."

While Rudy was lobbing grenades into the enemy's camp, Bobby Schwartz and another O'Melveny partner, Charles Reed, stood guard on either side of the boyish-looking, nervous Badagliacca in the room down the hall. A Harvard MBA, Badagliacca had the job of supervising the preparation of the studio's motion picture profit and loss statements. If anyone really knew whether Paramount's movies made money, it was supposed to be Badagliacca.

His testimony, which I'd read two weeks earlier, was breathtakingly brief— only 350 words. It was in fact shorter than a typical Art Buchwald column, but there was nothing humorous about it. Paramount's vice-president for motion picture planning stated "under penalty of perjury" that what he said was "true and correct." And what he said was the bulwark of Paramount's defense that its net profit contract was not unconscionable.

> From data maintained by Paramount as of February 1983, I have analyzed the profit and loss for each motion picture released by Paramount between the start of fiscal year 1978 and the end of fiscal year 1982. My work shows that of the 90 films released during this time period, almost two-thirds lost money. The 34 films which were profitable for Paramount generated $197 million over the period on total revenues of $1.9 billion which is a 10% profit margin. Aside from unprofitable pictures, the five most successful films contributed more than 50% of the profits earned by all successful pictures during the period. Therefore, it is obvious that for every successful motion picture, Paramount must retain a multiple of that picture's direct and indirect costs in order to show an overall profit from its motion picture business.

Several things had jumped out at me from these carefully chosen words that I was sure had been written by Paramount's lawyers and not the witness. Why was Paramount, as Badagliacca admitted, using stale numbers "as of February 1983" and not relying upon the most up-to-date information that would include all the money that the films had taken in after 1983? What did Badagliacca mean by the undefined term "lost money"? Was that more voodoo accounting?

In the next and last paragraph of his declaration, Badagliacca added a qualifier to his claim that two out of three movies "lost money."

> The statistics in the preceding paragraph take into account not only the direct costs in this time period (i.e., those charged to the picture's account as they are incurred) but also overhead costs incurred between 1978 and 1982 by the Motion Picture Group and each picture's allocated share of corporate costs which relate to the motion picture business of Paramount.

This was a big mouthful to swallow. How much was this overhead? What were the allocated corporate costs? What was the profitability of these ninety films without these costs that did not relate directly to the development, production and distribution of a picture?

None of these critical questions was answered by the declaration, and no supporting documentation had been furnished. I smelled cooked books and had demanded that Paramount give me hard documentary evidence to back up Badagliacca's claims that making movies was such a risky business. Paramount stalled until the night before the deposition, when its lawyers dumped a thick computer printout on my desk. Labeled "Paramount Pictures Corporation . . . Estimated Lifetime Revenues," the sheaf of papers was supposed to have satisfied my discovery demand.

What I got was 166 pages of barely legible ten-year-old financial statements and income projections that were unintelligible and would have taken at least a week for even the trained eye of a Finger or a Hacker to decipher. It was one of the oldest litigation tricks in the books: overwhelm your adversary with a mountain of incomprehensible information when it is too late for him to get expert advice.

Ordinarily, I would have postponed the deposition and asked Sid and Phil to help me sort out the mess. But we were under an excruciatingly tight deadline, and I was afraid that I might never get to examine Badagliacca. That appeared to be what Paramount wanted.

Instead, I canceled long-standing plans to have dinner with Connie and friends and retired to my study. Alternately making pots of coffee and performing complex mathematical computations with my hand-held calculator, I stayed up all night tearing apart Paramount's numbers.

As the sun rose on the Fourth of July, I was wide awake. The 166 pages of financial data were dog-eared and coffee-stained, and my legal pad was full of handwritten notes. I had a lot of questions for Mr. Badagliacca.

But he had very few answers.

In all my years, I have rarely seen a witness so ill prepared for a deposition. Badagliacca had been given an assignment to massage the numbers to support Paramount's claim that winners must pay for losers, and he had no idea that he was about to face someone who understood his figures. Throughout the proceeding, he kept checking his watch. He seemed in a hurry to get out of there. I didn't blame him.

According to Badagliacca, Exhibit 329—the hodgepodge of computer runs

—represented estimated lifetime revenues and expenses of the studio's productions for the five years ended in July 1982. While it purported to be a five-year explanation of Paramount's estimated profits and losses on a per-picture basis, the story was told strictly from the studio's point of view with absolutely no supporting documents.

As I quickly established, Badagliacca had not prepared the original estimates, didn't know who had and wouldn't even tell me the names of the ninety movies.

"You refuse to tell me the titles?" I asked. Exhibit 329 had used code numbers for the movies instead of the actual names. Naturally, I wanted the witness to match up the numbers with a particular movie so that I could do my own investigation about the accuracy of the figures.

Badagliacca glanced at Reed for guidance.

Movie titles were "extremely sensitive, competitive, and proprietary information," Reed said. We had the numbers and would have to be happy with that. I wasn't.

Fortunately, I had cracked some of the code during my all-nighter, using some information that Jay Shapiro and Dennis Landry had given me about Paramount movies from 1978 to 1982.

"*An Officer and a Gentleman* opened on July 28, 1982. Since it was a very, very successful film, I want to know whether it was one of the titles included in the column labeled '1982,' " I asked.

Reed rubbed his temples hesitantly, then nodded.

"Okay. I'll indicate to you that it is," he said.

I pushed harder. What about *Raiders of the Lost Ark*, which was released on June 12, 1981?

"The key information you want is whether or not it's in the data, and it is. That's as far as we're going to go," Reed stonewalled.

"I've got to find it, is that what you're saying?" I asked.

"That's correct."

"Sort of like a contest."

"That's right."

"Do I get a prize if I find it?"

"It's possible."

My duel with Badagliacca was turning out to be more a war of words than numbers. As the quintessential corporate numbers cruncher, he did not seem to be able to answer the simplest question unless the proper label was attached to the proper set of numbers. When he insisted that money was "recognized" rather than earned, I asked him if "recognized" meant "accrued."

"Means financially recognized," said Badagliacca.

"And what does that mean?"

He stared at me blankly, as if I'd hit him with a water balloon.

"I have to think," said Badagliacca. After several seconds, he threw his hands up and cast me a defeated look.

"It means it was recognized," he said.

For the next fifteen minutes it was more of the same, and when I had finally had enough I exploded. Badagliacca maintained that the studio risked millions, but he couldn't show where. He said its profit margin was slim at best, but he couldn't explain why or how. He held that most movies were money losers, but he couldn't even tell me which ones they were.

Even *Reds*, the Warren Beatty picture about the Russian Revolution and one of the most notorious money losers in recent history, was buried somewhere among the ninety unnamed movies on his computer printout. But it was impossible to identify, and he would not reveal which one it was.

"I think your position is outrageous!" I barked at Reed. "This witness states conclusions that I think on their face are wrong, and I can't have the underlying data. I think the judge is going to compel it. If we have to come back here after he's compelled it, we'll come back here. I think you're wrong. I think these documents are very misleading. We've just seen it in fifteen minutes."

Badagliacca fidgeted with his copy of Exhibit 329. Reed stuck his chin out defiantly but said nothing.

"Also, I've got a witness who doesn't know what some of these things mean! He doesn't know how the estimate was made, who made it, on what basis, what computations were done . . ."

Throwing up my hands in mock frustration, I declared the deposition concluded only five hours after I had started. For the record, I was furious. Actually, I was delighted. Badagliacca could play dumb, he and Reed could stonewall me and play games with the numbers. But in a short while Judge Schneider would be reading this transcript and could demand answers to the questions I'd asked, as well as production of the backup data withheld from me. In fact, he could even order an audit of Paramount's books.

When I called Sid Finger to inform him that Bennett Newman, his former partner, had agreed to testify for Paramount, Sid was shocked and disappointed. Neither of us could figure out why Newman had done this.

He began his career as an attorney but, like so many others in the industry, he moved early into the financial side of the business. Sid Finger's thin, shrewd former partner had been involved in the entertainment industry for over thirty-five years, in the course of which he had advocated the cause of such profit participants as Steven Spielberg, Warren Beatty, Jack Nicholson, Clint Eastwood, Jane Fonda and Gregory Peck. In 1980, he had even been drafted by the Screen Actors Guild to assist the 24,000-member union in negotiating with the Alliance of Motion Picture and Television Producers a fairer standard net profit definition.

But Newman had now gone over to the other side. In support of Paramount's claim that our clients could not have reasonably expected better treatment, Newman turned his years of experience fighting for profit participants against Alain and Art. In his declaration, he denigrated our claims as old hat—"a 'standard' complaint about motion picture accounting that participants have voiced for years. The Court should understand that plaintiffs have not stumbled on any accounting practice or secret contract provision that agents and attorneys were not long aware of in 1983, and which participants with greater leverage are able to ameliorate or negotiate out of their agreements."

As for our contention that the standard net profit formula was nonnegotiable for all but a few participants, Newman stated that many of the more than one hundred contingent compensation contracts that he had seen "contained modifications of so-called studio 'standard' deals. . . . The wide variations in fixed and contingent compensation packages are a function of the experience and success of the participant, as well as the studio's interest in the specific project. . . . It seems that the plaintiffs' real complaint reduces to the proposition that, in retrospect, the studio did not give them a more generous deal."

The contents of Newman's declaration were not particularly damaging to our case. What bothered me was that he would betray the cause that he had championed for so long. We were at war, and he became in my mind a traitor.

In his testimony the afternoon of July 5, Newman slammed Phil Hacker for attempting "to rewrite the contract" in violation of his professional and ethical responsibilities, ignoring that it was the plaintiffs' lawyers and not accountants who were making the unconscionability claims. I jumped all over him, pressing for some supporting citation to a specific professional accounting standard or code of conduct that Hacker had violated.

"Can you cite to me any standard of the AICPA [American Institute of Certified Public Accountants] that supports your statement?"

"Objection," Schwartz interjected. "Mr. Newman is not being offered here as a spokesman or expert witness on behalf of the AICPA."

"But he is impugning the integrity of Phil Hacker," I fired back.

"This is argumentative," Schwartz countered. "Is that a question? Are you asking him whether he is impugning Hacker's integrity?"

"No," I bellowed. "The pending question is: Can you cite to me any standard of the AICPA that supports these statements?"

"No, I cannot," Newman meekly answered.

"Can you cite to me a standard of any professional governing body of certified public accountants that supports your statements?

"I can't, because I don't know."

We were loaded for bear with prior damaging statements by Newman about how studios shafted net profit participants. Thanks to modern computer technology, Dennis Landry had done a comprehensive search of hundreds of periodicals, and in Newman's case, he found some pure gold.

I confronted Newman with his quote in the February 20, 1978 issue of *Newsweek* in an article about David Begelman's embezzlement:

"The studio has the books and records, it interprets the contract, computes the profit and decides how much should be paid out. There's a certain amount of screwing going on all the time, but it's a mixed bag of inadvertent and intentional screwing."

Newman was ready for questioning about his statement, but I wasn't prepared for his answer.

"I take pride in that statement, though, because I look at myself, as do Hacker and Finger, as being the elite in this field . . . as bringing religion to the studios. They cleaned up their acts in good part because of that. And I found that what represented a reasonable statement in 1978 . . . at the time I retired [in 1985], no longer would be made."

This was absurd. What's more, it wasn't true, and Newman had been quoted as saying as much in Kathleen Neumeyer's scathing article about the studios' accounting practices in the May 1989 *Los Angeles* magazine.

> In virtually every film where artists, directors or writers are promised a percentage of the net or the gross, a dispute arises in which auditors have to be called on to see what fell into the cracks. Lawyers and accountants say every studio in town appears to have trouble with arithmetic.
>
> "I wouldn't put a halo on any one of them," says Bennett Newman, a retired tax attorney and CPA who has audited the books of hundreds of movies and TV series, including "The Exorcist," "Star Wars," "All in the Family," "M*A*S*H," and, more recently, "On Golden Pond."
>
> "Any television series that lasts five years is audited," Newman says. "Some audits don't pay for themselves, but that's rare. We would do what is known as a 'desk audit' and every once in a while, we would advise a client that it wouldn't be worthwhile to ask for an audit.
>
> "But when the firm did go in to scrutinize the studio's books, it invariably found evidence of underreporting."

With this knowledge in hand, I went on the attack.

"By the time you retired," I asked Newman, "were you prepared to put a halo on any of the motion picture studios in terms of the fairness of their accounting practices?"

"I think there was enormous improvement in their accounting practices," he said.

"Were you prepared to put a halo on them?"

"What is that supposed to mean?" Bobby demanded.

"Have you ever used, in a printed article, the term 'halo'?" I continued.

"Halo?" Newman asked.

"Halo. H-A-L-O. Like angels wear, or at least some of us believe they do."

"I must say, I don't know what you mean by that question," said Newman, shaking his head in bewilderment. "Put a halo on a studio."

"Do you remember giving an interview for the *Los Angeles* magazine?"

"I do."

"Do you remember being quoted in that magazine?"

"I don't know what—I don't know the quotes, but I remember being quoted—not necessarily quoted, but interviewed. I don't know what quotes she got."

" 'I wouldn't put a halo on any of them.' Did you say that to the reporter?"

"I may have."

"When you made these statements to the reporter for *Los Angeles* magazine, you believed them to be true and accurate at the time you made them?"

By now, Newman was rattled. He sagged in his chair, and he took on a defensive air.

I had one more big surprise for him.

Newman had not seen his ex-partner Sid Finger for several years. Sid's deposition was scheduled for the next morning, and he had come to town for a final preparation session as soon as I finished with Newman. During a break in Newman's deposition, I brought Sid into the conference room. They embraced, and after some pleasantries were exchanged, Sid leaned over and kissed Ben on the cheek. Stepping back, Sid stood there in silence, looking Newman squarely in the eyes for several seconds, and then left.

After that emotional moment, Newman was not worth much to Paramount. By the end of the day, he was admitting that it would be "unique" and "sad" if Bernheim and Buchwald never got any net profits from a movie that was as successful as *Coming to America*. Whether Finger's presence was a painful reminder to Newman of his past allegiances or whether Newman feared that Finger, the dean of profit participant accountants, would contradict him the next day, I will never know. But what I do know is that Newman never recovered from the kiss of Finger.

Sid Finger's Parkinson's seemed less severe as he took a seat in my conference room on the morning of July 6. He was calm, almost placid when he faced Bobby Schwartz.

Finger's ten-page declaration was the foundation for our unconscionability claims. Based on his review of 2,500 profit participation agreements, Finger was the ranking expert in America on Hollywood accounting. If Judge Schneider believed Finger, we had the evidence to prevail.

Bobby Schwartz is an able young lawyer, but he was no match for Sid Finger. This was the deposition that Finger had been waiting for all his career. It was his big chance to help right the imbalance between the greedy money men and creative talent.

For five hours, Schwartz probed, attacked and then retreated. Everywhere he turned, Sid was there to meet him and repel the assault as he persuasively made the case for judicial reform of Hollywood's accounting abuses. It was a marvel to observe—which is all I had to do. That day, I did not defend Sid Finger; I held his coat.

At one point, Schwartz asked Finger about his 1977 UCLA speech, which Sid had given me when I first met him in early 1990.

"Can you explain what you meant by the last sentence, 'It is my firm belief that this trend can well serve the conscientious profit participant who is willing to master complexity and make it his servant'?"

"Well, what I was trying to say there is please get to know all of the provisions that make up these definitions and the many pages devoted to the accounting section of that agreement. . . ."

"Based on your observations in the years after 1977, do you have an opinion as to whether the audience that you were addressing and people to whom these materials were furnished heeded your advice?"

"Not a hell of a lot of them listened, I don't think. Well, maybe they listened, but they didn't hear. But I'm sure some did, and I think some could have been educated by some of what they heard. But by and large, nothing really changed. If anything, it got worse . . . at least from the profit participant's point of view."

"What do you mean? What got worse?"

"I think it's harder today based on the standard net profits definition for a picture to reach net profits than it was then."

One reason that the profit participants were more short-changed today than thirteen years earlier was the shifting source of gross receipts from movies. Back in the 1970s, the free TV market was a lucrative source of revenues after the initial theatrical run (often as much as $20 million in license fees for a single movie), and the studio took only a 25 to 30 percent distribution fee on those ancillary revenues. But a decade later, home video had not only supplanted network TV and pay cable as the primary ancillary source of movie revenues, the studios "probably take in more from the sales of videocassettes than they do from film rental. . . . Relative to what the studios end up with, the profit participant gets very little. The studios only report a 20 percent royalty, charge him with distribution fees, and then charge against that balance very substantial guild fees and residuals. This has been a major reason why net profit participants find it harder to achieve net profits as defined."

Not only do the studios systematically deprive their creative "partners" of a fair share of profits through the standard net profit formula, they also engage in outright fraud. Sid explained:

"We have had numerous situations where marketing people or salespeople, when selling or licensing a package of films to TV stations, get one price for a whole package and have to allocate internally to each of the films. . . . The distributors have allocated generously to those pictures that did not require profit participation payments. . . . It's being done as we speak."

Touching on our evidence that the studios' standard net profit contracts were indistinguishable, Finger summed up his own feelings:

"It defies logic that all distribution fees have been the same virtually as long as I have been in this business."

And thanks to the hefty distribution fees and other charges in the "grossly unfair" net profit agreements, *Coming to America* would never pay any net profits.

"What do you mean by 'unfair'?" Schwartz asked.

"I mean they give [the profit participants] an agreement that makes it extremely difficult even with a successful picture to come out with any net profits. The picture virtually has to be a runaway success to achieve the point at which they can share in the back end."

Between the end of Finger's deposition and the start of the final witness, Sidney Sapsowitz, I took a ten-minute break. As Finger and I relaxed in my office near the conference room, there was a knock at the door. It was Bobby Schwartz.

"Excuse me, Pierce, is Sid Finger still with you?"

"Yes."

"May I see him for a moment?"

By then, Sid was standing next to me in the doorway.

"Mr. Finger, now that your deposition is over, I want to tell you something. You have been a hero of mine for some time."

"Really?" Sid said.

"Yes, you have. My father, Bernard Schwartz, is a movie producer who was a client of yours."

"Of course," Sid said. "He's your father?"

"Yes. You audited Universal on *Coal Miner's Daughter*."

"I remember it very well. Your dad was the producer. We got him some money, didn't we?"

"You sure did," Bobbie agreed. "I went to law school on what you recovered for my father."

Paramount's final witness was a heavy hitter. Literally. At over three hundred pounds, Sidney Sapsowitz filled his chair. Smart and well coached, he was a thirty-year veteran of the motion picture industry. As Kirk Kerkorian's senior motion picture financial aide during the Las Vegas entrepreneur's ill-fated stewardship of MGM, Sapsowitz aided and abetted the destruction of one of the great Hollywood studios.

"In the 1970s MGM decided . . . that it was only going to make four or five pictures," he recalled. "It was going to cut its overhead. It was not going to maintain a studio per se. It was not going to maintain a distributional organization per se, and it was only going to make hit pictures.

"History has shown that that was not possible, particularly—I should say in light of the way Kerkorian and MGM and UA attempted to do it. Certainly experience there has been that less than 10 percent of the pictures have been what you depict as big hits."

This "risky business" thesis was the thrust of Sapsowitz's 15-page declaration, which was a stream of unrelenting conclusory statements, clichés and half truths unsubstantiated by any hard evidence or concrete data. The more you read, the more you doubted the prospects of these impoverished giants surviving the next crop of new movies. "A studio could not afford to stay in business if it did not retain a multiple of its total capital investment in a successful picture," he protested. Around our office, Sapsowitz was dubbed "Mr. Doom and Gloom."

I had not originally planned to take Sapsowitz's deposition since I was preoccupied with preparing for and defending Sid Finger's deposition. However, I finally decided that an all-out attack on Sapsowitz's slick testimony was essential to expose the fallacy of the risky business defense. Since I had deposed Badagliacca only days earlier and had figured out that Paramount's claim of two out of three losers was a sham, I was the natural candidate to deflate Sapsowitz. With Zazi at my side, I wasted no time.

Whatever might be said about overall industry averages, Paramount had been a successful studio over the past decade—in fact, the most successful of all the studios in terms of earnings, I pointed out.

As I later forced Sapsowitz to admit, Paramount had fifteen of the fifty-six top-grossing films from 1972 to 1990. Universal was the next highest with nine, then Fox with six, and Warner Bros. with seven. And of the fifteen Paramount titles, the majority had paid net profits.

Sapsowitz had claimed in his declaration that everyone in the motion picture industry knew that " 'Net profit' is a misnomer—that a 'net profit participation' is not intended to be a share in the studio's profits. Representatives of the creative community have long known that, as a rule of thumb, a participant's 'net profits' were distributable only after a defined 'breakeven' and that such 'breakeven' occurred only after the studio had retained some multiple of negative cost."

The problem was that neither Paramount's nor any other studio's net profit contract disclosed these supposedly well-known, brutal realities.

"Have you ever seen a major motion picture studio that starkly presented it in that manner in a net profit definition?" I asked.

"No."

And as for why studios would use such a misleading "misnomer" as "net profits" in its contracts, Sapsowitz conceded that the term was an "arbitrary convention." I thought it was worse than that—a false suggestion of a reasonable expectation that the net profit participant would share in the success of a successful motion picture. When Sapsowitz gave me a cute answer that he had never been a profit participant, I unloaded on him.

"Under the Buchwald/Bernheim agreement, it's more likely that Buchwald and Bernheim would get hit by a bolt of lightning than to receive any profit under the profit definition, given the 25 percent participations to Murphy and Landis; isn't that true?"

Sapsowitz wouldn't answer.

I read from his declaration: "the 'net profits' definition counterbalances this risk, by enabling the studio to recover the costs (direct and indirect) and lost profit of the many unsuccessful films from the revenues generated by the few successful ones."

"Another way of putting that is that the profits of the winners will help cover the costs of the losers," I said. "Is that correct?"

"Yes."

"Now, did you see anywhere in Buchwald's and Bernheim's net profit contracts any disclosure to that effect?

"No."

In his sworn statement, Sapsowitz had noted that the average development cost per picture at all the studios was in the six figures. That comment gave me an opening to probe further my mounting evidence of collusion among the studios to restrain competition.

"How did you know the development costs of other studios when you were at MGM-UA?"

"We generally exchange general kinds of information as to averages and whatnot, but not specifics with regard to a particular project."

"When do these exchanges occur?"

"From time to time."

"On the golf course or—"

"Maybe."

"Industry meetings?"

"Not at industry meetings."

"Lunch or dinner?"

"Lunch or dinner on occasion."

Another occasion for these "exchanges" that Sapsowitz failed to mention was when Paramount, Universal and MGM-UA executives met to discuss the film marketing activities of United International Pictures (UIP)—a joint venture of the three studios that distributes their films in sixty-two foreign markets. Shrouded in secrecy, this lucrative network, conceived by Kirk Kerkorian, Lew Wasserman and Charlie Bluhdorn in the early 1980s, was beyond the reach of inquisitive federal investigators. But its decisions on which films to promote and on allocations among films in a package—sensitive judgments rife with potential conflicts of interest—had a direct impact on profit participants.

In his declaration, Sapsowitz had predicated the survival of modern motion picture studios solely on the perpetuation of the net profit caste system— balancing the studios' books on the backs of net profit participants. I had a few other ideas.

"It would certainly help, wouldn't it, if they made better movies with less losses, right?"

"Certainly."

"And I guess you have seen in your career that from time to time, when studios have a string of losses, they change top management."

"On occasion."

"Well, that's one of the truisms in this town, isn't it?"

"That is."

"I guess another way to improve your profits is to control your costs better if you can, right?"

"Certainly."

Then I asked him, "If Judge Schneider agreed with our challenges to the fairness of the net profit formula, and Paramount had $10 million less to pay its shareholders because it had to pay that amount to Bernheim and Buchwald, would that result in an unreasonable return on investment for Paramount?"

"Probably not." But, Sapsowitz insisted, "It would have a material effect."

"Would it jeopardize the survival of Paramount Pictures Corporation?" I asked.

"It might."

"How?"

"Because I think the question here isn't as it pertains to this one client, but as it pertains to an industry practice and an industry set of standards and what repercussions that might have through gross participants, adjusted gross participants and the whole contingent compensation practice in the industry."

"So you see dire consequences for the industry if the Court upholds our contentions in this case?

"Conceivably. . . . The feeling throughout the industry is . . . that it would have a dire effect."

36

Debunking Myths

— — — — — — — — —

"WELL, LADIES AND GENTLEMEN, I brought you here because our game plan isn't working," said a perturbed Harvey Schneider to Zazi, Chuck, Bobby and me on the morning of July 13. A week earlier, lawyers for both sides in *Buchwald v. Paramount* had given new meaning to the phrase "weight of the evidence." We and Paramount had wheeled into Department 52 two bulging boxes—more than two thousand pages of depositions, declarations and exhibits.

Schneider explained that his crowded docket already caused him to work six and a half days a week. When did we think he was going to find the time to wade through the record that we had submitted?

"There's no way. There is just—I don't have the time. I have to sleep. It's just a requirement that I have acquired over the years, and so I have to do that."

He was leaning heavily toward appointing a retired judge to slog through the morass and make recommendations to him. I was strongly opposed to anyone hearing the case except Judge Schneider. We had spent months sensitizing him to the issues, and he had ruled in our favor on Paramount's misappropriation of Art's story. A new judge was a wild card, whereas Schneider was a known commodity.

I whispered to Diamond that I preferred to stay in Department 52 and pare down the depositions and exhibits to a manageable size for Schneider to digest. Happily, Chuck concurred.

The judge agreed to let us focus the mountain of evidence. He then gave us thirty-five questions that he wanted answered by citations to the declarations, transcripts and exhibits. And he wanted them in ten days.

It took our side fifteen days and fifty-six pages, but we came up with a "brief" that boiled our position down to a repudiation of three of Hollywood's big myths:

That everything is negotiable at Paramount and the other studios; that moviemaking is a risky business in which losers outnumber winners; and that studio survival depends on winners subsidizing losers through huge, flat fees and arbitrary charges unrelated to actual value or costs.

In its own forty-five-page brief, Paramount argued that we were living in a dream world.

"Ignoring reality, plaintiffs ask the Court for a new deal that they had no chance of getting at the bargaining table," Diamond wrote. "There is no basis in law, in equity or the facts of this case to justify this unprecedented request."

The fight now came down to five issues:

- Whether net profits were a scam foisted on gullible talent.
- Whether the standard net profit contract was a contract of adhesion.
- Whether contract terms were unconscionable.
- Whether studios needed these terms to survive the risky business of moviemaking.
- Whether Bernheim forfeited financial interest in the project because he had accepted the turnaround clause in his contract.

Turnaround seemed the least important of the five issues.

According to Paramount, after the studio abandoned *King for a Day* in the spring of 1985, Bernheim had one year to "turn around" the project by getting another studio to adopt the project and pay Paramount its $500,000 in development costs. But we believed turnaround was a frivolous argument at best. It became irrelevant six months earlier, when Judge Schneider ruled that Art wrote the story upon which *Coming to America* was based. From that day forward, Paramount was equally obligated to pay Alain for failing to hire him to produce any movie based upon *King for a Day*.

Not so, according to Chuck Diamond.

"Turnaround gives a producer a free one-year option to take someplace else everything owned by the studio—the scripts, the years of development effort and expense, as well as any underlying rights," he wrote. "It is a practical alternative to a studio simply 'warehousing' a project after it loses interest."

The producer has one year. If he fails and the project is subsequently revived, the producer loses his right to participate in the profits, according to Paramount.

Legally and morally, Paramount should have renegotiated with Buchwald and Bernheim in 1987, when Murphy renewed interest in the project. Even the studio's Richard Zimbert admitted to us that Paramount "would not even think about" going behind Bernheim's back to negotiate with Buchwald. Yet the studio held that Bernheim, who brought the project to the studio and nursed it through development for two years, was out in the cold.

Based on Zimbert's testimony as well as Schneider's own earlier ruling, I thought the judge would dismiss turnaround out of hand. But I had sorely miscalculated.

For the moment, our big problem was convincing the judge that Paramount's standard 26-page, single-spaced net profits pact was legally "adhesive": containing provisions prepared by a stronger party with no recourse for meaningful negotiation by the weaker party.

Preprinted apartment leases, insurance contracts and the waiver of liability terms printed on the back of parking lot tickets are classic examples of adhesive contracts. They can be enforced, but courts will occasionally strike unduly harsh terms. That's what we wanted Judge Schneider to do with the notorious Exhibit A.

In all, there were eighteen unfair, unconscionable and adhesive provisions in Exhibit A. They included expense items such as the studio's distribution fees, overhead charges and other flat charges that bore no relationship to actual costs and, in fact, were "sources of enormous profit to the studio, especially on a high-grossing film like *Coming to America*."

The most lucrative hidden profit was the distribution fee. Sapsowitz testified that the studio earned a profit of 20 to 27 percent of its gross receipts on a hit like *Coming to America*. On this one film, the distribution fee alone more than covered the cost of Paramount's worldwide distribution network for an entire year and made the $63 million in distribution fees the studio collected on its other 1987 releases pure profit.

Paramount might need its exorbitant distribution fee to offset its risks, but that didn't explain why the studio needed even more money for studio overhead, advertising, interest and video manufacturing and distribution costs. These and other contractual charges bore "no relationship to actual cost and are in fact hidden sources of profit to the studio," we argued.

Paramount didn't even bother with any point-by-point defense of its fees and charges. Instead, Diamond asserted that Art and Alain could not obtain damages even if the net profit contract were unconscionable. Unconscionability can only be used as a shield to defend against oppressive contract terms, not as a sword to invalidate overly harsh provisions, he said.

"Instead of preventing oppression, a court would, in effect, make a better bargain for one of the parties than actual bargaining could produce," Diamond wrote.

Diamond tried to use the testimony of Roger Davis against us, claiming that the William Morris agent "believed that the contracts were fair and reasonable when signed and he did not try to negotiate better compensation terms because in his opinion, his clients did not deserve them."

But Davis also testified that he knew Bernheim lacked sufficient clout to get Paramount to agree to any changes in Exhibit A. Paramount's own experts —Ben Newman, Mel Sattler and Sid Sapsowitz—agreed that our clients wouldn't have been able to negotiate anything beyond the boilerplate.

Paramount maintained, however, "that the terms of Exhibit A are wide open to negotiation." No subject was off limits. Zimbert testified that, at one time or another, a whole catalog of various standard terms in Exhibit A had been modified. The fact that Davis negotiated none was immaterial. If his clients had clout, things might have been different.

Yet Davis and Newman both admitted net profit participants rarely got any changes in the studios' standard form agreements. The most damaging testimony of all came from Paramount's Sapsowitz, who admitted that a net profit participant relegated to that inferior status remained there. Only a minuscule number ever climbed out of the net profit basement.

According to Paramount, clout, or lack of it, was just one of those inevitable inequities of life.

"This only proves that in the movie industry, as elsewhere, an employee's salary depends on his bargaining power," Diamond wrote.

Paramount was right about one thing. The inequity did seem to be inevitable. It was interesting, however, that the studio lawyers did not address the question of whether or not the inequity was fair.

"The risk of failure in the motion picture business is ever present, immense, and unmitigable," Diamond claimed in hyperbole that even made me blanch.

The contract *was* fair in that, as a whole, it struck a fair balance between the studio's enormous risk and its rewards, he argued.

According to Sapsowitz, when Bernheim signed his contract, fewer than one of fifteen projects placed in development were ever made into motion pictures. Out of these, seven in ten "failed to earn back their actual direct and indirect costs of production, promotion and distribution."

Badagliacca had testified that Paramount's actual track record was two losers out of three. Our own Roger Davis had admitted that, even as practiced by the studios, moviemaking was "a crap shoot" on a film-by-film basis.

But the net profits formula accommodated this "fundamental economic reality of the motion picture business," Paramount argued. Since most motion pictures lost money, the occasional winner had to subsidize the frequent losers. Otherwise, the studios would go broke.

This net profit formula had become almost a tradition. Who the hell were Bernheim and Buchwald to challenge it? They bore no risk. If the film flopped, they had no obligation. Yet Paramount spent $40 million to produce and committed another $35 million to distribute Coming to America "with no assurance that a single theater admission would be sold," Diamond wrote.

But it was never a matter of striking a balance between a studio's risks and rewards. According to Youngstein's and Petersdorf's depositions, at least for the last decade, revenue from video, cable and pay television made it very difficult for a studio to lose money. By our reckoning, the vast majority of films made by Paramount and the other studios made money—"thus demystifying the bogus 'winners must pay for losers' justification for huge studio profits and no net profits."

The real question was whether moviemaking was so risky that studios were justified in gouging net profit participants for the greater good of the studio's survival. Badagliacca's deposition and financial "analysis" turned out to be our single biggest aid in defeating that argument. They supported our arguments that the alleged risks of moviemaking do not justify radically shifting the balance against plaintiffs' ever receiving any net profits, I wrote.

Badagliacca's "analysis" was the underpinning to Paramount's "risky business" defense. Yet, from where I sat, it looked like a result-oriented hodgepodge of financial mumbo jumbo.

For twenty hours a day over three days, I sat at my office computer systematically destroying Badagliacca's testimony. In order to determine what movies actually cost and earned, I had to analyze twenty-three years of Gulf & Western annual reports and motion picture industry data from over fifty other sources and perform more than a hundred and fifty calculations.

But it was worth the effort.

I was able to prove that, in his five-year analysis of ninety films from 1978 to 1982, Badagliacca lowballed revenues, overstated expenses and depressed profits in order to arrive at the conclusion that two out of three movies lost money. In our brief, I accused Paramount of "startling fabrication," "financial chicanery," and "playing games with the numbers to deceive the Court and the public about the riskiness of modern filmmaking." Even for a trial lawyer who struggled through calculus, the defects in the studio's presentation were glaring:

- Badagliacca never explained his terminology. "Profit and loss," "lost money," "indirect costs" and "overhead costs" were never defined.
- He selectively excluded future video and foreign TV revenues and arbitrarily allocated indirect and overhead costs to each picture, never offering an explanation.
- He did not know how the numbers that he used had been prepared or even who prepared them.
- Badagliacca used a mix of estimated and actual figures which artificially depressed profitability by almost $100 million over the five years analyzed in his printouts. Instead of a 10 percent profit margin, my calculations showed that Paramount earned 15 percent, which would have made two out of three movies profitable rather than the other way around. If I added in the correct overhead figures, my analysis showed an even higher success ratio: three out of four films were profitable.

A footnote Bruce Margolius found buried in the financial section of the 1989 annual report of Paramount Communications Inc. seemed to confirm my marathon calculations. The footnote said that 94 percent of Paramount's films became profitable within three years of release.

Badagliacca's "most shocking deception," I wrote, may have been his failure to include at least $217.5 million from video, cable and television syndication in his profit study. When all the omitted future profits were factored into his analysis, Paramount's profit margin skyrocketed to 38.3 percent.

The studio's motion picture division had an operating income margin more than double the margin of the entire company. Rather than a drag on profits, the studio so boosted Gulf & Western's profitability that the shareholders would have been "far better off liquidating the rest of the company and pouring all of the proceeds into its 'risky' motion picture division," I wrote.

In fact, that is exactly what Gulf & Western did from 1983, when Charles Bluhdorn died and Martin Davis took over, through 1989. By the time *Buchwald v. Paramount* went to trial, Gulf & Western was reduced from a diversified conglomerate to a media company concentrated in just three commodities: books, TV and movies.

"Far from the doom and gloom scenario that Paramount's lawyers are painting in this courtroom, the Paramount brain trust has looked into the future, and they have seen celluloid," I wrote.

While any one film might flop, the explosion of foreign markets and VCRs had provided an added safety net. In addition, studios had fat film libraries that produced a steady profit stream for decades after a movie's initial release.

"In truth, movies are not a risky business—and Paramount, more than anyone else, knows it," I concluded.

Paramount would not let us look at their books, so my attack was a calculated guess at best. If I could pique Judge Schneider's interest, though, I might persuade him to order an independent audit of the ninety movies.

The outcome might very well dramatically affect how Paramount and the rest of Hollywood conducted their business for years to come. As the industry watched the unfolding struggle, no one understood why Paramount had let the case spin so perilously out of control.

No one except Martin Davis.

Davis had gotten tough. Increasingly, as the summer wore on, Art and I heard from Davis associates that the Paramount Communications chief was determined to defeat his former friend for causing him such personal embarrassment.

"With my last breath and my last lawyer, I will beat Art Buchwald," Davis was said to have fumed.

And word filtered back to us that Paramount would never settle on any terms.

Suing studios was becoming a growth industry for Kaye, Scholer.

While Zazi and Bruce filed our trial brief, I took off for a one-day business trip to New York to work on a $100 million lawsuit I filed in Manhattan federal court against Columbia Pictures. In the fall of 1988, producers Lester Persky and Richard Bright accused the studio of failing to pay millions of dollars of profits on twelve movies their partnerships owned which were being distributed by Columbia. The list included *Shampoo*, *Funny Lady*, *The Front* and *The Last Detail*.

It was another in my expanding docket of suits against studios charging creative accounting, illegal marketing activities and abuse of trust. In the months ahead, I would sue Universal on behalf of the Mae West estate for failing to pay net profits on the 1940 comedy *My Little Chickadee*. I would also take on Warner Bros. for not paying any net profits on *Batman* to executive producers Benjamin Melnicker and Michael Uslan—despite the fact that that movie had worldwide sales in excess of $600 million and was ranked the sixth highest-grossing movie of all time.

After I finished in New York, I shuttled to Martha's Vineyard to visit Art and Ann Buchwald.

"What about this 'risky business' stuff?" Art wanted to know one afternoon as we lunched at a plain picnic table on the aging front porch of the Vineyard Haven Yacht Club—the least exclusive club in America, once described by the New York *Times* as "a shack on a dune." "It sounds like a lot of crap to me. Who are they kidding?"

"I agree, Art. I just hope that the judge read my cross-examination of Paramount's chief financial planner, Badagliacca. It's buried in a couple thousand pages of transcripts, exhibits and legal briefs."

"And if he didn't?" Art asked.

"You and I will have a lot more time for tennis this fall."

A week after both sides filed their briefs, I was back in Los Angeles. Judge Schneider set up a conference call for August 1, during which he told us he wanted us back in court on August 6. He had some preliminary conclusions for us. We might want to notify the media, he suggested.

I was unnerved. The buzz around town was that the judge wasn't buying "unconscionability" and that he was calling the hearing to deliver the death blow to our case. On Monday morning, Department 52 was packed with reporters, lawyers and observers.

Taking the bench promptly at eight-thirty, Judge Schneider launched into his preliminary answers to the thirty-five questions on which we had submitted evidence two weeks earlier. Right away, Bruce Margolius and I were heartened.

"Were the Buchwald and Bernheim contracts take-it-or-leave-it contracts? That is, did plaintiffs and defendant negotiate in this case? . . . The entire contract was drafted by Paramount. Mr. Davis testified that no negotiation was made or attempted by him on the net profit contract because Bernheim lacked the clout for him to negotiate a better deal for net profits. And he knew from prior experience that Paramount did not negotiate any change in its net profit agreement. . . . There was really no negotiations . . . with respect to the net profit agreement."

We had won the contract of adhesion argument. We were hardly home free, but we were still alive.

"Issue No. 8: Is contingent compensation in the form of net profits an important part of a talent's compensation package? The short answer to this question is yes.

"Issue No. 9: Are net profit participations ever generated by a film? The evidence on this issue is not conclusive. . . . As I indicated, this is one of the major issues in the case, it seems to me. And since the evidence is not conclusive, I want to take testimony from . . . Badagliacca, Sapsowitz, Newman, Petersdorf and Leedy.

"Issue No. 10: Did *Coming to America* generate any profits? I need to take testimony on this, gentlemen. And I want to hear from at least Mr. Desiderio and the accountants."

Schneider ticked off his thoughts on two dozen other issues, and Bruce and I liked what we were hearing.

"Whether intentional or not, it is clear that the net profit definition that permits gross participations to be given substantially reduces the chances of net profit participants receiving any money. This is particularly true since the shares given to gross profit participants can effectively wipe out net profit participants' hope of ever seeing any money on a film.

"There is . . . a difference between a studio's risks on a particular film and a studio's risks in being in the movie business in general. A particular movie, depending on the star, may or may not present a risk. It seems clear, however, that the studios wouldn't be in the business if they continually lost money. The bottom line is that I don't have enough information on this issue and I need to take testimony from the same witnesses that I've indicated above."

Paramount had not convinced him that "winners must subsidize losers," and he wanted live testimony.

Then Judge Schneider dropped a ticking time bomb in Diamond's lap.

The judge had indeed read my cross-examination of Badagliacca, and he was skeptical of Paramount's claim that two out of three movies actually lose money—so skeptical that he wanted the documents that Paramount had refused to give me.

"Mr. Badagliacca says that there are internal profit and loss statements that do not go to profit participants. I would be very interested in seeing those, gentlemen."

"So would I, your honor," I blurted out.

"Would you repeat that?" a stunned Diamond asked.

Schneider obliged, and Diamond insisted that the statements were "part of the record."

"I don't think so," Schneider replied, raising his voice slightly for emphasis. "I'm very seriously thinking of ordering the production of these internal documents."

"I'd like to be heard on that," Diamond insisted.

But Schneider was adamant. He was so exercised about "the profitability of pictures at Paramount, the issue of actual versus contract accounting, and the point at which *Coming to America* will achieve net profits" that he was also thinking about appointing his own expert "to thoroughly examine the books and records of Paramount. . . . It's not clear to me that I have all the facts that I need with respect to those issues."

Bruce passed me a note: "Schneider has figured out that Paramount is lying about its profitability. Paramount will never submit to an audit. They'll have to settle."

This inquiry could "open up Pandora's box," Diamond ominously warned. "I suggest that the Court is ranging far afield, and . . . not dealing with the issues relevant to the questions of unconscionability."

The judge would not be bullied.

"In the vernacular of the movie industry, I'm giving you a preview of coming attractions. . . . It is entirely possible, after taking the testimony, that I may well ask for the production of those internal documents, and I may well appoint my own expert to do whatever we all can agree is appropriate under the circumstances. The parameters of the investigation are not established in my mind—at this time."

Despite his carefully chosen words, the judge was clearly not buying Paramount's act on its perilous profitability.

"You don't have to be a Rhodes scholar to figure out that these folks aren't in business to continually lose money. Even I'm smart enough to realize that. So, what's the answer to all these problems? I'd like to know. . . . I haven't been given conclusive evidence that this is a risky business."

The rest of the hearing was devoted to the judge giving his tentative views on the remaining questions. One answer further buoyed our spirits: distribution fees, overhead charges and other flat fees have no relation to actual costs. This finding was the essential prerequisite to declaring the contract unconscionable. All that stood in our way, I thought, was Paramount's tenuous risky business defense, some lingering questions in the judge's mind about whether we could use unconscionability as "a sword instead of a shield," and the effect of Bernheim's turnaround clause.

Paramount won one issue that it cared about dearly. Schneider had concluded that outside of giving them an honest accounting, the studio had no fiduciary duty to Art and Alain. That is, it had been under no obligation to keep its expenses down on *Coming to America* in order to maximize Art's and Alain's profit position. According to Schneider, essentially that meant Paramount didn't have to "spend money wisely." As I described the judge's thinking later to the media, Paramount was legally within its rights to be an unimaginably lousy money manager.

Schneider also made it clear during the hearing that he was not very interested in interpreting a boilerplate contract either. What interested him was whether he did, in fact, have the legal discretion to rewrite all or part of Art's and Alain's net profit agreements.

"One way or another, I'm going to get to the bottom of this," he warned as the hearing ended.

Outside the courtroom, both Diamond and I went on at length about how we'd triumphed. Depending upon which side you were rooting for, we both had reason to crow.

"It was a very good day for us in this case," said Diamond, pointing to the defeat of our fiduciary duty argument. "We are very happy."

I admired Chuck's spin control abilities.

"We're very euphoric," I said. "Paramount, by its own defense, has put the film industry's profitability on trial—something I don't think the other studios are very happy about."

And with good reason, I learned later that day when I picked up *Daily Variety.*

Suing studios had become a popular Hollywood avocation. At the same time Diamond and I were making our latest appearance before Judge Schneider, two brand-new net profit lawsuits were being filed in Los Angeles Superior Court. Actress Sigourney Weaver and director James Cameron joined producer Walter Hill and several others in a suit charging Twentieth Century Fox with failing to pay net profits on the 1986 science fiction thriller *Aliens.* At the same time, actors/writers Renee Taylor and Joe Bologna sued Columbia/Tri-Star for using their screenplay as the basis for the 1989 release, *See No Evil, Hear No Evil,* and failing to pay them net profits.

Outrage over studio profiteering was spreading. Creative people were no longer afraid of the anonymous executives behind the studio gates. Buchwald and Bernheim had let the genie out of the bottle, and now it refused to go back inside. Whether we won or lost, Hollywood would never be the same again.

37

The Envelope, Please

IN THE WAKE of the August 6 hearing, I pondered strategy for the next phase of the case. Ordinarily I'd have hashed this out with my colleagues, but Zazi was on her honeymoon in Bora Bora, and Bruce and Dennis were on vacation too.

We had to persuade Judge Schneider that he ought to examine Paramount's books and records and appoint his own auditor. He was leaning in that direction, but I needed something to push him over. By the time Dennis returned, I had thought of that something. I reached him at home on a Saturday.

"Dennis, I have an idea."

"I'm sure you do." He knew that he was about to be sent on a mission.

"Is there a computerized data base that contains *Daily Variety?*"

"No, you have to read the back issues when you want to find something. There isn't even a topical index for researching back issues."

"Well, Dennis, ol' boy, you are about to spend a lot of time in the library."

"Risky business?"

"You bet. I have a hunch that former Paramount executives couldn't resist the temptation to brag about their financial success in the trades. I want every quote that anyone at the studio ever uttered about film profitability."

"How far back?"

"Say fifteen years."

"That's a lot of reading. Fifteen years times 260 issues per year. Several thousand issues averaging over thirty pages per issue."

"I know, and we have a lot riding on it. Thanks, Dennis."

Landry went to the Academy of Motion Picture Arts and Science's Margaret Kettrick Library and read through fifteen years' worth of *Variety*, culling out the incessant reports of Paramount's ever escalating movie receipts. Dennis and I also pored through twenty-three years of Gulf & Western financial statements. We found several gems, including a 1984 statement from Frank Mancuso about Paramount's standing policy on earning studio profits:

"Our challenge is to squeeze every potential revenue-dollar out of every movie we make. It's a 52-week-a-year challenge."

According to the company's own annual reports, one of the chief ways the corporation was meeting that challenge was through its rapidly expanding videocassette operations. In 1983, Paramount marketed over 176,000 copies of *Flashdance*, "enough to make it potentially the largest selling video cassette in history." Two years later, *Flashdance* cassette sales were already chicken feed. The company's 1985 report was boasting sales of 1 million copies of *Raiders of the Lost Ark* and pulling in 1.2 million preorders for *Beverly Hills Cop II*. In that year's annual report, the corporation also reported:

"Home video, a market that didn't exist five years ago, has become an important and growing source of revenue for Paramount and other motion picture studios. Industry sales of prerecorded videocassettes are expected to reach an estimated $2 billion in calendar 1985 and $2.5 billion in 1986."

So what could that add up to by 1990? Perhaps $5 billion? Or more?

By 1988, Paramount reported to its shareholders that more than 52 million American households had VCRs. Outside of the United States, another 100 million VCRs were in use. For Paramount, that meant that hits like *Crocodile Dundee*, *Coming to America* and *Fatal Attraction* could rake in even more abroad. Even a domestic box office flop like *The Presidio* could actually turn out to be an international hit. Paramount's prognosticators predicted that, by 1994, half of all foreign film revenue would come from video.

"While we have long had an international audience, it has never been so large and we have never had so many ways to reach it," Paramount's management wrote in the company's 1989 annual report—the first in which "home video" was accorded its own separate section.

But Art and Alain, and every other creative person who ever signed a studio contract, would never see more than a small slice of 20 percent of that video pie. In 1990, the studios and their distributors still kept eighty cents of every dollar, plus "expenses."

While Landry was digging up proof that Paramount's was anything but a risky business, Bruce chased evidence that Paramount borrowed regularly from Security Pacific Bank, using film packages as collateral. While Diamond stood in the courtroom, telling Judge Schneider and the rest of the world that most Paramount movies didn't earn a dime, the company's money men were seeking—and getting—millions in bank loans on the strength of their movie profits!

Our sleuthing remained a risky business for us, though. We were digging up proof that Paramount's risks were minimal and profits enormous, but the judge, already buried in a mountain of transcripts, exhibits and "briefs," did *not* want any more paper. Yet that was precisely what we were generating—a persuasive record of newly discovered evidence that Paramount was lying about its profitability.

Diamond and I continued to tilt over "unconscionability," filing rival briefs on the subject the first week of September. But I saw little hope for us if we simply wheeled in another cartload of documents and dumped them on the Court's desk by our October 15 trial deadline. Worse yet, Judge Schneider had forbidden any more filings without his prior permission. I had to do something dramatic to get the judge's attention.

Risking his ire, I sat down and wrote him a letter on September 24. In eight single-spaced pages I told him I wanted to reopen discovery, but the real reason for sending the letter was to show the judge that Paramount was playing fast and loose with its financial figures. I laid out in detail our findings from a broad range of sources, including filings with government agencies, annual reports, newspaper and magazine articles, and knowledgeable third parties.

The one thing the studio had fought tooth and nail was to keep us—and the Court—from seeing its true profit and loss records. I told Judge Schneider that those records were *precisely* what I demanded to see. Furthermore, I wanted to fly to New York and depose Martin Davis himself, as well as his two top financial officers. I wanted them to explain to the Court, under oath, how risky their business really was—and explain contrary statements about Paramount's high profitability that they had made to shareholders over the years.

I also proposed to call five current and former Paramount film executives to the stand to explain risky business, including Barry Diller, Frank Yablans, Sid Ganis, Don Simpson and Frank Mancuso. I cited Diller, who served as Paramount's chairman from 1974 to 1984, as just the kind of witness who could offer firsthand evidence of Paramount's profitability. During an eighteen-month stretch in 1977 and 1978, Paramount released twenty profitable movies in a row and the studio's impressive profitability was not attributable to a single blockbuster, he had once told *Business Week*.

"When you release twenty films and do not lose money on a single one, it isn't just luck," he said at the time.

Similarly, I planned to ask Simpson what he meant when he told *Reel Power* author Mark Litwak that, while he worked at Paramount from 1972 to 1983, the studio made thirty-seven profitable movies in a row:

"The truth is that with ancillary sales . . . very few pictures lose money. Most break even. . . . The studio can't lose. I've been at Paramount for 11 years and I can only remember two pictures losing money. . . . People don't understand how this business works. You go out and get guarantees. . . .

[The misconceptions] are all publicity shit. [The studios] try to make *Time* and *Newsweek* believe in the poor beleaguered movie business."

In a 1980 interview with the *Christian Science Monitor*, Sid Ganis, the president of Paramount's motion picture group in the fall of 1990, had likewise boasted of a studio's ability to make a profit even on box office disappointments.

"A major [studio] will make some money on a picture whether or not it is successful. They get distribution fees on every picture they sell."

Margolius and Landry had discovered that, as far back as the early seventies, Paramount also minimized its risk through joint ventures, partnerships and lease-back arrangements, and raked in huge profits. In its 1973 annual report, then Paramount president Yablans spelled out exactly how this risk-sharing maneuver worked with a hit film that had been independently financed but distributed through Paramount the previous year:

"*Lady Sings the Blues*, in which Paramount has a substantial profit participation that involved no dollar investment, has generated rentals so far totalling approximately $9 million."

And when the studio released *Reds* in 1981, Paramount did not gamble a penny of its own money. The movie's record $33.5 million production price tag was underwritten in a complex tax shelter arrangement with a subsidiary of Barclays Bank. As part of an overall deal for $105 million worth of films, Barclays bought *Reds* and leased it back to Paramount so that the studio reaped the profits but assumed none of the risk. Just fragmentary evidence alone, I told the judge, indicated that "Paramount has substantially reduced its financial risk in moviemaking by means of off balance sheet financing, cofinancing, and other programs by which outside investors contributed some or all of the money for producing and/or distributing the films. . . . In 1978–82 alone, these sources contributed at least 20% of Paramount's direct production costs."

Diamond's response was swift and predictable. In a lengthy September 28 letter to Judge Schneider, he accused me of trying "to bring in a new line-up of witnesses to bolster a sagging case. . . . Corralling Paramount's former creative executives as trial witnesses and rummaging through ancient memoranda and correspondence will not serve any legitimate fact-finding purpose," he told Judge Schneider.

"The number and percentage of movies that produced profits for Paramount is a matter for accountants—exactly the witnesses the Court has asked to hear from and whom Paramount will produce. The bravado of studio executives, perhaps 'hyping' their track record, even if accurately reported (which, in the case of Simpson, it was not), cannot impeach audited financial statements."

Laying open Paramount's entire financial history simply because Buchwald and Bernheim wanted net profits from one movie was "perverse," said Diamond.

But not so perverse in Harvey Schneider's opinion.

The judge convened a special October 1 conference in his chambers. Right off the bat, he strongly disagreed with Diamond's claim, first raised in his letter a few days earlier, that the law of unconscionability did not authorize us to put Paramount's profitability on trial. "Profitability is an issue in this case," Judge Schneider assured Diamond several times. And if Paramount disagreed, he self-assuredly told Diamond, it could take an emergency appeal (called a "writ of mandate") to the Court of Appeal.

Judge Schneider then zeroed in on Badagliacca's 166-page computer printout that Diamond insisted was all the internal Paramount financial records that the judge needed to see.

"Badagliacca was not convincing," he told us. "There are documents he mentioned, like the internal profit statements that say 'for Paramount's eyes only,' that have not been made public.

"I want as much information as I can get. I want to get to the bottom of every scrap of paper that is relevant to the profitability issue, and I'm inclined to require the production of every document that has a reasonable probability of being relevant. . . . If Paramount is right, it is entitled to be vindicated. But plaintiffs are entitled to prove that they are right."

Rejecting Diamond's suggestion that former Paramount executives were just "puffing" when they bragged about the studio's string of profitable movies, the Court ruled that we would also be able to examine witnesses under oath, starting with Barry Diller. And Schneider had a lot of his own questions that he wanted to ask. He was now convinced that he had to bring in his own accountant to help him sift through fifteen years of Paramount's finances. "Whomever you choose is fine with me," the judge indicated.

As we prepared to leave, Judge Schneider reached in his drawer, pulled out a brochure and let the air out of my balloon.

"One more thing, gentlemen. I see that both of you are hitting the lecture circuit a little prematurely here," he said, tossing the brochure across his desk.

The pamphlet advertised a November 3 symposium, sponsored by the Los Angeles County Bar Association, titled " 'The Back End': A Look at Gross and Net Participation in the Wake of *Buchwald v. Paramount*." Inside, headlining the daylong seminar, were Charles Diamond and Pierce O'Donnell.

"How can you have a conference about the wake of the Buchwald decision when we're in the middle of it?" Schneider asked.

Chuck and I had been invited to participate six months earlier and, at the time, both Diamond and I, as well as Judge Schneider, thought the whole thing would be over in a few months. That was before unconscionable contracts and risky business. After he had us squirm for a while, the judge threw the brochure back into the drawer.

"Well, let's not jump the gun," he said.

For the first time in months, Chuck and I agreed on something: we canceled our appearances before the bar association. The message from Judge Schneider was loud and clear: this was his show right now. And the way things were going, that was just fine with me.

. . . .

The question of an accountant or "Special Master" for Judge Schneider was still open. I wanted someone with an entertainment industry accounting background who had experience auditing motion picture studios and who would be fair and impartial. That was a tall order because most accountants worked either the studio or profit participant side of the street but not both. After talking to Finger, Hacker and Shapiro and interviewing several people, I found that ideal figure.

A senior partner of Price Waterhouse, Franklin R. Johnson is a certified public accountant with a reputation as one of the leading motion picture industry accountants in the country. He had conducted studio audits on behalf of profit participants and had done auditing work for MCA/Universal, Twentieth Century Fox and Disney. The fact that his clients included studios did not bother me at all. I had recently worked with Frank on a legal and financial audit of New World Pictures on behalf of our mutual client, General Electric Capital, and I had a high regard for his integrity and professionalism.

Johnson was an attractive candidate for another reason. Price Waterhouse is the accounting firm that for decades has supervised the annual balloting for the Academy Awards. Every Oscar buff knows that it is a Price Waterhouse accountant, decked out in his tuxedo, who hands over the winning name when the presenter says, "The envelope, please." And it is Frank Johnson who is in charge of Price Waterhouse's handling of the Academy Awards balloting and telecast appearances. What better accountant, I thought, to hand Judge Schneider the envelope containing an audit of Paramount's books.

Now I had to sell Johnson to Diamond and his client. Paramount had proposed two other accountants to Judge Schneider, and I had nominated Frank Johnson and another accountant. But I knew something that put Diamond and his law firm in an awkward position: O'Melveny & Myers was one of the major outside law firms that regularly represented Price Waterhouse. How would it look if Diamond trashed one of the firm's major clients and deprived its top movie accounting partner of this high-visibility appointment in the most publicized Hollywood accounting case ever?

What Diamond did not know was that I had been reliably informed that Frank Johnson, in an unpublished press interview, had criticized the studios for sharing only 20 percent of the videocassette revenues with profit participants. That told me that he was not in the studios' pockets. And it was conceivable that Judge Schneider might ask Johnson to advise him on other aspects of the case, including the fairness of the 80-20 video split that I had attacked as unconscionable. Without ever having spoken a word to Johnson about any of the issues in our case, I was certain he would be inclined to recommend a more evenhanded split of videocassette revenues.

While I was jockeying to get Frank Johnson named Special Master, Howard Weitzman called during the second week in October. One of the preeminent trial lawyers in America, Howard is also an old friend of mine and a law school classmate of Harvey Schneider's.

Howard's call did not come as a surprise. Several months earlier, when I helped Howard work out a complicated settlement in the "Blue Jeans Wars" between Guess? and Jordache, I'd hinted that he might reciprocate and broker a settlement between Paramount and my clients. Now he was representing David Kirkpatrick, who had recently left Disney and was returning to Paramount as its newly named head of production. Ironically, Disney was now doing to Kirkpatrick what Paramount had done when Kirkpatrick jumped ship for the Weintraub Entertainment Group four years earlier: suing him for breach of contract.

Howard was friendly with Robert Pisano, Paramount's general counsel, and his engagement by Kirkpatrick had given him the opening he needed to take on the mediator role I'd envisioned for him.

His call, Howard told me, had been authorized by Pisano and Frank Mancuso.

"How does $1.3 million sound?" he asked almost immediately.

It was our first solid offer from Paramount since the eve of trial. I guessed that the studio's legal department had probably done a rough in-house analysis and come up with $1.3 million as a number that would just about cover our legal fees. They were wrong of course. We had passed the $1.3 million mark way back in March and were fast approaching $2 million. We were spending time at the rate of $100,000 per month, and I had only half as many lawyers as Paramount was throwing against us. Little wonder then that we had already exceeded my revised prediction to the Kaye, Scholer billing committee that our total fees would be only $1.75 million.

Weitzman interpreted my silence as a somewhat less than lukewarm response. "I know they're on another planet, Pierce," he said. "I know that you can't settle for $1.3 million. But let's get the ball rolling."

I had $5 million in mind. That was the original figure in our complaint, it was reasonable recompense for what Paramount had done to my clients, and the math worked out right: our share of the take would be $2 million and Alain and Art would get $3 million. By rights, we were entitled to make more than merely the normal value of our time in light of the results and our contingent fee risk. But the firm wasn't in the case to make a killing.

I countered with $8 million.

"Look, Howard, it's your job to sell a number in between $1.3 million and $8 million. You know that I will take less than $8 million, but $1.3 million is insulting. I have $2 million in time charges and a 40 percent contingency fee. Your client is smart enough to figure it out." And I gave him a bone: I said that we would issue a joint press release, and I would make nice about the studio settling the case in the interest of minimizing tensions within the creative community.

"I'll be back with a counteroffer," Howard signed off.

After I hung up, I immediately called Washington and tracked Buchwald down at the Jockey Club where Ann and he were dining with Washington *Post* editor Ben Bradlee and his columnist wife, Sally Quinn.

"Art, this is just you and me talking," I told him. "This is very sensitive."

After hearing me out on the settlement offer, Art repeated his one caveat to me: no gag order. He was agreeable to a fair settlement, but not if Paramount conditioned its payment on silence.

"Weitzman never mentioned a confidentiality clause, and he knows from my prior conversations with him that you won't be muzzled about the terms of any deal. So I assume that Paramount is prepared to forget about it."

Also, I mentioned the idea of a joint press release, and he said, "Yeah, I have never used my column to argue our case. And I won't do it in the future. That would be a breach of ethics for a newspaperman. You can tell them they don't have to worry about that."

"I will, Art. You know what the timing of the call tells me?"

"What?"

"Paramount's running scared. They didn't bamboozle Schneider with all those numbers and accounting double-talk. In a few days, the judge is about to appoint an accountant to audit Paramount's books for five years and then make the results public. That's the last thing the studio wants. They haven't been able to derail the audit, so the only way out is to settle."

"Sounds great," Art told me. "Keep me posted."

When Buchwald got back to his table, Bradlee asked what was so important that Art got called away from the dinner table. Art shrugged. It was his lawyer in Los Angeles, he said, calling about possibly settling the case. Nothing more was said, and the diners returned to their meals and talk of the upcoming fall elections.

The following day, the Washington *Post's* John Richardson called me, saying he had heard a rumor that a settlement might be in the offing.

"I have no comment," I said, my mind racing about how to head off this unwelcome intrusion of the free press just as Paramount and I were starting to have the first serious settlement talks in over two years. I wouldn't lie to a reporter, so I said "no comment" to each of his questions.

"You know, Pierce, when you say no comment, there must be something going on. You haven't ever missed a chance to take a shot at Paramount. It's almost newsworthy that Buchwald's spin doctor won't talk to the media."

"Come on, John. Give me a break. You know that's one subject that no lawyer talks about while it's going on, and I'm not confirming that anything is going on."

"Okay. I understand," he said. "But help me out here. Who should I talk to?"

"Why don't you call Robert Pisano at Paramount?"

The next call I got was from Weitzman.

"The talks are off, Pierce. Some reporter from the *Post* called Pisano and they went nuts," he said. "They said that you turned the press loose on them to increase the pressure for settlement. So then they figured that it was your client who tipped off his buddy Bradlee at the *Post*. It doesn't really matter, though. The settlement talks are over."

I sat back, feeling an odd mix of disappointment and exhilaration. I laughed out loud.

"You know, Howard, if you'd called to tell me this a month ago, I would have gone over to Harry's, ordered up a tumbler of Old Bushmill's and drunk myself slowly into a stupor. But I'm telling you now, after what I heard in Schneider's chambers last week, your client—well, now your former client—is goddam crazy. Those guys don't have a clue what they're facing. And the hawks over there used Richardson's phone call as an excuse to scuttle settlement talks. They deserve whatever happens to them."

"I know," he said with a deep sigh. "I told them that Schneider's going to lower the boom and that they were facing a disaster, putting the industry's net profit contracts on the line. I don't know who's calling the shots over there. They're walking right into a bottomless pit with their eyes wide open. And they don't seem to care."

Paramount eventually accepted Frank Johnson as the Court's independent expert, and at the October 17 hearing Schneider formally appointed him as his Special Master and ordered us to schedule a hearing with Johnson to come up with a "game plan."

But the judge resisted another attempt by Diamond to prevent the audit.

"The doctrine of unconscionability focuses on the allocation of risks, and I don't see how I can make a determination as to the allocation of risks unless I know something about Paramount's profits," Schneider said. And then he made this ominous observation:

"It is only if Paramount is right . . . that these contract provisions are required because of the nature of the allocation of risks, that Paramount prevails . . . on the unconscionability issue."

Schneider then denied Paramount's request to throw out our unconscionability claim. We were not using the doctrine improperly, he ruled. And, he announced, he was planning on writing a formal decision "as I did the first time around."

I certainly hoped it was just like the first time around.

The only sour note during the hearing was the judge's failure to rule on the turnaround issue. "I'm having a little bit of a problem with turnaround. . . . The application of the language to this case I find somewhat difficult. . . . The turnaround provision would seem to suggest that Bernheim's rights, all of his rights, terminated at the end of turnaround."

The sole consolation was that the judge said he had not made up his mind. But I should be prepared to convince him that Bernheim's rights—and almost all of our damages—had not been forfeited back in 1986 when Alain failed to set up the project at another studio and reimburse Paramount for its half million dollars in development costs.

Schneider seemed energized by the prospect of having his own auditor look at Paramount's books. The fact that the inquiry may have been unprecedented did not faze him in the least.

"We're sort of blazing new trails here and there and we can invent the wheel as we go along," he commented.

Toward the end of the hearing I suggested that, in light of statements made by Diamond in recent letters to the judge, Paramount might be abandoning its risky business justification for his unconscionable contract terms. At first, Diamond's response seemed to indicate that he agreed with my observation.

"It's our view that, regrettably, we marched, albeit hand in hand with the plaintiffs, down the wrong path of analysis. I don't think, as a matter of law, the magnitude of the risks that we take in making movies probably is germane to the question of whether the contracts with the plaintiffs are substantively fair."

But as he kept arguing, Diamond talked himself out of conceding that his client was no longer defending the unconscionable contract terms on the grounds that they were essential for the studio's survival.

"It's not clear, but I guess the answer to my question is that at this point they are not abandoning the defense," I noted.

"I guess not," a bemused Judge Schneider agreed.

Down on the first floor of the courthouse, Howard Weitzman was quietly filing a completely unrelated lawsuit that, ironically, confirmed much of the uglier side of Hollywood I had described just one year earlier during the first phase of *Buchwald v. Paramount*.

It turned out that Weitzman was representing Robert Wachs, who had hired him to sue Arsenio Hall for fraud and malicious breach of contract. The talk show host Wachs had helped raise to superstar status had fired him as his manager on August 2.

Wachs demanded $25 million in damages.

On October 25, Zazi and I met for an hour with screenwriter Larry Ferguson and his attorney, Jamie Mulholland, to discuss suing the Writers Guild over its mishandling of a credits arbitration for *Beverly Hills Cop II*. Ferguson, who cowrote the screenplay for the Paramount hit with Warren Skaaren, maintained that the story was his alone, but Robert Wachs and Eddie Murphy convinced Paramount and the WGA otherwise. Thus, the screen credits proclaimed to the world that Wachs and Murphy were the creative forces who conceived the story for the movie while Ferguson and Skaaren merely wrote it up in screenplay form. The whole affair bore a striking similarity to Buchwald's case, and that's why Ferguson came to see me.

The grab for the story credit was typical of Bob Wachs, Ferguson told us. He had power and money, but, like his client, he wanted more. Ferguson, who is one of the industry's most talented screenwriters and whose writing credits include *The Hunt for Red October*, is a ruggedly handsome, articulate and disarmingly blunt person. Halfway through our meeting, when our discussion had shifted for a moment to *Buchwald v. Paramount*, Ferguson knocked me off my chair.

"I really like you, Pierce, so I feel I can tell you this story," he said as he leaned forward on the couch in my office and looked me straight in the eye with a gaze so intense that I blinked.

One day in the late spring or early summer of 1987, Ferguson ran into Wachs on the Paramount lot. They of course knew each other from Ferguson's recent work on *Beverly Hills Cop II* which Murphy and Wachs greatly admired. Ferguson asked Wachs what Eddie Murphy was up to, and Wachs went into a lengthy rapture about the latest movie idea that Murphy had conceived himself, according to Wachs.

It was about a black African prince who comes to America and winds up in the ghetto, he told him.

"Now, I had been on the Paramount lot in 1983 and 1984, and I had read the Buchwald treatment because I was one of the writers being considered for that project," Ferguson told me.

"So I said to Bob: 'Bob, come on, that's Art Buchwald's story. I read it myself when Paramount had it in development a few years ago.'

"Bob got real defensive and said, 'No, it's not. What are you talking about?'

" 'Bob,' I said again, 'that's Buchwald's story.' At which point Bob said to me: 'Don't worry. They'll never know the difference.' "

After Ferguson and his lawyer left, I sat in my office with Zazi. I was angry.

"If Ferguson's telling the truth—and I have absolutely no doubt about his veracity—Wachs lied under oath," I told Zazi.

"Well, I believe Larry," my colleague said. "He has a lot to lose by telling us what he just said. He still works on the Paramount lot, and we know how vindictive the studio can be."

"Think about it, Zazi. If Wachs testified falsely, what about the other witnesses like Eddie and Arsenio? How high up the pecking order did this perjury go? How many Paramount executives knew that Buchwald's *King for a Day* was in fact the source of Murphy's inspiration and conspired to cover up the theft back as early as 1987?"

"Well, that's the smoking gun for punitive damages that we needed at the trial," Zazi noted. "What are you going to do with this new evidence?"

"For now, there's nothing we can do. I don't want to hurt Larry's career. What's more, we are in the fight of our lives right now over unconscionability. We have months of Johnson's audit work and wrangling with Paramount about what it all means. If we surface Ferguson now, it will look like we are desperate, and we're not. Let's hold him in reserve."

Diamond and I were back in court on November 8 with Frank Johnson sandwiched between the two of us at a table in the center of Judge Schneider's courtroom. The room was nearly vacant. After all, it was to be a simple status conference, during which Schneider was planning to tell the accounting expert from Price Waterhouse precisely what he wanted from Paramount's front office.

That was exactly how the hearing started out.

"Desiderio testified that within the last fifteen years Paramount has paid in excess of $150 million in net profits using the standard net profit definition, or something close to it," Schneider began. "What would be involved in determining the accuracy of that statement?"

"Well, that would be a relatively time-consuming job. . . . It's capable of being done," Johnson answered. He estimated forty to ninety hours inside the Paramount books for the twenty-nine films which the studio claimed had paid net profits.

Schneider also wanted to know about break even. Sid Finger testified that *Coming to America* might break even at $238 million, and Carmen Desiderio told us it would break even at $168 million, he said. Could Johnson find out when the film would generate a profit under the net profit definition and based on "actual expenses"?

Diamond interrupted. Desiderio *projected* break even at $168 million, he corrected. The Paramount accountant didn't flatly *say* when the movie would or would not move into net profits. Schneider scowled, and Johnson jumped in as a referee.

"Your honor, I guess my reaction to this issue is that there would be in existence at Paramount estimates of ultimate revenues on *Coming to America*, as to what at the end of its lifetime it will earn," said Johnson in an impromptu attempt to mediate this disagreement. "What is relevant is what the most current information at Paramount indicates as to what is likely *Coming to America* will achieve. Those numbers would be available, presumably. . . . It would just be a mathematical exercise of applying those numbers to contractual terms."

Schneider seemed satisfied.

The judge introduced the next item on his agenda by reiterating one of the key conclusions he had announced at the early August hearing.

"I have already concluded that these flat expenses [15 percent for overhead and 10 percent for advertising surcharge] do not bear any relationship to actual cost. I don't think Paramount contends otherwise."

I looked over at Diamond, but he did not object to Judge Schneider's characterization of his position. And if he did, I knew from over nine months of hand-to-hand combat with him that he would speak up.

Judge Schneider then instructed his Special Master to take a side-by-side look at *Coming to America*'s bottom line: how much did it earn under GAAP accounting, and how much did it earn using the standard net profit definition?

"The film is already profitable—there is no question about that," said Diamond, interrupting again. "There's never been a dispute about that. The film reached profits some period of time ago."

Johnson refereed again, promising that he could come up with the two separate profit/loss statements. All he would need would be total access to all of Paramount's receipts and expenses for the movie, including home video records. I looked at Zazi and Bruce, and they smiled. Johnson was going after the huge profits that, in his words to the judge, "reside in a home video subsidiary or division." If these profits alone were restored to the picture's account, the entire $18 million net loss that Paramount was claiming would be wiped out, and there would be millions of net profits. The hoarding of these immense profits was one of the studio's largest Achilles' heels and a source of outrage in the creative community. And Judge Schneider had just ordered a full-blown investigation.

Schneider seemed to be smiling too. After nearly a year of dickering over very basic dollars and cents issues, he was finally getting somewhere. But he was far from finished. He had a lot on his "laundry list" that he wanted Johnson to examine.

"Paramount has taken the position that its standard net profit definition is necessary because Paramount runs a risk on each picture because there are so many more pictures that lose money than make money," he said. "They argue that it's necessary in order for the continued existence of Paramount and, I guess by implication, all other people involved in this business that winners pay for losers. I'm interested in knowing, as of the time the contracts involved in this case were entered into, whether Paramount's assertions are correct."

Diamond shook his head and raised his voice.

"It's not my position that it is necessary for Paramount to have net profit contracts to do anything," he said. "It's not Paramount's position that we have to have net profit contracts."

"Really?" asked a dumbfounded Schneider.

"Really, absolutely, your honor," Diamond fired back. "What we have said since the beginning of the case is that more pictures lose money than make money. The necessary implication of that fact is that, on pictures that are successful, the studio has to reach enough profits to defray the losses that it makes on the pictures that are unsuccessful."

"What is different from what you just said and what I said?" Schneider wanted to know.

"It is not necessary that we split profits with net profit participants in the fashion we do. What we have said is, historically, the way the industry has grown up, that is the fact." But the studio did not have to treat profit participants like Alain and Art the way they did to survive; it could find other ways to make up the deficits on the losing pictures.

Schneider stopped short and stared at Diamond for two uncomfortable seconds. He blinked like a man who had just been informed that the moon was composed of Roquefort. Noting that Diamond's statements were "a revelation," Judge Schneider was incredulous. He asked Chuck point-blank: was it his position that the studio's flat distribution fees and costs "are not required for the future existence of Paramount or the industry? Is that what you are telling me?"

The answer was yes, Diamond replied. "We could do business any number of different ways. We could try to negotiate a better split with the theater owners and add more revenues. We could pay gross participants less. We could pay studio executives less. Shareholders could settle for less dividends." The only reason Buchwald and Bernheim had such a definition in their contracts was because the pacts had been negotiated that way.

But Diamond did not stop at making the concession that I had suggested three weeks earlier he was making. He went on to argue that he had never claimed that Paramount needed the net profit formula for its survival! That was too much for an already perturbed Schneider to take without comment.

"But that's what you have continuously told me."

"I have never said that," Diamond angrily replied.

"I think that you ought to go back and look at your documents," the judge scolded him. "Let me see if I further understand your position. You don't need the provisions but you have them in this contract because they were negotiated. That's the end of story."

"End of story," Diamond shot back. "We have them in the contract because they were negotiated and are fair. Our defense to unconscionability is that . . . they were represented by a powerhouse of a talent agent and the deal is competitive. It's what they would have gotten."

Schneider sat back in his chair and rocked in stunned silence for a moment.

"This case has become incredibly more simple in the last ten minutes," he said finally.

"Indeed," I agreed, "my heart leaps for joy."

Then Schneider leaned forward, pointing an accusatory finger at Diamond.

Diamond had filed "mountains of paper," but the Court had assumed, as I had, that Paramount was arguing that because of the great risks that the studio assumed, its net profit contract was not unconscionable. The judge noted that he and I "must be incredibly dense."

"I won't speak for the Court. Obviously, Mr. O'Donnell isn't dense," said Diamond.

Schneider's face darkened. He carefully folded his hands in front of him and raised his voice a notch, refusing to explode.

I saw my opportunity and jumped into the fray.

"I'm heartened that we have finally returned to planet earth," I said. They were dropping risky business as a defense because they did not want Schneider or Johnson peeking into their "historic" profitability, I suggested.

Schneider was still steamed but kept his cool as he ran down the rest of the questions on his list. What he quickly discovered, however, was that the whole investigation of Paramount's books was moot because of Diamond's abandonment of a defense that he was now claiming that the studio had never asserted. The lawfulness of Paramount's—and every other studio's—net profit contract would rise or fall based on whether or not it was fair. We were on the verge of an unimaginably spectacular victory.

By the end of the judge's recitation, it was clear that Johnson was no longer needed. Schneider was ready to hear our final arguments and make a ruling, he said. He thanked Johnson for his truncated service, apologized for any inconvenience, ordered us to be ready for final arguments in December and returned to his chambers. I could only imagine the explosion that took place once his door was safely closed behind him.

38

Net Profits
Are Dead

FOR THE THIRD YEAR in a row, Buchwald made a post-Thanksgiving appearance on "Larry King, Live!" to discuss "the lawsuit that will not die."

Art acknowledged right off the bat that he was not planning on retiring on the strength of any windfall profits he might collect in *Buchwald v. Paramount.* Instead, he would be satisfied just to show the world what a sham a studio net profit contract really was.

"Are you ticked at the system?" King asked about the case dragging on for three years.

"No, I'm not ticked at anything," said Art.

Still bearing the year-old scars from the trial, Buchwald reserved his bitterness for Paramount's lawyers.

"They tried to make me into a plagiarist. They tried to use the racist thing on me. And they really try to smear you. . . . They want to destroy you as a person."

"That's the adversarial nature of the system, though, right?" King asked.

"Yeah, and I don't like any of it. . . . I have nothing but ill feeling for Paramount."

Art went on to say that the case stood a better than even chance of being trivialized into merely a case of sour grapes by Paramount's lawyers and its publicity department. If he had not been a public figure, the suit might well have been tossed out of court before he had ever been able to give his side of the story to a judge.

"I had the power that other people don't have to be able to deny [falsehoods] publicly and get the story out. The average person doesn't have the power. I feel very sorry for them."

"What about if this script had been written by 'Louis Smith' of Fayetteville, North Carolina?"

"I don't know the answer to that. What's happened to me—this is the downside of this whole suit—is I've gotten over a hundred scripts and scenarios from people who feel they have been cheated by the studios and want me to help them. I send them all to Pierce O'Donnell."

At my request, Art flew into Los Angeles for the December 6 hearing to determine the outcome of Phase II. Although he would not testify, I wanted Art sitting with Alain to symbolize the significance of the judge's decision on the fairness of Paramount's net profit contract and to remind everyone that this case was about two creative people who had twice been shafted by a studio. As I expected, the newspaper and magazine photos and TV clips all featured my two clients sitting together in the front row of the courtroom spectator gallery.

I'd spent several weeks preparing and had done two moot courts in New York and Los Angeles as a final dress rehearsal for the December 6 showdown. Many people mistakenly believe moot court is a "Let's Play Lawyer" game for second-year law students. For trial lawyers, however, moot court is a regular exercise in courtroom preparation and self-restraint.

The dry runs in front of my brilliant colleagues Michael Malina and Joel Katcoff on the nineteenth floor of 425 Park Avenue were often more exacting than the real thing, with my partners playing judge and adversary hour after grueling hour. The questions were rarely kind and my inquisitors' attitudes ranged from coldly contemplative to scornful. For my part, I went in and out of character more often than Eddie Murphy.

Joel Katcoff was particularly brutal about turnaround. It was the one argument I had always played down because I interpreted Judge Schneider's interest in the other issues—particularly contract of adhesion and unconscionability—as disinterest in turnaround. And I believed that Judge Schneider's summary adjudication ruling in our favor in the fall of 1989 had effectively foreclosed any such argument by Paramount.

Katcoff warned me not to take the issue for granted. Turnaround was a major threat: we could win every round and still lose the money if Paramount could show that Bernheim was not entitled to his 17.5 percent of net profits because his rights had expired one year after Paramount abandoned *King for a Day* in 1986. Following Katcoff's warning, I started sweating more about turnaround.

Paramount was right. Alain did not set up *King for a Day* at another studio within the standard one year required by virtually all turnaround provisions.

But what did that mean? Paramount maintained that all its ties with Bernheim were severed as of March 1986—fourteen months before Eddie Murphy first offered *The Quest* idea to Paramount.

I decided to stick to the argument that Buchwald and Bernheim were a package deal: Paramount couldn't pay one of them without paying the other, and it had already been decreed that the studio *had* to pay Buchwald.

But Paramount was fond of trying to use against us our staunch ally, Roger Davis. Chuck Diamond kept returning to Davis's June deposition testimony that, even if the studio had decided to purchase Buchwald's story long after the original option expired, it would not have any obligation to rehire and pay Bernheim as the producer of the movie based upon that story.

We had won the first trial, but we would come up almost empty-handed if we did not knock out Paramount's net profit accounting. Nevertheless, my mood was upbeat. Whatever happened, I was prepared for the most important argument in my career. Now it was a question of how well I executed.

On December 6, the moment of truth arrived. Chuck Diamond faced me from across Harvey Schneider's courtroom in the style of the Nixon-Kennedy debates. Diamond had a podium and so did I.

Before we got started, I initiated a conference with Judge Schneider in his chambers, ostensibly to help a *Variety* reporter. Dave Robb, who had doggedly covered the entire second phase of the case with balanced and insightful reporting of complex legal and accounting issues, wanted to tape the proceedings and, as was her custom, Judge Schneider's bailiff said no. Pointing out that the pool TV camera in the courtroom had an unfair advantage because it was making a live "video transcript" of the proceedings, I asked Schneider to waive the usual rules for audio taping. The judge granted my request.

"My, Mr. Diamond, do we have a new do?" Schneider asked, admiring Chuck's hair. Not only had Diamond styled his hair differently, he wore a new, expensive-looking tailored outfit complete with shoulder pads. He was ready for the TV cameras. On the other hand, I was now forty pounds heavier than I had been when we summed up at the close of the first trial a year earlier. If Chuck was Harry Hamlin, I was, as Sharam Victory of the *American Lawyer* described me, John Candy playing Uncle Buck in a baggy, pinstriped Brooks Brothers suit.

Before stepping back out into the courtroom, I asked the question that was my primary reason for wanting a chambers conference: did the judge want to hear our prepared arguments or, as I expected from the last closing argument, did he want to start right off the bat with questions?

"I don't need speeches, but if you feel you need to do it for your clients or for the media, go ahead," he said.

I swallowed hard. I had spent weeks preparing elaborate outlines for answering the written questions that the judge had given counsel several weeks earlier. Working from that familiar material would make it easier for me to tick off my points. In a debate, you have to improvise—especially when your real opponent is not opposing counsel but a brilliant judge who relishes intellectual sparring and relentlessly presses you for concessions that could doom your chances for victory.

"Okay. Let's can the speeches," I said, dismissing the easy way out.

Diamond jabbed first. The only reason Art and Alain wanted the old contract upheld was so they could angle for a new one, he alleged. Their lawsuit had metamorphosed into a demand to strike a new bargain "to give them more money." *Coming to America* screenwriters Barry Blaustein and David Sheffield also had a net deal and had earned no net profits, but they hadn't sued Paramount. How were Buchwald and Bernheim any different?

"There would probably be fewer people here," Schneider said. Once again, the courtroom was packed with reporters, Paramount executives, supporters like Lynn Roth, and spectators. Even the jury box was brimming with attorneys from Paramount, O'Melveny & Myers, and Kaye, Scholer who wanted ringside seats for a live presentation of "L.A. Law." Only a few feet to my right was Joshua Wattles, Zimbert's protégé and one of the architects of Paramount's defense strategy.

The law did not give Schneider the right to rewrite Buchwald's and Bernheim's contracts, Diamond insisted. But Schneider squinted at him like a one-eyed traffic cop and read aloud to him from the California Civil Code:

> "The court may refuse to enforce the contract without the unconscionable clause, or it may so limit the application of any unconscionable clause as to avoid any unconscionable result."

Setting aside the Civil Code, he glared down from the bench at Diamond.

"It sure seems to me that is talking about doing a little rewriting of the contract," said the judge.

But Diamond's army of researchers had found case law that they believed held otherwise. An investor had sued Dean Witter Reynolds several years earlier on grounds that the stockbrokerage house imposed unconscionable fees upon him in its standard contract. The trial court's dismissal of the lawsuit was later upheld on appeal. Diamond told Schneider that the investor was trying to protect himself from unfair fees Dean Witter imposed without any negotiation, but the California Court of Appeal had held that the plaintiff could use unconscionability only as a "shield" if the brokerage firm sued him to enforce the provision and collect the fees and not as a "sword" in a lawsuit to invalidate the provision and collect damages. In the Buchwald case, Diamond insisted, Art and Alain were in effect trying to use unconscionability as a sword to get money and not as a "shield" to protect themselves from paying unfair fees. What my clients wanted, Diamond urged, was more profit out of their contract than they had originally bargained to receive—and more than Paramount would ever have agreed to pay.

While Judge Schneider was hammering Diamond with the California Supreme Court's decision in favor of concert promoter Bill Graham that had implicitly approved how we were using the unconscionability doctrine, I stood there biting my tongue and gripping the podium tightly, waiting for an opening to join the fray. Mike, Joel, Bruce and Zazi had drilled me for hours on this point. When it was finally my turn, I pointed out the obvious.

"You know swords and shields are metaphors of war, implements of war, your honor," I said.

"This is a kind of war," Schneider mused.

"This is a kind and gentle war," I said, casting an unkind glance at my opponent at his podium on the opposite side of the courtroom.

Paramount had put my clients on the defensive with its own "sword," I pointed out: the standard net profits contract.

"When the contract is put in my face and Mr. Diamond says, 'Here. See? Your clients were literate. They were adults and they had William Morris. Tough luck.' "—*that* was offensive, I said.

But it was, in fact, tough luck, according to Diamond. He stuck his chin out and literally challenged me "to cite a single case decided in the annals of Anglo-American jurisprudence" where a contract was rewritten to force one party to pay the other more money than it ever bargained to pay or ever *would* have bargained to pay in the first place.

"There is no such case," Diamond scoffed. "If Mr. O'Donnell has one, let him speak now."

"Do you wish to speak now, Mr. O'Donnell?" asked Schneider, enjoying the lively give and take.

"Yes, I wouldn't like my silence to be held against me, your honor," I said. "The fact of the matter is, that's a phony question. False hypothesis. That's not, as I just said a moment ago, what we are seeking to do here. We had a contract that was imposed on us, as we have alleged. We hope the Court will find that. We didn't have any meaningful choice. . . ."

Ours was not a case about swords and shields. It was a case that came down to a single question: Is it a fair and reasonable contract?

And rising to Diamond's challenge, I pointed to four cases in black notebooks that I had given the judge and Chuck at the beginning of the argument. Turning to address Diamond directly, I noted that in each instance "the Court actually looked at the fairness of the price which the seller had imposed upon the buyer and . . . the Court had no temerity whatsoever—Mr. Diamond—in deciding this was an unfair bargain struck by parties of unequal bargaining power. The Court leveled the playing field."

Before I could tell whether Schneider was buying my argument, he switched gears, and hit me with Joel Katcoff's turnaround specter. Perhaps because I had been conditioned to worry about this issue, I reeled, even though I knew the punch was coming. When I tried lamely to convince him that he'd already ruled that Bernheim and Buchwald were a package deal and that Bernheim's contract could not be severed from Buchwald's by a turnaround clause in his contract, Schneider looked at me sternly and said:

"I am now telling you that I did *not* focus on turnaround in making that ruling. That is why I have told you turnaround is open as far as I'm concerned."

Cold sweat trickled slowly down my backbone. Just a moment earlier, I had felt as though I was beating Diamond's pants off. Now, ten feet away, he was smiling as if he had me on the ropes and was ready to finish me off. Katcoff's words reverberated in my head: *"We could win every round and still lose the money on turnaround."*

I had a couple of cards up my sleeve, but even I wasn't sure they would be enough.

First, I argued that *King for a Day* never went into turnaround because Paramount didn't pay $50,000 before May 1, 1985, to exercise its option to buy all rights to Buchwald's treatment.

"Wait. It never went into turnaround?" Schneider asked incredulously.

"No, sir," I said.

I had memos from Alexandra Denman and another studio official, Virginia Briggs, stating that Bernheim's turnaround expired at the same time as Art's option, which Paramount had failed to renew. That, I said, indicated that Bernheim's *King for a Day* project had never gone into turnaround.

But two years later, I continued, Paramount "unabandoned the abandonment.

"They resuscitated *King for a Day* through the evolutionary process I proved in the first trial, and they made *King for a Day* into *Coming to America*," I explained. "*King for a Day* was like a phoenix. It was resurrected."

What's more, I argued, the purpose of the turnaround provision was to enable a studio to recoup its investment in an abandoned project. "Paramount did more than recoup its investment," I added, alluding to the tens of millions of dollars of profits that Paramount conceded it had earned on *Coming to America*. "The intent of turnaround was accomplished here."

Then Diamond proceeded to astonish me by conceding part of my argument.

"We did resurrect the project. So what? The turnaround provision says we have the right to resurrect the project."

This was a damning admission because it allowed me to argue that Paramount was using turnaround as a sword to cut off Bernheim's rights when its purpose was merely to shield the studio from a producer walking off with an abandoned project and not reimbursing the studio for its investment.

"How cynical could we be?" I asked rhetorically. "Let's assume after just one year and a day they get together in May 1986 in Mr. Mancuso's office and say, 'Okay, we took care of Bernheim. Bring in Wachs. Let's get this sucker going again.' That's what happened here in effect."

"Let me ask you this question," Schneider said. "Assume the turnaround forecloses Mr. Bernheim. Mr. Buchwald still has some residual interest?"

"Right," I agreed nervously. But everyone in the courtroom knew that would mean that we would get only Buchwald's 1.5 percent of a net profit that Paramount had been maintaining for a year equaled less than zero. Schneider read my mind when I added, "I'd like to have known that back in January, to be very candid with the Court."

"I am not interested in who wins," Schneider patiently explained. "I'm trying to reach the right result."

"I have a less academic interest," I replied testily.

The judge turned to Diamond and told him he could have "the last word on this issue."

"I can't believe my ears," Diamond said.

"Is that it?" Schneider asked.

Diamond pointed an accusing finger at me.

"He wants the Court not to enforce [the contract]. He wants the Court to require Paramount to pay pursuant to a formula which has lines drawn through it. He wants Paramount to pay pursuant to a formula which says we can charge a distribution fee, but he wants the Court to add, '. . . but only up to the point of our actual distribution expenses.' Clearly, that's what he's asking."

I shrugged. He was right. I was even willing to give Paramount a little more than that.

"Plus a reasonable profit," I said, turning to Diamond and again addressing him directly. "Indeed, I will give you an *unreasonable* profit. I just want a little bit of profit."

The audience laughed, the judge smiled, but Diamond was shaken. At least for the moment, the judge seemed to be agreeing with our "unbelievable" request that he rewrite for the parties a fairer deal that would give us a piece of the net profit pie. Things began to look a little better.

We were not past the turnaround bogeyman by any means, but *if* we prevailed, Diamond would have to come up with a fallback position to minimize the damages Paramount would have to pay. Diamond's suggestion was to "look to the market" to establish the going price for a producer and writer like Bernheim and Buchwald.

"The price cases tell you how to do that. . . . You look at the law of supply and demand. You look at what other similar buyers and sellers agree to pay and accept for similar goods and services."

Had he stuck to the "market value" argument, instead of slipping back into the risky business defense he'd abandoned a month earlier, Diamond would have avoided a stormy clash with Judge Schneider that seriously hurt his credibility. The determination of unconscionability, he argued, "doesn't turn on how much money we made or didn't make. What it turns on is what did we contribute [and] what did they contribute? They contributed a kernel of an idea."

"What did we contribute to this? Forget what profits we may have made. We got the star, we got the director, we got the screen writers. We came up with the scripts. We provided the 55-acre lot on which to make the film.

"We provided the 6,000 employees to work on it. We provided the 95,000 transactions that constituted it. We provided the distribution organization. We provided the advertising expertise and, your honor, we provided the money. We provided $70 million going out the door.

"Now, I don't want to get into a fight with Mr. O'Donnell about what our risks were, but it's sufficient to say, and I don't think anybody in this courtroom would disagree, that there was an element of risk we wouldn't get our money back."

"Why is risk analysis important?" Judge Schneider wanted to know.

Diamond blinked, caught like an opossum crossing a four-lane highway after dark. It wasn't important, he said. It was just that Paramount put up the money. Therefore, the studio's contribution was greater than Art's and Alain's.

"You know what it sounds like?" Schneider said. "It sounds like you are injecting risk analysis into the analysis but you don't want to have an examination of your books and records. That's what it sounds like to me."

Diamond beat a quiet retreat, conceding that Paramount would accept my conclusion that at least three out of four movies did make money. But the concept of risk was so ingrained in his thinking that he could not bring himself to abandon totally this defense. As I looked over at this talented lawyer struggling with his demon, I thought of the scene in *Dr. Strangelove* where Peter Sellers as the title character cannot stop his arm from involuntarily straightening out in a salute.

"We put up the money," he finally said in exasperation.

"If you get me back into risk analysis, the whole game is going to change again," Schneider warned.

"I won't get you back to risk analysis," Diamond said. "I like this game."

For the next several minutes, Schneider and Diamond dueled. I stood there quietly, marveling at the judge's grasp of the facts and law as he allowed Diamond to dig a deep hole and then gently pushed him into it. There was nothing for me to say. So, when the judge finally remembered that I was not, as my former colleague Brendan Sullivan quipped about himself at the Oliver North Iran-Contra hearings, a "potted plant," and invited my comments, I replied, "I couldn't have said it better myself, your honor."

Following a brief recess during which I huddled with Bruce and Zazi, who was now four months pregnant, the judge got Diamond to acknowledge that both the negotiated contracts that Art and Alain signed and the standard form Schedule A stapled to them were inseparable. That gave me another shot at Paramount when it came my turn to speak again.

"Let's assume the contract said, 'You will get net profits—40 percent of net profits—if the cow jumps over the moon. Take it or leave it.' Now, Mr. Diamond would have you rule that I can't challenge that term as being unconscionable."

Diamond shot back that my "cow-jumped-over-the-moon" analogy was an illusory contract—a ploy any first-semester law student knows is a bogus argument.

"That's not unconscionability!" he said. "We paid out X million dollars [in net profits] over the last number of years. Nobody's saying it was an illusory promise! The question here is whether the promise, the package, to pay the money was just shocking to the conscience."

Then, for the first time, Diamond showed his frustration. He held out both his palms and asked:

"Judge, how can you cut [the net profit contract] into pieces? We agreed to pay up to 41 1/2 percent of something. We did *not* agree to pay 41 1/2 percent of the profits. You found that we didn't agree to do that! How can you force that bargain on us by rewriting the formula?"

Diamond's Dean Witter case, which had been one of Paramount's big hopes for a knockout going into the closing argument, seemed to be crumbling. Our "sword" was fast becoming a "shield" in Harvey Schneider's eyes. He hung on to Diamond like a prickly thistle, peppering him with the same question in a dozen different guises: why couldn't he find the standard net profits contract legally unconscionable?

"You are telling me I really can't look at the outrageous nature of the net profit formula because it was all part of the package. Is that what you're saying?" asked the judge.

"You look at that as well as everything else," said Diamond.

When Diamond then suggested that the net profit formula was not a contract of adhesion because it was "subject to negotiation," Judge Schneider jumped on his attempt to avoid a serious factual problem for Paramount.

"Do you have any evidence in this record that Paramount has ever *negotiated* the net profit formula? Point it out to me."

All Diamond had was Richard Zimbert's declaration. The Paramount executive had testified that the formula was negotiable, Diamond said.

"Just point me to the part of the record which says that the net profit formula *has been* negotiated. I'd be very interested in seeing that," Schneider persisted with bulldog tenacity.

But Diamond had no evidence, beyond the sworn statements from Zimbert, Denman and Hahn that it could be possible to negotiate better terms. He brought up the old sore point that William Morris, not Paramount, had fallen down on its job of negotiating a better deal for their clients.

"Mr. Davis testified that the reason he didn't ask for any more was because he didn't think the idea that he was hawking in 1982 was worth any more," Diamond said.

Not true, I countered. The key point was that my clients had no meaningful choice. Davis testified that it was impossible for people with no clout to negotiate any changes in the standard net profit contract. And even if some aspects of a contract were negotiated, that did not preclude a finding of contract of adhesion. After all, I reminded the judge as I turned and pointed to Bernheim and Buchwald a few feet away, Bill Graham, the prominent rock concert promoter, "had a heck of a lot more clout—no offense, fellows—than my two clients, and the Court had no problem in *Graham* saying that still does not preclude an inquiry into the substantive fairness of the arbitration term in that case."

At one point, as the judge was talking, Diamond abruptly cut him off and started arguing.

But not for long.

"Mr. Diamond, I am not interrupting you. Please do not interrupt me," Schneider demanded in a tone of voice that would melt steel.

No sooner had I started to relax than Schneider turned to me.

"I want to go back to something that is troubling me on turnaround," he said.

The chill returned to my spine.

"What if, Mr. O'Donnell, the year passes and it is the day after the [end of the turnaround] year? The turnaround period is over. Paramount now says, 'I think . . . maybe we want to make that movie.' Why can't it do so?"

It was Judge Schneider's now familiar interrogation technique—leading lawyers down one path and suddenly switching to another.

Fixing my gaze on Schneider's eyes, I mentally steeled myself to give the answer that I was now convinced, after one and a half hours of debate, would spell the difference between victory and defeat in our uphill battle to knock out the net profit system in Hollywood.

Paramount had the right to use Tab Murphy's script or Francis Veber's script, I began. But they did not have the right to make the movie *King for a Day*. And *King for a Day* became *Coming to America*, the Court had already ruled.

By my calculations, Paramount officially abandoned Bernheim's *King for a Day* project on March 29, 1985. The studio let its option on Art's story lapse on May 1, 1985. If Art and Alain were a package deal, as I had argued, Paramount's turnaround rights ended the same day Art's option lapsed.

I saw the judge tuning out. I wasn't registering. My heart sank. I could see that he was about to switch gears again. In a split second, I decided to be bold.

"Here is my point," I continued. "If I could just finish, your honor. Thank you."

It worked. The judge settled back in his chair and gave me his undivided attention. Now I had to deliver.

As I resumed my argument, Schneider got interested. He interrupted me, bombarding me with questions. We were having a dialogue. The process of persuasion was under way.

"You have not heard Mr. Diamond argue that he had anything other than ownership interests in two sterile scripts he couldn't use," I told the judge.

"I guess the trouble I'm having is in linking up the rights that Bernheim has in connection with the ownership in the script," Schneider interjected. "I don't see the link."

I pushed ahead, pointing out that it was Bernheim who had originally held the option to Buchwald's material and relinquished it to Paramount. Moreover, Zimbert had testified that he would never have gone behind Bernheim's back to make a deal with Buchwald after Paramount's option expired.

Judge Schneider was still skeptical.

"How are Bernheim's rights affected by who owns the scripts? That's the part I'm missing."

It was a Mexican standoff, I answered. After the option expired, Paramount couldn't make a movie based on Buchwald's treatment without going back to Buchwald and renegotiating to acquire the rights.

"They might well have had to go back to Mr. Buchwald and do things," the judge observed. "But how does that affect Bernheim?"

I had one last point to persuade him.

Bernheim and Buchwald were "linked at the hip contractually," I maintained.

His curiosity piqued, the judge wanted to know what contract provision supported my "Siamese twin theory."

I directed him to a clause buried in Alain's contract:

" 'If the picture is produced . . . artist . . . shall be employed by Paramount Pictures,' " I read. "And 'the Picture' is of course *King for a Day*. That's why they were linked at the hip. If they made the picture which was *King for a Day*, they had to employ Bernheim as the producer for the movie."

As the judge turned to another topic, I still could not tell whether I had persuaded him. The near-permanent skeptical look told me that he might be unconvinced. Or this shrewd jurist may have been testing me, forcing me to push the outside of the envelope and give him the best possible arguments for rejecting Paramount's turnaround defense.

But I wasn't sure. And when I'm uncertain, I assume the worst. In this case, that meant that Art was going to win and Alain was going to lose. What Judge Schneider might see as classic Solomonic justice was going to leave Buchwald, Bernheim and my firm with just 1½ percent of whatever revised net profit or net loss figure emerged from a favorable ruling knocking out Paramount's net profit contract.

We would win—the net profit contract would be declared unconscionable —but Kaye, Scholer would wind up eating $2 million in legal fees and my clients wasting $500,000 in costs. Robert Draper's taunting words at his press conference a year earlier haunted me: "O'Donnell has won a Pyrrhic victory!"

Judge Schneider was almost finished with us, but he still wanted to know what he was supposed to do if he threw out the decades-old net profit contract. How was he supposed to figure out what to order Paramount to pay?

"I don't recommend you go to Delphi," I answered, referring to the ancient Greek practice of consulting an oracle near the foot of Mount Parnassus for advice on difficult questions.

"That is in chambers," Schneider said, smiling. "I don't have to go far."

As long as the judge wanted to be his own oracle, I suggested he start by striking the oppressive, unreasonable, one-sided fees and charges Paramount salted through its contracts. Things like excessive overhead, advertising surcharges, exorbitant interest, hoarding 80 percent of video revenue and the other items on my laundry list of eighteen unconscionable provisions. Then, with the advice of experts such as Price Waterhouse's Frank Johnson, the Special Master, the judge could establish reasonable profit levels for Paramount on its fees and charges.

"I think there is no dodging the bullet that the Court in the third phase—the true accounting if you will—will have to set numbers. That is a judicial function," I said.

An ashen-faced Chuck Diamond refused even to respond to Schneider's request for guidance on setting a payoff amount for Buchwald and Bernheim. He simply went into another—and final—tirade.

"You don't have the authority to rewrite the contract, to change the economic terms. . . . We made a deal. We agreed to pay a price. The Court can't suddenly say, 'Paramount, you have to pay more,' because it is clear on the face of this record we voluntarily wouldn't have agreed to pay more."

By now Diamond was in high dudgeon.

"If Roger Davis had asked for what Mr. O'Donnell is asking for, we would have kicked him out of the office and said, 'Are you crazy? You want 40 percent of the profits? Get lost!'" said Diamond, furious at the suggestion that he might lose. "How can you force that deal on my client? How can you do that?"

Judge Schneider sat back and stroked his chin, looking more than ever like an oracle.

"I don't know if I can do it or not as we speak," he replied cryptically. "I'll let you know in a little while."

Diamond realized too late that he had painted himself into a corner by abandoning the risky business defense. He may have kept the judge from looking at Paramount's books, but it left him and his client nowhere to run. Still, the studio wouldn't have to fork over much if Art was the only one the judge ordered Paramount to pay.

As I left the courtroom for the ritualistic hallway interviews with the media, I was as equivocal as Diamond. On the one hand, I was optimistic about our contract of adhesion and unconscionability attack. But the judge had savaged me on turnaround. It was a dark cloud that hung over our prospects for success.

For his part, Art was his old ebullient self. Out in the hallway, while Diamond and I each struggled to put a good face on the day's proceedings, Art characteristically saw the potential significance of the case.

"If the judge rules they can't write contracts like this, that affects everybody," Buchwald told the gathered reporters. "That's good. That's what matters."

If what happened after the first trial was any measure, it would be several weeks before we knew Judge Schneider's decision. He'd asked for more written arguments, and they would take a few more days to prepare. And then he had an opinion to write.

Once again, it was time to wait. Yuletide was fast approaching. And this year Harvey Schneider would play Santa Claus or the Grinch Who Stole Christmas.

It had been almost two and a half years since I had met Art in Connie's hometown. On December 21, I was back in New Orleans with my family for the holidays. With some final Christmas shopping to complete, I dropped off Connie, Meghan and Brendan at a children's museum. I had brought my compact portable cellular telephone so that I could stay in touch with the office when I was not near a regular phone, and on the way to a shopping mall on the edge of the French Quarter, I called Zazi, who was on duty back in Los Angeles.

"Your timing's perfect," she said excitedly. "I just got off the phone. The judge is releasing the opinion at 1:30 P.M.!"

All I could think to say was: "That's after the New York Stock Exchange closes."

I hadn't had any alcohol, but I felt oddly tipsy as I set the phone back down on the seat next to me. I steered the car to the curb, took some deep breaths, and then climbed out and went to a restaurant. With the portable phone on the bar, I quickly downed two Cokes to pump some caffeine into my system. I would have to wait at least an hour before I would know.

I wanted to talk to somebody, but I didn't dare use the portable phone because I knew Zazi would be calling me within seconds of getting Judge Schneider's decision.

Unless it was bad news.

Then she might not call for some time. I stared at the gray, lifeless phone lying in front of me like a large, dead roach. I ordered another Coke and made small talk with the bartender. A watched phone never rings.

In fact, it didn't ring until ninety minutes later. I'd picked up Connie and the kids and was approaching an on ramp for the I-10 freeway near the Superdome.

"We won!" Zazi shrieked.

"You're kidding! You're kidding!" I exclaimed at the top of my voice. I had put up a good front, but privately I had prepared myself for the worst.

Connie knew instantly what was happening. "Congratulations!" she whispered in my ear as she kissed me on the cheek and squeezed my right arm. For twenty years, she had been my good luck charm—not to mention the best thing that had ever happened to me. She had coincidentally been with me when I heard from Zazi that we had won the first trial. She was with me again when I learned we had won twelve months later. I vowed not to let her out of my sight in the future whenever I was waiting for a verdict.

By this point, I was so out of it that I missed the ramp for the interstate.

With one hand on the steering wheel and the other pressing the cellular phone to my ear, I listened to Zazi's breathless summary of the decision.*

This time our victory was total.

Judge Schneider ruled Art and Alain's standard form contract was a contract of adhesion, all the other studios' contracts were virtually identical, and seven provisions were unconscionable. But the icing on the cake was his verdict on turnaround. Adopting the arguments that I had pressed at oral argument, the Court ruled emphatically that Paramount was not protected by the turnaround clause in Bernheim's contract.

"It is clear Paramount was required to employ Bernheim as producer on *Coming to America* and that Paramount breached its contract with Bernheim by failing to do so," Schneider wrote.

I arranged to have Zazi fax the decision to a Kinko's copy store near my mother-in-law's house. Less than thirty minutes later, I inhaled each page as it came out of the machine. The other customers weren't sure what to make of a grown man standing over a fax chanting "Right on!" every minute or so. When one of the employees asked me why I was so happy, I told him.

"David just beat Goliath—again!"

When I got back to the house, I sat down and savored every word of Schneider's meticulously crafted, thirty-six-page decision. Paramount's contract was an illegal contract of adhesion, according to Schneider, who relied heavily on Bill Graham's case in the California Supreme Court. "There is not the slightest doubt that [boilerplate terms] were presented to Bernheim on a 'take it or leave it' basis. Indeed, the evidence reveals that Bernheim did not have the 'clout' to make a better deal."

As for Paramount's claim that it freely negotiated with talent, the judge was "not impressed with Paramount's evidence." Nor was he impressed with the argument that my clients could have gone elsewhere for a better deal. "There is evidence in the record that Paramount's net profit formula is standard in the film industry," Schneider wrote. "Further, there is evidence in the record to support the conclusion that essentially the same negotiations are conducted at all studios and that when one studio revises a provision of its net profit formula, that revision is adopted by the other studios."

In words that would be ominous to studio heads and their lawyers, Judge Schneider made a finding that demonstrated the wisdom of our strategy of attacking the seven studios as an oligopoly that restrained competition in the motion picture industry.

"Contractual relations between certain talent and studios, at least talent such as Bernheim who lack the 'clout' of major stars, do not take place in a freely competitive market. Rather, it is clear that if a talent such as Bernheim wishes to work in the film industry, he must do so on terms substantially dictated by the studio. This is particularly true with respect to the net profit formula contained in the contract involved in this case."

* Judge Schneider's decision on Phase II is reproduced in full in Appendix B.

As I expected, Judge Schneider made short shrift of Paramount's contention that we were improperly using unconscionability as a sword rather than a shield. As for Paramount's argument that he could not strike down portions of the net profit contract, but had to decide its fairness in its entirety because the various terms were "financially interrelated," the Court pointed to a specific provision of the California Civil Code that explicitly authorized him to strike down an entire contract or any portions. And to ensure that Paramount did not later try to rewrite the history of Phase II, the judge devoted four pages to documenting that, because Paramount had "remarkably" abandoned its risky business argument at the November 8 hearing, the Court did not follow through on the audit of Paramount's books for the ninety movies whose dismal earnings, the studio had argued, substantiated the claim that losers outnumbered winners.

Turning to the specific items challenged in the net profit formula, Judge Schneider found that "with respect to a number of provisions plaintiffs have sustained their burden of proving such provisions are 'overly harsh' and 'one-sided.' . . . Indeed, in light of Paramount's 'all or nothing' approach to unconscionability, plaintiffs' evidence stands unrefuted."

The judge found seven provisions unconscionable:

(1) *Fifteen Percent Overhead on Eddie Murphy Productions Operational Allowance.*

"The court finds this provision unconscionable because an additional 15% charge is made for overhead 'on top of' this item. In effect, this results in charging overhead on overhead. The court is able to perceive no justification for this obviously one-sided double charge and Paramount has offered none."

(2) *Ten Percent Advertising Overhead Not in Proportion to Actual Costs.*

"This flat overhead charge, which has no relation to actual costs, adds significantly to the amount that must be recouped by Paramount before the picture will realize net profits. Again, the court is able to discern no justification for this flat charge and Paramount has offered none."

(3) *Fifteen Percent Overhead Not in Proportion to Actual Costs.*

"Paramount's charge of a flat 15% for overhead yields huge profits, even though the overhead charges do not even remotely correspond to the actual costs incurred by Paramount. In this connection, it should be observed that although Paramount originally contended that this charge was justified because 'winners must pay for losers,' this justification was abandoned by Paramount during the November 8, 1990, hearing held in this case."

(4) *Charging Interest on Negative Cost Balance Without Credit for Distribution Fees.*

"Paramount accounts for income on a cash basis, while simultaneously accounting for cost on an accrual basis. This slows down the recoupment of negative costs and inflates the amount of interest charged. The court finds this practice to be 'one-sided' in the absence of a justification for the practice."

(5) *Charging Interest on Overhead.*

"Paramount receives revenues in the form of distribution fees and overhead charges, neither of which are taken into account in determining whether costs have been recouped. This results in 'interest' becoming an additional source of unjustified profit. The court finds this practice to be 'overly harsh' and 'one-sided' and thus unconscionable."

(6) *Charging Interest on Profit Participation Payments.*

"Paramount charges the payments made to gross participants to negative costs. In fact, these payments are not paid until the film has derived receipts. Accordingly, Paramount has not in any real sense advanced this money. Nevertheless, Paramount charges interest on gross participation shares. This is unconscionable."

(7) *Charging an Interest Rate Not in Proportion to the Actual Cost of Funds.*

"Paramount charges an interest rate which can be as much as 20 to 30%, even when no funds have been laid out by Paramount. This is a one-sided, and thus unconscionable, provision."

The judge did not make any specific findings concerning the other provisions that we had attacked. Two months later, he would explain that, after he found the first seven items unconscionable, he didn't carefully analyze the remainder because the entire net profit contract was hopelessly permeated with unconscionability and unenforceable. Accordingly, the net profit contract, as it had been framed and forced on countless writers, actors, directors and producers for more than a half century, was dead.

In Judge Schneider's stirring words, "The net profit formula as written no longer exists."

As for the remedy in the wake of his ruling, the judge deferred a final decision pending further proceedings. My clients would not be allowed to reap "a windfall"—"an award far beyond the reasonable expectations of the parties when the contract was executed"—but they were entitled to an "equitable award" of "fair and reasonable" damages, Judge Schneider indicated. For now, however, I was content to savor this special moment.

One of the first calls Zazi received after getting the decision was from Chuck Diamond, congratulating the Kaye, Scholer team. Even though he disagreed with Schneider all the way down the line, Chuck still called it a phenomenal victory for us in a case that he thought he had won.

"[Schneider] was giving them a Christmas present," he sarcastically told the press. "We're quite perplexed as to which way to go. None of us know what the new contract will look like until the judge gets done writing it. We'll all look forward with great curiosity to see how he intends to work this magic."

The studio was equally outraged by the ruling. Ironically, the judge's bombshell exploded in the middle of Paramount's annual Christmas party. In a prepared release, read in a dull monotone to the press, Paramount's publicity department chief said:

"Regarding today's ruling in the case of *Buchwald v. Paramount*, we believe that Judge Schneider has gone far beyond existing law in permitting Buchwald and Bernheim unilaterally to rewrite their contracts to suit themselves. That is what is really unconscionable.

"The court has permitted sophisticated and experienced businessmen to gain in the courtroom what they were unable to obtain at the bargaining table. Here plaintiffs were represented in their negotiations by senior executives at the William Morris Agency and understood fully the terms and conditions of the contracts they eagerly signed."

Calling the ruling a threat to the free-market system, Paramount vowed to appeal the decision of this outsider who had set himself up as "the Commissar of Industry contracts" in Hollywood.

While Zazi handled the media in Los Angeles, Alain appeared on television on the West Coast, and Art went on CNN in the East, I played media spinmeister in the Deep South for two hours straight. Many of the reporters congratulated me on what they instantly perceived as another landmark victory for creative people in the motion picture industry.

"This is a fantastic victory," I told *Variety*'s Dave Robb. "What Judge Schneider's decision does is help level the playing field for negotiations between the all-powerful studios and the creative talent who make their hit movies possible."

The media reached the same verdict. The next day's New York *Times* article by Larry Rohter called it "a decision likely to force sweeping changes in the way Hollywood negotiates its contracts and does its bookkeeping." The Christmas Eve story in the *Wall Street Journal* by Amy Stevens and Amy Dockser Marcus observed that the ruling, "one of the few times a court has thrown out a standard movie contract," "is expected to shake the Hollywood studio hierarchy and its decades-old system of net profit deal making."

A week later, in its year-end edition, the New York *Times* did a month-by-month analysis of the most significant events of 1990 in the motion picture business. In January, according to the review, Art Buchwald and Alain Bernheim stunned Hollywood by proving that Art's story was the basis for the hit comedy *Coming to America*. At year's end, the *Times* noted, Buchwald and Bernheim did it again by proving that the standard net profits contract, used to cheat thousands of creative people before them out of countless millions, was illegal.

All that was left to decide was how much money my clients would get.

39

War

of Attrition

——— ——— ——— ——— ——— ——— ——— ——— ———

"I'D PAY YOU $10 million today if you could put that genie back into Judge Schneider's bottle," my breakfast guest told me on January 14, 1991, at the Century Tower Hotel, a few blocks from my office. He was John Schulman, a tall, ruggedly handsome and affable former trial lawyer who had left private practice in the mid-1980s to take over the reins of the Warner Bros.' legal department. I had known the savvy general counsel from Democratic political circles and played tennis with him.

I was once again on the prowl for allies to force Paramount to settle. Profound concern about our dramatic victory a few weeks earlier was shared that morning by every motion picture studio executive who did not work on the Paramount lot. For example, Lew Wasserman, the chairman of MCA/Universal and godfather of studio moguls, called the decision "a cancer." He told friends that Paramount "should have paid Buchwald the five dollars"—referring to our well-known demand for $5 million. For the survivor of countless threats to the studios' hegemony in the motion picture industry over the past half century and a man who had just sold his company for $6.6 billion to the Japanese giant Matsushita, $5 million was pocket change. More importantly, Wasserman had instinctively perceived the potential threat of our frontal assault on the net profit contract.

The anxieties of the studio bosses had been underlined in a December 31, 1990 column by *Weekly Variety*'s editor-in-chief, Peter Bart, a former

MGM/UA executive, who described Buchwald and Schneider as "two unlikely heavies" who had ended the "feudal system" in Hollywood. Another article in the same issue noted that "the ruling represents a stunning rebuke to studios' longstanding business practices. . . ." And according to *California* magazine, the decision "may have changed the center of gravity" and "may result in the reinvention of how Hollywood does business."

"Look, Pierce, you did too good a job this time," John told me over coffee and cereal. "That decision affects all of us, not just Paramount. We can't let it stand."

"Well, John, if you don't like the decision, then you and the other studios, in an act of enlightened self-interest, have to make it go away. The decision is not yet final. Chuck Diamond got an extra month until the end of January to file objections. We still have some time."

"What are you proposing?" he asked. In the motion picture community, straight-shooting Schulman was a breath of fresh air. If anyone could get the message to Paramount, he could.

"You're one of the most respected lawyers in this business, John," I said. "I know that there's no love lost between Warner Bros. and Paramount because of Marty Davis's last-minute attempt to take over *Time* after Warners and *Time* had negotiated a merger."

"You've got that right. That stunt cost us over $9 billion in additional debt that is like a ball and chain on Time Warner. I'm not sure that I'm the best messenger."

"I hear you, but Dick Zimbert and you get along well, from what you've told me. Go talk to him. You know the arguments to make better than I do. Paramount is on a kamikaze mission. I didn't file this lawsuit over two years ago to invalidate Hollywood accounting methods. While I'm happy that we did it, Paramount brought this disaster on itself out of sheer arrogance."

"What do you want?"

"I want money, no gag order on the terms of settlement, and that's all."

"How much?"

"Look, John, I'm not going to quote a figure at this point. I'm not trying to be coy, but Paramount has treated us like dirt in the past when it came to settlement. I told you earlier about the abortive Howard Weitzman initiative last fall. I've still got mud on my face with the clients over that one. I first want to know whether there's any sincere interest in discussing settlement."

My instincts were right.

A week later, Schulman reported back: no interest whatsoever. It was now "a matter of principle," according to Zimbert. Harvey Schneider was an "ignorant civilian" who had no idea what he was doing, Zimbert told Schulman. Paramount was going to tough it out.

I got the same message from Frank Mancuso.

A former colleague of mine, Robin Russell, who had worked as a lawyer at Paramount and followed Eisner, Katzenberg, and Hahn to become the top motion picture lawyer at Disney, volunteered in January to call her friend

David Kirkpatrick. Back in September, Kirkpatrick had returned to Paramount from Disney to head up movie production under Mancuso. Robin, who thought that Paramount should have thrown in the towel long ago, saw an opportunity for Kirkpatrick to score valuable points with the creative community if he could get the credit for brokering a settlement with us.

Robin called me a few days after our conversation.

David had talked to Mancuso and Bob Pisano, the general counsel. Mancuso instructed David to relay this message: "Tell Pierce that we're not in the least bit interested."

Paramount told the same thing to the other studios in private discussions in 1990 and 1991 in which their executives urged Martin Davis, Mancuso and others to settle with us and avoid the risk that an appellate court might affirm Judge Schneider's ruling that the motion picture industry is not competitive and that the net profit contract is unconscionable. At one point, Warner Bros. and other studios were so eager for Paramount to abort its threatened appeal that they offered to chip in to help pay the settlement. Paramount said thanks but no thanks.

That was also the studio's public position: Paramount would not settle and would appeal as soon as the damages were awarded in what had become known as Phase III of our case.

The promise to appeal the unconscionability decision was predictable. What shocked me and many in the legal and entertainment communities were the vitriolic attacks in the media on Judge Schneider. The judge had now joined the ranks of Buchwald, Bernheim and their lawyers as a target.

"This decision doesn't have a snowball's chance in hell of being upheld," Diamond defiantly predicted to *Business Week* reporter Ronald Grover. "What the judge seems to want to do is regulate us like a public utility." This was tough, as well as undiplomatic, talk about a judge in a pending case.

But Chuck Diamond is no fool, I told my colleagues. Paramount's and Diamond's attacks on the judge's decision appeared to me to be part of an orchestrated public relations campaign to disparage this gutsy jurist in the eyes of the public and his judicial peers, including the Court of Appeal and Supreme Court judges who would eventually hear the appeal. In numerous articles the first few weeks after the December 21 ruling, a chorus of Hollywood "insiders"—many of them speaking without attribution—savaged Judge Schneider's decision.

A New Year's Eve piece in *Weekly Variety* by Henry Kissinger's son David contained a potpourri of paranoia and poison.

• " 'The worst possible scenario is that everyone will now sue and there will just be chaos,' claimed one entertainment attorney."

• " 'Most lawyers who work in this area every day think the decision was just plain dumb,' said one prominent entertainment attorney who asked not to be named."

• "In the long term, most entertainment attorneys predicted the decision will be overruled. 'Usually I rate the chances of winning on an appeal at somewhere around 10%,' said one Paramount attorney. 'This time I'd put our chances of getting this decision reversed at over 90%.' "

• " 'I don't know what precedent there is for a judge overruling an entire industry's way of doing business,' said Eric Weissman, a prominent Hollywood attorney. 'People have spent their entire careers writing these kinds of contracts. All of a sudden someone comes along and tells them their lives have been meaningless.' "

Peter Dekom, a lawyer representing major stars like Sylvester Stallone and Bruce Willis who had the bargaining clout of an Eddie Murphy, issued one of the nastiest blasts. In the same one-sided *Weekly Variety* article that offered no balancing comments from me or anyone applauding the ruling, Dekom tried to make Judge Schneider look like an enemy of the "little people" on whose behalf Buchwald and Bernheim had waged their lonely battle.

"It's a disaster. This judge clearly doesn't understand the entertainment industry. If this decision stands, the repercussions are going to be catastrophic for everyone in the industry. [The studios] may now simply refuse to give profit participations altogether."

As Alain and Art read the mounting attacks on the judge's decision, they became incensed and wanted to know what I was going to do about it. Realistically, there was little I could do while the case was still pending other than what I was doing—defending the judge in the media and supporting his decision when Paramount appealed. I told my clients that the judge and we would have to tough it out until vindicated by the appellate courts several years down the road. Like it or not, Paramount and its allies had a First Amendment right to express their disagreement with Judge Schneider's opinion.

"If they're free to trash the judge, then I'm at liberty to defend him publicly, aren't I, Pierce?" an upset Art Buchwald asked me in an early morning call on January 9, 1991.

Art had just read an op-ed article in that day's *Wall Street Journal* by L. Gordon Crovitz, titled "Coming to America: The End of Contracts." An attorney and award-winning *Journal* columnist whose beat included law, lawyers and the legal system, Crovitz had a reputation as a conservative who had little regard for the judicial system and even less for plaintiffs and their attorneys. *Buchwald v. Paramount* was made to order for this scold.

Crovitz's column was by far the harshest criticism of Judge Schneider's decision. Suggesting that Buchwald was a "court jester" who "brought a hilarious lawsuit," Crovitz chastised the judge for agreeing with "Buchwald's mischievous argument that contracts are meaningless." At the heart of Crovitz's defense of Paramount's net profit contract was the familiar argument, abandoned by Paramount before Judge Schneider's ruling, that "since movies that are hits pay for the flops, studios need to recoup more than the costs of each moviemaking film." I had no doubt that Crovitz had been thoroughly indoctrinated by Diamond, who was quoted in the column debunking Schneider's opinion.

In a sweeping, apocalyptic assessment that gave new meaning to overkill, Crovitz predicted no less than the demise of contract law as it had developed over the centuries. Why? Because Buchwald took Paramount to court, had the audacity to challenge the economic caste system in Hollywood, and found a judge willing to throw out the net profit contract.

"A California appeals court could rescue contracts by reversing Judge Schneider's attack on their sanctity," Crovitz suggested. "Or maybe Mr. Buchwald will come clean and announce that his lawsuit was all a big joke that got out of hand."

After Art hung up, he immediately called the editor of the *Journal*'s op-ed page and asked her to print his rebuttal in the form of a full column instead of an abbreviated letter to the editor. She told him that printing a response in this form was unprecedented. But, Art replied, Crovitz had attacked him personally—something that didn't happen every day.

To its credit, the *Journal* ran Art's rebuttal, titled "Paramount's Funny Books Are No Laughing Matter," as a featured column on the op-ed page in the January 23, 1991 edition. Crovitz had picked on the wrong plaintiff. With his unique blend of humor, fact and sarcasm, Buchwald skewered him:

> On Jan. 9 I woke up to discover that I had been pilloried by The Wall Street Journal [Buchwald began]. This was an unusual experience for me because I am paid to pillory others. My attacker . . . wrote a long op-ed piece taking me to task for not only suing Paramount Pictures, but for winning.
>
> The judge ruled that I did write [the original story for *Coming to America*], and told Paramount to observe the terms of our contract, which included a net share in the profits.
>
> This decision made Paramount very sad and it came back by saying that the picture, which grossed over $350 million, made no net for us. It lost $18 million. Paramount's lawyers accused me of being a crybaby because I had signed such a lousy contract.
>
> Once again the judge ruled in our favor. He called the Paramount contract unconscionable. He said Paramount did a lot of funny things with its books that prevented anyone from getting net profits. At this moment the judge is trying to come up with a figure that will compensate us for Paramount's creative bookkeeping. This has Paramount and, apparently, Mr. Crovitz very upset.

Taking issue with "those who object to talent (even humorists) suing over contracts because they believe they have been shafted by major studios," Art offered his own assessment of the decision's significance.

> Thanks to our victory over Paramount, there is now hope this decision will make studios more careful when sticking it to the people they work with.

Meanwhile, as I awaited a third round, my patience was being sorely tested. In an annual ritual at Kaye, Scholer, I met again in January with the billing committee in New York to discuss the case. The legal fees now exceeded $2 million, the firm had advanced several hundred thousands of dollars of cost for expenses (including Xeroxing), the clients were out of pocket for over $200,000 in costs and expert witness fees, and Paramount had still not been ordered to pay my clients the price of a postage stamp. And there was no end in sight.

Judge Schneider's latest ruling did not specify what standard he would use to award damages. All we knew in January 1991 was that he would not slavishly apply Paramount's net profit contract. Nor did we know when the judge would set a trial date for damages.

This time I was not asked by my billing committee to make any more predictions about how long the case would last or how much it would cost. Notwithstanding the fact that the legal fees were now a multiple of my original estimate and no end was in sight, my partners once again commended my team and me for winning another round in the battle and told me to go finish the job—regardless of what it cost or how long it took.

On January 31, 1991, Paramount stunned Judge Schneider and us. Instead of objecting as expected to particular aspects of the December 21 decision, Paramount's lawyers filed a request that the Court reopen Phase II and allow the studio to relitigate the unconscionability of its net profit contract. Diamond argued in his papers that Paramount never had a chance to defend the eighteen separate contract provisions that we had challenged and that he had held evidence in reserve that would justify these terms. All Paramount had agreed to submit for decision, he claimed, was whether the net profit contract, taken as a whole, was defensible because it had been negotiated by sophisticated parties and was fair and reasonable on its face.

Zazi, Bruce and I filed a tough opposition, pointing out that Paramount's counsel, when he unequivocally abandoned the risky business defense at the November 8, 1990 hearing and thereby averted a court-supervised audit of the studio's books by Price Waterhouse, had told the Court that his client was not relying upon Paramount's risk or the reasonableness of individual charges or fees. Like the Ghost of Christmas Past, the "winners must pay for losers" defense was being resurrected in a different form. What Paramount was trying to do, we noted, was to get a second bite of the apple on risky business.

Not surprisingly, Judge Schneider hardly needed our help in sorting out what Paramount was trying to do.

At an early morning hearing on February 11, 1991, Schneider got right to the point.

"Well, I must say I'm perplexed by your filing, Mr. Diamond. I have read and reread the transcript of the November 8 hearing. And I have a very difficult time understanding how you can make the contentions that you have made. . . ."

Diamond, impeccably dressed in a crisp black suit, answered that he had been relying upon three lines in the 13-page, June 11, 1990 "stipulation and proposed order"—an agreement between the parties' attorneys submitted for the judge's approval—concerning the issues that would be tried as part of

Phase II. That language provided that one of the Phase II issues would be whether "the following alleged practices [are] unconscionable, absent justification or other defense, which, if necessary, will be adjudicated in the next phase." Unfortunately for Diamond, Judge Schneider never agreed to and did not sign the stipulation and it therefore never became a binding order in the case. More importantly, as the judge pointed out to Diamond that morning, the subsequent events of the case—particularly Diamond's concessions at the hearing on November 8, 1991, that he was not claiming that the eighteen provisions were necessary for the studio's survival and that his only "justification or other defense" was that the terms had been negotiated and were fair and reasonable on their face—rendered moot the proposed stipulation and unsigned order.

"I had my expert here and we were ready to go into all the various aspects of Paramount's books and records," the judge observed. "I ultimately sent him home."

But Diamond was adamant, protesting that he never abandoned a defense of the individual items but only of the contract as a whole. Judge Schneider then started reading back to Chuck his admissions in the November 8 hearing transcript, leaning forward and hurling his words directly at Diamond with a forcefulness and emphasis that I had never before seen from him or any other jurist.

Yet Diamond did not back down. His voice rising, he continued to maintain that Paramount had reserved the right to present further evidence if its contract was found to be unconscionable. His argument and disrespectful tone convinced me that he knew he was going to lose this battle but was trying to bait the judge and get him to blow his cork so that he could cite this judicial intemperance as a ground for reversal on appeal.

"My client should have a constitutional right to present [relevant evidence]," said Diamond.

"Don't wave the flag at me, Mr. Diamond, please," Schneider responded.

At one point, Judge Schneider threatened to grant Diamond's request to reopen Phase II, noting that Diamond was trying to interject a risk analysis back into the case. Making clear what I had suspected—that he had not ruled on the eleven provisions that he had not analyzed in his opinion because "I thought when I got to seven that was enough"—he warned Diamond that he would recommission his accounting expert, Frank Johnson of Price Waterhouse, to audit Paramount's books for "a thorough, complete review of risk" as to all eighteen provisions.

"I won't limit it to those seven provisions [that he had invalidated]," Schneider stressed. "That I promise you."

For my part, I told the judge I was torn: on the one hand, I would like to see Paramount finally come clean and produce *all* the financial information it had kept confidential; on the other, it seemed clear that Diamond was playing a stalling game and "trying to salt the record for an appeal," and that reopening Phase II would simply prolong the case another six months to a year.

"I think it's unfair to the Court and particularly the plaintiffs, who are spending extraordinary sums of money on legal fees and expert witness fees. . . . I'm between a rock and a hard place as Mr. Buchwald's and Bernheim's counsel."

Scowling at Diamond, Schneider shook a finger at him like an outraged schoolteacher.

"Let me tell you: it seems to me, Mr. Diamond, with all due respect, you're doing what every litigant would love to do," said Schneider. "You argue a point of view, lose, and then say, . . . 'I'll come back and try a new theory.' That's what it appears to me you are doing."

Diamond blithely responded that Schneider's December decision had been premature and that the studio demanded a new trial.

"I thought it was absolutely crystal clear that on November 8 you had abandoned all this risk stuff and we were going to focus on the agreement—the fairness of the agreement on its face," Schneider said, his face beginning to redden.

Throughout the half-hour hearing, Schneider lashed out at Diamond over Paramount's disingenuous attempt to resurrect risky business despite his clear abandonment of the defense at the November 8 hearing and the December 6 closing argument.

"We seem to have a difficulty with the English language in this case," the judge sarcastically noted toward the end of the hearing. "I might say a difficulty I have never had with any other case I've been involved in."

Finally, at my suggestion, the judge agreed to let Paramount make a "proffer of evidence" and tell him in detail what additional evidence the studio wanted to offer to defend its eighteen net profit provisions. As I told the judge, "I think this is a bluff. I think we should call their bluff. I have consulted with my experts. I don't think there is any chance at all they're going to be able to show what Mr. Diamond [claimed in his request to reopen Phase II]. . . . I don't think that they can even make a proffer."

In ordering Diamond to make the proffer, Judge Schneider warned that he was still not allowing Paramount to reopen its case. Diamond asked for six weeks to prepare his proffer, but the judge told him to file it in four weeks.

"This case has been going on forever," Schneider said. "I thought we were getting near the end of this case. Apparently we're just beginning."

I asked for two weeks to respond to whatever Diamond submitted.

"That means we will meet again April 1," Schneider said as he dismissed us. "Highly appropriate under the circumstances."

While Diamond and I prepared for April Fool's Day, Hollywood and Paramount—as we had both come to know them—were undergoing wrenching changes.

The box office tallies were in for 1990. Paramount, which finished right behind Disney as the top-grossing studio of 1990, took in $634.7 million at the box office for the year. Disney had taken in $663.6 million. Nevertheless, both studios were publicly admitting that they and the entire motion picture industry were on shakier financial ground than at any time in recent history. Indeed, by the end of the year, MGM/UA would be in a death spiral, Orion would be bankrupt, Sony would be wondering how much it overpaid for Columbia/Tri-Star and the Guber-Peters management team, and a financial malaise would be gripping Hollywood.

In a 28-page "confidential" memo to key Disney executives that Jeffrey Katzenberg crafted during his 1990 Christmas vacation on Maui, the Disney Studios chairman summed up many of the financial problems that faced all eight major studios. Recession, rising production costs and studio bidding wars that had jacked up the price of star vehicle scripts beyond the $1 million mark, all contributed to the crunch. The biggest problem, however, was the Blockbuster.

Titled "The World Is Changing: Some Thoughts on Our Business," his memo read like a State of the Industry address and focused on the most expensive, and disappointing, release among Disney's nineteen films of 1990: *Dick Tracy*.

"As profitable as it was," Katzenberg wrote, " 'Dick Tracy' made demands on our time, talent and treasury that, upon reflection, may not have been worth it."

It was, he admitted, intended to be a blockbuster. A net profit statement published in *Variety* disclosed that Disney spent $46.5 million to produce the Warren Beatty-Madonna comic book fantasy and another $54.7 million to advertise and distribute *Dick Tracy*. By year's end, however, the *Dick Tracy* grosses totaled only $103.7 million. It seemed clear that—like *Coming to America*—*Dick Tracy* would *never* earn a net profit. The film remained an object lesson in why high production costs, wholesale hype and stellar gross-point contracts were not the prudent way to make movies in the nineties.

In fact, according to Katzenberg, 1990 marked "steady decline for all of Hollywood . . . a year that was capped off by a disastrous Christmas for nearly everyone." The movie business was *not* "recessionproof" as conventional wisdom had long maintained. Pay TV and home video, among other forms of entertainment, were ending the former monopoly of first-run movies as the most popular form of entertainment in hard times.

Unless studios gave up their blockbusters as well as the overpriced talent who made them, they seemed as doomed as dinosaurs.

A prescient, anonymous Disney employee got hold of Katzenberg's memo in mid-January and began faxing it all over the planet. By the end of February, everyone in and out of the industry had heard of "the Katzenberg memo." And everyone who worked in Hollywood had read it.

In March, the Los Angeles *Times*'s Dennis McDougal had once again laid his hands on a revealing studio net profit participation statement, this time for *Batman*—the sixth highest grossing movie of all time. Like *Coming to America* and *Dick Tracy*, however, it was a disaster on paper. As of September

30, 1990, it had grossed $253.4 million for the studio—but it was still $35.8 million in the red!

All three movies were predisposed to financial ruin . . . at least for the net profit participants. The formula was always the same: high-priced talent who refused to accept anything less than gargantuan salaries and hefty gross points (Jack Nicholson, Warren Beatty, Eddie Murphy), plus extravagant advertising budgets that often exceeded the actual cost of production, combined with enormous overhead and interest charges guaranteed to eat up receipts as soon as they came into the studio accounting office.

By now, this fatal subtraction and the net profit fiasco—first given broad national exposure by *Buchwald v. Paramount*—was an open joke. The only thing that changed in emcee Billy Crystal's caustic remarks about Hollywood accounting during the March 1991 Academy Awards telecast was that *Batman* had replaced *Coming to America* as the butt of the jokes. As Frank Mancuso knew only too well, however, declining profits and skyrocketing star costs were no laughing matter.

Despite Paramount's second-place box office finish in 1990 and its *Ghost* finishing as the year's top hit, Martin Davis was not pleased with the overall performance of his studio. The Eddie Murphy relationship was sorely strained, Mancuso's team had produced such disasters as *Almost an Angel*, *Two Jakes*, *Air America*, *Days of Thunder* and Eddie Murphy's *Another 48 HRS.* and *Harlem Nights*. Over the past year, production costs had spiraled out of control. For example, *The Godfather, Part III* had reportedly cost at least $55 million to make and close to that much to advertise, but it had not earned back Paramount's out-of-pocket investment when it disappeared from United States theaters only two months after its release.

The trend for 1991 was already dismal. By mid-March, Paramount stood in seventh place in the annual box office derby—ahead only of lowly MGM/UA. Thanks to tens of millions of dollars of write-offs from film flops, the parent company had reported a first quarter loss of $7.3 million compared to a profit of $21.2 million for the same period a year earlier. With costs escalating and profits plummeting, the studio was fast becoming an Achilles' heel. Forgotten were Mancuso's glory years such as 1986 when Paramount totally dominated the competition, grabbing an astounding 32 percent share of the year's domestic box office with such hits as *Star Trek IV*, *Top Gun* and *Crocodile Dundee*.

Davis was unhappy for still another reason.

As he had told Buchwald in June 1990, Paramount was getting clobbered in the courtroom and the court of public opinion, and the events of the succeeding nine months had only made matters a lot worse. Industry insiders and mutual friends had continued to press Davis to settle with Buchwald, but he stubbornly refused. Davis blamed one person for not winning: Frank Mancuso.

Two years of bad news and personal humiliation were just too much for

Buchwald's prickly former pal. So, in an ironic reprise of his appointment of Mancuso instead of Michael Eisner to replace Barry Diller in 1984, Davis surprised everyone in mid-March when he appointed Stanley Jaffe instead of Mancuso as the new president and chief operating officer of the studio's parent company, Paramount Communications Inc. Jaffe, the tough-minded, fifty-year-old executive producer of such hits as *Fatal Attraction* and *The Accused* and the former president of production at Paramount in the early 1970s, was given total control over the studio and publishing operations. And Mancuso would now report to Jaffe.

Mancuso, who thought he had been in the running for the presidency, found out about the Jaffe appointment by fax. According to his business associates, the usually soft-spoken Mancuso went into an immediate rage. Two days later, Mancuso abruptly departed as chairman and chief executive of Paramount Pictures, sending a shock wave of job insecurity through the studio and prompting widespread criticism of Martin Davis's insensitivity.

The day after he left, the furious fifty-seven-year-old executive slapped a $45 million breach-of-contract lawsuit against the studio he had called home for twenty-nine years. Mancuso claimed that Paramount had in fact fired him, Davis had negotiated with Jaffe behind his back, and his five-year contract did not allow anyone to be insinuated in the chain of command between Davis and him. Rebutting any notion that he was fired for incompetence and taking a chapter out of our Phase II litigation strategy, Mancuso quoted Paramount Communications Inc.'s most recent annual report to show that the studio was in fact prospering under his leadership.

"There is absolutely no basis in fact to the lawsuit," Paramount responded in an echo of the terse comment that greeted the filing of Buchwald's and Bernheim's lawsuit two and a half years earlier.

Upon hearing the news, Buchwald called me and suggested that Mancuso and he could form a club—people shafted by Paramount's breaches of contract. As it turned out, however, Mancuso wouldn't have remained a member for very long: according to the Los Angeles *Times*, Paramount and he settled within two months for more than $20 million! But Mancuso wouldn't talk about the settlement terms: he had acquiesced in the standard Hollywood gag agreement that Buchwald had vowed he would never sign.

The lesson of the Mancuso/Paramount falling out and quick settlement was not lost on me. Frank Mancuso was a member of The Club; my clients were outsiders. The Club took care of its own—and punished interlopers who threatened to upset this tidy arrangement.

Mancuso was not the only victim on the Paramount lot of Martin Davis's displeasure over the mishandling of *Buchwald v. Paramount*. The same day that Mancuso's exit was announced, *Daily Variety* disclosed that Robert Pisano, the studio's general counsel since 1985 and a former O'Melveny & Myers partner, had been "fingered for major responsibility for the chaotic aftermath of the Art Buchwald suit seeking multimillion dollar compensation from Paramount. . . ." And on May 9, 1991, it was announced that Paramount had terminated Pisano as well as Ken Suddleson, an attorney and executive vice-president who had worked for Mancuso since 1987. *Daily Variety* reported:

> One Paramount source suggested that the termination of Pisano and Suddleson goes deeper than their ties to Mancuso—that it is a way of holding them accountable for company unhappiness at the outcome of the Art Buchwald "Coming To America" suit.
> "Buchwald," states the source, "is everyone's pink slip."

Pisano's duties, including overseeing *Buchwald v. Paramount*, were assigned on an interim basis to my nemesis, Richard Zimbert. Despite their instrumental role in fashioning Paramount's defense, Zimbert and his protégé, Joshua Wattles, didn't get a "Buchwald pink slip." Nor did the studio's outside trial lawyers. What that told me was that the firings of Mancuso, Pisano and Suddleson were high-profile acts of retribution for losing—not punishment for waging the war in the first place. Martin Davis had removed some of the furniture, but he had no intention of cleaning house.

Neither the breathtaking changes in management at the very apex of Paramount Pictures nor the widening fiscal turmoil within the studio system in general had any discernible effect on Paramount's litigation strategy. Even though Jaffe was in and Mancuso was out, it was "risky business" as usual within the studio walls at 5555 Melrose Avenue.

On March 11, Diamond filed a 39-page proffer of how he would defend the studio's movie profit participation formula if the judge allowed him. It was long on strident language but short on convincing proof.

"In Plaintiffs' May 1990 statement of contentions, invective and hyperbole took the place of evidence to support their claim that Paramount's Net Profits formula is unfair to participants," Diamond began his argument. In a rhetorical flourish that put me to shame, Diamond added:

"The truth has been the victim of this rush to overturn decades of established and accepted business practices and fashion for plaintiffs a lucrative remedy."

Contrary to Judge Schneider's instructions, Paramount dished up old wine in a new bottle. The justification for each of the individual provisions was a rehash of evidence offered in Phase II back in June and July 1990. Ultimately, however, Paramount's main defense remained that "the motion picture business was and is high risk, and those who run studios can attest to the fact that more films lose money than make it." Try as it may, Paramount just could not exorcise the "R" word from its lexicon.

"Tonight the motion picture community gathers to confer its Academy Awards," we began in our 100-page response to Paramount's proffer filed two weeks later.

Based on its latest deceit, Paramount should be awarded a special Oscar—for most outrageous performance in a courtroom. Rarely has a litigant been so deserving of such opprobrium.

Mad as hell, I didn't pull any punches:

Paramount apparently believes that litigation is a recreational sport for the rich and powerful to play games with their poorer and weaker adversaries and the court. If you are a well-heeled Goliath, you do not have to honor the rules; only the little people play by the rules. You can say anything you want and change your position when it suits your convenience; only the little people must take consistent positions. And when you are defeated, you can cry foul and ask for a new trial; only the little people get one bite at the apple. . . . Paramount's delaying tactics and shifting positions have cost the Plaintiffs dearly in time and money.

Judge Schneider shared our sentiments.

"It seems to me this is a case, as I indicated last time, where a party has decided by way of strategy and tactics, to adopt the [new] position when the Court ruled against it," he said, choosing his words carefully but his indignation evident at the thirty-minute, April 1 hearing on Paramount's bid to reopen Phase II.

As usual, the courtroom was packed with reporters, lawyers, Alain and his two sons, and Paramount's regulars, Josh Wattles and publicist Harry Anderson. Deborah Rosen, who had handled Paramount's public relations on the case for two years, was noticeably absent. Diamond was flanked by Bobby Schwartz and Lon Sobel. To my right were Bruce Margolius and Zazi Pope, who was only weeks from delivery but had stayed on the job to battle Paramount's new trial bid. In the audience was a new recruit, Greg Dovel, an energetic, brilliant 1986 Harvard Law School graduate who would replace Zazi while she was on maternity leave. Greg, who had clerked for Supreme Court Justice Antonin Scalia, represented the latest tangible evidence of Kaye, Scholer's commitment to Buchwald and Bernheim.

Paramount "now seeks another bite of the apple by attempting to resurrect an unsigned stipulation," Judge Schneider continued, intermittently reading from notes on a legal pad and transcripts of prior hearings where Diamond had made fatal admissions. "By way of comment, if this were permitted, there would be no end of litigation. Every party that loses would come in and say, 'Whoops! I have another theory I would like to explore.' That could go on ad infinitum. I'm not going to permit that to happen. I'm ready for Phase III, gentlemen."

Judge Schneider's ruling was a flat repudiation of Diamond's claim that he reasonably relied on the stipulation and proposed order that the Court never signed. His argument, the judge noted, was "highly suspect" and "stretches credulity to the breaking point." What had happened, the judge found, was that "the defendants and counsel knew that the stipulation was invalid and created the so-called justification evidence after the fact and after hearing the Court's [adverse] decision on Phase II."

Looking a few feet to my left, I could see that Diamond, who had informed the judge and me that his client might immediately file an emergency appeal called a "petition for writ of mandate," was livid. His credibility as a lawyer had just been shattered before a half dozen reporters whose millions of readers, viewers and listeners would soon learn that Paramount had been caught red-handed playing fast and loose with the truth. Worse yet, Diamond was stuck with a factual record that substantially lessened Paramount's chances for an appellate reversal of Judge Schneider's unconscionability ruling. As we walked out of the courtroom, I wondered if Chuck was rethinking his cocky prediction three months earlier that the judge's decision "doesn't have a snowball's chance in hell of being upheld."

Out in the hallway, both Diamond and I were besieged by the usual retinue of reporters whom we had gotten to know on a first-name basis. While I stood a couple yards away from Diamond's mini-press conference, waiting my turn, I could not help overhearing this unbelievable exchange:

"You're saying that the judge's action is unprincipled?" one of the reporters asked.

"We view it so, yes, unprincipled and outrageous," said Diamond calmly, in a torrent of measured abuse that I sensed might be rehearsed and not inspired by the passion of the moment.

"The judge has come off the bench and joined opposing counsel. He has decided to renege on an agreement to allow us to introduce further evidence. Having brokered that deal, the judge walks away from it and joins Mr. O'Donnell in denying it ever existed, with the effect that Paramount's been denied its day in court. We have been blindsided by this frankly foolish action. The Court has indulged in petulance, making judgments before all the information is really before him. The decision is factually baseless and unfathomable."

When the media turned to me for a response, I glared at Diamond, and he stared back with daggers. Pausing for a second until I was under control, I then made the statement I had planned before I heard Diamond's scurrilous personal attack on Judge Schneider.

"We are thrilled with the judge's decision. Paramount's defense is in shambles. You almost have to feel sorry for Paramount's lawyers. They never know from one day to the next who their client's management is going to be. We look forward now to the damages trial."

With the denial of its bid to reopen Phase II, Paramount had no upside left in the case; it was now only a question of how much money the studio would be ordered to pay my clients. After conferring with Art and Alain, I decided to make one last effort to settle the marathon case. Based on how rudely we had been treated in the past, I was not sanguine. But the studio had new management, the disaster was attributable to the discredited Mancuso regime, and I owed it to my clients and the firm to swallow my pride and take another shot.

Art had only one condition. He did not think that I should call Diamond directly because it would appear that we were too eager to settle. I had my own reasons for avoiding Diamond: I was so angry at him for slamming Judge Schneider that I was afraid that I couldn't be effective.

By this time, I had run out of entrees into the Paramount hierarchy. Alain suggested that we try to enlist his longtime friend and tennis partner, Eric Weissman, one of the deans of entertainment law in Hollywood who had publicly questioned the judge's unconscionability ruling.

A gracious, courtly lawyer and Austrian by birth, Weissman readily agreed with me that perpetuation of *Buchwald v. Paramount* and the escalating antagonism between creative talent and studios was bad for the motion picture industry. He agreed to call Richard Zimbert, whom he had represented when he came to Paramount over fifteen years earlier. Over the past year Zimbert had been sending me taunting messages via our mutual accountant, Robert Goldberg. My personal favorite: "Tell Pierce I'll be in a walker before Paramount pays him any money."

Late in the afternoon of April 3, Eric phoned me to give a detailed report of his one-hour meeting with Zimbert at Paramount.

"Well, Pierce, I failed," he began. "It was a pleasant meeting. Dick said many flattering things about you and your lawyering in the case, but that's about it. After the preliminaries, I told him that you wanted $8 million, and he said that Paramount would not pay one tenth of that amount."

"That's absurd," I exploded. "Their last offer was for $1.3 million—$500,000 higher!"

"I know. But Dick was intransigent. I couldn't budge him. He told me that you would come out fine from this case with all your publicity and referrals. Art would do well too. It was Alain that he was concerned about. He liked Alain, and wishes that there was a way to compensate him. He quickly added that he was not trying to divide and conquer."

"Sure," I interjected.

"Dick reserved his anger and harshest words for the judge. He was most unflattering. He thinks Judge Schneider is a nut case and that they will get him reversed on appeal. I told him that I did not like the judge's decision either, but Paramount should be concerned about the precedent if the case is affirmed on appeal. Dick said that he didn't care about the precedent."

"Eric, ever since the decision last December, Paramount has told countless people that the reason they will not settle is that they do not want a precedent and they must take an appeal to make sure that Judge Schneider's decision is obliterated from the annals of jurisprudence. Now they're saying that they don't care about precedent. Well, I now have the picture. They don't give a damn about principle or precedent. As Art has always suspected, this case is about power. Period. We know what has to be done now."

"Pierce, Dick also said that they expected to get clobbered in the damages phase by Judge Schneider. And, oh yes, he told me that he, Dick, would personally bring the check to you if your judgment is upheld on appeal."

"Anything else?"

"There was one other thing. When it was clear that he didn't want to talk about settlement, I asked him why they had not gone ahead with the risky business defense. Dick told me that they had in fact made a lot of money in those five years and they couldn't let the Court examine their books."

"Thank you for your efforts on behalf of the industry and us. Let's play tennis soon."

"I wish I could have brought better news. Take care."

When I hung up the phone, I was seething. What troubled me more than anything else was that I now knew that Diamond was doing the bidding of his client and that his remarks were part of a deliberate campaign to impugn the integrity of an outstanding judge who had the gall to stand in Paramount's way. As far as I was concerned, Diamond was really no different than his predecessor Draper, who stooped to conquer with his knowingly false charges of racism and plagiarism.

I needed someone to talk to, someone who would understand and be able to counsel me. Zazi was not home, Bruce was not reachable, and my buddy Ron Silverman, one of Los Angeles's top trial lawyers and my frequent sounding board on the case, was out to dinner.

I dialed a number that I had dialed many times before.

"Hello, Danny. This is Pierce. I hope I'm not bothering you."

"No, not at all," Arnold replied. "What's up, ol' boy?"

"I need to talk with you . . . right now. Do you have a few minutes?"

"Of course I do. What's bothering you?"

"It's those bastards at Paramount. You probably saw in the trades today that the judge slammed them again, denying their attempt to retry the accounting issues."

"I saw that, and Alain called me. Congratulations. You're destroying them."

"I know, and that's why I'm so frustrated. Never before have I so convincingly trounced an adversary, and yet been treated with such contempt."

"What's the latest indignity?" Danny asked.

I told him about the failed Eric Weissman mission and Zimbert's admission about why Paramount pulled the risky business defense.

"That's outrageous," Danny told me. "But listen, Pierce, don't let 'em get you so upset. That's exactly what they're trying to do. They know how badly you have hurt them—in court and in the public's eye. They're playing with your mind. They will deny you the ultimate satisfaction—settling—because they know that's what you want."

"Yeah," I agreed. Danny's soothing voice and ice-cold logic were already calming me down.

"I know how hard it is on you—how intense this whole thing is—but you can't let them get to you like this. Go finish the job. Nail 'em with a big damages verdict. You'll win the appeal. You're a winner, never forget that. Your cause is just. Just hang on."

"You know, ol' boy, you're the one who got me into this mess," I reminded him. "If I hadn't taken your damn call that day back in 1988—"

Danny started laughing. It was infectious. I started howling too. We continued to laugh as we reminisced about our own past battles against the studios. The laughter, the mutual affection, was the best tonic of all.

"Thank you, dear friend."

"Pierce, get a good night's sleep."

Diamond kept his promise. In yet another brief (this one, 47 pages long), a petition for writ of mandate was filed with the California Court of Appeal on April 12. Diamond managed to refrain from repeating his accusation that Schneider was unprincipled, but he did say that Hollywood would be paralyzed if Schneider's decision were allowed to stand. Paramount demanded an immediate reversal.

After reviewing a blistering opposition from us, the appellate court returned a one-sentence reply to Diamond's brief on April 24, 1991:

"The petition for writ of mandate-prohibition is denied."

Paramount's prepared press release sounded like it came from Dick Zimbert's dictating machine:

> We are disappointed that the Court of Appeal chose not to step in at this stage of the proceedings because we believe the decision is fundamentally wrong. However, we are confident that ultimately we will prevail on the merits.

Nearly five months after the end of Phase II, risky business was finally dead. But Paramount wasn't. The battle was just beginning.

40

Fair Market Value

——— ——— ——— ——— ——— ——— ——— ——— ———

"WHETHER IT IS A NOVEL, a television episode, a textbook or a film, nearly everything we do starts with ideas from creative people," Stanley Jaffe told a group of Wall Street security analysts, gathered in midtown Manhattan for their annual Paramount Communications Inc. briefing in the spring of 1991. With Martin Davis sitting next to him, Paramount's new studio boss was trying to reassure his skeptical listeners—jittery over Paramount's $200 million in movie write-downs during the previous year and steady decline in box office prominence since 1986—that Paramount's real strength and value were not in cash flow but in ideas.

On the other coast, I was telling Judge Schneider the same thing as we began the battle over how much money Paramount should pay Buchwald and Bernheim. My clients had helped the studio make at least $85 million in profits from *Coming to America*, I reminded the judge in a brief filed in mid-May. After the swift appellate court rejection of Paramount's effort to get the Phase II unconscionability decision reversed before the case was even finished in the trial court, the judge asked the lawyers to submit their views on what standards should guide him in awarding damages.

To no one's surprise, Paramount urged the judge merely to focus on the seven provisions of the net profit formula that he had found unconscionable. Under the studio's preferred approach, the judge would simply reform the contract by substituting lower "actual cost" figures for the invalidated overhead, interest rate and other charges and then compute the net profit. "To do any more than to scale back these provisions so that they are 'in proportion' to Paramount's 'actual' costs would be judicial overkill . . . [and] would result in the windfall that this Court has pledged to avoid," Diamond argued in his brief. But as I told Judge Schneider at a hearing on June 6, 1991, Paramount's method of computing damages would result in a windfall for Paramount.

"Bluntly, Mr. Diamond has done the math, and he knows that if you follow his lead on tinkering with the seven [provisions], there probably still wouldn't be a net profit. . . ."

We had argued that the judge should refuse to enforce the net profit contract altogether and, in its place, award my clients either a fair share of the actual profits of Coming to America or the fair market value of their contributions to the success of the movie. Under our approach, the Court would hear expert testimony about what Alain's and Art's services were worth and consider what other similarly situated producers and creators had earned on successful movies. Consequently, the odds on our receiving a respectable damages award would be infinitely greater.

On June 14, Judge Schneider issued a five-page order on the legal standard that he would employ in Phase III. To our delight, he rejected Paramount's recommendation and would not try to rehabilitate the flawed net profit formula. "The court declines to become involved in a wholesale rewriting of the contract between the parties."

Instead, the judge opted, as authorized by the California statute on unconscionable contracts, to throw out the entire net profit contract because it was hopelessly "permeated with unconscionability." It was time to stop beating a dead contract. Instead, the judge adopted one of our proposals and Paramount's fall-back position.

"The Court concludes that, under the circumstances presented by this case, it would be appropriate to measure the recovery by the fair market value of plaintiffs' contributions to 'Coming To America.' . . . Paramount benefitted from plaintiffs' work and should pay for it. In effect, Paramount would be unjustly enriched if it was not required to do so."

To Paramount's chagrin, the judge even left the door open to showing that the huge amount of Paramount's profits on the movie based on Buchwald's story was some evidence of the fair market value of my clients' contributions to its success.

Adoption of the fair market value test was another key victory for us on the road to recovering an equitable damages award. Like so many of our successes, however, the bitter was mixed with the sweet. Privately, I had told Alain and Art in the spring that I hoped for an early fall trial, lasting about a week, and a final decision from Judge Schneider by Halloween. But the judge declined to set a firm trial date and ordered us back in ninety days for another status conference after we had depositions of the battery of experts on Hollywood compensation practices that each side had nominated.

While Art was disappointed that the damages trial was postponed for at least another six months, he didn't need the money and remained stoical about the legal process and cynical about the motives of Paramount's lawyers.

"Well, that assures another good year for O'Melveny & Myers," he commented.

"And another several hundred thousand dollars in legal fees for your lawyers," I added. "Except we're not getting paid by the hour."

"But think about all the great experience you're getting," Art replied.

For Bernheim, however, the delay was devastating. More than any of us, Alain daily bore the brunt of uncertainty and delay. "I just don't understand why a defendant can get away with dragging out a case so long," he told Zazi and me. "It wouldn't be tolerated in France." We had triumphed twice, but we had nothing to show for it, and no end in sight.

And while Alain was a bona fide hero in Hollywood, Art and I began to wonder whether he was becoming a victim of the Big Chill—silent ostracism by studios for daring to challenge their supremacy. Except for two projects with Danny Arnold under the auspices of Danny's overall deal with Disney, Alain had not made a production deal of his own with a major studio since we had filed suit, and it was starting to hurt financially. Stanley Jaffe, his old friend and colleague from *Racing With the Moon*, put out the word that he was not welcome at Paramount. And when he did get Fox interested in a project with Bette Midler attached, the studio's business affairs executive told Alain's agent, "No back end for Bernheim."

Art was very distressed about what the case was doing to his dear friend—"the real hero of this fight," Art frequently reminded me. Yet despite the extraordinary burdens and stress imposed by the case, Alain kept on fighting: reading scripts, optioning material and nursing along Danny's and his projects at Disney.

Meanwhile, back in the Los Angeles courtroom that none of Paramount's new leaders seemed to want to acknowledge publicly, the legal team that Pisano had hired from his old law firm to defeat Buchwald and Bernheim was finally wrestling with the same issue that my Kaye, Scholer colleagues and I had been trying to address since the beginning of 1991:

What was "fair market value" for Art and Alain's contributions to Paramount's 1988 Eddie Murphy blockbuster?

Chuck Diamond got the debate off to a shocking start at a June 28 hearing when, after I again demanded access to Paramount's books, he conceded—publicly and for the first time—that *Coming to America* made "tens of millions of dollars" in actual profits for Paramount Pictures. Our figures showed that it was at least $85 million and would probably top $100 million well before the turn of the century.

"People in this industry are not compensated on the profitability of a film to a studio," he later explained out in the courthouse hallway. "They are compensated on the basis of a net profit point or an adjusted gross point or a gross point. But nobody is paid a part of the studio's actual profits."

The only reason he made the admission in open court, he said, was to convince Judge Schneider to drop any further threat of a court-supervised audit of Paramount's books. Now that it was clearly understood that *Coming to America* had, in fact, earned a sizable profit for the studio, Diamond reasoned that we could get on with establishing Buchwald and Bernheim's "fair market value" for their services.

That value, he maintained, equaled zero.

We had a different figure in mind. In a July 3 follow-up letter that Bruce Margolius sent to Diamond, we spelled out our vision for the third and final phase of the case. We would call about a half dozen witnesses, including the legendary Hollywood literary agent Swifty Lazar and producers Paul Maslansky *(Police Academy)* and David Brown *(The Sting, Jaws, The Verdict, Driving Miss Daisy)*. We also planned to call again Rudy Petersdorf, Dr. Howard Suber of the UCLA Film School, Jay Shapiro (whose former accounting firm Laventhol & Horwath had gone bankrupt), and Jeffrey Robin, the William Morris Agency's West Coast business affairs chief. The idea was to get each of them to testify that our clients' contributions to *Coming to America*, and especially Bernheim's, were worth several million dollars.

Based on Diamond's preliminary witness list, we figured Paramount would be calling a similar number to the stand.

Then, a week later, Diamond played his hand. On July 17, Paramount hit William Morris with a massive subpoena, demanding all contracts, deal memos, options and profit participation statements for the agency's clients who received creator or producer fees between the years of 1975 and 1987. Diamond said Paramount needed the documents in order to prepare for the deposition of our expert, Jeffrey Robin. But an infuriated William Morris executive committee chairman, Roger Davis—the man who had represented Alain back in 1983 and had testified in our behalf in Phase II—believed otherwise. If Diamond succeeded, William Morris would be obliged to open up its confidential files of former and current clients, including such luminaries as Barbra Streisand, Robert Redford, Clint Eastwood, Sylvester Stallone, Arnold Schwarzenegger, Goldie Hawn, Chevy Chase, Jane Fonda, Michael Douglas, Sam Shepard and Sally Field. For a firm whose clients cherish privacy about their deals and finances, compulsory disclosure of these secrets —to a major studio with whom their clients regularly negotiated—could be disastrous.

Davis instructed his lawyers to file a motion to quash the oppressive subpoena. William Morris attorney Peter Smoot, a tall, lanky pro who talked slowly but thought quickly, estimated that it would take four to six paralegals several thousand hours to sift through 4,000 boxes of documents to come up with what Paramount demanded. In his brief, Smoot called the subpoena "a transparent attempt to dissuade Mr. Robin from testifying against [Paramount]." I agreed. Paramount's move on William Morris reminded me of the not very subtle intimidation of Laventhol & Horwath in the spring of 1990 after Jay Shapiro and Sid Finger agreed to testify for us as accounting experts in Phase II. In both instances, the good will of the firms' clients was essential to their existence. While Diamond's subpoena had all the subtlety of a runaway Mack truck on a steep incline, it understandably rattled William Morris. If the subpoena were not thrown out, Smoot told the Court, William Morris would have no choice but to withdraw Jeffrey Robin as one of our key experts.

Not since Draper's racism and plagiarism charges had I seen Art so upset. I saw him every day during the month of August while my family and I vacationed on Martha's Vineyard, and more than once he said, "How the hell can the Court allow this blatant harassment? Paramount didn't subpoena CAA or ICM or the other studios for the net profit information about other producers and writers. They singled out William Morris for special treatment because they had the guts to stand up to Paramount and support us. Well, damn it, I hope that you are not going to let them get away with it?"

One day I mentioned in passing that Chuck Diamond had injured his ankle badly playing tennis. Art jumped on me.

"How can you be concerned about Diamond after all that he and his law firm have done to us and you and now William Morris?"

"Art, I just said I felt sorry for the guy hurting his ankle at the beginning of his family vacation."

"You're getting soft on Diamond, Pierce. You're losing the fire in your belly about winning this case."

"Art, all I said was—"

"I know, but you have to stay tough. We haven't finished the fight yet."

Art cracked a smile after a minute of this teasing. But I knew that he really didn't see anything funny about Paramount's tactics.

His passion about the William Morris subpoena inspired me.

"Paramount is waging a war on Plaintiffs and their allies," I charged in the opening salvo of my brief in support of William Morris's motion to quash the subpoena that I wrote on Martha's Vineyard and faxed back to Greg Dovel in Los Angeles. "For Plaintiffs, who have been battling Paramount for almost three years, it is a war of attrition. But for the William Morris Agency, whose lifeblood is its clients' confidence in the confidentiality of their contracts, it is nuclear war. . . . William Morris's commendable courage to stand up for the rights of creative talent like Art Buchwald and Alain Bernheim should not be chilled by Paramount's bullying tactics."

Diamond maintained he was not trying to terrorize William Morris and its clients. After all, the agency had negotiated Bernheim's and Buchwald's deals and stood to receive 10 percent of any damages awarded. And that was not the only justification Diamond advanced: "Paramount [subpoenaed] these documents from the William Morris Agency . . . because market value must be established by reference to the market. As the world's largest talent agency, the William Morris Agency's producer and writer deals are undoubtedly representative of the prevailing price for these services."

In July, as the battle over the William Morris client records was looming, Stanley Jaffe had installed a new studio chairman: Brandon Tartikoff, the forty-two-year-old wunderkind president of NBC. The week after Jaffe was hired in March, Paramount Communications Inc.'s stock tumbled three points. But the day after Tartikoff's appointment was announced, the stock jumped up $1.75 a share.

The boyish Tartikoff affected a public image of an amiable but driven executive with populist tastes who had triumphed over Hodgkin's disease and other personal tragedies, including his young daughter's paralysis in a 1990 auto accident. But he was also known among his business subordinates as tough, brash and hard-nosed.

The successor to Michael Eisner and Frank Mancuso seemed determined to put Paramount's fat movie budgets on a TV production diet. Among his first executive decisions was the addition to the 1991 holiday release schedule of *All I Want for Christmas*—a $12-million family feature shot on an NBC movie-of-the-week schedule of thirty days. He also gave the green light to *Wayne's World*, a movie based on a "Saturday Night Live" comedy skit about two teen airheads who have their own public access TV show.

At the same time, Tartikoff pulled the plug on a Harrison Ford period piece about the turn-of-the-century Pullman train strike, titled *Night Ride Down*. It might have been a big screen story, but it was too expensive at over $46 million just for production costs.

The new studio chief also claimed that he encouraged a new respect for writers. Their opinions would be solicited during the making of movies and their scripts would not be "cannibalized" for other projects, he said.

Despite the rolling heads, tightened budgets and Tartikoff's promise of a new day, plenty of the old Paramount philosophy remained. Old enemies were punished and old friends rewarded, regardless of talent, attitude or track record.

Producer Robert Evans—the former head of Paramount movie production who had run afoul of the law with a misdemeanor cocaine conviction and had been implicated in a murder case involving his last movie, the 1984 flop *Cotton Club*—was effusively welcomed back to the studio with a new five-year contract. Eddie Murphy, who had spent much of the previous two years shoveling foul-mouthed abuse on Paramount, extended his exclusive contract to include another two movies beyond the two he still owed the studio from his last five-picture deal. Neither his *Harlem Nights* ego trip nor his wooden walk through *Another 48 HRS.* was held against him. Murphy's per picture fee soared to $15 million, plus, of course, his 15 percent piece of gross receipts.

"I can't think of any other star-studio relationship that has been this successful," gushed Paramount motion picture president David Kirkpatrick, "and the arrival of Brandon Tartikoff from NBC with whom Eddie has a terrific relationship dating back to his 'Saturday Night Live' days no doubt provided him with an additional comfort level."

Less than two months later, Kirkpatrick and Paramount production president Gary Lucchesi would be purged by Tartikoff. When Tartikoff put *Night*

Ride Down into turnaround, its executive producer, Ned Tanen, also left and ended up at Columbia/Tri-Star as an independent producer. Another Mancuso holdover, Deborah Rosen, Paramount's executive vice-president for worldwide publicity, was also shown the door. Zimbert and Wattles remained at their posts.

As for *Buchwald v. Paramount*, the only public statement Tartikoff made was that the studio would not settle.

August 22 was the day Judge Schneider said he would decide whether William Morris had to hand over its confidential files to Paramount. It also marked the thousandth day since we first filed suit against Paramount Pictures. As it turned out, the most difficult assignment that day was getting to Los Angeles.

Three days before the hearing, Hurricane Bob wreaked havoc on Cape Cod and Martha's Vineyard. Art had to arrange for a private plane to get me off the island to Boston where I caught a commercial airliner to Los Angeles.

From the beginning of the hearing on the William Morris subpoena, Judge Schneider made it clear that he didn't want fifteen years' worth of net profit contracts from the agency's vaults. All he wanted was some idea of the going rate for producers and writers associated with "a movie that turned out to be very successful."

Diamond seized the opportunity to return, once again, to the net profit formula as a means of low-balling the "fair market value" of Buchwald's and Bernheim's services.

Airplane! was a very successful Paramount picture that didn't cost much to make because it had no major stars and relatively unknown producer/writers, Diamond told Judge Schneider. Those producers wound up earning more than $2 million in net profits.

But *Fatal Attraction*, another box office smash, earned almost no net profits because it had stars like Michael Douglas and executive producers like Stanley Jaffe and Sherry Lansing with large gross positions. The net profit participants got almost nothing.

"The circumstances of those films differed," explained Diamond. "People who produce pictures that only cost $1.79 to make and earn $60 to $70 million get a lot more than people who are involved in pictures like 'Coming To America.' It's determined by the formula. And how can you escape the formula? The formula produces that result."

Judge Schneider was neither fooled nor moved. He saw "risky business" creeping back into Diamond's rhetoric under a different rubric, and he would have nothing to do with it.

"I've already escaped the formula," he wryly noted. "I'm not going back."

Peter Smoot pressed hard his defense of his client's privacy. Instead of asking William Morris for financial information on its clients, Paramount ought to subpoena all the other studios for their contracts, Smoot suggested.

"What's wrong with Mr. Smoot's suggestion that you lay a subpoena on

Twentieth Century Fox and Columbia and all these other folks?" Schneider asked Diamond. "Why don't you do that?"

"Because I want to go to one place that's representative," Diamond answered. "One-stop shopping."

He stopped, pulled himself up and cocked his head just slightly in the direction of the bench.

"And, Judge, I think the record should reflect that you're making faces at my argument."

Schneider blinked, his mouth dropping open.

"You are," Diamond said again.

"I don't think the record should reflect anything like that because I wasn't making any faces at your argument," Schneider snapped.

"Your honor," I said, "I want the record to reflect I saw no such facial expression whatsoever."

Bruce and I were dumbfounded. Diamond remained bent on baiting the judge into error. He next launched into a tirade against the futility of subpoenaing studios, independent production houses, movie-of-the-week producers . . .

"I'll go looking, journeying the countryside looking for defunct producers," as Diamond put it, urging each of them to reveal to Paramount the market price for producer services, when all he had to do was rummage through the William Morris archives.

But Smoot maintained that Paramount was guilty of "strong-arm" tactics, knowing that disclosure would spark outrage and perhaps a mass exodus of the agency's clients.

"Your honor, can we talk about what's *really* going on?" asked Smoot.

"What's really going on is . . . I'm not going to permit this discovery because I think it's not going to assist the Court in any fashion and it's not going to be relevant or calculated to lead to the discovery of admissible evidence," Schneider said with finality.

While William Morris client contracts were off limits, the judge did leave the door open for Paramount to refile a demand for a limited number of William Morris's profit participation statements. And out in the hallway after court, Diamond left no doubt that he would barge right through that door.

"Are we still hot on the trail of William Morris?" he said to reporters. "Yes, but they'll be looking through a different set of 400 boxes."

The next day, Diamond filed an amended subpoena, asking for the agency's compensation records for film producers like Bernheim and creators like Buchwald. This time, he only requested confidential information on Morris clients involved in box office hits produced for $20 million or more in the mid-1980s.

And, once again, William Morris moved to quash the subpoena.

By October, Judge Schneider saw the pattern and ordered us all back into Department 52.

"Gentlemen and lady," said Schneider on October 7, nodding at Zazi Pope, who had recently returned from her maternity leave, the proud mother of a healthy boy. "I have read all the papers that have been filed and the bottom line is I do not think I have enough information to rule on this motion. It also occurs to me that the issues involved in this motion may arise again if, for example, other studio documents are subpoenaed. And so I intend to do the following: I intend to refer this motion to retired Justice Richard Amerian."

Amerian was a fifty-four-year-old former associate justice of the California Court of Appeal who had resigned to return to private practice and served as a "rent-a-judge" like Jerry Pacht, who had adjudicated our discovery disputes on the eve of the first trial. In a procedure that had become routine in Los Angeles in recent years, Schneider was simply shifting a time-consuming discovery headache to a retired judge to solve.

This was a shrewd move by Judge Schneider. A respected jurist, Amerian had no ties to the case or to Hollywood. He was a registered Republican but had been elevated to the Court of Appeal by Governor Jerry Brown, a Democrat, so he couldn't even be charged with political bias. Nor could he be accused of harboring ill will against Paramount and its lawyers. I was eager to see if Diamond's act played any better out of town.

It didn't.

Within two weeks of his appointment and studying a new wave of briefs, Amerian scheduled a six-hour "trial" on the William Morris subpoena, to be conducted in the Kaye, Scholer moot courtroom, located just two floors below my office suite. Six months earlier, I had designed and built the moot courtroom—replete with a bench, witness stand, jury box, counsel table, spectator section, podium and the Great Seal of California—as a place for our litigators, clients and witnesses to practice for depositions and trials and for hearings and trials in cases where a private judge was presiding.

As Alain, his son Daniel, several reporters, and I watched, Amerian listened to Diamond's arguments on behalf of Paramount and Zazi's arguments on behalf of our clients. Occasionally, Peter Smoot got a chance to speak too.

The most interesting revelation during the October 23 "trial" was Paramount's latest figures on receipts and expenses for *Coming to America*. The studio had remained mum since March 1990, when Paramount reported a $125 million gross for the studio. Since then, Diamond told Amerian, the movie's revenues had climbed another $14 million.

Did that mean it was no longer in the red?

Hardly.

The $18 million deficit had shrunk by only $5 million or so, according to Diamond. As Sid Finger had predicted, the gross points granted Eddie Murphy and John Landis had eaten up most of the $14 million. Amazingly, *Coming to America* was still somewhere between $11 million and $13 million in the hole! While the movie originally cost about $40 million to make, subsequent payouts to Murphy and Landis, as well as the studio's other expenses, raised the film's cost to $106 million, according to Diamond.

It was not enough, therefore, just to examine the William Morris files on producers' paychecks, Diamond argued. If Amerian wanted to be fair, he had to limit Judge Schneider's comparison of compensation to a producer's earnings on those big-budget movies with the same revenue-to-cost ratio as *Coming to America*. Diamond proposed a revenue-to-cost ratio of 1.3:1—a formula that virtually guaranteed that there would be no comparable films and arguably no extra money for Bernheim and Buchwald.

Zazi suggested that the Court expand the relevant universe to profit participation statements of films with budgets of only $10 million or more and gross receipts of $100 million and higher. Our research had identified potentially a dozen films in the 1980s that had exceeded this threshold and paid handsome net profits to the producers. This was a pivotal issue for us, one that could spell the difference between payday and Pyrrhic victory.

But Peter Smoot held to his position that Paramount didn't have any need, or right, to rifle through the William Morris confidential files at all. He pointed out that five days earlier, on October 18, Paramount had served subpoenas for Paul Maslansky's files at Warner Bros. and David Brown's at Universal. Paramount promptly received the profit participation statements for Brown's *Jaws* and Maslansky's *Police Academy* in preparation for Diamond's deposition of those two Buchwald witnesses. Why couldn't Paramount do the same with similar films at other studios? Why, Smoot asked, was it so necessary to get into William Morris's files?

At the close of the hearing, Amerian thanked us and promised a fast decision.

He kept his word.

On November 5, he submitted a 23-page report to Judge Schneider, recommending that he limit his attention to films released between 1980 and 1988 and adopting our proposal that the relevant films have budgets over $10 million and domestic grosses over $100 million. Amerian also rejected Paramount's revenue-to-cost ratio straitjacket. Whether the information came from William Morris or elsewhere, the financial statements Judge Schneider examined should not be for movies that were sequels of other movies, Amerian added.

The film producers whose compensation packages Judge Schneider should use to decide how much to award Bernheim ought to have had three prior film producer credits and should have received $100,000 to $300,000 in upfront fees as well as 15 to 50 percent of the net profits, Amerian recommended. As for Buchwald, Amerian suggested that Judge Schneider compare any idea or treatment that earned its creator between $35,000 and $65,000 in up-front fees and 1 to 3 percent of the net.

William Morris would have to produce those limited records but did not have to reveal the names of either the producers or the movies.

"What is important is the raw statistical data about films and their net profit," he concluded. "What should matter little is the name of the talent and the name of the film."

And, with minor modifications, Judge Schneider adopted Justice Amerian's recommendation in early December.

It was another critical victory, one that enabled us to present relevant evidence of what comparable producers and creators had been paid for successful movies. It was also a sweet success for our gutsy ally, William Morris, which had lately been battered by major defections of top agents in its movie department. Despite internal pressure to withdraw Jeff Robin as an expert witness for us and appease Paramount, Roger Davis stuck to his guns. It was a profile in courage in a community of cowards.

As 1991 drew to a close, I began to wonder if there would be much left of Paramount by the time the case was finally over. Hemorrhaging losses, the studio had dropped from fifth to eighth place in domestic box office share. Tartikoff's first pet project, *All I Want for Christmas*, barely recouped its production costs. *The Addams Family* was doing well during the busy holiday season, raking in over $80 million, but Paramount had purchased that whole package from Orion. The only original Paramount production among the top ten at year's end was the last in its franchise series: *Star Trek VI*, but there would be no more of them.

The entire nation was in the worst recession since the 1930s, but Paramount seemed to be faring exceptionally poorly. In a year-end edition, *Weekly Variety* reported that no film division employee at Paramount would receive bonuses or salary increases in the current fiscal year, that fewer executives would be placed under contract than in the past and that those who did win contracts would get shorter-term deals with options to renew that favored the studio. Some existing middle management vice-presidents would get no contracts at all. They would simply work day to day as "at will" employees, the same as the secretaries, janitors and guards at the front gate.

But Eddie Murphy was doing all right.

He was working on his first Paramount project in two years: *Boomerang*, a comedy about a ladies' man who finally meets his match. In April, he would be loaned out to Disney for *The Distinguished Gentleman*, a story about a con man who scams his way into Congress. When I read the notice in the trades, I remembered Wachs talking at length in our deposition two years earlier about Eddie's complete lack of interest in doing anything remotely connected with politics. Eddie was supposedly no more interested in *King for a Day* than he would have been in a remake of *Mr. Smith Goes to Washington*.

It occurred to me that Ronald Reagan had been in the White House when I first filed Art's lawsuit. I wondered if someone other than George Bush would be occupying the Oval Office when the case was finally resolved. Yet there was light at the end of the tunnel—at least at the trial court level. At my urging, Judge Schneider had finally set a trial date, March 2, 1992, to decide how much my clients got out of *Coming to America*.

Meanwhile, Paramount and Kaye, Scholer came close to making a deal.

But not to settle the *Buchwald* case.

The Washington *Post* reported the story on November 22, 1991:

> Here's a case of motion pictures making for strange bedfellows: The producers of the Eddie Murphy comedy "Boomerang," in which Murphy's co-stars include Robin Givens, Grace Jones and Eartha Kitt, recently asked for permission to shoot some scenes in the New York law offices of Kaye, Scholer, Fierman, Hays & Handler. That's the law firm representing Art Buchwald in his lawsuit against Paramount Pictures over Murphy's "Coming To America"; "Boomerang" is a Paramount picture. The law firm turned the moviemakers down.

And speaking of strange bedfellows, Eddie Murphy and John Landis approached our accountant, Phil Hacker, about auditing Paramount's books for *Coming to America*. Even gross participants were starting to think that they could be the victims of fatal subtraction.

This was the first Christmas in three years that I was not in trial on *Buchwald v. Paramount*. Two days after Christmas, I took my family skiing for a week in Park City, Utah. And on New Year's Eve, I was mugged—by Paramount's desperate lawyers.

I'd returned from the slopes late that afternoon, and for some unknown reason, I called the office. My assistant Celine was on vacation, Zazi, Bruce and I were out of town. The alert receptionist, Christy Marin, gave me my messages and then added, "Oh, by the way, you just got a package from O'Melveny & Myers which I put on your desk." My suspicions immediately aroused, I asked her to give it to Greg Dovel, who was at the office preparing a case for trial.

My family and I went out for dinner, and when we got back, a 15-page fax was waiting for me at the front desk. It was a motion that Chuck Diamond and Bobby Schwartz had filed late in the day. Styled an Ex Parte Application for an Order Precluding Certain Evidence at Trial, it requested that Judge Schneider—without a hearing and without any response—prevent us from offering any evidence of Bernheim's damages at the March 2, 1992 damages trial other than financial data of what comparable producers and creators were paid. In other words, the expert testimony of our distinguished producers, David Brown and Paul Maslansky, as well as Jeffrey Robin and Rudy Petersdorf, would be totally barred. If Paramount's gambit succeeded, our chances of getting a respectable recovery would be greatly reduced.

This type of ex parte motion is customarily reserved for emergency matters such as temporary restraining orders to prevent violence or preserve property. By no stretch of the imagination were any such pressing matters involved here. This was nothing other than harassment.

It was also another personal—and baseless—attack on my colleagues and me. Paramount's lawyers alleged that we had deceived Judge Schneider about evidence we would offer at trial, distorted the judge's remarks at a prior hearing, and welshed on promises to the Court. The charges were pure fantasy, but they could not go unanswered.

I canceled our New Year's Eve celebration with friends and wrote a letter to Judge Schneider that was faxed to our New York office, typed into our global computer, printed out New Year's Day in Los Angeles, and delivered to Judge Schneider at 8:30 A.M. on January 2.

> Paramount's sneak attack on New Year's Eve is totally unjustified. The damages phase of this case entered its second year on December 21, 1991. . . . Paramount has been given every indulgence in Phase III by the Court and Plaintiffs' counsel in terms of scheduling, extensions, and even a stay pending the resolution of Paramount's abortive petition for writ of mandate. . . .
>
> What conceivable justification can there be for this gamesmanship?
>
> Paramount cites no exigency or other compelling reason for an ex parte filing. The trial is over two months away. . . .
>
> As offensive as the filing of the Ex Parte Application is, I am more outraged by the contents of this pleading. It is nothing other than a frontal assault on the integrity of Plaintiffs' counsel based on half-truths, innuendo, and outright falsehoods. This is hardly the first time in this case that Paramount has sought to poison the Court's mind by means of a preemptive attack on Buchwald's and Bernheim's counsel.

On January 3, Judge Schneider summarily denied Paramount's Ex Parte Application without requiring us even to file an opposition. The big losers continued to be Paramount itself—and the stockholders whom Martin Davis purported to champion. As one respected entertainment lawyer told Bernheim at year's end, "Paramount took a $250,000 case and bought $100 million of ill will and bad publicity."

Even by Hollywood accounting standards, that was a lot of money.

41

A Higher Justice

___ ___ ___ ___ ___ ___ ___ ___ ___

MONDAY, MARCH 2. I WAS IN MY STUDY at the computer screen, putting the final touches on my opening statement in the third and final phase of *Buchwald v. Paramount* that would start in a few hours.

This week we would try to persuade Judge Schneider to award millions of dollars to Buchwald and Bernheim as damages for Paramount's use of Buchwald's treatment and refusal to allow Bernheim to produce *Coming to America*.

When he heard about our multimillion-dollar claim two months before trial, Bobby Schwartz told the Associated Press:

"Buchwald and Bernheim must be floating in Never-Never Land."

A week later, in their own official answer to our claim, Paramount's lawyers promised to put expert witnesses on the stand who would testify that Buchwald should have earned no more than $65,000 and that Bernheim's services were worth something between $100,000 and $225,000. After the longest-running civil trial in the history of Los Angeles Superior Court, Paramount wanted Judge Schneider to award as little as $165,000 to my two clients—and no money for their net profit shares that we had spent a year proving were a cruel hoax.

In a series of preliminary rulings, Judge Schneider set the ground rules for our March showdown. In determining how much Art and Alain would get in "fair market value" compensation, he would listen to what experts thought was fair and consider what the writers and producers of comparable films earned between 1980 and 1988. The judge would also hear testimony about how much of the profits from *Coming to America* were attributable to Art's story and Alain's producing.

I was worried. Did that mean Judge Schneider was about to go back on his own Phase II ruling and bring back the standard net profits contract in order to calculate what Art and Alain should get?

Apparently not.

Just five days before trial, the Court added one more condition to the trial ground rules that was a setback for Paramount: its witnesses couldn't base their testimony on the unconscionable net profit formula.

The piercing ring of the phone interrupted my musings about the week ahead.

"Pierce, this is Allan Pepper." Allan is the normally calm, administrative partner of Kaye, Scholer and my fellow executive committee member.

"What's up?"

"The Office of Thrift Supervision just sued the firm for $275 million and has issued an order freezing the firm's assets."

Allan went on to relate the latest developments in Kaye, Scholer's tense dealings with the federal government in the wake of our representation of Lincoln Savings & Loan in the mid-1980s. In adversary bank examinations, we had defended Charles Keating's notorious institution, which the feds had closed in early 1988 and whose bailout would cost the federal taxpayers at least $2 billion. Spearheaded by the firm's then chairman Peter Fishbein, our aggressive defense of the charges leveled against Lincoln by the Federal Home Loan Bank Board in San Francisco had forestalled the government's eventual takeover of the S&L and arguably increased the bailout cost. The regulators vowed that they would get even.

They got their chance several years later.

Looking for scapegoats and deep pockets, the Office of Thrift Supervision (OTS) in the Department of the Treasury—the new federal S&L regulator and home for many former Federal Home Loan Bank Board officials—had already sued several law and accounting firms for allegedly aiding and abetting the collapse of the thrifts for whom they had rendered professional services. But the new suit against Kaye, Scholer had two novel twists—the OTS claimed that the firm had a duty to disclose to the bank examiners potentially adverse information traditionally protected by the attorney-client privilege, and the OTS issued a unilateral administrative freeze order that threatened to put us out of business. And all this was done without notice, a hearing, or any proof that the firm had done anything wrong!

I couldn't believe it. The precedent was staggering: the government was saying that a defense lawyer was as guilty as his client merely because he kept the client's confidences in strict conformity with the code of ethics. And, as a partner in the firm, I, too, was potentially on the hook for something predating my arrival at Kaye, Scholer.

After I hung up, I did some simple math: my share of the $275 million liability that now hung like a pall over Kaye, Scholer and its 106 partners was more than I would likely get from Paramount in damages for Art and Alain. I was anxious for my family as well as my colleagues and employees at a law firm that had become my home and had been incredibly supportive for the past three and a half years as we battled Paramount. But I couldn't let this personal calamity affect my performance. I had a job to do.

I smiled confidently at Zazi, Bruce, Greg Dovel, Chuck Diamond and Bobby Schwartz as I set my briefcase on the conference table an hour later. Department 52 was once again packed. At least half the gallery was filled with reporters from the local and national press. The new cable television channel, Court-TV, set up an unobtrusive camera in the back left corner of the courtroom and broadcast the entire proceeding live. Carl Nagin, an aggressive reporter from PBS's "Frontline," conducted spot interviews for a documentary on the case that would be aired in the fall.

One of Nagin's interviewees was well-known publicist John Scanlon, whose clients had included Ivana Trump during the breakup of her marriage with "The Donald," and CBS, during General William Westmoreland's libel trial against that network. This time, Scanlon's client was Paramount, and his job was to act as a "spin doctor," putting the best face on things for Paramount by getting to the press before they wrote their stories. Scanlon had already spoken with Los Angeles *Times* reporter Terry Pristin. In her Monday morning story about the opening of the trial, she quoted Scanlon's dire warning:

"We would advise [Buchwald] not to buy a house in the south of France. This is far from over, no matter what the decision of the judge is."

This was a retread of Paramount's tired old admonition. As far back as Robert Draper and Phase I, Paramount had been vowing that the case would be appealed. It was, quite simply, a precedent that the studio could not allow to stand. And, since his loss in Phase II, Diamond had made no secret that a big part of his strategy was putting on the best and most thorough case he could so that Paramount could overturn all of Judge Schneider's verdicts.

Buchwald v. Paramount was nearing an end. But in a sense it would probably never be over. The studios could not allow it to be over. Too much was at stake. In three and a half years of nonstop news stories about Paramount's "unprofitable" $350-million-grossing movie, the studios had been found out —not just in midtown Manhattan and Beverly Hills, but all across America wherever people paid their $5, $6, or $7 to see a mulitmillion-dollar celluloid story whose very creators often wound up with less than the price of a box of popcorn.

With that thought in mind, I launched into my opening statement.

"This trial began over two years and two months ago. That's longer than the run of most television series and Broadway plays. . . .

"Now, fourteen months after our victory in Phase II, we are here to see whether these were pyrrhic victories, as Paramount now claims, or whether, as we urge, the services and contributions of Art Buchwald and Alain Bernheim were valuable and they should be awarded far more than the paltry $250,000 that Paramount insists at most they are worth."

We were ready to put people on the stand who would corroborate our position. I reeled off our witness list:

- Jay Shapiro, an industry auditor for nineteen years;
- David Brown, former co-head of production at Fox and Warner Bros. and producer of *Jaws, The Sting, Cocoon, The Verdict,* and several other hits during an illustrious quarter century in the movie business;
- Paul Maslansky, producer of *The Russia House* and creator of the six *Police Academy* movies which had worldwide revenues of more than $1 billion;
- Jeffrey S. Robin, senior vice-president of the William Morris Agency;
- Dr. Howard Suber, chairman of UCLA's film and television producers program with over twenty years' experience in dissecting the elements that make a movie popular.

Finally, I pared down our demands. We didn't want a windfall. We didn't want to take a shellacking either. What we wanted was the value-in-fact of Art's and Alain's contribution to *Coming to America.*

"The Court, we believe, must negotiate between the Scylla of windfall and the Charybdis of unjust enrichment," I said. "And we believe that range is bracketed by $5 million on the low side and $10 million on the high side."

After my Scylla and Charybdis allusion, I heard a collective groan from the gallery and Judge Schneider rolled his eyes. Whether it was because of my literary flourish or my asking for such a high amount of money, I'll never know.

Now it was Diamond's turn. And he went a bit overboard too.

"Your honor, this is not about personal views of fairness and it's not about lofty metaphysical concepts of intrinsic value, reasonableness and a new term Mr. O'Donnell just coined: 'value in fact.' It's about what somebody gets paid for doing a job."

Then Diamond posed a set of rhetorical questions that made my Homeric reference seem mild.

"Mr. O'Donnell's arguments this morning come down to notions of fairness, but there are two sides to that coin, your honor. Is it fair that motion picture producers earn more than a policeman? Is it fair that Mr. Bernheim will walk out of this courtroom with at minimum roughly ten times what we pay those who educate our children?"

Bruce Margolius wrote me a note:

"Brace yourself. He's going to bring up Mother Theresa's salary next."

Diamond didn't have Mother Theresa lined up to testify, but he did have a formidable set of experts to match each of ours, including:

- Producer David V. Picker, whose list of winners included *Tom Jones, Midnight Cowboy,* and the James Bond series and who, at various times

throughout his long career had run four different studios: Paramount, United Artists, Lorimar and Columbia;
- Martin Ransohoff, whose thirty-five film credits included production of *The Americanization of Emily*, *The Cincinnati Kid*, *The Jagged Edge*, *Silver Streak* and *Catch 22*;
- UCLA economics professor Benjamin Klein, who had years of experience testifying as an expert in contract damages trials;
- Michael Medved, cohost of the PBS show "Sneak Previews" and author of "The Golden Turkey Awards," featuring the worst motion pictures ever made;
- Jack Freedman, an independent producer who ran Warner Bros. business affairs for ten years before going out on his own in 1985 to make movies;
- Barry Blaustein, coscreenwriter with David Sheffield of *Coming to America*; and
- Richard Walter, a screenwriting instructor at UCLA and one of the uncredited original writers of *American Graffiti*.

"Mr. Walter will tell you that everybody has an idea for the hit movie," Diamond told the judge. "The taxi driver who took me to the court this morning. Probably your courtroom clerk. I know Mr. O'Donnell has a bunch in his pocket. But good ideas don't make good movies. Good ideas frequently lead to very bad movies. And he will tell you that there is no such thing as a good idea."

That Art had a good idea and Alain developed it into three scripts for Paramount over a two-and-a-half-year period meant very little, according to Diamond.

"Ultimately, the success of a movie and the success of this movie . . . was due to the way the idea was developed and its execution, not the Buchwald two-and-one-half-page treatment."

In the end, he said, Schneider's nullification of the net profits contract meant that the judge could only award damages based on "the fair market value of the services actually rendered: what people like the plaintiffs get for doing the job that they ostensibly contributed to on 'Coming To America.'

"Our witnesses will opine that in the real world, not in fantasyland, people like that could be expected to earn $300,000; not more," he said. "We will ask for your judgment in accord with that evidence."

I smiled to myself. Diamond had come up $50,000 from Paramount's original claim that Art and Alain deserved no more than $250,000. That was a start —even if the increase wouldn't pay our photocopying costs.

I called Jay Shapiro to the stand first to get our six comparable movies on the record. Adjusted to 1988 dollars, producer earnings under standard net profit deals on the six movies ranged from $900,000 to $15 million—a point I wanted established at the very outset. This range made my proposal look reasonable.

Under the criteria set by Judge Schneider following the referral to Justice Amerian, each comparable movie had to have been released between 1980 and 1988 and have earned at least $75 million in studio gross receipts and cost at least $10 million to make. That meant eliminating a whole range of similar hits, including three of David Brown's biggest moneymakers from the seventies: *The Sting* (1973), which took in $78.2 million; *Jaws* (1975), $129.5 million; and *Jaws II* (1978), $50.4 million.

While the identity of the films were confidential under a pretrial stipulation, the Los Angeles *Times* got ahold of court records and identified them as:

- *Beverly Hills Cop* (1984), which grossed $234.7 million for Paramount and earned $3 million for the producers Don Simpson and Jerry Bruckheimer;
- *An Officer and a Gentleman* (1982), which grossed $129.7 million for Paramount and earned $2.5 million for Martin Elfand;
- *Nine to Five* (1980), which grossed $103.3 million for Twentieth Century Fox and earned $3 million for Bruce Gilbert;
- *Stir Crazy* (1980), which grossed $101.3 million for Columbia and earned $4 million for Hannah Weinstein;
- *Terms of Endearment* (1983), which grossed $108.4 million for Paramount and earned $3 million for James L. Brooks; and
- *Robocop* (1987), which grossed $78 million for Orion and earned $900,000 for the producers.

If Alain's contract terms were applied to those six comparable movies, his paycheck ought to have totaled between $3.4 million and $10.7 million, Shapiro had calculated. That would then set the stage for our witnesses to place the range for Alain's damages between $4.7 million and $7.5 million. As Jay went through his calculations, I could tell that Judge Schneider was unimpressed with these high figures. It was going to be a long week.

David Brown was our first expert. One of the classiest persons ever in the motion picture business, Richard Zanuck's suave, deep-voiced partner for nearly twenty years was last year's winner (along with Zanuck) of Hollywood's highest producer honor, the Irving Thalberg Award for a body of work reflecting the highest-quality movie production. But before David even got on the stand to give a $4 million damages figure, Diamond was up moving to exclude any opinion about fair market value under a pretrial ruling barring us from offering any testimony based on the assumption that Buchwald and Bernheim could have forced Paramount, which needed the rights to Buchwald's story, to renegotiate their deal on the eve of production in 1987. Although I succeeded in getting Brown on the stand, Judge Schneider, after reading his deposition over the lunch recess, ruled that he could not express an opinion on fair market value because he had offered no other basis in his deposition other than the prohibited hypothetical renegotiation. We had gotten caught in a time warp because David's deposition had preceded the judge's ground rules for trial testimony.

In any event, David had valuable testimony about the critical role of a movie producer, whose most important attribute is "an ability to identify a story that will make a successful motion picture." And Bernheim, he testified, had "a particularly keen sense of story values."

Next on the list was "sheer dogged perseverance. An unreal view of the world. Ability to take rejection on a daily basis and still survive in some way."

A producer had to know screenwriters, actors and directors, have a sense of the marketplace, understand how to develop a fragmentary notion into a screenplay, motivate writers and "bring a film project to the eve of production by identifying directors, actors and other main participants in the production process."

A movie's financial success, Diamond insisted in his cross-examination, depends on many factors other than the producer's contributions. "Pictures that do better in terms of costs to receipts pay off bigger bucks," Diamond told the judge. Later, out in the hallway, Diamond, with John Scanlon at his side, told reporters, "*Coming to America* was not the gold cow" because it was costly to make. Maybe, I pointed out to those same reporters, but the largest of those costs was the $50 million to $60 million distribution fee that Paramount paid to itself, even before Eddie Murphy was cut in on the action. The studio *was* the cost.

My next witness was Paul Maslansky, a thirty-one-year veteran of the movie business who had produced over thirty movies. Once again, Diamond was on his feet trying to prevent him from offering an opinion on fair market value. This time, Judge Schneider went our way, ruling that Paul's deposition had fairly revealed the basis for his opinion that Art and Alain should receive the same total compensation as the director John Landis.

Maslansky, a balding law school dropout, learned his first lesson in Hollywood as far back as 1964, when he produced Donald Sutherland's first movie, *Castle of the Living Dead*. If you wanted to work for the studios, you turned the other cheek and kept your complaints to yourself. They made the money; you made the movies. But you always kept your eyes open for your big chance.

Maslansky's chance came one morning in 1983, while he was overseeing a ticker tape parade scene in San Francisco for the movie, *The Right Stuff*. Three or four busloads of "very motley-looking" police officers showed up to help control the crowds. Some were fat, some were anemic, some were wild-eyed and some were so laid back they looked like they were sleepwalking.

They were police cadets, he was told by the sergeant in charge, but they would not necessarily become police officers because they could be flunked out of the academy at any time.

"And it sort of triggered an idea," Maslansky continued. "What if they wanted to stay in and banded together as a group and fought the authority of the academy?"

Maslansky went back to his hotel that night and wrote a one-and-a-half-page treatment. He showed it to a studio executive who suggested he take it to Alan Ladd, Jr., then production chief at Warner Bros. "Laddy" gave

Maslansky a production deal with up-front compensation of $125,000 and a range of 15 to 40 percent of the net profits—a deal that was not as good as Bernheim's for *King for a Day* despite Maslansky's far better track record.

Maslansky eventually earned over $14 million in net profits for creating and nurturing the series.

Together, all six *Police Academy* films had world-wide revenues of about $1 billion, and Warner Bros. made a fortune.

Maslansky called ideas "our true currency." For having come up with the unique idea for *Coming to America* and nurturing it through the studio development process, he said, Art and Alain were entitled to just as much as John Landis: $6.2 million.

"Without Buchwald and Bernheim there would have been no 'Coming to America,' " Maslansky said flatly. "The contribution of Bernheim and Buchwald was equally as significant as the contribution of Mr. Landis in this particular case."

Maslansky's quick wit was evident in Diamond's brief cross-examination. When Chuck pointed out that "ultimately under Mr. Bernheim's stewardship the project died at Paramount," Paul replied:

"Yes, it did, but apparently the idea didn't."

"And, well, that is subject to differing opinions," Diamond shot back.

"Not according to the judge," Paul replied, with a nod toward Schneider.

Coming to America was successful because of its unique concept and star, said our next witness, tight-lipped, bespectacled Dr. Howard Suber, a distinguished UCLA film professor for a quarter of a century and chairman of the school's independent film and television producers program. The film was a box office hit because of the "twin pillars"—Buchwald's unique idea and Eddie Murphy's persona: they made an equal contribution to the movie's popularity. He didn't feel qualified, however, to put a dollar value on Art's concept.

As for Art's story, it was "high concept": a phrase credited to Barry Diller during his days as an ABC-TV programming executive in the seventies and carried over to Paramount where movie concepts were increasingly being reduced to one-liners—the film industry's equivalent of the politician's sound bite. Essentially, high concept in comedy meant a new twist on a familiar element, and fish-out-of-water stories like *King for a Day* were among the most popular high-concept comedies.

Eddie Murphy without a strong concept could not carry a movie, Suber noted, pointing to *Harlem Nights*. And the importance of Buchwald's concept to *Coming to America*'s success was confirmed by Paramount in its promotional materials—the "one-sheet" (theater lobby poster) of Eddie in royal African garb bestriding Park Avenue like a Colossus, the movie theater "trailer" (preview), and the artwork and copy on the videocassette box. In each, Eddie Murphy as an African prince in the urban American ghetto was "Paramount's own perception of what it had to sell."

Bobby Schwartz's uneventful cross-examination only enhanced Suber's credibility as a ranking expert in analyzing the popularity of films. Judge Schneider seemed impressed with the academic approach to putting a value on Art's concept. At one point, Suber told Schwartz that a black prince from a South Pacific island would not have been as successful a movie. Judge Schneider wanted to know why. Choosing his words carefully, Suber answered:

"It was quite well known and commented on at the point when Paramount was contemplating Eddie's new film that Eddie was being criticized . . . for insufficient blackness, shall we say, [and] that it was important that he hire more black people. . . . By allowing Eddie to make a film which was [cast almost] entirely [with] black people, . . . he got . . . a kind of double whammie out of it. Black royalty coming to the black ghetto from the South Pacific would not be seen by . . . the black American audiences, who were a significant core of his audience, in the same light."

Our last witness, Jeffrey Robin, was a thoughtful, handsome, bearded lawyer who had been in the entertainment business since 1971. He had been a lawyer-negotiator in private practice for clients like Billy Crystal, Sally Field and Jason Robards and a business affairs executive at Capitol Records, Paramount and most recently the William Morris Agency. In January, Robin had been promoted to senior vice-president in charge of William Morris's motion picture department worldwide. Under questioning by Bruce Margolius, Robin told the Court that, in light of the fact that Paramount had green-lighted the project, Landis and Murphy were committed and the studio needed Buchwald's rights to make the movie, the fair market value for Buchwald's contributions and Bernheim's work as producer was worth around $7 million—fees of between $475,000 and $800,000 and one and a half times Landis's contingent compensation or $6.3 million.

But the judge was restless and frustrated after two days of testimony.

"I suspect I could line up thirty folks like you," he told Robin, his voice booming across the courtroom. "And Mr. Diamond could line up thirty folks, and they're each going to have an opinion. And you say $2 million or $8 million or $137 million or a dollar and a half! These are just *numbers* to me! Without foundational facts to support them, they're not very meaningful. . . . And it's going to work both ways."

Judge Schneider was looking for "all of the ingredients upon which you base your conclusions. . . . I need to have some basis for any conclusions that I reach. That is the exercise that we have been attempting to go through. Period."

I was frustrated too. There was no simple formula for trying to put a dollar value on a movie concept that had been misappropriated five years earlier and a producer's services that had never been rendered because of Paramount's breach. All we had were the opinions of competing experts. The whole damages phase was inherently unfair to my clients because, as Roger Davis had testified in Phase II, they had been cheated out of the ability to exploit normal market forces and negotiate for a better deal in 1987 when Paramount resurrected their project.

Out in the hallway after Day Two, Art, who had arrived Monday evening and had quickly neutralized Paramount's spin doctor Scanlon, was already claiming victory.

"The only thing we're discussing now is how much we've won, and that has nothing to do with the fact that they will never be able to use the same accounting system again," he told the assembled press.

"I don't give a damn about the money," he said. "My lawyer cares, but I make a very good living at what I do. I'd be very happy to receive a nice settlement for one reason: people judge in this country by how much money you get."

"Paramount made a huge amount of money and what I feel we deserve is a small share of the cake," Alain said softly to the same news people.

As I stood on the fringe of the pack of reporters and listened to Art and Alain, I had no doubt that independent-minded Judge Schneider would not accept either side's position. The final damages award was now a crapshoot. Whatever the amount, I had to get more than the $300,000 figure being pushed by Diamond. Otherwise, without some element of damages for the worthless 19 percent of net profits, the entire three-and-a-half-year struggle would be worse than a Pyrrhic victory—it would be a resounding defeat! Art could tell the world that we had already won, but my job wasn't by any means finished.

When we returned to court Wednesday morning, Bobby Schwartz grilled Jeff Robin on his lack of experience. As an agent/attorney, Robin made deals, not movies. How could he testify to what Bernheim deserved if he'd never even produced a movie himself?

Once Schwartz had finished, Diamond tried to have Robin's entire testimony stricken.

Schneider refused.

Instead, he kept his views of our final witness's opinions to himself and told Paramount to call its first witness.

UCLA economics professor Benjamin Klein had never produced a movie either, but he was an old hand at producing high-priced market analyses and mind-boggling rows of comparative numbers. Using five of the seven movies that Jay Shapiro had cited in his assessment that Art and Alain should get something between $3.4 million and $10.7 million, Klein concluded by a process he called "regression analysis" that Alain was due $252,000 and Art should receive only between $22,000 and $82,000. Even if overhead and interest charges were dropped and estimated videocassette revenue was doubled, Bernheim still wouldn't be entitled to more than $347,000, Klein testified.

As I began my cross-examination, I couldn't resist tweaking Klein, a highly respected economist whom my law firm was using for a multinational corporate client in another case. It was no small irony, I pointed out, that Paramount paid Klein more to testify than the amount he said that the studio owed Art for conceiving the idea for *Coming to America.*

For over an hour I hammered away at Klein, pointing out the numerous ways in which his opinion depended "directly and inexorably" on the unconscionable net profit formula. At one point, I asked Klein a rhetorical question to remind the judge why he had invalidated the net profit formula: explain to me, as an economist, how Paramount could have recouped all of its direct and indirect costs, made tens of millions of dollars of profits, and yet there would never be any net profits? The answer, of course, was the insidious net profit formula by which another $20 million of gross receipts could have been collected by Paramount since Phase II and the deficit was reduced by only $2 million, from $18 million to $16 million.

When I asked Klein how he had arrived at many of the dollar figures he had plugged into his charts, he admitted they had come not from court exhibits but from a summary of contract terms and a phone call to Paramount's accounting chief, Carmen Desiderio. I quickly objected to the testimony as hearsay, and Judge Schneider concurred, disallowing many of the numbers in the professor's charts. Klein apologized to Diamond from the witness stand for failing to get his numbers into the court record.

"No apology necessary," Diamond said testily, visibly upset that I had succeeded in preventing him from getting this evidence in the record so that Paramount could use it on appeal to undermine Judge Schneider's Phase II unconscionability decision.

When Diamond attempted to rehabilitate Klein, we all got some overdue comic relief. Chuck asked his expert to restate his opinion on Buchwald's damages.

"Well, as I testified—it was in a range between $22 and $82 million."

I shot a look back at Art and Alain, who had joined everyone else in the courtroom in laughing at Klein's mistake. Art nodded, signaling that he liked the number.

"You mean thousand?" asked the judge, coming to the rescue.

"I mean—sorry, thousand," an embarrassed Klein replied, adding that he was tired.

Diamond moved to strike the answer, but when I stood to inform the Court that my client would take the $22 to $82 million, Diamond amended his motion:

"I move to strike the witness."

Bearded and bald except for a fringe of shoulder-length blond hair, screenwriting instructor Richard Walter looked and sounded like a time traveler from the sixties. He had taught at UCLA since 1977 and authored a textbook on screenwriting. He'd also written the two earliest drafts of *American Graffiti*, but lost out in arbitration when he sought screen credit. His only actual feature-writing credits were for *The Return of Zorro* and another screenplay about a character known as "The Dynamite Lady."

But Walter was no stranger to practical moviemaking. He had written several industrial and educational films, consulted with studios on story structure questions and once ate a hot dog on camera with Charles Durning in a 1986 Columbia comedy called *Big Trouble.* In his opinion, Buchwald's concept was "not worth very much at all [and] certainly it's not worth anything resembling the contribution of Eddie Murphy." Walter's opinion seemed to proceed from a bias that "the idea, the concept is the single most overappreciated entity in the whole entertainment industry."

High concept alone did not mean success, Walter claimed, citing *Howard the Duck, My Stepmother Is an Alien* and *Radio Flyer* as movies developed from high concepts that laid eggs at the box office. It was the execution of *Coming to America* that made it a success, he maintained.

Greg Dovel, my gifted associate whom Walter repeatedly and loudly referred to as "Mr. Doe-vall!," took on the cross-examination. The witness moved back and forth in his seat like a cobra and often spoke so rapidly that the court reporter had to ask him to slow down. Walter insisted that *Coming to America* was a romantic fairy tale about a charming young man's coming of age with scant resemblance to Buchwald's treatment. In the end, he could not give Judge Schneider a magic formula to figure damages for Art and Alain.

The judge was growing as impatient with Paramount's witnesses as he had been with ours. Most of what he had been hearing, an exasperated Schneider told us, was "fluff."

Paramount next paraded three producers to the stand. David Picker, Martin Ransohoff and Jack Freedman all had the same thing to say: Buchwald and Bernheim should not get any money beyond the fixed fees in their contracts. Under no circumstances, they said in a chorus most of Thursday, should the pair get any net profits because *Coming to America* had not yet earned any net profits under the unconscionable formula.

It was my gut instinct that these opinions would not win the day for Paramount. In our cross-examinations, Zazi, Bruce and I stressed their arbitrary and capricious assumptions in placing the value in 1983 instead of 1987 when the contract was breached and in failing to put any value on the contributions that Art and Alain actually made to the movie's success. The judge himself signaled how he felt when he said during Picker's testimony, "The fact that the net profit formula is being used as a base for this kind of testimony . . . is troublesome from the outset."

Paramount's next witness late Thursday afternoon was a self-assured, self-appointed arbiter of popular taste. Michael Medved pointed out almost immediately upon taking the witness stand that he could rarely go anywhere without being recognized as the Groucho look-alike, cohost of the PBS series "Sneak Previews," seen on 180 stations every week.

"People come up to me all the time, I mean as recently as a few moments ago in the hallway of this courthouse," said the Yale-educated critic. "People come up because they know you're a movie critic and say, you know, 'You liked such and such a movie. I didn't like it. How could you recommend it to me?' Or alternatively they say, 'Thank you for sending me to "Wayne's World," ' to mention a Paramount release."

"Dumb movie," muttered Judge Schneider, wrinkling his nose.

"Actually, your honor, I think it's not," said Medved.

Bobby Schwartz tried steering the questioning away from the recently released Paramount comedy about a pair of rock 'n' roll misfits. *Wayne's World* wasn't particularly subtle or memorable, yet after three weeks in the theaters it had already earned $46 million. This was a mystery that Judge Schneider wanted to probe further.

"Would you permit me, Mr. Schwartz?" he asked. Then he peered down at the hapless Medved. "How did *you* review 'Wayne's World'?" the judge demanded.

"With pleasure," Medved answered. "Actually, I thought that, for what it was, it achieved its goals admirably."

"What were its goals?" Judge Schneider persisted.

"It was, your honor, what we call a critic-proof movie. In other words, the dumber it is, the more it achieves its basic intentions which is to be the dumbest thing around."

Judge Schneider gave up and turned the witness back over to Schwartz, who walked Medved through yet another list of story elements to illustrate why, in Medved's view, *Coming to America* was neither based upon Art's story nor dependent in any way upon the three *King for a Day* scripts that Alain had developed for Paramount. Buchwald's and Bernheim's contributions "were at best minimal to the final success" of *Coming to America*, Medved asserted.

On Friday morning Zazi wasted no time attacking Medved, characterizing him as "an expert on bad films." She established that, at $200 an hour, Medved had already earned between $8,000 and $10,000 from Paramount as an expert witness—not the best position for an allegedly unbiased movie critic to find himself in.

Her most damning line of questions, however, dealt with an even more suspect quid pro quo practice among film critics:

"Sir, it's very common, is it not, for studios to call up film critics and ask them to provide quotes for the studio to use in their newspaper ads, isn't it?"

"There is a common practice in the industry that, after a critic has seen a screening of a film in advance, the publicist for the studio will call the critic to get a reaction," said Medved. "If the reaction is positive, the publicist for the studio will frequently—much too frequently as I have commented publicly and in the press—much too frequently, the publicist for the studio will ask the critic to grant the use of that positive opinion. . . ."

"Sir, you recently described yourself as a veteran quote whore, did you not?"

Zazi held up an interview in which Medved spoke out self-deprecatingly about the practice of film critics cozying up to studios by delivering raves about their latest films. Medved squirmed.

"That is out of context," Medved snapped. "I think if you were to take a look at that article, what I was saying in the article was I felt that many television critics, including myself, had been tarnished by what I consider to be a lamentable practice."

But the die had been cast. Medved found himself on the defensive from that moment on. Following his testimony, in which he also admitted advising studios on how to market movies before they were released, other critics across the country attacked his objectivity, citing his acknolwedged relationships with Hollywood studios as compromising his independence.

In a six-page statement he sent out to the media in the days following the trial, Medved pointed out that he had reviewed several Paramount films unfavorably in the past.

"This record hardly indicates a critic whose support has been 'purchased' by Paramount," Medved argued.

But the damage to his reputation had already been done.

"He sold his soul to the devil," said the Washington *Post*'s television critic, Tom Shales. "I think it's completely without any argument immoral. I don't see any possible mitigating circumstances."

Paramount's final witness had been subpoenaed at the last minute by the studio: Barry Blaustein, the man credited with coauthoring the *Coming to America* screenplay. As recently as twenty-four hours earlier, Diamond's team had been unsure whether Blaustein would appear. Had it been left to Blaustein, he would not have shown up. He was a most reluctant witness.

"I have extremely mixed feelings about testifying," he said. A tall, rangy man with curly brown hair, a broad sense of humor and an equally broad, toothsome smile, he added, "I am also a profit participant in this movie and I have not yet received a dime. . . ."

Though they held five net points between them, Blaustein and his collaborator, David Sheffield, had never earned any more than their $400,000 upfront fee. Indeed, as profit participants on the second in Paul Maslansky's *Police Academy* series, the two screenwriters had earned nearly $1 million each from their five net profit points, even though *Police Academy* 2 had less than a third of *Coming to America*'s box office.

But Blaustein and Sheffield also blamed Buchwald for alternately belittling their screenplay and then claiming credit for the story that the screenplay was based upon. Too much weight in the industry is given to bare-bones ideas, Blaustein complained.

Ideas are important, but not nearly so important as the screenplay itself, he testified. If ideas alone were enough, "my mailman would be a screenwriter," said Blaustein.

"There is never an idea that writes itself, nor is there a trial that tries itself," he continued. "It takes hours of work and preparation."

Blaustein said he had never seen Buchwald's treatment. Diamond handed him a copy and he quickly read through it. When he finished, he held up a half-inch-thick, bound screenplay in his right hand.

"This is 'Coming to America,' " he said.

Then, holding up the *King for a Day* treatment in his left hand, he said: "This is a three-page outline. They have nothing to do with each other."

Outside of about forty handwritten pages of notes that Murphy had written and four days of talks with Murphy and Hall in New York, Blaustein and Sheffield were on their own, Blaustein testified. For seven weeks the pair worked six days a week, approximately eight to ten hours a day, writing the screenplay.

"We put Mr. Hall and Mr. Murphy's name on it because we figured it would be harder for Paramount to turn down a script with their names on it in addition to ours," he claimed. "But there was never any question, I know, in Mr. Murphy's mind, that we were the writers of the screenplay."

Outside in the hallway following his testimony, Blaustein called Paramount's accounting "creative." But he had also found himself caught between a studio he believed had cheated him out of profits, a fellow writer whose cause he believed in and his own integrity as a writer.

Blaustein criticized Buchwald for going on television and talk shows with the charge that *Coming to America* was a "stinker." Art was sympathetic and, perhaps, even a little embarrassed by his disparagement of the movie during the years of battle with Paramount.

"You have a right to feel the way you do," he told Blaustein in their first-ever face-to-face meeting in the hallway. Blaustein promised to return the money Art had spent on his ticket to see *Coming to America* if Buchwald would agree to pay Blaustein back for the ticket he had bought as a kid in New York to see Art's only Broadway play, *Sheep on the Runway*.

What began as a rancorous first meeting between two writers ended with a united message for the reporters gathered in the hallway outside Department 52.

"I hope Mr. Buchwald makes a lot of money off this case," said Blaustein.

In my forty-five-minute closing argument on Friday afternoon, I asked the judge to adopt Maslansky's $6.2 million calculation in awarding damages because Art and Alain's contribution was at least equivalent to the director's. My argument on fair market value broke down into three themes: the great value of my clients' contributions, the market for producer contingent compensation that showed the $6.2 million was within the range of what comparable producers earned on the six comparable films, and why it was fair for Buchwald and Bernheim to earn at least a fraction of the profits that Paramount had reaped from their efforts. I blasted Paramount's argument that, in assessing fair market value, Judge Schneider should stick to the unconscionable net profit formula—"Hollywood's equivalent of a politician's promise that he won't raise taxes." Even though it was among the thirty-five top-grossing films of all time Paramount knew the film would never return net profits. *Coming to America* should have been renamed *From Here to Infinity*, I argued.

"I do not mean to suggest that the 'King for a Day' treatment ranks with 'Beowulf' as a priceless contribution to Western culture," I conceded. Nevertheless, it did turn out to be a $350 million idea and Paramount had robbed my clients of any chance of putting their idea on the market by going ahead with the film before securing the rights to Art's treatment. But the studio "did far more and far worse than that. Paramount destroyed any readily ascertainable fair market value of Plaintiffs' asset by taking and using their property without consent."

As I approached the end of my argument, I had some parting thoughts for Judge Schneider and the millions who had followed the marathon case for three and a half years.

"As a lawyer and officer of the court . . . I'm proud to have represented these two determined men who stood up for their rights and fought for what they think is just. Whether they get a dollar or millions of dollars, that's not what this case is really all about. . . .

"Your honor, no damages award, no matter how high or low, can enhance or detract from my clients' dogged pursuit of justice against a powerful foe. For my clients and me and my colleagues, there is a higher justice than dollars and cents. A higher justice than box office receipts or gross points or net profits. A higher justice that this case, this court, and these plaintiffs have recalled for a hopeful creative community of artists, writers, directors and actors—the men and women, the creative talent, who make the movies.

"Regardless of what happens on Paramount's appeal, this case will endure forever in the hearts and minds of people who put a higher value on principles than profits. . . .

"As this bruising battle in this court comes to an end and we fade out, please keep one thing in mind. When all is said and done, 'Coming to America' is based upon the creative genius of Art Buchwald. And there would be no 'Coming to America' but for Alain Bernheim's creative efforts and determination in marrying Buchwald's concept with Paramount's Eddie Murphy.

"Somewhere, your honor, in all that pile of money, there must be something left over for Alain Bernheim and Art Buchwald. How much is, of course, for you to decide. We have given you our evidence. We entrust it to your judgment."

When I turned away from the bench and looked out at the jam-packed courtroom, I saw Alain in the front row of seats, putting a handkerchief to his eyes. Art sat beside him, his comforting arm around his old friend's shoulders, while his own bulldog lower lip stuck out a bit further than usual, holding his own emotions in check.

Chuck Diamond delivered his own closing with a surgical, businesslike detachment that nonetheless carried undertones of cold fury. Fair market value should be based on the "real world" as it existed in 1983, he said, rather than "pure conjecture" as to what might have happened had Paramount been forced to buy *King for a Day* in 1987.

"Everything else is marshmallows," Diamond told the judge. "If you grab it, it disappears between your fingers."

Art and Alain were entitled to no more than the fixed fees in their contract, he said. Even if the contract had "unconscionable" elements, we were not automatically entitled to more money.

"Plaintiffs in this case don't want fair market value. They want 'just compensation,'" he said.

Art and Alain were like home sellers who try raising the selling price of a house that's already been sold after oil has been discovered on the property. If everyone involved in making a film could similarly determine their cut after the fact, the result would be "economic anarchy.

"You can't create an award that is greater than the reasonable expectations of the parties at the time the contract was made," Diamond said.

But I could tell that the judge was not moved by my able adversary's plea that he should ignore his Phase II ruling and award no contingent compensation. Judge Schneider found "troublesome" Paramount's argument that my clients should get no benefit after they "go to the . . . legal trouble of knocking down the net profit formula. . . .

"Well, gentlemen, this ends a long ordeal," a relaxed Judge Schneider remarked after Chuck and I had finished. "And I want to make a couple of observations. The case has been fun, even though Mr. Diamond and I have earlier on had some differences of opinion that were indeed spirited. I considered that to be in the nature of advocacy and tried not to be—certainly tried not to have it carry over from day-to-day. And I don't think it has.

"I want to thank both of you for acting—all of your staff, but I'm addressing Mr. Diamond and Mr. O'Donnell specifically—for acting professionally, acting cooperatively in your presentation. It makes my job incredibly easier, especially in a case where there is a certain amount of publicity attached to it and we have a cooperative environment. . . .

"I know I enjoyed very much the give and take that we had. . . . And I hope to see you both soon."

Then it ended, at 3:47 p.m., March 6, 1992.

"My long nightmare is over," Buchwald told reporters outside the courtroom.

When the case first went to court, Art had expected a quick settlement. The trial went forward because Bernheim and he had publicly and unwittingly challenged the status quo and Martin Davis couldn't allow that to happen, he told the media.

"Marty said he couldn't stop it," Art remembered. "He can buy Warner Bros. with one phone call but he can't stop a lawsuit.

"No matter what happens here, we've changed what's going on in Hollywood and the writers, actors and producers are going to have a better shot. But not for long because they'll find another way to screw them."

As for Hollywood in general, Art had one line to deliver.

"It's a nice place to visit," he said.

Then he left.

That night I hosted a "wrap party" at Tutto Bene on La Cienega Boulevard in West Los Angeles. Virtually everyone who had been involved in the case attended, from Danny Arnold (whom I kiddingly reviled for getting me involved in the first place) to Howard Suber, who had only recently joined our cause as an expert witness. My assistant, Asaf Cohen, collected $5.00 each from the forty guests, who placed bets as to what final damages would be; all proceeds from this pool were to go to the person with the number closest to the award.

While I knew otherwise in my heart, I predicted $5 million, the figure that I had put in the complaint back in November 1988. Almost everyone else came up with multimillion-dollar numbers. Except for Art. His pool slip called for only a $1 million award.

"In the long run, all of us will be better off if the judge doesn't give us too much money," he told me.

"Why? What are you talking about?" I said, pouring another glass of wine.

"We just will. Believe me," Buchwald said.

Then I got lost in another conversation, hands slapping my back and cocktail laughter drowning out Art's words.

Halfway through the evening, an unanticipated guest arrived. By sheer happenstance, Barry Blaustein had also come to Tutto Bene for dinner and had run into Art. They talked privately for a long time; Art repeated his apologies from that afternoon in the courtroom hallway, and Barry graciously accepted. Noting that the studio was trying to divide and conquer writers, they reconciled. Art was visibly relieved.

Art and Barry then joined us in the back room where we all clinked glasses and drank to the end, forever, of the studio net profit scam.

On Monday, March 16, ten days after the trial, I was closeted in an office overlooking San Francisco Bay with fifteen other lawyers from around the country who were helping me with strategy for a case I'd be arguing later that year before the California Supreme Court. The meeting broke up shortly before 4 P.M., and I phoned Zazi.

This time Connie wasn't with me when I got the news.

"We got $900,000," Zazi said, "$150,000 for Art and $750,000 for Alain."

"Excuse me," I said. "Did you say $900,000, Zazi?"

"Yes, Pierce. The judge wrote a fourteen-page opinion. As we expected, he didn't accept either side's damages theory. He came up with his own."*

I felt like I'd just been hit across the face with a crowbar. All that hard work, I thought. Two major victories in two years, and now a reward of less than $1

---

* Judge Schneider's decision on Phase III is reproduced in full in Appendix C.

million. God damn it, it wasn't fair! How could Harvey Schneider do this? The judge *knew* what bastards Paramount's faceless executives were. He'd been personally attacked and ridiculed himself. And now the studio could gloat that it had kept down the damages at least to a point where Kaye, Scholer would get little or no fees for its efforts on behalf of Art, Alain and the creative community.

As I wallowed in self-pity, Art's observation the night of the party that we would be better off with a low award echoed in my head. Once again, Buchwald was right.

The case had stopped being about money months, even years, earlier.

We had spent over $1 million just to prove the breach of contract in January 1990. I knew our chances of recouping legal fees were slim, but I also knew we couldn't quit. We had a tiger by the tail. To let go was to admit failure, not just for us, but for every writer who has ever had his story stolen and every producer who has ever seen his net profits eroded to nothing by a larcenous net profit formula.

As the months passed and our costs mounted, my team of lawyers and I had worked even harder, motivated by a shared feeling that what we were doing was right and would someday make a difference.

Money was how Paramount and the other studios defined value. We couldn't fall into that trap. My own closing argument came back to me.

"This case will endure forever in the hearts and minds of people who put a higher value on principles than profits."

I came out of my stupor and realized I'd left Zazi hanging on the other end of the line.

"Well, kid, it's not what we asked for, but it doesn't come as a surprise either," I said with a sigh.

"No, Pierce, it doesn't," Zazi said in a calm, clear voice. "We've known since Phase II that the damages award would be conservative so that the unconscionability ruling would have a better chance of standing up on appeal."

"Well, I told Judge Schneider in closing argument that the case wasn't about money," I said. "I guess he took me at my word."

We both started laughing. Besides our sense of outrage, all we had had to sustain us for over three and a half years was our sense of humor. We would need it during the next few hours as we explained our take on the third and final decision to the rest of the world.

"I'm sure Paramount has already declared victory," I said.

"You bet," Zazi answered. "We spent $2.5 million to get $900,000. That's their line. Sound familiar?"

It was exactly the same in-your-face statement Bob Draper had delivered to the media after Phase I, when he first revealed to the world that *Coming to America* had never turned a net profit and probably never would.

"And, to add insult to injury, they've announced that they are appealing. It could be another two years and hundreds of thousands of dollars in fees for us."

"I know. Believe me, I know," I said in almost a whisper. "But at this point it doesn't make any difference. Whatever it takes, no matter how long or expensive, we'll stick with Art and Alain and see our victories through the appellate gauntlet."

"And we'll win," Zazi said confidently.

"Where's Alain?" I asked.

"He'll be here in a minute. The press is on the way over. I just spoke to Art. He's really upbeat about the whole thing."

"And Alain?" I asked.

"Relieved. At peace. He thanked us again for everything we've done and is proud of what we accomplished."

"That's the best news you could have given me. Alain was the one I was always worried about. He had so much of himself invested in this project and, then, the lawsuit. I'll talk to him when he gets to the office. Now—how many reporters do we have to call?"

"At least thirty."

"Okay, let's divide up the list and go at it. Art, Alain, you and I will teach John Scanlon a thing or two about spin control."

For the next three hours the four of us kept stressing the obvious: that Buchwald's award was 250 percent of what Paramount wanted to pay and Bernheim's share was almost four times what the studio had insisted he should receive. The total verdict was nine times the only no-strings-attached settlement offer that Paramount had ever made, back in the summer of 1988 before I even took the case.

Art put the whole case in perspective.

"Paramount and the other studios have to change every contract they ever made. And they call that a victory? Look, the decision might stop those guys from stealing—but I doubt it."

When told by a TV reporter that Paramount had already declared a victory and announced that it was appealing, Art looked into the camera and spoke to the rest of America outside jaded Hollywood:

"They say they won, and they're appealing. We're not appealing. Now you tell me who won."

I told the media that Judge Schneider had been "Solomonic": neither side got what it wanted, but he had vindicated our position. Our clients shared in the financial success of *Coming to America*, even if Kaye, Scholer did not.

"The whole case is a great victory for the creative community," I told Robert Welkos of the Los Angeles *Times*.

I praised Chuck Diamond for his skillful lawyering, but he remained uncharacteristically quiet. All calls were referred to Paramount's public relations chief, Harry Anderson. Diamond did tell Zazi that it was not his decision as to whether the studio would appeal Schneider's decision. Sober-minded studio executives and their lawyers were hoping that Paramount would not appeal.

Warner Bros. general counsel John Schulman had told me back in January 1991 that he would pay me $10 million to put Judge Schneider's genie back in the bottle. If an appellate court affirmed his unconscionability ruling, every studio and every movie whose talent worked under the standard net profits contract would be affected. Peter Dekom, an entertainment lawyer with an unabashed pro-studio bias, told the Los Angeles *Times*:

"If Paramount loses on appeal, it will encourage anyone who has a similar financial situation with movies to file a lawsuit. And if the appellate ruling is certified for publication, it will set a precedent for other courts to follow that the net profit definition is inherently suspect."

In my heart of hearts, I hoped that Paramount did appeal. Judge Schneider's ruling on the misappropriation of Art's treatment was so factually and legally sound that the chances for reversal were not great. The Phase II decision—that the take-it-or-leave-it net profit formula was a contract of adhesion and several of its key terms were unenforceable—was based on unambiguous statutory and case law. Paramount's withdrawal of its risky business defense—to avoid a court-supervised audit by Price, Waterhouse—left the industry's net profit contract virtually defenseless.

On the morning of March 17, in deference to the patron saint of Ireland, Art Buchwald finished wrapping a package destined for New York's Columbus Circle. It was addressed to Martin S. Davis, care of Paramount Communications, Inc. Inside was an unopened bottle of Dom Perignon and a note that read:

> Marty—
> I believe this belongs to you. You need a drink.
>   Art

Aftermath

A SIMPLE breach-of-contract suit that should have been settled in the summer of 1988 for a few hundred thousand dollars and a microwave oven, as Buchwald loved to say, became a worldwide cause célèbre about the artistic and financial rights of creative talent in the motion picture industry. Thanks to the arrogance of Paramount and its chairman, what started as a brush fire became a conflagration that was allowed to burn out of control for almost four years.

The man who precipitated the affair was one of the losers. Notwithstanding Judge Schneider's diplomatic comments in his first decision, millions mistakenly believed that Eddie Murphy "stole" Art Buchwald's story. And despite Paramount's refusal to settle in order to curry favor with its Golden Child, Murphy, apparently ignoring his failure to show up at trial to explain the origins of Coming to America, irately attributed his tarnished image to the studio's mishandling of the case.

His career seemed to be in an artistic tailspin. Harlem Nights, which he conceived, wrote, directed and produced, was a disaster. Another 48 HRS. was hardly a box office triumph. Murphy's next movie, Boomerang, written by Coming to America writers Barry Blaustein and David Sheffield, and scheduled for release later in 1992, will tell a lot about whether the thirty-one-year-old is still bankable.

Robert Wachs opened up his own talent management company in Beverly Hills. After Arsenio Hall fired him in 1990, Wachs hired Howard Weitzman and sued Hall for 50 percent of the profits from "The Arsenio Hall Show" (over $6 million) plus another $75 million in damages. Represented by Buchwald's and Bernheim's first lawyer, Howard King, Hall countersued Wachs, claiming that Wachs was not entitled to any money because he had been practicing as an agent without a license. Wachs retorted with a lawsuit in federal court seeking a declaration that the California law governing the licensing of agents was unconstitutional. Eventually, these suits will settle, and the big winners will be the lawyers for both sides.

Since his cameo appearance as his pal Eddie's surrogate in the first Buchwald v. Paramount trial, Arsenio Hall has continued to flourish. His top-rated late night talk show, owned by Paramount, remains popular with young, hip audiences, although critics have lamented his fawning interview style and lack of substance. In late 1990, Hall signed a new contract with Paramount, giving him a four-movie deal and the chance to produce movies and television shows. Whether Hall learned any lessons from his best friend's trials and tribulations in dealing with fame and fortune might very well dictate how brightly and how long his star will burn.

John Landis was hired by Disney in 1991 to direct Oscar, a critical and financial bomb starring Sylvester Stallone. The same year, Landis also directed Michael Jackson's music video "Black or White" for Jackson's "Dangerous" album. Shortly before the music video was released, however, four minutes—featuring scenes in which the pop icon for teenagers smashed a car with a crowbar and mimed masturbation—were cut when broadcasters threatened not to air the spot.

Martin Davis continues to rule his Paramount media empire with an iron hand. Despite the billions of cash in the company's coffers, Davis had failed to pull off any major acquisition or merger by the spring of 1992. Jesse Kornbluth suggested in Vanity Fair that Davis "may be, all by himself, Paramount's poison pill."

Nearing retirement age, Davis remains active in charity work, including his beloved Multiple Sclerosis Society and a more recent cause, the Barbara Bush Foundation for Family Literacy.

In the three and a half years that Davis tangled with Buchwald, Paramount's profits plummeted, largely owing to the movie studio's sagging performance. For fiscal year 1988, Paramount reported earnings of $384.7 million—the highest in the company's history. Three years later the earnings had dropped by 68 percent to $122.2 million. In the same three-year period, the market value of Paramount's stock price remained stagnant at about $45 per share.

Meanwhile, Michael Eisner and Jeffrey Katzenberg, whom Davis had forced out of Paramount in late 1984, have helped guide the Walt Disney Company to dizzying new heights of profitability, stock market value and movie market share. For example, in the summer of 1988, Disney stock sold in the low 60s, but by March 1992 a Disney share was trading as high as $157. Earnings went from $522 million in 1988 to $636 million in 1991.

Frank Mancuso, the man whom Davis blamed for the studio's nose dive, put his $20 million lawsuit settlement in the bank. By the time the Buchwald trial ended, Mancuso had still not announced any new studio affiliation or career plans.

A. Robert Pisano, Paramount's general counsel who got his "Buchwald pink slip" for his role in the debacle, returned to his former law firm O'Melveny & Myers.

.   .   .   .

Richard Zimbert, the mastermind behind Paramount's strategy, was effectively demoted when Brandon Tartikoff, Stanley Jaffe's choice to run the studio, brought in respected William Bernstein, former president of bankrupt Orion, to serve as his right hand in the post of executive vice-president in charge of business affairs, legal, finance and studio administration. Zimbert, who has "retired" almost as many times as Frank Sinatra, is to retire for good this time, although he has promised that, even if he's in a walker, he will personally bring me Paramount's check for Buchwald and Bernheim.

Joshua Wattles, Zimbert's protégé and Paramount's deputy general counsel and day-to-day liaison with its litigation counsel, is still on the job. The consummate office politician, who did not hesitate to tell people that Pisano, and not he, had chosen Robert Draper to defend Paramount in the first phase of the trial, once remarked to Bernheim, "I'm a survivor—like a cockroach."

After leaving Paramount as an independent producer/consultant, Ned Tanen landed at Columbia Pictures in a similar capacity. David Kirkpatrick, ousted by Tartikoff, remains a member of The Club as an independent producer on the Paramount lot. Ricardo Mestres is top executive at Disney's Hollywood Pictures.

After the death of Tony Liebig in August 1991, Ken Kulzick and Lon Sobel joined another law firm. Robert Draper is still at O'Melveny & Myers, his star dimmed by his courtroom performance in the first round. Charles Diamond, on the other hand, escaped a similar fate, in part because it was widely perceived that the extreme positions he was forced to advocate were dictated by the client. His law firm's stature in the entertainment and legal communities, however, was tarnished by Buchwald v. Paramount.

Roger Davis, after thirty years with the William Morris Agency, announced his retirement, effective at the end of the year. His successor will be Jeffrey Robin. Thanks to its courage in standing up for Buchwald and Bernheim and resisting pressure to stay on the sidelines, William Morris has earned the well-deserved respect of the creative community.

Lynn Roth and David Rintels are busy turning out movie scripts. As a member of the Writers Guild of America West Board of Directors, Rintels continues in his long-running role of loyal opposition to Brian Walton's continuing domination of the Board. The Writers Guild itself, with its timorous leadership and passive membership, has little hope of elevating the economic or creative status of writers in the Hollywood pecking order, leading some to believe that a new, bolder collective bargaining unit is necessary.

Under an overall deal with Disney, Danny Arnold is creating new television series, producing movies and writing a screenplay. Disaffected with American

politics, and declining standards and values in society in general and the enter-
tainment industry in particular, the self-proclaimed "paranoid with proof" is
threatening to pull up stakes and move to the south of France.

Living in idyllic Ojai, California, Rudy Petersdorf has stayed busy consulting
on the motion picture industry and occasionally serving as an expert witness.
Now well into his late seventies, Max Youngstein, is thinking about taking the
California bar examination so that he can sue all the studios for a massive
antitrust conspiracy to cheat actors, writers, directors and producers. To no one's
surprise, Phil Hacker's studio auditing business and Jay Shapiro's consulting on
entertainment industry lawsuits are flourishing. Still the accounting guru for
Silver Screen Partners, Sid Finger is also scheduled to appear as an expert wit-
ness for me in a Manhattan federal trial in which the Persky-Bright partnerships
are suing Columbia Pictures for tens of millions of dollars for cheating on
accountings for profits and other misconduct in connection with the distribution
of a dozen films, including Shampoo *and* Funny Lady.

This case was not for the fainthearted. Kaye, Scholer reviewed over 1,000,000
pages of documents, filed over 100 pleadings and compiled over 10,000 pages of
sworn testimony. It's not hard to run up a $2.5 million legal bill and over
$500,000 in costs when it takes three and a half years to complete a case.
Paramount threw against us three law firms with at least fifteen lawyers on the
case, its huge in-house legal and accounting departments, a major national
accounting firm, thirty expert witnesses, four publicists and the bulging bank
account of one of the world's largest media corporations, whose $5 to $7 million
in estimated costs were being partially underwritten by a gargantuan insurance
company.
Somehow we won.
In the wake of Judge Schneider's damages verdict, the firm received kudos from
lawyers and creative talent for its dogged prosecution of its clients' claims and
its huge commitment of resources in the face of overwhelming odds and opposi-
tion. "The firm's unrecouped $2.5 million in legal fees benefited every writer,
director, actor and producer in the motion picture business," David Brown reas-
sured me. "Look at your historic efforts as an investment in good will that could
never have been purchased in equivalent advertising dollars."

Two days after the Buchwald trial ended, Kaye, Scholer, prompted by urgings
from its banks and major clients not to engage in a long, drawn-out battle that
might destroy the firm despite its innocence, entered into a settlement with the
Office of Thrift Supervision for $41 million, over half of which was covered by
insurance and the rest payable over five years. Lawyers and judges, while prais-
ing the firm for honoring its clear ethical duty to be a zealous advocate for its
client and not to betray client confidences to government regulators, blasted the
government for its strong-arm tactics. "If the government can hammer a firm as
powerful and prestigious as Kaye, Scholer into submission," remarked Angelo T.

Cometa, immediate past president of the New York State Bar Association, "it can do it to anybody."

Zazi Pope, the earnest rookie who came of age in the cross fire and was the most dedicated, talented colleague with whom anyone could ever hope to work, is back at her desk doing routine commercial litigation. In her "spare time," she is working on a death penalty appeal and human rights causes in Latin America and Asia.

Marsha Durko, the reliable, behind-the-scenes coordinator of the year-long discovery leading up to the first trial, is working with me on entertainment litigations for such clients as Dino De Laurentiis, the Mae West Estate, Julia Phillips, and Miramax. Suzanne Tragert, the other eager novice who tried the first phase with me, went on maternity leave, had a baby boy, and has returned to the office; she still enjoys riding motorcycles on the weekend. Dennis Landry continues to work out every day and to dazzle everyone with his encyclopedic knowledge of the entertainment industry.

Michael Malina and Joel Katcoff, the team's New York brain trust, have gone back to representing major corporations in complex cases involving antitrust, patent infringement and securities law. Bruce Margolius is establishing a law practice in Park City, Utah, when he's not hunting gophers for relaxation in Montana. Greg Dovel is volunteering as a part-time prosecutor to sharpen his trial skills.

Relieved that the emotionally draining trial is over, Alain Bernheim has thrown himself full time into his movie projects. After a long drought that raised suspicions about possible blackballing by the studios, Alain, who became a U.S. citizen during the trial, has one movie set to go into production and others in development.

Art Buchwald is busy completing his memoirs. "They only go up to 1962 when Ann and I returned from Paris," Buchwald tells friends. "Nothing interesting happened to me after I came back." The lower-than-hoped-for damages award prompted these consoling words from my client: "Not getting $5 million in Hollywood sounds like a death in the family."

Judge Harvey Schneider has returned to the daily routine of handling over 500 cases on his "fast track" docket, keeping a tight rein on lawyers in his courtroom and insisting that they maintain the highest standards of professionalism. He continues to teach his innovative program in trial practice for lawyers.

Dennis McDougal voluntarily took himself off the Buchwald story at the Los Angeles/Times when he agreed to coauthor Fatal Subtraction *with me. For the last year of* Buchwald v. Paramount, *he wrote chiefly about the television indus-try for the* Times. *He is currently at work on his third book.*

And as for me, I have managed to lose the forty pounds gained during the second and third phases of the trial.

Only ten days after the damages verdict, Thomas Girardi, one of the nation's leading trial lawyers, and I filed an $8 million suit against Warner Bros., alleg-ing that the studio had cheated Benjamin Melnicker and Michael Uslan, the creators and executive producers of Batman, out of their contractual 13 percent share of net profits. Despite collecting over $425 million in gross receipts from all sources, the studio claimed that the fifth-highest-grossing movie of all time was over $20 million in the red (according to the same net profit formula invali-dated by Judge Schneider) and would never generate a net profit. The next, logical reform effort after Buchwald v. Paramount, *the* Batman *suit focused on the eleven net profit terms—including the siphoning off of 80 percent of the lucrative video revenues—that Judge Schneider did not adjudicate.*

Hollywood is a different place after Buchwald v. Paramount.

By forcing a prolonged, high-visibility confrontation with surrogates of the creative community, Paramount exacerbated the historically strained relations between the buyers and sellers in Hollywood. Resentment of the studios—partic-ularly for their disdain of the "little people" who lack the clout to protect their ideas and pocketbooks—reached fever pitch as Paramount pulled out all the stops to overwhelm Buchwald and Bernheim in a war of attrition.

For now at least, Paramount and the other studios—economic dinosaurs in a rapidly changing market climate that will eventually punish them for their inef-ficiency and excesses—will survive their close encounter with the pundit and his producer. Their immediate survival was never the issue in Buchwald v. Para-mount. Art Buchwald is not Joshua, and the walls of Hollywood are still intact. But it's no longer business as usual either.

As Terry Pristin of the Los Angeles Times observed during the damages trial, the case "has already had a profound impact on the way business is conducted in Hollywood."

Freddie Fields, a producer, former agent and once head of MGM, told the Los Angeles Times after the damages verdict: "The suit has opened up a keg of worms. It makes everyone look at things from both angles."

Their consciousness raised, all writers are now aware of the risks in exposing movie ideas to the unscrupulous and the need to be vigilant about how projects are pitched to potential buyers. Studios have implemented tighter procedures for preventing a reprise of what happened at Paramount with Buchwald's treatment. And an award of nearly $1 million for a movie idea has given agents new ammunition in negotiating for writers.

On the compensation front, talent are no longer accepting the glib reassur-ances of their agents and lawyers that "We got you a great deal—a share of net profits." Empowered with the knowledge that net profits are worthless, they are *insisting on more up-front compensation, fairer, easily enforceable back-end deals (such as deferred payments at a certain level of domestic box office receipts), or a combination of the two.*

The power that comes from knowing how Hollywood really does business may not materially increase the net worth of the creative community. After all, even with a fairer surrogate for net profits, most movies will not generate big payoffs for the participants because of out-of-control costs and gross participations for overpaid stars. But at least writers will know what to expect and be forewarned. Jack Mathews, Newsday's film critic, offered this tongue-in-cheek postmortem a week after the ruling:

> Maybe the lessons of the Buchwald Case could be codified as the Buchwald version of the Miranda rights and read to every newcomer who shows up at a studio to pitch an idea.
>
> You have the right to remain silent.
>
> Any statement that you make can and will be stolen from you.
>
> You have the right to talk to an attorney before and during any meeting.
>
> If you cannot afford an attorney, you can use one of ours. (Just kidding, babe.)
>
> And if we make a deal, expect us to try to beat you out of every dime we can. We can't help ourselves. It's our nature.

Epilogue

"OKAY, WE HAVE A DEAL," I told Bertram Fields, the famed Hollywood lawyer hired by Paramount to handle its appeal of the judgment for $1,021,466 entered in favor of my clients by Judge Harvey Schneider on June 10, 1992.

With those words uttered over a telephone in late June 1995, *Buchwald v. Paramount* was finally over, settled after seven years of hand-to-hand combat with one of the most powerful media companies in the world. It would take another three months of back-and-forth negotiating over the wording of the settlement agreement and joint press release and the entry of an appellate court order before the case was officially concluded. Emotionally, however, this was the climax.

Since our $900,000 damages award in March 1992, the case had followed a tortuously slow path to the California Court of Appeal, the next stop on the judicial marathon. After the damages award, Paramount unsuccessfully sought a new trial and then agreed to pay certain "costs of suit" allowed by statute to the prevailing party. Unfortunately, this allowance of slightly over $120,000 covered only a fraction of our $750,000 in litigation expenses for expert witnesses, deposition transcripts, photocopying, and travel. What it particularly did not cover was the tab of over $4 million in legal fees that Kaye, Scholer had amassed in fighting Paramount. (Unlike England, the loser rarely has to pay the winner's attorney's fees in federal and state courts in this country.)

By the time I reached a settlement with Fields in the early summer of 1995, three more years in the life of *Buchwald v. Paramount* had elapsed. The first two years were spent correcting the hundreds of errors in the trial transcripts, finding exhibits misplaced by court personnel, getting the clerk's office to inventory the massive volumes of exhibits and other court documents for the record on appeal, and drafting numerous appeal briefs. Then in the fall of 1994, while we awaited the scheduling of an oral argument date before three appellate justices, Paramount unexpectedly decided to give up the fight. But nothing about this case was ever easy or routine—it took almost another year to negotiate a decent settlement.

Along the way, my clients had become frustrated and, at times, angry over the prolonged delays. "This kind of thing would never be tolerated in France,"

Alain Bernheim would remind me with a slightly superior tone in his voice. No matter how many times I tried to explain that Paramount had the legal right to several appeals and that the shorthanded clerk's office—decimated by staff cuts thanks to Proposition 13—had to prepare a bulging record comprised of 37,000 pages of transcripts and exhibits *before* Paramount's opening appeal brief could be filed, my clients understandably complained that they were victims of slow motion justice. After I wrote Art and Alain in January 1993 and gave them a timetable predicting up to two to four more years for Paramount to exhaust its appeals to the California Court of Appeal, California Supreme Court, and United States Supreme Court, Alain, now in his seventies and stunned by this possibility, sent me the only letter that I can recall receiving from him in all the years of the case:

> Never in a million years did I think the appeal could drag on that long. I realize that you are not responsible but nonetheless it is extremely depressing and has thrown me for a loop. I wish I had known more about American law when I first got started. I now have to keep my fingers crossed that at least we win before I get too old to enjoy something out of it!

Buchwald was also growing weary of the case's glacial pace. He was especially furious about the delays caused by the poor state of the trial transcripts replete with typos, garbled sentences, and missing words. After he testified at the first phase in December 1989 and read the botched transcript of his own testimony, he fumed: "Imagine if this were a capital case and someone's life was on the line!" Perhaps sensing the irony, Art fired off a letter to his Irish-American lawyer on St. Patrick's Day, 1993, complaining bitterly about the incompetent court reporter who had "wreaked so much damage" on the "critical trial record." "This trial has taken a toll on all of us," Art continued, "and it seems so sad that after all this time there doesn't seem to be an end in sight."

Art got so upset that, on September 22, 1993, he actually wrote to Judge Schneider, copying Chuck Diamond and me.

> I don't know what the protocol is about writing to the judge in a case in which one is a party, but I am very concerned at what happened once the case left your court.
>
> First of all I want to say that I thought you were a fair and honorable justice and we don't have any complaints about your decision. We all spent four years of our lives on this case and you gave it tremendous attention and assiduously applied the facts to the law.
>
> Unfortunately, while the case was going on, the court reporter screwed up the transcripts something awful. The personnel in the Clerk's office responsible for assembling the record have been unconscionably slow. We have spent over an entire year trying to get the record straight.
>
> There is something terribly wrong with the system when scant attention is paid to the transcripts. It appears that everyone wasted their time when the official record does not accurately reflect the proceedings. . . .

I am told that we may not have a decision on the appeal until 1994—two years after you finished your work. No appeal should drag on for so long.

You did your job, we did ours, yet we find that we have to pay a high price for people who didn't do theirs.

Judge Schneider did not appreciate my client's frank correspondence. The stern jurist promptly wrote back to Diamond and me, noting that he had no control over the transcript and asking that our clients be "instructed [that] it is inappropriate for any of the parties to send a letter to the court." When I ran into Chuck in our building's parking garage shortly after the exchange of letters, he remarked: "Doesn't Harvey have a sense of humor?"

The clients' and my frustrations notwithstanding, there were moments of comic relief. One of my favorites was the letter that Art received from a lawyer, Victor A. Motley, in Richmond, Virginia, two months after our $900,000 verdict. Mr. Motley claimed that he represented one "Bernard Elam aka Alain Bernheim."

Dear Mr. Buckwald (sic):

Please be advised that I have been retained by the above-referenced with respect to the lawsuit with Paramount concerning the movie 'Coming to America.'

Please advise of the status of collecting the $750,000 judgment [awarded to Bernheim].

Art and I had a lot of fun with this one. We first interrogated poor Alain about his identity, suggesting that he might be an imposter and that Mr. Elam was the true Alain Bernheim. Next, we had Zazi Pope telephone Victor Motley. Zazi reported back that, after her conversation with him, Motley suspected that his client may be an escapee from a local mental hospital.

One of the other reasons for the delay was Paramount's decision to replace Diamond and O'Melveny & Myers with Fields. Bert was the fourth lead opposing counsel whom we had faced in this case. Serving as Marty Davis' lawyer was hazardous duty.

A few months after the verdict, I was handling a case for producer Dino DiLaurentiis against Universal Studios. My opposing counsel was Bert Fields, perhaps the most influential and successful lawyer in Hollywood over the past several decades. A legendary figure in the entertainment business, Bert is a suave, affable gentleman in his sixties who prefers a cardigan to a suit, champagne to beer, and whose butler presides over the family dinner. Part dealmaker and part litigator, he has managed to pull off a lawyer's coup in a town that divides sharply between those who represent talent and those who defend management: he simultaneously defends studios and negotiates against them on behalf of such clients as Tom Cruise, Dustin Hoffman, Warren Beatty, Michael Jackson, the Beatles, and Mike Nichols. (Bert also represents two of the three founders of DreamWorks—Jeff Katzenberg and David Geffen.) After my first-round victory in Buchwald v. Paramount, Bert and I found ourselves opposing each other in high-profile Hollywood cases such as Dino's lawsuit against Universal over the sequel rights to *Silence of the Lambs.*

As Bert and I talked one day during a break in Dino's deposition, Bert said matter-of-factly: "We're going to have a lot more fun together. Paramount has hired me to handle the Buchwald appeal."

"Great," I said, trying not to reveal my true feelings.

It was a smart move by the studio that had not displayed a lot of imagination during the four-year battle in the trial court. Fields is brilliant, articulate, and knows every nuance of how business is done in Hollywood. He was the perfect choice for the job.

Bert Fields is also a class act. A formidable foe yet always a professional, he is charming, honest, and reliable. When I needed a sounding board for legal strategy in my representation of Faye Dunaway against Andrew Lloyd Webber, Bert was generous with his time and advice. Ironically, in *Buchwald v. Paramount,* Bert recommended Howard Suber, who had given helpful expert testimony in Phase III of the trial on the important contribution made by Art's original idea to the commercial success of *Coming to America.*

Bert and I shared a common interest—lawyers who enjoyed writing for a popular audience. After *Fatal Subtraction* was published, I had embarked on a second career as a writer. Using the pseudonym "D. Kincaid," Bert had published two novels, *The Sunset Bomber* and *The Lawyer's Tale,* both of which are fast-paced and laced with Hollywood characters and sex. His writing had a serious side, too. Bert's latest work-in-progress was a scholarly book about King Richard III with a dramatically different take on the hunchbacked and despotic murderer as portrayed by Shakespeare.

Bert had one quality, however, that put off some people: an abundance of self-confidence which could be taken as arrogance. When *California Lawyer* magazine did a profile of Bert and me in connection with the Buchwald appeal, Bert told the author that he had never lost a trial or appeal in 30 years of practice and that he expected to continue his winning streak against me. "There's a first time for everything," I thought to myself.

Buchwald could not resist the opportunity to tease me.

"They say that Bert Fields is going to wipe the courthouse floor with you," Art bellowed from Martha's Vineyard early one morning when he had nothing better to do than to harass his lawyer. "Maybe we should just dismiss the case right now, before all the embarrassment of losing the appeal."

"You're right, Art," I meekly replied. "The man's a legend, a Hollywood titan on a white horse, who has come to the rescue of Paramount and all the studios to save them from having all their form contracts invalidated. We should bow to the inevitable. But if you want to continue your appeal, let me see if I can get a legal aid lawyer appointed for you."

By now we were both laughing as we had so many times before while riding the emotional rollercoaster of this case. Buchwald had an uncanny knack of finding my hot button. I am sure that I worked even harder on the appeal after that phone call—and after he sent me the following note in March 1994:

"Just received the Paramount appeal brief. They really have some top-flight people on this. I just don't see how you can beat them."

Art loved to satirize lawyers, and the case had given him years' worth of new material for his columns.

"I have no quarrel with Quayle and Bush when it comes to the elimination of lawyers," Art wrote in late August 1992, on the heels of their well-publicized attacks on trial lawyers. "But I do have some questions to pose to them." Art proceeded to ask the President if he was prepared to abolish the right to counsel for "one of your sons [who] is involved in a Savings and Loan scandal in Colorado and could be indicted for it"?

Art continued by noting that he was qualified to speak on the subject of the need for lawyers since he had spent four years in court.

> I was very much in favor of my lawyers, and very skeptical about the opposition's lawyers. My lawyers were brave, honest people who only believed in justice for their client. The lawyers that opposed us were crafty, double-dealing skunks who were only concerned with earning their enormous fees and showing the Judge they were smarter than he was. Many times my sympathies were with Shakespeare because I wanted to kill all the lawyers. . . . The trouble with all the [lawyer-killing] ideas is that when you bury three lawyers, eight new ones spring up in their place.

Two years later, after his case had entered its seventh year, Art would return to the same theme in his syndicated column:

> Where William Shakespeare and I parted company was when he wrote, 'The first thing we do let's kill all the lawyers.'
> I don't believe that you should kill **all** the lawyers. I think you should only kill those on the opposing side.

Art then proceeded to explain that the reason for Shakespeare's famous quote about lawyers was his financially ruinous lawsuit against Christopher Marlowe for plagiarism, libel, and defamation of character over his claim that he, not the Bard on Avon, had authored *Henry VI*. Borrowing from a familiar complaint that he frequently made to me about his own legal bills, Buchwald wrote:

> Ironically, what enraged Shakespeare was not the legal fees, but the expenses his lawyers billed him for. For example, they had every one of Shakespeare's plays and sonnets xeroxed fifty times, and then bound in a rare goatskin leather book to present to the judge. . . . When Shakespeare received the bill for these expenses, he went into a rage and screamed, 'First, let's kill all the lawyers.'

In truth, Art was an appreciative client.

When I was doing my book tour for the hardcover edition of *Fatal Subtraction* in September 1992, Art kindly agreed to appear with me on CNN's hit show, "Larry King Live." King was Art's long-time pal and a close friend of my late mentor, Edward Bennett Williams. The charming host with the world's most conspicuous suspenders was very gracious and served up soft pitches for Art and me. For the last segment of the show, I left the set so that Art and

Larry could shift gears and talk about the upcoming Presidential election. Art spontaneously praised Kaye, Scholer and me for sticking with Alain and him for four years even though we had not been paid a dime.

After I had concluded the settlement with Paramount in the summer of 1994, Art phoned me from Martha's Vineyard where he was spending the first summer in three decades without his wife Ann, who had recently died from lung cancer. I fully expected to get the classic ribbing to which I had grown accustomed and, candidly, relished. Not that day.

Art was serious.

"Now that the case is almost over, I want to tell you something from the bottom of my heart," he began. "You and your colleagues have fought for us for seven years. You never quit, never despaired, no matter how tough things got. Right up to the end, you were our fearless champions. And then you go and give us all the money. Thank you, Pierce."

For a trial lawyer, there is no fee that could ever come close to making you feel as good about your profession and yourself as I felt that day. At Danny Arnold's suggestion, I had easily persuaded the firm's billing committee to let the clients keep all of the $825,000 in settlement, less $225,000 that we had advanced for experts and other out-of-pocket costs on their behalf. Kaye, Scholer waived its right to over $300,000 in legal fees and gave it to the clients. That speaks volumes about Kaye, Scholer.

But this happy ending almost did not happen. Marty Davis was determined to beat his former friend Buchwald at any cost, and under no circumstances would he ever settle. It was a struggle to the death. Ironically, it was Davis' mean-spirited, stubborn refusal to settle early that created the opportunity for the landmark case of *Buchwald v. Paramount*. And it was Davis' demise that created the opportunity for cooler heads to prevail eventually at Paramount.

The Buchwald appeal was a momentous legal event for the entire entertainment industry. Daily commerce is conducted by means of boilerplate form contracts that are forced on talent without negotiation. Actors, musicians, singers, song composers, writers, directors, cinematographers, and producers —all of them routinely sign the same kinds of "take-it-or-leave-it" standardized contracts that Judge Schneider found "unconscionable" in Phase II.

By pressing its appeal and adamantly refusing to settle with us, Paramount was raising the stakes. A loss would not only doom the net profits contract used by Paramount, the other studios, independent distributors, television networks, and virtually every production company, but it would jeopardize literally tens of thousands of other entertainment industry contracts. It would be the legal equivalent of Armageddon. As my friend and veteran studio lawyer Ronald Olson told me: "You never risk in litigation a fundamental industry-wide business practice."

California Lawyer, the official magazine for the California bar, summarized the consensus view about the case:

[A] historic battle over Hollywood finance . . . the most sensational, potentially precedent-setting case in the entertainment industry. . . . The case goes to the heart of how Hollywood does business. . . . If Buchwald wins, it will set a far-reaching precedent affecting not just film studios but any business in which contracts are drawn up.

The insanity of it all was that this confrontation had always been—and remained—so utterly avoidable. Buchwald and Bernheim had filed suit because they felt cheated out of the right to participate in and benefit from a valuable movie idea that they had brought to Paramount. Neither they nor I ever dreamed that the case would spiral out of control, forcing us to litigate for seven years with the most powerful studio and star of the times, at a cost of $4 million dollars to my law firm, and requiring us to challenge the fairness of one of Hollywood's most sacred cows—the customary net profit definition. We were always willing to settle, but Paramount, controlled by a spiteful and selfish Martin Davis, was never seriously interested in an honorable peace.

The other studios wanted Paramount to settle, to the point where they were prepared to chip in to make the case go away. But Marty Davis told them to pound sand. The quip by Warner Bros. astute General Counsel John Schulman—he would pay $10 million to put "the genie" (Judge Schneider's unconscionability ruling) back in the bottle—typified the Hollywood Establishment's reaction to Paramount's decision to appeal.

I remained confident that we would win the appeal. Our team produced an excellent response brief to Paramount's 86-page opening brief filed by Bert Fields. The studio made no new legal arguments, and no matter how skillfully he advocated, Bert could not change the factual record in the trial court which was largely devoid of any evidence justifying the net profit contract. As Bert confided to me one day: "They didn't give me a hell of a lot to work with, did they?"

Notwithstanding our optimism, there was an appreciable chance that we would lose the unconscionability ruling.

To be sure, Judge Schneider had faithfully followed a California Supreme Court precedent, and our unfairness charges had not been rebutted by Paramount for its own strategic reason of avoiding a Price, Waterhouse audit of its books and unprecedented public disclosure of its true movie-making profitability. Nevertheless, the unconscionability doctrine had never before been applied to a contract for services in the entertainment industry, particularly where the two parties were as sophisticated as Art and Alain and represented by such a savvy agent/lawyer as Roger Davis of the powerful William Morris Agency. A similar unconscionability challenge by the creators and executive producers of *Batman*—this time to a virtually identical net profit contract imposed by Warner Bros.—had recently failed in the trial court. (The judge ruled that while it was a nonnegotiable contract of adhesion, but the plaintiffs had failed to show that the challenged terms were unjustified.) While we mustered some scholarly support in law school circles, the betting was heavily in favor of Paramount winning the unconscionability issue on appeal. As the Association of Talent Agents predicted in its bulletin for October 1994: "Smart money and a lot of good lawyers in this town are betting on a reversal."

Paramount was taking no chances on appeal. The redoubtable Bert Fields had to make at least two trips to New York to meet with Marty Davis and his top lawyer, Donald Oresman. Davis wanted to be sure that he was hiring the right man for the job. Fields was grilled about his legal theories and strategy for securing a reversal of the judgment. Davis made Fields promise that he would win. In his public statements about the appeal, Fields was supremely confident, if not cocky.

Throughout the Buchwald case, conventional wisdom had predicted that we would lose, yet we had always prevailed. I delighted in being cast as the underdog—it made me work harder and made the victories all the more glorious. In my heart, I believed that we would win the appeal. If the decision were mine alone, I would not have settled until we had won in the California Court of Appeal.

In the final analysis, however, we had to take seriously the possibility that we might lose the unconscionability victory. (There was never a realistic chance that we would lose on the issue of whether *Coming to America* was based upon Buchwald's treatment.) If we lost on the unfairness of the net profit formula and we did not get a reversal in the California Supreme Court, we would be forced to return to the trial court and relitigate damages under the reinstated contract. While we still had some unresolved claims such as breach of the duty of good faith and fair dealing, we might not get any more money than our contractual fixed compensation of $265,000. My already low enthusiasm for trying the damages phase a second time turned to dread when I learned that Judge Schneider had been reassigned from the civil to the criminal bench and would not preside if the case were remanded for a new damages trial.

More important than all this legal analysis was the emotional welfare of my clients. The snail's pace of the appellate process was alienating Art and Alain, sapping their passion for the case and creating tension in our attorney-client relationship. No matter how often or much I explained the reasons for the delay, I could tell that, month-by-month, year-by-year, even these strong and resolute men were losing heart.

"Even when you win, you lose by having to wait forever for a final resolution," Buchwald told me on the second anniversary of the verdict. In his frequent public appearances, Art usually made some reference to the case and how it was languishing on appeal. His audiences would roar in laughter as Art, his eyes twinkling impishly, claimed that his case started about the time Adolph Zukor founded Paramount during World War I.

For Alain, the interminable delays were no laughing matter. It was still hard for him to find work—movie production deals kept falling through for him, almost as if a curse had been put on him since he filed suit back in late 1988.

Not one of his projects had been greenlighted in the seven years that he had been trying to get Paramount to do the right thing. As Art had frequently acknowledged, Alain was the real hero and victim because he had to work in Hollywood. While Alain never tried to get us to settle the case cheaply, Art and I knew that a settlement would be best for Alain.

As for Kaye, Scholer, the firm continued to be spectacularly supportive, despite the fact that there was no hope that the firm would ever get back any meaningful portion of its humongous legal fees. By the time we had to start working on our appeal briefs, the original trial team was gone. Wanting more time with her newborn son, Zazi Pope went to work for John Schulman on the first-rate studio legal staff at Warner Bros. Zazi had been the heart and soul of our rebel band, and I missed her very much.

Marsha Durko went to work for another firm, and Suzanne Tragert left to teach at UCLA Law School, taking away two more outstanding lawyers who had contributed significantly to our victories. My brilliant partners, Michael Malina and Joel Katcoff, remained available for consultation, but they were busy on major litigations in the firm's New York office. That left Dennis Landry, my ace paralegal, and me.

Without any questions from my partners, I was able to cherry pick two of our young stars—again both women—to work on the appeal. Renee Wolf, a superb lawyer with a master's degree from the London School of Economics, is an exceptionally bright and gifted writer whose calm manner and indefatigable spirit would help get us through the challenge of writing a half dozen briefs on appeal. Ann Marie Mortimer, a feisty, younger lawyer with great presence and keen analytical skills, drew the assignment of doing a lot of the legal research and first drafting. "Morty," as she is affectionately known, worked tirelessly in her notoriously cluttered office and mastered a totally unfamiliar record. We also got superb assistance from Professor Clark Kelso of McGeorge School of Law who is a leading scholar on California contracts, a light opera singer, and an uncanny handicapper of appeals. (Clark and I had teamed up on several cases, we had never lost working together, and he predicted that we would win on appeal.) Finally, while Dennis Landry supplied all of the countless record citations that we needed for our briefs, retired California Supreme Court Justice Cruz Reynoso, my friend and colleague for a decade, offered shrewd advice on strategy.

In high-profile appeals like *Buchwald v. Paramount* where the decision will have broad ramifications beyond the immediate parties to the case, it is not uncommon for other interested parties to file *amicus curiae* ("friend of the court") briefs on behalf of one of the parties to the appeal. Our case attracted an unusually high number of *amicus curiae* briefs.

In one sense, this was surprising. Taking sides in public is not common in Hollywood. This is the place where the anonymous quote was perfected. "A source close to," "a Hollywood insider," "a veteran studio observer"—these are your faceless accusers who dish out negative statements confident that they will inflict injury without accountability. Art, Alain, and I had many well-wishers, but few who would go public.

So it came as no surprise that the Writers Guild of America, West, led by its Executive Director Brian Walton, a notorious chameleon and coward in my opinion, never came to our support in the trial court. When Paramount was able to get supporting briefs on appeal from the California Manufacturers Association, California Chamber of Commerce, Association of American Publishers, and the influential Alliance of Motion Picture and Television Producers, we needed to counteract their arguments and sheer numbers with our own support groups. Fortunately, we were able to get *amicus curiae* briefs from the Authors Guild, Producers Guild, Screen Actors Guild, American Federation of Television and Radio Artists, and Art's own guild, the Writers Guild of America, *East*. Despite my respectful written request and the valiant efforts of Danny Arnold and our pal Lynn Roth who had been elected a director of the west coast writer's guild, the Walton-dominated board still refused to file anything on our behalf.

This was the third time that the Writers Guild of America, West had refused to come to our assistance. For Art, it was the last straw. On October 1, 1994, he let Frank Pierson, the President, know how he felt:

Dear Frank,

Thank you for your letter. Even though it didn't say what I would have liked it to, I appreciate you taking so much time and space to tell us why the Guild could not support us. For eight years we've been fighting this battle alone so we're getting used to it.

I'm not going to fight it again in this letter.

No matter how the Guild sees this case, we have done a tremendous amount of good for all talent in business dealings with the studios.

Whether we win or lose in the State Supreme Court, the members of the Guild will have benefitted by our case.

For one thing the IRS now has a task force in Hollywood for the first time to make sure that what producers write off in their films are legitimate. I know we are responsible for that because we supplied them with a great deal of information on how studios operate. Thanks to the task force it will certainly make it a little easier for all talent in entertainment-land to collect promises of net.

For another thing, thanks to Bernheim and myself, the whole business of promising net when the studios know there will never be a net has changed. Studio lawyers are rewriting contracts, agents are examining these deals and making studios spell out what they mean by net, and people with money are now hiring accountants to audit the studio books. Eddie Murphy referred to net as 'monkey points.' It was a joke before our suit. . . .

The truth of the matter, Frank, whether you believe the Judge's decision or not, is that Hollywood may now be a safer, saner place for writers to work in. . . .

Ever since we started down this road, most wise men warned us we couldn't win. So far we have. The reason is that with or without a brief from the Guild we know that God is on our side.

Sincerely,
Art Buchwald

Not surprisingly, Pierson never replied to Art's letter. The conspicuous absence of the Writers Guild of America, West was not lost on Paramount. In a footnote to one of its appellate briefs, Paramount noted that while other guilds had come to Buchwald's defense as *amicus curiae*, the writers guild had not. Fortunately, we were able to cure that problem thanks to Mona Mangan and her gutsy east coast writers guild which filed a supportive brief.

While hundreds of pages of briefs were being cranked out by both sides, an event occurred that had the greatest influence on the ultimate resolution of the case. For over a decade, Marty Davis had been at the helm of media conglomerate Paramount Communications, Inc, but he had failed to find a strategic partner to make Paramount a key player in the brave new world of global media giants. Meanwhile, other companies were looking covetously at cash-rich Paramount Communications, Inc. In 1993, all hell broke loose over who would end up owning Paramount.

In mid-1993, Davis announced that his board of directors had approved a merger with the entertainment giant Viacom which distributes *The Cosby Show* and *Roseanne* and owns MTV, Nickleodeon, Nick At Nite, VH-1, Showtime, and the Comedy Channel. But Barry Diller, who ran Paramount studios for ten years before clashing with Davis whom he loathed, launched a hostile bid on behalf of QVC, the home shopping channel, backed by John Malone who heads Liberty Media and its affiliated group, TCI, the world's largest cable tv company. The Delaware courts blocked the friendly Paramount-Viacom merger, finding that Marty Davis and his board had breached their duties to shareholders by rejecting the higher bid of QVC.

The Delaware Supreme Court singled out Davis for criticism, noting that he had systematically kept important information from his board. It was a bitter irony for Davis who had long claimed that he was his shareholder's best friend. (Buchwald couldn't resist writing a satirical column about Marty's woes in which he expressed his concern that Davis might misuse Buchwald's $900,000 award "to save his company from a most unfriendly bid from Barry Diller.")

The fallout of the Paramount-Viacom-QVC court battle was a nasty proxy fight—the biggest takeover battle in the 1990s so far—from which Viacom ultimately emerged the "winner" in early 1994 by paying close to $10 billion for Paramount Communications, Inc. With over $12 billion in revenues, the combination of the two media conglomerates yielded the planet's second-largest media company, surpassed only by Time Warner with $13.3 billion in annual revenues. In the wake of Viacom's acquisition, Martin Davis was out of a job. No tears were being shed in Hollywood or at Davis' bank. Marty received $142 million worth of stock options and cash—reportedly the biggest golden parachute in corporate history.

The new leader of Viacom/Paramount (and its largest stockholder with 61% of the voting stock) is visionary Sumner Redstone, the 75-year-old chairman of Viacom who a decade ago was a relatively unknown Wall Street investor and part-time law lecturer from Boston who launched his media career by parlaying a few drive-in movie theatres into pioneering multi-screen cinema complexes. Redstone was reputed to be a hard-nosed, determined business-man whom the *London Sunday Times* claimed "files lawsuits about like con-fetti and keeps his enemies tied up in depositions and court appearances for months on end." He seemed like the least likely person in the world to end Paramount's hostilities with Buchwald and Bernheim.

Although his star fell from the Paramount firmament when he was sud-denly fired by Redstone near the end of 1995, Redstone's right hand man was initially Frank Biondi, Viacom's 50-year-old chief executive officer. Biondi and Buchwald knew each other socially on Martha's Vineyard. At a charity auc-tion, Biondi had purchased a dinner for himself, his wife and some friends hosted by Buchwald at his home on the island. While I was visiting in the summer of 1994 following the Viacom-Paramount marriage, Buchwald hosted the party for the Biondis, but I did not attend.

"Nothing personal, Pierce, but I want to keep our business out of this evening. If you're there, it will be a red flag."

The morning after the Biondi soiree, as we ate homemade pastry at the charming Deux Noisettes bed and breakfast in Vineyard Haven where I was staying, Art told me that the evening was a social success.

"Biondi is a very bright, nice guy," Art reported. "I especially liked his wife."

At about the same time that Buchwald and Biondi were sharing a mellow evening on Martha's Vineyard, I asked Peter Fishbein, my partner and the former chairman of Kaye, Scholer's Executive Committee, if he would feel comfortable talking to Sumner Redstone about possibly settling the case. Fishbein knew Redstone professionally and personally, having served as coun-sel to the National Association of Theatre Owners when Redstone was build-ing his fortune in the theatre business. Peter agreed, and a short time later, he reported that he had spoken with Sumner who had promised to investigate the matter. One of the points that I asked Peter to pass along to his former client was that the new Viacom/Paramount management team could earn some much-needed good will with the Hollywood creative community if it gracefully put the Buchwald case behind them.

Whether it was Buchwald's schmoozing and/or Fishbein's conversation with Redstone, or some other reason, Paramount's historic hard-line position —"millions for defense but not one cent for settlement"—changed dramati-cally. In September 1994, while I was in New York on business, I received a call from Bert Fields.

"Pierce, the new owners at Paramount have taken a close look at the case," Bert began after ostensibly calling me about another one of our cases. "They have nothing against Art and Alain, and they want to have good relations with talent. Now, of course, everyone on our side still believes that we will prevail on appeal, but they are prepared to settle for a reasonable amount."

I waited for the other shoe to drop.

"By reasonable, we're talking about some token amount, like $100,000," Bert added.

My mind was racing. I actually could not believe my ears. Paramount was talking the "S word"—SETTLEMENT. That was a shocker. I never thought that I would hear that word from a Paramount lawyer in this case. As gleeful as I was, I could not let Bert know how I really felt.

"Bert, that was the original offer to my clients in the summer of 1988 before I took the case. Don't you think a mere $100,000 offer is insulting after all these years?"

"Well, it was not intended to be insulting. There may be some room for movement."

"I will relay the offer to my clients and get back to you," I replied. "But I wouldn't hold out a lot of hope that this case will settle with such a low-ball number."

I immediately communicated the offer to Art and Alain.

"Sounds like they may want to settle but don't know how to do it," I told them.

"Why do you think they are making settlement overtures now?" Alain asked from Paris.

"My best guess is that Viacom thinks they might lose the appeal," I answered.

There had been some rumors that Viacom had engaged independent counsel to review the case. What I did not know at the time was that new management had made settling the case a top priority. What is most remarkable is that it took *ten* months of negotiations to get Paramount to offer enough money to settle the case. The reason I learned shortly before the final deal was made was that Bert Fields did not want to settle the case. Bert strenuously advised against settlement, to the point where it appeared to us that he was dragging his feet in responding to my counter-offers. At the very end, the case was settled against his recommendation.

The final settlement document did not contain a confidentiality clause—a point which Buchwald had insisted he would not compromise from the very first time that I met him in New Orleans in August 1988. But it did include a brief joint press release sounding the theme that Peter Fishbein had passed along to Sumner Redstone:

"A senior studio executive stated: 'Our settling has nothing to do with who was right or wrong in the case. Our new management is artist friendly. We want a successful working relationship with the creative community and to avoid disputes with them wherever possible. Art Buchwald is a great American humorist, and Alain Bernheim is a fine gentleman and respected producer. We want them as friends, not opponents.'"

Buchwald and Bernheim had a terse, one-line quote at the end of the press statement: "We're very pleased to have this behind us." While my clients were happy to have the whole ordeal over and bore no ill feelings toward the new Paramount/Viacom team, they could not bring themselves to say anything more in the joint press release. Seven years of bitter, hard-fought litigation had left scars. "The fewer the words, the better," Art told me as we were hammering out the statement. "We've won with dignity, and we never compromised our principles. The record speaks for itself."

Buchwald v. Paramount consumed seven years of a lot of people's lives. World War II lasted less time than what began as what one magazine called a "fairly minor breach of contract case." In that seven years, both sides and their allies spent over $12 million in legal fees and costs, careers were made and ruined, and there was no "final" resolution of the precedent-settling legal rulings in the trial court.

Over the course of the litigation, much changed for many of the key characters, the motion picture industry, and me.

When the case started, Ronald Reagan was President, O.J. Simpson was doing Hertz commercials, and Sumner Redstone had only recently taken over Viacom. There was no war in former Yugoslavia, the Soviet Union still existed, and Eddie Murphy and Paramount were on top of Hollywood. And no one was worried about the fat and cholesterol content of popcorn at local movie theatres.

Hollywood has gone through wrenching changes. Sony bought Columbia/Tri-Star and lost billions. Matshusita bought MCA/Universal, never figured out how to manage the asset, and sold 80% to Seagrams. Fox launched a successful fourth television network, and Paramount and Warner Bros. were locked in mortal combat to see which would emerge with the fifth commercial network. Disney acquired Capital Cities/ABC, Westinghouse and CBS announced a merger, and Time Warner acquired Ted Turner's media empire. (In the wave of media merger mania, Buchwald announced that he was merging with Russell Baker and was not afraid of Antitrust Division interference since it was now a museum.)

The William Morris Agency, which had fearlessly supported its clients in their battle with Paramount, was successfully rebuilding its film business after several years of painful defections. Roger Davis was enjoying retirement in Florida. Creative Artists Agency, the dominant talent firm in the 1980s and 1990s, suddenly became vulnerable with the departure of founders Michael Ovitz (off to run Walt Disney Company for Eisner) and Ron Meyer (off to help run MCA/Universal).

Paramount slipped from its domination of film distribution revenues in the 1980s as it struggled to find the magic touch that it had during Frank Mancuso's illustrious reign. (Mancuso was running MGM/UA for Credite Lyonnaise, and he hired me to be his chief litigation counsel in battles with Arnon Milchan and Honda.) Eddie Murphy's film career had not yet pulled out of a nose dive. (Once again demonstrating a chronic death wish in script selection, Eddie Murphy starred in *A Vampire in Brooklyn*, voted by many critics as one of the worst movies in 1995.) His pal Arsenio Hall lost his television show.

Robert Wachs, fired by Murphy and Hall, was trying to find a new Eddie Murphy to manage.

Buchwald v. Paramount was like Halley's Comet for the entertainment industry. The occasions when talent successfully challenge the established order are rare and fleeting. The case's lasting implications remain to be seen, however.

In the short term, studio lawyers have tinkered with their net profit contracts by deleting references to "net profits" and substituting some euphemism like "contractual contingent compensation." (I have seen a studio contract with a powerful producer that explicitly disclaims the applicability of Judge Schneider's unconscionability ruling because the parties were represented by counsel and the material terms were negotiated.) Some talent have begun bargaining for bonus payments (deferments) based on easily-verifiable benchmarks such as studio gross receipts. Others are demanding higher guaranteed compensation and telling the studios to forget about net profits. At a minimum, net profits as defined by the studios have gotten the bad name that they so richly deserve.

In the longer term, the case may signal a greater willingness on the part of talent to challenge how Hollywood does business. With the recent spate of media mergers, the concentration of power on the buyers' side has intensified. Only seven studios still have a stranglehold on movie distribution, controlling over 90% of the revenues and setting the harsh terms by which everyone must operate. Attempts to launch new major movie distribution companies have been singularly unsuccessful. Not surprisingly, this starkly noncompetitive market has prompted a class action antitrust by the estate of Lloyd Garrison, whose book was the basis of Oliver Stone's *JFK*, against Warner Bros. and the other six studios, alleging a price-fixing conspiracy to use the same unconscionable net profit definitions.

The public's dismay at the outrages of Hollywood accounting exposed in our case was heightened by disclosures made as we were winding up settlement negotiations with Paramount. In May of 1995, I was retained by Winston Groom, the author of the book *Forrest Gump* on which the Academy Award-winning movie was based. Groom, who had been given 3% of the net profits, was skeptical about his first accounting statement from Paramount that showed a $62 million net *loss* despite grossing over $657 million at box offices around the world. When the story broke, the media had a field day. *Forbes* ran a headline, "Now You See It, Now You Don't," that typified the derision over Paramount's claim.

Paramount fared no better when the *Los Angeles Times*, *Variety*, and the *Hollywood Reporter* wrote prominent stories about *Indecent Proposal*—ironically, on the very same day the studio proudly announced its settlement with Buchwald and Bernheim. Despite grossing more than $350 million worldwide, Paramount's accounting statement claimed that the hit movie was $37.5 million in the red. These negative stories will continue so long as studios account for net profits in the same unconscionable way they have for decades and continue to make expensive movies (average cost of over $30 million), to spend so much money on advertising (sometimes as much as the movie costs), and to give away so much of the gross receipts to actors and directors.

Alain Bernheim had not produced a movie since *Racing With The Moon* which he did with Sherry Lansing and Stanley Jaffe. Lansing, the movie production head of Paramount, had remained friendly toward Alain. Informally, I was assured by Bert Fields that "Alain is always welcome at Paramount," but my dear friend and client was not holding his breath waiting for Paramount to buy one of his projects. In early 1996, Alain was able to make a deal to produce a movie that has been in development for years. Alain's sons were budding writers in their own right, and Margie was as effervescent as always.

Stanley Jaffe sued Viacom-Paramount for allegedly cheating him out of stock options after Viacom took control. (The case was dismissed.) Jaffe and Paramount were in turn sued by David Kirkpatrick. "Davey the K" had become an independent movie producer on the Paramount lot after Jaffe, whom Marty Davis hired to oversee studio operations, had David removed as head of film production at the studio. Paramount terminated David before his three-year producer contract expired. With much justification, David believed that Jaffe was the Wizard of Oz who orchestrated his embarrassing ouster because of an old grudge stemming from David's attempt while production chief to reign in cost overruns on a film being made by Jaffe who was then an independent producer on the Paramount lot. As soon as the roles were reversed, Jaffe let everyone know that David was *persona non grata* at the studio.

In one of many ironic twists involving protagonists in the case, Kirkpatrick, who had been a star witness for us at the first trial because he told the truth about Eddie Murphy's extensive exposure to Buchwald's story, hired me to litigate against Paramount after the sudden death of his first lawyer, Howard King. Howard, who had become a friend of mine, had initially attempted to settle Art's and Alain's claim against Paramount in the spring of 1988. Paramount hired Bert Fields to defend Kirkpatrick's suit. The case was favorably settled without trial in early 1995.

I would never have represented Art and Alain if it were not for a referral by Danny Arnold. Danny was my first client when I came to Los Angeles in 1978, and I remained his lawyer until he died on August 19, 1995. No one ever had a better friend and critic, a bigger fan or more perceptive advisor. I loved Danny like a father, and he treated me like a son.

Some people thought Danny Arnold was a curmudgeon who had fallen out of love with the world. I knew differently: Danny Arnold saw things that no one else saw. He was kind-hearted, a sucker for a friend in trouble, and very generous to charity. He set impossible standards of excellence for himself and demanded the best from those who collaborated with him on hundreds of television shows and movies. His courage in fighting for principle is legendary. Danny was, in his own words, "a paranoid with proof." I miss him dearly.

Art Buchwald continued to be Art Buchwald. I am convinced that this plain-speaking humorist is one of the most beloved public figures in America.

Everywhere I go, people speak affectionately of the Pundit on the Potomac, and they applaud his courage for standing up for what he believed was right. The publication of the first volume of his critically-acclaimed, bestselling memoirs, *Leaving Home,* only enhanced his stature because of the touching vulnerability in his recollections of his early years as an orphan, would-be young Romeo, and Marine in World War II. More than anything else, Art has become a dear friend whose unfailing decency and integrity, as well as his wit and charm, made him an implacable plaintiff and inspiration for all of us.

After a decade of distinguished reporting on the entertainment industry, Dennis McDougal left the *Los Angeles Times* to become a full-time author. *In the Best of Families,* his next book after *Fatal Subtraction,* earned him a coveted Edgar Award nomination as one of the best crime books of 1994. *Mother's Day,* a chilling account of a mother forcing two of her children to kill two of her other children, is in its second printing. Dennis is busy at work on a biography of one of Hollywood's most powerful figures. In his spare time, he loves fly fishing.

I am still a trial lawyer representing people in trouble. I have developed a passion for writing. In hawking my screenplays, I use a pseudonym since I have sued most of the studios at one time or another. I have this recurring dream that Paramount will produce and distribute one of my movies.

Years of travel and late nights at the office eventually took their toll. After two years of separation, my 25-year marriage with Connie ended in early 1995 as amicably as can be expected under the circumstances. Connie and I have joint custody of Brendan and Meghan, both of whom seem to be doing very well, sustained by the daily knowledge that their mother and father love them dearly.

On St. Patrick's Day, I remarried. My new wife, Dawn Donley, is a bright, bubbling personality who was trained and initially practiced as a lawyer but who spent the last several years as a legal recruiter. After a gala wedding attended by 400 of our family and friends at the home of powerhouse attorney Tom Girardi, we honeymooned in Italy and Ireland for two weeks. Dawn and I are recently the proud parents of a blonde-haired, blue-eyed daughter, Courtney, who is endowed with her mother's beauty and her father's lungs. I have never been happier.

After eight years, I left Kaye, Scholer in early 1996 to start my own law firm again in downtown Los Angeles. I wanted to spend more time in court and with my family and less time managing lawyers and commuting over an hour to the office. The new firm, O'Donnell, Reeves & Shaeffer, LLP., started with ten lawyers, seven paralegals and all of my clients. The parting with Kaye, Scholer was amicable but bittersweet. I have many friends at that great law firm, and without Kaye, Scholer's unflinching commitment, *Buchwald v. Paramount* would have never happened. Yet the *Buchwald* case whetted my appetite for high-profile litigation, and I will now be freer to do what I love.

I learned a lot of lessons from *Buchwald v. Paramount.* For one thing, I should never predict how long a litigation is going to take or how much it will cost. A few others: the true measure of character is grace under pressure; the courts, while they can occasionally strike a blow for justice, are inadequate forums for resolving weighty public policy issues; and no one really wins in any lawsuit because the process takes its toll on the litigants in ways that are not readily obvious to those who have not endured such an ordeal.

Of all the many lessons learned, however, the most valuable one is something that they do not teach you in law school: nothing worth anything comes without a struggle; and fighting for what we believe is right, no matter the sacrifice, is ennobling. For teaching me that lesson, I will always be indebted to Art and Alain.

Pierce O'Donnell

Appendices

Appendix A

ART BUCHWALD, et al.,

    Plaintiffs,

v.

PARAMOUNT PICTURES CORPORATION,
etc., et al.,

    Defendants.

C 706083

STATEMENT OF
DECISION [FIRST PHASE]

Statement of Facts

In early 1982 Art Buchwald (Buchwald), an internationally renowned writer and humorist, prepared an eight page screen treatment entitled "It's a Crude, Crude World." (Exhibit 500A) Buchwald testified that he wrote this treatment by himself without help from anyone. (RT 441; 464) The inspiration of the principal character came from Buchwald's observance of a state visit by the Shah of Iran. Alain Bernheim (Bernheim), a close friend of Buchwald and co-plaintiff in this action, or Louis Malle, a prominent film director, suggested that the principal character be made a black man. (RT 442)

In March 1982, Buchwald sent his treatment to Bernheim. (Exhibit 2) Bernheim registered the treatment with the Writers Guild of America (Exhibits 3 and 4)

Subsequently, Bernheim suggested to Buchwald that the latter reduce his eight page treatment to a shorter version, which Buchwald did. (Exhibit 500B) The shorter treatment is basically a condensed version of the eight page treatment, except for the ending.

In late 1982, Bernheim met with Jeff Katzenberg (Katzenberg), the head of motion picture production at Paramount Pictures Corporation (Paramount)(RT 96), for the purpose of "pitching" Buchwald's story to Paramount for development into a movie starring Eddie Murphy. Murphy was then under contract to Paramount. In fact, Bernheim apparently retyped Buchwald's three page treatment and inserted Eddie Murphy's name after the name of the emperor. (Exhibit 6) Katzenberg read Buchwald's treatment and had a high regard for the concept as a movie. (RT 100; 106) Katzenberg described Buchwald's treatment as "a succinct, smart, straightforward idea with a lot of potential to it." (RT 106)

In late 1982 and early 1983 Paramount was extremely anxious to develop a project for Eddie Murphy. (Exhibits 11; 14) Buchwald's treatment, the title of which had by this time been changed to "King for a Day" by Paramount, was a project in which Paramount was interested. (Exhibit 15; RT 703–704) In fact, in January 1983 Paramount registered the title "King for a Day" with the MPAA. (Exhibit 16) Bernheim and Katzenberg remained in communication and a search for a writer began. (Exhibit 17) During this period of time, there was no doubt Paramount considered "King for a Day" a possible project for Eddie Murphy. (Exhibit 18) In fact, Paramount's creative executives loved Buchwald's story and concept and thought it would be a terrific vehicle for Eddie Murphy. Paramount envisioned Murphy playing at least two roles in Buchwald's story. (RT 707)

On February 24, 1983, Paramount and Bernheim entered into an agreement pursuant to which Bernheim was to produce and be entitled to certain payments if Paramount entered into an agreement with Buchwald acquiring Buchwald's story idea. (Exhibit 507) After the Bernheim-Paramount agreement was executed, the search for a writer for "King for a Day" continued. (Exhibit 22) On March 22, 1983, Buchwald and Paramount entered into an agreement pursuant to which Paramount purchased the rights to Buchwald's story and concept entitled "King for a Day." (Exhibit 506) According to Paramount creative executive David Kirkpatrick (Kirkpatrick), in his ten years at Paramount, Buchwald's treatment was the only one optioned by Paramount. Paramount did, of course, frequently option screenplays.

On March 28, 1983, Kirkpatrick and Ricardo Mestres (Mestres), another Paramount creative executive, sent a memorandum to Jeff Katzenberg.[1] In this memorandum it was indicated that a search for a writer for "King for a Day" was continuing. The same memorandum indicated that the project was being developed for Eddie Murphy "based on Art Buchwald." (Exhibit 25) On the same day "King for a Day" was listed as a project "potentially committed or active in development." (Exhibit 26) On April 2, 1983, in a handwritten note, Katzenberg indicated to Kirkpatrick and Mestres that he wanted a "full court press" on the "King for a Day" project. Several persons, including Buchwald himself, were being considered as potential screenplay writers. (Exhibits 27; 30; 31; 32; 33; 34; 35) Other persons were under consideration as possible directors. (Exhibit 28)

In the spring of 1983, Kirkpatrick met at the Ma Maison Restaurant with Eddie Murphy and others to discuss various potential movie development projects for Murphy. Katzenberg was present, as was Robert Wachs (Wachs), one of Murphy's managers. During this dinner meeting, ten or twelve potential movie projects were discussed. The Paramount executives went through the ten or twelve projects with Murphy and talked basically about characters or people involved. One of the stories that was discussed was Buchwald's "King for a Day." Murphy was positively responsive to the "King for a Day" presentation. At the same meeting Murphy indicated that he liked playing the African character in "Trading Places." (RT 552–555)

On March 23, 1983, Kirkpatrick sent a status report to Wachs, in which Wachs was advised that Paramount was still searching for a writer for the potential Eddie Murphy project "King for a Day." (Exhibit 36) Katzenberg testified that he spoke regularly with Wachs during 1983, both in person and on the telephone. They discussed projects that were in development for Murphy at Paramount. Katzenberg had similar conversations with Murphy's other manager, Richie Tienkin. (RT 122) On June 6, 1983, Kirkpatrick sent Wachs a short outline of Buchwald's "King for a Day." (Exhibit 39)

On July 9, 1983, a meeting was held at Paramount's office. Present were Kirkpatrick, Katzenberg, Mestres, Bernheim and Tab Murphy, who ultimately wrote the first screenplay for "King for a Day." After receiving a synopsis of Buchwald's treatment,

[1] It is important to note that Katzenberg had both a close professional and social relationship with Eddie Murphy. (RT 98)

Katzenberg suggested a number of changes. These changes included making the Eddie Murphy character more likable, having the Murphy character change in a cultural, rather than financial way, and having Murphy play a number of different roles. (Exhibit 41) On June 13, 1983, Kirkpatrick reported that the first draft of "King for a Day" was due on July 22, 1983. (Exhibit 42) Four days later, in a memorandum, "King for a Day" was described as the "Art Buchwald idea" that Paramount was "now developing for Murphy." (Exhibit 46) In late June the "Eddie Murphy picture" "King for a Day" was described as a possible project for direction by John Landis. (Exhibit 48) On July 1, 1983, Kirkpatrick wrote a letter to Landis which was accompanied by a description of a number of projects that were being proffered by Paramount for consideration by Landis. The description for "King for a Day" stated in pertinent part:

"KING FOR A DAY is high-styled political satire inspired by Art Buchwald. The movie is intended for Eddie Murphy, who is familiar with the idea and likes it very much. If necessary, however, I believe any one of several comedy stars could be excellent in the role. The writer is Tab Murphy, who has proven in another project that he has a terrific sense for Eddie Murphy's style. We expect a first draft in about four weeks."
(Exhibit 49; RT 120–121; 556)

In a memorandum dated July 12, 1983, the budget for "King for a Day" was estimated to be in the ten to twelve million dollar range by Mestres and Kirkpatrick. (Exhibit 51) In late July, 1983, an agreement was reached between Paramount and Tab Murphy, pursuant to which the latter was hired to do the first screenplay for "King for a Day." (Exhibit 53)

In August 1983, "King for a Day" was still being considered by Paramount as a possible project for Landis. (Exhibits 55; 56) As of August 19, 1983, it was anticipated by Kirkpatrick that Tab Murphy's first draft would be ready on September 2, 1983. (Exhibit 57) This date was later changed to September 23, 1983. (Exhibit 59) In mid-September 1983 the budget for "King for a Day" was still estimated at ten million dollars. (Exhibit 60) The date for submission of the first draft of "King for a Day" was later extended to September 30, 1983. At this time "King for a Day" was still identified among "potential Eddie Murphy projects." (Exhibit 62)

On September 30, 1983, Tab Murphy submitted his first draft of "King for a Day." (Exhibits 63; 64) The script was not well received by Paramount, Bernheim or, apparently, anyone else. (RT 599–600) As a result, the search for a writer for "King for a Day" continued. (Exhibits 66; 68) In the meantime, Paramount paid $2500 to Buchwald to extend its option on "King for a Day." (Exhibit 67)

In late October 1983 the search for a writer focused on the French writer and director, Francis Veber. (Exhibits 69; 70; 71; RT 601) At the same time, "King for a Day" was still being thought of by Paramount as a possible project for John Landis. (Exhibit 72) Additionally, Paramount was still referring to "King for a Day" as a high-styled political satire inspired by Art Buchwald. (Exhibit 73) On December 6, 1983, Kirkpatrick reported that Paramount was negotiating with Veber to write the script for "King for a Day" and that the deal might close that day. A copy of this memorandum was sent to Wachs, Murphy's manager. (Exhibits 75; 77) In December, Paramount indicated that a screenplay draft was expected by March 16, 1984, and that "King for a Day" was targeted for release in the summer of 1985. (Exhibit 76) On December 8, 1983, Wachs was sent a review of one of Veber's movies. (Exhibit 80) On December 12, 1983, Katzenberg sent a letter to Brandon Tartikoff, President of NBC Entertainment. In this letter, "King for a Day" was identified as a "priority development" that "Eddie Murphy will star in." (Exhibit 81; RT 128)

On January 4, 1984, Kirkpatrick reported that negotiations with Veber were still ongoing with respect to "King for a Day"—a potential Eddie Murphy project. A copy of this report was sent to Wachs and Murphy's agent, Hildy Gottlieb. (Exhibit 83) On

January 17, 1984, "King for a Day" was still listed as an "active" project. (Exhibit 84) Negotiations with Veber were still ongoing as of January 23, 1984. (Exhibit 85) On January 24, 1984, Katzenberg was notified that the title "King for a Day" had been cleared for use by Paramount. (Exhibit 86) In late January, Paramount's financial agreement with Bernheim was amended. (Exhibit 87) At the same time it was again reported that the deal with Veber was nearly closed. (Exhibit 88) On February 14, 1984, it was reported at Paramount that a draft for "King for a Day" was due to be submitted by Veber by May 30, 1984. (Exhibit 92) In a February 17, 1984, memorandum relating to "Eddie Murphy projects," "King for a Day" was described as a "political satire inspired by Art Buchwald" that was an excellent candidate for release in summer 1985. (Exhibit 93; see also Exhibit 99)

Sometime in 1984, Veber went to Washington, D.C., where he was shown around the ghetto by Bernheim and Buchwald.

On March 20, 1984, Paramount exercised its second option on Buchwald's work. (Exhibit 98)

In a memorandum dated May 14, 1983, Katzenberg informed Frank Mancuso, the head of Paramount, that "King for a Day" was one of the top three projects under development for Eddie Murphy at the time. Katzenberg stated: "Francis Veber, who is set to direct, will deliver his script [on "King for a Day"] mid-June. This is an excellent idea, and the marriage of Murphy and Veber could be something very special." (Exhibit 103)

On June 20, 1984, Kirkpatrick reported to Katzenberg that Veber's script should be ready by mid-August and that Veber would like "to shoot in the spring."[2] Wachs is shown as receiving a copy of this memorandum. (Exhibit 105)

On July 30, 1984, Katzenberg informed Kirkpatrick that Paramount should obtain a one-year extension on its option from Buchwald "for cheap money." (Exhibit 107)

On August 1, 1984, Bernheim reported to Katzenberg that Veber had read his script to him (Bernheim) and that Bernheim was very impressed. Bernheim stated that Veber had "captured" Buchwald's idea and that "Eddie is, I believe, in for a treat." (Exhibit 108)

In a memorandum dated August 3, 1984, Darlene Chan of Paramount reported "King for a Day" was scheduled for a summer 1985 release. (Exhibit 109) On August 15, 1984, the Paramount-Buchwald agreement was amended to provide for a third option. (Exhibit 110)

On October 1, 1984, Katzenberg was informed by Michael Besman, a member of Paramount's creative group, that Veber had "unofficially submitted the first draft of his screenplay." Besman reported that the "feeling was that the material was good, but it was hard to digest because of the format of the script." (Exhibit 114)

On October 3, 1984, Katzenberg informed Mancuso that Kirkpatrick had read the first third of Veber's screenplay, that Veber was coming to America the end of November and that there was a deal in place for Veber to direct "King for a Day." (Exhibit 115)

On October 10, 1984, Bernheim wrote Mancuso and informed him that he (Bernheim) had "been working with Francis Veber on our Eddie Murphy project (King for a Day)." Bernheim stated that he hoped Veber would arrive in Los Angeles by the end of November with the completed script. (Exhibit 116)

On October 16, 1984, Paramount exercised its third option on Buchwald's work. (Exhibit 117) On October 19, 1984, Ned Tanen, who by this time had taken over as President of Paramount, authorized payment of an additional $10,000 to Bernheim by reason of the latter's efforts in holding the "King for a Day" project together. (Exhibits 118; 119; RT 869)

---

[2] Veber was paid $300,000 by Paramount to write the script for "King for a Day." This was a large sum of money for such a script. (RT 148–149)

In mid-November Veber's first draft screenplay was submitted.

On January 1, 1985, Kirkpatrick directed a memorandum to Eddie Murphy's agents and managers—Gottlieb, Tienkin and Wachs. "King for a Day" was identified as one of the two strong development projects that would be "coming down the pike at the end of the month." In his memorandum Kirkpatrick reported that Veber was unhappy with his first script and wanted to revise it before it was shown to " 'Eddie's people.' " (Exhibit 123) Veber produced his revised draft in January 1985. (Exhibit 627) On February 1, 1985, it was reported that May 1, 1985, was the final date for Paramount to exercise its option on "King for a Day." (Exhibit 125) On the same date Bernheim wrote Tanen and inquired whether "Eddie [was] still interested in the basic Buchwald premise." Bernheim noted that he had been told that "Eddie and his associates were very high on the idea." (Exhibit 126)

On February 7, 1985, Bernheim again wrote Tanen. Bernheim indicated he had had a recent telephone conversation with Kirkpatrick in which the latter hung up on him. Bernheim also referred to the fact that they were "on the verge of signing a new writer (John See)." (Exhibit 128; see also Exhibit 127)

On February 20, 1985, Richard Fowkes of Paramount reported that a deal had been made with the writing team of Mierson and Krikes to do a rewrite on "King for a Day." (Exhibit 129; see also Exhibit 131) However, one week later it was reported that the deal with Mierson and Krikes "has been aborted." (Exhibit 132)

On March 6, 1985, Kirkpatrick sent a copy of the "King for a Day" script to Wachs, with copies to Gottlieb and Tamara Rawitt (of Eddie Murphy Productions). (Exhibit 134; RT 636) Wachs received the script and read at least part of it. (RT 766)

On March 29, 1985, Bernheim was informed that Paramount was abandoning "King for a Day." (Exhibit 135) On April 18, 1985, Paramount confirmed that "King for a Day" was "in turnaround."[3] (Exhibit 136) On April 3, 1985, Virginia Briggs of Paramount confirmed that "King for a Day" had been abandoned as of March 29, 1985. "King for a Day" was described as: "First draft screenplay by Tab Murphy; first draft and set of revisions by Francis Veber; both based upon original story and concept by Art Buchwald." (Exhibit 137) However, on May 5, 1985, in a report identifying the "state of potential Eddie Murphy projects," "King for a Day" was listed as one of the "projects in abeyance/on hold." (Exhibit 138) This memorandum was sent to Wachs, Tienkin, Rawitt and Gottlieb. (RT 787–788)

On August 14, 1985, a "coverage"[4] was written for the title "Ambassador at Large." The person who prepared this coverage likened "Ambassador at Large" to a story that Paramount had optioned from Art Buchwald. (Exhibit 139)

After Paramount abandoned "King for a Day," Bernheim became interested in finding another production company for the project. He was informed that Paramount had invested in excess of $418,000 in developing "King for a Day." (Exhibit 140) Although Bernheim attempted to purchase an option on the screenplay from Paramount (Exhibit 141), he was unsuccessful. (Exhibit 142; RT 882–883)

In May 1986, Buchwald optioned his treatment "King for a Day" to Warner Brothers (Exhibits 144; 146) Bernheim also entered into an agreement with Warner Brothers on the same project. (Exhibit 145)

In the summer of 1987, Paramount began the development process of a property called "The Quest," which was reported to be based upon a story by Eddie Murphy. (Exhibits 156; 508) The director selected for this project was John Landis. (Exhibits 157; 162) Barry Blaustein and David Sheffield were chosen to collaborate on the screenplay with Eddie Murphy and Arsenio Hall. (Exhibit 158) The shooting script for

---

[3] The term "turnaround" means that a producer is given the right to "take the project, call it his own, and try to set it up at another studio or third party financing." (RT 639)

[4] A "coverage" is a document in which the story is broken down, synopsized and explained. This document permits a reader to obtain a quick understanding of the story being synopsized. (RT 877)

"Coming to America," the subsequent title for "The Quest," is dated October 21, 1987. (Exhibit 171) In the meantime, Warner Brothers was still involved in developing the Buchwald treatment. (Exhibit 172) A script entitled "King Jomo" by Allan Katz was ready in revised form in November 1987. (Exhibit 173)

In early November 1987, after Bernheim learned that Paramount was going to begin shooting a movie in which Eddie Murphy was to play a black prince who comes to America to find a wife, Bernheim and Tanen met for lunch. Tanen became angry when Bernheim suggested that Paramount's movie was based on a character close to the one suggested by Buchwald. Tanen insisted Paramount's film had nothing to do with Buchwald's story. (Exhibit 605)

In January 1988, Warner Brothers cancelled the "King for a Day" project. Warner Brothers executive Bruce Berman made it clear that the cancellation was due, at least in part, to Warner's discovery of the fact that Paramount was shooting "Coming to America" starring Eddie Murphy. (RT 726–728; 732–736)

When "Coming to America" was released, the screenplay credit was given to Sheffield and Blaustein and Eddie Murphy received the story credit. (Exhibits 180; 183)

On June 29, 1988, Michael Batagglia of Paramount reported on "Coming to America" field publicity and promotions. One of the promotions was the use of a "King for a Day" concept, where a prize winner was afforded the opportunity to go on a shopping spree. (Exhibit 184)

Discussion

Introduction

At the outset the Court desires to indicate what this case is and is not about. It is *not* about whether Art Buchwald or Eddie Murphy is more creative. It is clear to the Court that each of these men is a creative genius in his own field and each is an uniquely American institution. This case is also *not* about whether Eddie Murphy made substantial contributions to the film "Coming to America." The Court is convinced he did. Finally, this case is *not* about whether Eddie Murphy "stole" Art Buchwald's concept "King for a Day." Rather, this case is primarily a breach of contract case between Buchwald and Paramount (not Murphy) which must be decided by reference to the agreement between the parties and the rules of contract construction, as well as the principles of law enunciated in the applicable legal authorities.

The Contract Between Buchwald and Paramount

As indicated, the starting point for the analysis of this case is the contract between Buchwald and Paramount.[5] Pursuant to this agreement (Exhibit 507) Buchwald transferred to Paramount "the sole and exclusive motion picture and other rights" to the "original story and concept written by Art Buchwald . . . tentatively entitled "KING FOR A DAY," also known as "It's a Crude, Crude World" (which material, as defined in said Standard Terms is hereinafter called the 'Work')." (Exhibit 506, p. 1) In the agreement Buchwald warranted "[t]hat the Work is original with Author; that neither the Work nor any part thereof are taken from or based upon any other material or any motion picture. . . ." (Exhibit 506, p. 3) As is pertinent to the present case, the agreement provided that:

" 'Work' means the aforementioned Material and includes all prior, present and future versions, adaptations and translations thereof (whether written by Author

[5] Although the Court intends to focus on the agreement between Buchwald and Paramount, there appears to be no dispute between the parties that co-plaintiff Bernheim's entitlement to damages under his agreement with Paramount (Exhibit 507) is dependent upon the outcome of the dispute between Buchwald and Paramount.

or by others), its theme, story, plot, characters and their names, its title or titles and subtitles, if any, . . . , and each and every part of all thereof. 'Work' does not include the material referred to in paragraph 2 (f) above, written or prepared by Purchaser or under Purchaser's Authority." (Id. at 15)

Finally, the agreement entitled Buchwald to certain "contingent consideration" "[f]or the first theatrical motion picture (the 'Picture'): If, but only if, a feature length theatrical motion picture shall be produced *based upon* Author's Work." (Emphasis added.) (Exhibit 506, p. 18)

The Meaning of "Based Upon"

Since the agreement provided Buchwald was entitled to payment only if Paramount produced "a feature length theatrical motion picture" "based upon Author's Work," the threshold inquiry in this case is what is meant by the term "based upon." Because the term is not defined in the contract, it was the Court's hope that the term had a specific meaning in the entertainment industry and that the experts who testified would so indicate. Unfortunately, there was as little agreement among the experts concerning the meaning of this term as there was between plaintiffs and Paramount concerning whether "Coming to America" is based upon Buchwald's treatment. For example, David Kirkpatrick testified that his understanding of "based upon," as used in the entertainment industry, is that "there exists some underlying antecedents that triggered the realization of the story in a screenplay." (RT 515) Kirkpatrick amplified his answer to state that "based upon" has two aspects—"the studio or production company had purchased or had access to [the author's work]. And two, that the antecedents were of a significant story nature to claim a based upon credit." (RT 646) In other words, Kirkpatrick opined that a movie is based upon a writer's work if it "was created out of significant elements from the underlying materials." By significant elements, Kirkpatrick meant "that there were character similarities, story similarities as it relates to the Act One, to (sic) Two, Three structure." (RT 647)

Helene Hahn, a Paramount attorney, testified (by way of deposition) that, in her opinion, "based upon" meant that the "screenplay of the motion picture had been derived from and incorporated the elements of author's work as herein defined." (Depo. Tr., p. 32) Alexandra Denman, another Paramount attorney, testified (by way of deposition) that "based upon" meant that the screenplay was written "with the elements of Mr. Buchwald's story, I mean the specific elements of the story, which is the work." (Depo. Tr., p. 50)

David Rintels, a writer, testified (by way of deposition) that "based upon" means "intent." (Depo. Tr., p. 115) Mr. Rintels further testified: "Before you get into plot you'll be able to see, just because you've been doing it for 30 years yourself, or I'll be able to see that—if I think that there is a similarity in spirit over—regardless of details, I think that's a factor, for something to be based on." (Depo. Tr., p. 127)

Edmund H. North, another writer, testified (by way of deposition) that he believed the focus in making the "based upon" determination should be whether there is an overriding similarity to plot, theme and characters. (Depo. Tr., pp. 91–92) Lynn Roth, another writer, defined "based upon" as meaning "something came from something else." Miss Roth conceded that "because we're dealing with so many kinds of material, you could not put it into a specific or as neat a definition as you can other credits in the industry, because we are dealing with, as I said before, different things. . . ." (Depo. Tr., p. 69) In determining whether one work came from an earlier work, according to Miss Roth, one looks at the essence of the material, i.e., "the basic theme" (Depo. Tr., p. 69) but not plot, characters and motivation because these relate to the "development of the project," not its theme (i.e., nucleus). (Dep. Tr., p. 71)

Since the Court found the testimony of the entertainment experts, both individually and collectively, to be of little value with respect to the "based upon" issue, the

Court turned to the appellate decisions of this State for guidance. Fortunately, that guidance existed. Indeed, as will be discussed more fully below, the Court believes these decisions provide a road map through the "based upon" mine field.

Access and Similarity

In cases involving infringement, which this case is not, it has been held that an inference of copying may arise where there is proof of access to the material with a showing of similarity. *Golding v. R.K.O. Pictures, Inc.*, 35 Cal.2d 690, 695 (1950). "Where there is strong evidence of access, less proof of similarity may suffice." (Id.) These same rules have been applied in a case involving a cause of action alleging breach of an express contract. *Fink v. Goodson-Todman Enterprises, Ltd.*, 9 Cal. App. 3d 996, 1013 (1970).

Access

In the present case, there is no real issue concerning Eddie Murphy's access to Buchwald's concept. Indeed, the evidence is that Murphy *knew* about Buchwald's concept. Specifically, it is undisputed that in the spring of 1983, Paramount creative executives Kirkpatrick and Katzenberg met with Murphy and his manager, Robert Wachs, at the Ma Maison Restaurant and discussed Buchwald's concept with them. In fact, it was reported that Murphy was positively responsive to the "King for a Day" presentation and indicated that he liked playing the African character in the movie "Trading Places." Murphy himself testified (by way of deposition) that he had "a very vague recollection, maybe of Jeff [Katzenberg] going into the 'King for a Day' thing. 'You'd be great in it.' " (Depo. Tr., p. 91) Murphy further testified that Katzenberg "liked the idea of it, I guess, 'cause I remember." (Id.)

There is other, persuasive evidence on the issue of access. For example, on June 6, 1983, Kirkpatrick sent Wachs a short outline of Buchwald's "King for a Day." (Exhibit 39) Wachs admitted that he read at least part of Buchwald's treatment. (RT 768)

Finally, there is evidence that Kirkpatrick discussed "King for a Day" with Eddie Murphy on at least three occasions subsequent to the meeting at the Ma Maison Restaurant in the spring of 1983. (RT 556–558)

Similarity

Since there is no real issue concerning access, the focus must then be on the question of similarity. Similarity is, of course, a question of fact for the trier of fact to determine. *Stanley v. Columbia Broadcasting System*, 35 Cal.2d 653, 660 (1950).

The parties have directed a substantial amount of their attention to the issue of similarity. Paramount contends that there must be *substantial* similarity between Buchwald's treatment and "Coming to America" in order for Buchwald to succeed in this case.[6]

Paramount also relies on *Teich v. General Mills, Inc.*, 170 Cal. App. 2d 791 (1959), *Henried v. Four Star Television*, 266 Cal. App. 2d 435 (1968) and *Whitfield v. Lear*, 582 F. Supp. 1186 (E.D.N.Y. 1984), *rev'd*, 751 F. 2d 90 (2nd Cir. 1984).

The Court believes Paramount's reliance on the cases cited above is misplaced because none of these cases involves an express contract with language similar to that involved in the Buchwald-Paramount contract. This point is cogently made by Nimmer in his classic work "Nimmer on Copyright":

[6] In Paramount's Trial Brief it is stated: "In order to sustain a finding of breach of contract under the contention that Coming to America was 'based upon' It's a Crude, Crude World, there must be a finding of significant or substantial similarity between the two works." (At 3)

"However, the copyright requirement that similarity between plaintiff's and de-fendant's work be 'substantial' . . . *is not applicable in idea cases.* If the only similarity is as to an idea then by definition such similarity is not substantial in the copyright sense. *Whitfield v. Lear,* 582 F. Supp. 1186 (E.D.N.Y. 1984) (Trea-tise quoted), *rev'd,* 751 F. 2d 90 (2nd Cir.) (1984). (Although the appellate deci-sion in *Whitfield* refers to a requirement of 'some substantial similarity' the hold-ing is that the district court's finding of 'no similarities' is unsupported in the record on appeal. 751 F. 2d at 93–94.) *If there is a contractual or other obligation to pay for an idea, the defendant cannot avoid such liability by reason of the fact he did not copy more than the abstract or basic idea of plaintiff's work.* [Citations omitted.] *Contra: Henried v. Four Star Television,* 72 Cal. Rptr. 223 (Cal. App. 1968). The result in the *Henried* case may be justified on the ground that the only element of similarity between the plaintiff's and defendant's works ('both heroes travel in chauffeur-driven Rolls Royces') was so well known as to preclude a trier of fact from concluding that defendant copied this element from plaintiff . . . *[b]ut the Henried court appears to be in error in affirming the sustaining of defen-dant's demurrer to plaintiff's implied contract count on the ground that the similar-ity between the two works was not 'substantial.' This principle of law would be equally applicable even if a non-substantial element of similarity were clearly copied by defendant from plaintiff, thus doing violence to the principles of contract law discussed above . . . and articulated in Weitzenkorn v. Lesser,* 40 Cal. 2d 778 (1953)." . . . [Emphasis added.] (Vol. 3, § 16.08[B], pp. 16–64, 65, fn. 58)

Although the Court believes the cases relied upon by Paramount are inapplicable to the issue of the extent of similarity that is required in this case, the Court has con-cluded the two controlling cases with respect to this issue are *Fink supra,* and *Weitzen-korn, supra.*

In *Fink,* as in the present case, the contract between the parties obligated the defendant to compensate the plaintiff if the defendant created a series "based on Plaintiff's Program or any material element contained in [it]." (9 Cal. App. 3d at 1002)[7] The Court stated that a " '[m]aterial element' could range from a mere basic theme up to an extensively elaborated idea, depending upon what might be proved as the concept of the parties." (Id. at 1008, fn. 15) With respect to the contract cause of action, the Court framed the issue: "[W]hether . . . defendants have *based* their series *on a* material element of plaintiff's program." (Id. at 1007) (Emphasis added.) The Court noted that its "based on any material element" test was "quite close to the concept of 'inspiration for' which was the key to the upholding of an implied contract count in *Minniear v. Tors,* 266 Cal. App. 2d 495, 505 [72 Cal. Rptr. 287]." (Id. at 1008)

Similarly, in *Weitzenkorn, supra,* the contract obligated the defendants to pay for plaintiffs' composition "if they used it or any portion of it, regardless of its originality." (40 Cal.2d at 791)

Based on the decisions in *Fink* and *Weitzenkorn,* and the contract involved in this case, the Court concludes that Paramount's obligation to pay Buchwald arose if "Com-ing to America" is based upon a material element of or was inspired by Buchwald's treatment. As the Court in *Fink* noted, this determination is to be made by searching for "points of similarity" both quantitatively and qualitatively. (9 Cal. App. 3d at 1010) It is to this search that the Court now turns.

[7] This contract language appears to be virtually identical to the language in the Buchwald-Paramount contract, which requires Paramount to compensate Buchwald if it produced a motion picture based upon Buchwald's work, which is defined as "its theme, story, plot, characters and their names . . . and each and every part of all thereof."

The Comparison of Buchwald's Treatment and "Coming to America"

Before engaging in a comparison of "King for a Day" and "Coming to America," the Court wishes to state the obvious. Specifically, plaintiff has the burden of proving similarity by a preponderance of the evidence. " 'Preponderance of the evidence' means evidence that has more convincing force than that opposed to it." (BAJI 2.60)

In Buchwald's treatment, a rich, educated, arrogant, extravagant, despotic African potentate comes to America for a state visit. After being taken on a grand tour of the United States, the potentate arrives at the White House. A gaffe in remarks made by the President infuriates the African leader. His sexual desires are rebuffed by a black woman State Department officer assigned to him. She is requested by the President to continue to serve as the potentate's United States escort. While in the United States, the potentate is deposed, deserted by his entourage and left destitute. He ends up in the Washington ghetto, is stripped of his clothes and befriended by a black lady. The potentate experiences a number of incidents in the ghetto, and obtains employment as a waiter. In order to avoid extradition, he marries the black lady who befriended him, becomes the emperor of the ghetto and lives happily ever after.

In "Coming to America" the pampered prince of a mythical African kingdom (Zamunda) wakes up on his 21st birthday to find that the day for his prearranged marriage has arrived. Discovering his bride to be very subservient and being unhappy about that fact, he convinces his father to permit him to go to America for the ostensible purpose of sowing his "royal oats." In fact, the prince intends to go to America to find an independent woman to marry. The prince and his friend go to Queens, New York, where their property is stolen and they begin living in a slum area. The prince discovers his true love, Lisa, whose father—McDowell—operates a fast food restaurant for whom the prince and his friend begin to work. The prince and Lisa fall in love, but when the King and Queen come to New York and it is disclosed who the prince is, Lisa rejects the prince's marriage invitation. The film ends with Lisa appearing in Zamunda, marrying the prince and apparently living happily ever after.

There are, to be sure, differences between Buchwald's "King for a Day" and "Coming to America." However, as noted above, where, as here, the evidence of access is overwhelming, less similarity is required. Moreover, " [e]ven if the similar material is quantitatively small, if it is qualitatively important . . . the trier of fact . . . may properly find substantial similarity.' " (*Fink, supra,* at 1013)

In his opening statement, counsel for plaintiffs made the following comparison of "King for a Day" and "Coming to America":

> "Both are modern day comedies. The protagonist is a young black member of royalty from a mythical African kingdom, pampered and extremely wealthy, well educated. They both come to a large city on the American East Coast. And they arrive as a fish out of water from this foreign kingdom.
>
> Abruptly, finding themselves without royal trappings of money and power, they end up in the black, urban American ghetto, about as far culturally as they could ever hope to be from their pampered, royal status in their mythical kingdom. Each character abandons his regal attitudes. Both live in the ghetto as poor blacks experiencing the realities of ghetto life.
>
> Each takes a menial job as (sic) a series of harrowing and comedic adventures in the ghetto, is humanized and enriched by his experiences. Love always triumphing over all, each meets and falls in love with a beautiful young American woman whom he will marry and make his Queen and live happily ever after in his mythical African kingdom." (RT 45)

The Court agrees with this comparison. In fact, the Court believes that these similarities alone, given the language of the contract involved in this case and the law that liability in a contract case can arise even if a non-substantial element is copied, might well be sufficient to impose contract liability on Paramount. (*Fink, supra; Weitzenkorn, supra; Minniear, supra*) The fact is, however, that other compelling evidence of similarity exists.

In the original script written by Tab Murphy that was indisputably based upon Buchwald's treatment, the king ends up as an employee of a fast food restaurant where he ultimately foils a robbery attempt by use of a mop. In "Coming to America" the prince is also employed by a fast food restaurant and foils a robbery attempt by use of a mop. These similar "gimmicks" provide compelling evidence that the evolution of plaintiffs' idea provided an inspiration for "Coming to America." (*Minniear v. Tors, supra,* at 505)[8]

The Court has found an item of documentary evidence significant with respect to the similarity issue. In early September, 1984, a writer by the name of Jim Harrison sent a treatment to Robert Wachs, Murphy's manager, which he suggested was "closely aligned with Murphy's talents." (Exhibit 111) This treatment envisioned Eddie Murphy playing an aide to a powerful Southern senator. The aide ultimately becomes the King of Somaili. (Exhibit 112) In rejecting this idea, Wachs wrote Harrison in pertinent part as follows:

"Unfortunately, there is a project under development at Paramount for Eddie entitled 'King for a Day', based on an unpublished Art Buchwald story, which is fairly close to your story line, hence I really can't give you a go-ahead on this one." (Exhibit 113; RT 794–796)

When asked what he meant by "fairly close," Wachs replied "that an ordinary person would find that any two items had more similarities than dissimilarities." (RT 799) If Murphy's manager thought that the Harrison treatment had more similarities than differences to Buchwald's treatment, it seems to the Court that a substantially stronger case can be made with respect to the similarities between Buchwald's treatment and "Coming to America."[9]

There are other factors that are present in this case that strongly support plaintiffs' position that Buchwald's original concept and its subsequent development at Paramount was the inspiration for "Coming to America." For example, the evidence is overwhelming that for two years Paramount considered "King for a Day" to be a project that was being developed for Eddie Murphy. In fact, when "Coming to America" was made, its star was Eddie Murphy. Additionally, during the development of "King for a Day" it was contemplated Murphy would portray multiple characters. In "Coming to America" he did.

Moreover, when "King for a Day" was under development, Paramount sought to interest John Landis in directing the movie. On July 1, 1983, David Kirkpatrick of Paramount sent to Landis a description of "King for a Day." In fact, Landis directed "Coming to America". The fact that Landis was aware of Buchwald's concept for

---

[8] During the trial of this case, an issue arose concerning whether the similarity comparison must be made between Buchwald's treatment and "Coming to America" or Buchwald's treatment as it evolved in the Tab Murphy and Veber's scripts and "Coming to America." The Court believes it is the latter comparison that must be made for several reasons. First, the contract between Buchwald and Paramount specifically authorized Paramount to "adapt, use, dramatize, arrange, change, vary, modify, alter, transpose . . . the Work and any parts thereof." (Exhibit 506, p. 4) Second, it is not just Buchwald's treatment, but the subsequent Tab Murphy and Veber's scripts, to which Murphy had access. Third, even though the contract provided that " 'Work' does not include the material referred to in paragraph 2 (f) above, written or prepared by Purchaser or under Purchaser's Authority" (Exhibit 506, p. 15), that provision simply means that the subsequent adaptations of Buchwald's treatment became the property of Paramount. It does not mean that Buchwald was not entitled to "based upon" compensation if the evolution of his treatment resulted in a motion picture produced by Paramount.

[9] Much the same may be said of the review of a work entitled "Ambassador at Large" which was prepared by a Paramount employee in August, 1985. (Exhibit 139)

"King for a Day" is important. Since the evidence revealed that Landis had creative input into "Coming to America," it is his access and knowledge, in addition to Eddie Murphy's, that is relevant to the issue of similarity.

It is also important to observe that one of the promotional ideas utilized in connection with "Coming to America" was a "King for a Day" concept where a prize winner was afforded the opportunity to go on a shopping spree. (Exhibit 184)

As indicated above, there are differences between Buchwald's treatment and "Coming to America." One of the principal differences is that the king in Buchwald's original treatment was despotic, while the prince in "Coming to America" is kind and naive. The fact is, however, that early in the development process Paramount desired to make Buchwald's king more likable. (Exhibit 41) Indeed, by the time Francis Veber submitted his second script, which was clearly based upon Buchwald's original treatment, the king had none of his despotic characteristics. As indicated above (fn. 8), the Court believes that "Coming to America" must be compared with the Buchwald treatment as it was developed in the Tab Murphy and Veber scripts.

The other significant difference between Buchwald's treatment and "Coming to America" is the motivation that brought the principal character to America. In Buchwald's treatment the motivation was to obtain military weapons from the United States. In "Coming to America" it was to find an independent wife. This dissimilarity does not, however, require a finding that "Coming to America" is not "based upon" Buchwald's work.

In many ways, the decision in *Weitzenkorn, supra,* is similar to the present case. *Weitzenkorn* was a breach of contract case in which the plaintiff sued to recover damages by reason of the defendant's use of her Tarzan/Fountain of Youth idea. Although both plaintiff's idea and the defendant's movie involved Tarzan, there were striking dissimilarities between the two. In plaintiff's story, Tarzan entered the area where the Fountain of Youth was located because he was captured by the evil persons who dwelled in the area. By contrast, in the defendant's version Tarzan voluntarily entered the area which was occupied by a king who was a friend of Tarzan. In plaintiff's version, Tarzan undertook his journey to rescue Boy. In defendant's version, Tarzan was on a mission of mercy to find a missing aviatrix. In plaintiff's version, the evil queen and her subjects disintegrated when Tarzan destroyed the Fountain of Youth. In defendant's version, the ending was totally different.

In *Weitzenkorn* the Court found no similarity as to form and manner of expression between plaintiff's composition and defendant's movie. Although both works included the same characters in Africa being involved with a mythical Fountain of Youth, the moral of each was entirely different. Specifically, the moral of plaintiff's work was that eternal youth was not a blessing. The moral of defendant's work was that eternal youth was a reward for good.

In spite of the significant differences between plaintiff's and defendant's work, the Court concluded that the trial court had erroneously sustained the demurrers of the defendants without leave to amend. Because the defendants had expressly agreed to compensate the plaintiff if they used plaintiff's composition, or any portion of it, the Court concluded that plaintiff's complaint stated a cause of action "no matter how slight or commonplace the portion which" the defendants used. (40 Cal. 2d at 792)

Finally, *Blaustein v. Burton,* 9 Cal. App. 3d 961 (1970) is also instructive. In this case plaintiff's idea of using Richard Burton and Elizabeth Taylor as the stars of "Taming of the Shrew," together with several ideas with respect to how and where the movie should be made, was held to give rise to contract liability.

Based upon the authorities discussed above and the provisions of the contract involved in this case, the Court concludes that "Coming to America" is a movie that was "based upon" Buchwald's treatment "King for a Day."[10] "Bearing in mind the unlimited access . . . [proved] in this case and the rule that the stronger the access the less striking and numerous the similarities need be . . . [the Court concludes that Paramount has] appropriated and used a qualitatively important part of the plaintiff's material in such a way that features discernible in . . . [Paramount's] work are substantially similar thereto. (Fink, supra, at 1013)[11]

Finally, the Court wishes again to emphasize that its decision is in no way intended to disparage the creative talent of Eddie Murphy. It was Paramount and not Murphy who prepared the agreement in question. It is Paramount and not Murphy that obligated itself to compensate Buchwald if any material element of Buchwald's treatment was utilized in or inspired a film produced by Paramount. "Coming to America" is no less the product of Eddie Murphy's creativity because of the Court's decision than it was before this decision was rendered.

The Issue of the Originality of Buchwald's Treatment

As indicated, in the agreement between Buchwald and Paramount, the former sold to Paramount his "original story and concept" and warranted that his work was original and not taken from or based upon any other material or motion picture. During the trial, Paramount was permitted to introduce into evidence a movie made in the 1950's by Charlie Chaplin entitled "A King in New York." Although the Court understood it to be Paramount's position during trial that Buchwald's treatment was not original in that it was based upon "A King in New York," it appears that this position was abandoned by Paramount during oral argument. Paramount's present position, as the Court understands it, is that if the Court concludes "Coming to America" is based upon Buchwald's treatment, it must similarly conclude that Buchwald's treatment is based upon "A King in New York" since the same degree of similarity exists between Buchwald's treatment and each of the two movies. The Court does not agree.

It is true that Buchwald testified that he saw "A King in New York" in Paris in the 1950's and wrote a column concerning his review of the movie after seeing it. Besides these facts, there is not a scintilla of evidence that Buchwald's treatment was in any way based on "A King in New York." Indeed Buchwald testified that his treatment was an original document and that he could not remember anything about the Chaplin movie. Moreover, the Court has viewed "A King in New York." Besides the fact that this movie involves a king who comes to America, there is not the slightest resemblance between "A King in New York" and "King for a Day." In Chaplin's movie the king is an elderly caucasian who is already married and deposed by the time he comes to America. Although he loses his fortune, he spends the entire movie living in luxury at the Ritz Hotel. Moreover, and most significantly, the movie is a satirical look at the McCarthy era and the American mentality during that period of time.

In sum, to the extent Paramount still intends to advance the argument, the Court rejects the contention that Buchwald's treatment was not original and that it was in any way based upon "A King in New York." Stated another way, while plaintiffs have proved by a preponderance that "Coming to America" is "based upon" "King for a Day," plaintiffs have also proved by a preponderance of the evidence that "King for a Day" is not "based upon" "A King in New York."

[10] The Court wishes to add that to the extent there is an ambiguity with respect to interpreting the "based upon" provision of the contract, that ambiguity must be resolved against Paramount as the drafter of the agreement. (Civ. Code § 1654; Glenn v. Bacon, 86 Cal. App. 58 (1927)

[11] The statement by Judge Learned Hand in Fred Fisher, Inc. v. Dillingham, 293 F.145 (1924) is appropriate to quote at this point. Judge Hand stated: "Everything registers somewhere in our memories, and no one can tell what may evoke it." Eddie Murphy, with commendable candor, admitted as much when he testified (by way of deposition) that he did not know "what triggers my subconscious." (Depo. Tr., p. 92)

Plaintiffs' Tort Claims

In addition to their contract claims, plaintiffs have advanced several tort theories of recovery, namely, bad faith denial of existence of contracts, bad faith denial of liability on their contracts, tortious breach of the implied covenant of good faith and fair dealing, breach of fiduciary duty, fraudulent concealment by a fiduciary and constructive trust. The obvious reason plaintiffs have asserted tort causes of action is to recover punitive damages since, absent such damages, the Court is able to discern no difference between any tort damages plaintiffs might recover and their contract damages.

The Court has concluded, as indicated, that "Coming to America" was based upon Buchwald's treatment. The Court is unable to find, however, any tortious conduct on the part of Paramount or any of its representatives. In order to award punitive damages to plaintiffs the Court would be required to find by clear and convincing evidence that defendant was guilty of fraud, oppression or malice, as those terms are defined in Civil Code Section 3294. While the Court rejects Paramount's contention that "Coming to America" is not "based upon" "King for a Day," the Court is unable to conclude that Paramount's conduct was in bad faith, let alone fraudulent, oppressive or malicious. Accordingly, while plaintiffs are entitled to recovery on their breach of contract claims, the Court finds the defendant is entitled to judgment on plaintiffs' tort claims.

Since neither party has requested a Statement of Decision, the Tentative Decision (as corrected herein) shall constitute the Statement of Decision. The Court understands there will now be an accounting phase of this case. The Court desires to make it clear that, depending on the evidence adduced during the accounting phase, the possibility exists that Paramount's accounting practices may make the imposition of tort damages appropriate.

DATED: JAN 31 1990

HARVEY A. SCHNEIDER
Judge of the Superior Court

Appendix B

SUPERIOR COURT OF THE STATE OF CALIFORNIA
FOR THE COUNTY OF LOS ANGELES

ART BUCHWALD, et al.,

    Plaintiff,

v.

PARAMOUNT PICTURES CORPORATION, etc., et al.,

    Defendants.

No. C 706083

TENTATIVE DECISION
(SECOND PHASE)

I. PRELIMINARY STATEMENT

In the first phase of this case, this Court ruled that Paramount's film *Coming to America* was "based upon" the screen treatment written by plaintiff Art Buchwald. In the second phase of the case, the Court has been presented with numerous issues, including whether: (i) The contract between plaintiff Bernheim and Paramount is a contract of adhesion; (ii) the contract, or any provision thereof, is unconscionable; (iii) the relationship between Bernheim and Paramount was that of co-venturers; (iv) Paramount owed a fiduciary duty to Bernheim; and (v) conduct on the part of Paramount breached the implied covenant of good faith and fair dealing. The Court has also been presented with the task of interpreting other contract provisions, including the so-called "consultation" clause; the "turnaround" provision; and paragraph D.2.b. of the Bernheim Deal Memo.

II. THE CONTRACT

In order to understand the issues presented to the Court in this phase of the proceeding, it is important to identify the components of the contract that present those issues. These components are:

1. The February 24, 1983, Deal Memo (consisting of six pages) entered into between Alma Productions, Inc. (Alain Bernheim's loan-out company)[1] and Paramount;

2. The so-called "turnaround" agreement (consisting of three pages);

3. Additional Terms and Conditions (consisting of six pages); and

4. Paramount's standard net profit participation agreement (consisting of 23 pages), with two attachments relating to royalties.

III. DISCUSSION

A. *Contract of Adhesion*

A "contract of adhesion" " 'signifies a standardized contract, which, imposed and drafted by the party of superior bargaining strength, relegates to the subscribing party only the opportunity to adhere to the contract or reject it.' (Citation omitted.)" *Graham v. Scissor-Tail, Inc.*, 28 Cal. 3d 807, 817 (1981). As the Court in *Graham* stated:

> "Such contracts are, of course, a familiar part of the modern legal landscape, in which the classical model of 'free' contracting by parties of equal or near-equal bargaining strength is often found to be unresponsive to the realities brought about by increasing concentrations of economic and other power. They are also an inevitable fact of life for all citizens—businessman and consumer alike. While not lacking in social advantages, they bear within them the clear danger of oppression and overreaching. It is in the context of this tension—between social advantage in the light of modern conditions on the one hand, and the danger of oppression on the other—that courts and legislatures have sometimes acted to prevent perceived abuses." (*Id.* at 817–818)

In the present case, the Court finds that Bernheim's compensation package, as set forth in the Deal Memo, was negotiated by Bernheim's agent and Paramount's representative, as were other provisions of the Deal Memo not relevant to this case. The Court finds, however, that the "boilerplate" language of the Deal Memo was not negotiated.

The Court further finds that the "turnaround" provision, the Additional Terms and Conditions, and the net profit participation agreement were not negotiated. With respect to the latter three parts of the Bernheim-Paramount contract, there is not the slightest doubt that they were presented to Bernheim on a "take it or leave it" basis. Indeed, the evidence reveals that Bernheim did not have the "clout" to make a better deal.

It is true Paramount has submitted evidence that it freely negotiates its net profit formula with the talent with which it deals. The Court is not impressed with Paramount's evidence. To the contrary, the Court concludes plaintiffs have proved by a

---

[1] In this Tentative Decision, for ease of reference, Bernheim will be referred to as the contracting party.

preponderance of the evidence that Paramount negotiates its net profit formula with only a relatively small number of persons who possess the necessary "clout," and even these negotiations result in changes that are cosmetic, rather than substantive. Indeed, if, as Paramount contends, it freely negotiates with respect to its net profit formula, the Court presumes it would have been inundated with examples of contracts where this was done. Succinctly stated, this has not occurred.

The evidence also discloses that the entire contract was drafted by Paramount and that the "turnaround" and net profit participation provisions were standard, form provisions. Indeed, there is evidence in the record that Paramount's net profit formula is standard in the film industry. Further, there is evidence in the record to support the conclusion that essentially the same negotiations are conducted at all studios and that when one studio revises a provision of its net profit formula, that revision is adopted by the other studios.

The above factors lead to the inescapable conclusion that the Bernheim-Paramount contract is a contract of adhesion. The fact that a portion of the contract was negotiated, i.e., Bernheim's compensation package in the Deal Memo, does not require a different conclusion. In *Graham, supra*, the Court held that the contract before it was a contract of adhesion, even though some of the terms were negotiated between the parties. (28 Cal.3d at 807)

B. *Unconscionability*

In *Graham, supra*, the Court stated:

"To describe a contract as adhesive in character is not to indicate its legal effect. It is, rather, 'the beginning and not the end of the analysis in so far as enforceability of its terms is concerned.' (Citation omitted.) Thus, a contract of adhesion is fully enforceable according to its terms (citations omitted) unless certain other factors are present which, under established legal rules—legislative or judicial—operate to render it otherwise.

"Generally speaking, there are two judicially imposed limitations on the enforcement of adhesion contracts or provisions thereof. The first is that such a contract or provision which does not fall within the reasonable expectations of the weaker or 'adhering' party will not be enforced against him. (Citation omitted.) The second—a principle of equity applicable to all contracts generally—is that a contract or provision, even if consistent with the reasonable expectation of the parties, will be denied enforcement if, considered in its context, it is unduly oppressive or 'unconscionable.' (Citations omitted.)" (28 Cal. 3d 807 at 819–820)

1. *Unconscionability—Sword or Shield*

Before addressing the issue of whether the Bernheim-Paramount contract, or any provision thereof, is unconscionable, it is necessary to discuss several contentions advanced by Paramount. First, relying primarily on *Dean Witter Reynolds, Inc. v. Superior Court*, 211 Cal. App. 3d 758 (1989), Paramount argues that plaintiffs are impermissibly using the doctrine of unconscionability as a "sword." Paramount claims that Civil Code section 1670.5,[2] as interpreted by *Dean Witter*, permits the doctrine to be utilized only as a "shield," i.e., by a defendant who has been sued. The Court does not agree.

In *Dean Witter* the plaintiff brought a class action attacking certain fees charged by

[2] Civil Code section 1670.5 provides in pertinent part as follows: "(a) If the Court as a matter of law finds the contract or any clause of the contract to have been unconscionable at the time it was made the Court may refuse to enforce the contract, or it may enforce the remainder of the contract without the unconscionable clause, or it may so limit the application of any unconscionable clause as to avoid any unconscionable result."

Dean Witter. Three of plaintiff's causes of action were the subject of defendant's petition for writ of mandate: The first cause of action for unfair competition; the third cause of action for unconscionability under Civil Code section 1670.5; and the fourth cause of action for unconscionability under the Consumer's Legal Remedy Act (CLRA). (*Id.* at 763)

In *Dean Witter* the Court of Appeal held, *inter alia*, that no affirmative cause of action for unconscionability was created by Civil Code section 1670.5. In reaching this conclusion the Court found that section 1670.5 merely codified the defense of unconscionability and did not support an affirmative cause of action based on that doctrine.

In the present case, plaintiffs have not violated the holding in *Dean Witter* by bringing an affirmative cause of action based on the doctrine of unconscionability. Rather, plaintiffs have raised the doctrine of unconscionability in response to Paramount's reliance on the contract between the parties as written. Several California appellate decisions support the use of the unconscionability doctrine in the manner in which plaintiffs seek to use that doctrine in this case.

In *Graham v. Scissor-Tail, Inc., supra*, plaintiff sued for breach of contract, declaratory relief and rescission. Defendant attempted to invoke the arbitration provision contained in the contract. Plaintiff claimed, however, that this provision was unconscionable. The Court not only permitted the plaintiff to assert the unconscionability doctrine, but found the arbitration provision unconscionable and struck it.

In *A & M Produce Co. v. FMC Corporation*, 135 Cal. App. 3d 473 (1982), the buyer of a tomato processing machine sued the seller for breach of express warranties, breach of implied warranty of fitness for a particular use and misrepresentation (although this last cause of action was dismissed by plaintiff at trial). The contract sued upon contained both a disclaimer of warranties and a limitation on the buyer's ability to recover consequential damages. Plaintiff attacked both of these provisions as unconscionable, after the defendant relied on the contract between the parties as written. Both the trial and appellate courts agreed and struck the unconscionable provisions.

In *Perdue v. Crocker National Bank*, 38 Cal. 3d 913 (1985), plaintiff claimed that his bank's "non-sufficient funds" charges were unconscionably high. He alleged five causes of action: (i) declaratory relief (that the signature card was not a contract authorizing non-sufficient funds charges); (ii) declaratory relief (that the non-sufficient funds charges were unconscionable); (iii) damages for unjust enrichment; (iv) to enjoin unfair and deceptive practices; and (v) to recover the difference between the non-sufficient funds charges and the bank's actual expenses (incurred in processing an NSF check).

Although the trial court sustained the bank's demurrer to all causes of action, the Supreme Court reversed on the second and third causes of action and reversed with leave to amend on the first and fourth causes of action. By validating plaintiff's second and third causes of action, the Supreme Court effectively held that an affirmative cause of action for unconscionability exists if it is brought as an action for declaratory relief and that unconscionable fees may be recovered under the rubric of unjust enrichment.

A careful review of *Dean Witter*, *Graham*, *A & M* and *Perdue* reveals no inconsistency. To the contrary, the following conclusions can be gleaned from these cases:

1. A cause of action for damages based on the doctrine of unconscionability (in the absence of a CLRA-type statute) is impermissible. *Dean Witter Reynolds, supra.*

2. A plaintiff may commence an action, even one for damages, based on the implicit assumption that the unconscionable provision does not exist. *A & M Produce, supra* (cause of action for breach of warranty; *Graham, supra* (suing in civil court, rather than arbitrating); *Perdue, supra* (suing for unjust enrichment).

3. In the kind of cases described in paragraph 2, when the defendant relies on the contract as written, e.g., *A & M Produce, supra* (disclaimer of warranty); *Graham, supra* (arbitration clause); *Perdue, supra* (bank rules allowing non-sufficient fund fees), then

plaintiff can counter with the claim the provisions are unconscionable. It also appears that a plaintiff may bring a cause of action for declaratory relief to have a contract provision declared unconscionable, without violating the principles enunciated in the cases referred to above. (*Perdue, supra*)[3]

To summarize, in the present case plaintiffs have not attempted to allege a cause of action based on the doctrine of unconscionability. To the contrary, plaintiffs have alleged three causes of action for breach of contract in which they seek damages. Paramount, by contrast, seeks to defend against plaintiffs' contract damage claims by invoking the provisions of the agreement between the parties as written. Plaintiffs, as is permitted by the cases referred to above, have countered by claiming certain contractual provisions are unconscionable. The Court finds that plaintiffs' use of the doctrine of unconscionability comports with the decisions in *Graham, supra; A & M Produce Co., supra*, and *Perdue, supra*.

2. Unconscionability—Surprise

Paramount also argues that the provision of the net profit formula cannot be found to be unconscionable because similar provisions have existed in the film industry for years and that all of the provisions were well known to Bernheim. In other words, Paramount argues the contract provisions, particularly the provisions of the net profit formula, cannot be unconscionable because Bernheim was in no way surprised by them.

It is no doubt true that the prevention of surprise is one of the two principal purposes of the doctrine of unconscionability. *A & M Produce Co., supra*, at 484. " 'Surprise' involves the extent to which the supposedly agreed-upon terms of the bargain are hidden in a prolix printed form drafted by the party seeking to enforce the disputed terms." *A & M Produce Co., supra*, at 486. It is equally true that, except perhaps for the amount of gross participation shares given to Murphy and Landis, Bernheim was not surprised by the provisions of the contract in question in this case, i.e., the contract provisions were not contrary to Bernheim's reasonable expectations.

The absence of surprise, however, does not render the doctrine of unconscionability inapplicable. Indeed, in *Graham, supra*, the trial court specifically found that the plaintiff was not surprised by the contract provision that was being attacked as unconscionable. (28 Cal. 3d at 821) Nevertheless, the trial court found the provision unconscionable and the California Supreme Court affirmed.

3. Unconscionability—Oppression

The other principal target of the unconscionability doctrine is oppression. *A & M Produce Co., supra*, at 484. " 'Oppression' arises from an inequality of bargaining power which results in no real negotiation and 'an absence of meaningful choice.' " *A & M Produce Co., supra*, at 486. This has been referred to as the procedural aspect of unconscionability. (*Id.*, at 486)

Unconscionability also has a substantive aspect. In *A & M Produce Co., supra*, the Court stated:

> "Commercial practicalities dictate that unbargained-for terms only be denied enforcement where they are also *substantively* unreasonable. (Citations omitted.) No precise definition of substantive unconscionability can be proffered. Cases have talked in terms of 'overly harsh' or 'one-sided' results. (Citations omitted.) One commentator has pointed out, however, that '. . . unconscionability turns

[3] The Court's analysis also appears to be consistent with the decision in *Cowin Equipment Co., Inc. v. General Motors Corporation*, 734 F.2d 1581 (11th Cir. 1984), another case relied upon by Paramount. In *Cowin* the Court held that unconscionability can be used to counter an affirmative defense but cannot be used as a "sword of restitution." (*Id.* at 1583)

not only on a "one-sided" result, but also on an absence of "justification" for it' (citation omitted), which is only to say substantive unconscionability must be evaluated as of the time the contract was made. (Citation omitted.) The most detailed and specific commentaries observed that a contract is largely an allocation of risks between the parties, and therefore that a contractual term is substantively suspect if it reallocates the risks of the bargain in an objectively unreasonable or unexpected manner. (Citations omitted.) But not all unreasonable risk allocations are unconscionable; rather, enforceability of the clause is tied to the procedural aspects of unconscionability (citation omitted) such that the greater the unfair surprise or inequality of bargaining power, the less unreasonable the risk allocation which will be tolerated." (Citation omitted.) (*Id.* at 487)

4. Unconscionability—All or Any Provision of the Contract

There is no question that the law relating to the doctrine of unconscionability permits a court to strike down an entire contract or any provision thereof. Indeed, Civil Code section 1670.5, quoted in footnote 2 hereof, so provides. See also *Perdue, supra*, at 925–926.

Paramount, while apparently recognizing the above quoted law, argues that it would be impermissible to apply the unconscionability doctrine to this case. As the Court understands it, Paramount's argument has two prongs. First, Paramount argues that a court may strike an unconscionable clause of a contract only where that clause is "divisible." (Memorandum of Points and Authorities of Defendant Paramount Pictures Corporation Re Phase II Hearing on Legal and Contract Interpretation Issues, filed July 24, 1990, at p. 15) (hereinafter referred to as "7/24/90 Memo.") Paramount contends that in the present case, plaintiffs are impermissibly attacking "financially interrelated provisions" and demanding "an individual defense of each." (*Id.*) Second, relying on a number of so-called "price" cases, Paramount argues that "profitability is not relevant to unconscionability." (Letter from Paramount's counsel dated October 10, 1990, attached to Notice of Filing Prior Correspondence to Court, filed November 9, 1990)

Addressing the last argument first, it is apparent that the events that occurred at the November 8, 1990, hearing in this case have rendered Paramount's second argument moot. A little discussion of the history of this case is required in order to validate this conclusion.

In many documents filed with the Court prior to November 8, 1990, Paramount argued that its net profit formula was justified, and indeed required, in order to permit it to remain in business. For example, in the Response of Defendant Paramount Pictures Corporation to Plaintiffs' Preliminary Statement of Contentions, filed May 21, 1990 (hereinafter referred to as "5/21/90 Memo"), Paramount argued:

> "In agreeing to underwrite what it could thus anticipate to be a $66.5 million investment, Paramount alone bore the risk that the Picture (sic) would not be produced or, if produced, would not commercially succeed and that its investment would be lost. In contrast, Bernheim and Buchwald risked nothing. Not surprisingly, Paramount obtained from Buchwald and Bernheim, as it does in varying degrees of all net participants, the right to attain gross receipts in excess of its direct out-of-pocket costs before it began sharing those receipts with participants. This simply reflects an attempt by the studio to balance the enormous economic risks attendant to motion picture production by insuring that the studio will reap a fair portion of the rewards resulting from a commercial success. As a means for compensating for an allocation of risks in the motion picture industry that places all the uncertainties on the studio, Paramount's contracts with Bernheim and Buchwald are not unconscionable. . . ." (at 12)

Similarly, in its 7/24/90 Memo Paramount stated:

"As forty years of studio-talent bargaining has established, a studio is entitled to a return commensurate with the risks of movie-making. *Otherwise, it could not remain a viable business.* (Citations omitted.) There is nothing unfair or unreasonable about how the 'Net Profits' formula strikes this balance. . . .

"The level of return allowed to Paramount under its 'Net Profits' formula is more than offset by the risks that the studio alone takes. As plaintiffs' experts readily conceded, 'Net Profits' participants bear no risk; if a film flops, participants have no obligation to take up the shortfall and their up-front fee is guaranteed. (Citations omitted.)

"In contrast, the studio's risks are enormous. When it signed the Buchwald and Bernheim contracts, Paramount assumed the risk that, despite substantial script development costs (nearly $500,000), the picture might never be made and that, even if made, the picture would not make money. Paramount spent $40 million to produce 'Coming to America' and committed another $35 million to an advertising and a promotional campaign with no assurance that a single theater admission would be sold. (Citation omitted.)

"The risk of failure in the motion picture business is ever-present, immense, and unmitigable. . . ." (Emphasis added.) (at 19–21)

The Court interpreted the above quoted statements of Paramount, and many others like them, to mean that Paramount was attempting to justify its net profit formula on the ground that this formula was necessary for Paramount's survival. Indeed, when Paramount's counsel stated, "[o]therwise it could not remain a viable business" (7/24/90 Memo at 19), the Court understood Paramount to mean what its counsel had stated.

It was because Paramount argued that its net profit definition was justified by the exigencies of the film industry that the Court decided to appoint its own accounting expert, pursuant to Evidence Code section 730. Indeed, the November 8, 1990, hearing was scheduled for the specific purpose of defining the tasks to be performed by the Court's expert. This would have included, of course, an examination of Paramount's books and records to determine the accuracy of Paramount's representation with respect to its profitability, the number of films that make and lose money, and whether it was necessary for successful films to subsidize unsuccessful films.[4] Remarkably, it was at this same hearing that counsel for Paramount abandoned the argument that Paramount's net profit formula was required by the nature of the motion picture business.

Paramount's abandonment of its "justification" argument rendered inquiry into Paramount's profitability moot and the appointment of the Court's expert unnecessary. This abandonment also renders inapplicable the so-called "price" cases relied upon by Paramount. These "price" cases were submitted to the Court, according to Paramount, to establish the point that "profitability" is not relevant to unconscionability." (October 10, 1990, letter, *supra*, at p. 1) Since Paramount no longer seeks to

[4] So long as Paramount maintained its net profit formula was justified by the nature of the motion picture industry, the Court felt an inquiry into Paramount's profitability was necessary and proper. In effect, Paramount was arguing that the net profit formula was justified in order to properly allocate the risks between Paramount and Bernheim, Paramount's position being that it bore substantially all of the risks. The Court reasoned that if Paramount's representations as to its profitability were untrue, i.e., if it really ran no meaningful risk because of the profit structure of its business, then its argument that the net profit formula was justified would fall by its own force. The Court concluded it was required to engage in an allocation of risk analysis because, as noted in *A & M Produce Co., supra,* "[a] contract is largely an allocation of risks between the parties, and therefore . . . a contractual term is substantively suspect if it reallocates the risks of the bargain in an objectively unreasonable or unexpected manner." (135 Cal. App. 3d at 487)

defend its net profit formula on the ground it is justified by the nature of its business, it is clear Paramount's profitability is irrelevant to the determination of whether the contract involved in this case is unconscionable.

As indicated above, Paramount also argues that the Court may not strike down all or any portion of the net profit definition because that definition is part of the entire compensation package between Paramount and Bernheim. Paramount further argues that it would not have paid Bernheim as much "up-front" money if it had known many of the components of the net profit formula would be invalidated, and that Bernheim will reap a windfall if the Court finds unconscionable portions of the net profit formula.

Paramount's argument is based on the proposition that the dispute between the parties is one over price. The Court is not convinced that this is the case. However, even if Paramount is correct, it is "clear that the price term, like any other term in a contract, may be unconscionable." *Perdue, supra,* at 926. In fact, in *Perdue* the Court stated:

> "The courts look to the basis and justification for the price (citation omitted), including 'the price actually being paid by . . . other similarly situated consumers in a similar transaction.' (Citation omitted.) The cases, however, do not support defendant's contention that a price equal to the market price cannot be held unconscionable. While it is unlikely that a court would find a price set by a freely competitive market to be unconscionable (citation omitted), the market price set by an oligopoly should not be immune from scrutiny. Thus courts consider not only the market price, but also the cost of the goods or services to the seller (citations omitted), the inconvenience imposed on the seller (citation omitted), and the true value of the product or service (citation omitted)." (38 Cal. 3d at 926–927)

In the present case, the Court has already found the Bernheim-Paramount contract to be adhesive. Moreover, it is clear, as the Court has already found, that contractual relations between certain talent and studios, at least talent such as Bernheim who lack the "clout" of major stars, do not take place in a freely competitive market. Rather, it is clear that if a talent such as Bernheim wishes to work in the film industry, he must do so on terms substantially dictated by the studio. This is particularly true with respect to the net profit formula contained in the contract involved in this case. As previously indicated, Paramount simply does not negotiate with respect to its net profit formula with talent such as Bernheim.

Additionally, Paramount's argument that it would be unfair if the Court found any part of the net profit formula unconscionable is based on the faulty premise that the only thing that mattered to Bernheim was the "up-front" money. While it is true Bernheim's agent, Roger Davis, testified that "up-front" money was important to Bernheim, he also testified that the other important consideration was "to get the project developed into a form where it could be made the basis of a motion picture." (Davis depo at 54) Presumably, Bernheim wanted to make a picture so that he could profit from it. (See Davis depo at 33; see also Youngstein depo at 121–122)

Moreover, Paramount's argument that net profits represented a relatively insignificant part of Bernheim's total compensation package flies in the face of other evidence in the record. For example, in his Supplemental Declaration, Carmen Desiderio, Paramount's Vice-President of Contract Accounting, testified that Paramount had paid more than $150 million in net profits over the past 15 years, using the net profit formula contained in Bernheim's contract, or one similar to it. Additionally, Paramount itself admitted in its 7/24/90 Memo, at 25, that " 'Net Profits' are a valuable form of contingent compensation, not the 'cruel hoax' that plaintiffs insinuate." Indeed, *Paramount's* "turnaround" provision provides for *Paramount* to receive net profits in the event Bernheim was successful in convincing another studio to make a film based on Buchwald's treatment. (Bernheim Deal Memo, at p. 2)

Further, the doctrine of unconscionability would be rendered nugatory if a contracting party could escape its application by negotiating some monetary provisions, while at the same time imposing unjustifiably onerous provisions with respect to other contract provisions. Yet, that is precisely what Paramount argues is permissible.

Paramount has referred the Court to four cases[5] which, it is contended, supports Paramount's position that the Court may not strike down certain provisions of its net profit formula while enforcing the remainder of the contract with Bernheim. Paramount's argument is totally refuted by the provisions of Civil Code section 1670.5, which specifically permits the Court to "enforce the remainder of the contract without the unconscionable clause" or to "limit the application of any unconscionable clause so as to avoid any unconscionable result." Moreover, none of the four cases relied upon supports Paramount's argument, and at least one refutes it.

In York, Sykes and Chow the respective courts did not address the question of whether a provision of a contract may be struck as unconscionable, while the balance of the contract is enforced. Indeed, if either of the two out-of-state cases had answered that question in the negative, the result would have been contrary to the express provisions of Civil Code section 1670.5.[6]

Furthermore, the other California case cited by Paramount, IMO Development, at least by implication refutes Paramount's argument. In IMO Development, the Court specifically held that a contract cannot be partially rescinded, i.e., a party cannot seek to rescind part of a contract and seek enforcement of the remainder. The Court in IMO Development never addressed the doctrine of unconscionability because it had never been pled. The language utilized by the Court strongly suggests, however, that if unconscionability had been pled, the result under that doctrine might well have been different than the decision reached on the issue of partial rescission. The Court in IMO Development stated:

> "What IMO does allege is that its consent was obtained by economic duress. Business or economic duress '. . . exists when threats to business or property interests by way of coercion and/or wrongful compulsion are present.' (Citation omitted.) That, however, is not tantamount to a showing of unconscionability. In other words, the presence of a supposed unconscionable contract provision, such as would admit to differential enforcement, does not logically provide for differential rescission." (Emphasis in original.) (Id. at 460)

In sum, the Court concludes that there is nothing about the contract involved in this case, or the circumstances surrounding its execution, which precludes the Court from addressing the issue of whether certain component parts of the net profit definition are unconscionable. The next issue that must be addressed is the appropriate manner of applying the doctrine of unconscionability to the contract involved in this case.

5. Unconscionability—The Doctrine Applied

Plaintiffs have challenged as unconscionable a number of provisions of Paramount's net profit formula. The challenged provisions include: 15 percent overhead on Murphy and Landis participation; 15 percent overhead on Eddie Murphy Productions operational allowance; 10 percent advertising overhead; 15 percent overhead; interest on

[5] These cases are York v. Georgia-Pacific Corp., 585 F. Supp. 1265 (N.D. Miss. 1984); Sykes v. Perry, 162 Kan. 365 (1947); IMO Development Corp. v. Dow Corning Corp., 135 Cal. App. 3d 451 (1982); and Chow v. Levi Strauss, 49 Cal. App. 3d 315 (1975).

[6] Chow, supra, was decided before Civil Code section 1670.5 was enacted. It is obvious, therefore, that the Court in that case could not have considered the applicability of that section.

negative cost balance without credit for distribution fees; interest on overhead; interest on profit participation payments; the interest rate not being in proportion to actual cost of funds; exclusion of 80 percent of video cassette receipts from gross receipts; distribution fee on video royalties; charging as distribution costs residuals on 20 percent video royalties; charges for services and facilities in excess of actual costs; no credit to production cost for reusable items retained or sold; charging taxes offset by income tax credit; charging interest in addition to distribution fees; 15 percent overhead in addition to distribution fees; and 10 percent advertising overhead in addition to distribution fees.

Paramount has never argued that any of these provisions are individually fair and reasonable. Rather, as has been indicated, Paramount has argued that the Bernheim-Paramount contract must be considered as a whole, that that contract is fair and reasonable and, therefore, the Court is not permitted to focus on individual provisions of the net profit formula to determine if such provisions are unconscionable. As discussed above, the Court rejects the argument that it is impermissible for it to focus on individual provisions of the net profit formula.

Plaintiffs, by contrast, have presented evidence which they argue supports their position that each of the challenged provisions are unconscionable. The Court is not persuaded that plaintiffs have sustained their burden of proof with respect to *each* challenged item. In fact, with respect to a number of challenged items it appears plaintiffs would like the Court to make a finding of unconscionability based upon the mere description of the item and without supporting evidence. This the Court is not prepared to do. However, with respect to a number of provisions plaintiffs have sustained their burden of proving such provisions are "overly harsh" and "one-sided." A & M Produce Co., supra, at 487. Indeed, in light of Paramount's "all or nothing" approach to unconscionability, plaintiffs' evidence stands unrefuted.

The Court finds the following provisions of Paramount's net profit formula unconscionable for the reasons indicated:

1. *Fifteen Percent Overhead on Eddie Murphy Productions Operational Allowance.* The Court finds this provision unconscionable because an additional 15 percent charge is made for overhead "on top of" this item. In effect, this results in charging overhead on overhead. The Court is able to perceive no justification for this obviously one-sided double charge and Paramount has offered none.

2. *Ten Percent Advertising Overhead Not in Proportion to Actual Costs.* This flat overhead charge, which has no relation to actual costs, adds significantly to the amount that must be recouped by Paramount before the picture will realize net profits. Again, the Court is able to discern no justification for this flat charge and Paramount has offered none.

3. *Fifteen Percent Overhead Not in Proportion to Actual Costs.* Paramount's charge of a flat 15 percent for overhead yields huge profits, even though the overhead charges do not even remotely correspond to the actual costs incurred by Paramount. In this connection it should be observed that although Paramount originally contended that this charge was justified because "winners must pay for losers" (Sapsowitz Deposition at 65), this justification was abandoned by Paramount during the November 8, 1990 hearing held in this case.

4. *Charging Interest on Negative Cost Balance Without Credit for Distribution Fees.* Paramount accounts for income on a cash basis, while simultaneously accounting for cost on an accrual basis. This slows down the recoupment of negative costs and inflates the amount of interest charged. The Court finds this practice to be "one-sided" in the absence of a justification for the practice.

5. *Charging Interest on Overhead.* Paramount receives revenues in the form of distribution fees and overhead charges, neither of which are taken into account in determining whether costs have been recouped. This results in "interest" becoming an addi-

tional source of unjustified profit. The Court finds this practice to be "overly harsh" and "one-sided," and thus unconscionable.

6. *Charging Interest on Profit Participation Payments.* Paramount charges the payments made to gross participants to negative costs. In fact, these payments are not paid until the film has derived receipts. Accordingly, Paramount has not in any real sense advanced this money. Nevertheless, Paramount charges interest on gross participation shares. This is unconscionable.

7. *Charging an Interest Rate Not in Proportion to the Actual Cost of Funds.* Paramount charges an interest rate which can be as much as 20 to 30 percent (Zimbert Deposition at 172), even when no funds have been laid out by Paramount. This is a one-sided, and thus unconscionable, provision.

In sum, the Court concludes that the foregoing provisions of Paramount's net profit formula are unconscionable. The conclusion that these provisions are unconscionable is by no means the end of the analytic trail. While this conclusion does actuate the Court's powers under Civil Code section 1670.5, it remains to be decided how those powers should be invoked.

As noted in *A & M Produce Co., supra,* "unconscionability is a flexible doctrine designed to allow courts to directly consider numerous factors which may adulterate the contractual process." (135 Cal. App. 3d at 484) Similarly, in *Frostifresh Corporation v. Reynoso,* 274 N.Y.S. 2d 757, 759 (1966) the Court stated that paragraph 2–302 of the Uniform Commercial Code, upon which Civil Code section 1670.5 is based, gives "the courts power 'to police explicitly against the contracts or clauses which they find to be unconscionable.' "

This Court interprets the cases dealing with the doctrine of unconscionability as authorizing the Court to use its powers under Civil Code section 1670.5 to produce an equitable result. Indeed, "equitable" would appear to be the antithesis of "unconscionable." In *Graham v. Scissor-Tail, Inc., supra,* the Court specifically recognized that the doctrine of unconscionability involves "a principle of equity applicable to all contracts generally— . . . that a contract or provision, even if consistent with the reasonable expectation of the parties, will be denied enforcement if, considered in its context, it is unduly oppressive or 'unconscionable.' " 28 Cal. 3d at 820. See also *Slaughter v. Jefferson Federal Savings and Loan Association,* 361 F. Supp. 590, 602 (D.C.D.C. 1973), in which the Court, after concluding the provisions of a contract were unconscionable, stated that in such circumstances "[t]he Court has broad discretion to fashion relief appropriate to the situation presented. . . ."

Since it is the task of the Court to achieve an equitable result, the question before the Court is: What decision is necessary in order to produce such a result? Plaintiffs answer this question by arguing that Bernheim is entitled to receive the compensation provided for in paragraph D.2.b of the Bernheim Deal Memo, after all of the unconscionable provisions are stricken and after permitting Paramount to recoup its actual costs plus a reasonable rate of return on its investment. Counsel for Paramount, although specifically asked by the Court during oral argument on December 6, 1990, stated he had no position with respect to this issue in light of his view that the Court could not determine that individual provisions of the net profit formula were unconscionable.

After careful consideration, the Court has concluded plaintiffs' approach must be rejected because it does not produce an equitable result. There are a number of reasons for the Court's conclusion.

If the Court were to strike all of the challenge provisions of the net profit formula that it has found to be unconscionable and permit Paramount only to recover its costs, plus a reasonable rate of return, the result would be an inequitable windfall to Bernheim. Stated another way, accepting plaintiffs' argument would result in Bernheim receiving a profit far beyond the contemplation of the parties at the time the contract was entered into and, apparently, far beyond the profit a producer with Bernheim's experience and track record would reasonably have been expected to earn.

The Court believes it does not have sufficient facts to fix the amount that Paramount should be required to pay Bernheim in this case. The Court intends, therefore, to defer to the third phase of this trial the amount of damages to which Bernheim is entitled and the manner in which such damages should be calculated. The Court anticipates that expert testimony may be required. Further, the Court desires to hear argument from counsel concerning these issues, particularly with respect to the factors that the Court should consider in arriving at an equitable award. Although counsel for Paramount has heretofore declined to take a position with respect to these issues, the Court assumes that, in light of the views expressed by the Court herein, counsel will now proffer Paramount's position.

The Court also desires to emphasize that its focus in the third phase will be on awarding damages to Bernheim which are fair and reasonable, but which will not result in Bernheim receiving a windfall, i.e., an award far beyond the reasonable expectations of the parties when the contract was executed.

The Court also intends to defer ruling on the amount to which Buchwald is entitled until after the amount due Bernheim is fixed. The Court observes, however, that under the contracts as written, Buchwald was to receive only a fraction of the net profits to which Bernheim would have been entitled (1 1/2 percent for Buchwald; 17 1/2 to 40 percent for Bernheim). The Court will in all likelihood be influenced by this fact in setting the amount due Buchwald.

C. The Juxtaposition of Unconscionability and the Consultation Clause

Paragraph D.2.b of the Bernheim Deal Memo contains the so-called "consultation clause." That clause provides that Bernheim "will be consulted on gross- and net-profit participations granted by PPC to third parties, but PPC's decision shall be final."

Bernheim contends that Paramount breached the consultation clause by not consulting with him. Paramount argues that the consultation clause is not significant since Paramount retained the right to make the final decision with respect to granting gross- and net-profit participations. The Court finds it unnecessary to resolve this dispute.

If Bernheim is correct, the result would be that he is entitled to receive 33.5 percent of the net profits on *Coming to America* under the net profit formula contained in the contract as written. This conclusion follows from Bernheim's position that, by reason of Paramount's breach of the "consultation" clause, he is entitled to the highest percentage of net profit permissible under paragraph D.2.b of the Deal Memo and Bernheim's concession that that highest percentage is 33.5 percent. If Paramount is correct, the result would be that Bernheim is entitled to receive only 17 1/2 percent of net profits (the floor established in Section D.2.b of the Bernheim Deal Memo) under the net profit formula contained in the contract as written.

In the preceding section of this Tentative Decision, however, the Court has concluded that a number of provisions of the net profit formula as written are unconscionable. The Court has also determined that it will follow a different path in arriving at equitable compensation for Bernheim and Buchwald in light of such unconscionability. Since, pursuant to the Court's ruling, the net profit formula as written no longer exists, it makes no difference whether Bernheim or Paramount is correct with respect to the percentage of net profits to which Bernheim is entitled. This factor also makes Paramount's alleged breach of the consultation clause irrelevant.

D. *The "Turnaround" Provision*

As indicated above, one of the component parts of the contract between Paramount and Bernheim is the so-called "turnaround" provision. The purpose of the "turn-around" provision is to permit a producer to take his project to another studio if the first studio is no longer interested in pursuing it, while at the same time permitting the first studio to recoup its development costs if the project is undertaken by the second studio. (Hahn Declaration, paragraph 19; Sattler Declaration, paragraph 53; Denman 6/28/90 Deposition at 55) Insofar as is pertinent to the present case, the "turnaround" agreement provides:

> "If, prior to the expiration of the turnaround period, the project is not placed elsewhere and/or if Lender has not complied with the conditions above, including, without limitation, complete reimbursement to Paramount, then at the end of the turnaround period, Lender's rights with respect to the project shall cease and Paramount's ownership thereof and all properties and rights encompassed therein shall be absolute."

The facts with respect to the application of the "turnaround" agreement to the present case are these: In March 1985 Paramount purported to give notice that it was abandoning the project that had been inspired by Buchwald's treatment. In May 1985 Paramount permitted its option with respect to the Buchwald material to expire. Paramount contends that since Bernheim failed to set up the project at another studio within the 12-month period ending in March 1986, the "turnaround" agreement extinguished any obligations Paramount had with respect to Bernheim.

It is true, as Paramount argues, that if the "turnaround" provision is considered in isolation, it would appear Bernheim's rights to compensation ended in March 1986. The vice of Paramount's argument is that the "turnaround" provision cannot be considered in isolation. Paragraph D.1 of the Bernheim Deal Memo provides, in pertinent part, that "[i]f the Picture is produced, Lender will furnish the services of Artist, who shall be employed by PPC to personally render all customary services as producer."

The Court has already concluded that the picture was made, i.e., that *Coming to America* was "based upon" Buchwald's treatment entitled "King for a Day." In light of this conclusion, it is clear Paramount was required to employ Bernheim as producer on *Coming to America* and that Paramount breached its contract with Bernheim by failing to do so. It would make no sense to conclude that Paramount breached the agreement by failing to employ Bernheim, while at the same time concluding Bernheim's right to compensation was terminated by application of the "turnaround" provision.

In reality, and the Court so finds, it was never contemplated that the "turnaround" provision would apply in a situation such as is presented by the facts of this case. Moreover, to the extent that there exists an ambiguity by reason of the existence of paragraph D.1 and the "turnaround" provision, it is clear that such ambiguity must be resolved against Paramount as drafter of the agreement. Civil Code section 1654; *Jacobs v. Freeman*, 104 Cal. App. 3d 177, 189 (1980).

Finally, the Court observes that one of the important purposes, perhaps the most important purpose of the "turnaround" provision, from Paramount's perspective, was to permit it to recoup its costs in the event Bernheim placed the project at another studio. In the present case that purpose has been satisfied since it is too clear to doubt Paramount has recovered all of its costs on *Coming to America*.

E. *The Co-Venturer and Fiduciary Duty Issues*

Bernheim contends that he and Paramount were co-venturers and that Paramount owed a fiduciary duty to him. With one exception to be discussed below, the Court is unable to agree with either of these contentions.

Whether or not the relationship between parties is that of co-venturer is essentially a question of fact. *Nelson v. Abraham* 29 Cal. 2d 745, 750 (1947). Few, if any, of the features that usually characterize a joint venture are present in this case. Bernheim did not have a right at all times to inspect and copy the purported venture's books and records (*Milton Kauffman v. Superior Court*, 94 Cal. App. 2d 8, 17 (1949)) and Paramount had pervasive control over the purported venture. Moreover, while there was an agreement between Bernheim and Paramount with respect to the sharing of profits (but not losses) (see *Howard v. Societa Di Unione, etc.* 62 Cal. App. 2d 842, 848 (1944)), Paramount retained the virtually unlimited power to determine whether Bernheim ever received any profit. The factors present in this case do not point to the existence of a joint venture between Bernheim and Paramount.

The Court is also unable to find the existence of a fiduciary relationship between Paramount and Bernheim, except with respect to Paramount's duty to render an accounting. *Waverly Productions v. RKO General, Inc.*, 217 Cal. App. 2d 721 (1963). In fact, the Court disposed of Bernheim's fiduciary duty claim in the Statement of Decision that was issued in the first phase of this case. In its Statement of Decision the Court stated:

"In addition to their contract claims, plaintiffs have advanced several tort theories of recovery, namely, bad faith denial of existence of contracts, bad faith denial of liability on their contracts, tortious breach of the implied covenant of good faith and fair dealing, breach of fiduciary duty, fraudulent concealment by a fiduciary and constructive trust. The obvious reason plaintiffs have asserted tort causes of action is to recover punitive damages since, absent such damages, the Court is able to discern no difference between any tort damages plaintiffs might recover and their contract damages.

"The Court has concluded, as indicated, that *Coming to America* was based upon Buchwald's treatment. The Court is unable to find, however, any tortious conduct on the part of Paramount or any of its representatives. In order to award punitive damages to plaintiffs, the Court would be required to find by clear and convincing evidence that defendant was guilty of fraud, oppression or malice, as those terms are defined in Civil Code section 3294. While the Court rejects Paramount's contention that *Coming to America* is not 'based upon' 'King for a Day,' the Court is unable to conclude that Paramount's conduct was in bad faith, let alone fraudulent, oppressive or malicious. Accordingly, while plaintiffs are entitled to recover on their breach of contract claims, the Court finds the defendant is entitled to judgment on plaintiffs' tort claims." (Statement of Decision (First Phase) at 33–34)[7]

In light of the Court's finding that Paramount's conduct was not tortious, the issue of whether a fiduciary duty existed between Bernheim and Paramount and, if so, whether Paramount breached that duty has been rendered moot. As indicated, however, the Court does find that a fiduciary duty exists with respect to Paramount's duty to render an accounting. *Waverly Productions v. RKO General, Inc.*, *supra*.

F. *The Covenant of Good Faith and Fair Dealing*

Plaintiffs argue that Paramount breached the implied covenant of good faith and fair dealing by improperly or excessively charging a number of different items as costs on *Coming to America*. Paramount has countered by arguing that plaintiffs will be given the opportunity to challenge these costs in the third (damage) phase of this trial.

In a preceding section of this Tentative Decision, the Court has ruled that a number

[7] In the same Statement of Decision the Court did indicate that "depending on the evidence adduced during the accounting phase, the possibility exists that Paramount's accounting practices may make the imposition of tort damages appropriate." Statement of Decision (First Phase) at 34.

of provisions of Paramount's net profit formula are unconscionable. The Court also indicated that it intends to fashion relief that will produce an equitable result in this case. In light of the Court's ruling, it appears to the Court that application of the doctrine of unconscionability will produce damages at least equal to damages that could be awarded for a breach of the covenant. The Court finds it unnecessary, therefore, to determine whether a breach of covenant has in fact occurred.

If a statement of decision is requested with respect to this phase of the trial, it shall be prepared by counsel for plaintiffs. This Tentative Decision shall be the statement of decision unless within ten days either party specifies controverted issues or makes proposals not covered in the Tentative Decision. Rule 232, Cal. Rules of Court. DATED: December 21, 1990.

HARVEY A. SCHNEIDER
Judge of the Superior Court

Appendix C

SUPERIOR COURT OF THE STATE OF CALIFORNIA FOR THE COUNTY OF LOS ANGELES

ART BUCHWALD, et al.,	
Plaintiffs,	No. 706083
v.	STATEMENT OF
PARAMOUNT PICTURES CORPORATION, etc., et al.,	DECISION [THIRD PHASE]
Defendants.	

Introduction

In the first phase of the trial of this case, the court concluded that Paramount's highly successful film "Coming to America" was "based upon," i.e., inspired by, a concept created by humorist Art Buchwald. In the second phase of the trial the court decided, *inter alia*, that certain provisions of Paramount's net profit formula were unconscionable. In a subsequent Order filed June 14, 1991, the court referred "to cases which indicate that 'unconscionability is a flexible doctrine' " (A&M *Produce Co. v. FMC Corporation*, 135 Cal. App. 3d 473, 484 (1982)) that gives the courts power "to police explicitly against the contracts or clauses which they find to be unconscionable." *Frostifresh Corporation v. Reynoso*, 274 N.Y.S. 2d 757, 759 (1966). The court then stated that it "interpreted these and other cases to mean that Civil Code Section 1670.5 permits the court to exercise the discretion granted by that section in a manner that produces an equitable result. *Graham v. Scissor-Tail, Inc.*, 28 Cal. 3d 807, 820 (1981)." (June 14, 1991, Order at 1–2.) In the same Order the court indicated that it was refusing to enforce the contract between the parties because it was permeated with unconscionability and that, as a result, "it would be appropriate to measure . . . [the recovery of plaintiffs] by the fair market value of plaintiffs' contributions to 'Coming to America.' " (*Id.* at 4.) The court further states that it was "able to discern no meaningful distinction between this approach, which was suggested by plaintiffs, and the *quantum meruit* approach which was alternatively suggested by Paramount." (*Id.* at 4.)

As a consequence of the court's decisions in the first two phases of this case and the June 14, 1991, Order, the third and final phase of this case was concerned with establishing the compensation to which plaintiffs Alain Bernheim and Art Buchwald are entitled.

Summary of the Evidence Presented

Plaintiffs approached the issue of the contributions of Bernheim and Buchwald to the success of "Coming to America" by assuming that in 1987 Paramount had given the go-ahead for a motion picture to be made based on Buchwald's concept, and that Paramount was already committed to pay Eddie Murphy and John Landis millions of dollars in compensation, whether or not the picture was actually made. Not surprisingly, under this "gun-to-the-head" approach to fair market value, one of plaintiffs' witnesses (Jeffrey Robin) opined that Bernheim and Buchwald were entitled to combined compensation in the amount of $6.2 million. (3/3/92 Tr. at 43.)[1]

The court rejects plaintiffs' approach to the issue of the compensation to which Bernheim and Buchwald are entitled, and specifically rejects as unfounded in fact the testimony of Mr. Robin. In rejecting this testimony, the court wishes to make it clear that it does not doubt Mr. Robin's good-faith belief in the opinion expressed by him.

Paramount, on the other hand, proffered the opinions of three experienced motion picture producers and executives, all of whom testified that Bernheim is entitled to "up-front" compensation in the range of $150,000–$200,000, and Buchwald in the range of $25,000–$65,000. All of these witnesses believe Bernheim and Buchwald are entitled to no additional contingent compensation because "Coming to America" has generated no net profits.

Paramount's economist, Benjamin Klein, utilizing a regression analysis, testified that Bernheim was entitled to compensation in the amount of $252,000. He also opined that Buchwald was entitled to compensation in the range of $22,000–$82,000.

Although the court believes Paramount's experts came closer to the mark in establishing the compensation to which plaintiffs are entitled than did plaintiffs' experts, the court is not prepared to accept the opinion of Paramount's experts *in toto*. Specifically, the court declines to accept in full the testimony of Paramount's motion picture producers and executives because, as discussed below, the court believes these witnesses failed to give sufficient consideration to factors which increase the compensation to which plaintiffs are entitled. The court declines to accept in full Professor Klein's analysis in part because, by his own admission, his opinion is based upon arbitrary assumptions (3/4/92 A.M. Tr. at 67; 72–73). Moreover, the court observes that even Professor Klein was required to admit that if certain adjustments were made for provisions of the net profit formula which the court found to be unconscionable, Bernheim's compensation would increase to $347,000 (3/4/92 A.M. Tr. at 74).

The Court's Approach to the Value of Bernheim's Services

Since the court declines to accept either plaintiffs' or defendants' evidence, is the court entitled to establish compensation within the parameters established by the evidence of the parties? Under established law, the answer to this question is clearly in the affirmative. Thus, in *People ex rel. Department of Public Works v. Peninsula Enterprises, Inc.*, 91 Cal. App. 3d 332, 346–347 (1979) the court stated:

[1] The court fully understands that in August 1991, it stated that the appropriate time frame for assessing damages was 1987. It was not the court's intention to suggest, however, that it would assess damages in 1987 based on a scenario that gave Paramount no choice but to pay large sums of money to Bernheim and Buchwald.

"In assessing the opinions of the valuation witnesses, however, the trier of fact is not required to accept the testimony of any one witness in total, but may instead, after balancing and reconciling the various opinions of the witnesses and their bases, decide upon a value which falls within the range of the opinion testimony. (Citations omitted.)"

Similarly, in *City of Pleasant Hill v. First Baptist Church*, 1 Cal. App. 3d 384, 409 (1969) the court made the following observations:

". . . 'However, "Upon the trier of fact rests the responsibility to reconcile, if possible, any apparent conflict, whether the same arises upon the entire case or in the testimony of a single witness, and to effectuate all the evidence, when the nature of the case will admit of such a disposition." ' (Citation omitted.) In this case the jurors after viewing the premises and hearing all the testimony may have determined that the property was not desirable for church purposes after the taking, but that the improvements which would be lost were not as valuable as the church contended; or they may have determined that the property could be used for church purposes after the taking, but would have a depreciated market value because any expansion would lead to crowded conditions."

See also *South Bay Irrigation District v. California-American Water Co.*, 61 Cal. App. 3d 944, 968–969 (1976).

Finally, the court notes that in eminent domain cases it is provided by statute that "[t]he fair market value of property taken for which there is no relevant market is its value on the date of valuation as determined by any method of valuation that is just and equitable." (Code of Civ. Proc. § 1263.320(b).) By analogy, the court believes the concept expressed in Code of Civil Procedure section 1263.320(b) may be applied in this case, since Civil Code section 1670.5 permits the court to fashion an equitable result.

As indicated, the court has rejected as unpersuasive plaintiffs' evidence of value. Moreover, while the court finds Paramount's evidence to be more persuasive, the court concludes that the opinions of value expressed by Paramount's experts are too low for the reason that such experts failed to ascribe sufficient value to factors which the court believes are important. It is these factors to which the court now turns.

At the outset, the court notes that under the contract entered into by Bernheim and Paramount, Bernheim was to received $200,000 in "up-front" compensation if a movie was made based upon Buchwald's concept and, in addition, contingent compensation in the amount of 33.5 percent of net profits reducible to 17.5 percent.[2] This deal, which was negotiated at a time when the parties believed the net profit formula was valid, is better than the amount some of Paramount's experts believe Bernheim is presently entitled to receive. In other words, Paramount's experts appear to ascribe no value to the kind of deal Bernheim might have been able to negotiate had both parties known the net profit formula was invalid.

The court also believes Paramount's experts have failed, in arriving at the value of Bernheim's compensation, to give sufficient consideration to the fact that Bernheim controlled Buchwald's concept—a concept that virtually everyone who testified at trial indicated was unique[3]—and that this control enhanced the value of Bernheim's services. Similarly, although several of Paramount's experts opined that the fact Buchwald's name was associated with the project would have resulted in increased media

[2] Although the contract between the parties actually provided that Bernheim was to receive 40 percent of net profits reducible to 17.5 percent, plaintiffs have stipulated that the actual percentage should be 33.5 percent.

[3] Plaintiffs' expert, Howard Suber, testified that he was aware of no other motion picture that involved a member of African royalty Coming to America and becoming involved in life in the urban ghetto. (3/3/92 Tr. at 99–100.)

attention, it appears to the court none of these ascribed any additional value to that fact.

Further, although the evidence revealed that Eddie Murphy and John Landis earned millions of dollars in "up-front" compensation for their respective roles in "Coming to America," and although plaintiffs' expert, Dr. Suber, testified that the twin pillars of the success of "Coming to America" were Buchwald's concept and Murphy's persona, none of Paramount's witnesses appeared to take these factors into consideration in arriving at Bernheim's compensation.[4]

Finally, and importantly, the court notes that although Paramount has earned tens of millions of dollars of profits from "Coming to America," none of Paramount's experts considered that fact in arriving at the compensation to be paid to Bernheim. The fact is, however, that it is entirely permissible for the court to consider the success of "Coming to America" in determining what compensation should be awarded Bernheim. Thus, in *How J. Ryan and Associates v. Century Brewing Association*, 55 P. 2d 1053, 1054 (1936) the Supreme Court of Washington observed:

> "The value of the property right or the value of the services each depend upon the value of the idea to the user and evidence as to the extent of the use and the volume of sales would be admissible in either case."

The same principle of law was enunciated by the California Supreme Court in *Stanley v. Columbia Broadcasting System*, 35 Cal. 2d 653, 667 (1950), wherein the court stated:

> "In the present case, both plaintiff and his expert witness testified as to the estimated worth of the program idea, and as to the custom in the industry to pay the author a certain percentage of the production costs based on the number of weeks the show was on the air. 'The fact that personal property which is injured or destroyed by the wrongful or negligent act of another, has no market value, does not restrict the recovery to nominal damages only; its value or the plaintiff's damages must be ascertained in some other rational way and from such elements as are attainable. In such case, the proper measure or damages is generally its actual value of its value to the owner. The value of an article may be shown by proof of such elements or facts as may exist—such as its cost, the cost of reproducing or replacing it, its utility and use. . . .' (Citation omitted.)"

Since the court has decided that the evidence of the parties sets the outside limits (i.e., the high and low) of the compensation to which Bernheim is entitled, but not the precise amount of that compensation, the question remains: To what compensation is Bernheim entitled? In reaching this decision, the court is fully mindful of the fact that its task is to produce a fair and equitable result—neither a windfall to Bernheim nor unjust enrichment for Paramount. Additionally, since the standard for an expert witness "is not mathematical exactness but only a reasonable approximation" (*Sheldon v. Metro-Goldwyn Pictures Corp.*, 309 U.S. 390, 408 (1940)), it is clear the trier of fact cannot be held to a stricter standard.

Having considered all the above, the court believes the fair and just compensation for Bernheim for his contribution to "Coming to America" is $750,000. The court observes that, given the fact it was stipulated that Paramount has earned tens of millions of dollars of profits from "Coming to America," the compensation awarded to Bernheim represents less than 1 percent of Paramount's profits (if "Coming to America" generated profits as high as $100 million) and less than 5 percent of Paramount's

---

[4] There was testimony adduced at trial that Bernheim's contribution to "Coming to America" was comparable to that of John Landis, the director. While the court seriously doubts this is true, the fact that Bernheim made a lesser contribution to "Coming to America" than Landis did not justify Paramount's experts in ascribing little value to Buchwald's concept and Bernheim's control of it.

profits (if "Coming to America" generated profits as low as $20 million). In awarding compensation to Bernheim, the court has also considered the fact that "Coming to America" was the product of creative efforts by many persons other than Bernheim and Buchwald, although that film was clearly based upon Buchwald's concept and Bernheim had a significant role in the early development of that concept.

The court's decision concerning the compensation to which Bernheim is entitled is buttressed by other evidence in the record. For example, Paramount's Exhibit 901 is entitled "Data on Films Meeting Court Specified Discovery Criteria."[5] This summary reflects that total producer compensation on five comparable films ranges between $150,000 and $4.3 million. The amount awarded to Bernheim falls within the range of total compensation paid to producers on the comparable films.[6]

The court also finds Exhibit 157, and the testimony of Jeffrey Robin (3/3/92 Tr. at 195–197), to be somewhat helpful in arriving at the compensation to which Bernheim is entitled. Mr. Robin testified:

"A: If one has gross participation, you're trying to determine how much net, in essence, you're giving away to third parties when you're converting gross to net. It's normal to do it at a two-to-one ratio, which is what Mr. Gelfan has done [in Exhibit 157]. If you look at Mr. Murphy's 15 percent of the gross, 29.5 percent of the net is approximately two times."

As the court interprets Exhibit 157 and Mr. Robin's testimony, Paramount and other studios consider 1 percent of gross profits to be the equivalent of 2 percent of net profits. In this case, Paramount's expert, David Picker, testified that Bernheim was entitled to receive contingent compensation of 10 percent of net profits reducible to 5 percent, and Paramount's other expert, Martin Ransohoff, testified that Bernheim was entitled to contingent compensation of 35 percent of net profits reducible to 12.5 percent. Taking the low number from each witness's testimony (Picker 5 percent and Ransohoff 12.5 percent) and utilizing the conversion factor of 1 percent of gross profits being equal to 2 percent of net profits, the result would be that 5 percent to 12 percent of net profits would be the equivalent of 2.5 percent to 6.25 percent of profits. Since Paramount has earned tens of millions of dollars of gross profits on "Coming to America," the range of gross profits to which Bernheim would be entitled, using these percentages and assuming a low gross profit figure of $20 million, would be $500,000 (2.5 percent of $20 million) to $1,250,000 (6.25 percent times $20 million). The amount awarded to Bernheim falls within this range.

The Court's Approach to the Value of Buchwald's Concept

If the evidence presented by the parties was less than persuasive with respect to the compensation to which Bernheim is entitled, it was even less so with respect to Buchwald. Paramount's experts did opine, however, that Buchwald was entitled to compensation in the range of $22,000 to $82,000. As indicated, Jeffrey Robin, the only one of plaintiffs' experts who ascribed a number to the compensation to which Buchwald and

[5] It is significant to note that Paramount's economist, Dr. Klein, testified at trial that he believed "the court did an excellent job in terms of standardizing for the quality of the producers in terms of the court's criteria." (3/4/92 Tr. at 44.)

[6] The court is fully aware that the costs on "Coming to America" were far greater than on any of the comparable films. One of the main reasons for this is that substantial gross profit participation shares were paid to Eddie Murphy and John Landis. The court was presented, of course, with no evidence concerning the contributions made by any of the producers on the comparable films. The court has been presented, however, with evidence of a number of factors which the court believes increases the compensation to which Bernheim is entitled, which factors were not given sufficient consideration by Paramount's experts. The court has concluded, therefore, that Bernheim is entitled to the compensation awarded in this decision, notwithstanding the substantial costs on "Coming to America."

Bernheim were entitled, opined that the plaintiffs were entitled to combined compensation of $6.2 million.

As stated above, the court is unable to accept plaintiffs' evidence with respect to the compensation to which Bernheim and Buchwald are entitled. On the other hand, the court believes Paramount's evidence with respect to Buchwald's entitlement to compensation is even closer to the mark than was its evidence with respect to Bernheim. As was the case with Bernheim, however, the court finds that Paramount's experts failed to give sufficient consideration to factors which have caused the court to conclude Buchwald is entitled to somewhat more compensation than testified to by Paramount's experts. These factors include the uniqueness of Buchwald's concept and the effect of that concept on the success of "Coming to America"; Buchwald's stature as a nationally known humorist and the media attention that would result from a film based upon a concept created by him; and the fact that Paramount has earned tens of millions of dollars of profits on "Coming to America." Considering all of these factors, the court concludes Buchwald is entitled to compensation in the amount of $150,000.

DATED: March 16, 1992

HARVEY A. SCHNEIDER
Judge of the Superior Court

Index